ירמיה

JEREMIAH

Hi Rick. Thank you for speaking
with me.

I just wanted to make amends
to you for not telling you
in person how I felt about
you.   860-465

I was wrong.   5090

I'm very sorry,
  not audible but in my heart).
(I hope you will someday)
   forgive me.

                    465- 5197
Hi, I'm a student of
     Dr. Hornung. May I
     speak to him?
   My name is Michelle.

I can forgive myself now.
Thank you, God.

SONCINO BOOKS OF THE BIBLE
EDITOR: REV. DR. A. COHEN M.A. Ph.D., D.H.L.

Jeremiah

HEBREW TEXT & ENGLISH TRANSLATION WITH AN INTRODUCTION AND COMMENTARY

by

RABBI DR. H. FREEDMAN, B.A., Ph.D.

Revised by

RABBI A. J. ROSENBERG

*Hear the word of the LORD, O ye nations,
And declare it in the isles afar off, and say :
'He that scattered Israel doth gather him,
And keep him as a shepherd doth his flock.'*

JEREMIAH XXXI. 9.

THE SONCINO PRESS
LONDON · JERUSALEM · NEW YORK

FIRST EDITION 1949 (Six Impressions)
REVISED EDITION 1985

© THE SONCINO PRESS LTD. 1985

ISBN 0-900689-29-3

PUBLISHERS' NOTE

*Thanks are due to the
Jewish Publication Society of America
for permission to use their beautiful
English text of the Scriptures*

PRINTED IN THE UNITED STATES OF AMERICA

PUBLISHERS' INTRODUCTION
TO THE REVISED SECOND EDITION

Just over thirty-seven years ago THE PSALMS, the first in a series of the SONCINO BOOKS OF THE BIBLE, saw the light of day, to be followed in the next six years by the remaining thirteen books. Whereas the earlier edition drew from various non-Jewish, as well as Jewish, sources, the publishers now feel there is a need to acquaint the reader with the pure Jewish view of these holy books, and this revised edition therefore limits its scope to the traditional classic Jewish commentaries and source material.

We are indebted to The Judaica Press for allowing us to use material from the Judaica Books of the Prophets.

FOREWORD BY THE GENERAL EDITOR TO THE FIRST EDITION

OF all the Hebrew prophets, with the exception of Moses, the fullest biography we possess is that of Jeremiah as contained in the Book that bears his name. It also provides valuable material which throws light upon the psychology of prophecy. The present volume is accordingly one of exceptional interest.

The series is distinctive in the following respects :

(*i*) Each volume contains the Hebrew text and English translation together with the commentary. (*ii*) The exposition is designed primarily for the ordinary reader of the Bible rather than for the student, and aims at providing this class of reader with requisite direction for the understanding and appreciation of the Biblical Book. (*iii*) The commentary is invariably based upon the received Hebrew text. When this presents difficulties, the most probable translation and interpretation are suggested, without resort to textual emendation. (*iv*) It offers a *Jewish* commentary. Without neglecting the valuable work of Christian expositors, it takes into account the exegesis of the Talmudical Rabbis as well as of the leading Jewish commentators.

All Biblical references are cited according to chapter and verse as in the Hebrew Bible. It is unfortunate that, unlike the American-Jewish translation, the English Authorized and Revised Versions, although made direct from the Hebrew text, did not conform to its chapter divisions. An undesirable complication was thereby introduced into Bible study. In the Hebrew the longer headings of the Psalms are counted as a separate verse; consequently Ps. xxxiv. 12, e.g., corresponds to verse 11 in A.V. and R.V. It is also necessary to take into account a marginal note like that found against 1 Kings iv. 21, 'ch. v. 1 in Heb.', so that the Hebrew 1 Kings v. 14 tallies with iv. 34 in the English.

It is hoped that this Commentary, though more particularly planned for the needs of Jews, will prove helpful to all who desire a fuller knowledge of the Bible, irrespective of their creed.

A. COHEN

CONTENTS

INTRODUCTION

THE period of Jeremiah's ministry extends from the thirteenth year of Josiah's reign (625 B.C.E.) until after the destruction of the Temple and the overthrow of the Judean State in 586.

[Josiah had come to the throne at the tender age of eight, after the fifty-two years' reign of his father, Manasseh. He did not succeed him directly, but followed his brother Amon who was assassinated after being on the throne less than two years (637).] Manasseh's reign had been marked by political and religious retrogression. Politically the country was forced to submit to the suzerainty of Assyria. Religiously the reforms inaugurated by Hezekiah had lost their effect and the people reverted to idolatry, with all its impure orgies and gruesome rites practised at the rural sanctuaries *on every high hill and under every leafy tree.* Superstition ran riot: augury and divination raised their heads again, and human sacrifice was re-introduced, Manasseh himself making his own son pass through the fire to Molech. The Mosaic religion was vigorously suppressed. Small wonder, then, that the Torah, the Mosaic Book of the Law, completely disappeared.

Such was the sorry state of affairs which obtained at the time of Josiah's accession. The Assyrian power, though on the decline, was still to be reckoned with. Western Asia had suffered an invasion by Scythian hordes, and it is probable that some of the pictures of devastation in the Book of Jeremiah were occasioned by this event.

In the eighteenth year of Josiah's reign (621) the Temple was being repaired, when beneath an accumulation of rubbish a copy of the Torah was found by Hilkiah, the High Priest, who handed it to Shaphan the scribe, who in turn read it to the king. He was deeply stirred, because he now realized the full extent of the people's apostasy. He also feared the retribution of his outraged God, and forthwith determined to purify the land from its alien worship. All idolatrous symbols in the country were destroyed. The rural sanctuaries were dismantled and their priests disqualified from officiating in the Temple, though to prevent them from fomenting a religious secessionist party, and perhaps also on humanitarian grounds, they were granted an allowance. The Temple was purified and the Feast of Passover reinstituted.

It was a thorough reform, but it affected externals only. A royal fiat, even if made ostensibly with the agreement of the people (or rather, of their leaders), could not produce a change of heart and truly eradicate the popular form of religion, which was idolatry. Jeremiah had no doubt enthusiastically welcomed the reform, but he soon chagrined on realizing its superficial character and how quickly the people reverted to their idolatrous malpractices.

In the meantime the political scene had changed. In face of the Scythian peril, the ancient rivals, Egypt and Assyria, had joined hands. Moreover, a new Power was coming on the scene—Babylonia—which threatened both. Nineveh, the capital of Assyria, was overthrown in 612 by a coalition of Babylonians, Medes and Scythians. A new capital was established in Haran, but this too the Assyrian king was compelled to evacuate. In 609 Pharaoh-neco II joined forces with the Assyrians to march on Haran. The Egyptian army advanced up the coast of the Land of Israel. Josiah, who saw his independence endangered if the Assyrians regained power, sought to block their advance. Battle was joined at Megiddo: the Judeans were defeated and Josiah was mortally wounded. He was taken to Jerusalem and buried there (607). This event was more than a political reverse. The devotees of idolatry saw in it judgment upon Josiah of the gods banished by him, and so his defeat and death further undermined his reforms and gave renewed impetus to idol-worship.

He was succeeded by his son Jehoahaz,

who was placed on the throne by *the people of the land*. His reign was brief: after three months he was deposed by Pharaoh-neco and exiled to Egypt where he died. His brother Jehoiakim (607-597) was appointed his successor by the king of Egypt presumably because he was pro-Egyptian. Judea was politically in a dangerous situation, but official circles relied upon the sanctity of the Temple and Jerusalem which, they believed, would render the city and therefore the country inviolable. At the risk of his life Jeremiah proclaimed that so long as they persisted in their way of life, even the Temple might be destroyed like the shrine at Shiloh before it. For uttering such thoughts he was arraigned on the capital charge of treason, and but for the intervention of the princes would undoubtedly have been executed. Another prophet, Uriah by name, who preached the same doctrine, was in fact put to death.

Assyria had by now lost her pre-eminence, and Babylon was embarking upon her career of conquest. In 605 Nebuchadnezzar became king of the new empire. He was immediately hailed as *the servant of the LORD* by Jeremiah who, seeing in him God's chosen instrument for punishing Judea, declared that all nations must submit to him. Jehoiakim, appreciating that Egypt could no longer be relied upon for assistance, swore allegiance to him, but broke away after three years. He was immediately attacked by the armies of the neighbouring countries in conjunction with Babylonian troops and lost his life fighting against them (597). His son Jehoiachin continued the struggle, but when Nebuchadnezzar arrived in person three months later to direct operations, he surrendered and was deported to Babylon, accompanied by his court, the nobility, seven thousand citizens together with their families, and a thousand craftsmen (597). This was the first breach in the Judean State which was to lead to its ultimate collapse.

The final scene in this tragedy was enacted in the reign of his ill-fated successor, Zedekiah, another son of Jehoiakim, and the last king of Judea. He repeated the oath of fealty to Babylon;

and all might have been well had not Egypt continued to stir up trouble, aided from within by a pro-Egyptian party. Wishful thinking did the rest. A wave of optimism swept the nation: they had but to revolt and their hated subjection would be ended. In this dangerous delusion they were encouraged not only by many of the civilian leaders, but also by a prophetic group who, claiming to speak in God's name, assured them of success. They went even farther and raised false hopes of a speedy collapse of the Babylonian empire, and the return of the captives together with the sacred vessels which had been carried away at the same time. Jeremiah now appeared in the streets of Jerusalem with a wooden yoke around his neck, to symbolize the continued domination of Babylon. Hananiah, one of the false prophets, broke the yoke in sight of the people. Jeremiah countered by predicting that instead of a wooden yoke, the nation would soon have an iron yoke fastened upon them. About the same time he sent his famous letter (chapter xxix) to the captives in Babylon, counselling them to settle down in the land of exile, and even to pray for the welfare of the cities where they were residing. But his counsels in Judea were disregarded.

Ultimately Zedekiah, probably against his will, was induced to join an anti-Babylonian coalition consisting of Edom, Ammon, Moab, Tyre, Sidon and Judea. In vain Jeremiah implored him to keep aloof from foreign entanglements and remain faithful to his oath of allegiance: the pro-Egyptian party was too strong for the vacillating king. Nebuchadnezzar dealt energetically with the revolt. Despatching part of his army against Tyre, he laid siege in person to Jerusalem in the winter of 588-7. The advance of an Egyptian army compelled him temporarily to raise the siege. Jeremiah took advantage of this respite to leave Jerusalem for his home in Anathoth, but he was arrested and charged with desertion. In spite of his protestations of innocence, he was thrown into prison. Secretly visited by the king, he again urged him to make a timely surrender to save the city. But matters were gone too far, and it is doubtful whether the king had the necessary authority even if he so desired. The hopeless revolt moved to its inevitable conclusion.

The Egyptians were repulsed by Nebuchadnezzar who resumed the siege. On the ninth of Tammuz in the year 586 a breach was made in the wall of Jerusalem. Zedekiah fled but was overtaken at Jericho. He was conveyed to Riblah, the enemy's headquarters, where, after being compelled to witness the killing of his sons, he was blinded, put into chains and taken to Babylon. A month later Nebuzaradan, the Babylonian Commander-in-Chief, acting on orders, destroyed Jerusalem. The Temple, the royal palace, and many great mansions were set on fire, and the walls rased to the ground. A large part of the population was deported to Babylon (586), and the overthrow of the Jewish State was complete.

Gedaliah, son of Ahikam and grandson of Shaphan the scribe, was appointed governor over the remnant that was left behind. But the unhappy community was still not to have rest. Baalis, king of Ammon, who resented the existence even of this small and enfeebled community, probably because he had designs upon Judea himself, dealt the final blow. Using Ishmael son of Nethaniah, of the defunct royal house, as his tool, he had Gedaliah murdered. The assassination availed Ishmael but little, for he fled to Ammon; but it wrote an appendix, as it were, to the tragedy. Those who were left in Judea feared the vengeance of Nebuchadnezzar, and in spite of the urgent advice and even threats of Jeremiah, fled to Egypt, forcing the prophet to accompany them. This was the third (but this time voluntary) exile of the Jewish people, and it finally extinguished any sort of autonomous community in Judea. The lights had gone out and were not to be relit for many years.

LIFE AND CHARACTER OF JEREMIAH

Of all the prophets of the Bible Jeremiah is probably the most interesting, because the most self-revealing. None

have told us so much about themselves, their feelings and emotions, as this tragic figure, so strangely compounded of intrepid boldness, which makes him brave the fierce animosity and hatred of people and leaders alike, and a diffident shrinking from his task of telling them the doom which inexorably awaits them —a task which he fain would abandon altogether if he could, but must perform despite himself. Other prophets delivered their messages, but have revealed little of what they felt in doing so. Jeremiah goes farther: he reveals the psychology of the prophet, lays bare the emotion of the man singled out to be the mouthpiece of God. We might have expected a feeling of elation; instead Jeremiah feels poignant sorrow, at times even rebelliousness against his Divinely ordained mission.

The son of Hilkiah, of a priestly family in Anathoth in the land of Benjamin (i. 1), his ministry, as stated above, covered a period of black disaster, culminating in the greatest catastrophe which had as yet befallen the nation. It might well tax the courage of the bravest man to insist that the comforting messages of the popular prophets were false—that for her sins Jerusalem must drink the cup of bitterness to the dregs. Jeremiah was not made of stern stuff. Only the consciousness of having been predestined for his task, the sense of dedication, and the overpowering urge of God's word within him, enable him to rise to the heights of his call. Highly significant is the statement in the first chapter: *And the word of the LORD came unto me saying: Before I formed thee in the belly I knew thee, and before thou camest forth out of the womb I sanctified thee; I have appointed thee a prophet unto the nations . . . Then the LORD put forth His hand, and touched my mouth; and the LORD said unto me: Behold, I have put My words in thy mouth* (verses 4f., 9).

It is instructive to compare his reaction to his call with that of Moses and Isaiah. An overpowering conviction of man's unworthiness in the face of the awe-inspiring majesty and holiness of God fills the latter; yet when he hears the Divine voice say, *Whom shall I send, and who will go for us?* he unhesitatingly replies, *Here am I; send me* (Isa. vi. 8), although he had not been called by name. Moses, too, perhaps experienced similar feelings when God appeared to him at the Burning Bush, when he hid his face in fear of looking upon the Divine splendour. But here the similarity ends. He, unlike Isaiah, was called by name, and his first reaction was one of personal unfitness: *Who am I, that I should go unto Pharaoh, and that I should bring forth the children of Israel out of Egypt* (Exod. iii. 11). The same humility and distrust of his powers characterized Jeremiah's response: *Ah, Lord GOD! behold, I cannot speak; for I am a child* (i. 6).

Jeremiah, then, may have been the weaker vessel as compared with Isaiah, but his task was far more difficult. In the supreme moment of Judea's trial, when Sennacherib's army lay encamped about Jerusalem, Isaiah had the grateful duty of assuring Hezekiah that the city would *not* fall. It is pleasant to say what one's listener desires to hear. But when more than a century later the Holy City was again menaced, this time by Nebuchadnezzar's forces, Jeremiah had to face obloquy and hatred, taunts of cowardice and defeatism and an accusation of treason when he had to advise submission to the conqueror. The difference in the two messages was not due to difference of theological outlook, as is sometimes argued. Each spoke the words which God had put into his mouth, and each was corroborated by the outcome of events.

Small wonder, then, that Jeremiah movingly bewails his fate. He has no desire to be the harbinger of evil, but he must; and he laments his lot: *Woe is me, my mother, that thou hast borne me a man of strife and a man of contention to the whole earth! I have not lent, neither have men lent to me; yet every one of them doth curse me* (xv. 10). *For as often as I speak, I cry out, I cry: 'Violence and spoil'; because the word of the LORD is made a reproach unto me, and a derision, all the day ... Cursed be the day wherein I was born; the day wherein my mother bore me, let it not be blessed ... Where-*

fore came I forth out of the womb to see labour and sorrow, that my days should be consumed in shame? (xx. 8, 14, 18).

This outburst reminds one of Job's (Job iii. 2f.), and it was equally justified. True, he did not suffer the physical calamities which had crushed Job; but for a man of his shrinking temperament the mental anguish which seared his soul was no less overwhelming. He would have preferred to lay aside the mantle of prophecy and live the life of an ordinary citizen, seeing all and saying nothing. But a force stronger than himself drives him on: *O LORD, Thou hast enticed me, and I was enticed, Thou hast overcome me, and hast prevailed ... And if I say: 'I will not make mention of Him, nor speak any more in His name,' then there is in my heart as it were a burning fire shut up in my bones, and I weary myself to hold it in, but cannot* (xx. 7, 9).

How did a prophet feel when uttering the dire threats of doom which read so impressive in the pages of the Bible? Some picture these men as fierce and vindictive, joyfully contemplating the destruction of sinners, self-righteously exulting over the fate of the wicked. The Bible does not tell us much on this point, but what it does tell is sufficient to show that this picture is far from the truth. With heavy heart they uttered their predictions, and with still heavier heart did they see the fulfilment. The eleventh chapter of Ezekiel records how the prophet, then in Babylon, was lifted up by a spirit and brought to the Temple gate, where he was bidden to prophesy the destruction of the princes who had misled the people. Unlike most other prophecies, the fulfilment in this instance was immediate: *And it came to pass, when I prophesied, that Pelatiah the son of Benaiah* (one of the princes concerned) *died.* What was the prophet's reaction? Did he display exultation? *Then fell I down upon my face, and cried with a loud voice, and said: 'Ah Lord GOD! wilt Thou make a full end of the remnant of Israel?'* (Ezek. xi. 13).

In no prophet is this sympathy with the condemned seen so strongly as in Jeremiah. Taunted and jeered at, he avers that he does not desire the evil that he must foretell: *Behold, they say unto me: 'Where is the word of the LORD? let it come now.' As for me, I have not hastened from being a shepherd after Thee; neither have I desired the woeful day; Thou knowest it* (xvii. 15f.). Far from wishing it, he earnestly pleaded with God for leniency on behalf of the people, asserting that they had been deceived by false leaders. In a moment of rebelliousness he goes so far as almost to throw the blame upon the Almighty Himself: *Then said I : 'Ah, Lord GOD! surely Thou hast greatly deceived this people and Jerusalem, saying: Ye shall have peace; whereas the sword reacheth unto the soul'* (iv. 10). The theology may be faulty, but the humanity is remarkable.

In that spirit he laments for the people: *My bowels, my bowels! I writhe in pain! The chambers of my heart! My heart moaneth within me! I cannot hold my peace!* . . . *Destruction followeth upon destruction, for the whole land is spoiled; suddenly are my tents spoiled, my curtains in a moment* (iv. 19f.). Repeatedly he displays his tenderness, fervently praying for the people, agonizedly bewailing their cruel fate: *For the hurt of the daughter of my people am I seized with anguish; I am black, appalment hath taken hold on me. Is there no balm in Gilead? Is there no physician there? Why then is not the health of the daughter of my people recovered? Oh that my head were waters, and mine eyes a fountain of tears, that I might weep day and night for the slain of the daughter of my people!* (viii. 21-23; cf. ix. 16ff., etc.). He acknowledges the necessity of judgment, yet prays that it be tempered (x. 23). For His own sake God must help. In his simple and direct approach to God He is almost brought down to man's level, familiarly addressed as a Friend, rather than as an awe-inspiring Monarch: *O Thou hope of Israel, the Saviour thereof in time of trouble, why shouldest Thou be as a stranger in the land, and as a wayfaring man that turneth aside to tarry for a night?* (xiv. 8).

But the people, or rather the priests and prophets, were deaf to all this pleading. They heard only his predictions of woe, and they hated him. They plotted against his life. Jeremiah repeatedly speaks of these personal attacks. He became the object of nefarious schemes, and it is not surprising that mild and gentle though he was, he was goaded to execration and prayer for the death of his enemies. It must have been particularly distressing to him that his own class was foremost in these attacks. He was a priest and a prophet; yet against priest and prophet he had to inveigh, and they repaid him by scheming to take his life. His cup of bitterness was further added to when his own family joined the circle of conspirators, though it is not stated that they sought to kill him.

In fact, his life was more than once in danger. His blunt prophecies of the destruction of the Temple and Jerusalem led to his being arraigned and charged with a capital offence. In general it appears that, at least in the earlier stages of his career, his chief antagonists were the priests and prophets, whilst the princes were more ready to protect him. Charged with treason, he put up a bold defence, insisting that the Lord had sent him to prophesy thus, yet again pleading with them to repent, whereupon He would annul His intentions of evil. Quite simply he admitted that his life was in his accusers' hands, but warned them that should they take it, they would be committing murder (xxvi. 12ff.).

Although of a shrinking nature, he did not lack courage which he displayed not only in braving the fury of the people, but by his vigorous denunciation of their leaders, not even stopping at the king (viii. 1, xxii. 1-5). Allied to that courage was his faith in God in time of trouble, repeatedly expressed (xvi. 19, xvii. 5-11, etc.). In that faith he committed a symbolic act, viz. the purchase of land in the besieged country, though knowing —none better than he—that Judea must fall under the domination of the conqueror; but even as he had predicted disaster, so was he certain of ultimate restoration, and this certainty he manifested so signally by his act (xxxii. 6ff.).

On the other hand, this long-range faith did not blind him to the immediate hopelessness of the position. Concerning the first deportation in 597 false prophets gave a comforting assurance that the exile would be short. Jeremiah's endeavours to counter this view were of no avail: perhaps naturally, since men believe what they want to believe, the Judeans cherished hopes of the speedy return of the sacred vessels of the Temple and of the exiles then languishing in Babylon. In one of the most famous chapters of the Book, Jeremiah strongly counselled the exiles to make their peace with their captors, settle in the land of their captivity, and pray and work for the welfare of their new country (xxix. 1-7). This passage is often cited as proving the Jew's loyalty to and care for the land of his adoption, even though he regard himself as in exile. It does. But when Jeremiah wrote his letter the position was very different: the exile had only begun and the nation was locked in a life-or-death struggle with Nebuchadnezzar who had ordered it. The prophet must have known that his advice would render him liable to a charge of treason, and it needed tremendous courage, as well as unshakable conviction, to tender it.

During the period of his first imprisonment he committed his prophecies to writing through his amanuensis, Baruch the son of Neriah. He had them read to the people on a public fast day, in the hope that they might still effect a reformation, but in vain. When the words were read before Jehoiakim, one of his courtiers showed his anger by burning the scroll. Jeremiah had them rewritten.

In Zedekiah's reign the tragedy was drawing to its close. It is not surprising that as the siege dragged on and the position steadily worsened, his teachings were held to be dangerous, as they must have undermined the morale of the people, and he was imprisoned a second time. There he remained until the fall of the city. But long ere now his status as a man of God had been recognized, and Zedekiah secretly consulted him. Jeremiah once again counselled submission and all would yet be well. But the king was no longer master of the situation, and the war had to proceed to its inevitable dénouement.

Jeremiah was fated to see his prophecies fulfilled. When the city fell he was given the choice of going to Babylon, where he would be well treated, or remaining with the remnants of the people in the desolated country. A true patriot, he chose the latter. After the murder of Gedaliah he urged the people to stay instead of fleeing to Egypt. Even as he had earlier foretold disaster, so now, when his predictions were fulfilled, he comforted the people and assured them of restoration and rehabilitation in the land of their fathers. There was, of course, nothing contradictory in this assurance. The stern moralist must become the loving comforter when disaster has come to pass. His advice was disregarded, and he was forced to leave Judea with the remnants and fly to Egypt. There he made a last attempt to cure the people of their idolatrous practices, but to no effect.

At this point history loses track of him. Doubtless he died in Egypt.

Jeremiah has been called a pessimist. His very name has become symbolic of gloom. Yet nothing could be farther from the truth. His lines were not cast in pleasant places. He was fated to see the utter destruction of his beloved country, and his prophecies must be viewed in that light. It is more correct to describe him as a realistic optimist: 'realistic,' because he would not be lulled, nor allow the people to be lulled, into a false sense of security; 'optimist,' because beyond the immediate blackness he saw brightness for his people, spiritually purified by their sufferings, restored to their homeland, a reunited nation living on their own soil.

'Jeremiah is the spiritual heir of the great prophets that preceded him. He combines the tenderness of Hosea, the fearlessness of Amos, and the stern majesty of Isaiah. Like them, he is first of all a preacher of repentance: threatening judgment and, at the same time, holding out the promise of restoration. But even in his darkest moments, when he utterly despairs of the future of the Jewish State, his faith and trust in God do not desert him. . . . That (Israel) did not disappear (after his overwhelming disaster) was due to the activity of two men—Jeremiah and his disciple Ezekiel' (Hertz).

RELIGIOUS AND SOCIAL CONDITIONS

The Book of Jeremiah provides us with a very dark picture of the religious and social conditions of the time. Josiah's Reformation had been both incomplete and superficial. His reforms did not long survive him, and even during his lifetime the nation had not returned to God *with her whole heart, but feignedly* (iii. 10). Bitterly the prophet inveighed against the prevalent idolatry, contrasting the loyalty of other peoples to their deities, though these were not gods, with the faithlessness of Israel to the Lord (ii. 10f.). Incense was offered to the *queen of heaven*, primarily by women, but with the full connivance of their husbands. Indeed, the people attributed the misfortunes of the country to the cessation of these observances during the period of the Reformation; and when Jeremiah appealed to them in Egypt, whither they had fled after the overthrow of Judea, to cease these practices, they refused (xliv. 15-19). Superstition was rife: men worshipped the sun, moon and stars (viii. 2), and sought omens and portents for their guidance (x. 2ff.).

Apparently these abominations were not all committed in the name of idol-worship, but also through perversion of the true faith. Thus Jeremiah accuses the scribes of having falsified the Torah: *How do ye say: 'We are wise, and the Law of the LORD is with us'? Lo, certainly in vain hath wrought the vain pen of the scribes* (viii. 8; see note in the Commentary for the translation). This implies that some at least defended themselves against Jeremiah's indictment by insisting that they were obeying the Law of God. But there was even worse. Human sacrifices were offered, and the prophet's vigorous denunciation of them as a perversion of true religion suggests that they were defended on such grounds.

The social picture is no brighter. The people are stigmatized as adulterers and treacherous, false to God and man alike. Slander and deceit make it impossible for one to trust even a neighbour or a brother, for *one speaketh peaceably to his neighbour with his mouth, but in his heart he layeth wait for him* (ix. 7). They are strong, but only to commit falsehood and *proceed from evil to evil* (ix. 2).

What of the leaders? They were the *shepherds* of the people, and in their refusal to seek God had misled their charges; they themselves had not prospered, whilst their flocks were scattered (x. 21). Instead of warning the people of their plight, so as to rouse them to ward off the evil which threatened them, they adopted a complacent attitude, healing the grievous sickness of the nation by glibly denying that there was anything wrong: *They have healed also the hurt of My people lightly, saying: 'Peace, peace,' when there is no peace* (vi. 14). They had gone further: they had actively helped in the ruin of their country (xii. 10). Jeremiah's frequent castigation of the leaders suggests that his sympathies were strongly with the people, and at an early stage of his work he already looked forward to better leaders who would direct them in the will of God: *I will give you shepherds according to My heart, who shall feed you with knowledge and understanding* (iii. 15). But this was a vision for the ideal future. In the unhappy present, oppression and injustice marked the relationship of the rich and powerful toward the poor and defenceless (vii. 6, etc.).

The position of slaves was a special problem. The Mosaic law enjoined that slaves should be freed after six years of service. This law had been a dead letter; but apparently after strong agitation they had been freed, the princes, officials, priests and people having entered into a solemn covenant to that effect. But they had soon re-enslaved them, and because they had violated the liberty of their brothers God proclaimed *liberty unto the sword, unto the pestilence, and unto the famine* (xxxiv. 17).

Social injustice has often been the concomitant of a luxurious civilization. A small group, the Rechabites, recognized this fact, and in obedience to the command of their ancestor, Jonadab the son of Rechab, had forsaken the complicated urban life of their time, living in tents instead of houses, possessing *no vineyard, or field or seed* (xxxv. 9). Jeremiah commended their faithfulness to their founder's teachings, which example was powerless to stem the rampant evil and only threw it into bolder relief.

JEREMIAH'S RELIGIOUS TEACHINGS

GOD. Like all prophets, Jeremiah starts from the standpoint of God. At a time when the land was overrun with idolatry, to which his pages give mournful testimony, Jeremiah insists that He alone is deserving of worship, He alone is all-powerful, all-seeing and all-knowing, in contrast to the idols which are lifeless. He is the Lord of Nature, and as the universal Creator has the right to dispose of all nations as He wills. This is stressed not as a mere theological concept, but as a truth whose practical consequences are of world import. As universal Creator He now orders all nations to submit to Nebuchadnezzar (xxvii. 5f.), and woe betide them if they prove recalcitrant!

Notwithstanding His infinite might, He is no arbitrary Monarch ruling by whims and caprice. On the contrary, He delights in justice and righteousness whilst Himself practising love on earth (ix. 23). The dark days through which the nation was passing did not shake Jeremiah's faith in Divine justice, and sadly he asked the age-old question why the wicked prosper and are so firmly established (xii. 1f.). This problem did not shake his conviction that God sees all and rewards and punishes (xvi. 17f.). A careful study of the passages where this thought occurs reveals that the prophet was thinking of the nation as a whole rather than of the individual.

To know God is man's highest aim and supreme achievement, in which alone he may take pride (ix. 22f.). By this 'knowing' Jeremiah does not mean abstruse metaphysical profundities about Him, attainable only by the philosopher and scholar. The knowledge required

is of the simplest nature and accessible to all: the awareness that He exercises *mercy* (*chesed*, the better equivalent is 'love'), *justice and righteousness*, for in these virtues He delights.

It is the duty of the Jew to worship and reverence Him alone, and not the idols—but not only the Jew's duty. All peoples must acknowledge Him, otherwise they will inevitably be destroyed (x. 10). In doing this He would not be acting arbitrarily but according to the dictates of justice: *For the LORD hath a controversy with the nations, He doth plead with all flesh* (xxv. 31). The simile is of a law-court where the plaintiff must prove his charge against the defendant; and though God be the Accuser, as Judge He must act in righteousness before condemning or acquitting.

But there is a more tender side to His nature. Though Israel has sinned, He remembers the affection of better days when, in the infancy of their history, the people showed unquestioning love by following Him into the wilderness (ii. 2). If Israel will but return He will show Himself merciful, for He will not nurse His anger against them for ever. He is Father and Friend, and reminds the people how but yesterday they had called Him by these terms (iii. 4, 19).

As He is omnipotent, so is He omnipresent. He can be approached even in exile. In the famous letter to the exiles Jeremiah assured them that they could seek and find Him in captivity; He would hear their supplication and bring them back to their country (xxix. 12f.).

GOD AND ISRAEL. One of the most strongly marked of Jeremiah's teachings is that a bond exists between God and Israel. This bond is in the form of a covenant—an agreement whereby God has chosen Israel as His people in consideration of the latter's acceptance of Him in a peculiar sense as their Deity. It was the prophet's sad duty to urge Israel's submission to Nebuchadnezzar under penalty of utter defeat and destruction. Perhaps for that reason he emphasized the eternal nature of the bond between God and His people. It is certainly remarkable that Jeremiah and Ezekiel, the prophets of the exile, give most prominence to the idea of a covenant, just because the catastrophic nature of the time might have led people at that stage of religious immaturity to point to current events as proof that the bond was broken.

This covenant idea is developed along two lines. Firstly, it imposes a special obligation of loyalty upon Israel. Upon this concept Jeremiah repeatedly bases his appeal that they abandon idolatry and return to God. On the other hand, though the nations destroy Israel, the special relationship which this covenant implies will not be broken.

He begins his prophetic teaching by reminding Israel of this relationship. In a beautiful simile to which he often returns Israel is depicted as God's 'bride,' consecrated to Him: *Go, and cry in the ears of Jerusalem, saying: Thus saith the LORD: I remember for thee the affection of thy youth, the love of thine espousals; how thou wentest after Me in the wilderness, in a land that was not sown. Israel is the LORD'S hallowed portion, His first-fruits of the increase; all that devour him shall be held guilty. Evil shall come upon them, saith the LORD* (ii. 2f.).

This bond or covenant is urged on historical grounds. God's liberation of Israel from Egypt gave Him a claim on their gratitude and worship, which was reinforced by His care of them in the wilderness, *a land of deserts and of pits . . . a land of drought and of the shadow of death.* He had brought them unscathed through all those dangers *into a land of fruitful fields, to eat the fruit thereof and the good thereof* (ii. 6f.). How base, then, is their ingratitude and forgetfulness when they turn away from Him to serve idols! Moreover, the covenant made with the patriarchs and renewed at the exodus was an essential pre-requisite for the fulfilment of God's promise that the land would belong to their children (xi. 2-5).

The duties which the covenant entails are not enumerated in detail, but it involved refraining from the abomina-

tions of idolatry (xxii. 9) and observing God's *laws, statutes and judgments,* swearing by His name and in general showing allegiance to Him. Two matters, however, are singled out. One is the Sabbath (xvii. 21f.). 'Covenant' is not explicitly mentioned in that passage, but it strongly emphasizes that the land will remain intact only if Israel keep the Sabbath; and since Israel's possession of the land was part of the covenant, it may be regarded as implied. The other was the freeing of slaves after their six years of bondage, in accordance with the Mosaic law (Exod. xxi. 2). In a lengthy passage this is explicitly made part of the covenant, for the violation of which princes, officials, priests and people are all bitterly castigated and threatened with the destruction of their country (xxxiv. 13ff.). That this protection of the rights of the weak should be singled out for special mention is characteristic of prophetical teaching.

The covenant did not confer immunity. On the contrary, it is repeatedly stressed that precisely because they enjoyed God's favour they will be punished in the event of disobedience. One may cite Amos iii. 2: *You only have I known of all the families of the earth; therefore I will visit upon you all your iniquities.* Notwithstanding that *evil shall come upon them* who devour Israel, the nations have been called upon to attack Judah, for whose sins he shall be destroyed and his land laid desolate. This is a cardinal feature of Jeremiah's teaching; hence his Book abounds in predictions of calamity. Naturally such a view aroused violent resentment: the very thing upon which they relied was held up as a cause of their downfall! It was so revolutionary a concept that to many it appeared nothing less than blasphemy.

Yet from the point of view of the nations, that did not mean that the covenant was now obsolete; it was still valid. Although they were carrying out God's purpose (Nebuchadnezzar is actually referred to as *My servant*), they would be punished. The theological problem why the nations should be penalized for carrying out God's designs presented no difficulty to the prophets. God uses many instruments to bring His decrees to fruition, *for all things are Thy servants* (Ps. cxix. 91). But the delegated nations had no thought of a mission: they were nothing else than rapacious conquerors. Isaiah has given clearest expression to this view: *O Asshur, the rod of Mine anger . . . I do send him against an ungodly nation, and against the people of My wrath do I give him a charge . . . Howbeit he meaneth not so, neither doth his heart think so; but it is in his heart to destroy, and to cut off nations not a few* (Isa. x. 5ff.).

As with other great teachers, the theologian and the man are sometimes at war with each other, which is not surprising since emotions often triumph over strict logic. So Jeremiah insists that the covenant does not confer immunity; yet when the country was smitten with a drought of extraordinary severity, he eloquently appealed to God, as Israel's hope, to send relief *for Thy name's sake*, reminding Him that they are His people and that His name is called upon them, though they have sinned (xiv. 1ff.). The prophet plaintively asks, *Hast Thou utterly rejected Judah? Hath Thy soul loathed Zion?* (verse 19), and goes on to plead: *Do not contemn us, for Thy name's sake, do not dishonour the throne of Thy glory; remember, break not Thy covenant with us* (verse 21). The misfortunes of His people seemed to reflect upon His honour, for was He not bound to protect them? Moreover, the covenant is here apparently regarded as binding upon God though Israel had been faithless to it. From the theological standpoint this contradicts his other teaching that Israel did not enjoy immunity, and indeed his plea is answered uncompromisingly: *Though Moses and Samuel stood before Me, yet My mind could not be toward this people; cast them out of My sight, and let them go forth* (xv. 1; cf. xi. 8). That the plea was made at all is quite understandable, since Jeremiah's love for his people outweighed his consistency.

Notwithstanding this uncompromising attitude here and elsewhere, which after all is his final teaching, the covenant was an assurance that in spite of the people's coming overthrow, they would never be wholly destroyed. A terrible picture is given of the havoc which the invader will wreak, yet it is coupled with the assurance that Judah will not be annihilated: *And they shall eat up thy harvest and thy bread, they shall eat up thy sons and thy daughters, they shall eat up thy flocks and thy herds, they shall eat up thy vines and thy fig-trees; they shall batter thy fortified cities, wherein thou trustest, with the sword. But even in those days, saith the LORD, I will not make a full end with you* (v. 17f.).

The covenant had not been a success since Israel had broken it. And so God promises a new covenant, not like the one which He made with them when they left Egypt, but a more durable one which He would write upon their hearts, so that all, from the humblest to the greatest, would know Him (xxxi. 31ff.). God's bond was with Israel as a whole, and with David and the priesthood in particular; and Jeremiah repeated the assurance, in spite of his scathing criticism of the king and the priests, that God's covenant with both was as permanent as the phenomena of Nature (xxxiii. 20ff.).

When his dire threats were fulfilled, Jerusalem captured and the Temple gone up in flames, and the last vestige of independence lost with the deportation of the blinded king Zedekiah and the people to Babylon, he felt the necessity to inspire his countrymen with hope. And Jeremiah, the so-called pessimist, gave new life to them and lifted them out of their despair by assuring them that God would build the nation up again in their own land (xlii. 10ff.), if they would but remain there and not flee to Egypt. On their insisting, he warned them that destruction would overtake them; yet even then a remnant would escape the sword and return to the land of Judah (xliv. 28), because the bond between God and Israel could never be finally broken.

The eternal nature of this bond was not due to an arbitrary favouring of Israel over other peoples. Earlier he had taught that all nations would come to serve God, but this would only throw Judah's sin in stubbornly clinging to idolatry into bolder prominence (xvi. 19f.). In the final analysis Jeremiah, like all other prophets, was convinced that the people of Israel would refind its better self. If other nations suffer total destruction while Judah would arise out of his defeat, it was because in spite of everything Judah would know how to purify himself from sin in his hour of trial: this alone would ensure his restoration (xxxiii. 4-8).

GOD AND THE NATIONS. At the outset of his ministry Jeremiah strikes the note of universalism: *I have appointed thee a prophet unto the nations* (i. 5). Hence the Book contains a number of messages addressed to the non-Israelite peoples. From chapter xliv onwards it is almost entirely concerned with other nations and only in a minor degree with Judah and Israel. In the earlier chapters there are also several passages of this kind (cf. i. 10, ix. 25, xxv. 15f., xxvii. 2ff., etc.). In the main these are predictions of their ultimate fate, rather than, as in the case of Israel, ethical and religious messages and calls to repentance. It may well be that prophecies or messages of a similar nature were addressed also to them but have not been preserved, on the Rabbinical principle that only prophecies of value for all time were placed on permanent record.

Notwithstanding his teaching that the other nations, and particularly Babylon, had been summoned by God to punish Judah for his sins, Jeremiah naturally felt bitter towards them. He calls on God to pour out His wrath on the nations that know Him not, *for they have devoured Jacob . . . and have laid waste his habitation* (x. 25). That imprecation he follows with the threat that God will destroy the evil neighbours who have consumed Israel's heritage (xii. 14). Israel's oppressors are destined to be punished (xxx. 16). On the other hand, the nations would be built up amidst the people of Judah if they learn to swear by the name of the

Lord instead of Baal's (xii. 16). In a moment of exaltation Jeremiah confidently anticipates that eventually all peoples will recognize Him alone as God: *Unto Thee shall the nations come from the ends of the earth, and shall say: 'Our fathers have inherited nought but lies, vanity and things wherein there is no profit'* (xvi. 19).

In the last chapters he prophesies the doom of several nations, including the Philistines, Moab, Ammon and Elam. Contrary to what we might have expected, he displays deep sympathy with them; yet in speaking of the Philistines he insists that their doom is inevitable, since God has commanded it. Perhaps he had been finally convinced that they were past repentance and improvement. By contrast he tempers his prophecies against Elam by predicting its ultimate restoration (xlix. 39).

JERUSALEM, THE TEMPLE AND ITS SACRIFICES. In popular belief the inviolability of Jerusalem and the Temple was axiomatic. Both were sacred to the people and to Jeremiah. How else could he declare: *At that time they shall call Jerusalem The throne of the LORD; and all the nations shall be gathered unto it, to the name of the LORD, to Jerusalem* (iii. 17)—a prophecy which would be meaningless if he did not acknowledge its sanctity? Very movingly he represents God as saying: *I have forsaken My house, I have cast off My heritage; I have given the dearly beloved of My soul into the hand of her enemies* (xii. 7).

This belief, nevertheless, constituted a danger, material and spiritual. It gave the people a false sense of security: surely God will protect His own! It also gave them a sense of spiritual well-being, smug and complacent, which was wholly unjustified. Jeremiah energetically combated these illusions. The mere possession of the Temple and Jerusalem could not save them: *Trust ye not in lying words, saying: 'The temple of the LORD, the temple of the LORD, the temple of the LORD, are these'* (vii. 4). Since the people were so wedded to this belief, they must be taught that even the

Holy City was not inviolable; and his prophecy that the Temple would be destroyed even as Shiloh (verse 14) inflamed the populace who demanded his death. He had earlier preached to them of defeat and destruction, but only in general terms. To specify Jerusalem and the Temple savoured of treason, and the priests formally arraigned him on this charge (xxvi. 8f.). Notwithstanding his narrow escape he continued to teach in the same strain, saying bitterly of Jerusalem: *For this city hath been to Me a provocation of Mine anger and of My fury from the day that they built it even unto this day, that I should remove it from before My face* (xxxii. 31). This second attack was in the tenth year of Zedekiah's reign, much later than the first which occurred in the beginning of Jehoiakim's reign. Nevertheless we may assume that it too, like the first, was only conditional since repentance would avert the evil decree (cf. xxvi. 3).

To deduce, as many scholars have done, that Jeremiah was antagonistic to the ritual of the Temple, is to read into his words a thought which he would have indignantly repudiated. True he uttered the Divine message: *Your burnt-offerings are not acceptable, nor your sacrifices pleasing unto Me* (vi. 20). Isaiah, and long before him Samuel, had stressed that obedience was preferable to sacrifice (cf. 1 Sam. xv. 22f.; Isa. i. 11ff.). Much has been made of vii. 22: *For I spoke not unto your fathers, nor commanded them in the day that I brought them out of the land of Egypt, concerning burnt-offerings or sacrifices.* Some have gone so far as to maintain that this is a repudiation of the Levitical Code. It is certainly far-fetched to make such a sweeping claim on the basis of a single sentence. It should be remembered that national liberation from Egypt had been accompanied by the institution of the Paschal sacrifice: would it then be argued that Jeremiah rejected the version of the exodus? And if so, how did he look upon Josiah's reinstitution of the Passover rite? Did he consider it an innovation based on the falsification of history? It is clear that he, like the other teachers of Israel, denounced

sacrifices only when they were brought in the wrong spirit; but he certainly approved of them when offered in genuine contrition. Hence he looked forward to the permanence of the Priestly and Levitical houses (xxxiii. 18), whose function was the maintenance of the ritual of the Temple.

THE EXILE. A most prominent feature of Jeremiah's teaching is his frequent prediction that the Judeans were going into exile. In modern times this is sometimes interpreted as proving that he, and the other prophets of the period, had reached the stage of religious development where they saw that God could be worshipped equally well in all places, and so it was necessary for Israel to be driven from his land and scattered in order that the artificial barrier between God and His people, which was raised by the belief in a special spiritual virtue attaching to the land of Canaan, might be broken down. Thereby the people would be brought nearer to Him, and at the same time diffuse the knowledge of Him among all nations.

This is a distortion of the prophet's teaching. He predicted exile, not as something beneficial either to Israel or to other peoples (although it proved so to the latter), but solely as punishment which would be terminated as soon as Israel repented. Nothing would have been more alien and incomprehensible to Jeremiah than to think of exile as a blessing to other peoples or as a means of bringing Israel closer to God. In one of his earliest utterances he describes exile as divorce between God and Israel (iii. 8; cf. Isa. l. 1). It is a cause for shame, an occasion for lamenting, the destruction of the tent of Israel, a punishment for Israel's forsaking God and His Torah and the practice of idolatry (ix. 16ff., x. 19f., xvi. 12f.).

As strongly as he threatened exile he foretold a restoration. He could hold out no hope for the speedy termination of the captivity and insisted that it must run its full course (xxix. 8f.). Indeed, those already exiled (viz. Jehoiachin and the people deported with him in 597) would be more fortunate than those who had remained in Judea (xxix. 16ff.), since the full weight of God's wrath was yet to be experienced by the latter. But that was because he saw more hope in the former upon whom he trusted the exile would have a remedial effect (xxiv). He was certain that in captivity they would be purified and learn to seek God with all their heart (xxix. 12, xxxiii. 4-8, l. 4f.).

Another effect of the exile would be the repudiation of the doctrine of ancestral responsibility with the substitution of individual responsibility, according to which a man is punished only for his own sins and not for those of his parents. This idea is elaborated in Ezekiel xviii. Jeremiah declares more briefly: *In those days they shall say no more: 'The fathers have eaten sour grapes, and the children's teeth are set on edge.' But every one shall die for his own iniquity; every man that eateth the sour grapes, his teeth shall be set on edge* (xxxi. 28f.).

Beyond the exile he eagerly looked forward to the restoration, his faith in which he demonstrated so dramatically by buying land in the besieged area (xxxii). So deep rooted was this hope that, in contemplating the exile of Judah, his mind went back to that of the Northern Kingdom more than 130 years earlier, and he apparently expected its restoration too (xxx. 3, l. 4). The restoration would be preceded by a period of great distress and suffering (xxx. 7). Again and again he returns to this theme, which is most beautifully expressed in the picture of Rachel weeping for her children: *Thus saith the LORD: A voice is heard in Ramah, lamentation, and bitter weeping, Rachel weeping for her children; she refuseth to be comforted for her children, because they are not. Thus saith the LORD: Refrain thy voice from weeping, and thine eyes from tears; for thy work shall be rewarded, saith the LORD; and they shall come back from the land of the enemy. And there is hope for thy future, saith the LORD; and thy children shall return to their own border* (xxxi. 14ff.).

Not only from Babylon, but from all the countries of their exile, would they be brought up to dwell in their land (xxiii. 3). When later, in spite of his pleading, they insisted on fleeing to Egypt, he predicted a dire fate for them, but even of those a small number would be saved to return (xliv. 28).

The teeming life of the big cities, their restless surge, the craving for luxury and ease which was productive of oppression and misery—these were not conducive to the purity of worship and social justice which should be the remedial effects of the exile. Jeremiah therefore seems to look forward to a more simplified life after the restoration in the form of a pastoral rehabilitation, coupled with the purification of the House of David: *Thus saith the LORD of hosts: Yet again shall there be in this place . . . and in all the cities thereof a habitation of shepherds causing their flocks to lie down . . . In the cities of the hill-country, in the cities of the Lowland, and in the cities of the South, and in the land of Benjamin, and in the places about Jerusalem, and in the cities of Judah, shall the flocks again pass under the hands of him that counteth them . . . In those days, and at that time, will I cause a shoot of righteousness to grow up unto David; and he shall execute justice and righteousness in the land* (xxxiii. 12ff.).

JEREMIAH'S STYLE

The Book consists of both prose and poetry, the latter slightly exceeding the former in quantity. Jeremiah's style is clear and lucid, direct and concise, and easily understood. His poetry lacks the vigour and crispness of Isaiah, but makes up for it by a lyric quality which combines pathos with picturesque imagery. While he can be and often is fiercely denunciatory, as often as not much of his teaching is in the form of urgent appeals; and in spite of the dread predictions of disaster, one receives the impression that he speaks in sorrow rather than in anger.

His pathos and simplicity and tender appeal are evident in his earliest addresses: *Go, and cry in the ears of Jerusalem, saying: Thus saith the LORD: I remember for thee the affection of thy youth the love of thine espousals; how thou wentest after Me into the wilderness, in a land that was not sown* (ii. 2). It would be difficult to express Israel's early trust in God more beautifully and simply than by this picture of a loving bride trustfully following her bridegroom into unknown perils and known hardships for the love of him. Or again: *Thus saith the LORD: What unrighteousness have your fathers found in Me, that they are gone far from Me, and have walked after things of nought, and are become nought?* (verse 5). It is a simple appeal, all the more impressive because in it God, as it were, places Himself on the defensive.

The same elegiac and melting quality is shown in: *Thus saith the LORD of hosts: Consider ye, and call for the mourning women, that they may come; and send for the wise women, that they may come; and let them make haste, and take up a wailing for us, that our eyes may run down with tears, and our eyelids gush out with waters. For a voice of wailing is heard out of Zion: 'How are we undone!'* (ix. 16ff.).

Israel's love for God was reciprocated. This is stated with masterly simplicity: *Thus saith the LORD: The people that were left of the sword have found grace in the wilderness, even Israel, when I go to cause him to rest. 'From afar the LORD appeared unto me.' 'Yea, I have loved thee with an everlasting love; therefore with affection have I drawn thee'* (xxxi. 1f.). There is a lyric quality in the strongly anthropomorphic picture of the relationship between God and His people: *Is Ephraim a darling son unto Me? Is he a child that is dandled? For as often as I speak of him, I do earnestly remember him still; therefore My heart yearneth for him, I will surely have compassion upon him, saith the LORD* (verse 19). This, of course, is the familiar theme of God's Fatherhood, but what could so bring out the close intimacy of that relationship as the humanizing touch of God playing with His darling child, a Father Whose love triumphs over all other feelings so that, notwithstanding His child's waywardness, His heart yearns for him whenever He speaks of him? Another bold anthropomorphism, though in a dif-

ferent vein, is: *The LORD doth roar from on high, and utter His voice from His holy habitation; He doth mightily roar because of His fold; He giveth a shout, as they that tread the grapes, against all the inhabitants of the earth* (xxv. 30).

Similes and picturesque imagery abound. These are often drawn from Nature or from the daily scenes with which the people were familiar. Out of numerous instances only a few need be cited: *For My people have committed two evils: they have forsaken Me, the fountain of living waters, and hewed them out cisterns, broken cisterns, that can hold no water* (ii. 13, cf. xvii. 13). A similar idea, but drawn directly from Nature, is: *Doth the snow of Lebanon fail from the rock of the field? Or are the strange cold flowing waters plucked up? For My people hath forgotten Me* (xviii. 14f.). Again: *I will utterly consume them, saith the LORD; there are no grapes on the vine, nor figs on the fig-tree, and the leaf is faded* (viii. 13)—a simple yet vivid picture of desolation which eats up everything, while 'the faded leaf' adds just the touch of neglect and decay necessary to complete the picture.

From the similes of Nature in which the Book abounds the following illustrate his powers of graphic imagery and his intimate knowledge of animal life: *Know what thou hast done; thou art a swift young camel traversing her ways; a wild ass used to the wilderness, that snuffeth up the wind in her desire; her lust, who can hinder it? All they that seek her will not weary themselves; in her month they shall find her* (ii. 23f.). *Yea, the stork in the heaven knoweth her appointed times; and the turtle and the swallow and the crane observe the time of their coming; but My people know not the ordinance of the LORD* (viii. 7). *As the partridge that broodeth over young which she hath not brought forth, so is he that gathereth riches, and not by right; in the midst of his days he shall leave them, and at his end he shall be a fool* (xvii. 11).

Then there is a passage reminiscent of the first Psalm: *Cursed is the man that trusteth in man . . . For he shall be like a tamarisk in the desert, and shall not see when good cometh; but shall inhabit the parched places in the wilderness, a salt land and not inhabited. Blessed is the man that trusteth in the LORD . . . For he shall be as a tree planted by the waters, and that spreadeth out its roots by the river, and shall not see when heat cometh, but its foliage shall be luxuriant; and shall not be anxious in the year of drought, neither shall cease from yielding fruit* (xvii. 5-8).

As he is familiar with Nature, so is he also with the scenes of everyday life which he employs to advantage: *The bellows blow fiercely, the lead is consumed of the fire; in vain doth the founder refine, for the wicked are not separated. Refuse silver shall men call them, because the LORD hath rejected them* (vi. 29f.). His simile of the potter fashioning and refashioning his clay (xviii. 2ff.) is too well known to need quoting. This last is also an instance of how he taught directly from the things he saw. Other examples are the almond-rod (i. 11f., the play on words there is noteworthy), the seething pot (verses 13f.), the girdle and its marring (xiii. 1ff.), the bottles filled with wine (verse 12), the four modes of destruction (xv. 3, though this rather belongs to a different category), the straw and the wheat (xxiii. 28), and the basket of figs (xxiv. 1ff.).

Though he lacks the biting satire of Isaiah, he can be satirical when necessary: *And thou, that art spoiled, what doest thou, that thou clothest thyself with scarlet, that thou deckest thee with ornaments of gold, that thou enlargest thine eyes with paint? In vain dost thou make thyself fair; thy lovers despise thee, they seek thy life* (iv. 30). And finally, his powers of graphic vividness are well displayed in the following: *I beheld the earth, and, lo, it was waste and void; and the heavens, and they had no light. I beheld the mountains, and, lo, they trembled, and all the hills moved to and fro. I beheld, and, lo, there was no man, and all the birds of the heavens were fled. I beheld, and, lo, the fruitful field was a wilderness, and all the cities thereof were broken down at the presence of the LORD, and before His fierce anger* (iv. 23ff.). Or again: *For death is come up into our windows, it is entered into our palaces, to cut off the children from the street, and the young men from the broad places* (ix. 20).

SYNOPSIS OF THE BOOK

Jeremiah's prophecies cover a period of about forty years. They are not arranged in chronological order but according to subject matter. The following is a synopsis of the Book:

I. i-xlv. Prophecies dealing with current history and events at home. These may be subdivided thus:

i-xx. Prophecies between Jeremiah's call (625) and the fourth year of Jehoiakim (604).

xxi-xxv. 14. Prophecies concerning the kings of Judah and the false prophets.

xxv. 15-38. A brief summary of the prophecies against the other nations which appear in xlvi-li.

xxvi-xxviii. Prophecies of the fall of Jerusalem, with several historical notices.

xxix. Letter to the captives in Babylon, deported in 597.

xxx-xxxi. Messages of comfort.

xxxii-xliv. History of the two years before the downfall of the Judean State.

xlv. A message to Baruch.

II. xlvi-li. Prophecies relating to foreign nations. These may be subdivided as follows:

xlvi, against Egypt; xlvii, against the Philistines; xlviii, against Moab; xlix, against Ammon (1-6), Edom (7-22), Damascus (23-27), Kedar and Hazor (28-33), and against Elam (34-39).

l and li, against Babylon.

III. lii. A supplementary and historical appendix relating the collapse of Judea and ending with a message of comfort intended as *athchalta di-geulah,* 'the beginning of the redemption,' conveyed by the fact that in the thirty-seventh year of his captivity, Jehoiachin was freed from prison and shown favour by the king of Babylon who *set his throne above the throne of the kings that were with him in Babylon* (verse 32).

JEREMIAH

1. THE words of Jeremiah the son of Hilkiah, of the priests that were in Anathoth in the land of Benjamin, 2. to whom the word of the LORD came in the days of Josiah the son of Amon, king of Judah, in the thirteenth year of his reign. 3. It came also in the days of Jehoiakim the son of Josiah, king of Judah, unto the end of the eleventh year of Zedekiah the son of Josiah, king of Judah, unto the carrying away of Jerusalem captive in the fifth month.

1 דִּבְרֵי יִרְמְיָהוּ בֶּן־חִלְקִיָּהוּ
מִן־הַכֹּהֲנִים אֲשֶׁר בַּעֲנָתוֹת
2 בְּאֶרֶץ בִּנְיָמִן׃ אֲשֶׁר הָיָה
דְבַר־יְהֹוָה אֵלָיו בִּימֵי
יֹאשִׁיָּהוּ בֶן־אָמוֹן מֶלֶךְ יְהוּדָה
בִּשְׁלֹשׁ־עֶשְׂרֵה שָׁנָה לְמָלְכוֹ׃
3 וַיְהִי בִּימֵי יְהוֹיָקִים בֶּן־
יֹאשִׁיָּהוּ מֶלֶךְ יְהוּדָה עַד־־
תֹּם עַשְׁתֵּי־עֶשְׂרֵה שָׁנָה
לְצִדְקִיָּהוּ בֶן־יֹאשִׁיָּהוּ מֶלֶךְ
יְהוּדָה עַד־גְּלוֹת יְרוּשָׁלַָם
בַּחֹדֶשׁ הַחֲמִישִׁי׃

v. 1. הפטרת ואלה שמות וגם הפטרת ראשי המטות

CHAPTER I

1–3 INTRODUCTION

1. *words.* The Hebrew *dibrë* may also mean 'matters, incidents, affairs.' Kimchi renders accordingly, and the opening phrase indicates both the *words,* i.e. prophecies of Jeremiah, and historical incidents in his life.

Jeremiah. Various explanations have been given of the name, such as 'the Lord hurls,' 'the Lord founds,' 'appointed of the Lord.' Perhaps it is a shortened form of *yarum yah,* 'the Lord is exalted.' The name is borne by several other persons in the Bible (cf. 2 Kings xxiii. 31; Neh. x. 3; 1 Chron. v. 24) (see Daath Mikra).

Hilkiah. There was a High Priest of that name (2 Kings xxii. 4), believed by many commentators to have been Jeremiah's father (Kimchi, Abarbanel, Ibn Nachmiash, Malbim).

of the priests that were in Anathoth. Special cities were set aside for residence by the Levites and priests (cf. Josh. xxi). Anathoth is the modern Anata, a small village lying on the highway from Jerusalem about three miles to the northeast (Daath Mikra).

2. *in the thirteenth year of his reign.* From this year until the end of the period mentioned in the next verse was forty years. Josiah ascended the throne in 637 B.C.E.; so Jeremiah's call occurred about 625. Josiah reigned another eighteen years, and was followed by Jehoahaz (three months), Jehoiakim (eleven years), Jehoiachin (three months), and Zedekiah (eleven years). Jehoahaz and Jehoiachin are omitted in verse 3, doubtless because their tenure of the throne was negligible (Abarbanel).

3. *in the fifth month.* Of the year 586 B.C.E. In that month Nebuzaradan burnt

4. And the word of the LORD came unto me, saying:

5 Before I formed thee in the belly I knew thee,
And before thou camest forth out of the womb I sanctified thee;
I have appointed thee a prophet unto the nations.

6. Then said I: 'Ah, Lord GOD! behold, I cannot speak; for I am a child.'

7. But the LORD said unto me:
Say not: I am a child;
For to whomsoever I shall send thee thou shalt go,
And whatsoever I shall command thee thou shalt speak.

8 Be not afraid of them;
For I am with thee to deliver thee,

4 וַיְהִ֥י דְבַר־יְהֹוָ֖ה אֵלַ֥י לֵאמֹֽר׃

5 בְּטֶ֨רֶם אֶצָּרְךָ֤ בַבֶּ֨טֶן֙ יְדַעְתִּ֔יךָ
וּבְטֶ֨רֶם
תֵּצֵ֤א מֵרֶ֨חֶם֙ הִקְדַּשְׁתִּ֔יךָ
נָבִ֥יא לַגּוֹיִ֖ם נְתַתִּֽיךָ׃

6 וָאֹמַ֗ר אֲהָהּ֙ אֲדֹנָ֣י יֱהֹוִ֔ה הִנֵּ֥ה
לֹא־יָדַ֖עְתִּי דַּבֵּ֑ר כִּי־נַ֖עַר
אָנֹֽכִי׃

7 וַיֹּ֤אמֶר יְהֹוָה֙ אֵלַ֔י
אַל־תֹּאמַ֖ר נַ֣עַר אָנֹ֑כִי
כִּ֤י עַל־כָּל־אֲשֶׁ֤ר אֶֽשְׁלָחֲךָ֙
תֵּלֵ֔ךְ
וְאֵ֛ת כָּל־אֲשֶׁ֥ר אֲצַוְּךָ֖ תְּדַבֵּֽר׃

8 אַל־תִּירָ֖א מִפְּנֵיהֶ֑ם
כִּֽי־אִתְּךָ֥ אֲנִ֖י לְהַצִּלֶ֖ךָ

v. 5. ו' יתירה

the Temple and the houses in Jerusalem (2 Kings xxv. 8f.).

4–10 GOD'S CALL TO JEREMIAH

5. *before I formed,* etc. [Jeremiah commences his prophetic labours with the consciousness of having been predestined for his mission. This consciousness must have sustained him and enabled him to triumph over the moods of despondency to which he was subject.]

I knew thee. I had regard to and chose thee as My messenger. For the use of the verb in this sense, cf. Nahum i. 7; Ps. i. 6 (Daath Mikra).

6. *behold, I cannot speak.* It is not his youth and lack of experience that make him hesitate, for Samuel too was young

when he commenced to prophesy. It was his feeling of insignificance and his subordination to an older sage and prophet whom he thought more worthy for this mission (Kimchi).

7. *to whomsoever I shall send thee,* etc. [God gives His servants the strength to carry out their appointed tasks.] The translation *to whomsoever* is not found in Jewish commentaries, most of which follow Targum, rendering:

wherever I shall send thee. The Hebrew preposition *al* having here, as elsewhere in the Bible, the force of *el*. Metsudath David, however, renders: 'on whatsoever errand.'

8. *I am with thee.* God is with His servants in the mission He entrusts to them (cf. Exod. iii. 12).

Saith the LORD.

ç. Then the LORD put forth His hand, and touched my mouth; and the LORD said unto me:

Behold, I have put My words in thy mouth;

10 See, I have this day set thee over the nations and over the kingdoms,

To root out and to pull down, And to destroy and to overthrow; To build, and to plant.

11. Moreover the word of the LORD came unto me, saying: 'Jeremiah, what seest thou?' And I said: 'I see a rod of an almond-tree.'

12. Then said the LORD unto me: 'Thou hast well seen; for I watch over My word to perform it.'

9 וַיִּשְׁלַח יְהֹוָה אֶת־יָדוֹ וַיַּגַּע עַל־פִּי וַיֹּאמֶר יְהֹוָה אֵלַי הִנֵּה נָתַתִּי דְבָרַי בְּפִיךָ:

נְאֻם־יְהֹוָה:

10 רְאֵה הִפְקַדְתִּיךָ ׀ הַיּוֹם הַזֶּה עַל־הַגּוֹיִם וְעַל־הַמַּמְלָכוֹת לִנְתוֹשׁ וְלִנְתוֹץ וּלְהַאֲבִיד וְלַהֲרוֹס לִבְנוֹת וְלִנְטוֹעַ:

11 וַיְהִי דְבַר־יְהֹוָה אֵלַי לֵאמֹר מָה־אַתָּה רֹאֶה יִרְמְיָהוּ וָאֹמַר

12 מַקֵּל שָׁקֵד אֲנִי רֹאֶה: וַיֹּאמֶר יְהֹוָה אֵלַי הֵיטַבְתָּ לִרְאוֹת כִּי־שֹׁקֵד אֲנִי עַל־דְּבָרִי

---

9. *Then the* LORD *... my mouth.* An anthropomorphism; the action symbolized that henceforth he would speak with the tongue (authority) of God, the Divine holiness having been communicated to him by the contact (Alshich).

10. *to root out . . . and to plant.* Not that the prophet would himself have the power to do this, but it would be his mission to announce what God was about to do. The ultimate purpose of his prophecy would be *to build, and to plant*; but, as so often happens, much would have to be destroyed before reconstruction could commence (Alshich, Malbim).

11–12 VISION OF THE ALMOND-TREE

Following soon on his call, Jeremiah beholds two visions which create within him an awareness that momentous events affecting the Kingdom of Judah are imminent.

11. *'I see a rod of an almond-tree.'* He saw a bare branch of an almond-tree with neither leaf nor blossom, which he recognized through prophecy as a branch of an almond-tree (Kimchi).

12. *for I watch,* etc. The message of the vision is conveyed through the resemblance of the Hebrew for *almond-tree* (shakëd) and the verb meaning *watch* (or 'wakeful') (shokëd). Two thoughts are suggested: first, the almond-tree is the first to blossom; so will God *hasten* to perform His words (Rashi, Kimchi). Second, that God will watch over His word to fulfill it, that it should not be neglected or put off for the distant future (Daath Mikra).

The Midrash (Ecc. Rabbah 12:8) tells us that the almond-tree takes twenty-one days from the time it blossoms until

13. And the word of the LORD came unto me the second time, saying: 'What seest thou?' And I said: 'I see a seething pot; and the face thereof is from the north.' 14. Then the LORD said unto me: 'Out of the north the evil shall break forth upon all the inhabitants of the land. 15. For, lo, I will call all the families of the kingdoms of the north, saith the LORD; and they shall come, and they shall set every one his throne at the entrance of the gates of Jerusalem, and against all the walls thereof round about, and against all the cities of Judah. 16. And I will utter my judgments against them touching all their wickedness; in that they

13 לַעֲשֹׂתְוֹ : וַיְהִי דְבַר־יְהֹוָה |
אֵלַי שֵׁנִית לֵאמֹר מָה אַתָּה
רֹאֶה וָאֹמַר סִיר נָפוּחַ אֲנִי
רֹאֶה וּפָנָיו מִפְּנֵי צָפוֹנָה :
14 וַיֹּאמֶר יְהֹוָה אֵלָי מִצָּפוֹן
תִּפָּתַח הָרָעָה עַל כָּל־יֹשְׁבֵי
15 הָאָרֶץ : כִּי | הִנְנִי קֹרֵא לְכָל־
מִשְׁפְּחוֹת מַמְלְכוֹת צָפוֹנָה
נְאֻם־יְהֹוָה וּבָאוּ וְנָתְנוּ אִישׁ
כִּסְאוֹ פֶּתַח | שַׁעֲרֵי יְרוּשָׁלַם
וְעַל כָּל־חוֹמֹתֶיהָ סָבִיב וְעַל
16 כָּל־עָרֵי יְהוּדָה : וְדִבַּרְתִּי
מִשְׁפָּטַי אוֹתָם עַל כָּל־רָעָתָם

---

the almonds become completely ripe. This was symbolic of the twenty-one days from the seventeenth of Tammuz, when the city was broken into, until the ninth of Ab, when the Temple was destroyed (Rashi).

13–16 VISION OF THE BOILING CALDRON

13. *seething.* lit. 'blown.' This follows Rashi. Kimchi explains that this is a seething caldron from which steam ascends, resembling one who blows, emitting vapor from his mouth. Abarbanel interprets it as a pot under which the embers are fanned into flame.

from the north. The direction from which danger threatens Judah (Rashi).

14. *the evil.* [In the sense of calamity; here it denotes the invasion of the land.]

15. A similar prophecy of the gathering of the nations against Judah is contained in Isa. xvii. 12ff.

they shall set every one his throne. The prophet does not think of the siege of Jerusalem, but of the sequel when the city has been captured. The victorious chieftains will proceed to sit in formal judgment (for this use of *throne,* cf. Ps. ix. 5, cxxii. 5) upon the inhabitants, *at the entrance of the gates* where trials were held, to determine what was to be done to the defeated population and their towns. See below xxxix. 3 (Kimchi).

16. *I will utter my judgments.* The initial letter of *my* should be printed with a capital, the reference being to God Whose agents the conquerors are and Whose verdict they will execute (Malbim).

all their wickedness. Specified in the second half of the verse: desertion of the Lord is one sin. The second sin is sacrificing to false gods no matter how burdensome their worship. This sin was aggravated by the fact that they received

have forsaken Me, and have offered unto other gods, and worshipped the work of their own hands. 17. Thou therefore gird up thy loins, and arise, and speak unto them all that I command thee; be not dismayed at them, lest I dismay thee before them. 18. For, behold, I have made thee this day a fortified city, and an iron pillar, and brazen walls, against the whole land, against the kings of Judah, against the princes thereof, against the priests thereof, and against the people of the land. 19. And they shall fight against thee; but they shall not prevail against thee; For I am with thee, saith the LORD, to deliver thee.'

אֲשֶׁר עֲזָבוּנִי וַיְקַטְּרוּ לֵאלֹהִים
אֲחֵרִים וַיִּשְׁתַּחֲווּ לְמַעֲשֵׂי
17 יְדֵיהֶם: וְאַתָּה תֶּאְזֹר מָתְנֶיךָ
וְקַמְתָּ וְדִבַּרְתָּ אֲלֵיהֶם אֵת
כָּל־אֲשֶׁר אָנֹכִי אֲצַוֶּךָּ
אַל־תֵּחַת מִפְּנֵיהֶם פֶּן־
18 אֲחִתְּךָ לִפְנֵיהֶם: וַאֲנִי הִנֵּה
נְתַתִּיךָ הַיּוֹם לְעִיר מִבְצָר
וּלְעַמּוּד בַּרְזֶל וּלְחֹמוֹת נְחֹשֶׁת
עַל־כָּל־הָאָרֶץ לְמַלְכֵי
יְהוּדָה לְשָׂרֶיהָ לְכֹהֲנֶיהָ וּלְעַם
19 הָאָרֶץ: וְנִלְחֲמוּ אֵלֶיךָ וְלֹא־
יוּכְלוּ לָךְ כִּי־אִתְּךָ אֲנִי
נְאֻם־יְהוָה לְהַצִּילֶךָ:

no benefit therefrom since they worshipped the work of their own hands (Malbim). During Manasseh's reign, idolatry became more rampant than ever. The priests made images which they claimed were endowed with heavenly powers. The prophet ridicules them, telling them that they are merely the work of their hands, possessing no divine powers (Daath Soferim).

17–19 MESSAGE OF ENCOURAGEMENT TO JEREMIAH

17. *gird up your loins.* This is an expression of quickening like a man of valor (Rashi). We find that Elijah girded his loins in order to run swiftly before Ahab's chariot, in 1 Kings xviii. 46 (Kimchi). Since you are aware of the impending doom, gird your loins despite your youth and commence quickly to deliver My message to the people (Abarbanel).

18. Jeremiah would, indeed, have to plough a lonely furrow, with all sections of the nation against him. For that reason God assures him of the strength wherewith He will fortify him.

the kings of Judah. The plural, *kings,* signified that his career would extend through several reigns (Daath Soferim).

the princes. [i.e. officers of the State.]

the priests. Even from them he would meet with opposition (Malbim, Alshich).

19. *they shall not prevail against thee.* The meaning is, not finally prevail; he would suffer many setbacks, but they would be only temporary (Kimchi, xv. 20).

2   CHAPTER II   ב

1. And the word of the LORD came to me, saying: 2. Go, and cry in the ears of Jerusalem, saying: Thus saith the LORD:

> I remember for thee the affection of thy youth,
> The love of thine espousals;
> How thou wentest after Me in the wilderness,
> In a land that was not sown.

3 Israel is the LORD's hallowed portion,

> His first-fruits of the increase;

1 וַיְהִי דְבַר־יְהֹוָה אֵלַי לֵאמֹר׃
2 הָלֹךְ וְקָרָאתָ בְאָזְנֵי יְרוּשָׁלַ͏ִם
לֵאמֹר כֹּה אָמַר יְהֹוָה
זָכַרְתִּי לָךְ חֶסֶד נְעוּרַיִךְ
אַהֲבַת כְּלוּלֹתָיִךְ
לֶכְתֵּךְ אַחֲרַי בַּמִּדְבָּר
בְּאֶרֶץ לֹא זְרוּעָה׃
3 קֹדֶשׁ יִשְׂרָאֵל לַיהֹוָה
רֵאשִׁית תְּבוּאָתֹה

CHAPTER II

1–3   GOD REMEMBERS ISRAEL'S LOVE FOR HIM IN THE PAST

1. *the word of the* LORD *came to me.* This first prophecy of Jeremiah extends to the end of chapter vi. Its main theme is the implicit confidence which the people of Israel displayed in God during the early stage of the national existence and its contrast with the present state of backsliding.

2. *for thee.* i.e. in thy favour (Daath Mikra).

the love of thine espousals. By his trust in departing from Egypt, a land of comparative plenty (cf. Num. xi. 5), into the wilderness *(a land that was not sown),* Israel sealed his ties of close kinship with God. With beautiful and tender imagery that act of trust is described as Israel's *espousals,* comparable with a bride following her husband to a strange country. The loving confidence in God shown by the nation in its youth is remembered by God in its favour and leads to His promise in verse 3. It is unlikely that Jeremiah had forgotten, or desired to gloss over, the many instances of lack of faith in the wilderness when the Israelites murmured against God. But these could not efface their praiseworthy trust in embarking upon such a venture, even though the hardships of the desert subsequently dimmed their glowing faith (Daath Soferim).

3. *the* LORD's *hallowed portion.* In a special sense Israel is dedicated to God, just as the first-fruits belonged to the priests as His representatives. The people are therefore under His direct protection, and woe to them who seek to destroy them (Abarbanel). Though it is the prophet's thesis that these nations are carrying out God's designs, he knew that they are not actuated by any high or noble motive. For them it was simply a matter of aggression and lust for conquest, for which they would be punished (Ramban, Genesis xv. 14).

His first-fruits of the increase. As the first-fruits of a field are sacred, so is Israel, the 'first-fruits of humanity' (Philo), sacred to God. The mention of *first-fruits* implies that He expects a later harvest, i.e. while Israel is the first people whom He chose, God looks to the ingathering of all other peoples too,

All that devour him shall be held
guilty,

Evil shall come upon them,

Saith the LORD.

4 Hear ye the word of the LORD, O
house of Jacob,

And all the families of the house of
Israel;

5 Thus saith the LORD:

What unrighteousness have your
fathers found in Me,

That they are gone far from Me,

And have walked after things of
nought, and are become nought?

כָּל־אֹכְלָיו יֶאְשָׁמוּ

רָעָה תָּבֹא אֲלֵיהֶם

נְאֻם־יְהֹוָה׃

4 שִׁמְעוּ דְבַר־יְהֹוָה בֵּית

יַעֲקֹב

וְכָל־מִשְׁפְּחוֹת בֵּית יִשְׂרָאֵל׃

5 כֹּה | אָמַר יְהֹוָה

מַה־מָּצְאוּ אֲבוֹתֵיכֶם בִּי עָוֶל

כִּי רָחֲקוּ מֵעָלָי

וַיֵּלְכוּ אַחֲרֵי הַהֶבֶל וַיֶּהְבָּלוּ׃

v. 3. קמץ בז״ק   v. 3. ע״כ   v. 4. הפטרת מסעי

who in the fulness of time would come
to acknowledge Him (Hirsch).

evil shall come upon them. The assurance
given to the patriarchs (Gen. xii. 3,
xxvii. 29) held good also of their
descendants. 'Still the above promise,
declared thousands of years ago, has
always held good: — all those that
believed that they could "devour" Israel
will present to the retrospective historical eye the view of having been
guilty...; with the fate that they had
intended for Israel they had sealed their
own downfall' (Hirsch).

4-13   JUDAH'S UNGRATEFUL FOLLY

4. *Israel.* Only the Kingdom of Judah
was left, that of Israel having come to an
end more than a century earlier (in 722
B.C.E.). But Jeremiah regards Judah as
representative of the whole nation.
Moreover, he may intentionally have
addressed himself also to the exiles of
the Northern Kingdom, as well as to

some Israelite families who may have
been left in Samaria (Daath Mikra).

5. *what unrighteousness,* etc. [As often in
the Bible, the question expresses an
emphatic negative: no unjust act on
God's part can account for the nation's
infidelity.]

things of nought. [A strong and forth-
right characterization of idolatry: with
all its pomp and pageantry it is mere
nothingness, utterly futile and empty.]

and are become nought. The worship of
such futility inevitably renders the
worshippers like itself, emptying them
of all spiritual content (cf. Ps. cxv. 8)
(Ibn Nachmiash, Hirsch).

6f. Only by deliberately and ungrate-
fully shutting out from their minds
God's manifold favours, His deliverance of them from Egypt and His loving
protection in the wilderness, could they
have grown so unfaithful to Him
(Kimchi).

6 Neither said they:
   'Where is the LORD that brought
      us up
   Out of the land of Egypt;
   That led us through the wilder-
      ness,
   Through a land of deserts and of
      pits,
   Through a land of drought and of
      the shadow of death,
   Through a land that no man passed
      through,
   And where no man dwelt?'

7 And I brought you into a land of
   fruitful fields,
   To eat the fruit thereof and the
      good thereof;
   But when ye entered, ye defiled
      My land,
   And made My heritage an abomi-
      nation.

8 The priests said not: 'Where is the
      LORD?'
   And they that handle the law knew
      Me not,

6 וְלֹא אָמְרוּ
אַיֵּה יְהוָה הַמַּעֲלֶה אֹתָנוּ
מֵאֶרֶץ מִצְרָיִם
הַמּוֹלִיךְ אֹתָנוּ בַּמִּדְבָּר
בְּאֶרֶץ עֲרָבָה וְשׁוּחָה
בְּאֶרֶץ צִיָּה וְצַלְמָוֶת
בְּאֶרֶץ לֹא־עָבַר בָּהּ אִישׁ
וְלֹא־יָשַׁב אָדָם שָׁם:

7 וָאָבִיא אֶתְכֶם
אֶל־אֶרֶץ הַכַּרְמֶל
לֶאֱכֹל פִּרְיָהּ וְטוּבָהּ
וַתָּבֹאוּ וַתְּטַמְּאוּ אֶת־אַרְצִי
וְנַחֲלָתִי שַׂמְתֶּם לְתוֹעֵבָה:

8 הַכֹּהֲנִים לֹא אָמְרוּ אַיֵּה יְהוָה
וְתֹפְשֵׂי הַתּוֹרָה לֹא יְדָעוּנִי

---

6. *pits.* Holes in the treacherous sands which may cause serious accidents (Daath Mikra).

the shadow of death. The Hebrew word used in Ps. xxiii. 4. Its meaning is 'deep darkness' (so Rashi, Menachem, and Dunash). Ibn Ganah and Kimchi render as in our translation.

7. *a land of fruitful fields.* lit. 'a land of the Carmel.' The entire land is compared to the fertile Mount Carmel (Ibn Nachmiash).

ye defiled. 'By idol-worship' (Metsudath David).

My land . . . My heritage. The land chosen by God for His particular purpose (Kimchi) and therefore a consecrated land.

an abomination. [By pagan rites performed in it, the Holy Land is become loathsome in the sight of God.]

8. Jeremiah's indictment of the national leaders (whom he evidently holds responsible for the people's apostasy) is very comprehensive, and embraces both the spiritual and temporal rulers.

the priests. Whose duty is to teach the ways of God (cf. Mal. ii. 7) (Metsudath David).

they that handle the law. The religious officials who administer and interpret the Torah; i.e., the Sanhedrin (Metsudath David).

knew Me not. Men studied the Torah without the desire really to know and imitate the ways of God (Kimchi).

And the rulers transgressed against
Me;
The prophets also prophesied by
Baal,
And walked after things that do
not profit.
9 Wherefore I will yet plead with
you, saith the LORD,
And with your children's children
will I plead.
10 For pass over to the isles of the
Kittites, and see,
And send unto Kedar, and consider diligently,
And see if there hath been such
a thing.
11 Hath a nation changed its gods,
Which yet are no gods?
But My people hath changed its
glory
For that which doth not profit.
12 Be astonished, O ye heavens, at
this,

וְהָרֹעִים פָּשְׁעוּ בִי
וְהַנְּבִיאִים נִבְּאוּ בַבַּעַל
וְאַחֲרֵי לֹא־יוֹעִלוּ הָלָכוּ:
9 לָכֵן עֹד
אָרִיב אִתְּכֶם נְאֻם־יְהֹוָה
וְאֶת־בְּנֵי בְנֵיכֶם אָרִיב:
10 כִּי עִבְרוּ אִיֵּי כִתִּיִּים וּרְאוּ
וְקֵדָר שִׁלְחוּ וְהִתְבּוֹנְנוּ מְאֹד
וּרְאוּ הֵן הָיְתָה כָּזֹאת:
11 הַהֵימִיר גּוֹי אֱלֹהִים
וְהֵמָּה לֹא אֱלֹהִים
וְעַמִּי הֵמִיר כְּבוֹדוֹ
בְּלוֹא יוֹעִיל:
12 שֹׁמּוּ שָׁמַיִם עַל־זֹאת

---

the rulers. lit. 'the shepherds,' i.e. the
Kings (Rashi, Targum).

the prophets. i.e. the false prophets
(Kimchi).

prophesied by Baal. i.e. in the name of
Baal (Rashi, Targum).

things that do not profit. The idols
(Metsudath David). Abarbanel explains
that in this manner, with all their deeds
they followed things that do not profit.

9. *plead.* [i.e. contend. The Hebrew
verb *rib* always means 'to plead' in a
legal sense, i.e. contend, and never 'to
beseech' or 'make intercession.']

10. *isles of the Kittites.* Cyprus and the
neighbouring islands, including also the
coastlands of Italy and Greece. In Gen.
x. 4 *Kittim* is reckoned among the sons
of Javan (Greece).

Kedar. A son of Ishmael (Gen. xxv.

13), here denoting Arabia in general.
The sense is: Go wherever you will, east
or west, and you will find no parallel to
your conduct (Abarbanel).

11. *a nation.* i.e. a heathen nation
(Targum).

which yet are no gods. A reason why
these should have been changed
(Metsudath David).

its glory. The Almighty, Who is Israel's
glory (Rashi). Cf. *Thus they exchanged their
glory for the likeness of an ox that eateth grass*
(Ps. cvi. 20). Abarbanel explains the
verse in a slightly different manner: If a
nation exchanged its gods, it is because
they are no gods, but My people hath
changed its glory for that which does
not profit.

12. As Nature is summoned to attest
the prophetic admonition and Divine
arraignment of Israel (cf. Deut. xxxii. 1;

And be horribly afraid, be ye exceeding amazed,

Saith the LORD.

13 For My people have committed
two evils:

They have forsaken Me, the
fountain of living waters,

And hewed them out cisterns,
broken cisterns,

That can hold no water.

14 Is Israel a servant?

Is he a home-born slave?

Why is he become a prey?

15 The young lions have roared
upon him,

And let their voice resound;

And they have made his land
desolate,

וְשָׂעֲרוּ חָרְבוּ מְאֹד

נְאֻם־יְהֹוָה׃

13 כִּי־שְׁתַּיִם רָעוֹת עָשָׂה עַמִּי

אֹתִי עָזְבוּ מְקוֹר ׀ מַיִם חַיִּים

לַחְצֹב לָהֶם בֹּארוֹת

בֹּארֹת נִשְׁבָּרִים

אֲשֶׁר לֹא־יָכִלוּ הַמָּיִם׃

14 הַעֶבֶד יִשְׂרָאֵל

אִם־יְלִיד בַּיִת הוּא

מַדּוּעַ הָיָה לָבַז׃

15 עָלָיו יִשְׁאֲגוּ כְפִרִים

נָתְנוּ קוֹלָם

וַיָּשִׁיתוּ אַרְצוֹ לְשַׁמָּה

פתח בס״פ v. 14.

Isa. i. 2), so is she bidden to show her
horror at the people's faithlessness (see
Hirsch).

be ye exceedingly amazed. lit. 'be exceedingly dried up'; the heavens should lose
their moisture in horror of such perfidy
(Kimchi, Targum). Others render: See
that there will be desolation, storm, and
destruction because of this abomination
(Metsudath David).

13. *two evils.* i.e. a twofold evil,
counted as two (Metsudath David). Had
they forsaken their God for one His
equal, it would have been one evil. Now
that they have forsaken Me, the
fountain of living waters, to follow
idols, which are like cisterns of stored-
up water, and cracked as well, these are
two evils (Rashi).

the fountain of living waters. God is

compared to a spring of living waters in
two respects: He is the source of goodness just as the spring is the source of
the water. It does not originate from
any other source. Also, God's goodness
is unceasing, just as the spring water
does not cease to flow (Kimchi).

14–30 THE FAITHLESSNESS OF ISRAEL

14. *is Israel a servant?* The prophet is
thinking more particularly of the
Northern Kingdom which had been
devastated and the population taken as
captives to Assyria, and asks, 'Is their
servile condition natural to the people?'
The answer expected is negative; a different explanation accounts for their
lowly state (Abarbanel).

15. *the young lions.* Israel's enemies,
the Assyrians; for the imagery, cf. Isa.
v. 29.

10

His cities are laid waste,
Without inhabitant.

16 The children also of Noph and
Tahpanhes
Feed upon the crown of thy head.

17 Is it not this that doth cause it
unto thee,
That thou hast forsaken the Lord
thy God,
When He led thee by the way?

18 And now what hast thou to do in
the way to Egypt,
To drink the waters of Shihor?
Or what hast thou to do in the
way to Assyria,
To drink the waters of the River?

19 Thine own wickedness shall correct thee,

עָרָיו נִצְּתָה
מִבְּלִי יֹשֵׁב׃
16 גַּם־בְּנֵי־נֹף וְתַחְפְּנֵס
יִרְעוּךְ קָדְקֹד׃
17 הֲלוֹא־זֹאת תַּעֲשֶׂה־לָּךְ
עָזְבֵךְ אֶת־יְהוָה אֱלֹהַיִךְ
בְּעֵת מוֹלִכֵךְ בַּדָּרֶךְ׃
18 וְעַתָּה מַה־לָּךְ לְדֶרֶךְ מִצְרַיִם
לִשְׁתּוֹת מֵי שִׁחוֹר
וּמַה־לָּךְ לְדֶרֶךְ אַשּׁוּר
לִשְׁתּוֹת מֵי נָהָר׃
19 תְּיַסְּרֵךְ רָעָתֵךְ

v. 15. נצתו ק׳   v. 16. ותחפנחס ק׳

are laid waste. The verb may mean 'are
burnt' (so Rashi, Kimchi).

16. *Noph.* Memphis, near modern
Cairo; further alluded to in xliv. 1, xlvi.
14, 19 (Targum, Daath Mikra).

feed upon the crown of thy head. Even
Egypt, upon whom Israel relied for
help, was merely exploiting them for
her own benefit, and would not scruple
to rob them, when it suited her con-
venience (as happened in the reign of
Jehoiakim, 2 Kings xxiii. 35). The figure
seems to be of cattle grazing in a field.
This follows Ibn Kaspi.

17. *thou hast forsaken the Lord.* This
answers the question in verse 14
(Metsudath David).

when He led thee by the way. Either in the
way of the wilderness (so Kara), or in the
way of goodness and virtue (Rashi,
Kimchi).

18. *what hast thou to do. . .?* Why
should you go to Egypt and to Assyria
to seek aid? If you follow the straight
path, you will not have to travel to
distant places as if you wished to drink
the waters of the Shihor or the waters of
the river of the king of Assyria.
Jonathan renders: And now, why
should you befriend Pharaoh the king
of Egypt to cast your male children into
the river, and why should you enter into
a treaty with the Assyrians to exile you
to places past the Euphrates? (Kimchi).
Kara explains: Why should you go
down to Egypt for aid, to the country
where you suffered during your
sojournings there, and why should you
go to Assyria for aid, as Ahaz entered
into a treaty with Assyria so that they
assist him against Aram in 2 Kings
xvii. 7.

the River. The Euphrates, on which
Babylon was situated. It symbolizes the

And thy backslidings shall re-
prove thee:
Know therefore and see that it is
an evil and a bitter thing,
That thou hast forsaken the LORD
thy God,
Neither is My fear in thee,
Saith the Lord GOD of hosts.
20 For of old time I have broken
thy yoke,
And burst thy bands,
And thou saidst: 'I will not trans-
gress';
Upon every high hill
And under every leafy tree
Thou didst recline, playing the
harlot.
21 Yet I had planted thee a noble
vine,
Wholly a right seed;
How then art thou turned into
the degenerate plant
Of a strange vine unto Me?

וּמְשֻׁבוֹתַ֫יִךְ֙ תּוֹכִחֻ֔ךְ

וּדְעִ֣י וּרְאִ֗י כִּי־רַ֤ע וָמָר֙

עָזְבֵ֖ךְ אֶת־יְהֹוָ֣ה אֱלֹהָ֑יִךְ

וְלֹ֥א פַחְדָּתִ֖י אֵלַ֑יִךְ

נְאֻם־אֲדֹנָ֥י יֱהֹוִ֖ה צְבָאֽוֹת:

20 כִּ֤י מֵעוֹלָם֙ שָׁבַ֣רְתִּי עֻלֵּ֔ךְ

נִתַּ֖קְתִּי מוֹסְרוֹתַ֑יִךְ

וַתֹּאמְרִ֖י לֹ֣א אֶעֱב֑וֹד

כִּ֤י עַל־כָּל־גִּבְעָ֣ה גְּבֹהָ֔ה

וְתַ֖חַת כָּל־עֵ֣ץ רַעֲנָ֑ן

אַ֖תְּ צֹעָ֥ה זֹנָֽה:

21 וְאָֽנֹכִי֙ נְטַעְתִּ֣יךְ שֹׂרֵ֔ק

כֻּלֹּ֖ה זֶ֣רַע אֱמֶ֑ת

וְאֵיךְ֙ נֶהְפַּ֣כְתְּ לִ֔י

סוּרֵ֖י הַגֶּ֥פֶן נָכְרִיָּֽה:

v. 19.　קמץ בז״ק v. 20.　אעבור ק׳

aid they sought from Assyria (Metsudath David).

19. *wickedness . . . backslidings.* The bitter results of these acts will show them
the folly of their ways (Malbim).

My fear. i.e. fear of Me.

20. *I have broken . . . not transgress.* If
this rendering is correct, the meaning is
that God had delivered Israel on
various occasions in the past, and after
each of them Israel had promised no
more to transgress His word (Rashi,
Kimchi). R.V. margin reads 'thou hast

broken . . . I will not serve' *(shabarti* and
nittakti are then the archaic forms of the
second person feminine and not the
usual first person singular, whilst the
kethib, eëbod, is retained). This is preferred by modern commentators as
being more in keeping with the general
tenor of the context (Daath Mikra).

high hill. The location of idolatrous
worship (Daath Mikra).

under every leafy tree. In whose shade
lewd rites were practised (Daath Mikra).

21. *a noble vine, wholly a right seed.*

12

22 For though thou wash thee with
 nitre,
 And take thee much soap,
 Yet thine iniquity is marked be-
  fore Me,
 Saith the Lord GOD.

23 How canst thou say: 'I am not
 defiled,
 I have not gone after the Baalim'?
 See thy way in the Valley,
 Know what thou hast done;
 Thou art a swift young camel
 traversing her ways;

24 A wild ass used to the wilderness,
 That snuffeth up the wind in her
  desire;
 Her lust, who can hinder it?
 All they that seek her will not
 weary themselves;
 In her month they shall find her.

25 Withhold thy foot from being
 unshod,
 And thy throat from thirst;

22 כִּי אִם־תְּכַבְּסִי בַּנֶּתֶר
וְתַרְבִּי־לָךְ בֹּרִית
נִכְתָּם עֲוֹנֵךְ לְפָנַי
נְאֻם אֲדֹנָי יֱהֹוִה:

23 אֵיךְ תֹּאמְרִי לֹא נִטְמֵאתִי
אַחֲרֵי הַבְּעָלִים לֹא הָלַכְתִּי
רְאִי דַרְכֵּךְ בַּגַּיְא
דְּעִי מֶה עָשִׂית
בִּכְרָה קַלָּה מְשָׂרֶכֶת דְּרָכֶיהָ:

24 פֶּרֶא ׀ לִמֻּד מִדְבָּר
בְּאַוַּת נַפְשׁוֹ שָׁאֲפָה רוּחַ
תַּאֲנָתָהּ מִי יְשִׁיבֶנָּה
כָּל־מְבַקְשֶׁיהָ לֹא יִיעָפוּ
בְּחָדְשָׁהּ יִמְצָאוּנְהָ:

25 מִנְעִי רַגְלֵךְ מִיָּחֵף
וּגְרוֹנֵךְ מִצִּמְאָה

v. 24. וגרונך ק׳   v. 25. נפשה ק׳

Israel was descended from Abraham;
from such seed good fruit might assuredly have been expected; cf. Isa. v.
1–7 (Kimchi).

unto Me. [To My sorrow.]

22. Even though you perform righteousness outwardly, this does not conceal from Me your secret iniquity
(Metsudath David).

23. *I have not gone . . . Valley.* Probably
in self-defence the Israelites maintained
that the rites they observed were performed in the service of God, not of the
false gods, Baalim. To this the prophet
retorts that by their horrible nature
these rites, which included human sacrifice in the Valley of Hinnom (cf. vii. 31),

could be ascribed to nought else than
the cult of Baalim (Daath Mikra).

traversing her ways. lit. 'entangling her
ways': running hither and thither,
crossing and recrossing her own path,
driven by lust. So Israel eagerly sought
one god after another (Kimchi).

24. *a wild ass.* Cf. the description of
this animal in Job xxxix. 5–8, distinguished by refusal to be restrained.

will not weary . . . find her. In the month
of mating, her sires need not weary
themselves in seeking her; on the
contrary, she eagerly seeks them out.
Similarly Israel turns eagerly to idolatry
(Daath Mikra).

25. *withhold . . . thirst.* Do not become

But thou saidst: 'There is no hope;
No, for I have loved strangers,
and after them will I go.'

26 As the thief is ashamed when he
is found,
So is the house of Israel ashamed;
They, their kings, their princes,
And their priests, and their pro-
phets;

27 Who say to a stock: 'Thou art my
father,'
And to a stone: 'Thou hast
brought us forth,'
For they have turned their back
unto Me, and not their face;
But in the time of their trouble
they will say:
'Arise, and save us.'

28 But where are thy gods that thou
hast made thee?

וַתֹּאמְרִי נוֹאָשׁ
לוֹא כִּי־אָהַבְתִּי זָרִים
וְאַחֲרֵיהֶם אֵלֵךְ׃
26 כְּבֹשֶׁת גַּנָּב כִּי יִמָּצֵא
כֵּן הֹבִישׁוּ בֵּית יִשְׂרָאֵל
הֵמָּה מַלְכֵיהֶם שָׂרֵיהֶם
וְכֹהֲנֵיהֶם וּנְבִיאֵיהֶם׃
27 אֹמְרִים לָעֵץ אָבִי אַתָּה
וְלָאֶבֶן אַתְּ יְלִדְתָּנוּ
כִּי־פָנוּ אֵלַי עֹרֶף וְלֹא פָנִים
וּבְעֵת רָעָתָם יֹאמְרוּ
קוּמָה וְהוֹשִׁיעֵנוּ׃
28 וְאַיֵּה אֱלֹהֶיךָ אֲשֶׁר עָשִׂיתָ לָּךְ

v. 27. ילדתנו ק׳

---

barefooted and parched, do not spend
yourselves on journeys to other lands
seeking aid (Kimchi). Rashi and Metsudath David explain: Do not persist in
your idolatry, for which you will ultimately be punished by going into
captivity unshod and parched.

there is no hope. Israel retorts that it is
vain to try to turn him away from his
chosen paths. He is determined to
follow after strange gods (Metsudath
David).

26. *as the thief is ashamed when he is
found.* The Targum and Kimchi render: 'as one is ashamed when he is
found out as a thief, after having posed
as an honest man.' Malbim explains
that the thief is not ashamed of his
crime of stealing. He is ashamed of his
being found out in public. i.e. his
shame is not due to the theft, but to the
incident that befell him because of the

theft. He does, therefore, not regret his
sins.

so is the house of Israel ashamed. Shame
and confusion will cover them when
they ultimately realize the folly of their
ways. Kimchi renders: 'so should Israel
have been ashamed of his evil ways.'
Following Malbim's explanation: the
house of Israel suffers shame because of
the misfortunes that befell them because
of their sins.

they. The masses (Hirsch).

their kings, etc. See on i. 18.

27. *stock . . . stone.* From which their
idols are fashioned (Kimchi).

thou art my father. Standing in relation
to its devotee as guardian and protector
(Daath Mikra). Malbim explains that,
whereas in earlier generations, the
people had worshipped idols as

14

Let them arise, if they can save
    thee in the time of thy trouble;
For according to the number of
    thy cities
Are thy gods, O Judah.
29 Wherefore will ye contend with
    Me?
Ye all have transgressed against
    Me,
Saith the LORD.
30 In vain have I smitten your chil-
    dren—
They received no correction;
Your sword hath devoured your
    prophets,
Like a destroying lion.
31 O generation, see ye the word of
    the LORD:
Have I been a wilderness unto
    Israel?

יָק֧וּמוּ אִם־יוֹשִׁיע֖וּךָ
בְּעֵ֣ת רָעָתֶ֑ךָ
כִּ֚י מִסְפַּ֣ר עָרֶ֔יךָ
הָי֥וּ אֱלֹהֶ֖יךָ יְהוּדָֽה׃
29 לָ֥מָּה תָרִ֖יבוּ אֵלָ֑י
כֻּלְּכֶ֛ם פְּשַׁעְתֶּ֥ם בִּ֖י
נְאֻם־יְהוָֽה׃
30 לַשָּׁוְא֙ הִכֵּ֣יתִי אֶת־בְּנֵיכֶ֔ם
מוּסָ֖ר לֹ֣א לָקָ֑חוּ
אָכְלָ֧ה חַרְבְּכֶ֛ם
נְבִיאֵיכֶ֖ם כְּאַרְיֵ֥ה מַשְׁחִֽית׃
31 הַדּ֗וֹר אַתֶּם֙ רְא֣וּ דְבַר־יְהוָ֔ה
הֲמִדְבָּ֤ר הָיִ֙יתִי֙ לְיִשְׂרָאֵ֔ל

intermediaries between them and God
and believed that they had the power to
bring God's bounty upon them, in
Jeremiah's time, they sunk to the state
of believing that the idols had actually
created them, and they worshipped
them for their own powers.

28. according to the number, etc. The
Midrash depicts the origin of these idols
representing each city. At first, they
placed images in the fields. When no
one protested, they put them at the
beginning of the roads. When this was
allowed to remain, they put idols in the
cities. Daath Soferim explains that this
was not originally meant as idolatry, but
it was a vestige of the Canaanite culture
which the Jews had adopted, believing
that these images would bring them
luck. Since they were allowed to remain,
they were gradually placed in more and
more prominent places, only to be
eventually regarded as deities.

29. contend. Why do you expostulate
and complain that I desert you in your
crisis, seeing that you rebel against Me?
(Kimchi).

30. in vain . . . correction. God's punishment has been of no avail; they
refused to be instructed.

your prophets. The true messengers of
God to be distinguished from the false
prophets mentioned in verse 26. Rashi
and Metsudath David comment: This
alludes to Zechariah the son of Jehoiada
(cf. 2 Chron. xxiv. 20f.) and Isaiah (who,
according to tradition, suffered a
martyr's death in the reign of Manasseh).

**31–37 THREATENED PUNISHMENT OF
ISRAEL**

31. see ye the word of the LORD. Take
note of it; pay heed to it (Targum).

have I been a wilderness unto Israel? Have

Or a land of thick darkness?
Wherefore say My people: 'We
  roam at large;
We will come no more unto
  Thee'?

32 Can a maid forget her ornaments,
  Or a bride her attire?
Yet My people have forgotten
  Me
Days without number.

33 How trimmest thou thy way
  To seek love!
Therefore—even the wicked
  women
Hast thou taught thy ways;

34 Also in thy skirts is found the
  blood
Of the souls of the innocent poor;
Thou didst not find them break-
  ing in;
Yet for all these things

אִם־אֶרֶץ מַאְפֵּלְיָה
מַדּוּעַ אָמְרוּ עַמִּי רַדְנוּ
לוֹא־נָבוֹא עוֹד אֵלֶיךָ:
32 הֲתִשְׁכַּח בְּתוּלָה עֶדְיָהּ
כַּלָּה קִשֻּׁרֶיהָ
וְעַמִּי שְׁכֵחוּנִי
יָמִים אֵין מִסְפָּר:
33 מַה־תֵּיטִבִי דַרְכֵּךְ
לְבַקֵּשׁ אַהֲבָה
לָכֵן גַּם אֶת־הָרָעוֹת
לִמַּדְתִּי אֶת־דְּרָכָיִךְ:
34 גַּם בִּכְנָפַיִךְ נִמְצְאוּ דַּם
נַפְשׁוֹת אֶבְיוֹנִים נְקִיִּים
לֹא־בַמַּחְתֶּרֶת מְצָאתִים
כִּי עַל־כָּל־אֵלֶּה:

v. 31. למדת ק׳ v. 33. ב׳ טעמים

I failed to provide for his needs?
(Abarbanel).

we roam at large. At our own sweet will,
declining to accept direction from God
(Targum).

32. *attire.* The noun *kishshurim* occurs
in Isa. iii. 20 where it is translated *sashes.*
Some translate it there as 'hair ribbons'
(Rashi), and some as 'ribbons worn
around the neck' (Ibn Ezra).

33. *how trimmest thou thy way.* lit. 'how
makest thou thy way good,' i.e. how you
carefully plan your way to achieve your
evil object (Metsudath David).

therefore. Better, 'verily'; the Hebrew
lachen introduces an oath of affirmation,
explains Rashi.

even the wicked . . . ways. Thou art a
master in wickedness even to the
wicked. Rashi renders: 'verily to the
most evil of ways thou hast accustomed
thy way.'

34. *of the souls.* [i.e. the persons.]

thou didst, etc. This translation construes the verb *metsathim* as the poetic
form of the second person singular, not
the usual first person (Rashi).

breaking in. Which might have justified
an act of homicide (cf. Exod. xxii. 1).

yet for all these things. If this rendering is
correct, the clause has to be connected
with the next verse, as in A.J. (so also
Kimchi). R.V. has 'I have not found it at
the place of breaking in, but upon all
these'; the meaning is: I did not find

35 Thou saidst: 'I am innocent;
Surely His anger is turned away
from me'—
Behold, I will enter into judgment with thee,
Because thou sayest: 'I have not
sinned.'
36 How greatly dost thou cheapen
thyself
To change thy way?
Thou shalt be ashamed of Egypt
also,
As thou wast ashamed of Asshur.
37 From him also shalt thou go
forth,
With thy hands upon thy head;
For the LORD hath rejected them
in whom thou didst trust,
And thou shalt not prosper in
them.

וַתֹּאמְרִי כִּי נִקֵּיתִי 35

אַךְ שָׁב אַפּוֹ מִמֶּנִּי

הִנְנִי נִשְׁפָּט אוֹתָךְ

עַל־אָמְרֵךְ לֹא חָטָאתִי:

מַה־תֵּזְלִי מְאֹד 36

לְשַׁנּוֹת אֶת־דַּרְכֵּךְ

גַּם מִמִּצְרַיִם תֵּבשִׁי

כַּאֲשֶׁר בֹּשְׁתְּ מֵאַשּׁוּר:

גַּם מֵאֵת זֶה תֵּצְאִי 37

וְיָדַיִךְ עַל־רֹאשֵׁךְ

כִּי־מָאַס יְהוָֹה בְּמִבְטַחַיִךְ

וְלֹא תַצְלִיחִי לָהֶם:

their blood in a hidden place (where a
thief might attempt to break in), which
would have indicated that you were
ashamed of your misdeeds, but upon
your garments *(thy skirts)*, openly flaunted (Metsudath David).

35. *thou saidst.* Or, 'yet thou saidst'
(Metsudath David).

surely His anger, etc. All is well with
me: this proves my innocence, since I
evidently enjoy God's favour (Alshich).

36. *how greatly dost thou cheapen . . .
way?* Another translation is: 'Why
goest thou so much to change thy way?
(Kimchi).

to change thy way. To forsake God and
seek help from Egypt (Rashi). Or, ever

seeking different allies, now Egypt, now
Assyria (Kimchi).

thou shalt be ashamed of Egypt also. i.e.
disappointed in Egypt who will prove
treacherous; for the fulfillment of this
prophecy, cf. xxxvii. 5 (Kimchi).

as thou wast ashamed of Asshur. This
occurred in the reign of Ahaz, who
stripped the Temple and his own palace
of their treasures in order to enlist the
help of the king of Assyria, but with the
opposite result (cf. 2 Chron. xxviii. 20).

37. *him.* The king of Egypt (Metsudath David).

shalt thou go forth. Empty-handed at a
time when his help is required (Kimchi).

with thy hands upon thy head. In shame
and lamentation (cf. 2 Sam. xiii. 19).

3   CHAPTER III   ג

1   . . . saying:
If a man put away his wife,
And she go from him,
And become another man's,
May he return unto her again?
Will not that land be greatly pol-
luted?
But thou hast played the harlot
with many lovers;
And wouldest thou yet return to
Me?
Saith the LORD.

2 Lift up thine eyes unto the high
hills, and see:
Where hast thou not been lain
with?
By the ways hast thou sat for
them,

א לֵאמֹר
הֵן יְשַׁלַּח אִישׁ אֶת־אִשְׁתּוֹ
וְהָלְכָה מֵאִתּוֹ
וְהָיְתָה לְאִישׁ־אַחֵר
הֲיָשׁוּב אֵלֶיהָ עוֹד
הֲלוֹא חָנוֹף תֶּחֱנַף
הָאָרֶץ הַהִיא
וְאַתְּ זָנִית רֵעִים רַבִּים
וְשׁוֹב אֵלַי
נְאֻם־יְהֹוָה׃
2 שְׂאִי עֵינַיִךְ עַל־שְׁפָיִם וּרְאִי
אֵיפֹה לֹא שֻׁגַּלְתְּ
עַל־דְּרָכִים יָשַׁבְתְּ לָהֶם

v. 2. שכבת ק

CHAPTER III

1–5 THE CONSEQUENCE OF INFIDELITY

1. *saying.* Some commentators
explain: So did the Lord command me,
saying (Kara). Rashi renders: I have to
say. Metsudath David renders: It is
proper to say to Israel. Malbim explains
this verse as a debate between God and
the land, which desires to expel Israel
for her sins. She bases her argument on
the law of the Torah, forbidding a
former husband to remarry his wife
who was married to another after he
divorced her. He renders: Does not the
land lie, saying, 'If a man puts away his
wife . . . may he return unto her again?'
Kimchi connects *saying* with *the* LORD
hath rejected them, etc., in the preceding
verse.

and wouldest thou yet return to Me?

According to this translation the meaning is: Since you went after the Baalim,
your repentance cannot be accepted
until you go into exile for a long time
and you forget your old sins and your
idolatry. Then you will be able to return
(Kimchi). Yet, though this seems the
most natural rendering and fits in best
with the next verse, it apparently contradicts the urgent pleas of Jeremiah (as,
indeed, of all prophets) that, no matter
how deeply Israel has sunk, he should
repent and return to God. A.V. and R.V.
therefore seem preferable: 'yet return
again to Me'; in spite of everything,
God is ready to receive the people back,
although this would be unlawful in
marital relationship (so Rashi and
Metsudath David).

2. *high hills.* See on ii. 20 (Kimchi).

by the ways, etc. Like a harlot to lure

18

As an Arabian in the wilderness;
And thou hast polluted the land
With thy harlotries and with thy
wickedness.

3 Therefore the showers have been
withheld,
And there hath been no latter
rain;
Yet thou hadst a harlot's forehead,
Thou refusedst to be ashamed.

4 Didst thou not just now cry unto
Me: 'My father,
Thou art the friend of my youth.

5 Will He bear grudge for ever?
Will He keep it to the end?'
Behold, thou hast spoken, but hast
done evil things,
And hast had thy way.

6. And the LORD said unto me in
the days of Josiah the king: 'Hast

כְּעֲרָבִי בַּמִּדְבָּר
וַתַּחֲנִיפִי אֶרֶץ
בִּזְנוּתַיִךְ וּבְרָעָתֵךְ׃
3 וַיִּמָּנְעוּ רְבִבִים
וּמַלְקוֹשׁ לוֹא הָיָה
וּמֵצַח אִשָּׁה זוֹנָה הָיָה לָךְ
מֵאַנְתְּ הִכָּלֵם׃
4 הֲלוֹא מֵעַתָּה קָרָאתי לִי אָבִי
אַלּוּף נְעֻרַי אָתָּה׃
5 הֲיִנְטוֹר לְעוֹלָם
אִם־יִשְׁמֹר לָנֶצַח
הִנֵּה דִבַּרְתְּ
וַתַּעֲשִׂי הָרָעוֹת וַתּוּכָל׃
6 וַיֹּאמֶר יְהוָה אֵלַי בִּימֵי יֹאשִׁיָּהוּ

v. 4. יתיר י׳

men (cf. Gen xxxviii. 14; Prov. vii. 12)
(Metsudath David).

as an Arabian in the wilderness. Being out
in the open, he is ready to meet any
caravans or passers-by. So is Israel
eager to embrace every form of idolatry
(Kimchi).

3. *the showers.* Perhaps the opposite of
the latter rain, and therefore equivalent
to *the former rain* in Deut. xi. 14, which is
the heavy rains that occur about the end
of October (so Kimchi).

latter rain. Which falls during March
and April (Rashi).

a harlot's forehead. Brazen and shame-
less (Kimchi).

4. The meaning of A.J. is: You have
only just been appealing to Me, protesting your affection for Me, and
asserting your confidence that the for-

giving God will not always be angry; yet
you are, in fact, forsaking Me. But A.V.
(following Rashi) is preferable: 'Wilt
thou not from this time cry unto Me,
'My father . . . youth?' The prophet
appeals to Israel to acknowledge God
even at this late hour, and gives the
assurance that He will surely not retain
His anger for ever. Yet even as he makes
this appeal, he sadly adds that the
people have demonstrated their will to
persist in their wickedness.

5. *thou hast spoken.* i.e. thou hast
spoken words of repentance, but, in
reality, thou hast done evil things
(Kimchi, Metsudath David). Rashi
explains: Thou hast spoken never to
return to Me.

and hast had thy way. lit. 'and hast been
able.' The meaning is 'and hast prevailed' (as in Gen. xxxii. 29) in evil
(Rashi).

thou seen that which backsliding Israel did? she went up upon every high mountain and under every leafy tree, and there played the harlot. 7. And I said: After she hath done all these things, she will return unto Me; but she returned not. And her treacherous sister Judah saw it. 8. And I saw, when, forasmuch as backsliding Israel had committed adultery, I had put her away and given her a bill of divorcement, that yet treacherous Judah her sister feared not; but she also went and played the harlot; 9. and it came to pass through the lightness of her harlotry, that the land was polluted, and she committed adultery with stones and with stocks; 10. and yet for all this her treacherous sister Judah hath not returned unto Me

הַמֶּלֶךְ הֲרָאִיתָ אֲשֶׁר עָשְׂתָה
מְשֻׁבָה יִשְׂרָאֵל הֹלְכָה הִיא
עַל־כָּל־הַר גָּבֹהַּ וְאֶל־תַּחַת
כָּל־עֵץ רַעֲנָן וַתִּזְנִי־שָׁם:
7 וָאֹמַר אַחֲרֵי עֲשׂוֹתָהּ אֶת־כָּל־
אֵלֶּה אֵלַי תָּשׁוּב וְלֹא־שָׁבָה
וַתֵּרֶא בָּגוֹדָה אֲחוֹתָהּ
8 יְהוּדָה: וָאֵרֶא כִּי עַל־כָּל־
אֹדוֹת אֲשֶׁר נִאֲפָה מְשֻׁבָה
יִשְׂרָאֵל שִׁלַּחְתִּיהָ וָאֶתֵּן אֶת־
סֵפֶר כְּרִיתֻתֶיהָ אֵלֶיהָ וְלֹא
יָרְאָה בֹּגֵדָה יְהוּדָה אֲחוֹתָהּ
9 וַתֵּלֶךְ וַתִּזֶן גַּם־הִיא: וְהָיָה
מִקֹּל זְנוּתָהּ וַתֶּחֱנַף אֶת־
הָאָרֶץ וַתִּנְאַף אֶת־הָאֶבֶן
10 וְאֶת־הָעֵץ: וְגַם־בְּכָל־זֹאת
לֹא־שָׁבָה אֵלַי בָּגוֹדָה אֲחוֹתָהּ

ותרא ק' .7 v.

6–13 THE GUILT OF JUDAH

6. *in the days of Josiah.* For the years of his reign, see on i. 2. As the Northern Kingdom was overthrown and destroyed in 722 B.C.E., Israel had by then been in exile nearly a hundred years.

Israel. i.e. the ten tribes of the north. *Backsliding Israel* is a comparatively mild epithet, given the Ten Tribes because of their inability to learn a lesson from any who preceded them. Judah is given the harsher epithet, 'treacherous Judah,' since they should have learned from the downfall of the Ten Tribes (Rashi).

7. *and I said.* I hoped that, after all Israel's sinning, he would return to Me. I.e., after they had satisfied their desires, I hoped that they would repent of their sins and return to Me, but they did not do so (Malbim).

8. *given her a bill of divorcement.* Sent the people into captivity in Assyria. Since they were sent for an extended exile, never to return to sovereignty, the future king being of the house of David, their exile is called a bill of divorcement (Kimchi).

9. *the lightness of her harlotry.* i.e. she thought lightly of such infidelity to God (so the Targum).

with her whole heart, but feignedly,
saith the LORD—11. even the LORD
said unto me—backsliding Israel
hath proved herself more righteous
than treacherous Judah. 12. Go,
and proclaim these words toward
the north, and say:

Return, thou backsliding Israel,
Saith the LORD;
I will not frown upon you;
For I am merciful, saith the LORD,
I will not bear grudge for ever.

13 Only acknowledge thine iniquity,
That thou hast transgressed against
the LORD thy God,
And hast scattered thy ways to
the strangers
Under every leafy tree,
And ye have not hearkened to My
voice,
Saith the LORD.

יְהוּדָה בְּכָל־לִבָּהּ כִּי אִם־־
11 בְּשֶׁקֶר נְאֻם־יְהוָה: וַיֹּאמֶר
יְהוָה אֵלַי צִדְּקָה נַפְשָׁהּ מְשֻׁבָה
12 יִשְׂרָאֵל מִבֹּגֵדָה יְהוּדָה: הָלֹךְ
וְקָרָאתָ אֶת־הַדְּבָרִים הָאֵלֶּה
צָפוֹנָה וְאָמַרְתָּ
שׁוּבָה מְשֻׁבָה יִשְׂרָאֵל
נְאֻם־יְהוָֹה
לוֹא־אַפִּיל פָּנַי בָּכֶם
כִּי־חָסִיד אֲנִי נְאֻם־יְהוָֹה
לֹא אֶטּוֹר לְעוֹלָם:
13 אַךְ דְּעִי עֲוֺנֵךְ
כִּי בַּיהוָה אֱלֹהַיִךְ פָּשָׁעַתְּ
וַתְּפַזְּרִי אֶת־דְּרָכַיִךְ לַזָּרִים
תַּחַת כָּל־עֵץ רַעֲנָן
וּבְקוֹלִי לֹא־שְׁמַעְתֶּם
נְאֻם־יְהוָֹה:

10. *with her whole heart, but feignedly.*
A great religious reform took place
during the reign of Josiah, and an
earnest endeavour was made to stamp
out idolatry (cf. 2 Kings xxiii).
Nevertheless, as appears from this verse,
the people were not sincere in their
conversion (Rashi, Kimchi).

11. *more righteous.* Either, by comparison (Kimchi); or, since the Kingdom of
Israel did not have the example of
punishment before their eyes, as did
Judah in the destruction of the ten
tribes (Rashi).

12. *toward the north.* i.e. Assyria,

whither the ten tribes had been deported (Rashi).

I will not frown. lit. 'I will not cause
My face to fall,' paraphrased by Jonathan as 'I will not send forth My anger
upon you.'

13. *only acknowledge thine iniquity.* Ad-
mission of sin must be the first step to
repentance and recovery of God's
favour (Kimchi).

and hast scattered thy ways. The phrase is
usually understood as a variant of
traversing her ways (ii. 23). Here,
however, scattering denotes wandering
all over to worship many different

14. Return, O backsliding children, saith the LORD; for I am a lord unto you, and I will take you one of a city, and two of a family, and I will bring you to Zion; 15. and I will give you shepherds according to My heart, who shall feed you with knowledge and understanding. 16. And it shall come to pass, when ye are multiplied and increased in the land, in those days, saith the LORD, they shall say no more: The ark of the covenant of the LORD; neither shall it come to mind; neither shall they make mention of it; neither shall they miss it; neither shall it be made any more. 17. At that time they shall call Jerusalem The throne of the LORD; and all the nations shall be gathered unto it, to the name of the

14 שׁוּבוּ בָנִים שׁוֹבָבִים נְאֻם־
יְהֹוָה כִּי אָנֹכִי בָּעַלְתִּי בָכֶם
וְלָקַחְתִּי אֶתְכֶם אֶחָד מֵעִיר
וּשְׁנַיִם מִמִּשְׁפָּחָה וְהֵבֵאתִי
אֶתְכֶם צִיּוֹן: וְנָתַתִּי לָכֶם 15
רֹעִים כְּלִבִּי וְרָעוּ אֶתְכֶם דֵּעָה
וְהַשְׂכֵּיל: וְהָיָה כִּי תִרְבּוּ 16
וּפְרִיתֶם בָּאָרֶץ בַּיָּמִים הָהֵמָּה
נְאֻם־יְהֹוָה לֹא־יֹאמְרוּ עוֹד
אֲרוֹן בְּרִית־יְהֹוָה וְלֹא יַעֲלֶה
עַל־לֵב וְלֹא יִזְכְּרוּ־בוֹ וְלֹא
17 יִפְקֹדוּ וְלֹא יֵעָשֶׂה עוֹד: בָּעֵת
הַהִיא יִקְרְאוּ לִירוּשָׁלַם כִּסֵּא
יְהֹוָה וְנִקְווּ אֵלֶיהָ כָל־הַגּוֹיִם

---

deities, reminiscent of 'For according to the number of thy cities are thy gods, O Judah' (2:28) (Kimchi).

14–18   EXHORTATION TO REPENTANCE

14. *children . . . I am a lord.* The verb *baalti* is derived from the noun *baal* which means both 'lord' and 'husband'; R.V. 'I am a husband.' Malbim explains: Although the sinful fathers did not repent, I, nevertheless, call to the children to repent. Although I divorced the mother and gave her her bill of divorcement, I am your husband, and I will keep you as My wife.

one of a city, and two of a family. Family probably signifies here 'a clan,' hence a larger group than a city (see on i. 15 and cf. viii. 3, xxv. 9 where the term obviously means whole tribes or peoples). The intention is: even if only a very small number repent, God will not

let them be swallowed up in the exile, but bring them back to Zion (Kimchi).

15. *shepherds.* See on ii. 8.

16. *in those days.* [When a new covenant is made by God with the people.]

neither shall it be made any more. A tangible and visible symbol of God's Presence will no longer be necessary. Metsudath David comments: Though you be multiplied and increased, you will not arouse the envy of your neighbours, so that there will be no need for you to come and pray before the ark of the Lord for protection; such a petition will never be thought of again. Kimchi's interpretation is somewhat similar.

17. *The throne of the LORD.* Jerusalem, as the centre of God's kingdom and of His worship, will take the place of the ark, and all peoples will be attracted to it (Abarbanel).

LORD, to Jerusalem; neither shall
they walk any more after the stubbornness of their evil heart. 18. In
those days the house of Judah shall
walk with the house of Israel, and
they shall come together out of the
land of the north to the land that I
have given for an inheritance unto
your fathers.'

19 But I said: 'How would I put
thee among the sons,
And give thee a pleasant land,
The goodliest heritage of the
nations!'
And I said: 'Thou shalt call Me,
My father;
And shalt not turn away from
following Me.'

20 Surely as a wife treacherously
departeth from her husband,

לְשֵׁם יְהֹוָה לִירוּשָׁלִַם וְלֹא־
יֵלְכוּ עוֹד אַחֲרֵי שְׁרִרוּת לִבָּם
18 הָרָע: בַּיָּמִים הָהֵמָּה יֵלְכוּ
בֵית־יְהוּדָה עַל־בֵּית
יִשְׂרָאֵל וְיָבֹאוּ יַחְדָּו מֵאֶרֶץ
צָפוֹן עַל־הָאָרֶץ אֲשֶׁר
הִנְחַלְתִּי אֶת־אֲבוֹתֵיכֶם:
19 וְאָנֹכִי אָמַרְתִּי
אֵיךְ אֲשִׁיתֵךְ בַּבָּנִים
וְאֶתֶּן־לָךְ אֶרֶץ חֶמְדָּה
נַחֲלַת צְבִי צִבְאוֹת גּוֹיִם
וָאֹמַר אָבִי תִּקְרְאוּ־לִי
וּמֵאַחֲרַי לֹא תָשׁוּבוּ:
20 אָכֵן בָּגְדָה אִשָּׁה מֵרֵעָהּ

v. 19. תקראי ק׳   v. 19. תשובי ק׳

---

18. The reunion of Israel and Judah
was the fervent dream and hope of the
prophets, both before their overthrow
and after (cf. ii. 4; Isa. xi. 12; Ezek.
xxxvii. 16ff.; Hos. ii. 2).

**19–20 THE PEOPLE FRUSTRATED GOD'S
HOPES FOR THEM**

19. *but I said.* Better, 'now I had said.'
The verse describes God's intentions
and hopes concerning Judah which,
however, were not realized.

among the sons. God would single
Judah out from among His other sons,
viz. the other nations (Rashi). [The
words, incidentally, assert the univer-
sality of God's Fatherhood.] The verse is
differently explained by modern commentators. Judah is referred to in this
verse in the feminine. She is depicted as
God's only daughter, whereas the other

nations are depicted as His sons.
According to the Mosaic Law, a
daughter does not inherit if there are
sons. God wishes to make an exception
with Judah by giving her a portion of
His inheritance, and not only an inheritance, but 'the goodliest heritage of
the nations' (Daath Mikra).

the goodliest heritage of the nations.
Judah's heritage would be outstanding-
ly glorious, by having the Divine
Presence specially manifest in it (Metsudath David).

and I said. [Better, 'and I had said,' a
continuation of the first words of the
sentence.]

thou shalt call Me, My father. Cf. verse 4.

20. *surely.* Better, 'but surely,' 'but in
truth': the contrast between God's

23

So have ye dealt treacherously
with Me, O house of Israel,
Saith the LORD.

21 Hark! upon the high hills is heard
The suppliant weeping of the
children of Israel;
For that they have perverted their
way,
They have forgotten the LORD
their God.

22 Return, ye backsliding children,
I will heal your backslidings.—
'Here we are, we are come unto
Thee;
For Thou art the LORD our God.

23 Truly vain have proved the hills,
The uproar on the mountains;
Truly in the LORD our God
Is the salvation of Israel.

24 But the shameful thing hath devoured

בֵּן בְּגַדְתֶּם בִּי
בֵּית יִשְׂרָאֵל נְאֻם־יְהוָה:

21 קוֹל עַל־שְׁפָיִם נִשְׁמָע
בְּכִי תַחֲנוּנֵי בְּנֵי יִשְׂרָאֵל
כִּי הֶעֱווּ אֶת־דַּרְכָּם
שָׁכְחוּ אֶת־יְהוָה אֱלֹהֵיהֶם:

22 שׁוּבוּ בָּנִים שׁוֹבָבִים
אֶרְפָּה מְשׁוּבֹתֵיכֶם
הִנְנוּ אָתָנוּ לָךְ
כִּי אַתָּה יְהוָה אֱלֹהֵינוּ:

23 אָכֵן לַשֶּׁקֶר
מִגְּבָעוֹת הָמוֹן הָרִים
אָכֵן בַּיהוָה אֱלֹהֵינוּ
תְּשׁוּעַת יִשְׂרָאֵל:

24 וְהַבֹּשֶׁת אָכְלָה

v. 21. קמץ בז״ק   v. 22. כצ״ל

hopes and what actually happened
(Rashi).

21–25 ISRAEL'S REMORSE

A picture of the nation's repentance and
confession of sin. This is either a
description of what ought to happen
(Kimchi); or perhaps the prophet here
gives utterance to his conviction of
Israel's ultimate repentance, no matter
how unpropitious the signs in the
present (Abarbanel).

21. *the high hills.* The same place where
God had been faithlessly forsaken for
idolatry (verse 2) (Ibn Nachmiash).

22. *return, ye backsliding children.* [The
Hebrew words, though diametrical
opposites, are similar, and the idea

conveyed is: instead of being *shobabim*
(backsliding), let them be *shabim* (peni-
tents).]

23. *the hills . . . mountains.* Idolatry,
practised on the hills and mountains,
has been proved vain and futile (Metsudath David).

the uproar (hamon). The wild orgies
which accompanied idol-worship
(Daath Mikra). It may perhaps refer to
the 'multitudes' worshipping on the
mountains (Kimchi).

24. *the shameful thing.* viz. Baal-
worship, idolatry (cf. Hos. ix. 10)
(Rashi).

hath devoured, etc. As a punishment
for idolatry we and our fathers have lost

The labour of our fathers from
our youth;
Their flocks and their herds,
Their sons and their daughters.

25 Let us lie down in our shame,
And let our confusion cover us;
For we have sinned against the
LORD our God,
We and our fathers,
From our youth even unto this
day;
And we have not hearkened
To the voice of the LORD our
God.'

אֶת־יְגִיעַ אֲבוֹתֵינוּ מִנְּעוּרֵינוּ
אֶת־צֹאנָם וְאֶת־בְּקָרָם
אֶת־בְּנֵיהֶם וְאֶת־בְּנוֹתֵיהֶם:
25 נִשְׁכְּבָה בְּבָשְׁתֵּנוּ
וּתְכַסֵּנוּ כְּלִמָּתֵנוּ
כִּי לַיהֹוָה אֱלֹהֵינוּ חָטָאנוּ
אֲנַחְנוּ וַאֲבוֹתֵינוּ
מִנְּעוּרֵינוּ וְעַד־הַיּוֹם הַזֶּה
וְלֹא שָׁמַעְנוּ
בְּקוֹל יְהֹוָה אֱלֹהֵינוּ:

| 4 | CHAPTER IV | ד |

1 If thou wilt return, O Israel,
Saith the LORD,
Yea, return unto Me;
And if thou wilt put away thy
detestable things out of My
sight,
And wilt not waver;

1 אִם־תָּשׁוּב יִשְׂרָאֵל |
נְאֻם־יְהֹוָה
אֵלַי תָּשׁוּב
וְאִם־תָּסִיר שִׁקּוּצֶיךָ
מִפָּנַי וְלֹא תָנוּד:

all our possessions; or these had been
sacrificed to Baal (Daath Mikra).

their sons and their daughters. Cf. v. 17. It
possibly alludes to human sacrifice
(Daath Mikra).

25. *let us lie down in our shame.* Perhaps
on the ground in remorse (cf. 2 Sam.
xii. 16, xiii. 31).

let our confusion cover us. So intense will
the feeling of shame be that it will
appear to enshroud us; cf. *and shall put
on their own shame as a robe* (Ps. cix. 29)
(Metsudath David).

CHAPTER IV

1-4 THE CONSEQUENCE OF REPENTANCE

1. *return . . . return.* If you will return
(repent) and confess your guilt (this is a
continuation of iii. 22–25), then you will
return to your former splendour and be
My people once more (Rashi, Metsudath David).

detestable things. Idolatrous worship
and impure rites (Kimchi).

waver. Wander away from God. A.V.,
following Rashi and Kimchi, renders:
'then shalt thou not remove,' i.e.
wander into captivity. But A.J. correctly

2 And wilt swear: 'As the LORD
liveth'
In truth, in justice, and in righteousness;
Then shall the nations bless themselves by Him,
And in Him shall they glory.

3 For thus saith the LORD to the
men of Judah and to Jerusalem:
Break up for you a fallow ground,
And sow not among thorns.

4 Circumcise yourselves to the LORD,
And take away the foreskins of
your heart,
Ye men of Judah and inhabitants
of Jerusalem;
Lest My fury go forth like fire,

וְנִשְׁבַּ֙עְתָּ֙ חַי־יְהֹוָה֙ 2
בֶּאֱמֶ֖ת בְּמִשְׁפָּ֣ט וּבִצְדָקָ֑ה
וְהִתְבָּ֥רְכוּ ב֖וֹ
גּוֹיִ֔ם וּב֖וֹ יִתְהַלָּֽלוּ׃
כִּי־כֹ֣ה ׀ אָמַ֣ר יְהֹוָ֗ה 3
לְאִ֤ישׁ יְהוּדָה֙ וְלִירֽוּשָׁלִַ֔ם
נִ֥ירוּ לָכֶ֖ם נִ֑יר
וְאַֽל־תִּזְרְע֖וּ אֶל־קֹצִֽים׃
הִמֹּ֣לוּ לַֽיהֹוָ֗ה 4
וְהָסִ֙רוּ֙ עָרְל֣וֹת לְבַבְכֶ֔ם
אִ֥ישׁ יְהוּדָ֖ה וְיֹשְׁבֵ֣י יְרֽוּשָׁלָ֑͏ִם
פֶּן־תֵּצֵ֤א כָאֵשׁ֙ חֲמָתִ֔י

construes the clause as still governed by
the introductory *if* and part of the
protasis (Abarbanel).

2. and wilt swear. When the necessity
arises (Targum). The phrase does not
advocate swearing, even by the name of
God (Kimchi).

as the LORD liveth. Swearing by the
Lord (and not by an idol) implied
sincere allegiance to Him (cf. Deut. vi.
13) (Kimchi).

in truth, etc. Otherwise the oath would
be blasphemous. The Rabbis interpret:
Only when a man has truth, justice and
righteousness is he worthy of swearing
by the name of God (see Kimchi).

then shall the nations, etc. Israel's
genuine repentance will by force of
example lead the other nations also to
God. While Judaism does not advocate
active proselytization, it does look forward to the time when all people, spon-
taneously and of their own accord, will

acknowledge Him (cf. Isa. ii. 3, lxv. 16)
(Daath Soferim).

3. break up. Cf. Hos. x. 12. Plough up
the ground to remove the weeds and the
thorns. This will be explained in the
following paragraph.

and sow not among thorns. First abandon
your wickedness and idolatry, and then
approach Me in prayer (Targum, Rashi).
The metaphor is taken from real life.
Learn from the farmers, who plow their
fields in the winter to kill the roots of
the grasses lest they grow thorns in the
time of sowing in the winter (Rashi).

4. circumcise . . . your heart. Remove the
hard excrescence which has grown over
your heart and prevents you from being
influenced by God's exhortations (cf.
Deut. x. 16) (Malbim).

*ye men of Judah and inhabitants of Jeru-
salem.* You important people, the men
of Judah and especially the inhabitants
of the Holy City, Jerusalem, have pity
on your treasured possession before it is
too late (Daath Soferim).

And burn that none can quench it,
Because of the evil of your doings.

5 Declare ye in Judah, and publish
  in Jerusalem,
And say: 'Blow ye the horn in the
  land';
Cry aloud and say:
'Assemble yourselves, and let us
  go into the fortified cities.'

6 Set up a standard toward Zion;
Put yourselves under covert, stay
  not;
For I will bring evil from the
  north,
And a great destruction.

7 A lion is gone up from his thicket,
And a destroyer of nations

וּבְעֲרָה וְאֵין מְכַבֶּה
מִפְּנֵי רֹעַ מַעַלְלֵיכֶם:
5 הַגִּידוּ בִיהוּדָה
וּבִירוּשָׁלַםִ הַשְׁמִיעוּ
וְאִמְרוּ וּתִקְעוּ שׁוֹפָר בָּאָרֶץ
קִרְאוּ מַלְאוּ וְאִמְרוּ
הֵאָסְפוּ וְנָבוֹאָה
אֶל־עָרֵי הַמִּבְצָר:
6 שְׂאוּ־נֵס צִיּוֹנָה
הָעִיזוּ אַל־תַּעֲמֹדוּ
כִּי רָעָה אָנֹכִי
מֵבִיא מִצָּפוֹן וְשֶׁבֶר גָּדוֹל:
7 עָלָה אַרְיֵה מִסֻּבְּכוֹ
וּמַשְׁחִית גּוֹיִם

v. 5. תקעו ק׳ v. 5. המ׳ בפתח

5–31 JUDGMENT IMMINENT UPON JUDAH

A picture of the impending disaster.
Flight to the protection of the walled
cities; terror and dismay spread over the
land; the enemy swoops down on the
doomed country; the prophet's grief at
the horror of it all, particularly as it is
occasioned by the people's insensate
folly; a graphic vision of the earth waste
and void reeling under God's anger;
Zion cries out in the extremity of her
distress. This and the prophecies in the
following chapters may have been written with reference either to the Scythian
(c. 625 B.C.E.) or the Babylonian invasion. The latter is more probable; see
on verse 7.

5. *declare ye.* The danger is at hand;
warn the people to take refuge in the
fortified cities (Kimchi).

blow ye the horn. The signal of danger
and alarm (cf. Amos. iii. 6).

cry aloud. lit. 'cry, fill,' i.e. cry out with
the fulness of your strength (Kara).

let us go, etc.. Scholars quote as a parallel the crowding of the inhabitants of
Attica within the walls of Athens on the
occasion of a Spartan invasion.

6. *set up a standard.* As a signpost
(Kimchi).

toward Zion. To guide the fleeing refugees (Kimchi). *Zion* here denotes the city
of Jerusalem (Daath Mikra).

put yourselves under covert. The verb *hëiz*
means 'to bring one's family, or possessions, to a place of safety' (cf. Exod. ix.
19) (Kimchi, Daath Mikra).

7. *a lion.* A designation for Nebu-

27

Is set out, gone forth from his place;
To make thy land desolate,
That thy cities be laid waste, without inhabitant.

8 For this gird you with sackcloth,
Lament and wail;
For the fierce anger of the LORD
Is not turned back from us.

9 And it shall come to pass at that day,
Saith the LORD,
That the heart of the king shall fail,
And the heart of the princes;
And the priests shall be astonished,
And the prophets shall wonder.

10. Then said I: 'Ah, Lord GOD! surely Thou hast greatly deceived this people and Jerusalem, saying: Ye shall have peace; whereas the

נֹסֵעַ יָצָא מִמְּקֹמוֹ
לָשׂוּם אַרְצֵךְ לְשַׁמָּה
עָרַיִךְ תִּצֶּינָה מֵאֵין יוֹשֵׁב:
8 עַל־זֹאת חִגְרוּ שַׂקִּים
סִפְדוּ וְהֵילִילוּ
כִּי לֹא־שָׁב
חֲרוֹן אַף־יְהֹוָה מִמֶּנּוּ:
9 וְהָיָה בַיּוֹם־הַהוּא
נְאֻם־יְהֹוָה
יֹאבַד לֵב־הַמֶּלֶךְ
וְלֵב הַשָּׂרִים
וְנָשַׁמּוּ הַכֹּהֲנִים
וְהַנְּבִיאִים יִתְמָהוּ:
10 וָאֹמַר אֲהָהּ | אֲדֹנָי יֱהֹוִה אָכֵן
הַשֵּׁא הִשֵּׁאתָ לָעָם הַזֶּה
וְלִירוּשָׁלִַם לֵאמֹר שָׁלוֹם יִהְיֶה

chadnezzar, king of Babylon (Rashi, Kimchi).

a destroyer of nations. [The words emphasize both the might and ruthlessness of the attacker.]

8. *gird you with sackcloth.* [A mark of intense distress and mourning.]

is not turned back from us. God is still angry with His people because they have not repented, or their penitence has not been sincere (Kimchi).

9. *king . . . princes.* Who should be the first to encourage and strengthen the people in the crisis. *Heart* signifies 'courage' (Metsudath David).

astonished . . . wonder. They will be bewildered by the extent of the disaster,

and not know what advice to give to the stricken nation (Abarbanel).

10. *surely Thou hast greatly deceived . . . peace.* A very daring charge! Kimchi explains: The false prophets assured the people of peace, and God, as it were, must be held responsible, in that they were not immediately punished by Him. He suggests further that we render: Thou hast caused to greatly deceive. He complains that God had inspired the false prophets to announce their optimistic prophecy. Abarbanel objects that, were such the case, neither the prophets nor their followers could be blamed for misleading the people. Saadya Gaon renders: 'Thou hast revealed the deception of this people.' Abarbanel explains that the prophets' surprise and

sword reacheth unto the soul.'

11 At that time shall it be said of this
people and of Jerusalem:
A hot wind of the high hills in the
wilderness
Toward the daughter of My
people,
Not to fan, nor to cleanse;

12 A wind too strong for this shall
come for Me;
Now will I also utter judgments
against them.

13 Behold, he cometh up as clouds,
And his chariots are as the whirlwind;
His horses are swifter than
eagles.—
'Woe unto us! for we are undone.'—

14 O Jerusalem, wash thy heart from
wickedness,
That thou mayest be saved.

לָכֶם וְנָגְעָה חֶרֶב עַד־הַנָּפֶשׁ:

11 בָּעֵת הַהִיא יֵאָמֵר לָעָם־הַזֶּה
וְלִירוּשָׁלַ͏ִם
רוּחַ צַח שְׁפָיִם בַּמִּדְבָּר
דֶּרֶךְ בַּת־עַמִּי
לוֹא לִזְרוֹת וְלוֹא לְהָבַר:

12 רוּחַ מָלֵא מֵאֵלֶּה יָבוֹא לִי
עַתָּה גַם־אֲנִי
אֲדַבֵּר מִשְׁפָּטִים אוֹתָם:

13 הִנֵּה | כַּעֲנָנִים יַעֲלֶה
וְכַסּוּפָה מַרְכְּבוֹתָיו
קַלּוּ מִנְּשָׁרִים סוּסָיו
אוֹי לָנוּ כִּי שֻׁדָּדְנוּ:

14 כַּבְּסִי מֵרָעָה לִבֵּךְ יְרוּשָׁלַ͏ִם
לְמַעַן תִּוָּשֵׁעִי

bewilderment at the calamity will lead
the people to believe that 'surely Thou
hast greatly deceived this people,' that
they were indeed inspired by God to
announce this prophecy.

whereas the sword, etc. Or, 'and so the
sword,' etc.; because the people were so
beguiled, they are now in this terrible
plight (Metsudath David).

unto the soul. i.e. to the destruction of
life (Targum).

11. *at that time.* i.e. when the enemy
attacks (Kimchi).

not to fan, nor to cleanse. The foe will
swoop down on Israel, not like a gentle
wind separating the grain from the
chaff, but wholly destructive like *a hot
wind.* Abarbanel explains that the spirit
of his prophecy resembles a hot wind, a
wholly destructive one. He supports

God in maintaining that all the prophecy he received was of imminent doom.
It could not possibly be misconstrued to
mean that there would be peace. The
word *ruach* is used in two senses, as
'wind' and as 'spirit.' This is a play on
words.

12. *too strong for this.* i.e. for winnow-
ing (Daath Mikra).

for Me. In My service (Daath Mikra).

13. *he.* viz. the enemy. Similar com-
parisons are found in other prophets;
cf. Ezek. xxxviii. 16 for *cloud,* Isa. v. 28,
lxvi. 15 for *whirlwind,* and Hab. i. 8 for
eagle (better 'vulture') (Daath Mikra).

14. *that thou mayest be saved.* [There is
still time to avert the doom, for all
prophecies of punishment are conditional.]

How long shall thy baleful thoughts
Lodge within thee?

15 For hark! one declareth from Dan,
And announceth calamity from the hills of Ephraim:

16 'Make ye mention to the nations:
Behold — publish concerning Jerusalem—
Watchers come from a far country,
And give out their voice against the cities of Judah.'

17 As keepers of a field
Are they against her round about;
Because she hath been rebellious against Me,
Saith the LORD.

18 Thy way and thy doings have procured
These things unto thee;
This is thy wickedness; yea, it is bitter,
Yea, it reacheth unto thy heart.

עַד־מָתַי תָּלִין בְּקִרְבֵּךְ
מַחְשְׁבוֹת אוֹנֵךְ:

15 כִּי קוֹל מַגִּיד מִדָּן
וּמַשְׁמִיעַ אָוֶן מֵהַר אֶפְרָיִם:

16 הַזְכִּירוּ לַגּוֹיִם
הִנֵּה הַשְׁמִיעוּ עַל־יְרוּשָׁלַ͏ִם
נֹצְרִים בָּאִים מֵאֶרֶץ הַמֶּרְחָק
וַיִּתְּנוּ עַל־עָרֵי יְהוּדָה קוֹלָם:

17 כְּשֹׁמְרֵי שָׂדַי
הָיוּ עָלֶיהָ מִסָּבִיב
כִּי־אֹתִי מָרָתָה
נְאֻם יְהֹוָה:

18 דַּרְכֵּךְ וּמַעֲלָלַיִךְ
עָשׂוֹ אֵלֶּה לָךְ
זֹאת רָעָתֵךְ כִּי מָר
כִּי נָגַע עַד־לִבֵּךְ:

v. 18. קמץ בז״ק

---

15. *Dan.* On the northern border of Palestine (Kimchi).

the hills of Ephraim. The range that divides Ephraim from Judah, only about ten miles from Jerusalem. The force of the verse is: the sands are running out; the foe is rapidly approaching the capital, and repentance is urgent if the land is to be spared devastation (Daath Mikra).

16. *to the nations.* The Divine visitation which is about to take place has a universal significance, that retribution is

the sequel to sin; let the neighbouring peoples take heed (Daath Mikra).

watchers. In the sense mentioned in the following verse, where they are called *keepers of a field* (Ibn Nachmiash). Rashi renders: besiegers.

17. *as keepers of a field.* Who maintain a close guard upon it on all sides (Kimchi).

18. *thy wickedness.* i.e. the effect of thy wickedness (Kimchi).

it reacheth unto thy heart. It deals a fatal blow (Daath Soferim).

19 My bowels, my bowels! I writhe
in pain!
The chambers of my heart!
My heart moaneth within me!
I cannot hold my peace!
Because thou hast heard, O my
soul, the sound of the horn,
The alarm of war.

20 Destruction followeth upon de-
struction,
For the whole land is spoiled;
Suddenly are my tents spoiled,
My curtains in a moment.

21 How long shall I see the standard,
Shall I hear the sound of the
horn?

22 For My people is foolish,
They know Me not;
They are sottish children,
And they have no understanding;
They are wise to do evil,
But to do good they have no
knowledge.

19 מֵעַי ׀ מֵעַי ׀ אוֹחִילָה
קִירוֹת לִבִּי
הֹמֶה־לִּי לִבִּי
לֹא אַחֲרִשׁ
כִּי קוֹל שׁוֹפָר שָׁמַעַתְּ נַפְשִׁי
תְּרוּעַת מִלְחָמָה:
20 שֶׁבֶר עַל־שֶׁבֶר נִקְרָא
כִּי־שֻׁדְּדָה כָּל־הָאָרֶץ
פִּתְאֹם שֻׁדְּדוּ אֹהָלַי
רֶגַע יְרִיעֹתָי:
21 עַד־מָתַי אֶרְאֶה־נֵּס
אֶשְׁמְעָה קוֹל שׁוֹפָר:
22 כִּי ׀ אֱוִיל עַמִּי
אוֹתִי לֹא יָדָעוּ
בָּנִים סְכָלִים הֵמָּה
וְלֹא נְבוֹנִים הֵמָּה
חֲכָמִים הֵמָּה לְהָרַע
וּלְהֵיטִיב לֹא יָדָעוּ:

v. 19. קמץ בז״ק · v. 22. שמעת ק׳ · v. 19. אוחילה ק׳

19ff. Jeremiah's many prophesies of
disaster and punishment were not the
utterances of a vindictive and ruthless
moralist who derives a self-righteous
pleasure in contemplating the sufferings
of the wicked. His urgent warnings and
gloomy predictions were born of his
intense love for his people. He was a
true patriot; and here in an outpouring
of tenderness he identifies himself
completely with the agonies of his
country.

19. *my bowels*. Thought of by the
Hebrews as the seat of the emotions
(Daath Mikra).

20. *is spoiled*. The prophet envisages
the invasion as though it were actually
taking place (Daath Soferim).

21. *sound of the horn*. Urging the
people to flee from the oncoming
enemy (Kimchi). Other exegetes,
however, explain it as the sound of the
horn of the attacking enemy (Abarbanel, Isaiah da Trani, Metsudath
David).

22. *children*. They are indeed children
of God, but foolish. This verse is God's
reply to Jeremiah's question in the last
verse (Kimchi).

31

23 I beheld the earth,
And, lo, it was waste and void;
And the heavens, and they had
no light.

24 I beheld the mountains, and, lo,
they trembled,
And all the hills moved to and
fro.

25 I beheld, and, lo, there was no
man,
And all the birds of the heavens
were fled.

26 I beheld, and, lo, the fruitful field
was a wilderness,
And all the cities thereof were
broken down
At the presence of the LORD,
And before His fierce anger.

27 For thus saith the LORD:
The whole land shall be desolate;
Yet will I not make a full end.

רָאִ֙יתִי֙ אֶת־הָאָ֔רֶץ 23
וְהִנֵּה־תֹ֖הוּ וָבֹ֑הוּ
וְאֶל־הַשָּׁמַ֖יִם וְאֵ֥ין אוֹרָֽם׃

רָאִ֙יתִי֙ הֶֽהָרִ֔ים וְהִנֵּ֖ה רֹעֲשִׁ֑ים 24
וְכָל־הַגְּבָע֖וֹת הִתְקַלְקָֽלוּ׃

רָאִ֕יתִי וְהִנֵּ֖ה אֵ֣ין הָאָדָ֑ם 25
וְכָל־ע֥וֹף הַשָּׁמַ֖יִם נָדָֽדוּ׃

רָאִ֕יתִי וְהִנֵּ֥ה הַכַּרְמֶ֖ל הַמִּדְבָּ֑ר 26
וְכָל־עָרָ֗יו
נִתְּצוּ֙ מִפְּנֵ֣י יְהֹוָ֔ה
מִפְּנֵ֖י חֲר֥וֹן אַפּֽוֹ׃

כִּי־כֹה֙ אָמַ֣ר יְהֹוָ֔ה 27
שְׁמָמָ֥ה תִהְיֶ֖ה כָּל־הָאָ֑רֶץ
וְכָלָ֖ה לֹ֥א אֶעֱשֶֽׂה׃

23-28. The previous verse describes the spiritual and moral deterioration of the people. It is followed by a passage of singular power, describing vividly and graphically how, in the physical world, cosmos has reverted to chaos — the inevitable result of the former evil.

23. *waste and void.* The state of primeval matter before the spirit of God moulded it into order and form (Gen. i. 2).

24. *moved to and fro.* This follows Rashi. Perhaps A.V. 'moved lightly' comes nearer the meaning, the root of the verb signifying 'lightness.' Despite their massive weight, they swayed like something light. This follows Rabbi Joseph Kimchi.

25. *and all the birds,* etc. The last word in desolation (Metsudath David).

26. *the fruitful field ... the cities,* etc. Town and country alike are completely devastated.

27. *yet will I not make a full end.* This clause is apparently out of place in a picture of utter destruction, and, moreover, it breaks the connection between verses 27 and 28. Nevertheless, to regard it as an interpolation or spurious is to misunderstand the teachings of Jeremiah and, indeed, of the prophets in general. Even in their darkest predictions and gloomiest moments, they retained the profound conviction that no matter how widespread the destruction, a residue would be left to form the nucleus of a better people, faithful in their allegiance to God. Without this conviction their life's work would, in fact, be meaningless (cf. v. 10, 18; Isa. vi. 11-13; Amos ix. 8) (see Daath Soferim).

28 For this shall the earth mourn,
And the heavens above be black;
Because I have spoken it, I have
purposed it,
And I have not repented, neither
will I turn back from it.

29 For the noise of the horsemen
and bowmen
The whole city fleeth;
They go into the thickets,
And climb up upon the rocks;
Every city is forsaken,
And not a man dwelleth therein.

30 And thou, that art spoiled, what
doest thou,
That thou clothest thyself with
scarlet,
That thou deckest thee with
ornaments of gold,
That thou enlargest thine eyes
with paint?
In vain dost thou make thyself
fair;
Thy lovers despise thee, they seek
thy life.

עַל־זֹאת תֶּאֱבַל הָאָרֶץ 28
וְקָדְרוּ הַשָּׁמַיִם מִמָּעַל
עַל כִּי־דִבַּרְתִּי זַמֹּתִי
וְלֹא נִחַמְתִּי
וְלֹא־אָשׁוּב מִמֶּנָּה:
מִקּוֹל פָּרָשׁ וְרֹמֵה קֶשֶׁת 29
בֹּרַחַת כָּל־הָעִיר
בָּאוּ בֶּעָבִים
וּבַכֵּפִים עָלוּ
כָּל־הָעִיר עֲזוּבָה
וְאֵין־יוֹשֵׁב בָּהֵן אִישׁ:
וְאַתְּ שָׁדוּד מַה־תַּעֲשִׂי 30
כִּי־תִלְבְּשִׁי שָׁנִי
כִּי־תַעְדִּי עֲדִי־זָהָב
כִּי־תִקְרְעִי בַפּוּךְ עֵינַיִךְ
לַשָּׁוְא תִּתְיַפִּי
מָאֲסוּ־בָךְ עֹגְבִים
נַפְשֵׁךְ יְבַקֵּשׁוּ:

ואת ק' v. 30.

---

28. *for this.* The calamity which has befallen the land of Judah (Metsudath David).

the earth mourn. The soil will not produce its fruits (see Rashi, Kimchi).

the heavens above be black. [With dark clouds, as if in mourning.]

29. *the whole city.* City stands here for 'land' (Targum). Or, perhaps, it is used generically: the whole (of every and any) city (Kimchi).

30. Completely unimpressed by the seductive wiles of Zion's inhabitants,

their captors will not abate their harshness in the least.

enlargest thine eyes. A common practice in the East in Biblical times and later (cf. 2 Kings ix. 30; Ezek. xxiii. 40).

thy lovers. They whose friendship was courted (the Chaldeans) are now the implacable enemies of Judah. The Hebrew word *ogebim* is a term of scorn and denotes an adulterous paramour. Thus here, too, Jeremiah emphasized that in seeking alliances with Egypt and Asshur (ii. 33f.) they had, as it were,

31 For I have heard a voice as of a
woman in travail,
The anguish as of her that bring-
eth forth her first child,
The voice of the daughter of
Zion, that gaspeth for breath,
That spreadeth her hands:
'Woe is me, now! for my soul
fa_inteth
Before the murderers.'

כִּי קוֹל כְּחוֹלָה שָׁמַעְתִּי 31
צָרָה כְּמַבְכִּירָה
קוֹל בַּת־צִיּוֹן
תִּתְיַפֵּחַ תְּפָרֵשׂ כַּפֶּיהָ
אוֹי־נָא לִי
כִּי־עָיְפָה נַפְשִׁי לְהֹרְגִים:

5   CHAPTER V   ה

1 Run ye to and fro through the
streets of Jerusalem,
And see now, and know,
And seek in the broad places
thereof,
If ye can find a man,
If there be any that doeth justly,
that seeketh truth;
And I will pardon her.
2 And though they say: 'As the
LORD liveth,'
Surely they swear falsely.

שׁוֹטְטוּ בְּחוּצוֹת יְרוּשָׁלַם 1
וּרְאוּ־נָא וּדְעוּ
וּבַקְשׁוּ בִרְחוֹבוֹתֶיהָ
אִם־תִּמְצְאוּ אִישׁ
אִם־יֵשׁ עֹשֶׂה מִשְׁפָּט
מְבַקֵּשׁ אֱמוּנָה
וְאֶסְלַח לָהּ:
וְאִם חַי־יְהֹוָה יֹאמֵרוּ 2
לָכֵן לַשֶּׁקֶר יִשָּׁבֵעוּ:

v. 2. סבירין אכן

acted adulterously, since God was their
'Spouse' (iii. 1) (Kara).

31. *that spreadeth her hands.* Appealing-
ly, crying out in anguish, *Woe is me*
(Daath Mikra).

CHAPTER V

JERUSALEM'S DEPRAVITY

1–9 NO GROUND FOR GOD'S PARDON

1. *streets . . . broad places.* Men of
justice and truth were to be found in
Jerusalem; but they had to shut themselves up in their homes, afraid to
appear in the streets and public squares

for fear of the wicked (Kimchi). [It is an
exaggeration to interpret the verse as
declaring that there was not one God-
fearing man in the city, although it is so
understood by many moderns.]

a man. Worthy of being so called
(Kimchi).

truth. Or, 'faithfulness.' [This virtue
(*emunah*) unites in itself faithfulness
towards God (constancy), towards man
(integrity), towards oneself (genuineness).]

2. *and though . . . swear falsely.* Their
oaths are false, even when supported by
the most solemn mention of God's
name (Kimchi).

3 O LORD, are not Thine eyes upon
truth?
Thou hast stricken them, but
they were not affected;
Thou hast consumed them, but
they have refused to receive
correction;
They have made their faces harder
than a rock;
They have refused to return.
4 And I said: 'Surely these are poor,
They are foolish, for they know
not the way of the LORD,
Nor the ordinance of their God;
5 I will get me unto the great men,
And will speak unto them;
For they know the way of the
LORD,
And the ordinance of their God.'
But these had altogether broken
the yoke,
And burst the bands.

יְהֹוָה עֵינֶיךָ הֲלוֹא לֶאֱמוּנָה 3
הִכִּיתָה אֹתָם וְלֹא־חָלוּ
כִּלִּיתָם מֵאֲנוּ קַחַת מוּסָר
חִזְּקוּ פְנֵיהֶם מִסֶּלַע
מֵאֲנוּ לָשׁוּב:
וַאֲנִי אָמַרְתִּי אַךְ־דַּלִּים הֵם 4
נוֹאֲלוּ כִּי לֹא יָדְעוּ דֶּרֶךְ יְהֹוָה
מִשְׁפַּט אֱלֹהֵיהֶם:
אֵלְכָה־לִּי אֶל־הַגְּדֹלִים 5
וַאֲדַבְּרָה אוֹתָם
כִּי הֵמָּה יָדְעוּ דֶּרֶךְ יְהֹוָה
מִשְׁפַּט אֱלֹהֵיהֶם
אַךְ הֵמָּה יַחְדָּו שָׁבְרוּ עֹל
נִתְּקוּ מוֹסֵרוֹת:

surely. The Hebrew *lachen* means
'therefore.' A number of Hebrew MSS.
read *achen*, surely; according to
Masorah, however, the reading is *lachen*,
whereas the intention is *achen*, nevertheless (Minchath Shai). See Daath Mikra.
Though they swear by the name of God,
nevertheless they swear falsely.

3. *are not Thine eyes upon truth?* Thou
lookest for truth and faithfulness in
men. Rashi explains: dost Thou not
look for faithful men to deal well with
them? Kimchi's rendering is: 'Are not
Thine eyes upon what is enduring?' i.e.
God's acts are meant to be of lasting
and stable worth. But His punishment
of Judah has not been of enduring
value, because despite the fact that He
has stricken them, they were not
induced to repent. Why, then, persist in
smiting them?

Thou hast consumed them. God has

almost destroyed them completely
(Kimchi).

4. *poor.* The prophet is referring to the
mass of the people. Some excuse may be
made for them in that their poverty and
lack of education lead them to depart
from God's ordinance. It is more difficult to make them amend their ways
(Kimchi).

they are foolish, etc. Sin can only be due
to ignorance and folly, which keep men
from knowing the way of God. Cf. the
Talmudic maxim, 'No man sins unless a
spirit of folly has entered into him'
(Sotah 3a).

5. Perhaps, thinks the prophet, he may
have more success with *the great men,* the
leaders. They will surely listen, since
they must have a knowledge of *the way of
God.* With them, too, he is disappointed
(Kimchi, Ibn Nachmiash).

6 Wherefore a lion out of the forest
doth slay them,
A wolf of the deserts doth spoil
them,
A leopard watcheth over their
cities,
Every one that goeth out thence is
torn in pieces;
Because their transgressions are
many,
Their backslidings are increased.
7 Wherefore should I pardon thee?
Thy children have forsaken Me,
And sworn by no-gods;
And when I had fed them to the
full, they committed adultery,
And assembled themselves in
troops at the harlots' houses.
8 They are become as well-fed
horses, lusty stallions;
Every one neigheth after his neighbour's wife.

עַל־כֵּן הִכָּם אַרְיֵה מִיַּעַר 6
זְאֵב עֲרָבוֹת יְשָׁדְדֵם
נָמֵר שֹׁקֵד עַל־עָרֵיהֶם
כָּל־הַיּוֹצֵא מֵהֵנָּה יִטָּרֵף
כִּי רַבּוּ פִּשְׁעֵיהֶם
עָצְמוּ מְשֻׁבוֹתֵיהֶם׃
אֵי לָזֹאת אֶסְלַח־לָךְ 7
בָּנַיִךְ עֲזָבוּנִי
וַיִּשָּׁבְעוּ בְּלֹא אֱלֹהִים
וָאַשְׂבִּעַ אוֹתָם וַיִּנְאָפוּ
וּבֵית זוֹנָה יִתְגֹּדָדוּ׃
סוּסִים מְזֻיָּנִים מַשְׁכִּים הָיוּ 8
אִישׁ אֶל־אֵשֶׁת רֵעֵהוּ יִצְהָלוּ׃

v. 7. אסלח ק'   v. 7. קמץ בז"ק   v. 8. מיוזנים ק'

---

6. *lion . . . wolf . . . leopard.* Typical of
the various nations which from time to
time attacked and despoiled them. The
metaphor is suggested by the wild beasts
which were an actual danger in the land
(cf. 1 Sam. xvii. 34; 1 Kings xiii. 24).
Midrashically, the lion represents Babylon, the wolf Media, the leopard
Greece, and 'torn to pieces' Edom
(Rashi from Leviticus Rabbah 13. 2).
According to Targum, the lion represents the king of the invading nation,
the wolf its army, and the leopard the
officers.

7. *thy children.* The inhabitants of
Jerusalem. God addresses the nation
(Daath Mikra).

and sworn by no-gods. Swearing *by no-
gods* was a profession of belief in idolatry. For the term *no-gods (lo-elohim),* cf.
Deut. xxxii. 17 *(lo-eloah)* and 21 *(lo-el).*

when I had fed them to the full. Cf. the

Talmudic proverb: 'The lion does not
growl over a heap of straw, but over a
heap of flesh' (Ber. 32a), i.e. satiety
produces haughtiness. The prosperity
which God granted to them, instead of
making them grateful, led to depravity
(cf. Deut. xxxii. 15) (Kimchi).

they committed adultery. This may be a
metaphor for apostasy (cf. iii. 1), but
perhaps also to be understood in its
literal sense as all commentaries.

and assembled themselves in troops. Bereft
of shame, they make no attempt to
avoid publicity in their immoral conduct. The phrase may have an allusion
to the obscene orgies which characterized certain idolatrous cults (Daath
Mikra).

8. The first clause is variously translated. A.V. and R.V. have: 'they were as
fed horses in the morning' (so Rashi and
Metsudath David), i.e. having been

9 Shall I not punish for these things?
Saith the LORD;
And shall not My soul be avenged
On such a nation as this?

10 Go ye up into her rows, and
destroy,
But make not a full end;
Take away her shoots;
For they are not the LORD's.

11 For the house of Israel and the
house of Judah
Have dealt very treacherously
against Me,
Saith the LORD.

12 They have belied the LORD,
And said: 'It is not He,
Neither shall evil come upon us;
Neither shall we see sword nor
famine;

13 And the prophets shall become
wind,
And the word is not in them;

9 הַעַל־אֵלֶּה לוֹא־אֶפְקֹד
נְאֻם־יְהֹוָה
וְאִם בְּגוֹי אֲשֶׁר־כָּזֶה
לֹא תִתְנַקֵּם נַפְשִׁי:
10 עֲלוּ בְשָׁרוֹתֶיהָ וְשַׁחֵתוּ
וְכָלָה אַל־תַּעֲשׂוּ
הָסִירוּ נְטִישׁוֹתֶיהָ
כִּי לוֹא לַיהֹוָה הֵמָּה:
11 כִּי בָגוֹד בָּגְדוּ בִּי
בֵּית יִשְׂרָאֵל וּבֵית יְהוּדָה
נְאֻם־יְהֹוָה:
12 כִּחֲשׁוּ בַּיהֹוָה
וַיֹּאמְרוּ לוֹא־הוּא
וְלֹא־תָבוֹא עָלֵינוּ רָעָה
וְחֶרֶב וְרָעָב לוֹא נִרְאֶה:
13 וְהַנְּבִיאִים יִהְיוּ לְרוּחַ
וְהַדִּבֵּר אֵין בָּהֶם

filled with food in the night they are lustful in the morning. R.V. margin renders: 'roaming at large,' which derives *mashkim* from a root *shachah*. A.J., *lusty stallions* construes *mashkim* as an abbreviated form of *maashichim*, a denominative of *eshech*, 'testicle' (Malbim).

9. *shall not My soul be avenged?* [This is anthropomorphism: just retribution for sins which, as it were, affront God's purity and holiness is spoken of as Divine 'vengeance.']

10-19 THE DESTROYING ENEMY IS SUMMONED

10ff. Since the people have thrown off

their allegiance, God disowns them and bids the nations come and attack them.

10. *into her rows.* Of vines (Rashi). A.V. and R.V., 'go ye up upon her walls,' follow Menahem and Kimchi.

but make not a full end. See on iv. 27.

shoots. Continuing the metaphor of the vineyard; but A.V. has 'battlements' following Kimchi, and R.V. 'branches,' following Metsudoth.

12. *it is not He.* Who is responsible either for our well-being or for our ills. We need therefore fear nothing (Targum, Rashi, Kimchi).

13. *and the prophets,* etc. This con-

Thus be it done unto them.'

14 Wherefore thus saith the LORD,
the God of hosts:
Because ye speak this word,
Behold, I will make My words in
thy mouth fire,
And this people wood, and it
shall devour them.

15 Lo, I will bring a nation upon
you from far,
O house of Israel, saith the LORD;
It is an enduring nation,
It is an ancient nation,
A nation whose language thou
knowest not,
Neither understandest what they
say.

16 Their quiver is an open sepulchre,
They are all mighty men.

17 And they shall eat up thy harvest,
and thy bread,
They shall eat up thy sons and
thy daughters,

כֹּה יַעֲשֶׂה לָהֶם:

14 לָכֵן כֹּה־אָמַר יְהֹוָה
אֱלֹהֵי צְבָאוֹת
יַעַן דַּבֶּרְכֶם אֶת־הַדָּבָר הַזֶּה
הִנְנִי נֹתֵן דְּבָרַי בְּפִיךָ לְאֵשׁ
וְהָעָם הַזֶּה עֵצִים וַאֲכָלָתַם:

15 הִנְנִי מֵבִיא עֲלֵיכֶם גּוֹי מִמֶּרְחָק
בֵּית יִשְׂרָאֵל נְאֻם־יְהֹוָה
גּוֹי | אֵיתָן הוּא
גּוֹי מֵעוֹלָם הוּא
גּוֹי לֹא־תֵדַע לְשֹׁנוֹ
וְלֹא תִשְׁמַע מַה־יְדַבֵּר:

16 אַשְׁפָּתוֹ כְּקֶבֶר פָּתוּחַ
כֻּלָּם גִּבּוֹרִים:

17 וְאָכַל קְצִירְךָ וְלַחְמֶךָ
יֹאכְלוּ בָּנֶיךָ וּבְנוֹתֶיךָ

tinues the rejoinder of the people. The prophets of doom are empty windbags, falsely claiming to speak God's word, and their threatening predictions will be fulfilled only in themselves (Abarbanel).

14. *the God of hosts.* [A frequent designation of the Almighty, especially used by Isaiah. It represents His irresistible power as the Disposer of forces which none can withstand.]

thy mouth. i.e. Jeremiah's (Kara, Kimchi).

it shall devour them. The prophecies of woe will certainly be fulfilled (Metsudath David).

15. *from far.* Cf. Isa. v. 26.
house of Israel. [Used here of the whole nation, Judea included.]

an enduring nation. The adjective describes a stream whose waters do not fail; here it describes the enemy as a people which does not fail in the purpose it undertakes (Daath Mikra).

an ancient nation. Alluding to the antiquity of the Babylonians with their long record of military prowess (Kimchi).

whose language thou knowest not. They were 'barbarians' in the original sense of the term, a fact which increases the terror they arouse (cf. Deut. xxviii. 49; Isa. xxviii. 11).

16. *their quiver is an open sepulchre.* Their arrows are deadly (cf. Ps. v. 10).

17. *they shall eat up thy sons.* To be understood metaphorically. A.V. and R.V. render: 'which thy sons and thy

They shall eat up thy flocks and
thy herds,
They shall eat up thy vines and
thy fig-trees;
They shall batter thy fortified
cities,
Wherein thou trustest, with the
sword.

18 But even in those days, saith the
LORD,
I will not make a full end with
you.

19. And it shall come to pass, when
ye shall say: 'Wherefore hath the
LORD our God done all these things
unto us?' then shalt Thou say unto
them: 'Like as ye have forsaken Me,
and served strange gods in your land,
so shall ye serve strangers in a land
that is not yours.'

20 Declare ye this in the house of
Jacob,
And announce it in Judah, saying:

21 Hear now this, O foolish people,
and without understanding,
That have eyes, and see not,

יֹאכַל צֹאנְךָ וּבְקָרֶךָ
יֹאכַל גַּפְנְךָ וּתְאֵנָתֶךָ
יְרֹשֵׁשׁ עָרֵי מִבְצָרֶיךָ
אֲשֶׁר אַתָּה
בֹּטֵחַ בָּהֵנָּה בֶּחָרֶב׃

18 וְגַם בַּיָּמִים הָהֵמָּה נְאֻם־יְהֹוָה
לֹא־אֶעֱשֶׂה אִתְּכֶם כָּלָה׃

19 וְהָיָה כִּי תֹאמְרוּ תַּחַת מֶה
עָשָׂה יְהֹוָה אֱלֹהֵינוּ לָנוּ אֶת־
כָּל־אֵלֶּה וְאָמַרְתָּ אֲלֵיהֶם
כַּאֲשֶׁר עֲזַבְתֶּם אוֹתִי וַתַּעַבְדוּ
אֱלֹהֵי נֵכָר בְּאַרְצְכֶם כֵּן
תַּעַבְדוּ זָרִים בְּאֶרֶץ לֹא
לָכֶם׃

20 הַגִּידוּ זֹאת בְּבֵית יַעֲקֹב
וְהַשְׁמִיעוּהָ בִיהוּדָה לֵאמֹר׃

21 שִׁמְעוּ־נָא זֹאת
עַם־סָכָל וְאֵין לֵב
עֵינַיִם לָהֶם וְלֹא יִרְאוּ

---

daughters should eat' (so Metsudath
David).

18. See on iv. 27.

19. *in a land that is not yours.* The Babylonian captivity is evidently predicted.
The intention is that they will receive
payment in kind. They worshipped
foreign gods in their land; now they will
serve strangers in a land not theirs
(Kimchi).

20–31 CAUSE OF THE IMPENDING
CALAMITY

20. *Jacob . . . Judah. The house of Jacob* is
the Northern Kingdom; again the
whole nation is addressed (Daath
Soferim).

21. *understanding.* lit. 'heart.'

that have eyes, etc. lit. 'they have eyes,'
etc. The change from the second to the
third person indicates that this is a
parenthetical reflection by the prophet.

That have ears, and hear not:

22 Fear ye not Me? saith the LORD;
Will ye not tremble at My presence?
Who have placed the sand for the bound of the sea,
An everlasting ordinance, which it cannot pass;
And though the waves thereof toss themselves, yet can they not prevail;
Though they roar, yet can they not pass over it.

23 But this people hath a revolting and a rebellious heart;
They are revolted, and gone.

24 Neither say they in their heart:
'Let us now fear the LORD our God,
That giveth the former rain, and the latter in due season;
That keepeth for us
The appointed weeks of the harvest.'

25 Your iniquities have turned away these things,

אָזְנַיִם לָהֶם וְלֹא יִשְׁמָעוּ׃

22 הַאוֹתִי לֹא־תִירָאוּ
נְאֻם־יְהוָֹה
אִם מִפָּנַי לֹא תָחִילוּ
אֲשֶׁר־שַׂמְתִּי חוֹל גְּבוּל לַיָּם
חָק־עוֹלָם וְלֹא יַעַבְרֶנְהוּ
וַיִּתְגָּעֲשׁוּ וְלֹא יוּכָלוּ
וְהָמוּ גַלָּיו וְלֹא־יַעַבְרֻנְהוּ׃

23 וְלָעָם הַזֶּה הָיָה
לֵב סוֹרֵר וּמוֹרֶה
סָרוּ וַיֵּלֵכוּ׃

24 וְלֹא־אָמְרוּ בִלְבָבָם
נִירָא נָא אֶת־יְהוָה אֱלֹהֵינוּ
הַנֹּתֵן גֶּשֶׁם וְיוֹרֶה וּמַלְקוֹשׁ בְּעִתּוֹ
שְׁבֻעוֹת חֻקּוֹת קָצִיר
יִשְׁמָר־לָנוּ׃

25 עֲוֺנוֹתֵיכֶם הִטּוּ־אֵלֶּה

v. 22.   v. 24. קמץ בז״ק   יורה ק׳

The phrase occurs *verbatim* in Ps. cxv. 5f. where it refers to idols. Possibly it was proverbial, and is here applied by Jeremiah to the people, on the line of reasoning that idolatry (although we have no particular reference to it) makes its devotees like the idols themselves (see on ii. 5) (see Daath Mikra).

22. The omnipotence of God is so obviously attested by Nature; will it have no effect upon the people?

23. *but this people,* etc. Inanimate Nature, even when rebellious, cannot overstep its appointed bounds. Yet this people has defied God and ignored the

purpose for which He chose them! (Metsudath David).

24. As His infinite power does not arouse fear of Him within them (verse 22), they also blind themselves to their dependence upon Him for their sustenance.

that keepeth for us ... harvest. Who preserves the harvesting period (about the latter half of April and May) as a dry season, since rain at that time would harm the crops (Kimchi).

25. *these things ... good.* The aforementioned blessings (Malbim). Or, the understanding of these things (viz.

And your sins have withholden
good from you.
26 For among My people are found
wicked men;
They pry, as fowlers lie in wait;
They set a trap, they catch men.
27 As a cage is full of birds,
So are their houses full of deceit;
Therefore they are become great,
and waxen rich;
28 They are waxen fat, they are become sleek;
Yea, they overpass in deeds of
wickedness;
They plead not the cause, the
cause of the fatherless,
That they might make it to
prosper;
And the right of the needy do
they not judge.
29 Shall I not punish for these
things?
Saith the LORD;
Shall not My soul be avenged
On such a nation as this?

וְחַטֹּאותֵיכֶ֖ם
מָנְע֥וּ הַטּ֖וֹב מִכֶּֽם׃
26 כִּֽי־נִמְצְא֥וּ בְעַמִּ֖י רְשָׁעִ֑ים
יָשׁ֙וּר֙ כְּשַׁ֣ךְ יְקוּשִׁ֔ים
הִצִּ֙יבוּ֙ מַשְׁחִ֔ית אֲנָשִׁ֖ים יִלְכֹּֽדוּ׃
27 כִּכְל֣וּב מָלֵ֣א ע֔וֹף
כֵּ֥ן בָּתֵּיהֶ֖ם מְלֵאִ֣ים מִרְמָ֑ה
עַל־כֵּ֥ן גָּדְל֖וּ וַֽיַּעֲשִֽׁירוּ׃
28 שָׁמְנ֣וּ עָשְׁת֗וּ
גַּ֚ם עָֽבְר֣וּ דִבְרֵי־רָ֔ע
דִּ֣ין לֹא־דָ֗נוּ דִּ֤ין יָתוֹם֙ וְֽיַצְלִ֔יחוּ
וּמִשְׁפַּ֥ט אֶבְיוֹנִ֖ים לֹ֥א שָׁפָֽטוּ׃
29 הַֽעַל־אֵ֥לֶּה לֹֽא־אֶפְקֹ֖ד
נְאֻם־יְהֹוָ֑ה
אִ֚ם בְּג֣וֹי אֲשֶׁר־כָּזֶ֔ה
לֹ֥א תִתְנַקֵּ֖ם נַפְשִֽׁי׃

v. 25. ר׳ יתיר

God's power and bounty) and the good
sense to draw the right conclusions
from them (Metsudath David).

26. wicked men. i.e. wicked men who
trap their fellowmen and rob them
(Alshich).

they pry. The verb is singular; each one
of them pries (Kimchi).

as fowlers. Cf. Mic. vii. 2.

27. deceit. Ill-gotten wealth (Kimchi).

28. *that they might make it to prosper.* Or,
'and yet they prosper'; in spite of their
misdeeds (Kimchi).

29. Repetition of verse 9 as though it
were a refrain.

shall not My soul be avenged? [Such acts
of injustice are not merely a wrong
against one's fellow-men, but also an
affront to God which must be avenged.
That evil against man is also evil against
God was one of the great messages of
the prophets.] Although God is slow to
anger and waits for sinners to mend
their ways, there are, nevertheless, sins
whose retribution cannot be delayed
since the leniency to the sinner is harm
to the victim, and it is unjust to be
lenient to one at the expense of another
(Daath Soferim).

on such a nation as this? This appears to
imply very grave sins. This is, however
exaggerated. The complaint is to Israel,

41

30 An appalling and horrible thing
    Is come to pass in the land:
31 The prophets prophesy in the
    service of falsehood,
    And the priests bear rule at
    their beck;
    And My people love to have it so;
    What then will ye do in the end
    thereof?

30 שַׁמָּה וְשַׁעֲרוּרָה
נִהְיְתָה בָּאָרֶץ:
31 הַנְּבִאִים נִבְּאוּ בַשֶּׁקֶר
וְהַכֹּהֲנִים יִרְדּוּ עַל־יְדֵיהֶם
וְעַמִּי אָהֲבוּ כֵן
וּמַה־תַּעֲשׂוּ לְאַחֲרִיתָהּ:

6   CHAPTER VI   ו

1 Put yourselves under covert, ye
    children of Benjamin,
    Away from the midst of Jerusalem,
    And blow the horn in Tekoa,

ו הָעִזוּ | בְּנֵי בִנְיָמִן
מִקֶּרֶב יְרוּשָׁלַ͏ִם
וּבִתְקוֹעַ תִּקְעוּ שׁוֹפָר

who are people of God and who are expected to be superior to other nations (Daath Soferim).

30. The mode of life among the nation has become normal with them, but in the sight of God it is *an appalling and horrible thing.*

31. Not only the temporal rules (referred to in verse 28), but also the spiritual leaders, are corrupt. What hope is there then?

in the service of falsehood. They tell the people that there will be peace, and thereby lead them to evil ways (Kimchi). 'Falsehood' may be euphemistic for 'Baal,' meaning that the prophets prophesied in the name of Baal (Metsudath David). The prophets were people who supported their assertions upon divine inspiration. Hence, not subject to argument. The people were, therefore, inclined to believe them (Daath Soferim).

at their beck. In their interest and at their pleasure (Metsudath David).

My people love to have it so. The masses submitted without protest to the misrule (Kimchi).

in the end thereof. When retribution comes (Kimchi).

CHAPTER VI

1–8   SOUND THE ALARM!

1. *put yourselves under covert.* For the verb, see on iv. 6.

ye children of Benjamin. The city of Jerusalem was located in the territory of Benjamin, and for that reason the population was in special danger since the enemy would make for the capital. Possibly Jeremiah addressed himself to the Benjaminites because he belonged to that tribe (Kimchi).

Tekoa. About twelve miles south of Jerusalem. It was the home of Amos. The name involves a play on the verb *tikeu, blow* (the horn), and the town is probably specified for the assonance (Kimchi). For another example of this, cf. Zeph. ii. 4.

And set up a signal on Beth-
  cherem;
For evil looketh forth from the
  north,
And a great destruction.

2 The comely and delicate one,
  The daughter of Zion, will I cut
  off.

3 Shepherds with their flocks come
  unto her;
  They pitch their tents against her
  round about;
  They feed bare every one what is
  nigh at hand.

4 'Prepare ye war against her;
  Arise, and let us go up at noon!'
  'Woe unto us! for the day declineth,
  For the shadows of the evening are
  stretched out!'

וְעַל־בֵּית הַכֶּרֶם שְׂאוּ מַשְׂאֵת
כִּי רָעָה נִשְׁקְפָה מִצָּפוֹן
וְשֶׁבֶר גָּדוֹל:
² הַנָּוָה וְהַמְּעֻנָּגָה
דָּמִיתִי בַּת־צִיּוֹן:
³ אֵלֶיהָ יָבֹאוּ רֹעִים וְעֶדְרֵיהֶם
תָּקְעוּ עָלֶיהָ אֹהָלִים סָבִיב
רָעוּ אִישׁ אֶת־יָדוֹ:
⁴ קַדְּשׁוּ עָלֶיהָ מִלְחָמָה
קוּמוּ וְנַעֲלֶה בַצָּהֳרָיִם
אוֹי לָנוּ כִּי־פָנָה הַיּוֹם
כִּי־יִנָּטוּ צִלְלֵי־עָרֶב:

---

a signal. Perhaps 'a beacon' (cf. Judg.
xx. 38) (Kimchi).

Beth-cherem. Some identify it with En-
kerem, west of Jerusalem, and others
with Ramat-Rachel, south of Jerusalem
(Daath Mikra). It is mentioned again in
Nehem. iii. 14. It is mentioned there as
the name of a province in the period of
the return to Zion. This was the source
of the stones used for the altar and the
ramp leading up to it (Middoth iii. 4).

evil. The catastrophe of invasion
(Abarbanel).

from the north. See on i. 13.

2. *the comely and delicate one.* Zion is
compared to a beautiful and delicately
reared woman (so Kimchi, Metsudath
David, R.V., and some moderns). Rashi
explains the phrase as 'the meadow, yea
the luxuriant one.' This fits the image of
the invading shepherds (Malbim).

will I cut off. The tense of the Hebrew
verb is the prophetic perfect, literally 'I
have cut off'; so certain is the destruc-

tion that it is described as having taken
place (see Rashi).

3. *shepherds.* For this image of invaders, cf. xii. 10.

they feed bare, etc. Each commander
will ravage a part of the country
(Kimchi).

4. *prepare ye.* The verse is spoken to
the enemy. The verb is literally 'sanctify'; entry upon war was regarded as a
solemn act and observed by the offering
of sacrifices (Daath Mikra).

at noon. [The heat of the day when an
enemy on the march usually rests. It
denotes, therefore, a surprise attack.]

woe unto us! . . . stretched out! A.J. prints
this sentence with quotation marks,
understanding the words as spoken by
Israel, not the enemy, and as a lament at
nightfall over the destruction accomplished during the day, or an expression
of fear that, under cover of darkness,
the enemy will work even greater
destruction. Metsudath David construes

43

5 'Arise, and let us go up by night,
And let us destroy her palaces.'

6 For thus hath the LORD of hosts
said:
Hew ye down her trees,
And cast up a mound against Jeru-
salem;
This is the city to be punished;
Everywhere there is oppression in
the midst of her.

7 As a cistern welleth with her
waters,
So she welleth with her wickedness;
Violence and spoil is heard in her;
Before Me continually is sickness
and wounds.

8 Be thou corrected, O Jerusalem,

5 קוּמוּ וְנַעֲלֶה בַלָּיְלָה
וְנַשְׁחִיתָה אַרְמְנוֹתֶיהָ:
6 כִּי כֹה אָמַר יְהוָה צְבָאוֹת
כִּרְתוּ עֵצָה
וְשִׁפְכוּ עַל־יְרוּשָׁלַם סֹלְלָה
הִיא הָעִיר הָפְקַד
כֻּלָּהּ עֹשֶׁק בְּקִרְבָּהּ:
7 כְּהָקִיר בַּוֹר מֵימֶיהָ
כֵּן הֵקֵרָה רָעָתָהּ
חָמָס וָשֹׁד יִשָּׁמַע בָּהּ
עַל־פָּנַי תָּמִיד חֳלִי וּמַכָּה:
8 הִוָּסְרִי יְרוּשָׁלַם

v. 6. הה' רפה v. 7. בּיר ק'

the whole verse as the words of the enemy. The second half is, according to him, a lament of the soldiers that the day is already past and the destruction not yet complete. This interpretation is adopted by most moderns and accords better with the next verse.

5. by night. We will not wait until morning for the final assault (Metsudath David).

palaces. The Hebrew word may signify 'citadels, strongholds.' Kimchi (*Shorashim*) derives it from 'ram,' *high,* denoting a tall building.

6. hew ye down her trees. For the erection of bulwarks (cf. Deut. xx. 20).

a mound. Level with the walls of the city, to facilitate the attack (Metsudath David).

7. a cistern. The translation of A.J. follows the *kethib,* whereas the *kerë* means 'well' (so R.V.). According to the *kethib,* the intention is that Jerusalem

was a storehouse of evil, just as a cistern is used to store rain water (Abarbanel). According to the *kerë,* the intention is that, just as well water continues to flow without a stop, so does Jerusalem's evil constantly increase and renew itself (Rashi, Kimchi).

welleth. The meaning of the verb is uncertain; R.V. margin, 'keepeth fresh,' is probable.

violence and spoil. The phrase may be a cry of alarm (cf. xx. 8) (Metsudath David).

sickness and wounds. The sickness and wounds are the punishment for the violence and spoil mentioned earlier in the verse (Rashi, Targum). It is also possible that the violence and spoil cause sickness and wounds to the victims (Kimchi).

8. The prophet has already predicted the doom of the city. Yet, as so often, he makes a last-minute appeal.

Lest My soul be alienated from
thee,
Lest I make thee desolate,
A land not inhabited.

9 Thus saith the LORD of hosts:
They shall thoroughly glean as a
vine
The remnant of Israel;
Turn again thy hand
As a grape-gatherer upon the
shoots.

10 To whom shall I speak and give
warning,
That they may hear?
Behold, their ear is dull,
And they cannot attend;
Behold, the word of the LORD is
become unto them a reproach,
They have no delight in it.

11 Therefore I am full of the fury of
the LORD,
I am weary with holding in:
Pour it out upon the babes in the
street,

פֶּן־תֵּקַע נַפְשִׁי מִמֵּךְ
פֶּן־אֲשִׂימֵךְ שְׁמָמָה
אֶרֶץ לוֹא נוֹשָׁבָה:
9 כֹּה אָמַר יְהוָה צְבָאוֹת
עוֹלֵל יְעוֹלְלוּ כַגֶּפֶן
שְׁאֵרִית יִשְׂרָאֵל
הָשֵׁב יָדְךָ
כְּבוֹצֵר עַל־סַלְסִלּוֹת:
10 עַל־מִי אֲדַבְּרָה וְאָעִידָה
וְיִשְׁמָעוּ
הִנֵּה עֲרֵלָה אָזְנָם
וְלֹא יוּכְלוּ לְהַקְשִׁיב
הִנֵּה דְבַר־יְהוָה
הָיָה לָהֶם
לְחֶרְפָּה לֹא יַחְפְּצוּ־בוֹ:
11 וְאֵת חֲמַת יְהוָה ׀ מָלֵאתִי
נִלְאֵיתִי הָכִיל
שְׁפֹךְ עַל־עוֹלָל בַּחוּץ

v. 10. קמץ בז"ק

alienated. lit. 'pulled out.' God is interwoven with Israel, as it were, but sin will wrench Him away from the people — a striking metaphor expressing God's love on the one hand, and the powerful effect of sin on the other (Daath Mikra).

9–15 THE PEOPLE'S CORRUPTION

9. *turn again.* This is addressed to the enemy (Rashi).

as a grape-gatherer. Who seeks to leave nothing behind. So is the enemy bidden to be thorough in spoiling sinful Israel.

Alshich regards *turn again,* etc., as addressed to the prophet who is bidden to search whether any good grapes are concealed under the leaves, i.e. whether there are any righteous who deserve to be saved (cf. v. 1). On this interpretation, verse 10 is the despairing answer of the prophet: the search is vain.

10. *a reproach.* They treat the word of God with derision (Rashi).

11. *pour it out.* The verb is best parsed as the infinitive (so Rashi), 'to pour out,' i.e. this fury is to be poured out.

And upon the assembly of young
men together;
For even the husband with the
wife shall be taken,
The aged with him that is full of
days.

12 And their houses shall be turned
unto others,
Their fields and their wives together;
For I will stretch out My hand
upon the inhabitants of the
land,
Saith the Lord.

13 For from the least of them even
unto the greatest of them
Every one is greedy for gain;
And from the prophet even unto
the priest
Every one dealeth falsely.

14 They have healed also the hurt of
My people lightly,
Saying: 'Peace, peace,' when
there is no peace.

15 They shall be put to shame because they have committed
abomination;
Yea, they are not at all ashamed,
Neither know they how to blush;

וְעַל סוֹד בַּחוּרִים יַחְדָּו
כִּי־גַם־אִישׁ עִם־אִשָּׁה יִלָּכֵדוּ
זָקֵן עִם־מְלֵא יָמִים׃
12 וְנָסַבּוּ בָתֵּיהֶם לַאֲחֵרִים
שָׂדוֹת וְנָשִׁים יַחְדָּו
כִּי־אַטֶּה אֶת־יָדִי
עַל־יֹשְׁבֵי הָאָרֶץ
נְאֻם־יְהוָה׃
13 כִּי מִקְּטַנָּם וְעַד־גְּדוֹלָם
כֻּלּוֹ בּוֹצֵעַ בָּצַע
וּמִנָּבִיא וְעַד־כֹּהֵן
כֻּלּוֹ עֹשֶׂה שָּׁקֶר׃
14 וַיְרַפְּאוּ
אֶת־שֶׁבֶר עַמִּי עַל־נְקַלָּה
לֵאמֹר שָׁלוֹם ׀ שָׁלוֹם
וְאֵין שָׁלוֹם׃
15 הֹבִישׁוּ כִּי־תוֹעֵבָה עָשׂוּ
גַּם־בּוֹשׁ לֹא־יֵבוֹשׁוּ
גַּם־הַכְלִים לֹא יָדָעוּ

v. 15. קמץ בז"ק

12–15. These verses are largely repeated in viii. 10–12.

13. *greedy for gain.* They are guilty of
self-seeking even if it entail wrong upon
their neighbour (Daath Soferim).

14. *they have healed.* The subject is the
prophets and priests (Kimchi).

lightly. Simply by assuring them that
all is well (Rashi). Daath Soferim asserts
that the leaders did not intentionally
mislead the people. They wished to save

them from the panic of the impending
invasion. They attempted to bribe the
surrounding countries so that they
should be friendly to Israel and not
attack her. This solution, although
generally acceptable, was, in this case,
oversimplistic and superficial. The
prophet castigated them for engaging in
these simple solutions instead of repenting of their sins.

15. *they shall be put to shame.* A.V. and
R.V., based on Kimchi, construe as a

Therefore they shall fall among
  them that fall,
At the time that I punish them
  they shall stumble,
Saith the LORD.

16 Thus saith the LORD:
Stand ye in the ways and see,
And ask for the old paths,
Where is the good way, and walk
  therein,
And ye shall find rest for your
  souls.
But they said: 'We will not walk
  therein.'

17 And I set watchmen over you:
'Attend to the sound of the horn,'
But they said: 'We will not
  attend.'

18 Therefore hear, ye nations,
And know, O congregation, what
  is against them.

לָכֵן יִפְּלוּ בַנֹּפְלִים
בְּעֵת־פְּקַדְתִּים יִכָּשְׁלוּ
אָמַר יְהוָה׃

16 כֹּה אָמַר יְהוָה
עִמְדוּ עַל־דְּרָכִים וּרְאוּ
וְשַׁאֲלוּ ׀ לִנְתִבוֹת עוֹלָם
אֵי־זֶה דֶרֶךְ הַטּוֹב וּלְכוּ־בָהּ
וּמִצְאוּ מַרְגּוֹעַ לְנַפְשְׁכֶם
וַיֹּאמְרוּ לֹא נֵלֵךְ׃

17 וַהֲקִמֹתִי עֲלֵיכֶם צֹפִים
הַקְשִׁיבוּ לְקוֹל שׁוֹפָר
וַיֹּאמְרוּ לֹא נַקְשִׁיב׃

18 לָכֵן שִׁמְעוּ הַגּוֹיִם
וּדְעִי עֵדָה אֶת־אֲשֶׁר־בָּם׃

question: 'were they ashamed. . .?' Preference may perhaps be given to the interpretation of Rashi and Metsudath David: 'They should have been ashamed . . . but in fact are not at all ashamed.'

16–21 UNHEEDED WARNINGS

16. *stand in the roads.* i.e. in your speculation, 'stand' in the good road and in the evil road and seek to determine which is, indeed, the good road. In this, Jeremiah resembles Elijah, who exhorted the people to choose between worshipping God and worshipping Baal. He, too, confronts the people with this ultimatum. The true prophets tell you to repent of your evil ways lest you be delivered into the enemies' hands. The false prophets encourage you to continue on the way you are going and to ignore the warnings of the true prophets. They assure you that there

will be peace. Jeremiah exhorts the people to test the matter with their intelligence to determine which way is right. He tells them also to delve into the past. Ask for the paths the earlier generations have traversed, and you will find that those who followed the path of truth prospered and those who followed the path the false prophets encourage you to follow met only with disaster. Hence, there are two ways of determining which path to follow, the speculative approach and the traditional approach (Kimchi).

rest for your souls. Freedom from anxiety (Kimchi).

17. *watchmen.* Prophets who sought to waken you to the dangers of your apostasy from God (cf. Ezek. iii. 17, xxxiii. 7).

18. *congregation.* viz. of the Gentiles. Elsewhere the word *edah* always refers to

19 Hear, O earth:
Behold, I will bring evil upon this
   people,
Even the fruit of their thoughts,
Because they have not attended
   unto My words,
And as for My teaching, they
   have rejected it.
20 To what purpose is to Me the
   frankincense that cometh from
   Sheba,
And the sweet cane, from a far
   country?
Your burnt-offerings are not
   acceptable,
Nor your sacrifices pleasing unto
   Me.
21 Therefore thus saith the LORD:
Behold, I will lay stumbling-
   blocks before this people,
And the fathers and the sons
   together shall stumble against
   them,
The neighbour and his friend,
   and they shall perish.
22 Thus saith the LORD:
Behold, a people cometh from the
   north country,

19 שִׁמְעִי הָאָרֶץ
הִנֵּה אָנֹכִי מֵבִיא רָעָה
אֶל־הָעָם הַזֶּה
פְּרִי מַחְשְׁבוֹתָם
כִּי עַל־דְּבָרַי לֹא הִקְשִׁיבוּ
וְתוֹרָתִי וַיִּמְאָסוּ־בָהּ:
20 לָמָּה־זֶּה לִי לְבוֹנָה
מִשְּׁבָא תָבוֹא
וְקָנֶה הַטּוֹב מֵאֶרֶץ מֶרְחָק
עֹלוֹתֵיכֶם לֹא לְרָצוֹן
וְזִבְחֵיכֶם לֹא־עָרְבוּ לִי:
21 לָכֵן כֹּה אָמַר יְהֹוָה
הִנְנִי נֹתֵן
אֶל־הָעָם הַזֶּה מִכְשֹׁלִים
וְכָשְׁלוּ בָם אָבוֹת וּבָנִים יַחְדָּו
שָׁכֵן וְרֵעוֹ יֹאבֵדוּ:
22 כֹּה אָמַר יְהֹוָה
הִנֵּה עַם בָּא מֵאֶרֶץ צָפוֹן

v. 21. ואבדו ק'

Israel, but the parallelism with *nations*
makes it evident that the Gentiles are
here intended (Metsudath David).

what is against them. Better '(the evil)
that is in them' (Rashi, Kimchi).

19. *the fruit of their thoughts.* The results
of their wicked deeds, inspired by their
evil thoughts (Kimchi).

20. Sacrifice without good deeds is
unacceptable to God. There is nothing
to suggest that Jeremiah or the other
prophets opposed sacrifices as a religious institution; what they denounced

was conformity to the demands of the
Temple without observance of the
moral law.

21. This verse does not deny free will,
which all the pleadings, exhortations
and denunciations of the prophet
emphatically affirm.

stumbling blocks. This undoubtedly refers
to material misfortunes, not to moral
lapses (Alshich).

22–26 THE ENEMY DESCRIBED

22. *the north country.* See on i. 13.

48

And a great nation shall be roused
from the uttermost parts of the
earth.

23 They lay hold on bow and spear,
They are cruel, and have no
compassion;
Their voice is like the roaring sea,
And they ride upon horses;
Set in array, as a man for war,
Against thee, O daughter of Zion.

24 'We have heard the fame thereof,
Our hands wax feeble,
Anguish hath taken hold of us,
And pain, as of a woman in
travail.'

25 Go not forth into the field,
Nor walk by the way;
For there is the sword of the
enemy,
And terror on every side.

26 O daughter of my people, gird
thee with sackcloth,
And wallow thyself in ashes;
Make thee mourning, as for an
only son,

וְגוֹי גָּדוֹל
יֵעוֹר מִיַּרְכְּתֵי־אָרֶץ:

23 קֶשֶׁת וְכִידוֹן יַחֲזִיקוּ
אַכְזָרִי הוּא וְלֹא יְרַחֵמוּ
קוֹלָם כַּיָּם יֶהֱמֶה
וְעַל־סוּסִים יִרְכָּבוּ
עָרוּךְ כְּאִישׁ לַמִּלְחָמָה
עָלַיִךְ בַּת־צִיּוֹן:

24 שָׁמַעְנוּ אֶת־שָׁמְעוֹ
רָפוּ יָדֵינוּ
צָרָה הֶחֱזִיקַתְנוּ
חִיל כַּיּוֹלֵדָה:

25 אַל־תֵּצְאִי הַשָּׂדֶה
וּבַדֶּרֶךְ אַל־תֵּלֵכִי
כִּי חֶרֶב לְאֹיֵב
מָגוֹר מִסָּבִיב:

26 בַּת־עַמִּי חִגְרִי־שָׂק
וְהִתְפַּלְּשִׁי בָאֵפֶר
אֵבֶל יָחִיד עֲשִׂי־לָךְ

v. 26. קמץ בפשטא v. 25. תלכו ק׳ v. 25. תצאו ק׳

---

the uttermost parts of the earth. Cf. xxxi. 8 where the phrase is used of Babylon, the land of captivity.

23. *set in array.* Or, 'equipped.'

24. Jeremiah expresses the feelings of his countrymen about the enemy.

fame. i.e. report.

25. *go not forth.* Jeremiah warns them of the danger of going beyond the walls of the city (Malbim).

and terror. Omit *and* which is absent in the original, the word being in apposition to *the sword of the enemy.* The phrase is characteristic of Jeremiah; cf. xx. 3, 10, xlvi. 5, xlix. 29; cf. also Ps. xxxi. 14.

26. *daughter of my people.* The nation as a whole (cf. iv. 11).

as for an only son. The severest bereavement a Hebrew could suffer (cf. Amos. viii. 10; Zech. xii. 10).

Most bitter lamentation;
For the spoiler shall suddenly
   come upon us.

27 I have made thee a tower and a
   fortress among My people;
That thou mayest know and try
   their way.

28 They are all grievous revolters,
Going about with slanders;
They are brass and iron;
They all of them deal corruptly.

29 The bellows blow fiercely,
The lead is consumed of the fire;
In vain doth the founder refine,
For the wicked are not separated.

מִסְפַּד תַּמְרוּרִים
כִּי פִתְאֹם יָבֹא הַשֹּׁדֵד עָלֵינוּ:
27 בָּחוֹן נְתַתִּיךָ בְעַמִּי מִבְצָר
וְתֵדַע וּבָחַנְתָּ אֶת־דַּרְכָּם:
28 כֻּלָּם סָרֵי סוֹרְרִים
הֹלְכֵי רָכִיל
נְחֹשֶׁת וּבַרְזֶל
כֻּלָּם מַשְׁחִיתִים הֵמָּה:
29 נָחַר מַפֻּחַ
מֵאֵשְׁתַּם עֹפָרֶת
לַשָּׁוְא צָרַף צָרוֹף
וְרָעִים לֹא נִתָּקוּ:

v. 29. מאש תם ק׳

the spoiler. viz. Babylon (Metsudath David).

suddenly. [In view of Jeremiah's repeated warnings as well as the actual march of events, the invaders' attack could hardly be unexpected. But no matter how much we school ourselves to the thought of disaster, an inner hope makes us incredulous of final destruction, and whenever it comes, it is 'sudden.' Or: all your preparations will avail you nothing. When the invader attacks he will brush aside your defences as though you were caught unprepared.]

27-30 GOD HAS REJECTED JUDAH

27. *a tower and a fortress.* The words are spoken by God to Jeremiah: I have made you strong to resist all attacks from the people you denounce; therefore you can fearlessly *try their way,* i.e. pronounce judgment upon their evil (cf. i. 18f.).

and try. Hebrew *ubachanta* from the root *bachan;* the use of the verb, or the idea itself, is suggested by *bachon, tower,* in the first half of the verse (Kimchi).

28. *they are brass and iron.* The meaning is doubtful. A comparison with Ezek. xxii. 18-22 suggests that the point is that they are of inferior metal, as brass and iron are in comparison with silver (from the point of view of value). Rashi suggests: Going about with slanderers (strong as) brass and iron (to inflict injury upon their fellow-men).

29. The mention of brass and iron suggests a further simile. 'In refining, the alloy containing the gold or silver is mixed with lead, and fused in a furnace on a vessel of earth or bone-ash; a current of air is turned upon the molten mass (not upon the *fire*); the lead then oxidizes, and acting as a flux, carries away the alloy, leaving the gold or silver pure (I. Napier, *The Ancient Workers in Metal,* pp. 20, 23). In this case, the bellows wears out from constant blow-

30 Refuse silver shall men call them,
Because the LORD hath rejected
them.

בֶּסֶף נִמְאָס קָרְאוּ לָהֶם 30
כִּי־מָאַס יְהוָֹה בָּהֶם׃

7   CHAPTER VII   ז

1. The word that came to Jeremiah
from the LORD, saying: 2. Stand
in the gate of the LORD's house, and
proclaim there this word, and say:
Hear the word of the LORD, all ye
of Judah, that enter in at these
gates to worship the LORD. 3. Thus
saith the LORD of hosts, the God of
Israel:

Amend your ways and your doings,
and I will cause you to dwell in this
place. 4. Trust ye not in lying words,
saying: 'The temple of the LORD, the
temple of the LORD, the temple of

הַדָּבָר אֲשֶׁר־הָיָה אֶל־ 1
יִרְמְיָהוּ מֵאֵת יְהוָֹה לֵאמֹר׃
עֲמֹד בְּשַׁעַר בֵּית יְהוָֹה וְקָרֵאתָ 2
שָׁם אֶת־הַדָּבָר הַזֶּה וְאָמַרְתָּ
שִׁמְעוּ דְבַר־יְהוָֹה כָּל־
יְהוּדָה הַבָּאִים בַּשְּׁעָרִים
הָאֵלֶּה לְהִשְׁתַּחֲוֹת לַיהוָֹה׃
כֹּה־אָמַר יְהוָֹה צְבָאוֹת אֱלֹהֵי 3
יִשְׂרָאֵל הֵיטִיבוּ דַרְכֵיכֶם
וּמַעַלְלֵיכֶם וַאֲשַׁכְּנָה אֶתְכֶם
בַּמָּקוֹם הַזֶּה׃ אַל־תִּבְטְחוּ 4
לָכֶם אֶל־דִּבְרֵי הַשֶּׁקֶר
לֵאמֹר הֵיכַל יְהוָֹה הֵיכַל יְהוָֹה

ing, and yet the silver has not been
refined. It is still mixed with impurities,
and only impure silver remains. Kimchi
explains that the blower is the prophet,
the bellows his mouth and throat, and
the lead his efforts to admonish the
people by use of symbols and figures.
The impure silver symbolizes the wicked
of Israel. Despite all the prophet's
efforts, he is unsuccessful in separating
the wicked from their evil deeds.

30. *refuse . . . rejected.* In the Hebrew,
both words are derived from the same
root.

CHAPTER VII

THE prophecies in chapters vii-x were
delivered at the Temple gates. Scholars

disagree about their date, the reigns of
Josiah and Jehoiakim being the most
favoured.

2-15 CALL FOR AMENDMENT

2. *the gate.* The eastern gate (Kimchi).
Some identify it with *the new gate* mentioned in xxvi. 10 (Daath Mikra).

all ye of Judah. It has been suggested
that the occasion was one of the three
pilgrim-feasts when the city was
crowded with visitors (Daath Mikra).

gates. There were seven in all (Kimchi).

3. *in this place.* i.e. the land, as defined
in verse 7 (Daath Mikra).

4. *the temple of the* LORD, etc. The false
prophets maintain that the presence of

the LORD, are these.' 5. Nay, but if ye thoroughly amend your ways and your doings; if ye thoroughly execute justice between a man and his neighbour; 6. if ye oppress not the stranger, the fatherless, and the widow, and shed not innocent blood in this place, neither walk after other gods to your hurt; 7. then will I cause you to dwell in this place, in the land

5 הֵיכַל יְהוָה הֵמָּה : כִּי אִם־־
הֵיטֵיב תֵּיטִיבוּ אֶת־דַּרְכֵיכֶם
וְאֶת־מַעַלְלֵיכֶם אִם־עָשׂוֹ
תַעֲשׂוּ מִשְׁפָּט בֵּין אִישׁ וּבֵין
6 רֵעֵהוּ : גֵּר יָתוֹם וְאַלְמָנָה לֹא
תַעֲשֹׁקוּ וְדָם נָקִי אַל־תִּשְׁפְּכוּ
בַּמָּקוֹם הַזֶּה וְאַחֲרֵי אֱלֹהִים
אֲחֵרִים לֹא תֵלְכוּ לְרַע לָכֶם :
7 וְשִׁכַּנְתִּי אֶתְכֶם בַּמָּקוֹם הַזֶּה

the Temple of the Lord is a guarantee for the safety of the city (Kimchi). Alshich contrasts these people who come to prostrate themselves before God in His Temple with those encountered by Ezekiel (viii. 16), 'And He brought me into the inner court of the LORD's house, and behold, at the door of the temple of the LORD, between the porch and the altar, were about five and twenty men, with their backs toward the temple of the LORD, and their faces toward the east; and they worshipped the sun toward the east.' Only those who came to the temple to give it honour and to prostrate themselves before God, did God promise to allow to dwell in the Holy Land if they would improve their ways and repent of their sins. Those who came to the temple to defile it and disgrace it were given no such promise. The threefold repetition of the phrase is for emphasis (cf. xxii. 29; Isa. vi. 3). Rashi cites the explanation of the Targum that it alludes to the three times in the year when the Temple was visited by pilgrims (Deut. xvi. 16).

are these. viz. the Temple buildings to which Jeremiah points in his address (Metsudath David).

6. *the stranger.* Special consideration for the stranger, who was (and is) so frequently the object of dislike and active persecution, is a marked feature of the Mosaic legislation (cf. Exod. xxii. 20, xxiii. 9; Deut. xxiv. 17). 'In thirty-six places in the Torah we are commanded not to oppress the stranger' (Talmud Baba Metsia 59b). 'This law of shielding the alien from all wrong is of vital significance in the history of religion. . . The alien was to be protected, not because he was a member of one's family, clan, religious community; but because he was a human being. In the alien, therefore, man discovered the idea of humanity' (Hermann Cohen). [In the present passage, justice to the alien is made one of the conditions for Israel's continuing to enjoy the possession of his land; otherwise he would be driven into exile. This is a conception of nationality, dependent on and in the service of a wider humanity, which has never been surpassed and has still to be realized by the peoples of the world.]

the fatherless, and the widow. Solicitude for the weak and for those who have lost their natural protector is another distinguishing characteristic of Judaism, upon which, as here taught, the stability of the nation depends (Abarbanel). [Noteworthy is its inclusion in this verse with the exhortation to desist from murder and idolatry, showing the great importance attached to it.]

that I gave to your fathers, for ever and ever. 8. Behold, ye trust in lying words, that cannot profit. 9. Will ye steal, murder, and commit adultery, and swear falsely, and offer unto Baal, and walk after other gods whom ye have not known, 10. and come and stand before Me in this house, whereupon My name is called, and say: 'We are delivered,' that ye may do all these abominations? 11. Is this house, whereupon My name is called, become a den of robbers in your eyes? Behold, I, even I, have seen it, saith the LORD. 12. For go ye now unto My place which was in Shiloh, where

בָּאָרֶץ אֲשֶׁר נָתַתִּי לַאֲבוֹתֵיכֶם
8 לְמִן־עוֹלָם וְעַד־עוֹלָם: הִנֵּה
אַתֶּם בֹּטְחִים לָכֶם עַל־דִּבְרֵי
9 הַשֶּׁקֶר לְבִלְתִּי הוֹעִיל: הֲגָנֹב ׀
רָצֹחַ וְנָאֹף וְהִשָּׁבֵעַ לַשֶּׁקֶר
וְקַטֵּר לַבָּעַל וְהָלֹךְ אַחֲרֵי
אֱלֹהִים אֲחֵרִים אֲשֶׁר לֹא־
10 יְדַעְתֶּם: וּבָאתֶם וַעֲמַדְתֶּם
לְפָנַי בַּבַּיִת הַזֶּה אֲשֶׁר נִקְרָא־
שְׁמִי עָלָיו וַאֲמַרְתֶּם נִצַּלְנוּ
לְמַעַן עֲשׂוֹת אֵת כָּל־
11 הַתּוֹעֵבֹת הָאֵלֶּה: הַמְעָרַת
פָּרִצִים הָיָה הַבַּיִת הַזֶּה אֲשֶׁר־
נִקְרָא שְׁמִי־עָלָיו בְּעֵינֵיכֶם
גַּם אָנֹכִי הִנֵּה רָאִיתִי נְאֻם־
12 יְהֹוָה: כִּי לְכוּ־נָא אֶל־
מְקוֹמִי אֲשֶׁר בְּשִׁילוֹ אֲשֶׁר

v. 10. פתח באתנח

---

shed not innocent blood. An allusion to the murder of the prophet Zechariah in the temple (Alshich).

9. *will ye steal,* etc. The verbs in the Hebrew are infinitives; render: 'What! steal,' etc.

10. *and say: 'We are delivered.'* Through the mere fact of our presence in the Temple (Metsudath David).

that ye may do all these abominations. What a distortion of religion to imagine that the existence of the Temple automatically provides you with security, so that instead of exercising an ethical and wholesome influence, it even encour-

ages you to perpetuate all the evils enumerated! The dire threat in verse 13 follows logically from this reasoning.

11. *den of robbers.* Whither you retreat and in which you take refuge after criminal exploits! (Metsudath David).

have seen it. That this is how you regard the Temple (Rashi). Kimchi explains more simply: I see into your hearts, and know that even when you approach My Temple, you will intend to continue in your evil ways. Daath Mikra renders: 'Verily, *I* do look upon it as such.'

12. *in Shiloh.* In the early period of

I caused My name to dwell at the first, and see what I did to it for the wickedness of My people Israel.

13. And now, because ye have done all these works, saith the LORD, and I spoke unto you, speaking betimes and often, but ye heard not, and I called you, but ye answered not;

14. therefore will I do unto the house, whereupon My name is called, wherein ye trust, and unto the place which I gave to you and to your fathers, as I have done to Shiloh.

15. And I will cast you out of My sight, as I have cast out all your brethren, even the whole seed of Ephraim.

16. Therefore pray not thou for this people, neither lift up cry nor prayer for them, neither make intercession to Me; for I will not hear thee. 17. Seest thou not what they do in the cities of Judah and in the streets of Jerusalem? 18. The

שִׁכַּנְתִּי שְׁמִי שָׁם בָּרִאשׁוֹנָה
וּרְאוּ אֵת אֲשֶׁר־עָשִׂיתִי לּוֹ
מִפְּנֵי רָעַת עַמִּי יִשְׂרָאֵל:

13 וְעַתָּה יַעַן עֲשׂוֹתְכֶם אֶת־כָּל־
הַמַּעֲשִׂים הָאֵלֶּה נְאֻם־יְהֹוָה
וָאֲדַבֵּר אֲלֵיכֶם הַשְׁכֵּם וְדַבֵּר
וְלֹא שְׁמַעְתֶּם וָאֶקְרָא אֶתְכֶם

14 וְלֹא עֲנִיתֶם: וְעָשִׂיתִי לַבַּיִת ׀
אֲשֶׁר נִקְרָא־שְׁמִי עָלָיו
אֲשֶׁר אַתֶּם בֹּטְחִים בּוֹ
וְלַמָּקוֹם אֲשֶׁר־נָתַתִּי לָכֶם
וְלַאֲבוֹתֵיכֶם כַּאֲשֶׁר עָשִׂיתִי

15 לְשִׁלוֹ: וְהִשְׁלַכְתִּי אֶתְכֶם מֵעַל
פָּנָי כַּאֲשֶׁר הִשְׁלַכְתִּי אֶת־כָּל־
אֲחֵיכֶם אֵת כָּל־זֶרַע אֶפְרָיִם:

16 וְאַתָּה אַל־תִּתְפַּלֵּל ׀ בְּעַד־
הָעָם הַזֶּה וְאַל־תִּשָּׂא בַעֲדָם
רִנָּה וּתְפִלָּה וְאַל־תִּפְגַּע־בִּי

17 כִּי־אֵינֶנִּי שֹׁמֵעַ אֹתָךְ: הַאֵינְךָ
רֹאֶה מָה הֵמָּה עֹשִׂים בְּעָרֵי
יְהוּדָה וּבְחֻצוֹת יְרוּשָׁלָ͏ִם:

Israel's history the tabernacle was located in Shiloh; but it was destroyed in the days of Eli, after the battle of Ebenezer, when the ark was carried away by the Philistines (1 Sam. iv. 1ff.). The overthrow of Shiloh is alluded to again in xxvi. 6 (cf. Ps. lxxviii. 60).

13. *and I called you.* To repentance (Metsudath David).

15. *Ephraim.* i.e. the ten tribes of the Northern Kingdom (Kimchi).

16-20 JEREMIAH IS NOT TO INTERCEDE FOR THE PEOPLE

17. This verse states the reason why it would be useless for the prophet to pray to God to relent.

children gather wood, and the fathers kindle the fire, and the women knead the dough, to make cakes to the queen of heaven, and to pour out drink-offerings unto other gods, that they may provoke Me. 19. Do they provoke Me? saith the LORD; do they not provoke themselves, to the confusion of their own faces? 20. Therefore thus saith the Lord GOD: Behold, Mine anger and My fury shall be poured out upon this place, upon man, and upon beast, and upon the trees of the field, and upon the fruit of the land; and it shall burn, and shall not be quenched.

21. Thus saith the LORD of hosts,

18 הַבָּנִים מְלַקְּטִים עֵצִים
וְהָאָבוֹת מְבַעֲרִים אֶת־הָאֵשׁ
וְהַנָּשִׁים לָשׁוֹת בָּצֵק לַעֲשׂוֹת
כַּוָּנִים לִמְלֶכֶת הַשָּׁמַיִם וְהַסֵּךְ
נְסָכִים לֵאלֹהִים אֲחֵרִים
19 לְמַעַן הַכְעִסֵנִי: הַאֹתִי הֵם
מַכְעִסִים נְאֻם־יְהֹוָה הֲלוֹא
אֹתָם לְמַעַן בֹּשֶׁת פְּנֵיהֶם:
20 לָכֵן כֹּה־אָמַר | אֲדֹנָי יֱהֹוִה
הִנֵּה אַפִּי וַחֲמָתִי נִתֶּכֶת אֶל־
הַמָּקוֹם הַזֶּה עַל־הָאָדָם
וְעַל־הַבְּהֵמָה וְעַל־עֵץ
הַשָּׂדֶה וְעַל־פְּרִי הָאֲדָמָה
21 וּבָעֲרָה וְלֹא תִכְבֶּה: כֹּה
אָמַר יְהֹוָה צְבָאוֹת אֱלֹהֵי

v. 21. הפטרת צו

18. *children . . . fathers . . . and the women.* Young and old, male and female, participate in a form of worship which is an affront to God.

cakes. A special word is used, *kaw-wanim,* probably of foreign origin, which is found again only in xliv. 19, a description of the same cult. Daath Mikra claims that it originates from Assyrian. It means 'a cake.'

the queen of heaven. The consonants of the Hebrew word would ordinarily be read as *malkath, the queen of;* but the traditional pointing is *melécheth,* and many Hebrew MSS. insert the letter *aleph* which supports it. The translation should accordingly be 'the work of heaven,' i.e. the heavenly bodies. Even without the *aleph,* Kimchi explains it in this manner. Some Jewish commentators think of the sun, as the dominant planet; modern expositors favour the moon or the planet Venus.

that they may provoke Me. They know the futility of idolatry and engage in it deliberately to provoke Me (Metsudath David). To the prophet it was inconceivable that anybody could believe in the reality of an idol.

19. *do they provoke Me?* Their idolatry cannot injure God; it leads to their shame and confusion (Kimchi).

the God of Israel: Add your burnt-offerings unto your sacrifices, and eat ye flesh. 22. For I spoke not unto your fathers, nor commanded them in the day that I brought them out of the land of Egypt, concerning burnt-offerings or sacrifices; 23. but this thing I commanded them, saying: 'Hearken unto My voice,

יִשְׂרָאֵל עֹלוֹתֵיכֶם סְפוּ עַל־
22 זִבְחֵיכֶם וְאִכְלוּ בָשָׂר: כִּי
לְא־דִבַּרְתִּי אֶת־אֲבוֹתֵיכֶם
וְלֹא צִוִּיתִים בְּיוֹם הוֹצִיאִ֯א
אוֹתָם מֵאֶרֶץ מִצְרָיִם עַל־
23 דִּבְרֵי עוֹלָה וָזָבַח: כִּי אִם־
אֶת־הַדָּבָר הַזֶּה צִוִּיתִי אוֹתָם
לֵאמֹר שִׁמְעוּ בְקוֹלִי וְהָיִיתִי

ע. 22. הוֹצִיאִי ק'

21-28   FUTILITY OF SACRIFICES WITHOUT MORALITY

21. *add your burnt-offerings,* etc. Burnt-offerings were wholly consumed on the altar, whilst of other sacrifices parts were eaten by the priests and offerers. The meaning is: There is no sanctity in offerings brought by guilty men; they are merely *flesh* and so you might as well eat your burnt-offerings too! (Rashi, Metsudath David).

22. *for I spoke not,* etc. Sacrifices were only of secondary importance and subordinate to moral conduct. But neither Jeremiah nor the other prophets opposed sacrifices as a religious institution. This is made clear from the whole context of the passage. The question is dealt with from the Jewish standpoint in Hertz, *The Pentateuch and Haftorahs,* Soncino edition, pp. 56off. Some non-Jewish commentators have likewise recognized that Judaism has always given precedence to the moral over the ritual law. The prophet Samuel states (1 Sam. xv. 22), *Hath the Lord as great delight in burnt-offerings and sacrifices, As in hearkening to the voice of the Lord? Behold, to obey is better than sacrifice, And to hearken*

than the fat of rams. Indeed, this selection of the Prophets has been chosen to read along with Lev. vi-viii as the Haphtarah, to indicate that it is better to obey God rather than to sin and bring a sacrifice (Levush).

in the day ... Egypt. Most moderns interpret the phrase in such a way that it supports their hypothesis that the sacrificial system of 'the Priestly Code' is post-Mosaic. But the context makes it evident that a contrast is drawn between offerings on the altar and the moral laws enjoined in the Decalogue (verse 9); and it is true that there is no mention of sacrifices in the Ten Commandments. Daath Mikra sugggests a different rendering of the text: 'I spake not unto your fathers ... for the sake of (or, on account of) burnt-offerings,' i.e. I did not bring you out of Egypt because I wanted your sacrifices, although these are certainly part of the system of Divine worship.

23. *saying.* What follows is not a verbal quotation but a summary of God's frequent exhortation (cf. Exod. xix. 5; Deut. v. 30).

and I will be your God, and ye shall be My people; and walk ye in all the way that I command you, that it may be well with you.' 24. But they hearkened not, nor inclined their ear, but walked in their own counsels, even in the stubbornness of their evil heart, and went backward and not forward, 25. even since the day that your fathers came forth out of the land of Egypt unto this day; and though I have sent unto you all My servants the prophets, sending them daily betimes and often, 26. yet they hearkened not unto Me, nor inclined their ear, but made their neck stiff; they did worse than their fathers.

27. And thou shalt speak all these words unto them, but they will not hearken to thee; thou shalt also call unto them, but they will not answer thee. 28. Therefore thou shalt say unto them:

This is the nation that hath not hearkened

לָכֶם לֵאלֹהִים וְאַתֶּם תִּהְיוּ־
לִי לְעָם וַהֲלַכְתֶּם בְּכָל־
הַדֶּרֶךְ אֲשֶׁר אֲצַוֶּה אֶתְכֶם
24 לְמַעַן יִיטַב לָכֶם: וְלֹא שָׁמְעוּ
וְלֹא־הִטּוּ אֶת־אָזְנָם וַיֵּלְכוּ
בְּמֹעֵצוֹת בִּשְׁרִרוּת לִבָּם הָרָע
וַיִּהְיוּ לְאָחוֹר וְלֹא לְפָנִים:
25 לְמִן־הַיּוֹם אֲשֶׁר יָצְאוּ
אֲבוֹתֵיכֶם מֵאֶרֶץ מִצְרַיִם עַד
הַיּוֹם הַזֶּה וָאֶשְׁלַח אֲלֵיכֶם
אֶת־כָּל־עֲבָדַי הַנְּבִיאִים יוֹם
26 הַשְׁכֵּם וְשָׁלֹחַ: וְלוֹא שָׁמְעוּ
אֵלַי וְלֹא הִטּוּ אֶת־אָזְנָם וַיַּקְשׁוּ
אֶת־עָרְפָּם הֵרֵעוּ מֵאֲבוֹתָם:
27 וְדִבַּרְתָּ אֲלֵיהֶם אֶת־כָּל־
הַדְּבָרִים הָאֵלֶּה וְלֹא יִשְׁמְעוּ
אֵלֶיךָ וְקָרָאתָ אֲלֵיהֶם וְלֹא
יַעֲנוּכָה:
28 וְאָמַרְתָּ אֲלֵיהֶם
זֶה הַגּוֹי אֲשֶׁר לוֹא־שָׁמְעוּ

with you. The obedience which I demand is for your benefit, not Mine (Metsudath David).

24. *backward and not forward.* 'To desert the path of faithfulness and righteousness, no matter under what new or attractive name, is always to go backward' (Hertz).

26. *they did worse than their fathers.* Each generation was more sinful than the preceding (Kimchi).

27. *but they will not hearken to thee.* It was the prophet's heartbreaking experience to know in advance that his call would fall on deaf ears. To minister under such conditions, knowing that one's work would bear fruit only in the distant . future, calls for the highest degree of faith and deepest conviction (cf. Isa. vi. 9ff.).

28. *faithfulness (emunah) is perished.* The phrase sums up all their misdeeds.

To the voice of the LORD their
God,
Nor received correction;
Faithfulness is perished,
And is cut off from their mouth.

29. Cut off thy hair, and cast it away,
And take up a lamentation on the
high hills;
For the LORD hath rejected and
forsaken the generation of
His wrath.

30. For the children of Judah have
done that which is evil in My sight,
saith the LORD; they have set their
detestable things in the house whereon My name is called, to defile it.

31. And they have built the high
places of Topheth, which is in the
valley of the son of Hinnom, to burn
their sons and their daughters in the

בְּקוֹל יְהֹוָה אֱלֹהָיו
וְלֹא לָקְחוּ מוּסָר
אָבְדָה הָאֱמוּנָה
וְנִכְרְתָה מִפִּיהֶם׃
29 גָּזִּי נִזְרֵךְ וְהַשְׁלִיכִי
וּשְׂאִי עַל־שְׁפָיִם קִינָה
כִּי מָאַס יְהֹוָה
וַיִּטֹּשׁ אֶת־דּוֹר עֶבְרָתוֹ׃
30 כִּי־עָשׂוּ בְנֵי־יְהוּדָה הָרַע
בְּעֵינַי נְאֻם־יְהֹוָה שָׂמוּ
שִׁקּוּצֵיהֶם בַּבַּיִת אֲשֶׁר־נִקְרָא
31 שְׁמִי־עָלָיו לְטַמְּאוֹ׃ וּבָנוּ
בָּמוֹת הַתֹּפֶת אֲשֶׁר בְּגֵיא בֶן־
הִנֹּם לִשְׂרֹף אֶת־בְּנֵיהֶם וְאֶת־

Cf. the contrast in Hab. ii. 4, *the righteous
shall live by his faith (emunah)*, where *faith*
sums up all virtues. For the definition of
emunah, see on v. 1.

from their mouth. They have even ceased
pretending (Kimchi).

29–viii. 3   SIN OF THE PEOPLE AND
ITS PUNISHMENT

In this section the nation's hideous sin
of child-sacrifice is particularized and
their impending doom announced.

29. *cut off thy hair.* As a sign of mourning (cf. Mic. i. 16; Job i. 20). The verb is
feminine and indicates that the nation
(Kimchi) or Jerusalem (Daath Mikra) is
addressed. The Hebrew for *hair* is literally 'crown,' and several commentators
interpret: remove the insignia of thy
regal power (Rashi, Targum).

30. *their detestable things.* Their idols;
possibly an allusion to what is narrated
in 2 Kings xxi. 5 (Kimchi).

in the house, etc. Such an act of sac-
rilege is the crowning insult (Daath
Mikra).

31. *Topheth.* The meaning and etymo-
logy of the word are doubtful. It is now
usually regarded as akin to an Aramaic
word for 'fireplace'; in the Bible it signifies the pit in which human victims were
burned (see Kara).

valley of the son of Hinnom. The meaning
of *Hinnom* is uncertain. Possibly *the son of
Hinnom* was the name of the former
owner of the valley where the rites were
practised (cf. ii. 23) (Kimchi, 2 Kings
xxiii. 10).

to burn their sons. This was the essential
feature of Molech-worship (cf. xix. 5,

fire; which I commanded not, neither came it into My mind. 32. Therefore, behold, the days come, saith the LORD, that it shall no more be called Topheth, nor The valley of the son of Hinnom, but The valley of slaughter; for they shall bury in Topheth, for lack of room. 33. And the carcasses of this people shall be food for the fowls of the heaven, and for the beasts of the earth; and none shall frighten them away. 34. Then will I cause to cease from the cities of Judah, and from the streets of Jerusalem, the voice of mirth and the voice of gladness, the voice of the bridegroom and the voice of the bride; for the land shall be desolate.

בְּנֵיהֶם בָּאֵשׁ אֲשֶׁר לֹא צִוִּיתִי
32 וְלֹא עָלְתָה עַל־לִבִּי: לָכֵן
הִנֵּה יָמִים בָּאִים נְאֻם־יְהוָֹה
וְלֹא־יֵאָמֵר עוֹד הַתֹּפֶת וְגֵיא
בֶן־הִנֹּם כִּי אִם־גֵּיא הַהֲרֵגָה
וְקָבְרוּ בְתֹפֶת מֵאֵין מָקוֹם:
33 וְהָיְתָה נִבְלַת הָעָם הַזֶּה
לְמַאֲכָל לְעוֹף הַשָּׁמַיִם
וּלְבֶהֱמַת הָאָרֶץ וְאֵין מַחֲרִיד:
34 וְהִשְׁבַּתִּי ׀ מֵעָרֵי יְהוּדָה
וּמֵחֻצוֹת יְרוּשָׁלַם קוֹל שָׂשׂוֹן
וְקוֹל שִׂמְחָה קוֹל חָתָן וְקוֹל
כַּלָּה כִּי לְחָרְבָּה תִּהְיֶה
הָאָרֶץ:

xxxii. 35; Lev. xviii. 21). The victims were placed on the red-hot hands of the idol, and their moans were drowned out by the drums of the priests (Rashi).

which I commanded not. [The protagonists of human sacrifice deliberately or in ignorance perverted the meaning of such a command as that of Exod. xiii. 2, or God's command to Abraham to sacrifice Isaac, which they may have cited in support of their terrible act; hence the stern and emphatic repudiation in this clause.]

32. *The valley of slaughter.* It will become the scene of their slaughter by the enemy (Metsudath David).

for lack of room. The place will acquire such a fearful reputation that, although people would be loath to bury a dead body there, they would be forced to do so with the slain because all other burial places will be filled (Kimchi).

33. *none shall frighten them away.* Utter desolation will reign, with not a person to drive away the birds of prey from the carcasses (Rashi). With this verse, cf. the threat in Deut. xxviii. 26 (Daath Mikra). [The ancients regarded such treatment of the corpse and the lack of proper burial with the utmost horror.]

34. *for the land shall be desolate.* Therefore, instead of joyous sounds, there will be cries and wailing (Kimchi). Others explain that there will be no more joyous sounds since no one will remain in the land (Metsudath David).

1. At that time, saith the Lord, they shall bring out the bones of the kings of Judah, and the bones of his princes, and the bones of the priests, and the bones of the prophets, and the bones of the inhabitants of Jerusalem, out of their graves; 2. and they shall spread them before the sun, and the moon, and all the host of heaven, whom they have loved, and whom they have served, and after whom they have walked, and whom they have sought, and whom they have worshipped; they shall not be gathered, nor be buried, they shall be for dung upon the face of the earth. 3. And death shall be chosen rather than life by all the

1 בָּעֵת הַהִיא נְאֻם־יְהוָֹה
וְיוֹצִיאוּ אֶת־עַצְמוֹת מַלְכֵי־
יְהוּדָה וְאֶת־עַצְמוֹת שָׂרָיו
וְאֶת־עַצְמוֹת הַכֹּהֲנִים וְאֵת ׀
עַצְמוֹת הַנְּבִיאִים וְאֵת עַצְמוֹת
יוֹשְׁבֵי־יְרוּשָׁלָ͏ִם מִקִּבְרֵיהֶם׃
2 וּשְׁטָחוּם לַשֶּׁמֶשׁ וְלַיָּרֵחַ וּלְכֹל ׀
צְבָא הַשָּׁמַיִם אֲשֶׁר אֲהֵבוּם
וַאֲשֶׁר עֲבָדוּם וַאֲשֶׁר הָלְכוּ
אַחֲרֵיהֶם וַאֲשֶׁר דְּרָשׁוּם וַאֲשֶׁר
הִשְׁתַּחֲווּ לָהֶם לֹא יֵאָסְפוּ
וְלֹא יִקָּבֵרוּ לְדֹמֶן עַל־פְּנֵי
3 הָאֲדָמָה יִהְיוּ׃ וְנִבְחַר מָוֶת
מֵחַיִּים לְכֹל הַשְּׁאֵרִית

ע. 1. יוֹצִיאוּ ק׳   ע. 1. קמץ בטרחא

CHAPTER VIII

VERSES 1–3 continue the denunciation contained in the preceding section.

1. *they shall bring out.* The subject is Israel's enemies, acting as the instruments of Divine punishment. In addition to leaving the slain unburied, they will violate the graves of those who had been interred (Malbim).

the priests. Who ministered to Baal (Metsudath David).

the prophets. i.e. the false prophets (Targum). The actual account of the fall of Jerusalem, as related in chapter xxxix and 2 Kings xxv, does not record the fulfilment of this prediction. It is,

however, mentioned in the Apocrypha (Baruch ii. 24f.).

2. *and all the host of heaven.* [The heavenly bodies, which had been worshipped as gods, will look powerless upon the dishonour inflicted on their devotees.]

whom they have loved. As gods. In the sight of their deities they will suffer these degradations (Metsudath David).

3. *death shall be chosen rather than life.* In spite of the insults to which the dead will be exposed (Rashi). 'Fortunately, the prophet's worst apprehensions were not realized. Time softened the utter despair of the first exiles. Jeremiah himself was yet to advise them to build

residue that remain of this evil
family, that remain in all the places
whither I have driven them, saith
the LORD of hosts.

4. Moreover thou shalt say unto
them: Thus saith the LORD:
Do men fall, and not rise up
again?
Doth one turn away, and not return?

5 Why then is this people of Jeru-
salem slidden back
By a perpetual backsliding?
They hold fast deceit,
They refuse to return.

6 I attended and listened,
But they spoke not aright;
No man repenteth him of his
wickedness,

הַנִּשְׁאָרִים מִן־הַמִּשְׁפָּחָה
הָרָעָה הַזֹּאת בְּכָל־הַמְּקֹמוֹת
הַנִּשְׁאָרִים אֲשֶׁר הִדַּחְתִּים שָׁם
נְאֻם יְהֹוָה צְבָאוֹת׃

4 וְאָמַרְתָּ אֲלֵיהֶם
כֹּה אָמַר יְהֹוָה
הֲיִפְּלוּ וְלֹא יָקוּמוּ
אִם־יָשׁוּב וְלֹא יָשׁוּב׃

5 מַדּוּעַ שׁוֹבְבָה הָעָם הַזֶּה
יְרוּשָׁלַ͏ִם מְשֻׁבָה נִצַּחַת
הֶחֱזִיקוּ בַּתַּרְמִית
מֵאֲנוּ לָשׁוּב׃

6 הִקְשַׁבְתִּי וָאֶשְׁמָע
לוֹא־כֵן יְדַבֵּרוּ
אֵין אִישׁ נִחָם עַל־רָעָתוֹ

v. 5. קמץ בפשטא   v. 6. פתח באתנח

houses and rear families' (Hertz).
[Nevertheless, he need not be judged as
unduly pessimistic even when he for-
bodes ill. All prophecies are conditional; and the shock of exile must have
been so great as to bring about the
change of mind and heart which
warranted the non-fulfilment of these
dire threats.]

family. Obviously the whole people is
meant (see on iii. 14) (Daath Mikra).

that remain in all the places. A.J. follows
Metsudath David. Kimchi renders: 'in
all the places where they remain.'

4-17 IMPENITENCE WILL BRING RETRIBUTION

4. It is never too late for them to

repent, no matter how deeply they have
fallen and how far they have strayed
from God.

doth one turn away, etc. Kimchi interprets: 'if one turn back (from sin), shall
He not turn back (from His intention to
destroy)?'

5. *they hold fast deceit.* As one takes
possession of a field, so do they take
possession of deceit, not willing to
abandon it (Urim Vethummim). Others
render: 'they have become strong
through deceit.' i.e. they have built up
their wealth through deceit. Therefore,
they refuse to repent and abandon their
wealth (Alshich).

6. *not aright.* lit. 'not so,' which Metsudath David explains as: their words

61

Saying: 'What have I done?'
Every one turneth away in his
    course,
As a horse that rusheth headlong
    in the battle.

7 Yea, the stork in the heaven
    Knoweth her appointed times;
And the turtle and the swallow
    and the crane
Observe the time of their coming;
But My people know not
The ordinance of the LORD.

8 How do ye say: 'We are wise,
And the Law of the LORD is with
    us'?
Lo, certainly in vain hath wrought

לֵאמֹר מֶה עָשִׂיתִי
כֻּלֹּה שָׁב בִּמְרֻצוֹתָם
כְּסוּס שׁוֹטֵף בַּמִּלְחָמָה:
7 גַּם־חֲסִידָה בַשָּׁמַיִם
יָדְעָה מוֹעֲדֶיהָ
וְתֹר וְסִיס וְעָגוּר
שָׁמְרוּ אֶת־עֵת בֹּאָנָה
וְעַמִּי לֹא יָדְעוּ
אֵת מִשְׁפַּט יְהוָה:
8 אֵיכָה תֹאמְרוּ חֲכָמִים אֲנַחְנוּ
וְתוֹרַת יְהוָה אִתָּנוּ
אָכֵן הִנֵּה לַשֶּׁקֶר עָשָׂה

v. 6.   v. 7. במרוצתם ק׳ וסיס ק׳

---

give no indication that the people have
any intention of returning to God.

every one . . . battle. As a horse rushes
headlong into battle, recking nought
that it may lead to its destruction, so do
they rush thoughtlessly on their course,
sinning and turning away from God
(Daath Mikra).

7. Instinctively migratory birds know
the times of their coming and going,
which are the natural law of their being;
yet the people, though endowed with
reason, do not know God's ordinances
which are the natural law of their existence.

in the heaven. 'There is peculiar force in
the words *in the heaven,* for unlike most
other emigrants, the stork voyages by
day at a great height in the air'
(Tristram). The time of its appearance in
the Holy Land is in the month of March
and it departs northward in May.

the turtle. 'Its return in spring is one of
the most marked epochs in the ornitho-
logical calendar' (Tristram).

the swallow. The Hebrew *sis* is to be
identified with 'the swift' *(cypselus)*. 'In
Palestine, the swallow is only a partial
migrant, many remaining through the
winter. The swift, on the contrary, is a
regular migrant, returning in myriads
every spring, and so suddenly, that,
while one day not a swift can be seen in
the country, on the next they have
overspread the whole land' (Tristram).

the crane. 'It only visits the cultivated
region (of Palestine) at the time of its
spring migration, where a few pairs
remain in the marshy plains, as by the
waters of Merom, but the greater
number pass onwards to the north. In
the southern wilderness south of
Beersheba, it resorts in immense flocks
to certain favourite roosting-places
during the winter' (Tristram).

8. *the Law of the LORD is with us.* The
people (or their religious leaders)
probably denied Jeremiah's charges of
apostasy and maintained that they were
fulfilling God's Torah (Kara).

certainly in vain, etc. The labours of the

The vain pen of the scribes.

9 The wise men are ashamed,
They are dismayed and taken;
Lo, they have rejected the word of
the LORD;
And what wisdom is in them?

10 Therefore will I give their wives
unto others,
And their fields to them that shall
possess them;
For from the least even unto the
greatest
Every one is greedy for gain,
From the prophet even unto the
priest
Every one dealeth falsely.

11 And they have healed the hurt of
the daughter of My people
lightly,
Saying: 'Peace, peace,' when
there is no peace.

12 They shall be put to shame because they have committed
abomination;
Yea, they are not at all ashamed,
Neither know they how to blush;

עֵט שֶׁקֶר סֹפְרִים׃
9 הֹבִישׁוּ חֲכָמִים
חַתּוּ וַיִּלָּכֵדוּ
הִנֵּה בִדְבַר־יְהֹוָה מָאָסוּ
וְחָכְמַת־מֶה לָהֶם׃
10 לָכֵן אֶתֵּן אֶת־נְשֵׁיהֶם
לַאֲחֵרִים
שְׂדוֹתֵיהֶם לְיוֹרְשִׁים
כִּי מִקָּטֹן וְעַד־גָּדוֹל
כֻּלֹּה בֹּצֵעַ בָּצַע
מִנָּבִיא וְעַד־כֹּהֵן
כֻּלֹּה עֹשֶׂה שָּׁקֶר׃
11 וַיְרַפּוּ אֶת־שֶׁבֶר בַּת־עַמִּי
עַל־נְקַלָּה
לֵאמֹר שָׁלוֹם ׀ שָׁלוֹם
וְאֵין שָׁלוֹם׃
12 הֹבִישׁוּ כִּי תוֹעֵבָה עָשׂוּ
גַּם־בּוֹשׁ לֹא־יֵבֹשׁוּ
וְהִכָּלֵם לֹא יָדָעוּ

v. 9. קמץ בז״ק   v. 11. חסר א׳   v. 12. v קמץ בז״ק

scribes, who were occupied with the writing and the study of the Torah, have been to no purpose, since ye disregard it (Kimchi). R.V. renders: 'the false pen of the scribes hath wrought falsely.' This may refer to the people's accusation of the prophets of writing false reproof, claiming divine inspiration (Kara).

9. *and taken.* Ensnared by their folly. All the verbs in the first half of the verse

are prophetic perfect and announce what will happen to *the wise men* (Daath Mikra).

what wisdom is in them? No wisdom is wisdom when its source, the word of God, is rejected (Metsudath David).

10. Verses 10–12 have a close resemblance to vi. 12–15. Repetitions of this kind occur frequently in this Book.

Therefore shall they fall among
them that fall,
In the time of their visitation they
shall stumble,
Saith the LORD.

13 I will utterly consume them,
saith the LORD;
There are no grapes on the vine,
Nor figs on the fig-tree,
And the leaf is faded;
And I gave them that which they
transgress.

14 ' Why do we sit still?
Assemble yourselves, and let us
enter into the fortified cities,
And let us be cut off there;
For the LORD our God hath cut
us off,
And given us water of gall to
drink,
Because we have sinned against
the LORD.

15 We looked for peace, but no good
came;
And for a time of healing, and
behold terror!'

לָכֵן יִפְּלוּ בַנֹּפְלִים

בְּעֵת פְּקֻדָּתָם

יִכָּשְׁלוּ אָמַר יְהֹוָה׃

13 אָסֹף אֲסִיפֵם נְאֻם־יְהֹוָה

אֵין עֲנָבִים בַּגֶּפֶן

וְאֵין תְּאֵנִים בַּתְּאֵנָה

וְהֶעָלֶה נָבֵל

וָאֶתֵּן לָהֶם יַעַבְרוּם׃

14 עַל־מָה אֲנַחְנוּ יֹשְׁבִים

הֵאָסְפוּ וְנָבוֹא

אֶל־עָרֵי הַמִּבְצָר

וְנִדְּמָה־שָּׁם

כִּי יְהֹוָה אֱלֹהֵינוּ הֲדִמָּנוּ

וַיַּשְׁקֵנוּ מֵי־רֹאשׁ

כִּי חָטָאנוּ לַיהֹוָה׃

15 קַוֵּה לְשָׁלוֹם וְאֵין טוֹב

לְעֵת מַרְפֵּה וְהִנֵּה בְעָתָה׃

v. 13. הפטרת ט׳ באב 15 .v. ה׳ במקום א׳

---

13. The passage commencing with this
verse to ix. 23 is the Haphtarah
(prophetic lection) on the ninth of Ab,
the anniversary of the destruction of the
Temple and the overthrow of the
Jewish State.

and I gave them, etc. Better, 'that which
I gave them (viz. the Torah) they transgress' (so Rashi). Kimchi renders: 'and
what I gave them (viz. the produce of
their fields) shall pass away from them
(to the enemy).' This is adopted by A.V.
and R.V. and is preferable.

14. *why do we sit still?* So will the inhabitants of the countryside speak when

the enemy attacks, with the probable
meaning that in the fortified cities they
will at least be able to sell their lives
dearly. Metsudath David explains: '(The
people will say), *"Why . . . cities,"* to
which the prophet rejoins, "And there
(too) we will be cut off" — punishment
cannot be escaped, for though destruction will come ostensibly from the
enemy, in fact it is *the* LORD *our God*
(Who) *hath cut us off.'*

water of gall. A figure for bitterness;
again ix. 14, xxiii. 15 (Metsudath
David).

15. Repeated in the second half of xiv.
19 with very slight variation.

64

16 The snorting of his horses is
heard from Dan;
At the sound of the neighing of
his strong ones
The whole land trembleth;
For they are come, and have devoured the land and all that is
in it,
The city and those that dwell
therein.

17 For, behold, I will send serpents,
basilisks, among you,
Which will not be charmed;
And they shall bite you, saith the
LORD.

18 Though I would take comfort
against sorrow,
My heart is faint within me.

19 Behold the voice of the cry of the
daughter of my people
From a land far off:
'Is not the LORD in Zion?
Is not her King in her?'—
'Why have they provoked Me
with their graven images,
And with strange vanities?'—

16 מִדָּן נִשְׁמַע נַחְרַת סוּסָיו
מִקּוֹל מִצְהֲלוֹת אַבִּירָיו
רָעֲשָׁה כָּל־הָאָרֶץ
וַיָּבוֹאוּ וַיֹּאכְלוּ אֶרֶץ וּמְלוֹאָהּ
עִיר וְיֹשְׁבֵי בָהּ:

17 כִּי הִנְנִי מְשַׁלֵּחַ בָּכֶם
נְחָשִׁים צִפְעֹנִים
אֲשֶׁר אֵין־לָהֶם לָחַשׁ
וְנִשְּׁכוּ אֶתְכֶם נְאֻם־יְהֹוָה:

18 מַבְלִיגִיתִי עֲלֵי יָגוֹן
עָלַי לִבִּי דַוָּי:

19 הִנֵּה־קוֹל שַׁוְעַת בַּת־עַמִּי
מֵאֶרֶץ מַרְחַקִּים
הַיהֹוָה אֵין בְּצִיּוֹן
אִם־מַלְכָּהּ אֵין בָּהּ
מַדּוּעַ הִכְעִסוּנִי
בִּפְסִלֵיהֶם בְּהַבְלֵי נֵכָר:

16. *Dan.* See on iv. 15.

strong ones. The war-horses (Rashi).

17. *serpents,* etc. Descriptive of the
invading host (Targum).

which will not be charmed. No charm will
avail against them; so will the enemy
also be implacable (Metsudath David).

**18-23 LAMENT OVER THE PEOPLE'S
PLIGHT**

18. *though I would take comfort.* Exegetes interpret it as an expression of
strengthening oneself and suppressing
one's sorrow. 'Were I to suppress my
sorrow' (Rashi).

19. *from a land far off.* Jeremiah anticipates the captivity, as though it has
already taken place (Rashi).

is not the LORD . . . in her? The words of
the exiles: in captivity they acknowledge
the might of God, and ask wonderingly
why Zion has been so degraded
(Alshich).

why have they . . . vanities? God's reply
(Kimchi). Rashi and Metsudath David
interpret the whole verse as spoken by
God: Behold, My people are in exile *(a
land far off);* it was necessary for them to
go into captivity, for *is not the LORD in her*
Who could have protected them? But I
(changing from the third person to the

20 'The harvest is past, the summer
    is ended,
    And we are not saved.'

21 For the hurt of the daughter of
    my people am I seized with
    anguish;
    I am black, appalment hath taken
    hold on me.

22 Is there no balm in Gilead?
    Is there no physician there?
    Why then is not the health
    Of the daughter of my people re-
    covered?

23 Oh that my head were waters,
    And mine eyes a fountain of tears,
    That I might weep day and night
    For the slain of the daughter of
    my people!

20 עָבַר קָצִיר כָּלָה קָיִץ
וַאֲנַחְנוּ לוֹא נוֹשָׁעְנוּ׃

21 עַל־שֶׁבֶר בַּת־עַמִּי הָשְׁבָּרְתִּי
קָדַרְתִּי שַׁמָּה הֶחֱזִקָתְנִי׃

22 הַצֳרִי אֵין בְּגִלְעָד
אִם־רֹפֵא אֵין שָׁם
כִּי מַדּוּעַ לֹא עָלְתָה
אֲרֻכַת בַּת־עַמִּי׃

23 מִי־יִתֵּן רֹאשִׁי מַיִם
וְעֵינִי מְקוֹר דִּמְעָה
וְאֶבְכֶּה יוֹמָם וָלַיְלָה
אֵת חַלְלֵי בַת־עַמִּי׃

v. 21. פתח באתנח

first) did not save them, because *they
provoked Me*, etc.

20. The verse is possibly a proverbial
saying: time rushes by and yet we are
not saved (Metsudath David). R.V.
margin agrees with Kimchi: 'The harvest is past, and the ingathering of
summer fruits is ended.' One naturally
looked forward to these seasons as
providing essential food-supplies; but
they have passed without leaving provi-
sion for the future.

21. *for the hurt . . . seized with anguish.* A
more literal translation would be: 'For
the shattering of the daughter of my
people have I been shattered (in heart).'
It should be noted that although Jeremiah incessantly rebuked and up-
braided the people and foretold the
inevitable catastrophe, he fully identifies
himself with them in their trials
(Kimchi).

I am black. i.e. with sadness and confusion.

22. *is there no balm in Gilead?* Metaphorical for, are there no prophets and
righteous men among them to heal
their spiritual sickness? (Rashi, Kara).
The phrase has become proverbial.
Gilead was famous for its balm from
early times (cf. Gen. xxxvii. 25). Kimchi
identifies it with balsam as does Aruch.
This was used for its therapeutic pro-
perties as well as its being an ingredient
of the incense. Daath Mikra identifies it
as *styrax officinalis*. The choicest of this
tree grew in Gilead, as in Gen. xxxvii.
25.

the health . . . recovered. Most exegetes
explain this as an expression of healing.

23. In the English versions this is ix. 1.
It is obviously the climax to the fore-
going, and this division is an error.

oh that my head were waters. Would that
my head be like a stream of water and
my eyes like a flowing fountain
(Targum). Kimchi renders: 'Would that
my head were like a vessel full of water

9 CHAPTER IX ט

1 מִי־יִתְּנֵנִי בַמִּדְבָּר
מְלוֹן אֹרְחִים
וְאֶעֶזְבָה אֶת־עַמִּי
וְאֵלְכָה מֵאִתָּם
כִּי כֻלָּם מְנָאֲפִים
עֲצֶרֶת בֹּגְדִים׃

2 וַיַּדְרְכוּ אֶת־לְשׁוֹנָם
קַשְׁתָּם שֶׁקֶר
וְלֹא לֶאֱמוּנָה גָּבְרוּ בָאָרֶץ
כִּי מֵרָעָה אֶל־רָעָה ׀ יָצָאוּ
וְאֹתִי לֹא־יָדָעוּ
נְאֻם־יְהוָה׃

3 אִישׁ מֵרֵעֵהוּ הִשָּׁמֵרוּ
וְעַל־כָּל־אָח אַל־תִּבְטָחוּ

v. 2. קמץ בתביר   v. 2. קמץ בטרחא

1 Oh that I were in the wilderness,
In a lodging-place of wayfaring men,
That I might leave my people,
And go from them!
For they are all adulterers,
An assembly of treacherous men.

2 And they bend their tongue, their bow of falsehood;
And they are grown mighty in the land, but not for truth;
For they proceed from evil to evil,
And Me they know not,
Saith the LORD.

3 Take ye heed every one of his neighbour,
And trust ye not in any brother;

which would flow through my eyes as tears, and that my eyes be a fountain of tears that does not run dry.'

CHAPTER IX

1–8 THE NATION'S CORRUPTION

1. *wilderness . . . lodging-place.* Though desolate and dreary, these are still better than the city with its vices, which the prophet proceeds to enumerate (Daath Mikra).

an assembly of treacherous men. The Hebrew word *atsereth* may signify any 'assembly,' as here. It is more usually the term for a gathering for some religious purpose, e.g. to celebrate a festival. Malbim accordingly explains:

even when they assemble to pray they are treacherous.

2. *their tongue, their bow of falsehood.* R.V. is better: 'and they bend their tongue (as it were) their bow for falsehood.' As the archer bends his bow to aim, so do they make their tongue ready to shoot (and kill) with the arrows of falsehood (Kimchi).

and Me they know not. All sin is eventually traced back to wilful ignorance of God (cf. Judg. ii. 10; Hos. iv. 1). Possibly *know* is used in the sense of 'have regard to' (cf. Ps. i. 6) (see Daath Soferim).

3. *take ye heed every one of his neighbour.* Let them beware of revealing their

For every brother acteth subtly,
And every neighbour goeth about
  with slanders.
4 And they deceive every one his
    neighbour,
And truth they speak not;
They have taught their tongue to
  speak lies,
They weary themselves to commit
  iniquity.
5 Thy habitation is in the midst of
    deceit;
Through deceit they refuse to
  know Me,
Saith the LORD.
6. Therefore thus saith the LORD
    of hosts:
Behold, I will smelt them, and try
  them;
For how else should I do,
Because of the daughter of My
  people?

כִּי כָל־אָח֙ עָק֣וֹב יַעְקֹ֔ב
וְכָל־רֵ֖עַ רָכִ֥יל יַהֲלֹֽךְ׃
4 וְאִ֤ישׁ בְּרֵעֵ֙הוּ֙ יְהָתֵ֔לּוּ
וֶאֱמֶ֖ת לֹ֣א יְדַבֵּ֑רוּ
לִמְּד֧וּ לְשׁוֹנָ֛ם
דַּבֶּר־שֶׁ֖קֶר הַעֲוֵ֥ה נִלְאֽוּ׃
5 שִׁבְתְּךָ֖ בְּת֣וֹךְ מִרְמָ֑ה
בְּמִרְמָ֛ה מֵאֲנ֥וּ דַֽעַת־אוֹתִ֖י
נְאֻם־יְהוָֽה׃
6 לָכֵ֗ן כֹּ֤ה אָמַר֙ יְהוָ֣ה צְבָא֔וֹת
הִנְנִ֥י צֽוֹרְפָ֖ם וּבְחַנְתִּ֑ים
כִּי־אֵ֣יךְ אֶֽעֱשֶׂ֔ה
מִפְּנֵ֖י בַּת־עַמִּֽי׃

v. 4. הל׳ דגושה

secrets to their neighbours (Metsudath David).

acteth subtly. With guile; the Hebrew *akob yaakob* is doubtless an allusion to Gen. xxvii. 36 (Daath Mikra). He forgets his brotherhood and lays a trap for his brother (Abarbanel).

4. *they have taught their tongue to speak lies.* Man is naturally truthful and upright, and must school himself to falsehood before it comes easily to him. Cf. the Hebrew prayer beginning, 'O my God, the soul which Thou gavest me is pure' (A.D.P.B., p. 5). Kimchi and others explain the verb *taught* in the sense of 'accustomed.'

they weary themselves to commit iniquity. It is so much easier to live uprightly and obedient to God's will, but they labour

and toil in order to sin! (see Rashi, Metsudath Zion).

5. *thy habitation.* Addressed to the people as a whole (Targum, Rashi).

through deceit. Knowledge of God, Who is holy and recoils from everything unjust and impure, cannot be reconciled with a life of deceit; therefore they deliberately reject knowledge of Him (Daath Mikra).

6. *I will smelt them.* As the silver is purified from its dross by smelting, so I will purify the nation by making them pass through the crucible of suffering (Rashi).

try. i.e. test, to find out whether the dross has been removed (Kimchi).

for how else ... My people? I have no

7 Their tongue is a sharpened
   arrow,
   It speaketh deceit;
   One speaketh peaceably to his
   neighbour with his mouth,
   But in his heart he layeth wait for
   him.
8 Shall I not punish them for these
   things?
   Saith the LORD;
   Shall not My soul be avenged
   On such a nation as this?
9 For the mountains will I take up a
   weeping and wailing,
   And for the pastures of the wilder-
   ness a lamentation,
   Because they are burned up, so
   that none passeth through,
   And they hear not the voice of the
   cattle;
   Both the fowl of the heavens and
   the beast
   Are fled, and gone.
10 And I will make Jerusalem heaps,
   A lair of jackals;
   And I will make the cities of
   Judah a desolation,
   Without an inhabitant.

7 חֵץ שָׁחֵט
לְשׁוֹנָם מִרְמָה דִבֵּר
בְּפִיו שָׁלוֹם אֶת־רֵעֵהוּ יְדַבֵּר
וּבְקִרְבּוֹ יָשִׂים אָרְבּוֹ׃
8 הַעַל־אֵלֶּה לֹא־אֶפְקָד־בָּם
נְאֻם־יְהוָה
אִם בְּגוֹי אֲשֶׁר־כָּזֶה
לֹא תִתְנַקֵּם נַפְשִׁי׃
9 עַל־הֶהָרִים אֶשָּׂא בְכִי וָנֶהִי
וְעַל־נְאוֹת מִדְבָּר קִינָה
כִּי נִצְּתוּ מִבְּלִי־אִישׁ עוֹבֵר
וְלֹא שָׁמְעוּ קוֹל מִקְנֶה
מֵעוֹף הַשָּׁמַיִם וְעַד־בְּהֵמָה
נָדְדוּ הָלָכוּ׃
10 וְנָתַתִּי אֶת־יְרוּשָׁלַםִ
לְגַלִּים מְעוֹן תַּנִּים
וְאֶת־עָרֵי יְהוּדָה
אֶתֵּן שְׁמָמָה
מִבְּלִי יוֹשֵׁב׃

v. 7. שחוט קרי

---

other choice, says God. I cannot leave
them in their sin, for they were intended
to be a holy people; nor can I utterly
destroy them, for they are My people:
hence I must purge them by tribulation
(Kimchi).

7. a sharpened arrow. The *kethib, shochet,*
means 'a slaying arrow.' The *kerë,
shachut,* signifies 'sharpened,' drawn
over the grindstone (Kimchi).

8. Repeated substantially from v. 9, 29.

9–15   THE COMING PUNISHMENT

A detailed description of the destruction
and desolation which will overtake
Judea, and the cause of the catastrophe:
the abandonment of God's service for
idolatry.

9. wilderness. The Hebrew *midbar* here
and elsewhere denotes 'land to which
cattle is driven to graze' (cf. Exod. iii. 1).

10. Jerusalem . . . the cities of Judah.

69

11 Who is the wise man, that he may
understand this?

And who is he to whom the
mouth of the LORD hath
spoken, that he may declare it?

Wherefore is the land perished

And laid waste like a wilderness,
so that none passeth through?

12 And the LORD saith:

Because they have forsaken My
law which I set before them,

And have not hearkened to My
voice, neither walked therein;

13 But have walked after the stubbornness of their own heart,

And after the Baalim, which their
fathers taught them.

14 Therefore thus saith the LORD of
hosts, the God of Israel:

Behold, I will feed them, even
this people, with wormwood

מִי־הָאִישׁ הֶחָכָם 11
וְיָבֵן אֶת־זֹאת
וַאֲשֶׁר דִּבֶּר פִּי־יְהֹוָה
אֵלָיו וְיַגִּדָהּ
עַל־מָה אָבְדָה הָאָרֶץ
נִצְּתָה כַמִּדְבָּר מִבְּלִי עֹבֵר:
וַיֹּאמֶר יְהֹוָה 12
עַל־עָזְבָם אֶת־תּוֹרָתִי
אֲשֶׁר נָתַתִּי לִפְנֵיהֶם
וְלֹא־שָׁמְעוּ בְקוֹלִי
וְלֹא־הָלְכוּ בָהּ:
וַיֵּלְכוּ אַחֲרֵי שְׁרִרוּת לִבָּם 13
וְאַחֲרֵי הַבְּעָלִים
אֲשֶׁר לִמְּדוּם אֲבוֹתָם:
לָכֵן כֹּה־אָמַר 14
יְהֹוָה צְבָאוֹת אֱלֹהֵי יִשְׂרָאֵל
הִנְנִי מַאֲכִילָם
אֶת־הָעָם הַזֶּה לַעֲנָה

Desolation will also overtake the cities,
and jackals will haunt the ruins of the
buildings (Metsudath David).

a lair of jackals. A favourite simile of
Jeremiah (cf. x. 22, xlix. 33, li. 37).

11. *who is the wise man,* etc. Consider-
ing the frequency with which Jeremiah
reiterated his message that idolatry
must lead to just such a destruction as is
here described, the question is probably
rhetorical and expresses his fervent
prayer: would they were wise enough to
understand the cause of their downfall,
and acknowledge the truth of God's
warning! Possibly, too, his words are a

tilt against the false prophets who
sought the reasons for the nation's
disasters and their remedies in anything
but the truth (see Abarbanel).

12. *which I set before them.* [Originally at
Sinai and subsequently in the exhortations of the prophets.]

therein. viz. in *My law.*

13. *their fathers taught them.* Sin begets
sin; the present generation was suffering, partly at least, through the evil
heritage they had received from former
generations. It is in this sense that Exod.
xx. 5 must be understood: the iniquity

And give them water of gall to drink.

15 I will scatter them also among the nations,
Whom neither they nor their fathers have known;
And I will send the sword after them,
Till I have consumed them.

16 Thus saith the LORD of hosts:
Consider ye, and call for the mourning women, that they may come;
And send for the wise women, that they may come;

17 And let them make haste, and take up a wailing for us,
That our eyes may run down with tears,
And our eyelids gush out with waters.

18 For a voice of wailing is heard out of Zion:
'How are we undone!
We are greatly confounded, because we have forsaken the land,
Because our dwellings have cast us out.'

וְהִשְׁקִיתִ֖ים מֵי־רֹֽאשׁ׃

15 וַהֲפִֽצוֹתִים֙ בַּגּוֹיִ֔ם
אֲשֶׁר֙ לֹ֣א יָֽדְע֔וּ הֵ֖מָּה וַאֲבוֹתָ֑ם
וְשִׁלַּחְתִּ֤י אַחֲרֵיהֶם֙ אֶת־הַחֶ֔רֶב
עַ֥ד כַּלּוֹתִ֖י אוֹתָֽם׃

16 כֹּ֤ה אָמַר֙ יְהֹוָ֣ה צְבָא֔וֹת
הִתְבּוֹנְנ֛וּ
וְקִרְא֥וּ לַמְקוֹנְנ֖וֹת וּתְבוֹאֶ֑ינָה
וְאֶל־הַחֲכָמ֖וֹת שִׁלְח֥וּ
וְתָבֽוֹאנָה׃

17 וּתְמַהֵ֜רְנָה וְתִשֶּׂ֧נָה עָלֵ֛ינוּ נֶ֖הִי
וְתֵרַ֤דְנָה עֵינֵ֙ינוּ֙ דִּמְעָ֔ה
וְעַפְעַפֵּ֖ינוּ יִזְּלוּ־מָֽיִם׃

18 כִּ֣י ק֥וֹל נְהִ֛י
נִשְׁמַ֥ע מִצִּיּ֖וֹן אֵ֣יךְ שֻׁדָּ֑דְנוּ
בֹּ֤שְׁנוּ מְאֹד֙ כִּֽי־עָזַ֣בְנוּ אָ֔רֶץ
כִּ֥י הִשְׁלִ֖יכוּ מִשְׁכְּנוֹתֵֽינוּ׃

v. 17. חסר א'   v. 18. קמץ בז"ק

---

of the fathers lead the following generations to sin, and this naturally brings its punishment. For *the Baalim*, cf. ii. 23 (see Daath Mikra).

14. *wormwood . . . water of gall.* Metaphorical for the bitterness of affliction (see on viii. 14).

15. *till I have consumed them.* i.e. most of them (Kimchi).

16–21 WAILING AND LAMENT

16. *the mourning women.* Professional mourners; they were generally women who followed the bier of a dead person and lamented his death in elegiac measures. In Mishnaic times, this was standard practice at all funerals. Now a whole nation was to be bewailed!

the wise women. Skilled in lamenting (Kimchi).

18. *we have forsaken the land.* [Involuntarily, to go into exile. The verb is prophetic perfect.]

our dwellings have cast us out. Or, as A.V., 'because they (i.e. our enemies)

71

19 Yea, hear the word of the LORD,
O ye women,
And let your ear receive the
word of His mouth,
And teach your daughters wail-
ing,
And every one her neighbour
lamentation:

20 'For death is come up into our
windows,
It is entered into our palaces,
To cut off the children from the
street,
And the young men from the
broad places.—

21 Speak: Thus saith the LORD—
And the carcasses of men fall
As dung upon the open field,
And as the handful after the
harvestman,
Which none gathereth.'

22 Thus saith the LORD:
Let not the wise man glory in his
wisdom,

19 כִּֽי־שְׁמַ֨עְנָה נָשִׁים֙ דְּבַר־יְהֹוָ֔ה
וְתִקַּ֥ח אָזְנְכֶ֖ם דְּבַר־פִּ֑יו
וְלַמֵּ֤דְנָה בְנֽוֹתֵיכֶם֙ נֶ֔הִי
וְאִשָּׁ֥ה רְעוּתָ֖הּ קִינָֽה׃

20 כִּֽי־עָ֤לָה מָ֨וֶת֙ בְּחַלּוֹנֵ֔ינוּ
בָּ֖א בְּאַרְמְנוֹתֵ֑ינוּ
לְהַכְרִ֤ית עוֹלָל֙ מִח֔וּץ
בַּחוּרִ֖ים מֵרְחֹבֽוֹת׃

21 דַּבֵּ֗ר כֹּ֚ה נְאֻם־יְהֹוָ֔ה
וְנָֽפְלָה֙ נִבְלַ֣ת הָֽאָדָ֔ם
כְּדֹ֛מֶן עַל־פְּנֵ֥י הַשָּׂדֶ֑ה
וּכְעָמִ֛יר מֵאַחֲרֵ֥י הַקֹּצֵ֖ר
וְאֵ֥ין מְאַסֵּֽף׃

22 כֹּ֣ה ׀ אָמַ֣ר יְהֹוָ֗ה
אַל־יִתְהַלֵּ֤ל חָכָם֙ בְּחָכְמָת֔וֹ

have cast down our dwellings' (so also
Rashi).

19. *receive the word of His mouth.* Con-
ventional phrases of lamentation will
not be used; God will dictate the appro-
priate phrases (Malbim).

20. *death is come up into our windows.*
Though we have erected defences
against the enemy, death has penetrated
into our homes; all our precautions
have proved in vain. Many commentators understand the reference to be to a
fatal epidemic which resulted from the
conditions of the siege (Daath Mikra).

21. *speak: Thus saith the LORD.* Speak
and do not hesitate (Daath Mikra).

which none gathereth. Either through

fear of leaving his hiding place (Metsudath David), or because of the multitude of the slain and the fewness of the
survivors.

22–23 KNOWLEDGE OF GOD IS NEEDED
ABOVE ALL

Neither wisdom, strength nor wealth is
a ground for pride. One may justly be
proud only knowing and understanding
that the Lord is the God of love, justice
and righteousness, and that these are
His prime demands upon His creatures.

22. *the wise man.* Without the knowledge of God human wisdom is futile.
*The fear of the LORD is the beginning of
wisdom* (Ps. cxi. 10; cf. Prov. ix. 10).

Neither let the mighty man glory
in his might,

Let not the rich man glory in his
riches;

23 But let him that glorieth glory in
this,

That he understandeth, and
knoweth Me,

That I am the LORD who exercise
mercy,

Justice, and righteousness, in the
earth;

For in these things I delight,

Saith the LORD.

24. Behold, the days come, saith
the LORD, that I will punish all them
that are circumcised in their uncircumcision: 25. Egypt, and Judah,
and Edom, and the children of
Ammon, and Moab, and all that
have the corners of their hair polled,
that dwell in the wilderness;

וְאַל־יִתְהַלֵּל הַגִּבּוֹר
בִּגְבוּרָתוֹ
אַל־יִתְהַלֵּל עָשִׁיר בְּעָשְׁרוֹ:
23 כִּי אִם־בְּזֹאת
יִתְהַלֵּל הַמִּתְהַלֵּל
הַשְׂכֵּל וְיָדֹעַ אוֹתִי
כִּי אֲנִי יְהוָֹה עֹשֶׂה חֶסֶד
מִשְׁפָּט וּצְדָקָה בָּאָרֶץ
כִּי־בְאֵלֶּה חָפַצְתִּי
נְאֻם־יְהוָֹה:
24 הִנֵּה יָמִים בָּאִים נְאֻם־יְהוָֹה
וּפָקַדְתִּי עַל־כָּל־מוּל
25 בְּעָרְלָה: עַל־מִצְרַיִם וְעַל־
יְהוּדָה וְעַל־אֱדוֹם וְעַל־בְּנֵי
עַמּוֹן וְעַל־מוֹאָב וְעַל כָּל־
קְצוּצֵי פֵאָה הַיֹּשְׁבִים בַּמִּדְבָּר

v. 23. למדנחאי ומשפט עד כאן

might. The only might of which man
may truly boast is the moral strength to
withstand temptation. 'Who is mighty?
He who subdues his passions' (Aboth).

riches. Wealth cannot deliver a man
from his fate, and material riches are
inferior to spiritual treasures (Kimchi).

23. *knoweth Me.* 'Having acquired this
knowledge, he will then be determined
always to seek lovingkindness, judgment and righteousness and thus to
imitate the ways of God' (Maimonides).

mercy. Or, 'lovingkindness' (A.V.,
R.V., Hebrew *chesed*). This precedes
justice and righteousness. Elsewhere in
Scripture it even 'precedes "truth."
Truth, justice and righteousness must

all be spoken and acted in *lovingkindness*;
otherwise, they cease to be truth, justice
and righteousness' (Hertz).

**24-25   GOD'S JUDGMENT WILL EXTEND TO
OTHER NATIONS ALSO**

24. *circumcised in their uncircumcision.*
Though physically circumcised, they are
spiritually uncircumcised, their hearts
being closed to the understanding and
love of God and His teachings (Rashi).

25. *Egypt,* etc. The nations enumerated apparently practised circumcision
(Daath Mikra).

all that have the corners of their hair polled.
i.e. cut away from the temples, forbidden in Lev. xix. 27 and alluded to again

For all the nations are uncircumcised,
But all the house of Israel are uncircumcised in the heart.

כִּי כָל־הַגּוֹיִם עֲרֵלִים
וְכָל־בֵּית יִשְׂרָאֵל
עַרְלֵי־לֵב:

10   CHAPTER X   י

1. Hear ye the word which the
LORD speaketh unto you, O house of
Israel; 2. thus saith the LORD:
Learn not the way of the nations,
And be not dismayed at the signs
of heaven;
For the nations are dismayed at
them.
3 For the customs of the peoples are
vanity;
For it is but a tree which one
cutteth out of the forest,
The work of the hands of the
workman with the axe.

1 שִׁמְעוּ אֶת־הַדָּבָר אֲשֶׁר דִּבֶּר
יְהֹוָה עֲלֵיכֶם בֵּית יִשְׂרָאֵל:
2 כֹּה ׀ אָמַר יְהֹוָה
אֶל־דֶּרֶךְ הַגּוֹיִם אַל־תִּלְמָדוּ
וּמֵאֹתוֹת הַשָּׁמַיִם אַל־תֵּחָתּוּ
כִּי־יֵחַתּוּ הַגּוֹיִם מֵהֵמָּה:
3 כִּי־חֻקּוֹת הָעַמִּים הֶבֶל הוּא
כִּי־עֵץ מִיַּעַר כְּרָתוֹ
מַעֲשֵׂה יְדֵי־חָרָשׁ בַּמַּעֲצָד:

v. 2. קמץ בז"ק

in xxv. 23, xlix. 32. This is probably a
reference to certain Arab tribes with
whom the practice had some religious
significance, as recorded by Herodotus.
Rashi and Kimchi render: 'and all that
are in the uttermost corners (or, that are
separated in the extreme ends) who
dwell in the wilderness,' i.e. the Arabian
desert to the east of the Holy Land.

for all the nations, etc. The clause is difficult and seems to contradict what precedes. The probable meaning is:
although the heathen peoples practised
circumcision, they are in God's sight
uncircumcised since their lives lack
spirituality; and similarly the circumcision of the Israelites means nothing to
Him in that they are *uncircumcised in the
heart.* They will be judged like the
heathen peoples (see Nedarim 31b).

CHAPTER X

1-16   HELPLESSNESS OF IDOLS

2. *the signs of heaven.* Such as eclipses
and meteors, which other nations
regarded as portents of evil (Rashi).

3. *customs.* lit. 'statutes.' *Customs* here
denotes religious practices and beliefs.
Thus the previous verse tells of their
love for astrology, and this verse con-
demns these beliefs in general as vanity,
and proceeds to illustrate this by reference to the absurdity of idol-worship
(Kimchi).

vanity. Empty and without content.
For the description of the making of an
idol which follows, cf. Isa. xl. 19f., xliv.
12ff.

for it is. The subject is the manufac-

4 They deck it with silver and with
  gold,
  They fasten it with nails and with
  hammers, that it move not.

5 They are like a pillar in a garden
  of cucumbers, and speak not;
  They must needs be borne, because they cannot go.
  Be not afraid of them, for they
  cannot do evil,
  Neither is it in them to do good.

6 There is none like unto Thee, O
  LORD;
  Thou art great, and Thy name is
  great in might.

7 Who would not fear Thee, O
  King of the nations?
  For it befitteth Thee;
  Forasmuch as among all the wise
  men of the nations, and in all
  their royalty,
  There is none like unto Thee.

4 בְּכֶסֶף וּבְזָהָב יְיַפֵּהוּ
בְּמַסְמְרוֹת וּבְמַקָּבוֹת
יְחַזְּקוּם וְלוֹא יָפִיק:
5 כְּתֹמֶר מִקְשָׁה הֵמָּה
וְלֹא יְדַבֵּרוּ
נָשׂוֹא יִנָּשׂוּא כִּי־לֹא יִצְעָדוּ
אַל־תִּירְאוּ מֵהֶם
כִּי־לֹא יָרֵעוּ
וְגַם־הֵיטֵיב אֵין אוֹתָם:
6 מֵאֵין כָּמוֹךָ יְהֹוָה
גָּדוֹל אַתָּה
וְגָדוֹל שִׁמְךָ בִּגְבוּרָה:
7 מִי לֹא יִרָאֲךָ מֶלֶךְ הַגּוֹיִם
כִּי לְךָ יָאָתָה
כִּי בְכָל־חַכְמֵי הַגּוֹיִם
וּבְכָל־מַלְכוּתָם
מֵאֵין כָּמוֹךָ:

v. 5. כצ״ל

tured idol, to be understood from the
context (Metsudath David).

5. *like a pillar in a garden of cucumbers.*
This rendering agrees with R.V. margin
as against A.V. 'they are as upright as
the palm tree,' R.V. 'like a palm tree of
turned work,' and is certainly correct.
The idol is contemptuously compared
to a scarecrow, and the same imagery is
found in Baruch vi. 70, 'for as a scarecrow in a garden of cucumbers keepeth
nothing: so are their gods of wood, and
laid over with silver and gold.'

must needs be borne. In religious proces-
sions (Daath Mikra).

6. *there is none,* etc. Better, 'because
there is none ... (therefore) Thou art
great' (Kimchi).

7. *who would not fear Thee. . . ?* Cf. v.
22. The Hebrew is difficult. Perhaps
verses 7f. should be rendered: 'Who
should not fear Thee? ... yet they are
altogether brutish,' preferring to worship idols of wood (Malbim). [*Wise men*
is literally 'the wise of' and may refer to
the images which are reputed to have
superhuman wisdom; similarly *their
royalty* may indicate the pantheon of
heathen worship.]

O King of the nations. An affirmation of

8 But they are altogether brutish
and foolish:
The vanities by which they are
instructed are but a stock;

9 Silver beaten into plates which is
brought from Tarshish,
And gold from Uphaz,
The work of the craftsman and of
the hands of the goldsmith;
Blue and purple is their clothing;
They are all the work of skilful
men.

10 But the LORD God is the true
God,
He is the living God, and the
everlasting King;
At His wrath the earth trembleth,
And the nations are not able to
abide His indignation.

11. Thus shall ye say unto them:
'The gods that have not made the
heavens and the earth, these shall
perish from the earth, and from
under the heavens.'

8 וּבְאַחַת יִבְעֲרוּ וְיִכְסָלוּ
מוּסַר הֲבָלִים עֵץ הוּא:
9 כֶּסֶף מְרֻקָּע מִתַּרְשִׁישׁ יוּבָא
וְזָהָב מֵאוּפָז
מַעֲשֵׂה חָרָשׁ וִידֵי צוֹרֵף
תְּכֵלֶת וְאַרְגָּמָן לְבוּשָׁם
מַעֲשֵׂה חֲכָמִים כֻּלָּם:
10 וַיהוָה אֱלֹהִים אֱמֶת
הוּא־אֱלֹהִים חַיִּים
וּמֶלֶךְ עוֹלָם
מִקִּצְפּוֹ תִּרְעַשׁ הָאָרֶץ
וְלֹא־יָכִלוּ גוֹיִם זַעְמוֹ:
11 כִּדְנָה תֵּאמְרוּן לְהוֹם אֱלָהַיָּא
דִּי־שְׁמַיָּא וְאַרְקָא לָא עֲבַדוּ
יֵאבַדוּ מֵאַרְעָא וּמִן־תְּחוֹת
שְׁמַיָּא אֵלֶּה:

v. 11. פתח באתנח

God's universal rule: He is not a tribal
God, but Sovereign over all peoples
(Kimchi).

8. *the vanities by which they are instructed.*
lit. 'the instruction of (received from)
vanities.'

are but a stock. Even the wise men of the
nations are brutish and foolish. They
instruct the people to worship idols,
which are vanity, being but a stock, for
it is plated with silver and gold, and it
cannot move by itself (Kimchi, Metsudath David).

9. How the idol is manufactured and
robed.

Tarshish. Jonathan identifies Tarshish
as Africa, probably Carthage, as is

asserted by Abarbanel (1 Kings x. 22).
Malbim (ad loc.) identifies it with Tar-
tessus in Spain. Alshich, Isaiah 23:12,
identifies it as Tarsus, a city in Asia
Minor on the Mediterranean. According to Rashi, 1 Kings x. 22, it is the
name of a sea. Cf. Rashi, Ibn Ezra,
Jonah i. 3.

Uphaz. Unknown. It is also mentioned
in Dan. x. 5 in a similar connection.
Some ancient versions identified it with
Ophir, as does Targum.

10. In contrast to the falsity of idols,
God is truth; in contrast to their dead-
ness and powerlessness, He is alive and
the King of the universe.

11. This verse is in Aramaic. Rashi
suggests that it is the text of a letter sent

12 He that hath made the earth by
His power,
That hath established the world
by His wisdom,
And hath stretched out the
heavens by His understanding;

13 At the sound of His giving a
multitude of waters in the
heavens,
When He causeth the vapours to
ascend from the ends of the
earth;
When He maketh lightnings
with the rain,
And bringeth forth the wind out
of His treasuries;

14 Every man is proved to be
brutish, without knowledge,
Every goldsmith is put to shame
by the graven image,
His molten image is falsehood,
and there is no breath in them.

15 They are vanity, a work of delusion;
In the time of their visitation
they shall perish.

16 Not like these is the portion of
Jacob;

עֹשֵׂה אֶרֶץ בְּכֹחוֹ 12
מֵכִין תֵּבֵל בְּחָכְמָתוֹ
וּבִתְבוּנָתוֹ נָטָה שָׁמָיִם:

לְקוֹל תִּתּוֹ הֲמוֹן מַיִם בַּשָּׁמַיִם 13
וַיַּעֲלֶה נְשִׂאִים מִקְצֵה אָרֶץ
בְּרָקִים לַמָּטָר עָשָׂה
וַיּוֹצֵא רוּחַ מֵאֹצְרֹתָיו:

נִבְעַר כָּל־אָדָם מִדַּעַת 14
הֹבִישׁ כָּל־צֹרֵף מִפָּסֶל
כִּי שֶׁקֶר נִסְכּוֹ וְלֹא־רוּחַ בָּם:

הֶבֶל הֵמָּה מַעֲשֵׂה תַּעְתֻּעִים 15
בְּעֵת פְּקֻדָּתָם יֹאבֵדוּ:

לֹא־כְאֵלֶּה חֵלֶק יַעֲקֹב 16

v. 13. הארץ ק׳

by Jeremiah to Jehoiachin and the other exiles in Babylon, advising them how to answer those who sought to seduce them to idolatry.

the gods. viz. the idols.

12. Verse 11 was a digression interrupting the sequence of thought, and verse 12 logically follows on verse 10 (Metsudath David). Kimchi, on the other hand, regards this verse as the sequel to verse 11, although the prophet now reverts to Hebrew: whereas *the gods . . . the heavens,* we will serve Him *that hath made the earth by His power.*

His wisdom. Cf. Prov. viii. 22-31, where Wisdom (personified) is represented as presiding at the Creation.

13. *maketh lightnings with the rain.* Flashes of lightning pierce the clouds so

that they empty their contents upon the earth (cf. Ps. cxxxv. 7).

His treasuries. Cf. Job xxxviii. 22.

14. *every man.* Who engages in idol-worship (Metsudath David).

every goldsmith. The maker of the image (Kimchi).

15. *a work of delusion.* They who put their trust in idols find themselves deluded in a time of emergency (Metsudath David).

in the time of their visitation. When God 'visits,' i.e. punishes, the idols and their worshippers according to their deserts (cf. Isa. ii. 12, 18) (Rashi).

16. *the portion of Jacob.* viz. God (cf. Ps. xvi. 5). It is a bold thought: if God owns Israel as His *inheritance* (second half of

For He is the former of all things,

And Israel is the tribe of His inheritance;

The LORD of hosts is His name.

17 Gather up thy wares from the ground,

O thou that abidest in the siege.

18. For thus saith the LORD: Behold, I will sling out the inhabitants of the land at this time, and will distress them, that they may feel it.

19 Woe is me for my hurt!

My wound is grievous;

But I said: 'This is but a sickness,

And I must bear it.'

20 My tent is spoiled,

And all my cords are broken;

כִּי־יוֹצֵר הַכֹּל הוּא

וְיִשְׂרָאֵל שֵׁבֶט נַחֲלָתוֹ

יְהֹוָה צְבָאוֹת שְׁמוֹ:

17 אִסְפִּי מֵאֶרֶץ כִּנְעָתֵךְ

יֹשֶׁבֶת בַּמָּצוֹר:

18 כִּי־כֹה אָמַר יְהֹוָה הִנְנִי קוֹלֵעַ

אֶת־יוֹשְׁבֵי הָאָרֶץ בַּפַּעַם

הַזֹּאת וַהֲצֵרֹתִי לָהֶם לְמַעַן

יִמְצָאוּ:

19 אוֹי־לִי עַל־שִׁבְרִי

נַחְלָה מַכָּתִי

וַאֲנִי אָמַרְתִּי אַךְ

זֶה חֳלִי וְאֶשָּׂאֶנּוּ:

20 אָהֳלִי שֻׁדָּד

וְכָל־מֵיתָרַי נִתָּקוּ

v. 17. יושבת ק׳   v. 18. מלעיל   v. 20. קמץ בז״ק

the verse), then Israel can regard Him in a special sense as his *portion* (Kimchi).

17-25   EXILE IS AT HAND

The prophet laments the imminent fate of the people, and prays to God to remember man's natural weakness of character and temper His punishment accordingly.

17. *gather up thy wares from the ground.* The Hebrew word translated *thy wares (kin'athech)* occurs nowhere else. It has been connected with an Arabic verb which means 'to contract, fold the wings,' and the sense of the clause is 'pack thy bundle (to take it) from the land,' since thou art going into

captivity (see Daath Mikra). The exegetes, however, connect it with *kena'an,* a trafficker.

18. *sling out.* For this verb, cf. 1 Sam. xxv. 29.

that they may feel it. lit. 'that they may find.' Rashi and Metsudath David interpret: that they may find their just deserts.

19. The prophet, speaking for the nation, laments his misfortunes.

20. The land is likened to a tent which has now been overthrown. But the most severe disaster is that the children of the nation have gone forth into exile, so that there is none to rebuild the shat-

My children are gone forth of
  me, and they are not;
There is none to stretch forth my
  tent any more,
And to set up my curtains.

21 For the shepherds are become
  brutish,
And have not inquired of the
  LORD;
Therefore they have not pros-
  pered,
And all their flocks are scattered.

22 Hark! a report, behold, it cometh,
And a great commotion out of the
  north country,
To make the cities of Judah des-
  olate,
A dwelling-place of jackals.

23 O LORD, I know that man's way
  is not his own;
It is not in man to direct his steps
  as he walketh.

24 O LORD, correct me, but in
  measure;
Not in Thine anger, lest Thou
  diminish me.

25 Pour out Thy wrath upon the
  nations that know Thee not,

בָּנַי יְצָאֻנִי וְאֵינָם
אֵין־נֹטֶה עוֹד אָהֳלִי
וּמֵקִים יְרִיעוֹתָי:
21 כִּי נִבְעֲרוּ הָרֹעִים
וְאֶת־יְהוָה לֹא דָרָשׁוּ
עַל־כֵּן לֹא הִשְׂכִּילוּ
וְכָל־מַרְעִיתָם נָפוֹצָה:
22 קוֹל שְׁמוּעָה הִנֵּה בָאָה
וְרַעַשׁ גָּדוֹל מֵאֶרֶץ צָפוֹן
לָשׂוּם אֶת־עָרֵי יְהוּדָה
שְׁמָמָה מְעוֹן תַּנִּים:
23 יָדַעְתִּי יְהוָה כִּי
לֹא לָאָדָם דַּרְכּוֹ
לֹא־לְאִישׁ הֹלֵךְ
וְהָכִין אֶת־צַעֲדוֹ:
24 יַסְּרֵנִי יְהוָה אַךְ בְּמִשְׁפָּט
אַל־בְּאַפְּךָ פֶּן־תַּמְעִטֵנִי:
25 שְׁפֹךְ חֲמָתְךָ
עַל־הַגּוֹיִם אֲשֶׁר לֹא־יְדָעוּךָ

tered country. Cf. Isa. liv. 2 for the
reverse, and see on iv. 20.

21. *the shepherds.* The leaders (cf. ii. 8)
(Metsudath David).

have not inquired of the LORD. They
refused to be guided by His teachings
(Daath Mikra).

all their flocks are scattered. The people
are suffering through the misguidance
of their leaders. Although the exile had
not yet taken place, the prophet speaks
of it as an accomplished fact (Metsudath
David).

22. *the north country.* Babylon (Metsudath David).

23. Man is morally weak and does not
always possess the strength to overcome
temptation and direct his steps aright.
Jeremiah urges this plea on behalf of his
people in mitigation of punishment
(Rashi).

24. *in measure.* lit. 'with judgment,' i.e.
not with excessive severity (cf. xlvi. 28)
(Kimchi).

25. *the nations that know Thee not.* Even
if Israel has sinned, surely he is not to

And upon the families that call
not on Thy name;
For they have devoured Jacob,
Yea, they have devoured him and
consumed him,
And have laid waste his habitation.

וְעַל מִשְׁפָּחוֹת
אֲשֶׁר בְּשִׁמְךָ לֹא קֹרָאוּ
כִּי־אָכְלוּ אֶת־יַעֲקֹב
וַאֲכָלֻהוּ וַיְכַלֻּהוּ
וְאֶת־נָוֵהוּ הֵשַׁמּוּ׃

11   CHAPTER XI   יא

1. The word that came to Jeremiah from the LORD, saying: 2. 'Hear
ye the words of this covenant, and
speak unto the men of Judah, and to

1 הַדָּבָר אֲשֶׁר־הָיָה אֶל־
יִרְמְיָהוּ מֵאֵת יְהוָה לֵאמֹר׃
2 שִׁמְעוּ אֶת־דִּבְרֵי הַבְּרִית
הַזֹּאת וְדִבַּרְתָּם אֶל־אִישׁ

be punished more severely than the
heathens who never have 'known' (i.e.
recognized) God (Kimchi).

families. See on iii. 14.

for they have devoured Jacob. Though the
disasters of the people are due to their
sins, yet the nations who executed
God's judgment were animated by a
spirit of vindictiveness and exceeded
what He ordained; they should accordingly be punished. The verse is repeated
in Ps. lxxix. 6f. with slight variations
(Kimchi).

CHAPTER XI

FROM xi. 1 to xii. 6 is an exhortation to
the people to be faithful to God's
covenant with them and a warning of
coming judgments. Two views are held
on the date of this passage: *(i)* that it
belongs to Jehoiakim's reign, and falls
between the prophet's address in the
Temple courts and Nebuchadnezzar's
victory over Egypt at Carchemish in 605
B.C.E. (see Kimchi); *(ii)* that it was delivered soon after the discovery of the
Book of the Law by Hilkiah in the reign
of Josiah (621 B.C.E.), and is connected

with that king's reforms in consequence
of the discovery (2 Kings xxiif.). The
latter is now generally accepted (Daath
Mikra).

2-8 EXHORTATION TO JUDAH

2. *this covenant.* Which God made with
Israel when they left Egypt. The general
sense of what is meant by the *covenant* is
clear from the following verses: Israel
was to be loyal to God's commandments, thereby constituting himself
God's people, while He would be
Israel's God; and only upon this condition rested the claim to possess the
Promised Land. Kimchi refers it to the
blessings and curses pronounced in the
plains of Moab which are summed up as
the words of the covenant (Deut. xxviii. 69;
note the same phrase in verse 8 of this
chapter).

hear ye . . . and speak. The plural of the
verb denotes Jeremiah and other
prophets. At that time, Zephaniah
(Zeph. i. 1) prophesied, as well as
Huldah the prophetess (2 Kings xxix.
14, 2 Chron. xxxiv. 22). During Jehoiakim's reign, Uriah of Kiriath-jearim

the inhabitants of Jerusalem; 3. and say thou unto them: Thus saith the LORD, the God of Israel: Cursed be the man that heareth not the words of this covenant, 4. which I commanded your fathers in the day that I brought them forth out of the land of Egypt, out of the iron furnace, saying: Hearken to My voice, and do them, according to all which I command you; so shall ye be My people, and I will be your God; 5. that I may establish the oath which I swore unto your fathers, to give them a land flowing with milk and honey, as at this day.' Then answered I, and said: 'Amen, O LORD.'

6. And the LORD said unto me: 'Proclaim all these words in the cities of Judah, and in the streets

יְהוּדָה וְעַל־יֹשְׁבֵי יְרוּשָׁלָ͏ִם:

3 וְאָמַרְתָּ אֲלֵיהֶם כֹּה־אָמַר יְהֹוָה אֱלֹהֵי יִשְׂרָאֵל אָרוּר הָאִישׁ אֲשֶׁר לֹא יִשְׁמַע אֶת־

4 דִּבְרֵי הַבְּרִית הַזֹּאת: אֲשֶׁר צִוִּיתִי אֶת־אֲבוֹתֵיכֶם בְּיוֹם הוֹצִיאִי־אוֹתָם מֵאֶרֶץ־ מִצְרַיִם מִכּוּר הַבַּרְזֶל לֵאמֹר שִׁמְעוּ בְקוֹלִי וַעֲשִׂיתֶם אוֹתָם כְּכֹל אֲשֶׁר־אֲצַוֶּה אֶתְכֶם וִהְיִיתֶם לִי לְעָם וְאָנֹכִי אֶהְיֶה

5 לָכֶם לֵאלֹהִים: לְמַעַן הָקִים אֶת־הַשְּׁבוּעָה אֲשֶׁר־נִשְׁבַּעְתִּי לַאֲבוֹתֵיכֶם לָתֵת לָהֶם אֶרֶץ זָבַת חָלָב וּדְבַשׁ כַּיּוֹם הַזֶּה וָאַעַן וָאֹמַר אָמֵן | יְהֹוָה:

6 וַיֹּאמֶר יְהֹוָה אֵלַי קְרָא אֶת־ כָּל־הַדְּבָרִים הָאֵלֶּה בְּעָרֵי יְהוּדָה וּבְחֻצוֹת יְרוּשָׁלָ͏ִם:

prophesied, and Habakkuk, too, prophesied around that period (Daath Mikra).

3. *cursed be the man.* A very forceful opening to the address made necessary by the recalcitrance of the people (Kimchi).

4. *the iron furnace.* A furnace for smelting metal, made of iron, since iron has a higher melting point than other metals (Daath Mikra). Egypt was the scene of bitter suffering (cf. Deut. iv. 20).

do them. The commandments communicated by My voice (Kimchi).

5. *as at this day.* Even as you now enjoy (Metsudath David).

amen, O LORD. Spoken in confirmation of *cursed be,* etc. (verse 3), as in Deut. xxvii. 15ff. (Rashi, Metsudath David).

6. *in the cities of Judah, and in the streets of Jerusalem.* This was probably a proverbial expression, meaning throughout the length and breadth of the country.

of Jerusalem, saying: Hear ye the words of this covenant, and do them. 7. For I earnestly forewarned your fathers in the day that I brought them up out of the land of Egypt, even unto this day, forewarning betimes and often, saying: Hearken to My voice. 8. Yet they hearkened not, nor inclined their ear, but walked every one in the stubbornness of their evil heart; therefore I brought upon them all the words of this covenant, which I commanded them to do, but they did them not.'

9. And the Lord said unto me: 'A conspiracy is found among the men of Judah, and among the inhabitants of Jerusalem. 10. They are turned back to the iniquities of their forefathers, who refused to hear My words; and they are gone after other gods to serve them; the house of Israel and the house of Judah have broken My covenant

לֵאמֹר שִׁמְעוּ אֶת־דִּבְרֵי
הַבְּרִית הַזֹּאת וַעֲשִׂיתֶם אוֹתָם:
7 כִּי הָעֵד הַעִדֹתִי בַּאֲבוֹתֵיכֶם
בְּיוֹם הַעֲלוֹתִי אוֹתָם מֵאֶרֶץ
מִצְרַיִם עַד־הַיּוֹם הַזֶּה הַשְׁכֵּם
וְהָעֵד לֵאמֹר שִׁמְעוּ בְּקוֹלִי:
8 וְלֹא שָׁמְעוּ וְלֹא־הִטּוּ אֶת־
אָזְנָם וַיֵּלְכוּ אִישׁ בִּשְׁרִירוּת
לִבָּם הָרָע וָאָבִיא עֲלֵיהֶם
אֶת־כָּל־דִּבְרֵי הַבְּרִית־
הַזֹּאת אֲשֶׁר־צִוִּיתִי לַעֲשׂוֹת
9 וְלֹא עָשׂוּ: וַיֹּאמֶר יְהוָה אֵלַי
נִמְצָא־קֶשֶׁר בְּאִישׁ יְהוּדָה
10 וּבְיֹשְׁבֵי יְרוּשָׁלָ͏ִם: שָׁבוּ עַל־
עֲוֹנֹת אֲבוֹתָם הָרִאשֹׁנִים אֲשֶׁר
מֵאֲנוּ לִשְׁמוֹעַ אֶת־דְּבָרַי
וְהֵמָּה הָלְכוּ אַחֲרֵי אֱלֹהִים
אֲחֵרִים לְעָבְדָם הֵפֵרוּ בֵית־
יִשְׂרָאֵל וּבֵית יְהוּדָה אֶת־
בְּרִיתִי אֲשֶׁר כָּרַתִּי אֶת־

מלעיל v. 10.

---

7. betimes. lit. 'rising early,' i.e. incessantly, at all times (cf. vii. 13 and often in this Book).

8. yet they hearkened . . . heart. Repeated substantially from vii. 24.

the words. i.e. the penalties for disobedience announced in the covenant (Rashi, Kimchi).

9–14 THE EXHORTATION IS IGNORED

9. *a conspiracy.* i.e. it has been discovered that certain individuals have conspired to rebel against God by worshipping idols (Daath Soferim).

10. *they are turned back.* For a time they discontinued the sins of their forefathers in the wilderness and later, but now they resumed them (Kimchi).

which I made with their fathers.
11. Therefore thus saith the LORD:
Behold, I will bring evil upon them,
which they shall not be able to
escape; and though they shall cry
unto Me, I will not hearken unto
them. 12. Then shall the cities of
Judah and the inhabitants of Jerusalem go and cry unto the gods unto
whom they offer; but they shall not
save them at all in the time of their
trouble. 13. For according to the
number of thy cities are thy gods, O
Judah; and according to the number
of the streets of Jerusalem have ye
set up altars to the shameful thing,
even altars to offer unto Baal.
14. Therefore pray not thou for this
people, neither lift up cry nor prayer
for them; for I will not hear them in
the time that they cry unto Me for
their trouble.'

15 What hath My beloved to do in
    My house,

11 אֲבוֹתָם: לָכֵן כֹּה אָמַר יְהֹוָה
הִנְנִי מֵבִיא אֲלֵיהֶם רָעָה אֲשֶׁר
לֹא־יוּכְלוּ לָצֵאת מִמֶּנָּה
וְזָעֲקוּ אֵלַי וְלֹא אֶשְׁמַע
12 אֲלֵיהֶם: וְהָלְכוּ עָרֵי יְהוּדָה
וְיֹשְׁבֵי יְרוּשָׁלַם וְזָעֲקוּ אֶל־
הָאֱלֹהִים אֲשֶׁר הֵם מְקַטְּרִים
לָהֶם וְהוֹשֵׁעַ לֹא־יוֹשִׁיעוּ לָהֶם
13 בְּעֵת רָעָתָם: כִּי מִסְפַּר עָרֶיךָ
הָיוּ אֱלֹהֶיךָ יְהוּדָה וּמִסְפַּר
חֻצוֹת יְרוּשָׁלַם שַׂמְתֶּם
מִזְבְּחוֹת לַבֹּשֶׁת מִזְבְּחוֹת
14 לְקַטֵּר לַבָּעַל: וְאַתָּה אַל־
תִּתְפַּלֵּל בְּעַד־הָעָם הַזֶּה
וְאַל־תִּשָּׂא בַעֲדָם רִנָּה
וּתְפִלָּה כִּי | אֵינֶנִּי שֹׁמֵעַ בְּעֵת
קָרְאָם אֵלַי בְּעַד רָעָתָם:
15 מֶה לִידִידִי בְּבֵיתִי

---

11. *I will not hearken.* Although 'the
gates of tears are never shut' (Talmud,
Ber. 32b), that is only when the tears
express true penitence. Here they will
merely cry for mercy, but not in contrition for their sins.

12. *unto whom they offer.* The use of the
present participle may imply that even
when crying to God, they still practise
idolatry (see Daath Mikra).

13. *for according to the number,* etc.
Repeated from ii. 28.

the shameful thing. lit. 'the shame,' the

prophet's contemptuous designation
for Baal (Metsudath David).

14. *they cry unto Me.* Even if *they* prayed
I would not hearken, since they cleave
to their iniquity; I will certainly not
accept *thy* prayers on their behalf
(Metsudath David). Cf. vii. 16.

15–17 JUDAH'S INFIDELITY TO GOD

15. *My beloved.* viz. Judah; but now
Judah has no right in God's house,
since his conduct is an affront to Him
(Metsudath David).

Seeing she hath wrought lewd-
ness with many,
And the hallowed flesh is passed
from thee ?
When thou doest evil, then thou
rejoicest.

16 The LORD called thy name
A leafy olive-tree, fair with
goodly fruit;
With the noise of a great tumult
He hath kindled fire upon it,
And the branches of it are broken.

17. For the LORD of hosts, that
planted thee, hath pronounced evil
against thee, because of the evil of
the house of Israel and of the house
of Judah, which they have wrought
for themselves in provoking Me by
offering unto Baal.

18 And the LORD gave me knowledge of it, and I knew it;
Then Thou showedst me their
doings.

עֲשׂוֹתָהּ הַמְזִמָּ֫תָה הָרַבִּים
וּבְשַׂר־קֹ֫דֶשׁ יַעַבְר֣וּ מֵעָלָ֑יִךְ
כִּי רָעָתֵ֫כִי אָז תַּעֲלֹֽזִי ׃

16 זַ֫יִת רַעֲנָ֗ן יְפֵה פְרִי־תֹ֫אַר
קָרָא יְהֹוָה שְׁמֵ֑ךְ
לְק֣וֹל ׀ הֲמוּלָּ֣ה גְדֹלָ֗ה
הִצִּית אֵ֣שׁ עָלֶ֔יהָ
וְרָע֖וּ דָּלִיּוֹתָֽיו ׃

17 וַיהֹוָה צְבָאוֹת הַנּוֹטֵ֫עַ אוֹתָ֗ךְ
דִּבֶּר עָלַ֫יִךְ רָעָ֑ה בִּגְלַל רָעַת
בֵּית־יִשְׂרָאֵל וּבֵית יְהוּדָ֗ה
אֲשֶׁר עָשׂ֤וּ לָהֶם לְהַכְעִסֵ֫נִי
לְקַטֵּר לַבָּֽעַל ׃

18 וַיהֹוָה הוֹדִיעַ֫נִי וָאֵדָ֑עָה
אָ֖ז הִרְאִיתַ֫נִי מַעַלְלֵיהֶֽם ׃

v. 16. דגש אחר שורק

seeing . . . with many. The Hebrew is
difficult to translate. The word for *lewd-
ness (mezimmah)* may mean 'evil design'
and *with* is not in the original. The best
rendering that can be obtained from the
text is: 'seeing that the multitude perform it, viz. evil scheming.' Accordingly
we have a repetition of the teaching,
already familiar in this Book, that God
will not accept the service of the Temple
as long as the people act corruptly. This
follows Metsudath David.

and the hallowed flesh is passed from thee.
lit. 'and as for the holy flesh (i.e. the
offerings) let them pass from upon thee.'
Discontinue the sacrifices which you feel
your duty to bring, since they are of no
use to you and will not avert your doom
(Metsudath David).

16. *a leafy olive-tree.* Rich in foliage (cf.
Ps. lii. 10). Similar imagery is used of
the nation's prosperity in Hos. xiv. 6ff.
(Daath Soferim).

He hath kindled fire. [The prophetic
perfect.] Although in His love for His
people God described them as a luxuriant olive-tree, He finds it necessary to
destroy them (Metsudath David).

17. *the house of Israel . . . the house of
Judah.* [The branches of the olive-
tree.]

18–23   A PLOT TO SILENCE JEREMIAH

18. *it.* The punishment which was to
befall the nation.

Thou showedst me. This is an aside,

19 But I was like a docile lamb that
   is led to the slaughter;
   And I knew not that they had
   devised devices against me:
   'Let us destroy the tree with the
   fruit thereof,
   And let us cut him off from the
   land of the living,
   That his name may be no more
   remembered.'
20 But, O LORD of hosts, that
   judgest righteously,
   That triest the reins and the
   heart,
   Let me see Thy vengeance on
   them;
   For unto Thee have I revealed
   my cause.
21. Therefore thus saith the LORD
concerning the men of Anathoth,
that seek thy life, saying: 'Thou shalt
not prophesy in the name of the

19 וַאֲנִי כְּכֶבֶשׂ אַלּוּף
יוּבַל לִטְבוֹחַ
וְלֹא־יָדַעְתִּי
כִּי־עָלַי ׀ חָשְׁבוּ מַחֲשָׁבוֹת
נַשְׁחִיתָה עֵץ בְּלַחְמוֹ
וְנִכְרְתֶנּוּ מֵאֶרֶץ חַיִּים
וּשְׁמוֹ לֹא־יִזָּכֵר עוֹד׃
20 וַיהֹוָה צְבָאוֹת שֹׁפֵט צֶדֶק
בֹּחֵן כְּלָיוֹת וָלֵב
אֶרְאֶה נִקְמָתְךָ מֵהֶם
כִּי אֵלֶיךָ גִּלִּיתִי אֶת־רִיבִי׃
21 לָכֵן כֹּה־אָמַר יְהֹוָה עַל־
אַנְשֵׁי עֲנָתוֹת הַמְבַקְשִׁים אֶת־
נַפְשְׁךָ לֵאמֹר לֹא תִנָּבֵא בְּשֵׁם

perhaps implying: I could hardly have
credited their evil, hadst Thou not
shown it to me. Kimchi relates the verse
to the plot against Jeremiah's life, thus
linking it with what follows: God gave
me the knowledge of their evil machinations against me. This interpretation is
accepted by most moderns.

19. Jeremiah's predictions had aroused
the enmity of his own townspeople
(verse 21) who plotted to take his life (cf.
xviii. 18).

a docile lamb. The prophet compares
himself to a domesticated pet animal
which is ignorant of the owner's intention to slaughter it (Isaiah da Trani).

with the fruit thereof. lit. 'with the bread
thereof'; perhaps a proverbial equivalent of 'root and branch.' i.e. let us kill
Jeremiah and his offspring (Isaiah da
Trani).

20. *the reins and the heart.* i.e. the
innermost feelings and thoughts (Kimchi).

Thy vengeance. He does not seek personal vengeance, but vengeance for
God, Whose cause he pleads (Malbim).

on them. The men of Anathoth who
were plotting against him (Rashi).

for unto Thee, etc. Conscious of his
integrity, Jeremiah commits his cause to
God from Whom nothing is hidden
(Metsudath David).

21. *thou shalt not prophesy.* When evil
cannot justify itself even by the most
specious reasoning, it falls back upon
the weapon of tyrants in all ages:
suppression of freedom of speech by
brute force. For other instances to
silence the prophets, cf. Amos ii. 12, vii.
10ff.; Mic. ii. 6. The threat in this verse

LORD, that thou die not by our hand'; 22. therefore thus saith the LORD of hosts:

> Behold, I will punish them;
> The young men shall die by the sword,
> Their sons and their daughters shall die by famine;

23 And there shall be no remnant unto them;

> For I will bring evil upon the men of Anathoth,
> Even the year of their visitation.

יְהֹוָה וְלֹא תָמוּת בְּיָדֵנוּ:

22 לָכֵן כֹּה אָמַר יְהֹוָה צְבָאוֹת הִנְנִי פֹקֵד עֲלֵיהֶם הַבַּחוּרִים יָמֻתוּ בַחֶרֶב בְּנֵיהֶם וּבְנֹתֵיהֶם יָמֻתוּ בָּרָעָב:

23 וּשְׁאֵרִית לֹא תִהְיֶה לָהֶם כִּי־אָבִיא רָעָה אֶל־אַנְשֵׁי עֲנָתוֹת שְׁנַת פְּקֻדָּתָם:

---

12   CHAPTER XII   יב

1 Right wouldest Thou be, O LORD,

Were I to contend with Thee,

Yet will I reason with Thee:

1 צַדִּיק אַתָּה יְהֹוָה כִּי אָרִיב אֵלֶיךָ אַךְ מִשְׁפָּטִים אֲדַבֵּר אוֹתָךְ

---

apparently contradicts verse 19, but it may indicate a later stage in the conspiracy. The secret plan to kill him having failed, they try to close his mouth by menaces (Ibn Nachmiash).

22. The punishment will take a form which vindicates the prophet: the invasion he foretold will come to pass, and in it the sword and famine will take their toll.

23. The judgment on Jeremiah's birthplace is particularly severe, because he had the right to expect sympathy and help from the population.

no remnant. The Rabbis note that this decree was repealed when the people of Anathoth repented when the enemy captured the city (Kimchi from Pesikta d'Rav Kahana). It is recorded that 128

men of Anathoth returned to the Holy Land from the Babylonian captivity (Ezra ii. 23).

the year of their visitation. When Nebuchadnezzar would conquer the country (Kimchi).

CHAPTER XII

1–6 WHY DO THE WICKED PROSPER?

THE evil which prevailed among the ruling class and the personal attack upon him aroused in the prophet's mind this question. This question was already raised by Asaph (Psalms lxx). Koheleth, too (v. 7), mentions the problem, as well as Habakkuk (i) and Job (xxi. 7).

1. *right wouldst Thou be.* I know that in

Wherefore doth the way of the wicked prosper?
Wherefore are all they secure that deal very treacherously?

2 Thou hast planted them, yea, they have taken root;
They grow, yea, they bring forth fruit;
Thou art near in their mouth,
And far from their reins.

3 But Thou, O Lord, knowest me,
Thou seest me, and triest my heart toward Thee;
Pull them out like sheep for the slaughter,
And prepare them for the day of slaughter.

4 How long shall the land mourn,
And the herbs of the whole field wither?
For the wickedness of them that dwell therein, the beasts are consumed, and the birds;

מַדּוּעַ דֶּרֶךְ רְשָׁעִים צָלֵחָה
שָׁלוּ כָּל־בֹּגְדֵי בָגֶד:
2 נְטַעְתָּם גַּם־שֹׁרָשׁוּ
יֵלְכוּ גַּם־עָשׂוּ פֶרִי
קָרוֹב אַתָּה בְּפִיהֶם
וְרָחוֹק מִכִּלְיוֹתֵיהֶם:
3 וְאַתָּה יְהוָה יְדַעְתָּנִי
תִּרְאֵנִי וּבָחַנְתָּ לִבִּי אִתָּךְ
הַתִּקֵם כְּצֹאן לְטִבְחָה
וְהַקְדִּשֵׁם לְיוֹם הֲרֵגָה:
4 עַד־מָתַי תֶּאֱבַל הָאָרֶץ
וְעֵשֶׂב כָּל־הַשָּׂדֶה יִיבָשׁ
מֵרָעַת יֹשְׁבֵי־בָהּ
סָפְתָה בְהֵמוֹת וָעוֹף

---

any argument Thou must be right. A.V. and R.V. have: 'righteous art Thou,' i.e. God's righteousness is axiomatic; nevertheless the question is suggested: how can it be reconciled with the prosperity of the wicked? (Kimchi).

reason with. lit. 'speak judgments,' i.e. argue with, or complain unto (Kimchi).

the wicked. Some understand the term of the people of Anathoth (cf. verse 6), and some as referring to Nebuchadnezzar (Rashi, Abarbanel).

2. *Thou hast planted them.* This figure of fixed tenure and stability is met with frequently in the Bible (cf. 2 Sam. vii. 10, referring to the whole nation; Isa. xl. 24; Ps. i. 3). Their prosperity is not by chance, but due to God's decree (Kimchi).

they grow. For this use of the verb

halach, lit. 'to go,' cf. Hos. xiv. 7, *his branches shall spread.*

Thou art near, etc.   They constantly have the Divine name on their lips, but their simulated piety is sheer hypocrisy (cf. Isa. xxix. 13).

3. *triest my heart.* Therefore Thou knowest that I do not speak hypocritically (Kimchi).

pull them . . . slaughter. This is an impassioned plea for the destruction of his enemies, the men of Anathoth (cf. xi. 21). It raises a moral difficulty; but Kimchi explains that Jeremiah pleaded with God to bring about their immediate downfall so that the people know the wages of sin. If Nebuchadnezzar is the subject of his plea, there is no difficulty.

4. *how long shall the land mourn.* The

87

Because they said: 'He seeth not
our end.'

5 'If thou hast run with the footmen,
and they have wearied thee,
Then how canst thou contend
with horses?
And though in a land of peace
thou art secure,
Yet how wilt thou do in the
thickets of the Jordan?

6 For even thy brethren, and the
house of thy father,
Even they have dealt treacherously
with thee,
Even they have cried aloud after
thee;
Believe them not, though they
speak fair words unto thee.'

כִּי אָמְרוּ
לֹא יִרְאֶה אֶת־אַחֲרִיתֵנוּ:
5 כִּי אֶת־רַגְלִים | רַצְתָּה
וַיַּלְאוּךָ
וְאֵיךְ תְּתַחֲרֶה אֶת־הַסּוּסִים
וּבְאֶרֶץ שָׁלוֹם אַתָּה בוֹטֵחַ
וְאֵיךְ תַּעֲשֶׂה בִּגְאוֹן הַיַּרְדֵּן:
6 כִּי גַם־אַחֶיךָ וּבֵית־אָבִיךָ
גַּם־הֵמָּה בָּגְדוּ בָךְ
גַּם־הֵמָּה קָרְאוּ אַחֲרֶיךָ מָלֵא
אַל־תַּאֲמֵן בָּם
כִּי־יְדַבְּרוּ אֵלֶיךָ טוֹבוֹת:

soil is represented as 'mourning' when
it does not produce, probably through
lack of rain. This is a God-sent punishment for the wickedness of the inhabitants; but the righteous among them
have to share the penalty! How long,
then, will God tolerate this injustice?
(Kara).

He seeth not our end. The subject is
uncertain. Some understand it as God
Who is unconcerned about their actions
and so they can continue in their evil
ways with impunity (Kimchi). Others
refer it to Jeremiah of whom they say
that they will outlive him and he will not
see his predictions fulfilled (Kara).

5. GOD'S REPLY. The question remains
unanswered, but God demands faith
and patience, for the prophet's present
difficulties are as nothing compared
with what is yet to come.

the footmen . . . with horses? If you find the
opposition of the men of Anathoth too
difficult to bear, how will you stand up
to the enmity of more formidable men,
the leaders of the nation? (Rashi).

a land of peace. The phrase is to be
understood in a comparative sense, a
land cultivated and inhabited, in contrast to *the thickets of the Jordan,* i.e. the
jungle along the banks of the river, the
haunt of wild animals (Rashi).

6. *cried aloud after thee.* They raised a
hue and cry against Jeremiah as though
he were a criminal to be hunted down
(Kara).

though they speak fair words unto thee. In
xi. 21 they are pictured as threatening
him with death. Probably they varied
their tactics, now threatening, now
cajoling (see Daath Mikra).

7 I have forsaken My house,
  I have cast off My heritage;
  I have given the dearly beloved of
    My soul
  Into the hand of her enemies.
8 My heritage is become unto Me
  As a lion in the forest;
  She hath uttered her voice against
    Me;
  Therefore have I hated her.
9 Is My heritage unto Me as a
    speckled bird of prey?
  Are the birds of prey against her
    round about?
  Come ye, assemble all the beasts
    of the field,
  Bring them to devour.
10 Many shepherds have destroyed
    My vineyard,
  They have trodden My portion
    under foot,

7 עָזַ֙בְתִּי֙ אֶת־בֵּיתִ֔י

נָטַ֖שְׁתִּי אֶת־נַחֲלָתִ֑י

נָתַ֛תִּי אֶת־יְדִד֥וּת נַפְשִׁ֖י

בְּכַ֥ף אֹיְבֶֽיהָ׃

8 הָיְתָה־לִּ֥י נַחֲלָתִ֖י

כְּאַרְיֵ֣ה בַיָּ֑עַר

נָתְנָ֥ה עָלַ֖י בְּקוֹלָ֑הּ

עַל־כֵּ֖ן שְׂנֵאתִֽיהָ׃

9 הַעַ֨יִט צָב֤וּעַ נַחֲלָתִי֙ לִ֔י

הַעַ֖יִט סָבִ֣יב עָלֶ֑יהָ

לְכ֗וּ אִסְפ֛וּ כָּל־חַיַּ֥ת הַשָּׂדֶ֖ה

הֵתָ֥יוּ לְאָכְלָֽה׃

10 רֹעִ֤ים רַבִּים֙ שִֽׁחֲת֣וּ כַרְמִ֔י

בֹּסְס֖וּ אֶת־חֶלְקָתִ֑י

7–13 DEVASTATION OF THE LAND THREATENED

A plaintive lament by God that He has had to surrender His beloved into the hands of their enemies. Such a fate would be occasioned by a severe national disaster, and the date may be the first capture of Jerusalem in 597 B.C.E. But the verbs can also be construed as the prophetic perfect and the passage refer to a catastrophe in the future, spoken of as though it had already taken place. In that case, the passage may be a general answer to the prophet's questioning: even though the wicked seem to be secure, yet the time is approaching when widespread devastation will overtake them.

7. *My house.* This probably means the Temple which, however, is identified with the nation, since their fate is interwoven (Kimchi).

the dearly beloved of My soul. Though sinners, they are God's *dearly beloved*; nevertheless justice demands retribution, since God is no respecter of persons (Kimchi).

8. *as a lion,* etc. When a lion roars in the forest, and the passersby hear his voice, they leave the road of the forest and even the road near the forest. So have I forsaken My inheritance, for they were like a lion in the forest that roars at night (Kimchi).

uttered her voice against Me. Openly expressed defiance (Daath Mikra).

9. *a speckled bird of prey.* Which incurs the enmity of other birds of prey. Birds are wont to attack other birds of unfamiliar plumage, a habit which was noted by classical writers (Rashi).

10. *many shepherds.* viz. rulers, but the reference is not clear. It may mean the generals of the enemy as in vi. 3 (so

They have made My pleasant
   portion
A desolate wilderness.

11 They have made it a desolation,
   It mourneth unto Me, being
      desolate;
   The whole land is made desolate,
   Because no man layeth it to
      heart.

12 Upon all the high hills in the
      wilderness spoilers are come;
   For the sword of the Lord
      devoureth
   From the one end of the land
      even to the other end of the
      land,
   No flesh hath peace.

13 They have sown wheat, and have
      reaped thorns;
   They have put themselves to
      pain, they profit not;
   Be ye then ashamed of your
      increase,
   Because of the fierce anger of the
      Lord.

נָתְנוּ אֶת־חֶלְקַת חֶמְדָּתִי
לְמִדְבַּר שְׁמָמָה׃
11 שָׂמָהּ לִשְׁמָמָה
אָבְלָה עָלַי שְׁמֵמָה
נָשַׁמָּה כָּל־הָאָרֶץ
כִּי אֵין אִישׁ שָׂם עַל־לֵב׃
12 עַל־כָּל־שְׁפָיִם בַּמִּדְבָּר
בָּאוּ שֹׁדְדִים
כִּי חֶרֶב לַיהוָֹה אֹכְלָה
מִקְצֵה אֶרֶץ
וְעַד־קְצֵה הָאָרֶץ
אֵין שָׁלוֹם לְכָל־בָּשָׂר׃
13 זָרְעוּ חִטִּים וְקֹצִים קָצָרוּ
נֶחְלוּ לֹא יוֹעִלוּ
וּבֹשׁוּ מִתְּבוּאֹתֵיכֶם
מֵחֲרוֹן אַף־יְהוָֹה׃

v. 11. המ׳ בצרי   v. 13. קמץ בז״ק

Rashi, Kimchi); or, the leaders of Israel
as in ii. 8 who are misleaders and
responsible for the plight of the nation
(Alshich).

My vineyard. Figurative of the people
(cf. Isa. v. 1ff.).

11. *unto Me.* lit. 'upon Me,' i.e. to My
grief (cf. for the usage, Gen. xlviii. 7).

layeth it to heart. Even now no one
troubles about the pending disaster; all
shut their ears to My warnings (Daath
Mikra).

12. *the sword of the* Lord. In the hands
of the enemy, who is only God's tool
(Kimchi). For this mode of thought, cf.
Isa. x. 15.

no flesh hath peace. Not only Judah, but
other nations will also be torn by war
(Kimchi).

13. *they have sown wheat, and have reaped
thorns.* It is simplest to understand *they*
as referring to Israel: not only has disaster come from without, but from within
too; even his crops have disastrously
failed and his labour has been in vain
(Metsudath David).

be ye then ashamed of your increase. For its
poverty demonstrates that you are
under God's displeasure (cf. xiv. 3f.;
Joel i. 11). The verbs are the prophetic
perfect (Metsudath David).

14. Thus saith the LORD: As for all Mine evil neighbours, that touch the inheritance which I have caused My people Israel to inherit, behold, I will pluck them up from off their land, and will pluck up the house of Judah from among them. 15. And it shall come to pass, after that I have plucked them up, I will again have compassion on them; and I will bring them back, every man to his heritage, and every man to his land. 16. And it shall come to pass, if they will diligently learn the ways of My people to swear by My name: 'As the LORD liveth,' even as they taught My people to swear by Baal; then shall they be built up in the midst of My people. 17. But if they will not hearken, then will I pluck up that nation, plucking up and destroying it, saith the LORD.

כֹּה ׀ אָמַר יְהֹוָה עַל־כָּל־ 14
שְׁכֵנַי הָרָעִים הַנֹּגְעִים בַּנַּחֲלָה
אֲשֶׁר־הִנְחַלְתִּי אֶת־עַמִּי
אֶת־יִשְׂרָאֵל הִנְנִי נֹתְשָׁם מֵעַל
אַדְמָתָם וְאֶת־בֵּית יְהוּדָה
אֶתּוֹשׁ מִתּוֹכָם: וְהָיָה אַחֲרֵי 15
נָתְשִׁי אוֹתָם אָשׁוּב וְרִחַמְתִּים
וַהֲשִׁבֹתִים אִישׁ לְנַחֲלָתוֹ וְאִישׁ
לְאַרְצוֹ: וְהָיָה אִם־לָמֹד 16
יִלְמְדוּ אֶת־דַּרְכֵי עַמִּי
לְהִשָּׁבֵעַ בִּשְׁמִי חַי־יְהֹוָה
כַּאֲשֶׁר לִמְּדוּ אֶת־עַמִּי
לְהִשָּׁבֵעַ בַּבָּעַל וְנִבְנוּ בְּתוֹךְ
עַמִּי: וְאִם לֹא יִשְׁמָעוּ וְנָתַשְׁתִּי 17
אֶת־הַגּוֹי הַהוּא נָתוֹשׁ וְאַבֵּד
נְאֻם־יְהֹוָה:

14–17 FATE OF ISRAEL'S ENEMIES

Although these nations are God's instruments for the execution of His purpose, they will be punished by exile for destroying Israel, because 'benefit is brought through the instrumentality of the virtuous, whilst hurt is brought through the instrumentality of the evil.' Their exile will only be temporary if they repent, but permanent if they persist in their evil ways. Exactly the same prospect is frequently held out to Israel in the Bible, since God is an impartial Judge. From this may be seen how false is the interpretation of 'chosen people,' applied to Israel, as 'favoured people.'

14. *Mine evil neighbours.* viz. Ammon, Moab, etc. In *Mine* God identifies Himself with Israel (Kimchi).

15. *I will again have compassion on them.* The restoration of Moab is foretold in xlviii. 47 and of Ammon in xlix. 6.

16. *to swear by My name.* See on iv. 2.

be built up. Cf. if thou return to the Almighty, thou shalt be built up (Job xxii. 23).

in the midst of My people. i.e. as My people will be restored to their land, so will they. *In the midst* further implies a harmonious state of unity and peace, and the passage may well be a Messianic

13   CHAPTER XIII   יג

1. Thus said the LORD unto me: 'Go, and get thee a linen girdle, and put it upon thy loins, and put it not in water.' 2. So I got a girdle according to the word of the LORD, and put it upon my loins.

3. And the word of the LORD came unto me the second time, saying: 4. 'Take the girdle that thou hast gotten, which is upon thy loins, and arise, go to Perath, and hide it there

כֹּה־אָמַר יְהֹוָה אֵלַי הָלוֹךְ 1
וְקָנִיתָ לְּדֹ אֵזוֹר פִּשְׁתִּים וְשַׂמְתּוֹ
עַל־־מָתְנֶיךָ וּבַמַּיִם לֹא
תְבִאֵהוּ : וָאֶקְנֶה אֶת־הָאֵזוֹר 2
כִּדְבַר יְהֹוָה וָאָשִׂם עַל־מָתְנָי :
וַיְהִי דְבַר־יְהֹוָה אֵלַי שֵׁנִית 3
לֵאמֹר : קַח אֶת־הָאֵזוֹר אֲשֶׁר 4
קָנִיתָ אֲשֶׁר עַל־מָתְנֶיךָ וְקוּם
לֵךְ פְּרָתָה וְטָמְנֵהוּ שָׁם בִּנְקִיק

---

forecast of the peace and friendship which will one day reign among all peoples (see Kimchi).

CHAPTER XIII

1-11 SYMBOL OF THE LINEN GIRDLE

AT the command of God, the prophet deposits a linen girdle, after having worn it a short while, in a cavity on the banks of the Euphrates (but see on verse 4). After a long interval he takes it out, only to find it completely rotted and useless. This is 'an acted parable': like a girdle Israel had been closely attached to God, but had proved unworthy of the honour and will be discarded like a soiled garment. Modern commentators differ on the question whether this was actually carried out by the prophet, or whether he saw it in a vision which he then imparted to the people. They are also divided on whether the passage relates to an early period of Jeremiah's ministry, by which time idolatry was already rife, or falls in Jehoiakim's reign (see on verse 18).

1. *a linen girdle.* The Hebrew word *ezor* denotes a loin-cloth rather than what is

now understood as a girdle. Linen garments were worn by the priests (Exod. xxviii. 39). Hence the girdle fittingly symbolized the community which was intended to be *a kingdom of priests and a holy nation* (Exod. xix. 6) (see Malbim).

upon thy loins. Emblematic of Israel's close attachment to God (verse 11).

put it not in water. New linen is steeped in water to soften it and make it more comfortable for wearing. Abarbanel claims that soaking it in water strengthens the fibers and retards its decay. Rashi explains that washing it in water will cleanse it of sweat and prevent its decay.

4. *Perath.* If the Euphrates is meant (though generally this is prefixed by 'the river'), this would necessitate a double journey of about three hundred miles. Some hold that the Hebrew *perathah* means 'to Parah' (cf. Josh. xviii. 23), a town three miles north-east of Anathoth. It is the modern Wadi Farah which has a fountain flowing out of the fissure of a rock. Apparently, Scripture means this cleft. At the beginning, the prophet was commanded not to dip the

in a cleft of the rock.' 5. So I went, and hid it in Perath, as the Lord commanded me. 6. And it came to pass after many days, that the Lord said unto me: 'Arise, go to Perath, and take the girdle from thence, which I commanded thee to hide there.' 7. Then I went to Perath, and digged, and took the girdle from the place where I had hid it; and, behold, the girdle was marred, it was profitable for nothing.

8. Then the word of the Lord came unto me, saying:

9. Thus saith the Lord: After this manner will I mar the pride of Judah, and the great pride of Jerusalem, 10. even this evil people, that refuse to hear My words, that

5	הַסָּלַע: וָאֵלֵךְ וָאֶטְמְנֵהוּ בִפְרָת כַּאֲשֶׁר צִוָּה יְהוָה:
6	אוֹתִי: וַיְהִי מִקֵּץ יָמִים רַבִּים וַיֹּאמֶר יְהוָה אֵלַי קוּם לֵךְ פְּרָתָה וְקַח מִשָּׁם אֶת־הָאֵזוֹר אֲשֶׁר צִוִּיתִיךָ לְטָמְנוֹ־שָׁם:
7	וָאֵלֵךְ פְּרָתָה וָאֶחְפֹּר וָאֶקַּח אֶת־הָאֵזוֹר מִן־הַמָּקוֹם אֲשֶׁר־טְמַנְתִּיו שָׁמָּה וְהִנֵּה נִשְׁחַת הָאֵזוֹר לֹא יִצְלַח לַכֹּל:
8	וַיְהִי דְבַר־יְהוָה אֵלַי לֵאמֹר:
9	כֹּה אָמַר יְהוָה כָּכָה אַשְׁחִית אֶת־גְּאוֹן יְהוּדָה וְאֶת־גְּאוֹן
10	יְרוּשָׁלַםִ הָרָב: הָעָם הַזֶּה הָרָע הַמֵּאֲנִים ׀ לִשְׁמוֹעַ אֶת־

girdle in water, and now he was commanded to put it in a very damp place to hasten its decay (Daath Mikra). They who understand the word as Euphrates mostly regard the incident as visionary. So Rambam and Abarbanel. The latter explains the allegory in detail. The girdle represents the Jewish people, which clung to God as a girdle clings to the loins of its wearer. Moreover, just as a girdle is a garment indicating esteem, so was Israel caused to cling to God 'for name, and for praise, and for glory.' God commanded the prophet to buy the girdle, symbolizing that Israel is one of God's possessions, as in Aboth 6:10. It was made of linen, *pishtim* in Hebrew, to indicate that, although they were downtrodden and humbled in Egypt, they were, nevertheless, destined to expand (*pasah*) in the Promised Land. He commanded him to put the girdle on his loins since the girdle symbolized

the Jewish people and the prophet the Almighty, and just as the Almighty acquired Israel and caused them to cling to Him, so did the prophet purchase the girdle and put it on his loins.

5. *in Perath.* If the river is intended, the meaning must be a place near the Euphrates (Metsudath David).

7. *and digged.* He had originally covered it over with earth so that it should not be removed by a person who found it among the rocks (Metsudath David).

9. The rotting of the girdle denotes the humbling of Judah's pride as a punishment for his idolatry which rendered the people as useless as the soiled girdle. Alternatively, their pride will be broken as easily as the rotted girdle disintegrates.

the pride. It is unlikely that the word is

walk in the stubbornness of their heart, and are gone after other gods to serve them, and to worship them, that it be as this girdle, which is profitable for nothing. 11. For as the girdle cleaveth to the loins of a man, so have I caused to cleave unto Me the whole house of Israel and the whole house of Judah, saith the LORD, that they might be unto Me for a people, and for a name, and for a praise, and for a glory; but they would not hearken.

12. Moreover thou shalt speak unto them this word: Thus saith the LORD, the God of Israel: 'Every bottle is filled with wine'; and when they shall say unto thee: 'Do we not know that every bottle is filled with wine?' 13. Then shalt thou say unto them: Thus saith the LORD: Behold, I will fill all the inhabitants of this land, even the kings that sit upon

דִּבְרֵי הַהֹלְכִים בִּשְׁרִרוּת
לִבָּם וַיֵּלְכוּ אַחֲרֵי אֱלֹהִים
אֲחֵרִים לְעָבְדָם וּלְהִשְׁתַּחֲוֹת
לָהֶם וִיהִי כָּאֵזוֹר הַזֶּה אֲשֶׁר
לֹא־יִצְלַח לַכֹּל: כִּי כַאֲשֶׁר 11
יִדְבַּק הָאֵזוֹר אֶל־מָתְנֵי אִישׁ
כֵּן הִדְבַּקְתִּי אֵלַי אֶת־כָּל־
בֵּית יִשְׂרָאֵל וְאֶת־כָּל־בֵּית
יְהוּדָה נְאֻם־יְהֹוָה לִהְיוֹת
לִי לְעָם וּלְשֵׁם וְלִתְהִלָּה
וּלְתִפְאָרֶת וְלֹא שָׁמֵעוּ:
וְאָמַרְתָּ אֲלֵיהֶם אֶת־הַדָּבָר 12
הַזֶּה כֹּה־אָמַר יְהֹוָה אֱלֹהֵי
יִשְׂרָאֵל כָּל־נֵבֶל יִמָּלֵא יָיִן
וְאָמְרוּ אֵלֶיךָ הֲיָדֹעַ לֹא נֵדַע
כִּי־כָל־נֵבֶל יִמָּלֵא יָיִן:
וְאָמַרְתָּ אֲלֵהֶם כֹּה־אָמַר 13
יְהֹוָה הִנְנִי מְמַלֵּא אֶת־כָּל־
יֹשְׁבֵי הָאָרֶץ הַזֹּאת וְאֶת־
הַמְּלָכִים הַיֹּשְׁבִים לְדָוִד

---

used here in the sense of arrogance and conceit, but rather their material eminence, their strength and wealth which are the source of their pride (Targum).

12–14 PARABLE OF THE WINE-BOTTLE

12. When the Judeans saw Jeremiah's deeds or his words, how he bought the girdle and hid it, and how it rotted away, they ridiculed him, saying that he was drunk. Therefore, immediately fol-

lowing the episode of the girdle, God commanded him to tell them that every bottle would be filled with wine, and that they are the drunken ones for they will be drunk from their troubles, not the prophet (Abarbanel).

bottle. Made of earthenware, not of skin (cf. xlviii. 12) (Kimchi).

13. *upon David's throne.* [David is mentioned probably in order to emphasize the contrast between them and him, and show how low they have fallen.]

David's throne, and the priests, and
the prophets, and all the inhabitants
of Jerusalem, with drunkenness.
14. And I will dash them one against
another, even the fathers and the
sons together, saith the LORD; I will
not pity, nor spare, nor have compassion, that I should not destroy
them.

15 Hear ye, and give ear, be not
proud;
   For the LORD hath spoken.

16 Give glory to the LORD your
   God,
   Before it grow dark,
   And before your feet stumble
   Upon the mountains of twilight,

עַל־כִּסְאוֹ וְאֶת־הַכֹּהֲנִים
וְאֶת־הַנְּבִיאִים וְאֵת כָּל־
יֹשְׁבֵי יְרוּשָׁלָ͏ִם שִׁכָּרוֹן׃
14 וְנִפַּצְתִּים אִישׁ אֶל־אָחִיו
וְהָאָבוֹת וְהַבָּנִים יַחְדָּו נְאֻם־
יְהֹוָה לֹא־אֶחְמוֹל וְלֹא־
אָחוּס וְלֹא אֲרַחֵם מֵהַשְׁחִיתָם׃
15 שִׁמְעוּ וְהַאֲזִינוּ אַל־תִּגְבָּהוּ
   כִּי יְהֹוָה דִּבֵּר׃
16 תְּנוּ לַיהֹוָה אֱלֹהֵיכֶם כָּבוֹד
   בְּטֶרֶם יַחְשִׁךְ
   וּבְטֶרֶם יִתְנַגְּפוּ רַגְלֵיכֶם
   עַל־הָרֵי נָשֶׁף

v. 13. קמץ בטרחא

---

the priests. i.e. the priests of Baal
(Metsudath David).

the prophets. i.e. the false prophets
(Targum).

with drunkenness. Not to be understood
literally, but in the sense of mental
intoxication, confusion and bewilderment, which will lead them to collide
with each other in their helplessness
before the enemy (Abarbanel, Metsudath David). For this figure, cf. xxv. 15f.,
xlviii. 26.

14. *I will dash.* As intoxicated persons
collide and cause each other to fall, so
will the confusion sent by God be a
factor in the destruction of the Kingdom (Kimchi). Jonathan takes this as a
sign of the inner strife that will exist
between the inhabitants of this land.

**15–17 THE PEOPLE EXHORTED TO HEED
THE WARNING**

15. *be not proud.* Do not be too proud

to hearken to God's admonition
(Kimchi).

16. The prophet exhorts them to repent
before going into exile, when their
enemies will lead them upon mountains
that will appear as mountains of twilight
(Ibn Nachmiash). Kimchi explains these
mountains as symbolic of the aid they
expected to receive from Egypt. Just as
one hopes to gain refuge in the mountains, so do you hope to gain refuge
with the aid of Egypt. Instead, you will
bruise your feet on these very mountains, as one who walks at night bruises
his feet on the stones.

give glory. By humbling yourselves
before Him, acknowledging your sin
and yielding Him your obedience (cf.
Josh. vii. 19) (Kara, Metsudath David).

before it grows dark. As the mountain
traveller hastens to reach safety before
darkness overtakes him, so let Israel

And, while ye look for light,

He turn it into the shadow of
death,

And make it gross darkness.

17 But if ye will not hear it,

My soul shall weep in secret for
your pride;

And mine eye shall weep sore,
and run down with tears,

Because the LORD's flock is
carried away captive.

18 Say thou unto the king and to
the queen-mother:

וְקִוִּיתֶם לְאוֹר

וְשָׂמָהּ לְצַלְמָוֶת

יָשִׁית לַעֲרָפֶל:

17 וְאִם לֹא תִשְׁמָעוּהָ

בְּמִסְתָּרִים תִּבְכֶּה־נַפְשִׁי

מִפְּנֵי גֵוָה

וְדָמֹעַ תִּדְמַע

וְתֵרַד עֵינִי דִּמְעָה

כִּי נִשְׁבָּה עֵדֶר יְהֹוָה:

18 אֱמֹר לַמֶּלֶךְ וְלַגְּבִירָה

v. 16. ושית ק׳

return to God before the darkness of
disaster engulfs him (Daath Mikra).

the mountain of twilight. i.e. mountains
enveloped in the dusk of twilight (Daath
Mikra).

and, while ye look for light, etc. The very
source whence you hope for salvation
will become the means of your destruction — an allusion to the false hopes
they entertained of help from Egypt
(Kimchi).

17. Jeremiah might appear a stern
prophet — so harsh that he roused the
fierce hostility of many sections of the
people. But his harshness was motivated
by the driving force of duty, however
unpleasant; a yearning love for his
people inspired him with deep compassion for their woes. In a passage of great
tenderness the Talmud interprets the
verse of God as the Speaker: 'As a
loving father sorrowing over his son's
misdeeds for which he has had to
punish him, so God weeps in a secret
place over Israel's glory *(sic)* which has
been taken from him and given to
others' (Chag. 5b).

for your pride. Either your pride which

will be humbled (Rashi), or your pride
which causes you stubbornly to refuse
to heed God's word (Kimchi).

the LORD's *flock.* Though they have
sinned, they are still *the* LORD's *flock*
(Daath Soferim). For the simile, cf. Ps.
lxxiv. 1, lxxx. 2.

is carried. The prophetic perfect (Daath
Mikra).

18–19 DIRGE OVER THE KING AND
QUEEN-MOTHER

18. *the king.* Jehoiachin (cf. xxii. 26).

the queen-mother. Nehushta (2 Kings
xxiv. 8). [Eastern etiquette attached
great prominence to the queen-mother,
as is shown by the frequency with which
she is specifically named in the Bible
(cf., e.g., 1 Kings xv. 2, 10, xxii. 42). This
prominence would be enhanced in the
present instance, since Jehoiachin was
only eighteen years old. Since kings
usually had many wives, not all of them
of the same status, the identity of a
prince's mother was a matter of importance in the succession to the throne. It
is remarkable that the mother's name is
given only for the kings of Judah, not

'Sit ye down low;

For your headtires are come down,

Even your beautiful crown.'

19 The cities of the South are shut up,

And there is none to open them;

Judah is carried away captive all of it;

It is wholly carried away captive.

20 Lift up your eyes, and behold

Them that come from the north;

Where is the flock that was given thee,

הַשְׁפִּילוּ שֵׁבוּ

כִּי יָרַד מַרְאֲשֹׁתֵיכֶם

עֲטֶרֶת תִּפְאַרְתְּכֶם:

19 עָרֵי הַנֶּגֶב סֻגְּרוּ

וְאֵין פֹּתֵחַ

הָגְלָת יְהוּדָה כֻּלָּהּ

הָגְלָת שְׁלוֹמִים:

20 שְׂאוּ עֵינֵיכֶם וּרְאִי

הַבָּאִים מִצָּפוֹן

אַיֵּה הָעֵדֶר נִתַּן־לָךְ

v. 20. שאו ק' וראו ק' v. 20.

---

those of Israel. An exception was Jehoram, whose mother is not mentioned (cf. 2 Kings viii. 16). His wife was Ahab's daughter (verse 18), and as a true daughter of Jezebel she may have forced the queen-mother into the background who, for this reason, is not named. The queen-mothers after that are mentioned for Judah, but not for Israel. This seems to indicate that their prominence was confined to Judah, since Judaism has always paid honour to women. The Kingdom of Israel, on the other hand, which came more strongly under the influence of the surrounding peoples, may have held women in less esteem, in conformity with the general ancient attitude.]

sit ye down low. Descend from your throne (Kimchi).

your headtires. Your royal dignity will be humbled to the dust (Malbim, Kimchi).

19. *the cities of the South.* i.e. of the Negeb, the arid region in the south of Judah. Though remote from the invader these cities will not escape his fury, but be rendered desolate, no in-

habitants being left in them even to open their gates (Daath Mikra).

captive all of it. This is a rhetorical exaggeration. The complete captivity did not come until the reign of Zedekiah; nevertheless, the magnitude even of the present disaster warranted such a description. Moreover, Jehoiachin and the princes who were exiled represented the whole nation (Kimchi).

20-27 CONSEQUENCE OF THEIR GUILT

The people's sins are responsible for the disaster. What has now become of the nation? They whose friendship they courted are now their masters. The nation is so deeply dyed with evil, that it is doubtful whether it can ever be clean again.

20. *lift up your eyes.* The *kethib* is feminine singular whereas the *kerë* is masculine plural. In verse 23 M.T. is masculine plural, but in the rest of the passage M.T. is feminine singular. Jerusalem is addressed (cf. verse 27) and insensibly she merges into the nation (see Rashi).

the north. Babylon (Kara).

97

Thy beautiful flock?

21 What wilt thou say, when He
    shall set the friends over thee
    as head,

    Whom thou thyself hast trained
    against thee?

    Shall not pangs take hold of thee,

    As of a woman in travail?

22 And if thou say in thy heart:

    'Wherefore are these things be-
    fallen me?'—

    For the greatness of thine iniquity
    are thy skirts uncovered,

    And thy heels suffer violence.

23 Can the Ethiopian change his
    skin,

    Or the leopard his spots?

    Then may ye also do good,

    That are accustomed to do evil.

24 Therefore will I scatter them, as
    the stubble that passeth away

    By the wind of the wilderness.

צֹאן תִּפְאַרְתֵּךְ׃

21 מַה־תֹּאמְרִי כִּי־יִפְקֹד עָלַיִךְ
וְאַתְּ לִמַּדְתְּ אֹתָם עָלַיִךְ
אַלֻּפִים לְרֹאשׁ
הֲלוֹא חֲבָלִים יֹאחֱזוּךְ
כְּמוֹ אֵשֶׁת לֵדָה׃

22 וְכִי תֹאמְרִי בִּלְבָבֵךְ
מַדּוּעַ קְרָאֻנִי אֵלֶּה
בְּרֹב עֲוֺנֵךְ נִגְלוּ שׁוּלַיִךְ
נֶחְמְסוּ עֲקֵבָיִךְ׃

23 הֲיַהֲפֹךְ כּוּשִׁי עוֹרוֹ
וְנָמֵר חֲבַרְבֻּרֹתָיו
גַּם־אַתֶּם תּוּכְלוּ לְהֵיטִיב
לִמֻּדֵי הָרֵעַ׃

24 וַאֲפִיצֵם כְּקַשׁ עוֹבֵר
לְרוּחַ מִדְבָּר׃

the flock that was given thee. What have
you done with the people entrusted to
your care? Although Jerusalem, symbolizing the nation, is addressed in the
passage as a whole, Metsudath David
understands this verse as referring to the
king and queen-mother.

21. the friends. Those who you
thought were your friends, but in fact
you have made your masters, viz. the
Babylonians (Daath Mikra).

22. are thy skirts uncovered. The figure is
apparently taken from the public
shaming of a harlot (cf. verse 26; Hos.
ii. 12). Israel's unfaithfulness to God is
often likened to adultery, and the disasters which will overwhelm the people
are described under the imagery of an
adulteress' punishment (Metsudath
David).

and thy heels suffer violence. This would
seem to continue the same figure,
although its exact application is not
obvious. Kimchi renders: 'and thy heels
are bared.' After the skirts are uncovered, the feet become visible. [Jonathan,
too, renders: 'your disgrace was seen.']
This is figurative of the people of Israel,
who were hidden under the wings of
God and who were the most esteemed
among the nations, and now wander
about without shelter. Their disgrace is,
therefore, revealed to all the nations.

23. The meaning is that they are so
steeped in evil that it is almost impossible for them to return to righteousness.

24. Cf. iv. 11f.

25 This is thy lot, the portion
    measured unto thee from Me,
    Saith the LORD;
    Because thou hast forgotten Me,
    And trusted in falsehood.

26 Therefore will I also uncover thy
    skirts upon thy face,
    And thy shame shall appear.

27 Thine adulteries, and thy neigh-
    ings, the lewdness of thy
    harlotry,
    On the hills in the field have I
    seen thy detestable acts.
    Woe unto thee, O Jerusalem!
    thou wilt not be made clean!
    When shall it ever be?

25 זֶה גּוֹרָלֵךְ מְנָת־מִדַּיִךְ
מֵאִתִּי נְאֻם־יְהוָה
אֲשֶׁר שָׁכַחַתְּ אוֹתִי
וַתִּבְטְחִי בַּשָּׁקֶר:
26 וְגַם־אֲנִי חָשַׂפְתִּי שׁוּלַיִךְ
עַל־פָּנָיִךְ
וְנִרְאָה קְלוֹנֵךְ:
27 נִאֻפַיִךְ וּמִצְהֲלוֹתַיִךְ
זִמַּת זְנוּתֵךְ
עַל־גְּבָעוֹת בַּשָּׂדֶה
רָאִיתִי שִׁקּוּצָיִךְ
אוֹי לָךְ יְרוּשָׁלִַם לֹא תִטְהֲרִי
אַחֲרֵי מָתַי עֹד:

14   CHAPTER XIV   יד

1. The word of the LORD that
came to Jeremiah concerning the
droughts.

1 אֲשֶׁר הָיָה דְבַר־יְהוָה אֶל־
יִרְמְיָהוּ עַל־דִּבְרֵי הַבַּצָּרוֹת:

---

25. *thy lot.* i.e. thy fate, punishment.

falsehood. i.e. idolatry (cf. x. 14).

26. Cf. Nahum iii. 5. The subject in
therefore will I also is very emphatic. After
describing what the people had done,
God declares what He will do.

27. *thy neighings.* Cf. v. 8.

on the hills. Favourite places for the
practice of idolatry (cf. ii. 20).

when shall it ever be? lit. 'after how
long yet?' A reformation will take place,

but how long will it be delayed? (see
Daath Mikra).

CHAPTER XIV

1-6 DROUGHT AND FAMINE

1. *concerning the drought.* Apparently a
series of severe droughts is referred to,
whose intensity had so impressed the
people as to make them an extraordinary occurrence. 'The recent studies
in Central Asia have led to the view that
there are recurring periods of dryness,
which . . . cause frequent famine'
(Flinders Petrie).

2 Judah mourneth, and the gates
thereof languish,
They bow down in black unto the
ground;
And the cry of Jerusalem is gone
up.

3 And their nobles send their lads
for water:
They come to the pits, and find
no water;
Their vessels return empty;
They are ashamed and con-
founded, and cover their heads.

4 Because of the ground which is
cracked,
For there hath been no rain in the
land,
The plowmen are ashamed, they
cover their heads.

5 Yea, the hind also in the field
calveth, and forsaketh her
young,
Because there is no grass.

6 And the wild asses stand on the
high hills,
They gasp for air like jackals;

² אָבְלָה יְהוּדָה
וּשְׁעָרֶיהָ אֻמְלָלוּ
קָדְרוּ לָאָרֶץ
וְצִוְחַת יְרוּשָׁלַ͏ִם עָלָתָה:
³ וְאַדִּרֵיהֶם
שָׁלְחוּ צְעוֹרֵיהֶם לַמָּיִם
בָּאוּ עַל־גֵּבִים
לֹא־מָצְאוּ מַיִם
שָׁבוּ כְלֵיהֶם רֵיקָם
בֹּשׁוּ וְהָכְלְמוּ וְחָפוּ רֹאשָׁם:
⁴ בַּעֲבוּר הָאֲדָמָה חַתָּה
כִּי לֹא־הָיָה גֶשֶׁם בָּאָרֶץ
בֹּשׁוּ אִכָּרִים חָפוּ רֹאשָׁם:
⁵ כִּי גַם־אַיֶּלֶת בַּשָּׂדֶה
יָלְדָה וְעָזוֹב
כִּי לֹא־הָיָה דֶּשֶׁא:
⁶ וּפְרָאִים עָמְדוּ עַל־שְׁפָיִם
שָׁאֲפוּ רוּחַ כַּתַּנִּים

v. 2. צ׳ זעירא v. 3. צעיריהם ק׳

2. *the gates.* i.e. the cities and their
inhabitants (cf. Deut. xvii. 2) (Rashi).

they bow down in black unto the ground. In
deep distress and mourning (Abarbanel).

3. *lads.* i.e. servants (Targum).

ashamed and confounded. Disconcerted
and discomfited at their plight (Daath
Mikra).

cover their heads. As a sign of mourning
(cf. 2 Sam. xv. 30).

4. *cracked.* [The Hebrew verb may be
translated 'dismayed.']

5. *the hind.* Even the hind, which has
so much affection for her young, for-
sakes them as soon as they are born
(Kimchi).

6. *wild asses.* Cf. ii. 24.

they gasp for air. [Through heat and
thirst.]

like jackals. The Hebrew noun *tannim*
may perhaps be a variant of *tannin*, 'the

100

Their eyes fail, because there is
  no herbage.

7 Though our iniquities testify
    against us,
  O LORD, work Thou for Thy
    name's sake;
  For our backslidings are many,
  We have sinned against Thee.

8 O Thou hope of Israel,
  The Saviour thereof in time of
    trouble,
  Why shouldest Thou be as a
    stranger in the land,
  And as a wayfaring man that
    turneth aside to tarry for a
    night?

9 Why shouldest Thou be as a man
    overcome,
  As a mighty man that cannot save?
  Yet Thou, O LORD, art in the
    midst of us,
  And Thy name is called upon us;
  Leave us not.

10. Thus saith the LORD unto this
people:
  Even so have they loved to
    wander,

כָּלוּ עֵינֵיהֶם כִּי־אֵין עֵשֶׂב׃

7 אִם־עֲוֹנֵינוּ עָנוּ בָנוּ
יְהוָה עֲשֵׂה לְמַעַן שְׁמֶךָ
כִּי־רַבּוּ מְשׁוּבֹתֵינוּ
לְךָ חָטָאנוּ׃

8 מִקְוֵה יִשְׂרָאֵל
מוֹשִׁיעוֹ בְּעֵת צָרָה
לָמָּה תִהְיֶה כְּגֵר בָּאָרֶץ
וּכְאֹרֵחַ נָטָה לָלוּן׃

9 לָמָּה תִהְיֶה כְּאִישׁ נִדְהָם
כְּגִבּוֹר לֹא־יוּכַל לְהוֹשִׁיעַ
וְאַתָּה בְקִרְבֵּנוּ יְהוָה
וְשִׁמְךָ עָלֵינוּ נִקְרָא
אַל־תַּנִּחֵנוּ׃

10 כֹּה־אָמַר יְהוָה לָעָם הַזֶּה
כֵּן אָהֲבוּ לָנוּעַ

---

crocodile,' which comes out of the water
gasping for air (see Metsudath Zion).

their eyes fail. This may be meant literally, implying the failing of sight
through thirst. But the phrase may
idiomatically express despair caused by
hope unfulfilled (cf. Ps. lxix. 4; Lam. iv.
17) (Metsudath David).

7–9 JEREMIAH INTERCEDES

7. *our iniquities.* He identifies himself
with the nation even in their sinfulness
(Kimchi).

work Thou for Thy name's sake. To
preserve Thine honour by proving that
Thou art the Ruler over all, lest the
heathens boast that their gods are
greater than Thou (Rashi).

8. *hope.* Although they have turned
away from Thy ways, they hope for
Thee, and in every generation, wert
Thou the hope of Israel, and Thou art
their Saviour in time of trouble.
Although the trouble is a result of their
sins, Thou savest them and showest
them compassion. Now, too, at this
time, save them and have compassion
on them and let them not perish from
hunger (Kimchi).

as a stranger . . . and as a wayfaring man.
Who have no interest in the welfare of
the people among whom they dwell
temporarily (Kimchi, Kara, Metsudath
David).

9. *overcome.* lit. 'astonished,' taken by
surprise and incapable of meeting an
emergency (Metsudath David).

They have not refrained their
feet;
Therefore the Lord doth not
accept them,
Now will He remember their
iniquity,
And punish their sins.

11. And the Lord said unto me:
'Pray not for this people for their
good. 12. When they fast, I will
not hear their cry; and when they
offer burnt-offering and meal-offer-
ing, I will not accept them; but
I will consume them by the sword,
and by the famine, and by the
pestilence.' 13. Then said I: 'Ah,
Lord God! behold, the prophets say
unto them: Ye shall not see the
sword, neither shall ye have famine;
but I will give you assured peace in
this place.' 14. Then the Lord
said unto me: 'The prophets prophesy lies in My name; I sent them
not, neither have I commanded
them, neither spoke I unto them;

רַגְלֵיהֶם לֹא חָשָׂכוּ
וַיהֹוָה לֹא רָצָם
עַתָּה יִזְכֹּר עֲוֹנָם
וְיִפְקֹד חַטֹּאתָם׃

11 וַיֹּאמֶר יְהֹוָה אֵלָי אַל־
תִּתְפַּלֵּל בְּעַד־הָעָם הַזֶּה
12 לְטוֹבָה׃ כִּי יָצֻמוּ אֵינֶנִּי שֹׁמֵעַ
אֶל־רִנָּתָם וְכִי יַעֲלוּ עֹלָה
וּמִנְחָה אֵינֶנִּי רֹצָם כִּי בַּחֶרֶב
וּבָרָעָב וּבַדֶּבֶר אָנֹכִי מְכַלֶּה
13 אוֹתָם׃ וָאֹמַר אֲהָהּ ׀ אֲדֹנָי
יְהֹוִה הִנֵּה הַנְּבִאִים אֹמְרִים
לָהֶם לֹא־תִרְאוּ חֶרֶב וְרָעָב
לֹא־יִהְיֶה לָכֶם כִּי־שָׁלוֹם
אֱמֶת אֶתֵּן לָכֶם בַּמָּקוֹם הַזֶּה׃
14 וַיֹּאמֶר יְהֹוָה אֵלַי שֶׁקֶר
הַנְּבִאִים נִבְּאִים בִּשְׁמִי לֹא
שְׁלַחְתִּים וְלֹא צִוִּיתִים וְלֹא
דִבַּרְתִּי אֲלֵיהֶם חֲזוֹן שֶׁקֶר

10–12   GOD'S REPLY

10. *even so have they loved to wander.* To
other gods. If I have now abandoned
them, it is because they first abandoned
Me (Rashi).

doth not accept them. He no longer has
pleasure in them, and therefore rejects
their plea (Metsudath David). From *the*
Lord to the end of the verse is quoted
from Hos. viii. 13.

12. *when they fast,* etc. Ceremonial
forms of religion will be of no avail.

Only sincere repentance will avail to
prevent the calamity (Malbim).

13–18   A   SECOND   PLEA   AND   THE
RESPONSE

13. *assured peace in this place.* 'You will
not be expelled because *this place* (Jerusalem or Judea as a whole) is under
God's special protection and He will
surely defend it,' such had been the
message of the false prophets. Since the
people had been misled by their religious guides, they should be treated by
God leniently (Daath Soferim).

they prophesy unto you a lying
vision, and divination, and a thing
of nought, and the deceit of their
own heart. 15. Therefore thus
saith the Lord: As for the prophets
that prophesy in My name, and
I sent them not, yet they say:
Sword and famine shall not be in this
land, by sword and famine shall
those prophets be consumed; 16. and
the people to whom they prophesy
shall be cast out in the streets of
Jerusalem because of the famine and
the sword; and they shall have none
to bury them, them, their wives, nor
their sons, nor their daughters; for
I will pour their evil upon them.'

17. And thou shalt say this word
unto them:

Let mine eyes run down with
    tears night and day,
And let them not cease;
For the virgin daughter of my
    people is broken with a great
    breach,
With a very grievous blow.

וְקֶסֶם וֶאֱלֻיל וְתַרְמִת לִבָּם
הֵמָּה מִתְנַבְּאִים לָכֶם: לָכֵן ‏15
כֹּה־אָמַר יְהוָה עַל־הַנְּבִאִים
הַנִּבְּאִים בִּשְׁמִי וַאֲנִי לֹא־
שְׁלַחְתִּים וְהֵמָּה אֹמְרִים חֶרֶב
וְרָעָב לֹא יִהְיֶה בָּאָרֶץ הַזֹּאת
בַּחֶרֶב וּבָרָעָב יִתַּמּוּ הַנְּבִאִים
הָהֵמָּה: וְהָעָם אֲשֶׁר־הֵמָּה ‏16
נִבְּאִים לָהֶם יִהְיוּ מֻשְׁלָכִים
בְּחֻצוֹת יְרוּשָׁלַם מִפְּנֵי ׀
הָרָעָב וְהַחֶרֶב וְאֵין מְקַבֵּר
לָהֵמָּה הֵמָּה נְשֵׁיהֶם וּבְנֵיהֶם
וּבְנֹתֵיהֶם וְשָׁפַכְתִּי עֲלֵיהֶם
אֶת־רָעָתָם:
וְאָמַרְתָּ אֲלֵיהֶם ‏17
אֶת־הַדָּבָר הַזֶּה
תֵּרַדְנָה עֵינַי דִּמְעָה
לַיְלָה וְיוֹמָם
וְאַל־תִּדְמֶינָה
כִּי שֶׁבֶר גָּדוֹל נִשְׁבְּרָה
בְּתוּלַת בַּת־עַמִּי
מַכָּה נַחְלָה מְאֹד:

15. *shall those prophets be consumed.*
They will be the first to suffer, since they
are the prime cause of the coming retribution (Kimchi).

16. *and the people,* etc.   Though misled

by false prophets, they must be held
responsible for their misdeeds (Kimchi).

17. *the virgin daughter.* So described
because no enemy had conquered the

18 If I go forth into the field,
Then behold the slain with the sword!
And if I enter into the city,
Then behold them that are sick with famine!
For both the prophet and the priest are gone about to a land, and knew it not.

19 Hast Thou utterly rejected Judah?
Hath Thy soul loathed Zion?
Why hast Thou smitten us, and there is no healing for us?
We looked for peace, but no good came;
And for a time of healing, and behold terror!

20 We acknowledge, O Lord, our wickedness,
Even the iniquity of our fathers;
For we have sinned against Thee.

21 Do not contemn us, for Thy name's sake,

18 אִם־יָצָאתִי הַשָּׂדֶה
וְהִנֵּה חַלְלֵי־חֶרֶב
וְאִם בָּאתִי הָעִיר
וְהִנֵּה תַּחֲלוּאֵי רָעָב
כִּי גַם־נָבִיא גַם־כֹּהֵן
סָחֲרוּ אֶל־אֶרֶץ וְלֹא יָדָעוּ:

19 הֲמָאֹס מָאַסְתָּ אֶת־יְהוּדָה
אִם־בְּצִיּוֹן גָּעֲלָה נַפְשֶׁךָ
מַדּוּעַ הִכִּיתָנוּ וְאֵין לָנוּ מַרְפֵּא
קַוֵּה לְשָׁלוֹם וְאֵין טוֹב
וּלְעֵת מַרְפֵּא וְהִנֵּה בְעָתָה:

20 יָדַעְנוּ יְהוָה
רִשְׁעֵנוּ עֲוֹן אֲבוֹתֵינוּ
כִּי חָטָאנוּ לָךְ:

21 אַל־תִּנְאַץ לְמַעַן שְׁמֶךָ

---

nation heretofore (cf. the phrase 'virgin soil') (Kimchi).

18. *the prophet.* The false prophet (Kimchi).

are gone about to a land, and knew it not. The clause is obscure and the meaning doubtful. Rashi explains: they have gone to a (foreign) land to seek salvation and knew (it) not that that very land would destroy them. The comment of Metsudath David is: they travelled about the country (like a merchant seeking to sell his wares; cf. R.V. margin 'trafficked' which is the sense of the Hebrew verb elsewhere) prophesying and giving counsel on matters of which they were ignorant. Some modern commentators connect with a verb in

Syriac, 'they go as beggars into a land which they knew not.'

19–22 A FURTHER PLEA TO GOD

19. *we looked for peace . . . terror.* This clause occurred in viii. 15. Perhaps it was a current saying, reflecting the darkness and despair before the final disaster (see Daath Soferim).

20. *even the iniquity of our fathers.* There is a long record of disloyalty to God extending over many generations. It now reaches its culminating point when punishment can no longer be withheld; therefore they can only rely upon God's mercy (Kimchi).

21. *do not contemn us.* There is nothing corresponding to *us* in the text and the

Do not dishonour the throne of Thy glory;
Remember, break not Thy covenant with us.

22 Are there any among the vanities of the nations that can cause rain?
Or can the heavens give showers?
Art not Thou He, O Lord our God, and do we not wait for Thee?
For Thou hast made all these things.

אַל־תְּנַבֵּל כִּסֵּא כְבוֹדֶךָ
זְכֹר אַל־תָּפֵר בְּרִיתְךָ אִתָּנוּ׃
22 הֲיֵשׁ בְּהַבְלֵי הַגּוֹיִם מַגְשִׁמִים
וְאִם־הַשָּׁמַיִם יִתְּנוּ רְבִבִים
הֲלֹא אַתָּה־הוּא
יְהוָה אֱלֹהֵינוּ וּנְקַוֶּה־לָּךְ
כִּי־אַתָּה עָשִׂיתָ
אֶת־כָּל־אֵלֶּה׃

---

15   CHAPTER XV   טו

1. Then said the Lord unto me: 'Though Moses and Samuel stood before Me, yet My mind could not be toward this people; cast them out of My sight, and let them go forth. 2. And it shall come to pass, when they say unto thee: Whither shall we go forth? then thou shalt

1 וַיֹּאמֶר יְהוָה אֵלַי אִם־יַעֲמֹד
מֹשֶׁה וּשְׁמוּאֵל לְפָנַי אֵין נַפְשִׁי
אֶל־הָעָם הַזֶּה שַׁלַּח מֵעַל־
2 פָּנַי וְיֵצֵאוּ׃ וְהָיָה כִּי־יֹאמְרוּ
אֵלֶיךָ אָנָה נֵצֵא וְאָמַרְתָּ

---

object of the verb is *the throne* (Daath Mikra). Early exegetes, however, render as A.J.

for Thy name's sake. Thy name being 'the Merciful One' (Rashi).

the throne of Thy glory. i.e. Jerusalem, the site of the Temple (cf. xvii. 12). On the general thought, see on verse 7.

22. *the vanities.* The false gods (Targum).

that can cause rain. Cf. the Talmudic statement: 'Three keys have not been entrusted to an agent (but are kept in God's hand): the keys of birth, rain and resurrection' (Sanh. 113a). Only the Creator has that power.

CHAPTER XV

1–9 THE SUFFERING IN STORE

1. *Moses and Samuel.* Both had inter-

ceded with God on Israel's behalf, but only after they had induced Israel to repent; then He hearkened to their prayers. Thus when Israel sinned with the Golden Calf, they first destroyed the sinners and then Moses said, *And now I will go up unto the* Lord, *peradventure I shall make atonement for your sin* (Exod. xxxii. 30). Similarly, Samuel first persuaded Israel to remove idolatry and then prayed for them (1 Sam. vii. 2ff.). You, however, (so spoke God to Jeremiah), pray for Israel even before they have reformed. In such a case not even Moses and Samuel could succeed (Rashi).

toward this people. To be well-disposed towards them (Kimchi).

2. *whither shall we go forth?* If denied God's forgiveness (Daath Mikra).

tell them: Thus saith the LORD:
Such as are for death, to death; and
such as are for the sword, to the
sword; and such as are for the
famine, to the famine; and such as
are for captivity, to captivity. 3.
And I will appoint over them four
kinds, saith the LORD: the sword to
slay, and the dogs to drag, and the
fowls of the heaven, and the beasts
of the earth, to devour and to
destroy. 4. And I will cause them
to be a horror among all the kingdoms of the earth, because of
Manasseh the son of Hezekiah king
of Judah, for that which he did in
Jerusalem.

5 For who shall have pity upon thee,
   O Jerusalem?
   Or who shall bemoan thee?
   Or who shall turn aside to ask of
    thy welfare?

6 Thou hast cast Me off, saith the
   LORD,
   Thou art gone backward;
   Therefore do I stretch out My
    hand against thee, and destroy
    thee;

אֲלֵיהֶם כֹּה־אָמַר יְהֹוָה
אֲשֶׁר לַמָּוֶת לַמָּוֶת וַאֲשֶׁר
לַחֶרֶב לַחֶרֶב וַאֲשֶׁר לָרָעָב
לָרָעָב וַאֲשֶׁר לַשְּׁבִי לַשֶּׁבִי:
3 וּפָקַדְתִּי עֲלֵיהֶם אַרְבַּע
מִשְׁפָּחוֹת נְאֻם־יְהֹוָה אֶת־
הַחֶרֶב לַהֲרֹג וְאֶת־הַכְּלָבִים
לִסְחֹב וְאֶת־עוֹף הַשָּׁמַיִם
וְאֶת־בֶּהֱמַת הָאָרֶץ לֶאֱכֹל
4 וּלְהַשְׁחִית: וּנְתַתִּים לְזַעֲוָה
לְכֹל מַמְלְכוֹת הָאָרֶץ בִּגְלַל
מְנַשֶּׁה בֶן־יְחִזְקִיָּהוּ מֶלֶךְ
יְהוּדָה עַל אֲשֶׁר־עָשָׂה
בִּירוּשָׁלָ͏ִם:
5 כִּי מִי־יַחְמֹל עָלַיִךְ יְרוּשָׁלַ͏ִם
וּמִי יָנוּד לָךְ
וּמִי יָסוּר לִשְׁאֹל לְשָׁלֹם לָךְ:
6 אַתְּ נָטַשְׁתְּ אֹתִי
נְאֻם־יְהֹוָה אָחוֹר תֵּלֵכִי
וָאַט אֶת־יָדִי עָלַיִךְ וָאַשְׁחִיתֵךְ

v. 4. לזוֹעה ק'

---

for death. By pestilence (cf. xviii. 21)
(Metsudath David).

to death, etc. Each to the punishment
decreed for him. (Metsudath David).

3. *kinds.* lit. 'families,' i.e. modes
of punishment (Kimchi, Metsudath
David). The verse proceeds to enumerate them: even when slain, they will be
subjected to the further indignity of
having the corpses dragged by dogs or
devoured by wild beasts (cf. xix. 7,
xxxiv. 20).

4. *because of Manasseh.* i.e. because
they approved of and imitated his
wickedness (Metsudath David).

5. *who shall turn aside . . . welfare?* Who

I am weary with repenting.

7 And I fan them with a fan in the
gates of the land;
I bereave them of children, I
destroy My people,
Since they return not from their
ways.

8 Their widows are increased to Me
above the sand of the seas;
I bring upon them, against the
mother, a chosen one,
Even a spoiler at noonday;

נִלְאֵ֖יתִי הִנָּחֵֽם׃

7 וָאֶזְרֵ֥ם בְּמִזְרֶ֖ה בְּשַׁעֲרֵ֣י הָאָ֑רֶץ
שִׁכַּ֤לְתִּי אִבַּ֙דְתִּי֙ אֶת־עַמִּ֔י
מִדַּרְכֵיהֶ֖ם ל֥וֹא שָֽׁבוּ׃
8 עָֽצְמוּ־לִ֤י אַלְמְנֹתָו֙
מֵח֣וֹל יַמִּ֔ים
הֵבֵ֨אתִי לָהֶ֥ם עַל־אֵ֛ם
בָּח֥וּר שֹׁדֵ֖ד בַּֽצָּהֳרָ֑יִם

v. 8. אלמנותיו ק׳

will take the least trouble even to
inquire after thee? (Rashi).

6. *I am weary with repenting.* An
anthropomorphism (cf. Gen. vi. 6).
Many times God decreed Israel's
destruction but relented; He can do so
no more (Rashi).

7. *I fan them with a fan.* Fan is used
in the sense of 'winnow' and 'a
winnowing-fork.' The meaning apparently is that God will scatter them
(Metsudath David).

in the gates of the land. Even in captivity
they will not be together, but scattered
throughout the cities of the land of exile
(Kimchi).

I bereave them of children. i.e. their
young children (Malbim).

I destroy My people. i.e. the older ones
(Malbim).

since they return not. *Since* is not in the
original and has been added by A.J. (the
R.V. omits it). Kimchi interprets: 'and
yet they return not (in spite of My
chastisement).' Despite the fact that I
winnowed, bereft, and destroyed the
Ten Tribes, the tribe of Judah, which
saw all that, did not return from their
evil ways (Kimchi).

8. *their widows are increased to Me,*
etc. The reference is to the crushing
defeat in the days of Ahaz, when Pekah
slew 120,000 in one day (2 Chron.
xxviii. 6). I am troubled about them,
and they are, in My eyes, more than the
sand of the seas (Kimchi). Others
render: 'their widows are heavier to Me
than the sand of the seas.' i.e. the distress of the widows of Judah weighs
upon Me, so to speak, more heavily
than the sand of the seas (Abarbanel).

against the mother, a chosen one
(bachur). The phrase is difficult. There
seems no reason why *the mother* should
be singled out, unless it is an idiom
implying everybody, as we use the
phrase 'even women and children' to
denote that none are exempted (Daath
Mikra). Some Jewish commentators
understand *mother* as figurative of Jerusalem, citing 2 Sam. xx. 19: *seekest thou to
destroy a city and a mother in Israel?* where
mother is synonymous with *city.* Metsudath David explains that Jerusalem was
a metropolis around which smaller
towns were clustered. Kara theorizes
that Jerusalem was considered the
mother of all the cities of Israel. He
identifies the *chosen one* as Nebuchadnezzar. Malbim understands *mother* literally,

I cause anguish and terrors to fall
upon her suddenly.

9 She that hath borne seven lan-
guisheth;

Her spirit droopeth;

Her sun is gone down while it
was yet day,

She is ashamed and confounded;

And the residue of them will I
deliver to the sword before their
enemies,

Saith the LORD.'

10 Woe is me, my mother, that thou
hast borne me

A man of strife and a man of
contention to the whole earth!

I have not lent, neither have men
lent to me;

Yet every one of them doth curse
me.

11. The LORD said: 'Verily I will
release thee for good; verily I will
cause the enemy to make supplication unto thee in the time of evil and

הִפַּלְתִּי עָלֶיהָ פִּתְאֹם
עִיר וּבֶהָלֽוֹת׃

9 אֻמְלְלָה יֹלֶדֶת הַשִּׁבְעָה
נָפְחָה נַפְשָׁהּ
בָּאָה שִׁמְשָׁהּ בְּעֹד יוֹמָם
בּוֹשָׁה וְחָפֵרָה
וּשְׁאֵרִיתָם לַחֶרֶב אֶתֵּן
לִפְנֵי אֹיְבֵיהֶם
נְאֻם־יְהֹוָֽה׃

10 אֽוֹי־לִי אִמִּי כִּי יְלִדְתִּנִי
אִישׁ רִיב
וְאִישׁ מָדוֹן לְכָל־הָאָרֶץ
לֹֽא־נָשִׁיתִי וְלֹא־נָֽשׁוּ־בִי
כֻּלֹּה מְקַלְלַֽוְנִי׃

11 אָמַר יְהֹוָה אִם־לֹא שֵׁרוֹתִֽךָ
לְטוֹב אִם־לוֹא ׀ הִפְגַּעְתִּי
בְךָ בְּעֵת רָעָה וּבְעֵת צָרָה

v. 9. בא ק׳   v. 11. שריתך ק׳

---

explaining it as the widowed mothers.
Kimchi renders: *on the congregation of
youths,* denoting that even a group of
young men would be unable to protect
themselves against the spoilers at
noonday.

9. *she that hath borne seven.* For the
number *seven,* cf. 1 Sam. ii. 5; a woman
with numerous children. Such a woman
should be most happy, but now she is
wretched (Daath Mikra).

while it was yet day. i.e. in the prime of
life, prematurely (Metsudath David).

10–21 JEREMIAH'S LAMENT: GOD'S REPLY

10. *woe is me.* His fearless denunciations of the people's sins and his dark
forebodings about their future had
brought about no reform; their only
sequel was intense bitterness towards
him personally. In a mood of depression he bewails his lot and wishes that
he had never been born (Metsudath
David).

11. *I will release thee.* The reading of
the *kerë* derives from the root *sharah,* 'set
free.' It is uncertain what the *kethib*

in the time of affliction. 12. Can iron break iron from the north and brass? 13. Thy substance and thy treasures will I give for a spoil without price, and that for all thy sins, even in all thy borders. 14. And I will make thee to pass with thine enemies into a land which thou knowest not; for a fire is kindled in My nostril, which shall burn upon you.'

15 Thou, O LORD, knowest;
   Remember me, and think of me,
      and avenge me of my persecutors;
   Take me not away because of
      Thy long-suffering;
   Know that for Thy sake I have
      suffered taunts.

אֶת־הָאֹיֵב: הֲיָרֹעַ בַּרְזֶל | ¹²
בַּרְזֶל מִצָּפוֹן וּנְחֹשֶׁת: חֵילְךָ ¹³
וְאוֹצְרוֹתֶיךָ לָבַז אֶתֵּן לֹא
בִמְחִיר וּבְכָל־חַטֹּאותֶיךָ
וּבְכָל־גְּבוּלֶיךָ: וְהַעֲבַרְתִּי ¹⁴
אֶת־אֹיְבֶיךָ בְּאֶרֶץ לֹא יָדָעְתָּ
כִּי־אֵשׁ קָדְחָה בְאַפִּי עֲלֵיכֶם
תּוּקָד:
אַתָּה יָדַעְתָּ יְהוָֹה ¹⁵
זָכְרֵנִי וּפָקְדֵנִי
וְהִנָּקֶם לִי מֵרֹדְפַי
אַל־לְאֶרֶךְ אַפְּךָ תִּקָּחֵנִי
דַּע שְׂאֵתִי עָלֶיךָ חֶרְפָּה:

represents. The sense of the clause seems to be: in the catastrophe which is approaching God will deliver him (Rashi after Dunash).

the enemy. The opponents of Jeremiah are meant. In their distress they will appeal to him to intercede on their behalf. This happened on several occasions; cf. xxi. 1ff., xxxvii. 3, xlii. 1 ff. (Rashi).

12. Iron from the north is the best and the hardest. This and the following two verses are apparently a digression in which God (or, according to others, the prophet) addresses the people: can your iron break the iron of the north, viz. the armies of Babylon? (Rashi).

13. This and the next verse occur again with variations in xvii. 3f.

without price. You will receive nothing from the enemy for what he takes of your possessions (Kara, Metsudath David).

even in all thy borders. Because your sins have filled the whole land (Metsudath David).

14. *and I will make thee to pass. Thee* does not occur in the text and the object may be *thy substance and thy treasures* of the previous verse but more likely this verse matches Deut. xxviii. 36 (Daath Mikra). Many Hebrew MSS. and the Targum read here, as in xvii. 4, *I will cause thee to serve.*

for a fire ... nostril. Identical with Deut. xxxii. 22.

15. The prophet resumes his dialogue with God.

Thou, O LORD, *knowest.* How I have suffered in carrying out the commission entrusted to me (Kimchi).

take me not away. Let me not perish (Kimchi).

Thy long-suffering. Towards my opponents (Kimchi).

16 Thy words were found, and I did
    eat them;

    And Thy words were unto me a
        joy and the rejoicing of my
        heart;

    Because Thy name was called on
        me, O Lord God of hosts.

17 I sat not in the assembly of them
    that make merry, nor rejoiced;

    I sat alone because of Thy hand;

    For Thou hast filled me with
        indignation.

18 Why is my pain perpetual,

    And my wound incurable, so that
        it refuseth to be healed?

    Wilt Thou indeed be unto me as
        a deceitful brook,

    As waters that fail?

19 Therefore thus saith the Lord:

    If thou return, and I bring thee
        back,

    Thou shalt stand before Me;

נִמְצְא֣וּ דְבָרֶ֗יךָ וָאֹ֣כְלֵ֔ם 16

וַיְהִ֤י דְבָֽרְךָ֙ לִ֔י

לְשָׂשׂ֔וֹן וּלְשִׂמְחַ֖ת לְבָבִ֑י

כִּֽי־נִקְרָ֤א שִׁמְךָ֙ עָלַ֔י

יְהוָ֖ה אֱלֹהֵ֥י צְבָאֽוֹת׃

לֹֽא־יָשַׁ֥בְתִּי בְסֽוֹד־מְשַׂחֲקִ֖ים 17

וָֽאֶעְלֹ֑ז

מִפְּנֵ֤י יָֽדְךָ֙ בָּדָ֣ד יָשַׁ֔בְתִּי

כִּֽי־זַ֖עַם מִלֵּאתָֽנִי׃

לָ֣מָּה הָיָ֤ה כְאֵבִי֙ נֶ֔צַח 18

וּמַכָּתִ֖י אֲנוּשָׁ֑ה מֵֽאֲנָ֖ה הֵֽרָפֵ֑א

הָי֤וֹ תִֽהְיֶה֙ לִ֔י כְּמ֖וֹ אַכְזָ֑ב

מַ֖יִם לֹ֥א נֶֽאֱמָֽנוּ׃

לָכֵ֗ן כֹּֽה־אָמַ֣ר יְהוָ֔ה 19

אִם־תָּשׁ֥וּב וַאֲשִֽׁיבְךָ֙

לְפָנַ֥י תַּֽעֲמֹ֑ד

v. 16. דברך ק׳

---

16. *Thy words were found, and I did eat them.* Thy words descended to me in the spirit of prophecy, and I joyfully welcomed them as one has pleasure in eating something tasty (Kimchi). Cf. the symbolism in Ezek. iii. 1ff.

because Thy name was called on me. As a prophet of God, not as a false prophet (Kimchi).

17. *I sat alone ... indignation.* The prophetic spirit with which God endowed him set him apart. 'I could not rejoice and make merry with the rest,' he says, 'being filled with indignation over the people's sins' (Daath Mikra).

because of Thy hand. Laid upon the prophet to arouse his special powers (cf. 2 Kings iii. 15; Isa. viii. 11; Ezek. iii. 14).

18. *wilt Thou indeed ... fail?* The Hebrew does not necessarily imply a question, although it may do so. In that case we have to assume that the question is rhetorical. It may, however, be a positive statement: 'Thou art indeed unto me,' etc. (so Rashi and Kimchi). Such an allegation need not surprise us. The prophet is only human and in his mental anguish momentarily gives way to despair. Even God has seemingly failed him (cf. xvii. 18 where he prays to be saved from despair).

a deceitful brook. A wadi which dries up in the summer; an image of what is unreliable (cf. Job. vi. 15).

19. *if thou return.* Such doubts are sinful; yet if thou wilt repent of them and

And if thou bring forth the
precious out of the vile,
Thou shalt be as My mouth;
Let them return unto thee,
But thou shalt not return unto
them.

וְאִם־תּוֹצִיא יָקָר
מִזּוֹלֵל כְּפִי תִהְיֶה
יָשֻׁבוּ הֵמָּה אֵלֶיךָ
וְאַתָּה לֹא־תָשׁוּב אֲלֵיהֶם:

20 And I will make thee unto this
people a fortified brazen wall;
And they shall fight against thee,
But they shall not prevail against
thee;
For I am with thee to save thee
and to deliver thee,
Saith the LORD.

20 וּנְתַתִּיךָ לָעָם הַזֶּה
לְחוֹמַת נְחֹשֶׁת בְּצוּרָה
וְנִלְחֲמוּ אֵלֶיךָ
וְלֹא־יוּכְלוּ לָךְ
כִּי־אִתְּךָ אֲנִי
לְהוֹשִׁיעֲךָ וּלְהַצִּילֶךָ
נְאֻם־יְהֹוָה:

21 And I will deliver thee out of the
hand of the wicked,
And I will redeem thee out of the
hand of the terrible.

21 וְהִצַּלְתִּיךָ מִיַּד רָעִים
וּפְדִתִיךָ מִכַּף עָרִיצִים:

16   CHAPTER XVI   טז

1. The word of the LORD came also
unto me, saying:
2 Thou shalt not take thee a wife,

1 וַיְהִי דְבַר־יְהֹוָה אֵלַי לֵאמֹר:
2 לֹא־תִקַּח לְךָ אִשָּׁה

return to Me, I will receive thee and
thou shalt stand before Me, enjoying
My favour (Kimchi).

the precious out of the vile. If you make a
great effort to lead them to repentance
and you succeed to take the precious
out of the vile; i.e. if you are able to
bring the wicked, who are vile, to be
good and precious (Kimchi). Metsudath
David renders, *the precious out of the
glutton,* explaining *zolel* as 'glutton.'

My mouth. My spokesman (cf. Exod. iv.
16) (Daath Mikra).

let them return, etc. Although you are
one against many, you must persist until
you raise them and not allow them to
drag you down to their level (Rashi).

20f. A repetition of the substance of i.
18f.

21. *the terrible.* i.e. the influential men
of the kingdom who use their power
ruthlessly; [they are perhaps to be
identified with the *kings of Judah,* etc., in
i. 18.]

CHAPTER XVI

1–13 JEREMIAH COMMANDED TO
PRACTISE SELF-DENIAL

2. *thou shalt not take thee a wife.* Marriage was regarded as man's natural
state (cf. Gen. i. 28, ii. 18). To refrain
from marriage for the reason given
would make a deep impression on the
people (Abarbanel).

Neither shalt thou have sons or
daughters in this place.

3. For thus saith the LORD concerning the sons and concerning the
daughters that are born in this place,
and concerning their mothers that
bore them, and concerning their
fathers that begot them in this land:

4 They shall die of grievous deaths;
They shall not be lamented,
neither shall they be buried,
They shall be as dung upon the
face of the ground;
And they shall be consumed by
the sword, and by famine;
And their carcasses shall be meat
for the fowls of heaven,
And for the beasts of the earth.

5. For thus saith the LORD: Enter
not into the house of mourning,
neither go to lament, neither bemoan them; for I have taken away
My peace from this people, saith the

וְלֹא־יִהְיוּ לְךָ בָּנִים וּבָנוֹת
בַּמָּקוֹם הַזֶּה:

3 כִּי־כֹה ׀ אָמַר יְהֹוָה עַל־
הַבָּנִים וְעַל־הַבָּנוֹת הַיִּלּוֹדִים
בַּמָּקוֹם הַזֶּה וְעַל־אִמֹּתָם
הַיֹּלְדוֹת אוֹתָם וְעַל־אֲבוֹתָם
הַמּוֹלִדִים אוֹתָם בָּאָרֶץ
הַזֹּאת:

4 מְמוֹתֵי תַחֲלֻאִים יָמֻתוּ
לֹא יִסָּפְדוּ וְלֹא יִקָּבֵרוּ
לְדֹמֶן עַל־פְּנֵי הָאֲדָמָה יִהְיוּ
וּבַחֶרֶב וּבָרָעָב יִכְלוּ
וְהָיְתָה נִבְלָתָם לְמַאֲכָל
לְעוֹף הַשָּׁמַיִם
וּלְבֶהֱמַת הָאָרֶץ:

5 כִּי־כֹה ׀ אָמַר יְהֹוָה אַל־
תָּבוֹא בֵּית מַרְזֵחַ וְאַל־תֵּלֵךְ
לִסְפּוֹד וְאַל־תָּנֹד לָהֶם כִּי־
אָסַפְתִּי אֶת־שְׁלוֹמִי מֵאֵת
הָעָם הַזֶּה נְאֻם־יְהֹוָה אֶת־

---

in this place. Anathoth (Kimchi) or
Jerusalem (Abarbanel).

4. *grievous deaths.* lit. 'deaths of dis-
eases,' from epidemics caused by the
famine (Kimchi).

they shall not be lamented. So many will
be claimed by death that there will be
no time or thought for mourning or

even for burying the dead honourably
(Metsudath David).

5. *mourning.* The word *marzeach* means
'a shrill sound.' It is applied to revelry
in Amos. vi. 7, here to 'wailing for the
dead' (Kimchi) Judaism commands
visits to mourners to comfort them as
an act of piety; but the prophet is told
not to perform it because God has
'taken away His peace from this people.'

LORD, even mercy and compassion.
6. Both the great and the small shall
die in this land; they shall not be
buried; neither shall men lament for
them, nor cut themselves, nor make
themselves bald for them; 7. neither
shall men break bread for them in
mourning, to comfort them for the
dead; neither shall men give them
the cup of consolation to drink for
their father or for their mother.
8. And thou shalt not go into the
house of feasting to sit with them,
to eat and to drink. 9. For thus
saith the LORD of hosts, the God of
Israel:

> Behold, I will cause to cease out
>   of this place,
> Before your eyes and in your days,
> The voice of mirth and the voice
>   of gladness,
> The voice of the bridegroom and
>   the voice of the bride.

6 הַחֶ֖סֶד וְאֶת־הָרַחֲמִֽים׃ וּמֵ֨תוּ
גְדֹלִ֧ים וּקְטַנִּ֛ים בָּאָ֥רֶץ הַזֹּ֖את
לֹ֣א יִקָּבֵ֑רוּ וְלֹֽא־יִסְפְּד֣וּ לָהֶ֗ם
וְלֹ֤א יִתְגֹּדַד֙ וְלֹ֣א יִקָּרֵ֔חַ לָהֶֽם׃
7 וְלֹֽא־יִפְרְס֥וּ לָהֶ֖ם עַל־־
אֵ֑בֶל לְנַחֲמֹ֖ו עַל־מֵ֑ת וְלֹֽא־
יַשְׁק֤וּ אֹותָם֙ כֹּ֣וס תַּנְחוּמִ֔ים
8 עַל־אָבִ֖יו וְעַל־אִמֹּֽו׃ וּבֵית־
מִשְׁתֶּ֥ה לֹא־תָבֹ֖וא לָשֶׁ֣בֶת
9 אֹותָ֖ם לֶאֱכֹ֣ל וְלִשְׁתֹּֽות׃ כִּ֣י
כֹה֩ אָמַ֨ר יְהוָ֤ה צְבָאֹות֙ אֱלֹהֵ֣י
יִשְׂרָאֵ֔ל
הִנְנִ֨י מַשְׁבִּ֜ית מִן־הַמָּקֹ֣ום הַזֶּ֗ה
לְעֵינֵיכֶ֖ם וּבִֽימֵיכֶ֑ם
קֹ֤ול שָׂשֹׂון֙ וְקֹ֣ול שִׂמְחָ֔ה
קֹ֥ול חָתָ֖ן וְקֹ֥ול כַּלָּֽה׃

6. *the great and the small.* The old and
the young (Targum).

*nor cut themselves, nor make themselves
bald.* Both these mourning practices
were forbidden (Lev. xix. 28; Deut. xiv.
1 and particularly to priests, Lev. xxi. 5).
Nevertheless, in assimilation to heathen
customs, they were commonly practised
in defiance of the law. Now, however,
death would be so widespread that they
would perforce be neglected (Kimchi).

7. *neither shall men break bread for
them.* The noun *bread* is not stated
explicitly but is implicit in the verb
used. It was customary for the friends of
mourners to provide them with their

first meal after the funeral (cf. 2 Sam.iii.
35; Ezek. xxiv. 17; Hos. ix. 4).

the cup of consolation. A special cup of
wine, so designated, was drunk by the
mourner, in connection with which a
prayer for comfort was added in the
Grace after meals (Keth. 8b; A.D.P.B.,
pp. 282f.).

8. As he was to avoid houses of mourning, so he was to shun houses where
domestic joys, e.g. marriages, were
being celebrated.

9. *before your eyes.* The calamities
would happen in their lifetime. Most of
the verse is repeated from vii. 34.

10. And it shall come to pass, when thou shalt tell this people all these words, and they shall say unto thee: 'Wherefore hath the LORD pronounced all this great evil against us? or what is our iniquity? or what is our sin that we have committed against the LORD our God?' 11. then shalt thou say unto them: 'Because your fathers have forsaken Me, saith the LORD, and have walked after other gods, and have served them, and have worshipped them, and have forsaken Me, and have not kept My law; 12. and ye have done worse than your fathers; for, behold, ye walk every one after the stubbornness of his evil heart, so that ye hearken not unto Me; 13. therefore will I cast you out of this land into a land that ye have not known, neither ye nor your fathers; and there shall ye serve other gods day

10 וְהָיָה כִּי תַגִּיד לָעָם הַזֶּה אֵת
כָּל־הַדְּבָרִים הָאֵלֶּה וְאָמְרוּ
אֵלֶיךָ עַל־מֶה דִבֶּר יְהֹוָה
עָלֵינוּ אֵת כָּל־הָרָעָה
הַגְּדוֹלָה הַזֹּאת וּמֶה עֲוֹנֵנוּ וּמֶה
חַטָּאתֵנוּ אֲשֶׁר חָטָאנוּ לַיהֹוָה
11 אֱלֹהֵינוּ: וְאָמַרְתָּ אֲלֵיהֶם עַל
אֲשֶׁר־עָזְבוּ אֲבוֹתֵיכֶם אוֹתִי
נְאֻם־יְהֹוָה וַיֵּלְכוּ אַחֲרֵי
אֱלֹהִים אֲחֵרִים וַיַּעַבְדוּם
וַיִּשְׁתַּחֲווּ לָהֶם וְאֹתִי עָזָבוּ
וְאֶת־תּוֹרָתִי לֹא שָׁמָרוּ:
12 וְאַתֶּם הֲרֵעֹתֶם לַעֲשׂוֹת
מֵאֲבוֹתֵיכֶם וְהִנְּכֶם הֹלְכִים
אִישׁ אַחֲרֵי שְׁרִרוּת לִבּוֹ־־
הָרָע לְבִלְתִּי שְׁמֹעַ אֵלָי:
13 וְהֵטַלְתִּי אֶתְכֶם מֵעַל הָאָרֶץ
הַזֹּאת עַל־הָאָרֶץ אֲשֶׁר לֹא
יְדַעְתֶּם אַתֶּם וַאֲבֹתֵיכֶם
וַעֲבַדְתֶּם־שָׁם אֶת־אֱלֹהִים

---

v. 11. קמץ בז"ק

---

10. Cf. v. 19, xiii. 22. In spite of the denunciations of the prophets, the people apparently were still unconscious of guilt. To this complacent frame of mind the false prophets had undoubtedly contributed.

12. *ye have done worse than your fathers.* [Instead of being warned and deterred by the evil of former generations, they have wandered still farther along the

path of apostasy. Their guilt is therefore greater and the penalty more severe.]

13. *a land.* lit. 'the land,' [appointed for their captivity.]

there shall ye serve other gods. The words are ironical. Banished from the Holy Land to a country where idolatry was the religion of the native population, they would have greater facilities to

and night; forasmuch as I will show you no favour.'

14. Therefore, behold, the days come, saith the LORD, that it shall no more be said: 'As the LORD liveth, that brought up the children of Israel out of the land of Egypt,' 15. but: 'As the LORD liveth, that brought up the children of Israel from the land of the north, and from all the countries whither He had driven them'; and I will bring them back into their land that I gave unto their fathers.

16. Behold, I will send for many fishers, saith the LORD, and they shall fish them; and afterward I will send for many hunters, and they shall hunt them from every mountain, and from every hill, and out of the clefts of the rocks.

17 For Mine eyes are upon all their ways,
     They are not hid from My face;
     Neither is their iniquity concealed from Mine eyes.

אֲחֵרִים֙ יוֹמָ֣ם וָלַ֔יְלָה אֲשֶׁ֛ר
לֹא־אֶתֵּ֥ן לָכֶ֖ם חֲנִינָֽה׃ לָכֵ֛ן 14
הִנֵּֽה־יָמִ֥ים בָּאִ֖ים נְאֻם־יְהֹוָ֑ה
וְלֹא־יֵאָמֵ֥ר עוֹד֙ חַי־יְהֹוָ֔ה
אֲשֶׁ֧ר הֶעֱלָ֛ה אֶת־בְּנֵ֥י יִשְׂרָאֵ֖ל
מֵאֶ֣רֶץ מִצְרָֽיִם׃ כִּ֣י אִם־חַי־ 15
יְהֹוָ֗ה אֲשֶׁ֤ר הֶעֱלָה֙ אֶת־בְּנֵ֣י
יִשְׂרָאֵל֙ מֵאֶ֣רֶץ צָפ֔וֹן וּמִכֹּל֙
הָֽאֲרָצ֔וֹת אֲשֶׁ֥ר הִדִּיחָ֖ם שָׁ֑מָּה
וַהֲשִׁבֹתִים֙ עַל־אַדְמָתָ֔ם
אֲשֶׁ֥ר נָתַ֖תִּי לַאֲבוֹתָֽם׃ הִנְנִ֛י 16
שֹׁלֵ֛חַ לְדַוָּגִ֥ים רַבִּ֖ים נְאֻם־
יְהֹוָ֖ה וְדִיג֑וּם וְאַחֲרֵי־כֵ֗ן
אֶשְׁלַח֙ לְרַבִּ֣ים צַיָּדִ֔ים וְצָד֗וּם
מֵעַ֤ל כָּל־הַר֙ וּמֵעַ֣ל כָּל־
גִּבְעָ֔ה וּמִנְּקִיקֵ֖י הַסְּלָעִֽים׃
כִּ֤י עֵינַי֙ עַ֣ל־כָּל־דַּרְכֵיהֶ֔ם 17
לֹ֥א נִסְתְּר֖וּ מִלְּפָנָ֑י
וְלֹֽא־נִצְפַּ֥ן עֲוֹנָ֖ם מִנֶּ֥גֶד עֵינָֽי׃

v. 16. לדיגים ק׳

---

indulge in their partiality for pagan worship (Abarbanel).

14-15 BANISHMENT WILL NOT BE
FOREVER

Repeated substantially in xxiii. 7f. The verses are regarded by moderns as an interpolation which breaks the connection with verse 16; but it was a frequent practice of the prophets to temper their denunciations with a word of hope (Kimchi). The severity of the forthcoming exile and the exile after the destruction of the Second Temple will cause the subsequent redemption to overshadow even the deliverance from Egypt.

18 And first I will recompense their
iniquity and their sin double;
Because they have profaned My
land;
They have filled Mine inheritance
With the carcasses of their
detestable things and their
abominations.

19 O LORD, my strength, and my
stronghold,
And my refuge, in the day of
affliction,
Unto Thee shall the nations come
From the ends of the earth, and
shall say:
'Our fathers have inherited
nought but lies,
Vanity and things wherein there
is no profit.'

20 Shall a man make unto himself
gods,
And they are no gods?

21 Therefore, behold, I will cause
them to know,

18 וְשִׁלַּמְתִּי רִאשׁוֹנָה
מִשְׁנֵה עֲוֹנָם וְחַטָּאתָם
עַל חַלְּלָם אֶת־אַרְצִי
בְּנִבְלַת שִׁקּוּצֵיהֶם
וְתוֹעֲבוֹתֵיהֶם
מָלְאוּ אֶת־נַחֲלָתִי :

19 יְהוָֹה עֻזִּי וּמָעֻזִּי
וּמְנוּסִי בְּיוֹם צָרָה
אֵלֶיךָ גּוֹיִם יָבֹאוּ
מֵאַפְסֵי־אָרֶץ וְיֹאמְרוּ
אַךְ־שֶׁקֶר נָחֲלוּ אֲבוֹתֵינוּ
הֶבֶל וְאֵין־בָּם מוֹעִיל :

20 הֲיַעֲשֶׂה־לּוֹ אָדָם אֱלֹהִים
וְהֵמָּה לֹא אֱלֹהִים :

21 לָכֵן הִנְנִי מוֹדִיעָם

v. 19. הפטרת בחקותי   v. 19. קמץ בז״ק

16–18 THEIR GUILT IS KNOWN TO GOD

16. The rounding up of the population
is graphically described under the
imagery of fishing and hunting.

18. *first.* Before I decree their
redemption as promised in verses 14f.
(Aramah).

19–21 ULTIMATE REPUDIATION OF IDOLS

The mention of the idols makes the
prophet look forward to the time when
not only Israel, but the heathens also,
will disavow them. Then will the
uniqueness of God's might be univer-
sally acknowledged.

19. *unto Thee shall the nations come.* This

Messianic vision is a distinctive feature
of Biblical teaching, and flows from the
exalted concept of the Brotherhood of
Man which will be realized as the sequel
of all nations acknowledging the one
God. It is worthy of note that the
prophet conceived of this conversion as
a spontaneous act brought about
neither by compulsion nor even per-
suasion (see Kimchi, Malbim).

20. *shall a man,* etc. Kimchi construes
the verse as the continuation of the
avowal of the nations. They will say,
'How could we ever have believed the
work of our hands to be a god?'

21. *cause them to know.* viz. those who
do not return to Me (Kimchi).

This once will I cause them to
know
My hand and My might;
And they shall know that My
name is the LORD.

בַּפַּעַם הַזֹּאת אוֹדִיעֵם
אֶת־יָדִי וְאֶת־גְּבוּרָתִי
וְיָדְעוּ כִּי־שְׁמִי יְהוָה:

17   CHAPTER XVII   יז

1 The sin of Judah is written
With a pen of iron, and with the
point of a diamond;
It is graven upon the tablet of
their heart,
And upon the horns of your
altars.
2 Like the symbols of their sons are
their altars,
And their Asherim are by the
leafy trees,

1 חַטַּאת יְהוּדָה כְּתוּבָה
בְּעֵט בַּרְזֶל בְּצִפֹּרֶן שָׁמִיר
חֲרוּשָׁה עַל־לוּחַ לִבָּם
וּלְקַרְנוֹת מִזְבְּחוֹתֵיכֶם:
2 כִּזְכֹּר בְּנֵיהֶם מִזְבְּחוֹתָם
וַאֲשֵׁרֵיהֶם עַל־עֵץ רַעֲנָן

---

this once. On this occasion when My
punishment will be so conspicuously
severe (Kara).

and they shall know that My name is the
LORD. They will then be convinced
that I am indeed King and Ruler, able
to fulfil My promises and enforce My
decrees (Rashi).

CHAPTER XVII

1–4   THE NATION'S SIN IS INDELIBLE

1. Judah's sin is indelibly engraven
upon their hardened hearts. Metsudath
David connects this verse with the fore-
going: though the heathens will one day
acknowledge the true God (xvi. 19),
Judah is firmly rooted in transgression.

a pen of iron. Used for writing on the
hard surface of stones, etc. (cf. Job xix.
24). It and *the point of a diamond* are used
to indicate how deeply the sin has
penetrated into the nation's heart.

their heart . . . your altars. Their guilt
has penetrated deep into their *heart,*
their innermost nature. It is at the same
time openly flaunted, as though you

(here, as frequently, Jeremiah changes
suddenly to the second person, but
many MSS. read 'their') had written it
on the horns of your altars (Metsudath
David).

2. *like . . . their altars.* The phrase is
difficult. The Hebrew is literally 'as they
remember their children their altars,'
which Rashi and Kimchi interpret: even
as men remember their sons always and
with longing, so is their remembrance
of and yearning for their idolatrous
altars. The Hebrew can also be translated: 'when their children remember
their altars, and their Asherim by the
leafy trees, they go up to the lofty hillocks.' As soon as their children remind
themselves of their altars that they
erected for idol worship, they immediately go up to the lofty hillocks to
sacrifice (Kara).

Asherim. The *asherah* was a pole set up
by the altar and served as a pagan
symbol. Being associated with a heathen
cult, it was forbidden by the Torah
(Deut. xvi. 21) (Daath Mikra).

by the leafy trees, upon the high hills. See
on ii. 20.

Upon the high hills.

3 O thou that sittest upon the
mountain in the field,

I will give thy substance and all
thy treasures for a spoil,

And thy high places, because of
sin, throughout all thy borders.

4 And thou, even of thyself, shalt
discontinue from thy heritage

That I gave thee;

And I will cause thee to serve
thine enemies

In the land which thou knowest
not;

For ye have kindled a fire in My
nostril,

Which shall burn for ever.

5 Thus saith the LORD:

Cursed is the man that trusteth in
man,

And maketh flesh his arm,

And whose heart departeth from
the LORD.

6 For he shall be like a tamarisk in
the desert,

עַל גִּבְעוֹת הַגְּבֹהוֹת:

3 הֲרָרִי בַשָּׂדֶה
חֵילְךָ כָל־אוֹצְרוֹתֶיךָ
לָבַז אֶתֵּן
בָּמֹתֶיךָ
בְּחַטָּאת בְּכָל־גְּבוּלֶיךָ:

4 וְשָׁמַטְתָּה וּבְךָ מִנַּחֲלָתְךָ
אֲשֶׁר נָתַתִּי לָךְ
וְהַעֲבַדְתִּיךָ אֶת־אֹיְבֶיךָ
בָּאָרֶץ אֲשֶׁר לֹא־יָדַעְתָּ
כִּי־אֵשׁ קְדַחְתֶּם בְּאַפִּי
עַד־עוֹלָם תּוּקָד:

5 כֹּה | אָמַר יְהֹוָה
אָרוּר הַגֶּבֶר
אֲשֶׁר יִבְטַח בָּאָדָם
וְשָׂם בָּשָׂר זְרֹעוֹ
וּמִן־יְהֹוָה יָסוּר לִבּוֹ:

6 וְהָיָה כְּעַרְעָר בָּעֲרָבָה

---

3. *O thou that sittest,* etc. There is
nothing in the text corresponding to
sittest. More literally, it would be translated: 'O thou mountaineer,' similar to
the French word found in Rashi. More
literally is A.V. and R.V., 'O my
mountain in the field,' an allusion to
Jerusalem with its lofty elevation (see
Daath Mikra). Kimchi, disregarding the
accents, explains: 'O my people who
worship idols on the mountain, in the
field will I give thy substance,' etc., i.e. it
will be free to all to plunder. From *I will
give* to the end of the verse is reproduced with variants from xv. 13f.

4. *and thou . . . gave thee.* You will lose
hold on your inheritance (Kimchi).

5-8   TRUST IN MAN AND GOD CONTRASTED

5. *cursed is the man.* Kimchi explains
that *the man* refers to those who relied
on the support of Egypt in defiance of
God's warnings through Jeremiah.

maketh flesh his arm. Depends upon
mortal man for support (Metsudath
David).

from the LORD. As his Helper (Kimchi).

6. *a tamarisk (arar).* This tree has been

And shall not see when good cometh;
But shall inhabit the parched places in the wilderness,
A salt land and not inhabited.

7 Blessed is the man that trusteth in the LORD,
And whose trust the LORD is.

8 For he shall be as a tree planted by the waters,
And that spreadeth out its roots by the river,
And shall not see when heat cometh,
But its foliage shall be luxuriant;
And shall not be anxious in the year of drought,
Neither shall cease from yielding fruit.

9 The heart is deceitful above all things,
And it is exceeding weak—who can know it?

וְלֹא יִרְאֶה כִּי־יָבוֹא טוֹב
וְשָׁכַן חֲרֵרִים בַּמִּדְבָּר
אֶרֶץ מְלֵחָה וְלֹא תֵשֵׁב׃

7 בָּרוּךְ הַגֶּבֶר
אֲשֶׁר יִבְטַח בַּיהוָה
וְהָיָה יְהוָה מִבְטַחוֹ׃

8 וְהָיָה כְּעֵץ ׀ שָׁתוּל עַל־מַיִם
וְעַל־יוּבַל יְשַׁלַּח שָׁרָשָׁיו
וְלֹא יִרְאֶ כִּי־יָבֹא חֹם
וְהָיָה עָלֵהוּ רַעֲנָן
וּבִשְׁנַת בַּצֹּרֶת לֹא יִדְאָג
וְלֹא יָמִישׁ מֵעֲשׂוֹת פֶּרִי׃

9 עָקֹב הַלֵּב מִכֹּל
וְאָנֻשׁ הוּא מִי יֵדָעֶנּוּ׃

v. 8. ירֽאה ק׳   v. 8. קמץ בז״ק

variously identified as the tamarisk or the juniper (Kimchi, Shorashim).

Although the juniper, called *arar* in Arabic, seems to fit the description of the lone tree growing in the desert, Feliks rejects this definition on the grounds that 'it is not found in salty ground or in the wildernesses and deserts of Eretz Yisrael. . . . Following the LXX which renders *'ar'ar* as *agriomyrike,* we suggest that the *'ar'ar* be identified with one of the species of tamarisk known in Arabic as *'arrah,* growing in salty soils and in the wilderness.'

shall not see when good cometh. It does not benefit from the rainfall (Kimchi).

9–10 THE HUMAN HEART

These verses have no apparent connection with what precedes and follows. Kimchi's interpretation is: The prophet, having contrasted trust in man with trust in God, goes on to say that it is a matter hidden in one's heart, which is deceitful: one may profess trust in God with his lips, whilst in his heart trusting to man. To this God replies, *I the* LORD *search the heart.*

9. *weak.* Or, connecting *anush* with *enosh,* 'man': 'and so very human!' (Malbim). If the heart is healthy, everything is healthy, but if the heart is sick, everything external is an empty dream. But who can look into the heart? Nobody can see into the heart, the feelings, the inner thoughts. Even if the heart is bad, who can test it? (Hirsch).

10 I the LORD search the heart,
    I try the reins,
    Even to give every man according
      to his ways,
    According to the fruit of his
      doings.

11 As the partridge that broodeth
    over young which she hath not
    brought forth,
    So is he that getteth riches, and
    not by right;
    In the midst of his days he shall
    leave them,
    And at his end he shall be a fool.

12 Thou throne of glory, on high
    from the beginning,
    Thou place of our sanctuary,

13 Thou hope of Israel, the LORD!

אֲנִי יְהֹוָה חֹקֵר לֵב 10
בֹּחֵן כְּלָיוֹת
וְלָתֵת לְאִישׁ כִּדְרָכָו
כִּפְרִי מַעֲלָלָיו׃
קֹרֵא דָגַר וְלֹא יָלָד 11
עֹשֶׂה עֹשֶׁר וְלֹא בְמִשְׁפָּט
בַּחֲצִי יָמָו יַעַזְבֶנּוּ
וּבְאַחֲרִיתוֹ יִהְיֶה נָבָל׃
כִּסֵּא כָבוֹד מָרוֹם מֵרִאשׁוֹן 12
מְקוֹם מִקְדָּשֵׁנוּ׃
מִקְוֵה יִשְׂרָאֵל יְהֹוָה 13

v. 10. כדרכיו ק׳   v. 11. קמץ בז״ק   v. 11. ימיו ק׳

---

10. *heart . . . reins.* Cf. xi. 20.

even to give, etc. This is an affirmation of the doctrine of Reward and Punishment, and is repeated in xxxii. 19; cf. also Ps. lxii. 13; Job xxxiv. 11. Perhaps *the fruit of his doings* suggests that good or evil automatically produces its sequel as cause and effect (Daath Soferim).

11   FATE OF THE UNSCRUPULOUS

the partridge. Based on the Midrash, many exegetes explain this verse as comparing the unscrupulous to the partridge that sits upon eggs that are not hers. When they hatch, however, they realize that they are not of the same species and desert their adopted parents. The meaning of the prophet is that the man who enriches himself by unjust means shall have as little enjoyment of his ill-gotten wealth, but shall leave it as prematurely as the partridge which sits on strange eggs, but is speedily robbed of her hopes of a brood.

a fool. In our verse, the word *nabal* is rendered as 'wicked' by Targum, or 'dishonoured' by Kimchi.

12–13   THEY WHO FORSAKE GOD ARE WITHOUT HOPE

12. *Thou throne of glory,* etc. *Thou* is not in the original. Its addition makes the two verses an invocation to God Who is addressed as the *throne of glory,* a name doubtless suggested by the Temple which was regarded as God's terrestrial throne. A.V. and R.V., less probably, make the verse a reference to Jerusalem: 'A glorious throne, set on high from the beginning, is the place of our sanctuary.'

Thou place of our sanctuary. God is, as it were, the place in which the Temple stands. Cf. 'He is the place of the universe, but the universe is not His place' (Talmud), i.e. the universe is contained in Him, but not He in it.

13. *hope of Israel.* See on xiv. 8.

All that forsake Thee shall be
  ashamed;
They that depart from Thee shall
  be written in the earth,
Because they have forsaken the
  LORD,
The fountain of living waters.

14 Heal me, O LORD, and I shall be
  healed;
Save me, and I shall be saved;
For Thou art my praise.

15 Behold, they say unto me:
'Where is the word of the LORD?
  let it come now.'

16 As for me, I have not hastened
  from being a shepherd after
  Thee;
Neither have I desired the woeful
  day; Thou knowest it;
That which came out of my lips
  was manifest before Thee.

17 Be not a ruin unto me;

כָּל־עֹזְבֶיךָ יֵבֹשׁוּ

יְסוּרַי בָּאָרֶץ יִכָּתֵבוּ

כִּי עָזְבוּ

מְקוֹר מַיִם־חַיִּים אֶת־יְהוָֹה׃

14 רְפָאֵנִי יְהוָֹה וְאֵרָפֵא

הוֹשִׁיעֵנִי וְאִוָּשֵׁעָה

כִּי תְהִלָּתִי אָתָּה׃ ·

15 הִנֵּה־הֵמָּה אֹמְרִים אֵלָי

אַיֵּה דְבַר־יְהוָֹה יָבוֹא נָא׃

16 וַאֲנִי

לֹא־אַצְתִּי ׀ מֵרֹעֶה אַחֲרֶיךָ

וְיוֹם אָנוּשׁ

לֹא הִתְאַוֵּיתִי אַתָּה יָדָעְתָּ

מוֹצָא שְׂפָתַי נֹכַח פָּנֶיךָ הָיָה׃

17 אַל־תִּהְיֵה־לִי לִמְחִתָּה

v. 13. וסורי ק׳   v. 14. עד כאן   v. 17. היו״ד בצרי

shall be written in the earth. Not in a
material which endures, like marble or
metal (Daath Mikra).

the fountain of living waters. See on ii.
13.

14–18 JEREMIAH PRAYS FOR
            VINDICATION

Many commentators treat this as a new
section, but verses 12f. may be the
introduction to it. Thus the prayer for
healing is introduced by the invocation
of God as the *throne of glory* and *the hope
of Israel;* hence it is natural to turn to
Him for healing and salvation.

14. *for Thou art my praise.* In Thee do I
glory that Thou art my Helper and wilt
deliver me from mine enemies (Rashi).

15. *let it come now.* They deride Jeremiah's prophecies and mockingly ask
for their fulfilment (Kimchi). According
to Malbim, Jeremiah was accused of
being a false prophet, a crime punishable by death.

16. *from being a shepherd.* The Hebrew
preposition has a privitive force, 'so as
not to be a shepherd': I had no intention of hastily abandoning the mission
entrusted by God to me because of the
suffering it has entailed (Ibn Nachmiash).

that which came out of my lips. My en-
treaties that the threatened doom may
be averted. (Rashi).

17. *a ruin.* Let not Thy mission be the
cause of my ruin (Rashi).

Thou art my refuge in the day of evil.

18 Let them be ashamed that persecute me, but let not me be ashamed;

Let them be dismayed, but let not me be dismayed;

Bring upon them the day of evil, And destroy them with double destruction.

19. Thus said the LORD unto me: Go, and stand in the gate of the children of the people, whereby the kings of Judah come in, and by which they go out, and in all the gates of Jerusalem; 20. and say unto them:

Hear ye the word of the LORD, ye kings of Judah, and all Judah, and all the inhabitants of Jerusalem,

מַחֲסִי אַתָּה בְּיוֹם רָעָה:

18 יֵבֹשׁוּ רֹדְפַי וְאַל־אֵבֹשָׁה אָנִי
יֵחַתּוּ הֵמָּה וְאַל־אֵחַתָּה אָנִי
הָבִיא עֲלֵיהֶם יוֹם רָעָה
וּמִשְׁנֶה שִׁבָּרוֹן שָׁבְרֵם:

19 כֹּה־אָמַר יְהֹוָה אֵלַי הָלֹךְ
וְעָמַדְתָּ בְּשַׁעַר בְּנֵי־עָם
אֲשֶׁר יָבֹאוּ בוֹ מַלְכֵי יְהוּדָה
וַאֲשֶׁר יֵצְאוּ בוֹ וּבְכֹל שַׁעֲרֵי

20 יְרוּשָׁלָ͏ִם: וְאָמַרְתָּ אֲלֵיהֶם
שִׁמְעוּ דְבַר־יְהֹוָה מַלְכֵי
יְהוּדָה וְכָל־יְהוּדָה וְכָל יֹשְׁבֵי
יְרוּשָׁלָ͏ִם הַבָּאִים בַּשְּׁעָרִים

v. 19. העם ק׳

18. *double destruction.* i.e. complete destruction. This verse apparently contradicts verses 16f., yet not necessarily. The prophet has indeed prayed that the people be spared; but now that they ask for the fulfilment of his prophecies of destruction, he prays for their complete discomfiture (cf. xviii. 18–23) (Kimchi).

19–27 SABBATH OBSERVANCE WILL RESTORE NATIONAL GLORY

The prophet exhorts the people to observe the Sabbath. Most modern commentators think of this section as detached; but if interpreted in the context, it would be pedantic to urge that Jeremiah has spoken in certain tones of the people's doom as inevitable. As already pointed out, prophecies, no matter how final in tone, are conditional, since God is always ready to receive the repentant sinner. Further-

more, it is the prophet's duty to indicate the remedy for current evils. It is therefore natural that Jeremiah should stress the importance of the Sabbath, a basic institution of Judaism. The hallowing of the Sabbath, with its intensive spiritual influence, would tend to wean the people from other malpractices and effect a reformation.

19. *the children of the people.* [This probably signifies the laity (the phrase is used in this sense in 2 Chron. xxxv. 5), including the royal house, as distinct from the priests and Levites.] This gate would be the entrance most frequently resorted to by them; so Jeremiah was to proclaim his message there first and repeat it in the other gates (Kimchi).

20. *ye kings of Judah.* Whereas in the previous verse the plural denotes successive kings, here it seems to mean the reigning monarch and the princes of his house (Kimchi).

that enter in by these gates; 21. thus
saith the LORD: Take heed for the
sake of your souls, and bear no
burden on the sabbath day, nor
bring it in by the gates of Jerusalem;
22. neither carry forth a burden out
of your houses on the sabbath day,
neither do ye any work; but hallow
ye the sabbath day, as I commanded
your fathers; 23. but they hearkened
not, neither inclined their ear, but
made their neck stiff, that they
might not hear, nor receive instruction. 24. And it shall come to pass,
if ye diligently hearken unto Me,
saith the LORD, to bring in no
burden through the gates of this
city on the sabbath day, but to
hallow the sabbath day, to do no
work therein; 25. then shall there
enter in by the gates of this city
kings and princes sitting upon the

21 הָאֵלֶּה: כֹּה אָמַר יְהֹוָה
הִשָּׁמְרוּ בְּנַפְשׁוֹתֵיכֶם וְאַל־
תִּשְׂאוּ מַשָּׂא בְּיוֹם הַשַּׁבָּת
וַהֲבֵאתֶם בְּשַׁעֲרֵי יְרוּשָׁלִָם:
22 וְלֹא־תוֹצִיאוּ מַשָּׂא מִבָּתֵּיכֶם
בְּיוֹם הַשַּׁבָּת וְכָל־מְלָאכָה
לֹא תַעֲשׂוּ וְקִדַּשְׁתֶּם אֶת־יוֹם
הַשַּׁבָּת כַּאֲשֶׁר צִוִּיתִי אֶת־
23 אֲבוֹתֵיכֶם: וְלֹא שָׁמְעוּ וְלֹא
הִטּוּ אֶת־אָזְנָם וַיַּקְשׁוּ אֶת־
עָרְפָּם לְבִלְתִּי שׁוֹמֵעַ וּלְבִלְתִּי
24 קַחַת מוּסָר: וְהָיָה אִם־שָׁמֹעַ
תִּשְׁמְעוּן אֵלַי נְאֻם־יְהֹוָה
לְבִלְתִּי ׀ הָבִיא מַשָּׂא בְּשַׁעֲרֵי
הָעִיר הַזֹּאת בְּיוֹם הַשַּׁבָּת
וּלְקַדֵּשׁ אֶת־יוֹם הַשַּׁבָּת
לְבִלְתִּי עֲשׂוֹת־בֹּה כָּל־־
25 מְלָאכָה: וּבָאוּ בְשַׁעֲרֵי הָעִיר
הַזֹּאת מְלָכִים ׀ וְשָׂרִים

v. 24. שמוע ק׳ v. 23. בו ק׳

---

21. *for the sake of your souls.* A.V. and
R.V. translate: 'take heed to yourselves.'
The intention is that they beware of
profaning the Sabbath, a sin punishable
by death (Metsudath David).

burden. Of merchandise, or more
particularly of produce from the agricultural districts (Kimchi).

22. *out of your houses.* Articles brought
from the house to carry outside the city
(Kimchi). It is also possible that he

warned them against carrying from
their houses into the street since it
involved the infraction of a Rabbinic
enactment, promulgated by Solomon
(Malbim).

23. Cf. vii. 26.

25. *kings and princes.* In a similar
passage (xxii. 4) *and princes* is omitted.

sitting. The subject is *kings,* [the *princes*
surrounding the throne] (Metsudath
David).

123

throne of David, riding in chariots and on horses, they, and their princes, the men of Judah, and the inhabitants of Jerusalem; and this city shall be inhabited for ever. 26. And they shall come from the cities of Judah, and from the places round about Jerusalem, and from the land of Benjamin, and from the Lowland, and from the mountains, and from the South, bringing burnt-offerings, and sacrifices, and meal-offerings, and frankincense, and bringing sacrifices of thanksgiving, unto the house of the LORD. 27. But if ye wil! not hearken unto Me to hallow the sabbath day, and not to bear a burden and enter in at the gates of Jerusalem on the sabbath day; then will I kindle a fire in the gates thereof, and it shall devour the palaces of Jerusalem, and it shall not be quenched.

יֹשְׁבִים֙ עַל־כִּסֵּ֣א דָוִד֮ רֹכְבִ֣ים
| בָּרֶ֣כֶב וּבַסּוּסִ֗ים הֵ֚מָּה
וְשָׂרֵיהֶ֔ם אִ֥ישׁ יְהוּדָ֖ה וְיֹשְׁבֵ֣י
יְרוּשָׁלָ֑͏ִם וְיָשְׁבָ֥ה הָעִֽיר־הַזֹּ֖את
26 לְעוֹלָֽם: וּבָ֣אוּ מֵעָרֵֽי־יְהוּדָ֡ה
וּמִסְּבִיב֣וֹת יְרוּשָׁלִַם֩ וּמֵאֶ֨רֶץ
בִּנְיָמִ֜ן וּמִן־הַשְּׁפֵלָ֣ה וּמִן־
הָהָ֣ר וּמִן־הַנֶּ֗גֶב מְבִאִ֛ים עֹלָ֥ה
וְזֶ֖בַח וּמִנְחָ֣ה וּלְבוֹנָ֑ה וּמְבִאֵ֥י
27 תוֹדָ֖ה בֵּ֣ית יְהֹוָֽה: וְאִם־לֹ֨א
תִשְׁמְע֜וּ אֵלַ֗י לְקַדֵּשׁ֙ אֶת־י֣וֹם
הַשַּׁבָּ֔ת וּלְבִלְתִּ֣י | שְׂאֵ֣ת מַשָּׂ֗א
וּבֹ֛א בְּשַׁעֲרֵ֥י יְרוּשָׁלַ֖͏ִם בְּי֣וֹם
הַשַּׁבָּ֑ת וְהִצַּ֧תִּי אֵ֣שׁ בִּשְׁעָרֶ֗יהָ
וְאָֽכְלָ֛ה אַרְמְנ֥וֹת יְרוּשָׁלַ֖͏ִם וְלֹ֥א
תִכְבֶּֽה:

26. *the land of Benjamin.* To the north of Judah.

the Lowland. The low hills and valleys stretching down towards the Philistine plain on the west and south-west of Judah.

the mountains. The hilly country south of Jerusalem.

the South. The Negeb (see on xiii. 19).

bringing burnt-offerings, etc. The prophet did not object to sacrifices as such.

and sacrifices. i.e. peace-offerings (Lev. iii. 1ff.).

meal-offerings. Cf. Lev. ii. 1ff.

frankincense. This is not a separate offering, but offered together with the meal-offerings (Lev. ii.1).

sacrifices of thanksgiving. Cf. Lev. vii. 11ff. These were also peace-offerings, perhaps the most highly esteemed of this class of offerings. 'In the time to come all sacrifices will cease, but the sacrifice of thanksgiving will not cease' (Talmud).

27. *a fire.* A symbol of destruction (cf. xxi. 14, xlix. 27, l. 32). The penalty resembles the refrain in Amos i. 4–ii. 5.

18   CHAPTER XVIII   יח

1 הַדָּבָר֙ אֲשֶׁ֣ר הָיָ֣ה אֶֽל־יִרְמְיָ֔הוּ
2 מֵאֵ֥ת יְהֹוָ֖ה לֵאמֹֽר׃ ק֗וּם
וְיָרַדְתָּ֙ בֵּ֣ית הַיּוֹצֵ֔ר וְשָׁ֖מָּה
3 אַשְׁמִֽיעֲךָ֖ אֶת־דְּבָרָֽי׃ וָאֵרֵ֖ד
בֵּ֣ית הַיּוֹצֵ֑ר וְהִנֵּה־ה֛וּא עֹשֶׂ֥ה
מְלָאכָ֖ה עַל־הָאָבְנָֽיִם׃
4 וְנִשְׁחַ֣ת הַכְּלִ֗י אֲשֶׁ֨ר ה֥וּא עֹשֶׂ֛ה
בַּחֹ֖מֶר בְּיַ֣ד הַיּוֹצֵ֑ר וְשָׁ֗ב

v. 3. והנה הוא ק׳

1. The word which came to Jeremiah from the LORD, saying: 2. 'Arise, and go down to the potter's house, and there I will cause thee to hear My words.' 3. Then I went down to the potter's house, and, behold, he was at his work on the wheels. 4. And whensoever the vessel that he made of the clay was marred in the hand of the potter, he made it again

---

CHAPTER XVIII

1-17 THE POTTER AND HIS CLAY

CHAPTERS XVIII-XX form a connected section. The familiar sight of the potter at work with his clay suggests to Jeremiah's mind a parallel to the working of God with His people. Chapter xviii describes the process of remaking a misshapen vessel and applies it to the fate of the nation. This is followed by the parable of the broken bottle with special reference to the persecution of the prophet by an official named Pashhur. The composition dates from the early years in the reign of Jehoiakim.

2. *go down.* Apparently, at that time, Jeremiah was in a place higher than the potter's house. Most likely, the potters' places of work were situated in the south of the city, which slopes downward toward the spring of the Shiloah, in order to be near water, which was needed for their work. Moreover, in that section there is clay, which served to make the earthenware vessels (Daath Mikra).

3. *the wheels.* The Hebrew noun has the dual formation and is literally 'the two stones.' The apparatus consisted of two circular stones; the lower was worked by the feet and connected 'with the upper, which supported the clay, by a vertical axis. The upper disc rotated when pressure was applied to the pedal, (Daath Mikra).

4. *of the clay.* The Hebrew editions and MSS. vary in the reading between *kachomer,* 'like the clay,' and *bachomer,* 'in (i.e. of) the clay.' The latter is preferable.

was marred. Thomson witnessed such a scene which he describes as follows: 'From some defect in the clay, or because he had taken too little, the potter suddenly changed his mind, crushed his growing jar instantly into a shapeless mass of mud, and beginning anew, fashioned it into a totally different vessel.' The application of the simile is not that the house of Israel is bound to be fashioned ultimately as God wishes, as might be concluded from verse 4, but that God disposes absolutely of the destinies of Israel and every other nation, in the same way that the potter does whatever he pleases with the clay. This is true notwithstanding pre-

another vessel, as seemed good to the potter to make it.

5. Then the word of the LORD came to me, saying: 6. 'O house of Israel, cannot I do with you as this potter? saith the LORD. Behold, as the clay in the potter's hand, so are ye in My hand, O house of Israel. 7. At one instant I may speak concerning a nation, and concerning a kingdom, to pluck up and to break down and to destroy it; 8. but if that nation turn from their evil, because of which I have spoken against it, I repent of the evil that I thought to do unto it. 9. And at one instant I may speak concerning a nation, and concerning a kingdom, to build and to plant it; 10. but if it do evil in My sight, that it hearken not to My voice, then I repent of the good, wherewith I said I would benefit it. 11. Now therefore do thou speak to the men of Judah, and to the inhabitants of Jerusalem, saying: Thus

וַיְּעֲשֵׂהוּ כְּלִי אַחֵר כַּאֲשֶׁר יָשַׁר
5 בְּעֵינֵי הַיּוֹצֵר לַעֲשׂוֹת: וַיְהִי
דְבַר־יְהוָה אֵלַי לֵאמְוֹר:
6 הֲכַיּוֹצֵר הַזֶּה לֹא־אוּכַל
לַעֲשׂוֹת לָכֶם בֵּית יִשְׂרָאֵל
נְאֻם־יְהוָה הִנֵּה כַחֹמֶר בְּיַד
הַיּוֹצֵר כֵּן־אַתֶּם בְּיָדִי בֵּית
7 יִשְׂרָאֵל: רֶגַע אֲדַבֵּר עַל־
גּוֹי וְעַל־מַמְלָכָה לִנְתוֹשׁ
8 וְלִנְתוֹץ וּלְהַאֲבִיד: וְשָׁב הַגּוֹי
הַהוּא מֵרָעָתוֹ אֲשֶׁר דִּבַּרְתִּי
עָלָיו וְנִחַמְתִּי עַל־הָרָעָה
אֲשֶׁר חָשַׁבְתִּי לַעֲשׂוֹת לוֹ:
9 וְרֶגַע אֲדַבֵּר עַל־גּוֹי וְעַל־
מַמְלָכָה לִבְנוֹת וְלִנְטוֹעַ:
10 וְעָשָׂה הָרָעָה בְּעֵינַי לְבִלְתִּי
שְׁמֹעַ בְּקוֹלִי וְנִחַמְתִּי עַל־
הַטּוֹבָה אֲשֶׁר אָמַרְתִּי לְהֵיטִיב
11 אוֹתוֹ: וְעַתָּה אֱמָר־נָא אֶל־
אִישׁ יְהוּדָה וְעַל־יוֹשְׁבֵי
יְרוּשָׁלַם לֵאמֹר כֹּה אָמַר יְהוָה

v. 10. הרע ק' v. 5. מלא ר'

---

vious predictions of blessings or disaster, because such are always conditional: the blessings will be forfeited if the people become unworthy of them, whilst the disaster may be averted if the people repent in time.

7. *a nation . . . a kingdom.* Although the moral is ultimately directed to the King-

dom of Judah (verse 11), *nation* and *kingdom* are an assertion of God's Sovereignty over all peoples (*Kimchi*).

8. *I repent.* An anthropomorphism, signifying not a change of mind (cf. Num. xxiii. 19), but in treatment occasioned by the change in the people's conduct (*Daath Mikra*).

saith the LORD: Behold, I frame evil against you, and devise a device against you; return ye now every one from his evil way, and amend your ways and your doings. 12. But they say: There is no hope; but we will walk after our own devices, and we will do every one after the stubbornness of his evil heart.'

13 Therefore thus saith the LORD:
Ask ye now among the nations,
Who hath heard such things;
The virgin of Israel hath done
A very horrible thing.

14 Doth the snow of Lebanon fail
From the rock of the field?

הִנֵּה אָנֹכִי יוֹצֵר עֲלֵיכֶם רָעָ֗ה
וְחֹשֵׁב עֲלֵיכֶם מַחֲשָׁבָה שׁוּבוּ
נָא אִישׁ מִדַּרְכּוֹ הָרָעָה
וְהֵיטִיבוּ   דַרְכֵיכֶם

12 וּמַעַלְלֵיכֶם: וְאָמְרוּ נוֹאָשׁ
כִּי־אַחֲרֵי מַחְשְׁבוֹתֵינוּ נֵלֵךְ
וְאִישׁ שְׁרִרוּת לִבּוֹ־הָרָע
נַעֲשֶׂה:

13 לָכֵן כֹּה אָמַר יְהֹוָה
שַׁאֲלוּ־נָא בַּגּוֹיִם
מִי שָׁמַע כָּאֵלֶּה
שַׁעֲרֻרִת עָשְׂתָה מְאֹד
בְּתוּלַת יִשְׂרָאֵל:

14 הֲיַעֲזֹב מִצּוּר שָׂדַי שֶׁלֶג לְבָנוֹן

11. *frame.* The verb, *yotser,* is identical with the word for *potter* and is deliberately chosen to suggest the connection (Kimchi).

12. *there is no hope.* It is too late: we have chosen our path and must continue in it. The same expression occurred in ii. 25 (Kimchi).

13. *the virgin of Israel.* See on xiv. 17. The people of Israel, like a virgin who keeps herself undefiled for her future husband, should have avoided contamination by foreign worship as the 'betrothed' of God (Metsudath David).

a very horrible thing. An action both unnatural and revolting, as the next verse explains (Kimchi, Rashi).

14. This is a difficult verse. As rendered by A.J., which agrees substantially with A.V. and R.V., the meaning is that

Nature pursues her course unchanged, whereas the nation has unnaturally changed its course. The Jewish commentators interpret the verse differently: shall one forsake the pure water coursing down the rock of the field from the melting snows (in favour of turbid waters), or should clear running water be abandoned for foul, stagnant waters?

doth . . . fail. The summit of Lebanon (lit. 'the white mountain') is clothed with perpetual snow, and nothing occurs to alter this (Ibn Nachmiash).

the rock of the field. The expression is strange. Daath Mikra suggests a translation in accordance with the alternative interpretation given above: 'Doth the ice-cold water (literally snow) of Lebanon fail (to stream down) upon the rocks in the nearby fields?'

Or are the strange cold flowing
waters
Plucked up?

15 For My people hath forgotten
Me,
They offer unto vanity;
And they have been made to
stumble in their ways,
In the ancient paths,
To walk in bypaths,
In a way not cast up;

16 To make their land an astonish-
ment,
And a perpetual hissing;
Every one that passeth thereby
shall be astonished,
And shake his head.

17 I will scatter them as with an
east wind
Before the enemy;
I will look upon their back, and
not their face,
In the day of their calamity.

אִם־יִנָּתְשׁוּ מַיִם
זָרִים קָרִים נוֹזְלִים:
15 כִּי־שְׁכֵחֻנִי עַמִּי לַשָּׁוְא יְקַטֵּרוּ
וַיַּכְשִׁלוּם בְּדַרְכֵיהֶם
שְׁבִילֵי עוֹלָם
לָלֶכֶת נְתִיבוֹת
דֶּרֶךְ לֹא סְלוּלָה:
16 לָשׂוּם אַרְצָם
לְשַׁמָּה שְׁרוֹקִת עוֹלָם
כֹּל עוֹבֵר עָלֶיהָ
יִשֹּׁם וְיָנִיד בְּרֹאשׁוֹ:
17 כְּרוּחַ־קָדִים אֲפִיצֵם
לִפְנֵי אוֹיֵב
עֹרֶף וְלֹא־פָנִים
אֶרְאֵם בְּיוֹם אֵידָם:

v. 15. שבילי ק׳   v. 16. שריקות ק׳

---

the strange cold flowing waters. Kimchi explains that the prophet takes an example of easily accessible water. He first mentions the water that flows from the rock of the field, which is easily accessible to all, and then he mentions the strange cold water, i.e. the water that is piped into the city or near the city from a long distance. Would anyone neglect to drink these easily accessible waters? Yet, I, Who am far from them according to My greatness, draw near to them to bring them benefit, but they have forgotten Me.

15. *vanity.* i.e. idols (Daath Mikra).

and they have been made to stumble. lit. as A.V. and R.V., 'and they have caused

them to stumble.' The subject may then be the false prophets, to be understood from the general context (Kimchi); or, *they* may simply be indefinite, in which case the sense approximates to 'and they (the people) have stumbled' (so LXX).

the ancient paths. Cf. vi. 16.

a way not cast up. A new way, not yet trodden out by travelers (Metsudath Zion).

16. *to make,* etc. That must be the inevitable result of abandoning the paths ordained by God (Kimchi).

hissing. An act indicative of amazement (Metsudath Zion).

17. *an east wind.* The sirocco, a hot

18 Then said they:
'Come, and let us devise devices
against Jeremiah;
For instruction shall not perish
from the priest,
Nor counsel from the wise, nor
the word from the prophet.
Come, and let us smite him with
the tongue,
And let us not give heed to any
of his words.'
19 Give heed to me, O LORD,
And hearken to the voice of them
that contend with me.
20 Shall evil be recompensed for
good?
For they have digged a pit for
my soul.
Remember how I stood before
Thee
To speak good for them,
To turn away Thy wrath from
them.

וַיֹּאמְרוּ ¹⁸
לְכוּ וְנַחְשְׁבָה עַל־יִרְמְיָהוּ
מַחֲשָׁבוֹת
כִּי לֹא־תֹאבַד תּוֹרָה מִכֹּהֵן
וְעֵצָה מֵחָכָם וְדָבָר מִנָּבִיא
לְכוּ וְנַכֵּהוּ בַלָּשׁוֹן
וְאַל־נַקְשִׁיבָה
אֶל־כָּל־דְּבָרָיו׃
הַקְשִׁיבָה יְהוָה אֵלָי ¹⁹
וּשְׁמַע לְקוֹל יְרִיבָי׃
הַיְשֻׁלַּם תַּחַת־טוֹבָה רָעָה ²⁰
כִּי־כָרוּ שׁוּחָה לְנַפְשִׁי
זְכֹר ׀ עָמְדִי לְפָנֶיךָ
לְדַבֵּר עֲלֵיהֶם טוֹבָה
לְהָשִׁיב אֶת־חֲמָתְךָ מֵהֶם׃

wind which springs up suddenly from the desert in the east (cf. xiii. 24).

18–23 JEREMIAH PRAYS FOR PUNISHMENT ON HIS ANTAGONISTS

18. *they.* Jeremiah's enemies.

for instruction shall not perish, etc. This may mean either *(i)* we are not dependent on him for instruction, counsel and prophecy; there are priests, wise men and prophets to guide us, and we can do without him (Kimchi); or *(ii)* if we do not rid ourselves of him, he will not cease to function as a priest, a wise man, or a prophet. As priest, he will not cease his instruction to the people, reproving them once concerning idolatry, once concerning immorality, once concerning profanation of the Sabbath,

for it is the function of the priest to instruct the people. If he is not instructing us, he will seek to advise us concerning political matters, contrary to our belief. If he is doing neither, he will prophesy his prophecies of doom (Abarbanel).

with the tongue. Let us lay charges against him which will encompass his destruction (Targum). The text may mean 'with (his) tongue' (so the Peshitta): let us use his own words to bring about his downfall through a charge of treason.

let us not give heed. We can ignore his threatenings of retribution (Abarbanel).

20. *for my soul.* i.e. for my life (Targum).

21 Therefore deliver up their
    children to the famine,
    And hurl them to the power of
    the sword;
    And let their wives be bereaved
    of their children, and widows;
    And let their men be slain of
    death,
    And their young men smitten of
    the sword in battle.

22 Let a cry be heard from their
    houses,
    When thou shalt bring a troop
    suddenly upon them;
    For they have digged a pit to
    take me,
    And hid snares for my feet.

23 Yet, LORD, Thou knowest
    All their counsel against me to
    slay me;
    Forgive not their iniquity,
    Neither blot out their sin from
    Thy sight;

21 לָכֵן תֵּן אֶת־בְּנֵיהֶם לָרָעָב
וְהַגִּרֵם עַל־יְדֵי־חֶרֶב
וְתִהְיֶנָה נְשֵׁיהֶם
שַׁכֻּלוֹת וְאַלְמָנוֹת
וְאַנְשֵׁיהֶם יִהְיוּ הֲרֻגֵי מָוֶת
בַּחוּרֵיהֶם
מְכֵּי־חֶרֶב בַּמִּלְחָמָה׃

22 תִּשָּׁמַע זְעָקָה מִבָּתֵּיהֶם
כִּי־תָבִיא עֲלֵיהֶם
גְּדוּד פִּתְאֹם
כִּי־כָרוּ שִׁיחָה לְלָכְדֵנִי
וּפַחִים טָמְנוּ לְרַגְלָי׃

23 וְאַתָּה יְהֹוָה יָדַעְתָּ
אֶת־כָּל־עֲצָתָם עָלַי לַמָּוֶת
אַל־תְּכַפֵּר עַל־עֲוֺנָם
וְחַטָּאתָם מִלְּפָנֶיךָ אַל־תֶּמְחִי

שׁוּחָה ק׳   v. 22.

21ff. The bitter imprecation is not hurled against the nation as a whole for refusing to accept his teachings, but is directed only against his enemies who plotted his death (Kimchi). Even so, the outburst does not represent Jeremiah at his highest and is uttered in a moment of exasperation. It should also be remembered that his anger was aroused not so much because he was being personally attacked as for the reason that his call from God was defied.

21. *hurl them to the power of the sword.* lit. 'pour them out upon the hands of the sword.' The expression occurs again in Ezek. xxxv. 5; Ps. lxiii. 11 and means that they should be thrust upon the sword so that their life-blood is poured out (so Kimchi and Metsudath David).

their men. The contrast in the next clause indicates that here are intended the men who are too old to fight on the battlefield, and *of death* signifies 'from pestilence' as in xv. 2 (Kimchi).

22. *their houses.* Broken into and plundered by the enemy (Daath Mikra).

23. *Thou knowest.* Although they schemed against Jeremiah in secret, their plot is known to God (Daath Mikra).

But let them be made to stumble
before Thee;
Deal Thou with them in the
time of Thine anger.

וְיִהְיוּ מֻכְשָׁלִים לְפָנֶיךָ
בְּעֵת אַפְּךָ עֲשֵׂה בָהֶם׃

---

19   CHAPTER XIX   יט

1. Thus said the LORD: Go, and
get a potter's earthen bottle, and
take of the elders of the people, and
of the elders of the priests; 2. and
go forth unto the valley of the son of
Hinnom, which is by the entry of the
gate Harsith, and proclaim there the
words that I shall tell thee; 3. and
say: Hear ye the word of the LORD,
O kings of Judah, and inhabitants of
Jerusalem; thus saith the LORD of
hosts, the God of Israel:

1 כֹּה אָמַר יְהֹוָה הָלֹךְ וְקָנִיתָ
בַקְבֻּק יוֹצֵר חָרֶשׂ וּמִזִּקְנֵי הָעָם
2 וּמִזִּקְנֵי הַכֹּהֲנִים׃ וְיָצָאתָ אֶל־
גֵּיא בֶן־הִנֹּם אֲשֶׁר פֶּתַח שַׁעַר
הַחַרְסוּת וְקָרָאתָ שָׁם אֶת־
הַדְּבָרִים אֲשֶׁר־אֲדַבֵּר
3 אֵלֶיךָ׃ וְאָמַרְתָּ שִׁמְעוּ דְבַר־
יְהֹוָה מַלְכֵי יְהוּדָה וְישְׁבֵי
יְרוּשָׁלָ͏ִם כֹּה־אָמַר יְהֹוָה
צְבָאוֹת אֱלֹהֵי יִשְׂרָאֵל הִנְנִי

v. 23. החרסית ק׳ v. 2. ויהיו ק׳

---

deal ... anger. At the time of Thy
anger wreak vengeance upon them so
that they will be unable to contain it
(Metsudath David).

CHAPTER XIX

1-3 PARABLE OF THE EARTHEN BOTTLE

IN the parable of the potter and his clay,
the point is the possibility of remaking a
vessel which has not met with approval;
here it is the destruction of a vessel
which proves useless.

1. *take.* Not in the Hebrew, but to be
understood (Targum).

the elders of the priests. Their chiefs
(again in 2 Kings xix. 2 and cf. 2 Chron.
xxxvi. 14).

2. *the valley of the son of Hinnom.* See on
vii. 31.

the gate Harsith. Or, 'the gate of pot-
sherds' (R.V. margin). It was perhaps
given that name because fragments of
pottery were cast there as refuse. It may
be identical with *the dung gate* (Neh. ii.
13) (Kimchi). Rabbi Joseph Kara
describes it as a place where earthenware vessels are made. As mentioned
above, the potters' establishments were
likely located in the southern part of the
city where clay is found. Also, it is near
water, needed for the manufacture of
earthenware vessels.

3. *kings.* See on xvii. 20.

this place. viz. Jerusalem (so again in
verse 4) (Abarbanel).

Behold, I will bring evil upon this place, which whosoever heareth, his ears shall tingle; 4. because they have forsaken Me, and have estranged this place, and have offered in it unto other gods, whom neither they nor their fathers have known, nor the kings of Judah; and have filled this place with the blood of innocents; 5. and have built the high places of Baal, to burn their sons in the fire for burnt-offerings unto Baal; which I commanded not, nor spoke it, neither came it into My mind. 6. Therefore, behold, the days come, saith the LORD, that this place shall no more be called Topheth, nor The valley of the son of Hinnom, but The valley of slaughter; 7. and I will make void the counsel of Judah and Jerusalem in this place; and I will cause them to fall by the sword before their

מֵבִיא רָעָה עַל־הַמָּקוֹם הַזֶּה
אֲשֶׁר כָּל־שֹׁמְעָהּ תִּצַּלְנָה
אָזְנָיו: יַעַן | אֲשֶׁר עֲזָבֻנִי 4
וַיְנַכְּרוּ אֶת־הַמָּקוֹם הַזֶּה
וַיְקַטְּרוּ־בוֹ לֵאלֹהִים אֲחֵרִים
אֲשֶׁר לֹא־יְדָעוּם הֵמָּה
וַאֲבוֹתֵיהֶם וּמַלְכֵי יְהוּדָה
וּמָלְאוּ אֶת־הַמָּקוֹם הַזֶּה דַּם
נְקִיִּם: וּבָנוּ אֶת־בָּמוֹת הַבַּעַל 5
לִשְׂרֹף אֶת־בְּנֵיהֶם בָּאֵשׁ
עֹלוֹת לַבָּעַל אֲשֶׁר לֹא־צִוִּיתִי
וְלֹא דִבַּרְתִּי וְלֹא עָלְתָה עַל־
לִבִּי: לָכֵן הִנֵּה־יָמִים בָּאִים 6
נְאֻם־יְהֹוָה וְלֹא־יִקָּרֵא
לַמָּקוֹם הַזֶּה עוֹד הַתֹּפֶת וְגֵיא
בֶן־הִנֹּם כִּי אִם־גֵּיא הַהֲרֵגָה:
וּבַקֹּתִי אֶת־עֲצַת יְהוּדָה 7
וִירוּשָׁלַםִ בַּמָּקוֹם הַזֶּה
וְהִפַּלְתִּים בַּחֶרֶב לִפְנֵי

---

his ears shall tingle. As in 1 Sam. iii. 11; 2 Kings xxi. 12.

4. *have estranged this place.* Made it strange to Me by practising hideous rites in it (see Kimchi).

innocents. Most probably the children who were sacrificed, as in the next verse (Metsudath David). Or, possibly, the allusion is to the blood of innocent people who were murdered (cf. 2 Kings xxi. 16).

5f. Almost identical with vii. 31f., on which see the notes.

5. *of Baal.* Corresponding to *of Topheth* in vii. 31.

7. *make void the counsel.* They will be emptied of counsel which might save them from the enemy (Metsudath David). The verb *bakkothi* is connected with *bakbuk, bottle,* in verse 1 and chosen because of it (Rashi). Modern commentators think that Jeremiah symbolically

enemies, and by the hand of them that seek their life; and their carcasses will I give to be food for the fowls of the heaven, and for the beasts of the earth; 8. and I will make this city an astonishment, and a hissing; every one that passeth thereby shall be astonished and hiss because of all the plagues thereof; 9. and I will cause them to eat the flesh of their sons and the flesh of their daughters, and they shall eat every one the flesh of his friend, in the siege and in the straitness, wherewith their enemies, and they that seek their life, shall straiten them. 10. Then shalt thou break the bottle in the sight of the men that go with thee, 11. and shalt say unto them: Thus saith the Lord of hosts: Even so will I break this people and this city, as one breaketh a potter's vessel, that cannot be made whole again; and they shall bury in Topheth, for want of room

אֽיְבֵיהֶ֔ם וּבְיַ֖ד מְבַקְשֵׁ֣י נַפְשָׁ֑ם
וְנָתַתִּ֤י אֶת־נִבְלָתָם֙ לְמַֽאֲכָ֔ל
לְע֥וֹף הַשָּׁמַ֖יִם וּלְבֶהֱמַ֥ת
8 הָאָֽרֶץ׃ וְשַׂמְתִּ֞י אֶת־הָעִ֣יר
הַזֹּאת֙ לְשַׁמָּ֣ה וְלִשְׁרֵקָ֔ה כֹּ֚ל
עֹבֵ֣ר עָלֶ֔יהָ יִשֹּׁ֥ם וְיִשְׁרֹ֖ק עַל־
9 כָּל־מַכֹּתֶֽהָ׃ וְהַֽאֲכַלְתִּ֗ים
אֶת־בְּשַׂ֤ר בְּנֵיהֶם֙ וְאֵ֖ת בְּשַׂ֣ר
בְּנֹֽתֵיהֶ֑ם וְאִ֛ישׁ בְּשַׂר־רֵעֵ֖הוּ
יֹאכֵ֑לוּ בְּמָצוֹר֙ וּבְמָצ֔וֹק אֲשֶׁ֧ר
יָצִ֣יקוּ לָהֶ֛ם אֹֽיְבֵיהֶ֖ם וּמְבַקְשֵׁ֥י
10 נַפְשָֽׁם׃ וְשָׁבַרְתָּ֖ הַבַּקְבֻּ֑ק
לְעֵינֵי֙ הָֽאֲנָשִׁ֔ים הַהֹֽלְכִ֖ים
11 אוֹתָֽךְ׃ וְאָֽמַרְתָּ֤ אֲלֵיהֶם֙ כֹּה־
אָמַ֣ר ׀ יְהֹוָ֣ה צְבָא֔וֹת כָּ֣כָה
אֶשְׁבֹּ֞ר אֶת־הָעָ֤ם הַזֶּה֙ וְאֶת־
הָעִ֣יר הַזֹּ֔את כַּֽאֲשֶׁ֤ר יִשְׁבֹּר֙
אֶת־כְּלִ֣י הַיּוֹצֵ֔ר אֲשֶׁ֛ר
לֹֽא־יוּכַ֥ל לְהֵֽרָפֵ֖ה ע֑וֹד
וּבְתֹ֣פֶת יִקְבְּר֔וּ מֵאֵ֥ין מָקֽוֹם׃

v. 11. ה׳ במקום א׳

emptied the vessel as he spoke these words.

and their carcasses, etc.   Based on vii. 33.

8. The verse repeats the substance of xviii. 16.

9. Their desperate straits will reduce them to cannibalism. This verse is derived from Deut. xxviii. 53. The fulfilment of the prediction is recorded in Lam. iv. 10.

10. *shalt thou break the bottle.* [It is still the practice in the East to break a jar near a person and express the hope that he will be similarly broken.]

11. *and they shall bury . . . to bury.* Based on vii. 32. The words are omitted in LXX but fit into the context. In the 'breaking' of the nation, the dead will be so numerous that even the unclean site of Topheth will have to be used for their burial (see Kara, Kimchi).

to bury. 12. Thus will I do unto
this place, saith the LORD, and to the
inhabitants thereof, even making
this city as Topheth; 13. and the
houses of Jerusalem, and the houses
of the kings of Judah, which are
defiled, shall be as the place of
Topheth, even all the houses upon
whose roofs they have offered unto
all the host of heaven, and have
poured out drink-offerings unto
other gods.

14. Then came Jeremiah from
Topheth, whither the LORD had sent
him to prophesy; and he stood in the
court of the LORD's house, and said
to all the people: 15. 'Thus saith the
LORD of hosts, the God of Israel:
Behold, I will bring upon this city
and upon all her towns all the evil
that I have pronounced against it;
because they have made their neck
stiff, that they might not hear My
words.'

12 לִקְבּוֹר: כֵּן־אֶעֱשֶׂה לַמָּקוֹם
הַזֶּה נְאֻם־יְהֹוָה וּלְיוֹשְׁבָיו
וְלָתֵת אֶת־הָעִיר הַזֹּאת
13 כְּתֹפֶת: וְהָיוּ בָּתֵּי יְרוּשָׁלַ͏ִם
וּבָתֵּי מַלְכֵי יְהוּדָה כִּמְקוֹם
הַתֹּפֶת הַטְּמֵאִים לְכֹל הַבָּתִּים
אֲשֶׁר קִטְּרוּ עַל־גַּגֹּתֵיהֶם לְכֹל
צְבָא הַשָּׁמַיִם וְהַסֵּךְ נְסָכִים
14 לֵאלֹהִים אֲחֵרִים: וַיָּבֹא
יִרְמְיָהוּ מֵהַתֹּפֶת אֲשֶׁר שְׁלָחוֹ
יְהֹוָה שָׁם לְהִנָּבֵא וַיַּעֲמֹד
בַּחֲצַר בֵּית־יְהֹוָה וַיֹּאמֶר
15 אֶל־כָּל־הָעָם: כֹּה־אָמַר
יְהֹוָה צְבָאוֹת אֱלֹהֵי יִשְׂרָאֵל
הִנְנִי מֵבִי אֶל־הָעִיר הַזֹּאת
וְעַל־כָּל־עָרֶיהָ אֵת כָּל־
הָרָעָה אֲשֶׁר דִּבַּרְתִּי עָלֶיהָ כִּי
הִקְשׁוּ אֶת־עָרְפָּם לְבִלְתִּי
שְׁמוֹעַ אֶת־דְּבָרָי:

v. 15. מביא ק׳

---

12. *as Topheth.* Which is filled with the
bones of the victims of human sacrifice
(Rashi); or it is a place which had been
defiled by Josiah (2 Kings xxiii. 10)
(Kimchi).

13. *roofs.* In the East the roofs of
buildings are flat and used for various
purposes (cf. Judg. xvi. 27; 1 Sam. ix.
26; 2 Sam. xi. 2).

14–15 SENTENCE ON JERUSALEM
REPEATED

From verse 14 to xx. 6 Jeremiah is

spoken of in the third person. The
passage may have been inserted from
Baruch's memoirs.

14. *from Topheth.* Where he had delivered his prophecy (verse 2). He now
presumably returns to the Temple area
and repeats God's message of doom
(Abarbanel).

15. *all her towns.* i.e. the other towns
of Judah (cf. xxxiv. 1) (Kimchi).

CHAPTER XX

20

ב

1. Now Pashhur the son of Immer the priest, who was chief officer in the house of the LORD, heard Jeremiah prophesying these things. 2. Then Pashhur smote Jeremiah the prophet, and put him in the stocks that were in the upper gate of Benjamin, which was in the house of the LORD. 3. And it came to pass on the morrow, that Pashhur brought forth Jeremiah out of the stocks. Then said Jeremiah unto him: 'The LORD hath not called thy name Pashhur, but Magor-missabib.

וַיִּשְׁמַע פַּשְׁחוּר בֶּן־אִמֵּר 1
הַכֹּהֵן וְהוּא־פָקִיד נָגִיד בְּבֵית
יְהוָה אֶת־יִרְמְיָהוּ נִבָּא אֶת־
הַדְּבָרִים הָאֵלֶּה: וַיַּכֶּה 2
פַּשְׁחוּר אֵת יִרְמְיָהוּ הַנָּבִיא
וַיִּתֵּן אֹתוֹ עַל־הַמַּהְפֶּכֶת אֲשֶׁר
בְּשַׁעַר בִּנְיָמִן הָעֶלְיוֹן אֲשֶׁר
בְּבֵית יְהוָה: וַיְהִי מִמָּחֳרָת 3
וַיֹּצֵא פַשְׁחוּר אֶת־יִרְמְיָהוּ
מִן־הַמַּהְפָּכֶת וַיֹּאמֶר אֵלָיו
יִרְמְיָהוּ לֹא פַשְׁחוּר קָרָא יְהוָה
שְׁמֶךָ כִּי אִם־מָגוֹר מִסָּבִיב:

CHAPTER XX

1-6 JEREMIAH ATTACKED BY PASSHUR

1. *Pashhur the son of Immer.* In later times these were apparently family names (Ezra ii. 37f., x. 20); here they are personal names. In xxi. 1 there is mention of Pashhur the son of Malchiah, and in xxxviii. 1 of Gedaliah the son of Pashhur; so the name seems to have been common.

chief officer. lit. 'overseer ruler' which some explain as 'deputy officer.' According to Jonathan, he was the assistant to the high priest. Daath Mikra conjectures that Pashhur's position was to preserve order in the Temple Court. See below xxix. 26. He considered Jeremiah a subversive element, and, therefore, smote him and imprisoned him. Since Pashhur was descended from a prominent priestly family, he dared attack the prophet of God without fear of punishment. His son, Gedaliah followed in his father's footsteps and

accused Jeremiah of weakening the war effort (xxxviii. 4) (Daath Soferim).

2. *smote.* Perhaps with *forty stripes* (Deut. xxv. 3) (see Targum).

the stocks. The Hebrew noun *mahpecheth* means literally 'causing distortion,' and denotes a pillory which forced the body into a cramped posture. It is mentioned again in xxix. 26, and 2 Chron. xvi. 10 refers to 'house of the stocks' (so lit., A.J. *prison-house*) (see Kimchi).

upper gate of Benjamin. Since the territory of Benjamin lay to the north of Jerusalem, this gate was on the north side of the Temple. The addition of *which was in the house of the* LORD serves to distinguish it from the city *gate of Benjamin* (xxxvii. 13, xxxviii. 7). The Temple stood on the slope of a hill so that parts of it were *upper* as compared with others (cf. *the upper court,* xxxvi. 10) (see Daath Mikra).

3. *Magor-missabib.* i.e. 'terror on every side.' The name is symbolic of the terror

4. For thus saith the LORD: Behold, I will make thee a terror to thyself, and to all thy friends; and they shall fall by the sword of their enemies, and thine eyes shall behold it; and I will give all Judah into the hand of the king of Babylon, and he shall carry them captive to Babylon, and shall slay them with the sword. 5. Moreover I will give all the store of this city, and all the gains thereof, and all the wealth thereof, yea, all the treasures of the kings of Judah will I give into the hand of their enemies, who shall spoil them, and take them, and carry them to Babylon. 6. And thou, Pashhur, and all that dwell in thy house shall go into captivity; and thou shalt come to Babylon, and there thou shalt die, and there shalt thou be buried, thou, and all thy friends, to whom thou hast prophesied falsely.'

7 O LORD, Thou hast enticed me, and I was enticed,

4 כִּי־כֹה אָמַר יְהוָֹה הִנְנִי נֹתֶנְךָ לְמָגוֹר לְךָ | וּלְכָל־אֹהֲבֶיךָ וְנָפְלוּ בְּחֶרֶב אֹיְבֵיהֶם וְעֵינֶיךָ רֹאוֹת וְאֶת־כָּל־יְהוּדָה אֶתֵּן בְּיַד מֶלֶךְ־בָּבֶל וְהִגְלָם בָּבֶלָה וְהִכָּם בֶּחָרֶב: 5 וְנָתַתִּי אֶת־כָּל־חֹסֶן הָעִיר הַזֹּאת וְאֶת־כָּל־יְגִיעָהּ וְאֶת־כָּל־יְקָרָהּ וְאֵת כָּל־אוֹצְרוֹת מַלְכֵי יְהוּדָה אֶתֵּן בְּיַד אֹיְבֵיהֶם וּבְזָזוּם וּלְקָחוּם וֶהֱבִיאוּם בָּבֶלָה: 6 וְאַתָּה פַשְׁחוּר וְכֹל יֹשְׁבֵי בֵיתֶךָ תֵּלְכוּ בַּשֶּׁבִי וּבָבֶל תָּבוֹא וְשָׁם תָּמוּת וְשָׁם תִּקָּבֵר אַתָּה וְכָל־אֹהֲבֶיךָ אֲשֶׁר־נִבֵּאתָ לָהֶם בַּשָּׁקֶר:

7 פִּתִּיתַנִי יְהוָֹה וָאֶפָּת

---

which the Babylonians will arouse among the people of Judah (Abarbanel).

4. *I will make thee a terror.* [It has been surmised that Pashhur was a leader of the pro-Egyptian party in Judea, and this fact may account for his fierce opposition to Jeremiah. His policy will result in his being the cause of the *terror* which was coming upon him and his followers.]

thine eyes shall behold it. [It will happen in his lifetime.]

and shall slay them. *And* is employed in the sense of 'or': he will either take them into captivity or slay them (Daath Mikra).

5. *the gains thereof.* The wealth acquired from their labours (Ibn Nachmiash).

6. *and there shalt thou be buried.* [This would be regarded as a severe penalty by one who loved his country. The fact that Jeremiah imposed it upon Pashhur seems to indicate that although he was by his wrong policy encompassing the nation's ruin and exile, he was a patriot at heart.]

prophesied falsely. He had acted as a prophet, speaking in the name of God without justification (cf. xiv. 14ff.).

Thou hast overcome me, and hast
  prevailed;
I am become a laughing-stock all
  the day,
Every one mocketh me.

8 For as often as I speak, I cry out,
I cry: 'Violence and spoil';
Because the word of the LORD is
  made
A reproach unto me, and a deri-
  sion, all the day.

9 And if I say: 'I will not make
  mention of Him,
Nor speak any more in His name,'
Then there is in my heart as it
  were a burning fire
Shut up in my bones,
And I weary myself to hold it in,
But cannot.

10 For I have heard the whispering
  of many,
  Terror on every side:
  'Denounce, and we will denounce
  him';

חֲזַקְתַּנִי וַתּוּכָל
הָיִיתִי לִשְׂחוֹק כָּל־הַיּוֹם
כֻּלֹּה לֹעֵג לִי׃

8 כִּי־מִדֵּי אֲדַבֵּר אֶזְעָק
חָמָס וָשֹׁד אֶקְרָא
כִּי־הָיָה דְבַר־יְהֹוָה לִי
לְחֶרְפָּה וּלְקֶלֶס כָּל־הַיּוֹם׃

9 וְאָמַרְתִּי לֹא־אֶזְכְּרֶנּוּ
וְלֹא־אֲדַבֵּר עוֹד בִּשְׁמוֹ
וְהָיָה בְלִבִּי כְּאֵשׁ בֹּעֶרֶת
עָצֻר בְּעַצְמֹתָי
וְנִלְאֵיתִי כַּלְכֵל
וְלֹא אוּכָל׃

10 כִּי שָׁמַעְתִּי דִּבַּת רַבִּים
מָגוֹר מִסָּבִיב
הַגִּידוּ וְנַגִּידֶנּוּ

v. 8. קמץ בז״ק

**7-18 JEREMIAH'S LAMENT OVER HIS
UNHAPPY LOT**

'Above xviii. 21, we read Jeremiah's first
prayer concerning his own situation.
The following is his second prayer. The
two prayers are very bitter, without
parallel except for Job's speeches
regarding his physical torments. Such
emotion due to personal spiritual suffering is astonishing. Possibly, this
describes what can happen even to the
greatest of prophets, but it is not
typical' (Daath Soferim).

7. *enticed.* To become Thy messenger
(Rashi). [The verb, as applied here to
God, signifies 'induced' and implies
that Jeremiah undertook his mission

under a Divine urge and not to express
his personal feelings.]

8. *violence and spoil.* The burden of his
message presages disaster, and it brings
upon him nought but reproach and
derision (Abarbanel).

9. The true prophet follows the Divine
call in spite of himself. An overpowering realization of his mission compels
him to speak words which he would
rather leave unsaid, but they burn
within him until he has given utterance
to them.

10. *the whispering.* The whispered plotting against him (Rashi).

terror on every side. He feels himself
surrounded by danger (Kimchi).

Even of all my familiar friends,
Them that watch for my halting:
'Peradventure he will be enticed,
and we shall prevail against
him,
And we shall take our revenge
on him.'

11 But the LORD is with me as a
mighty warrior;
Therefore my persecutors shall
stumble, and they shall not
prevail;
They shall be greatly ashamed,
because they have not prospered,
Even with an everlasting confusion which shall never be
forgotten.

12 But, O LORD of hosts, that triest
the righteous,
That seest the reins and the
heart,
Let me see Thy vengeance on
them;
For unto Thee have I revealed
my cause.

13 Sing unto the LORD,
Praise ye the LORD;
For He hath delivered the soul
of the needy
From the hand of evil-doers.

כָּל אֱנוֹשׁ שְׁלֹמִי
שֹׁמְרֵי צַלְעִי
אוּלַי יְפֻתֶּה וְנוּכְלָה לוֹ
וְנִקְחָה נִקְמָתֵנוּ מִמֶּנּוּ:

11 וַיהֹוָה אוֹתִי כְּגִבּוֹר עָרִיץ
עַל־כֵּן רֹדְפַי יִכָּשְׁלוּ
וְלֹא יֻכָלוּ
בֹּשׁוּ מְאֹד כִּי־לֹא הִשְׂכִּילוּ
כְּלִמַּת עוֹלָם לֹא תִשָּׁכֵחַ:

12 וַיהֹוָה צְבָאוֹת בֹּחֵן צַדִּיק
רֹאֶה כְלָיוֹת וָלֵב
אֶרְאֶה נִקְמָתְךָ מֵהֶם
כִּי אֵלֶיךָ גִּלִּיתִי אֶת־רִיבִי:

13 שִׁירוּ לַיהֹוָה
הַלְלוּ אֶת־יְהֹוָה
כִּי הִצִּיל אֶת־נֶפֶשׁ אֶבְיוֹן
מִיַּד מְרֵעִים:

---

denounce, and we will denounce him. They
urge each other to lay false charges
against him so that they may then
denounce him collectively (Ibn Nachmiash).

watch for my halting. They are on the
look out for him to make a false step to
take immediate advantage of it. (Kimchi).

enticed. Into an act or outburst of
words which will occasion a charge
against him (Abarbanel).

our revenge. [For his utterances which
impeded their pro-Egyptian policy.]

11. The gloom of his depression is

pierced by the light which comes from
the awareness that God is on his side.

they have not prospered. i.e. they have
failed in their schemes (Rashi).

12. Almost identical with xi. 20.

13. *sing unto the Lord.* Here he
addresses the pious in Jerusalem
(Kimchi).

for He hath delivered etc. By revealing to
him that they were plotting to poison
him so that he would not join them in
their meal (Kimchi).

the soul of the needy. He is obviously
referring to himself (Metsudath David).

14 Cursed be the day
  Wherein I was born;
  The day wherein **my** mother
    bore me,
  Let it not be blessed.

15 Cursed be the man who brought
    tidings
  To my father, saying:
  'A man-child is born unto thee';
  Making him very glad.

16 And let that man be as the cities
  Which the LORD overthrew, and
    repented not;
  And let him hear a **cry** in the
    morning,
  And an alarm at noontide;

17 Because He slew me not from
    the womb;
  And so my mother would have
    been my grave,
  And her womb always great.

18 Wherefore came I forth out of
    the womb
  To see labour and sorrow,
  That my days should be con-
    sumed in shame?

14 אָרוּר הַיּוֹם
אֲשֶׁר יֻלַּדְתִּי בּוֹ
יוֹם אֲשֶׁר־יְלָדַתְנִי אִמִּי
אַל־יְהִי בָרוּךְ:

15 אָרוּר הָאִישׁ
אֲשֶׁר בִּשַּׂר אֶת־אָבִי לֵאמֹר
יֻלַּד־לְךָ בֵּן זָכָר
שַׂמֵּחַ שִׂמֳּחָהוּ:

16 וְהָיָה הָאִישׁ הַהוּא כֶּעָרִים
אֲשֶׁר־הָפַךְ יְהוָה וְלֹא נִחָם
וְשָׁמַע זְעָקָה בַּבֹּקֶר
וּתְרוּעָה בְּעֵת צָהֳרָיִם:

17 אֲשֶׁר לֹא־מוֹתְתַנִי מֵרָחֶם
וַתְּהִי־לִי אִמִּי קִבְרִי
וְרַחְמָהּ הֲרַת עוֹלָם:

18 לָמָּה זֶּה מֵרֶחֶם יָצָאתִי
לִרְאוֹת עָמָל וְיָגוֹן
וַיִּכְלוּ בְּבֹשֶׁת יָמָי:

14–18. With this passage, cf. Job iii.
2–12. The consciousness of his hard lot
again comes to the fore in his mind.

14. *cursed be the day.* There is no
adequate reason for supposing that
actual personality was ascribed to time,
so that it could be blessed or cursed.
This is nothing more than a vehement
way of regretting that he was ever born
(see Kimchi).

15. *making him very glad.* [The language is probably ironical: the birth of

a son was the occasion of rejoicing to
the father, but how tragic for the son!]

16. *the cities.* viz. Sodom and Gomorrah (Rashi).

and repented not. Once He had decreed
their destruction (Rashi).

a cry. Of distress from persons
attacked (cf. xviii. 22) (Daath Mikra).

an alarm. Of war (cf. iv. 19).

17. *her womb always great.* lit. 'her
womb an everlasting conception.'

21   CHAPTER XXI   כא

1. The word which came unto Jeremiah from the LORD, when king Zedekiah sent unto him Pashhur the son of Malchiah, and Zephaniah the son of Maaseiah the priest, saying: 2. 'Inquire, I pray thee, of the LORD for us; for Nebuchadrezzar king of Babylon maketh war against us; peradventure the LORD will deal with us according to all His wondrous works, that he may go up from us.'

3. Then said Jeremiah unto them: Thus shall ye say to Zedekiah: 4. Thus saith the LORD, the God of Israel:

Behold, I will turn back the weapons of war that are in your

1 הַדָּבָר אֲשֶׁר־הָיָה אֶל־
יִרְמְיָהוּ מֵאֵת יְהוָה בִּשְׁלֹחַ
אֵלָיו הַמֶּלֶךְ צִדְקִיָּהוּ אֶת־
פַּשְׁחוּר בֶּן־מַלְכִּיָּה וְאֶת־
צְפַנְיָה בֶן־מַעֲשֵׂיָה הַכֹּהֵן
2 לֵאמֹר: דְּרָשׁ־נָא בַעֲדֵנוּ
אֶת־יְהוָה כִּי נְבוּכַדְרֶאצַּר
מֶלֶךְ־בָּבֶל נִלְחָם עָלֵינוּ אוּלַי
יַעֲשֶׂה יְהוָה אוֹתָנוּ כְּכָל־
נִפְלְאֹתָיו וְיַעֲלֶה מֵעָלֵינוּ:
3 וַיֹּאמֶר יִרְמְיָהוּ אֲלֵיהֶם כֹּה
4 תֹאמְרֻן אֶל־צִדְקִיָּהוּ: כֹּה־
אָמַר יְהוָה אֱלֹהֵי יִשְׂרָאֵל הִנְנִי
מֵסֵב אֶת־כְּלֵי הַמִּלְחָמָה

Would that I had never left it to enter the world! (Kara).

CHAPTER XXI

THIS chapter marks a new division of the Book. In the previous chapters the period was Jehoiakim's reign; now we pass to the siege of Jerusalem in 588 B.C.E. during the reign of Zedekiah, in which the Kingdom of Judah came to an end.

1–7 ZEDEKIAH'S APPEAL TO JEREMIAH

A similar incident is recorded in xxxvii. 3–10. It is possible that Zedekiah appealed twice to Jeremiah at different periods of the siege.

1. *Pashhur the son of Malchiah.* Not the same man mentioned in xx. 1.

Zephaniah. He is referred to again in xxix. 25. xxxvii. 3. In lii. 24, where the father's name does not appear, it may be a different man who is intended. Daath Mikra, however, identifies him with that Zephaniah, who was the deputy high priest.

2. *inquire.* Not in the sense of seeking information, but to pray on his behalf.

His wondrous works. Such as the one recorded in 2 Kings xix. 35. Neither Zedekiah nor his people had repented of their sins, but they begged Jeremiah to pray, thinking that their future depended upon him and that God would relent even if they did not repent of their sins (Abarbanel).

4. *turn back the weapons.* So that they are an ineffective defence against the besiegers (Kimchi).

hands, wherewith ye fight against the king of Babylon, and against the Chaldeans, that besiege you without the walls, and I will gather them into the midst of this city. 5. And I myself will fight against you with an outstretched hand and with a strong arm, even in anger, and in fury, and in great wrath. 6. And I will smite the inhabitants of this city, both man and beast; they shall die of a great pestilence. 7. And afterward, saith the LORD, I will deliver Zedekiah king of Judah, and his servants, and the people, and such as are left in this city from the pestilence, from the sword, and from the famine, into the hand of Nebuchadrezzar king of Babylon, and into the hand of their enemies, and into the hand of those that seek their life; and he shall smite them with the edge of the sword; he shall not spare them, neither have pity, nor have compassion.

8. And unto this people thou shalt say: Thus saith the LORD: Behold, I

אֲשֶׁר בְּיֶדְכֶם אֲשֶׁר אַתֶּם
נִלְחָמִים בָּם אֶת־מֶלֶךְ בָּבֶל
וְאֶת־הַכַּשְׂדִּים הַצָּרִים
עֲלֵיכֶם מִחוּץ לַחוֹמָה
וְאָסַפְתִּי אוֹתָם אֶל־תּוֹךְ
5 הָעִיר הַזֹּאת: וְנִלְחַמְתִּי אֲנִי
אִתְּכֶם בְּיָד נְטוּיָה וּבִזְרוֹעַ
חֲזָקָה וּבְאַף וּבְחֵמָה וּבְקֶצֶף
6 גָּדוֹל: וְהִכֵּיתִי אֶת־יוֹשְׁבֵי
הָעִיר הַזֹּאת וְאֶת־הָאָדָם
וְאֶת־הַבְּהֵמָה בְּדֶבֶר גָּדוֹל
7 יָמֻתוּ: וְאַחֲרֵי־כֵן נְאֻם־יְהוָה
אֶתֵּן אֶת־צִדְקִיָּהוּ מֶלֶךְ־
יְהוּדָה וְאֶת־עֲבָדָיו וְאֶת־
הָעָם וְאֶת־הַנִּשְׁאָרִים בָּעִיר
הַזֹּאת מִן־הַדֶּבֶר מִן־הַחֶרֶב
וּמִן־הָרָעָב בְּיַד נְבוּכַדְרֶאצַּר
מֶלֶךְ־בָּבֶל וּבְיַד אֹיְבֵיהֶם
וּבְיַד מְבַקְשֵׁי נַפְשָׁם וְהִכָּם
לְפִי־חֶרֶב לֹא־יָחוּס עֲלֵיהֶם
8 וְלֹא יַחְמֹל וְלֹא יְרַחֵם: וְאֶל־
הָעָם הַזֶּה תֹּאמַר כֹּה אָמַר
יְהוָה הִנְנִי נֹתֵן לִפְנֵיכֶם אֶת־

---

them. The Chaldeans (Kimchi). Others understand the word of the weapons (Rashi).

5. *I myself will fight against you.* By weakening your power of resistance

through disease which I will send as a visitation upon you (Kimchi).

7. *with the edge of the sword.* [An idiom meaning 'without quarter.']

set before you the way of life and the way of death. 9. He that abideth in this city shall die by the sword, and by the famine, and by the pestilence; but he that goeth out, and falleth away to the Chaldeans that besiege you, he shall live, and his life shall be unto him for a prey. 10. For I have set My face against this city for evil, and not for good, saith the LORD; it shall be given into the hand of the king of Babylon, and he shall burn it with fire.

11. And unto the house of the king of Judah: Hear ye the word of the LORD; 12. O house of David, thus saith the LORD:

Execute justice in the morning,

הֶרֶךְ הַחַיִּים וְאֶת־דֶּרֶךְ
9 הַמָּוֶת: הַיּשֵׁב בָּעִיר הַזֹּאת
יָמוּת בַּחֶרֶב וּבָרָעָב וּבַדָּבֶר
וְהַיּוֹצֵא וְנָפַל עַל־הַכַּשְׂדִּים
הַצָּרִים עֲלֵיכֶם יְחָיֶה וְהָיְתָה־
10 לּוֹ נַפְשׁוֹ לְשָׁלָל: כִּי־שַׂמְתִּי
פָנַי בָּעִיר הַזֹּאת לְרָעָה וְלֹא
לְטוֹבָה נְאֻם־יְהוָה בְּיַד
מֶלֶךְ־בָּבֶל תִּנָּתֵן וּשְׂרָפָהּ
11 בָּאֵשׁ: וּלְבֵית מֶלֶךְ יְהוּדָה
12 שִׁמְעוּ דְּבַר־יְהוָה: בֵּית דָּוִד
כֹּה אָמַר יְהוָה
דִּינוּ לַבֹּקֶר מִשְׁפָּט

v. 9. וחיה ק'

8-10　ADVICE TO THE PEOPLE

8. *the way of life,* etc. Reminiscent of Deut. xxx. 15ff. which the prophet doubtless had in mind. *Life* is, however, employed in a different sense: not 'a prosperous existence' but 'escape from death' (Daath Mikra).

9. *falleth away.* Like a man who hurriedly snatches up his prey, so will one snatch away his life from those who seek to take it (Rashi). Kara explains: If he saves his life, it will seem to him as though he has found spoil.

11-14　A MESSAGE TO THE KING

The verses seem out of place here, but may contain an eleventh-hour appeal for reformation which still might avert or mitigate the impending doom.

11. *king of Judah.* The addition of 'thou shalt say' is to be understood

(Kimchi). Alternatively, the translation is: 'and as for the house of the king of Judah,' and the words that follow are directly addressed to them (Malbim).

12. *O house of David.* He mentions David, who was conscientious in his performance of justice, as Scripture states, (2 Sam. 8:15) *And David executed justice and righteousness unto all his people.* So should his descendants and his household learn to emulate his good deeds (Kimchi).

in the morning. An expression denoting urgency: be swift to execute justice. Cf. 'The eager are early in the performance of God's precepts' (Talmud). Especially in execution of justice, before you occupy yourselves with eating and drinking and your personal needs, sit in the courthouse to judge anyone who comes to plead before you. Moses, too, sat to judge the people 'from morning until evening' (Kimchi). Alternatively,

And deliver the spoiled out of
the hand of the oppressor,
Lest My fury go forth like fire,
And burn that none can quench
it,
Because of the evil of your
doings.

13 Behold, I am against thee, O in-
habitant of the valley,
And rock of the plain, saith the
LORD;
Ye that say: 'Who shall come
down against us?
Or who shall enter into our
habitations?'

14 And I will punish you according
to the fruit of your doings,
Saith the LORD;
And I will kindle a fire in her
forest,
And it shall devour all that is
round about her.

וְהַצִּ֥ילוּ גָז֖וּל מִיַּ֣ד עוֹשֵׁ֑ק
פֶּן־תֵּצֵ֨א כָאֵ֤שׁ חֲמָתִי֙
וּבָעֲרָה֙ וְאֵ֣ין מְכַבֶּ֔ה
מִפְּנֵ֖י רֹ֥עַ מַעַלְלֵיהֶֽם׃
הִנְנִ֨י אֵלַ֜יִךְ יֹשֶׁ֧בֶת הָעֵ֛מֶק 13
צ֥וּר הַמִּישֹׁ֖ר נְאֻם־יְהֹוָ֑ה
הָאֹֽמְרִים֙ מִי־יֵחַ֣ת עָלֵ֔ינוּ
וּמִ֥י יָב֖וֹא בִּמְעוֹנוֹתֵֽינוּ׃
וּפָקַדְתִּ֧י עֲלֵיכֶ֛ם 14
כִּפְרִ֥י מַעַלְלֵיכֶ֖ם
נְאֻם־יְהֹוָ֑ה
וְהִצַּ֥תִּי אֵ֛שׁ בְּיַעְרָ֖הּ
וְאָכְלָ֥ה כׇּל־סְבִיבֶֽיהָ׃

מעלליכם ק׳ v. 12.

while it is still light, before the troubles
and darkness approach, execute justice,
as Isaiah (i. 27), *Zion shall be redeemed
with justice* (Malbim).

deliver the spoiled. [Solicitude for the
weak is characteristic of Bible teaching.]

from the hand of the oppressor. The word
'oppressor' includes one who receives
his friend's property as a depository, a
loan, or for hire, and refuses to return
it. The spoiler, who takes property by
force, will surely oppress, hence the
expression, *and deliver the spoiled from the
hand of the oppressor,* for the spoiler spoils
and oppresses (Kimchi).

and burn that none can quench it. For
other misdeeds there might be pallia-
tion; for social injustice there is none
(Malbim).

13. The reference is obviously to
Jerusalem, but it is difficult to understand the description since the city is not
situated in a *valley* nor upon a *rock*.

Kimchi explains that as Jerusalem was
on a hill, the surrounding land was
plain. Rashi explains midrashically that
the reference is to the depth of God's
plot against Jerusalem. Daath Mikra
describes Jerusalem's location as being
surrounded on three sides by valleys,
the Ben-Hinnom Valley on the west
and the south and the Kidron Valley on
the east. Also, Jerusalem was veritably
in a valley since the surrounding
mountains were higher than the one
upon which she is situated. These two
factors made it very difficult for the
enemies to gain entrance.

who shall come down against us? [This
would indicate an early stage of the
siege, when the people were still confident in their ability to withstand the
invader.]

14. *the fruit of your doings.* Jerusalem
may be strongly fortified, but the misdeeds of the inhabitants will bring
about their undoing (Malbim).

143

22   CHAPTER XXII   כב

1. Thus said the LORD: Go down to the house of the king of Judah, and speak there this word, 2. and say: Hear the word of the LORD, O king of Judah, that sittest upon the throne of David, thou, and thy servants, and thy people that enter in by these gates. 3. Thus saith the LORD:

Execute ye justice and righteousness, and deliver the spoiled out of the hand of the oppressor; and do no wrong, do no violence, to the stranger, the fatherless, nor the widow, neither shed innocent blood in this place. 4. For if ye do this thing indeed, then shall there enter in by the gates of this house kings

1 כֹּה אָמַ֣ר יְהֹוָ֔ה רֵ֖ד בֵּֽית־מֶ֣לֶךְ יְהוּדָ֑ה וְדִבַּרְתָּ֣ שָׁ֔ם אֶת־
2 הַדָּבָ֖ר הַזֶּֽה: וְאָ֣מַרְתָּ֘ שְׁמַ֣ע דְּבַר־יְהֹוָ֗ה מֶ֚לֶךְ יְהוּדָ֔ה הַיֹּשֵׁ֖ב עַל־כִּסֵּ֣א דָוִ֑ד אַתָּ֣ה וַעֲבָדֶ֗יךָ וְעַמְּךָ֙ הַבָּאִ֔ים
3 בַּשְּׁעָרִ֖ים הָאֵֽלֶּה: כֹּ֣ה ׀ אָמַ֣ר יְהֹוָ֗ה עֲשׂ֤וּ מִשְׁפָּט֙ וּצְדָקָ֔ה וְהַצִּ֥ילוּ גָז֖וּל מִיַּ֣ד עָשׁ֑וֹק וְגֵר֩ יָת֨וֹם וְאַלְמָנָ֤ה אַל־תֹּנוּ֙ אַל־תַּחְמֹ֔סוּ וְדָ֣ם נָקִ֔י אַל־תִּשְׁפְּכ֖וּ
4 בַּמָּק֣וֹם הַזֶּֽה: כִּ֤י אִם־עָשׂ֔וֹ תַּֽעֲשׂ֔וּ אֶת־הַדָּבָ֖ר הַזֶּ֑ה וּבָ֣אוּ בְשַׁעֲרֵ֣י הַבַּ֣יִת הַזֶּ֔ה מְלָכִים֩

CHAPTER XXII

THIS chapter and the following to verse 8 contain a series of judgments upon several kings of Judah, beginning with the reigning monarch. The separate sections were presumably uttered at different periods, and then brought together to form one consecutive passage.

1–9 EXHORTATION TO THE KING OF JUDAH

1. *go down.* From the Temple (Kimchi). The king's palace lay to the south of the Temple and was on lower ground (cf. xxxvi. 10ff.) (Daath Mikra).

2. Cf. xvii. 20.

3. Cf. xxi. 12.

do no wrong. Even by word of mouth (the Jewish commentators). The defenceless position of the classes mentioned demands special consideration.

do no violence. The prophet is referring to unjust exactions from the people to meet the cost of building luxurious palaces (verses 13ff.).

the stranger. [Whereas the nations of antiquity generally looked with suspicion and hostility upon the stranger, the Bible is particularly solicitous for his rights and feelings.]

neither shed innocent blood. For an instance of Jehoiakim's guilt in this respect, cf. xxvi. 20ff.

4. *then shall there enter.* Based substantially on xvii. 25.

sitting upon the throne of David, riding in chariots and on horses, he, and his servants, and his people. 5. But if ye will not hear these words, I swear by Myself, saith the LORD, that this house shall become a desolation.   6. For thus saith the LORD concerning the house of the king of Judah:

Thou art Gilead unto Me,
The head of Lebanon;
Yet surely I will make thee a wilderness,
Cities which are not inhabited.

7 And I will prepare destroyers against thee,
Every one with his weapons;
And they shall cut down thy choice cedars,
And cast them into the fire.

8. And many nations shall pass by this city, and they shall say every man to his neighbour: 'Wherefore hath the LORD done thus unto this

יֹשְׁבִ֥ים לְדָוִ֖ד עַל־כִּסְא֑וֹ
רֹכְבִים֙ בָּרֶ֣כֶב וּבַסּוּסִ֔ים ה֖וּא
5 וַעֲבָדָ֥ו וְעַמּֽוֹ׃ וְאִם֙ לֹ֣א תִשְׁמְע֔וּ
אֶת־הַדְּבָרִ֖ים הָאֵ֑לֶּה בִּ֤י
נִשְׁבַּ֙עְתִּי֙ נְאֻם־יְהֹוָ֔ה כִּֽי־
לְחָרְבָּ֥ה יִֽהְיֶ֖ה הַבַּ֥יִת הַזֶּֽה׃
6 כִּי־כֹ֣ה ׀ אָמַ֣ר יְהֹוָ֗ה עַל־בֵּית֙
מֶ֣לֶךְ יְהוּדָ֔ה
גִּלְעָ֥ד אַתָּ֛ה לִ֖י רֹ֣אשׁ הַלְּבָנ֑וֹן
אִם־לֹ֤א אֲשִֽׁיתְךָ֙ מִדְבָּ֔ר
עָרִ֖ים לֹ֥א נוֹשָֽׁבָה׃
7 וְקִדַּשְׁתִּ֧י עָלֶ֛יךָ מַשְׁחִתִ֖ים
אִ֣ישׁ וְכֵלָ֑יו
וְכָֽרְתוּ֙ מִבְחַ֣ר אֲרָזֶ֔יךָ
וְהִפִּ֖ילוּ עַל־הָאֵֽשׁ׃
8 וְעָֽבְרוּ֙ גּוֹיִ֣ם רַבִּ֔ים עַ֖ל הָעִ֣יר
הַזֹּ֑את וְאָֽמְרוּ֙ אִ֣ישׁ אֶל־רֵעֵ֔הוּ
עַל־מֶ֗ה עָשָׂ֤ה יְהֹוָה֙ כָּ֔כָה

v. 4. ועבדיו ק׳   v. 6. נושבו ק׳

---

upon the throne of David. lit. 'for (or, of) David upon his throne.' This wording, which differs from that of xvii. 25, emphasizes that David's descendants will reign; the same is implied in *he and his servants.*

5. *I swear by Myself.* A most solemn form of oath which occurs in several places (cf. xlix. 13; Gen. xxii. 16; Isa. xlv. 23). A similar expression occurs in li. 14 and Amos vi. 8.

6. *thou art Gilead . . . Lebanon.* Speci-

fied as well-wooded regions. As these might be denuded of trees and destroyed, so will God bring destruction upon the kingdom if iniquity continues therein (Daath Mikra).

7. *prepare.* lit. 'sanctify'; see on vi. 4.

choice cedars. An allusion to the princes and leaders, continuing the figure of Gilead and Lebanon (Metsudath David).

8f. A reminiscence of Deut. xxix. 23ff. and 1 Kings ix. 8f.

great city?' 9. Then they shall answer: 'Because they forsook the covenant of the LORD their God, and worshipped other gods, and served them.'

10 Weep ye not for the dead,
Neither bemoan him;
But weep sore for him that goeth away,
For he shall return no more,
Nor see his native country.

11. For thus saith the LORD touching Shallum the son of Josiah, king of Judah, who reigned instead of Josiah his father, and who went forth out of this place: He shall not return thither any more; 12. but in the place whither they have led him captive, there shall he die, and he shall see this land no more.

9 לָעִיר הַגְּדוֹלָה הַזֹּאת: וְאָמְרוּ
עַל אֲשֶׁר עָזְבוּ אֶת־בְּרִית
יְהוָֹה אֱלֹהֵיהֶם וַיִּשְׁתַּחֲווּ
לֵאלֹהִים אֲחֵרִים וַיַּעַבְדוּם:
10 אַל־תִּבְכּוּ לְמֵת
וְאַל־תָּנֻדוּ לוֹ
בְּכוּ בָכוֹ לַהֹלֵךְ
כִּי לֹא יָשׁוּב עוֹד
וְרָאָה אֶת־אֶרֶץ מוֹלַדְתּוֹ:
11 כִּי־כֹה אָמַר־יְהוָֹה אֶל־
שַׁלֻּם בֶּן־יֹאשִׁיָּהוּ מֶלֶךְ יְהוּדָה
הַמֹּלֵךְ תַּחַת יֹאשִׁיָּהוּ אָבִיו
אֲשֶׁר יָצָא מִן־הַמָּקוֹם הַזֶּה
12 לֹא־יָשׁוּב שָׁם עוֹד: כִּי
בִּמְקוֹם אֲשֶׁר־הִגְלוּ אֹתוֹ שָׁם
יָמוּת וְאֶת־הָאָרֶץ הַזֹּאת לֹא־
יִרְאֶה עוֹד:

9. *they forsook . . . other gods.* [Forsaking the covenant of God was not only a question of change in ritual, but as is shown by verse 3 a disregard of social justice and righteousness. The violation of right principles of conduct, not only the practice of revolting rites and the negation of monotheism, made idolatry the target of the fiercest denunciations by the prophets.]

10–12   THE FATE OF SHALLUM

This king succeeded his father Josiah on the throne. His reign was cut short after three months, when Pharaoh-neco took him prisoner and led him captive to Egypt where he died (2 Kings xxiii. 30ff.).

10. *the dead.* viz. Josiah, who was slain in battle at Megiddo when fighting against Pharaoh-neco. His fate was not as unhappy as his son's; reserve your lamentations for the latter (Daath Mikra).

goeth away. To Egypt as a prisoner (Daath Mikra).

he shall return no more, nor see. Better, in accordance with Hebrew idiom, 'he shall never again see.'

11. *Shallum.* From 1 Chron. iii. 15 we see that he is identical with Jehoahaz of 2 Kings (Ibn Ezra). Possibly this was his name before his accession. Rashi, following the Talmud, identifies him with

13 Woe unto him that buildeth his
   house by unrighteousness,
   And his chambers by injustice;
   That useth his neighbour's service without wages,
   And giveth him not his hire;
14 That saith: 'I will build me a
   wide house
   And spacious chambers,'
   And cutteth him out windows,
   And it is ceiled with cedar, and
   painted with vermilion.
15 Shalt thou reign, because thou
   strivest to excel in cedar?
   Did not thy father eat and drink,
   and do justice and righteousness?
   Then it was well with him.
16 He judged the cause of the poor
   and needy;
   Then it was well.

הוֹי בֹּנֶה בֵיתוֹ בְּלֹא־צֶדֶק 13
וַעֲלִיּוֹתָיו בְּלֹא מִשְׁפָּט
בְּרֵעֵהוּ יַעֲבֹד חִנָּם
וּפֹעֲלוֹ לֹא יִתֶּן־לוֹ:
הָאֹמֵר אֶבְנֶה־לִּי בֵּית מִדּוֹת 14
וַעֲלִיּוֹת מְרֻוָּחִים
וְקָרַע לוֹ חַלּוֹנָי
וְסָפוּן בָּאָרֶז וּמָשׁוֹחַ בַּשָּׁשַׁר:
הֲתִמְלֹךְ כִּי אַתָּה 15
מְתַחֲרֶה בָאָרֶז
אָבִיךָ הֲלוֹא אָכַל וְשָׁתָה
וְעָשָׂה מִשְׁפָּט וּצְדָקָה
אָז טוֹב לוֹ:
הֵן דִּין־עָנִי וְאֶבְיוֹן 16
אָז טוֹב

v. 14. קמץ בז"ק

king Zedekiah. Kimchi supposes him to be the same as Jehoiachin, understanding *son* of Josiah as 'grandson,' a usage not uncommon in the Bible. He is then referred to as *him that goeth away* of the preceding verse and *the dead* is Jehoiakim.

13-19 DENUNCIATION OF JEHOIAKIM

13. *by unrighteousness.* By methods contrary to the teachings of the Torah.

chambers. lit. 'upper chambers.' This may also be rendered, 'airy upper chambers.' These chambers were made for use in the hot summer season. As in verse 14, windows were made to allow the breeze to cool it (Kimchi).

without wages. [Forced labour was common amongst Oriental kings. The Hebrew prophets denounced it as an injustice; not even the king had a right to demand unpaid services from his subjects.]

14. *windows.* The form of the plural is unusual in the Hebrew, but is found in a number of places (Kimchi).

vermilion. The word occurs again only in Ezek. xxiii. 14.

15. *shalt thou reign . . . cedar?* [Should a king think only of surrounding himself with luxury!]

eat and drink, and do justice. Josiah enjoyed the material comforts of his regal status, but he also understood and performed the duties of kingship

Is not this to know Me? saith the
LORD.

17 But thine eyes and thy heart
Are not but for thy covetousness,
And for shedding innocent blood,
And for oppression, and for
violence, to do it.

18. Therefore thus saith the LORD
concerning Jehoiakim the son of
Josiah, king of Judah:
They shall not lament for him:
'Ah my brother!' or: 'Ah sister!'
They shall not lament for him:
'Ah lord!' or: 'Ah his glory!'

19 He shall be buried with the
burial of an ass,
Drawn and cast forth beyond the
gates of Jerusalem.

הֲלוֹא־הִיא הַדַּעַת אֹתִי
נְאֻם־יְהֹוָה׃

17 כִּי אֵין עֵינֶיךָ וְלִבְּךָ
כִּי אִם־עַל־בִּצְעֶךָ
וְעַל דַּם־הַנָּקִי לִשְׁפּוֹךְ
וְעַל־הָעֹשֶׁק וְעַל־הַמְּרוּצָה
לַעֲשׂוֹת׃

18 לָכֵן כֹּה־אָמַר יְהֹוָה
אֶל־יְהוֹיָקִים בֶּן־יֹאשִׁיָּהוּ
מֶלֶךְ יְהוּדָה
לֹא־יִסְפְּדוּ לוֹ
הוֹי אָחִי וְהוֹי אָחוֹת
לֹא־יִסְפְּדוּ לוֹ
הוֹי אָדוֹן וְהוֹי הֹדֹה׃

19 קְבוּרַת חֲמוֹר יִקָּבֵר
סָחוֹב וְהַשְׁלֵךְ
מֵהָלְאָה לְשַׁעֲרֵי יְרוּשָׁלָ͏ִם׃

(Kimchi). Or, possibly, the meaning is
that he was satisfied with plain living,
with ordinary food and drink, and spent
his energies in dispensing justice
(Rashi).

16. is not this to know Me? To execute
justice and righteousness, to protect the
poor and the oppressed — that is to
know God. The practical aim of religion
could not be defined more succinctly
(see Metsudath David).

**17. thy covetousness, and for shedding inno-
cent blood.** One led to the other;

innocent people were condemned to
death so that the king might confiscate
their estates (Malbim).

18. 'Ah my brother!' or: 'Ah sister!' The
usual form of lamentation (cf. 1 Kings
xiii. 30). 'Ah sister!' which is not applica-
ble here, is added for the sake of parallelism (see Kimchi).

'Ah lord!' or: 'Ah his glory!' The lament
of non-relatives over the death of a king
(Kimchi).

19. the burial of an ass. i.e. without
burial, the carcass of an animal being

20 Go up to Lebanon, and cry,
And lift up thy voice in Bashan;
And cry from Abarim,
For all thy lovers are destroyed.

21 I spoke unto thee in thy prosperity,
But thou saidst: 'I will not hear.'
This hath been thy manner from thy youth,
That thou hearkenedst not to My voice.

22 The wind shall feed upon all thy shepherds,
And thy lovers shall go into captivity;
Surely then shalt thou be ashamed and confounded
For all thy wickedness.

23 O inhabitant of Lebanon,
That art nestled in the cedars,

עֲלִי הַלְּבָנוֹן וּצְעָקִי 20
וּבַבָּשָׁן תְּנִי קוֹלֵךְ
וְצַעֲקִי מֵעֲבָרִים
כִּי נִשְׁבְּרוּ כָּל־מְאַהֲבָיִךְ:
דִּבַּרְתִּי אֵלַיִךְ בְּשַׁלְוֺתַיִךְ 21
אָמַרְתְּ לֹא אֶשְׁמָע
זֶה דַרְכֵּךְ מִנְּעוּרַיִךְ
כִּי לֹא־שָׁמַעַתְּ בְּקוֹלִי:
כָּל־רֹעַיִךְ תִּרְעֶה־רוּחַ 22
וּמְאַהֲבַיִךְ בַּשְּׁבִי יֵלֵכוּ
כִּי אָז תֵּבֹשִׁי וְנִכְלַמְתְּ
מִכֹּל רָעָתֵךְ:
יֹשַׁבְתְּ בַּלְּבָנוֹן 23
מְקֻנַּנְתְּ בָּאֲרָזִים

v. 20. ‏כצ"ל‏ v. 23. ‏ישבת ק'‏ v. 23. ‏מקננת ק'‏

left to rot. This prophecy was fulfilled when Jehoiakim died while being led in captivity by the Chaldeans. They did not allow his body to be buried (Kimchi).

20-30 THE FATE OF JEHOIACHIN

The prophet now, as an introduction to his lamentation over the next king Jehoiachin (Coniah), bewails the consequences of the policy of that king's father Jehoiakim. The people, depicted as a woman, is called upon to ascend the heights and to shout to their allies to come and assist them in the time of their catastrophe. The prophet selects the high mountains surrounding the land, from which one's voice carries. They are to call to their allies, only to find that they too are broken and are unable to help (Kimchi).

20. *go up.* Spoken to the people collectively; hence the use of the feminine in the Hebrew (Kimchi).

Abarim. From there, on mount Nebo, Moses viewed the Promised Land which he was not permitted to enter (Num. xxvii. 12; Deut. xxxii. 49).

21. *thy prosperity.* The Hebrew is plural: 'thy times of prosperity' (Kimchi).

22. *the wind . . . shepherds.* They shall quickly be broken as though they were devoured by the wind. This refers to the kings of Assyria and Egypt, who were to Judah as leaders and shepherds (Kimchi).

thy lovers. As in verse 20. They, too, will be driven into captivity; where, then, is thy hope?

23. *that art nestled in the cedars.* Like a bird in its nest among the cedars upon

149

How gracious shalt thou be when
    pangs come upon thee,
    The pain as of a woman in travail!
24. As I live, saith the LORD, though
Coniah the son of Jehoiakim king of
Judah were the signet upon My
right hand, yet would I pluck thee
thence; 25. and I will give thee into
the hand of them that seek thy life,
and into the hand of them of whom
thou art afraid, even into the hand of
Nebuchadrezzar king of Babylon,
and into the hand of the Chaldeans.
26. And I will cast thee out, and thy
mother that bore thee, into another
country, where ye were not born;
and there shall ye die. 27. But to
the land whereunto they long to
return, thither shall they not return.
28 Is this man Coniah a despised,
    broken image?

מַה־נֵּחַנְתְּ בְּבֹא־לָךְ חֲבָלִים
חִיל כַּיּוֹלֵדָה:

24 חַי־אָנִי נְאֻם־יְהוָה כִּי אִם־
יִהְיֶה כָּנְיָהוּ בֶן־יְהוֹיָקִים מֶלֶךְ
יְהוּדָה חוֹתָם עַל־יַד יְמִינִי

25 כִּי מִשָּׁם אֶתְּקֶנְךָּ: וּנְתַתִּיךְ
בְּיַד מְבַקְשֵׁי נַפְשֶׁךָ וּבְיַד
אֲשֶׁר־אַתָּה יָגוֹר מִפְּנֵיהֶם
וּבְיַד נְבוּכַדְרֶאצַּר מֶלֶךְ־
בָּבֶל וּבְיַד הַכַּשְׂדִּים:

26 וְהֵטַלְתִּי אֹתְךָ וְאֶת־אִמְּךָ
אֲשֶׁר יְלָדַתְךָ עַל הָאָרֶץ
אַחֶרֶת אֲשֶׁר לֹא־יֻלַּדְתֶּם שָׁם

27 וְשָׁם תָּמוּתוּ: וְעַל־הָאָרֶץ
אֲשֶׁר הֵם מְנַשְּׂאִים אֶת־נַפְשָׁם
לָשׁוּב שָׁם שָׁמָּה לֹא יָשׁוּבוּ:

28 הַעֶצֶב נִבְזֶה נָפוּץ
הָאִישׁ הַזֶּה כָּנְיָהוּ

the heights of Lebanon, secure from
attack, so had Judah thought herself
safe from invasion (Malbim).

how gracious shalt thou be, etc. Spoken
ironically: what grace and favour dost
thou think to find when the pangs come
upon thee, the horrors of invasion? The
LXX and Peshitta render: 'how wilt
thou groan!' as though the verb were
connected with the root *anach.* [The text
is perhaps to be translated, 'how art
thou to be pitied!']

24. *Coniah.* He is also named Jeconiah
(xxiv. 1, etc.) and Jehoiachin (lii. 31,
etc.).

26. *and thy mother that bore thee.* See on
xiii. 18.

there shall ye die. Cf. lii. 31ff.; 2 Kings
xxv. 27ff.

27. *whereunto they long,* etc. [This and
the following verses, which assume the
exile to have begun (whereas verses
24–26 speak of it as yet to take place),
are uttered in prophetic anticipation.]

28. *cast out.* The prophetic perfect.
The sympathetic tone of this verse
shows that, although Jeremiah was
constrained to utter predictions of a

Is he a vessel wherein is no
pleasure?
Wherefore are they cast out, he
and his seed,
And are cast into the land which
they know not?

29 O land, land, land,
Hear the word of the LORD.

30 Thus saith the LORD:
Write ye this man childless,
A man that shall not prosper in
his days;
For no man of his seed shall
prosper,
Sitting upon the throne of David,
And ruling any more in Judah.

אִם־כְּלִי אֵין חֵפֶץ בּוֹ
מַדּוּעַ הוּטְלוּ הוּא וְזַרְעוֹ
וְהֻשְׁלְכוּ עַל־הָאָרֶץ
אֲשֶׁר לֹא־יָדָעוּ:
29 אֶרֶץ אֶרֶץ אָרֶץ
שִׁמְעִי דְּבַר־יְהֹוָה:
30 כֹּה ׀ אָמַר יְהֹוָה
כִּתְבוּ אֶת־הָאִישׁ הַזֶּה עֲרִירִי
גֶּבֶר לֹא־יִצְלַח בְּיָמָיו
כִּי לֹא יִצְלַח מִזַּרְעוֹ
אִישׁ יֹשֵׁב עַל־כִּסֵּא דָוִד
וּמֹשֵׁל עוֹד בִּיהוּדָה:

23	CHAPTER XXIII	כג

1 Woe unto the shepherds that
destroy and scatter

1 הוֹי רֹעִים מְאַבְּדִים וּמְפִצִים

---

dark future, he was not actuated by
personal animosity (see Daath Soferim).

29. *O land, land, land.* The threefold
repetition denotes extreme affection (cf.
vii. 4).

30. *childless.* 1 Chron. iii. 17 records
that he did have children. Since none
succeeded him on the throne (although
Zerubbabel, his grandson, was one of
the leaders of the Return), with respect
to the monarchy he is regarded as childless. This is implied in the phrase, *for no
man of his seed,* etc. (Kara).

CHAPTER XXIII

1–8   PROMISE OF AN IDEAL RULER

AFTER the denunciation of the last kings
of Judah, an assurance is given that a
leader will arise after God's heart. He
will rule over a people restored to their
land.

1. *the shepherds.* The national rulers, as
in ii. 8, x. 21, etc. (Rashi, Kimchi).

that destroy and scatter. Under their evil
leadership the people abandoned the

The sheep of My pasture! saith the LORD.

2. Therefore thus saith the LORD, the God of Israel, against the shepherds that feed My people: Ye have scattered My flock, and driven them away, and have not taken care of them; behold, I will visit upon you the evil of your doings, saith the LORD. 3. And I will gather the remnant of My flock out of all the countries whither I have driven them, and will bring them back to their folds; and they shall be fruitful and multiply. 4. And I will set up shepherds over them, who shall feed them; and they shall fear no more, nor be dismayed, neither shall any be lacking, saith the LORD.

5 Behold, the days come, saith the LORD,

אֶת־צֹאן מַרְעִיתִי
נְאֻם־יְהֹוָה:

2 לָכֵן כֹּה־אָמַר יְהֹוָה אֱלֹהֵי
יִשְׂרָאֵל עַל־הָרֹעִים הָרֹעִים
אֶת־עַמִּי אַתֶּם הֲפִצֹתֶם אֶת־
צֹאנִי וַתַּדִּחוּם וְלֹא פְקַדְתֶּם
אֹתָם הִנְנִי פֹקֵד עֲלֵיכֶם אֶת־
רֹעַ מַעַלְלֵיכֶם נְאֻם־יְהֹוָה:

3 וַאֲנִי אֲקַבֵּץ אֶת־שְׁאֵרִית צֹאנִי
מִכֹּל הָאֲרָצוֹת אֲשֶׁר־הִדַּחְתִּי
אֹתָם שָׁם וַהֲשִׁבֹתִי אֶתְהֶן
עַל־נְוֵהֶן וּפָרוּ וְרָבוּ:

4 וַהֲקִמֹתִי עֲלֵיהֶם רֹעִים וְרָעוּם
וְלֹא־יִירְאוּ עוֹד וְלֹא־יֵחַתּוּ
וְלֹא יִפָּקֵדוּ נְאֻם־יְהֹוָה:

5 הִנֵּה יָמִים בָּאִים נְאֻם־יְהֹוָה

ways of righteousness and incurred exile. It is noteworthy that in the final analysis the misdeeds of the people are attributed to their leaders (Kimchi).

the sheep. [Such a simile could only have arisen among a people with a love for animals. At the same time the phrase *the sheep of My pasture* indicates God's solicitude for His people.]

2. *I will visit.* [The Hebrew verb, *pakad,* is the same as that translated *taken care* and is intentionally used: as the shepherds failed to look after their flock, God will not be concerned with their welfare.]

3. *the remnant.* A warning that the majority would be lost in captivity (Metsudath David).

4. *they shall fear no more.* The righteous ruler will ensure them tranquility and safety (Daath Mikra).

neither shall any be lacking. [He will also watch over them that none be lost, unlike sheep carried off by beasts of prey through their shepherd's neglect.]

5–8. In contrast to the unhappy past, a Messianic prophecy of hope for the future is spoken.

5. *behold, the days come.* A favourite

That I will raise unto David a
    righteous shoot,
And he shall reign as king and
    prosper,
And shall execute justice and
    righteousness in the land.
6 In his days Judah shall be saved,
    And Israel shall dwell safely;
And this is his name whereby he
    shall be called,
The LORD is our righteousness.

7. Therefore, behold, the days come,
saith the LORD, that they shall no
more say: 'As the LORD liveth, that
brought up the children of Israel out
of the land of Egypt'; 8. but: 'As the
LORD liveth, that brought up and
that led the seed of the house of
Israel out of the north country, and
from all the countries whither I had
driven them'; and they shall dwell
in their own land.

וַהֲקִמֹתִי לְדָוִד צֶמַח צַדִּיק
וּמָלַךְ מֶלֶךְ וְהִשְׂכִּיל
וְעָשָׂה מִשְׁפָּט וּצְדָקָה בָּאָרֶץ:
6 בְּיָמָיו תִּוָּשַׁע יְהוּדָה
וְיִשְׂרָאֵל יִשְׁכֹּן לָבֶטַח
וְזֶה־שְּׁמוֹ אֲשֶׁר־יִקְרְאוֹ
יְהוָה ׀ צִדְקֵנוּ:
7 לָכֵן הִנֵּה־יָמִים בָּאִים נְאֻם־
יְהוָה וְלֹא־יֹאמְרוּ עוֹד חַי־
יְהוָה אֲשֶׁר הֶעֱלָה אֶת־בְּנֵי
8 יִשְׂרָאֵל מֵאֶרֶץ מִצְרָיִם: כִּי
אִם־חַי־יְהוָה אֲשֶׁר הֶעֱלָה
וַאֲשֶׁר הֵבִיא אֶת־זֶרַע בֵּית
יִשְׂרָאֵל מֵאֶרֶץ צָפוֹנָה וּמִכֹּל
הָאֲרָצוֹת אֲשֶׁר הִדַּחְתִּים שָׁם
וְיָשְׁבוּ עַל־אַדְמָתָם:

v. 5. מלעיל

introduction by Jeremiah to a message
of reassurance; it occurs sixteen times in
the Book.

prosper. Or, as Abarbanel, 'deal wise-
ly'; he will carry on a policy which is
prudent and will bring happiness to his
land. It is the same verb as that found in
Isa. lii. 13 (see Abarbanel).

shall execute justice and righteousness.
This sums up the function of an ideal
ruler (cf. 2 Sam. viii. 15, of David).

6. *Israel shall dwell safely.* The exiles of
the Northern Kingdom will also be
redeemed and return to their land. A
reunion of the nation was hoped for by
the prophets (cf. Ezek. xxxvii. 19) (Abarbanel, Malbim).

the LORD *is our righteousness.* [Righ-
teousness will distinguish both ruler
and people, the source of that righteousness being God. It has been maintained that the name was suggested by
that of the last reigning king, Zedekiah
('the Lord is righteous'). In view of his
character (*he did that which was evil in the
sight of the* LORD, 2 Kings xxiv. 19), this is
improbable. If Jeremiah had him in
mind, it was only to mark a contrast
with him.] Rashi and Metsudath David
interpret the name, 'the Lord will justify
(i.e. vindicate) us'; and Kimchi understands the meaning to be, 'the righteousness of the Lord is with us.'

7f. The verses are substantially repeated
from xvi. 14f. Since the future redemp-

9 Concerning the prophets.

My heart within me is broken,

All my bones shake;

I am like a drunken man,

And like a man whom wine hath overcome;

Because of the LORD,

And because of His holy words.

10 For the land is full of adulterers;

For because of swearing the land mourneth,

The pastures of the wilderness are dried up;

And their course is evil,

And their force is not right.

11 For both prophet and priest are ungodly;

9 לַנְּבִאִים

נִשְׁבַּר לִבִּי בְּקִרְבִּי

רָחֲפוּ כָּל־עַצְמוֹתַי

הָיִיתִי כְּאִישׁ שִׁכּוֹר

וּכְגֶבֶר עֲבָרוֹ יָיִן

מִפְּנֵי יְהֹוָה

וּמִפְּנֵי דִּבְרֵי קָדְשׁוֹ:

10 כִּי מְנָאֲפִים מָלְאָה הָאָרֶץ

כִּי־מִפְּנֵי אָלָה אָבְלָה הָאָרֶץ

יָבְשׁוּ נְאוֹת מִדְבָּר

וַתְּהִי מְרוּצָתָם רָעָה

וּגְבוּרָתָם לֹא־כֵן:

11 כִּי־גַם־נָבִיא גַם־כֹּהֵן חָנֵפוּ

---

tion will be so much greater than the redemption from Egyptian bondage, the latter will not be given the importance it was given previously, but will be secondary to the later redemption when mentioned in oaths (Metsudath David).

9–40 DENUNCIATION OF THE PROPHETS

9. *like a drunken man.* Jeremiah is overcome by God's words concerning the false prophets. The pathos of the verse is most moving. Jeremiah, himself a prophet and charged with God's message, must have felt deeply the offence of the prophets who abused their calling and confirmed the people in their evil ways (see Metsudath David).

because of the LORD, *and because of His holy words.* God and His words are alike profaned by the false prophets. For the vices that prevailed in the land they must bear responsibility, because they

condoned, if not actually encouraged them (Kimchi).

10. *adulterers.* Probably to be interpreted literally and not figuratively of idol-worshippers (Ibn Nachmiash).

swearing. Using the Divine name in false oaths (Targum, Rashi, Kimchi).

the pastures of the wilderness. See on ix. 9.

and their course is evil. They run only to do evil, never to perform a precept or to do God's service (Rashi, Kara, Ibn Nachmiash).

their force is not right. They utilize their power for wrongful purposes (Kimchi).

11. *both prophet and priest.* From whom everyone learns (Rashi). Jonathan substitutes 'scribe' for 'prophet.' He sees *nabi* as 'speaker,' either one who speaks with divine inspiration or one who

Yea, in My house have I found their wickedness,
Saith the LORD.

12 Wherefore their way shall be unto them as slippery places in the darkness,
They shall be thrust, and fall therein;
For I will bring evil upon them,
Even the year of their visitation,
Saith the LORD.

13 And I have seen unseemliness in the prophets of Samaria:
They prophesied by Baal,
And caused My people Israel to err.

14 But in the prophets of Jerusalem I have seen a horrible thing:
They commit adultery, and walk in lies,
And they strengthen the hands of evil-doers,
That none doth return from his wickedness;
They are all of them become unto Me as Sodom,
And the inhabitants thereof as Gomorrah.

גַּם־בְּבֵיתִי מָצָאתִי רָעָתָם
נְאֻם־יְהֹוָה׃

12 לָכֵן יִהְיֶה דַרְכָּם לָהֶם
כַּחֲלַקְלַקּוֹת בָּאֲפֵלָה
יִדַּחוּ וְנָפְלוּ בָהּ
כִּי־אָבִיא עֲלֵיהֶם רָעָה
שְׁנַת פְּקֻדָּתָם
נְאֻם־יְהֹוָה׃

13 וּבִנְבִיאֵי שֹׁמְרוֹן רָאִיתִי תִפְלָה
הִנַּבְּאוּ בַבַּעַל
וַיַּתְעוּ אֶת־עַמִּי אֶת־יִשְׂרָאֵל׃

14 וּבִנְבִאֵי יְרוּשָׁלַ͏ִם
רָאִיתִי שַׁעֲרוּרָה
נָאוֹף וְהָלֹךְ בַּשֶּׁקֶר
וְחִזְּקוּ יְדֵי מְרֵעִים
לְבִלְתִּי־שָׁבוּ אִישׁ מֵרָעָתוֹ
הָיוּ־לִי כֻלָּם כִּסְדֹם
וְיֹשְׁבֶיהָ כַּעֲמֹרָה׃

v. 12. מלעיל

speaks lies like the false prophets; also the teacher of the people who speaks to them to admonish them (Kimchi).

priest. The Levitical priests who served in the Temple (Kimchi). Metsudath David interprets this as the priests of Baal.

12. *slippery places in the darkness.* The imagery is comparable with that of xiii. 16, and cf. Ps. xxxv. 6. Hitherto the corrupt prophets had pursued their evil course with assurance; but now the way

will be slippery and dark for them so that they stumble and fall.

13f. The prophets of Samaria had been guilty of *unseemliness* in that they openly practised idolatry. Those in Jerusalem, however, committed *a horrible thing* by addiction to adultery and falsehood, even encouraging the wrong-doers by their bad example.

14. *all of them.* The inhabitants of Judah (Metsudath David).

155

15. Therefore thus saith the LORD of hosts concerning the prophets:
Behold, I will feed them with wormwood,
And make them drink the water of gall;
For from the prophets of Jerusalem
Is ungodliness gone forth into all the land.

16 Thus saith the LORD of hosts:
Hearken not unto the words of the prophets that prophesy unto you,
They lead you unto vanity;
They speak a vision of their own heart,
And not out of the mouth of the LORD.

17 They say continually unto them that despise Me:
'The LORD hath said: Ye shall have peace';
And unto every one that walketh in the stubbornness of his own heart they say:
'No evil shall come upon you';

18 For who hath stood in the council of the LORD,
That he should perceive and hear His word?

15 לָכֵן כֹּה־אָמַר יְהֹוָה צְבָאוֹת
עַל־הַנְּבִאִים
הִנְנִי מַאֲכִיל אוֹתָם לַעֲנָה
וְהִשְׁקִתִים מֵי־רֹאשׁ
כִּי מֵאֵת נְבִיאֵי יְרוּשָׁלַם
יָצְאָה חֲנֻפָּה לְכָל־הָאָרֶץ׃

16 כֹּה־אָמַר יְהֹוָה צְבָאוֹת
אַל־תִּשְׁמְעוּ עַל־דִּבְרֵי
הַנְּבִאִים הַנִּבְּאִים לָכֶם
מַהְבִּלִים הֵמָּה אֶתְכֶם
חֲזוֹן לִבָּם יְדַבֵּרוּ
לֹא מִפִּי יְהֹוָה׃

17 אֹמְרִים אָמוֹר לִמְנַאֲצַי
דִּבֶּר יְהֹוָה שָׁלוֹם יִהְיֶה לָכֶם
וְכֹל הֹלֵךְ בִּשְׁרִרוּת לִבּוֹ אָמְרוּ
לֹא־תָבוֹא עֲלֵיכֶם רָעָה׃

18 כִּי מִי עָמַד בְּסוֹד יְהֹוָה
וְיֵרֶא וְיִשְׁמַע אֶת־דְּבָרוֹ׃

15. The first half of the verse is almost identical with ix. 14. There it is directed against the people, here against the priests and prophets.

ungodliness. Condonation of the evils of the people (Kimchi).

16. *unto vanity.* They buoy you up with false prophecies of peace. Or, it may be a denunciation of the general tenor of their teaching which was empty of spiritual content (see Kimchi).

17. *the* LORD *hath said.* The exact Hebrew expression does not elsewhere introduce the words of the Lord. It

therefore seems to be used here by Jeremiah as characteristic of the false prophets (Daath Mikra).

no evil shall come upon you. Cf. iv. 10, vi. 14, xiv. 13. The desire to hear such comforting prophecies was very strong; the people wanted them (cf. Isa. xxx. 10) and the false prophets supplied the popular demand to allay their fears instilled into them by the true prophets (Daath Mikra).

18. *for who hath stood ... word?* A rhetorical question: surely such corrupt men as these cannot claim to enjoy God's confidences! (Rashi).

Who hath attended to His word,
and heard it?

19 Behold, a storm of the LORD is
gone forth in fury,
Yea, a whirling storm;
It shall whirl upon the head of
the wicked.

20 The anger of the LORD shall not
return,
Until He have executed, and till
He have performed the purposes of His heart;
In the end of days ye shall consider it perfectly.

21 I have not sent these prophets,
yet they ran;
I have not spoken to them, yet
they prophesied.

22 But if they have stood in My
council,
Then let them cause My people
to hear My words,
And turn them from their evil
way,

מִי־הִקְשִׁיב דְּבָרִי וַיִּשְׁמָע׃

19 הִנֵּה ׀ סַעֲרַת יְהֹוָה חֵמָה יָצְאָה
וְסַעַר מִתְחוֹלֵל
עַל רֹאשׁ רְשָׁעִים יָחוּל׃

20 לֹא יָשׁוּב אַף־יְהֹוָה
עַד־עֲשֹׂתוֹ וְעַד־הֲקִימוֹ
מְזִמּוֹת לִבּוֹ
בְּאַחֲרִית הַיָּמִים
תִּתְבּוֹנְנוּ בָהּ בִּינָה׃

21 לֹא־שָׁלַחְתִּי אֶת־הַנְּבִאִים
וְהֵם רָצוּ
לֹא־דִבַּרְתִּי אֲלֵיהֶם
וְהֵם נִבָּאוּ׃

22 וְאִם־עָמְדוּ בְּסוֹדִי
וְיַשְׁמִעוּ דְבָרַי אֶת־עַמִּי
וִישִׁבוּם מִדַּרְכָּם הָרָע

v. 18. דברו ק׳

His word. The *kethib* has 'My word'
which R.V. adopts. The ancient Versions
fluctuate between the two readings.

19f. Repeated with slight variations in
xxx. 23f. These verses break the connection of the passage and are spoken
parenthetically: God's intentions are far
different from the peace smoothly
promised by these self-styled prophets.

20. *till He have performed.* God's purposes may be delayed in fulfilment, but
never thwarted by human action
(Metsudath David).

the end of days. A Messianic phrase
(Kimchi): when God will vindicate His
word and His Kingdom be established
on earth (cf. xlviii. 47, xlix. 39; Isa. ii.
2).

ye shall consider it perfectly. The Hebrew
verb is in the *hithpael* conjugation which
usually has a reflexive force. It might be
rendered: 'Ye shall consider yourselves
therein (with) understanding,' i.e. at
present you refuse to recognize this, but
in the end you will know it from
examining yourselves and from your
experience (see Daath Mikra).

21. *they ran.* In eagerness to deliver
messages which they had invented
(Kimchi).

22. *stood in My council.* Continuing verse
18.

and turn them from their evil way. For
they must have learned in *My council*
what I really desire (see Malbim).

And from the evil of their doings.

23 Am I a God near at hand, saith
the Lord,
And not a God afar off?

24 Can any hide himself in secret
places
That I shall not see him? saith
the Lord.
Do not I fill heaven and earth?
Saith the Lord.

25 I have heard what the prophets
have said,
That prophesy lies in My name,
saying:
'I have dreamed, I have
dreamed.'

26 How long shall this be?
Is it in the heart of the prophets
that prophesy lies,
And the prophets of the deceit
of their own heart?

27 That think to cause My people
to forget My name
By their dreams which they tell
every man to his neighbour,

וּמֵרֹעַ מַעַלְלֵיהֶם:

23 הַאֱלֹהֵי מִקָּרֹב
אָנִי נְאֻם־יְהֹוָה
וְלֹא אֱלֹהֵי מֵרָחֹק:

24 אִם־יִסָּתֵר אִישׁ בַּמִּסְתָּרִים
וַאֲנִי לֹא־אֶרְאֶנּוּ נְאֻם־יְהֹוָה
הֲלוֹא אֶת־הַשָּׁמַיִם
וְאֶת־הָאָרֶץ אֲנִי מָלֵא
נְאֻם־יְהֹוָה:

25 שָׁמַעְתִּי
אֵת אֲשֶׁר־אָמְרוּ הַנְּבִאִים
הַנִּבְּאִים בִּשְׁמִי שֶׁקֶר לֵאמֹר
חָלַמְתִּי חָלָמְתִּי:

26 עַד־מָתַי הֲיֵשׁ
בְּלֵב הַנְּבִאִים נִבְּאֵי הַשָּׁקֶר
וּנְבִיאֵי תַּרְמִת לִבָּם:

27 הַחֹשְׁבִים
לְהַשְׁכִּיחַ אֶת־עַמִּי שְׁמִי
בַּחֲלוֹמֹתָם
אֲשֶׁר יְסַפְּרוּ אִישׁ לְרֵעֵהוּ

---

23. *near at hand.* The false prophets accordingly cannot hide from God to escape their punishment (Rashi).

24. *do not I fill heaven and earth?* The equivalent of 'am I not omnipresent?' so that nobody can avoid My scrutiny (Kimchi).

25. *I have dreamed.* They claimed their dreams to be genuine revelations from God (Kimchi).

26. The verse is difficult. The probable meaning is: How long will this error continue? Do they really believe that their dreams are prophetic? No. They realize that a dream is not related to a prophetic vision, but they are deceitful (Abarbanel, Metsudath David).

27. *to forget My name.* Their sole intention of telling dreams is to cause the people to forget My name just as their forefathers forgot My name through their worship of Baal (Abarbanel, Metsudath David).

As their fathers forgot My name
 for Baal.
28 The prophet that hath a dream,
 let him tell a dream;
And he that hath My word, let
 him speak My word faithfully.
What hath the straw to do with
 the wheat?
Saith the LORD.
29 Is not My word like as fire?
 Saith the LORD;
And like a hammer that breaketh
 the rock in pieces?

30. Therefore, behold, I am against the prophets, saith the LORD, that steal My words every one from his neighbour. 31. Behold, I am against the prophets, saith the LORD, that use their tongues and say: 'He saith.' 32. Behold, I am against them that prophesy lying dreams, saith the LORD, and do tell them, and cause My people to err by their lies, and by their wantonness; yet

כַּאֲשֶׁר שָׁכְחוּ אֲבוֹתָם
אֶת־שְׁמִי בַּבָּעַל:
28 הַנָּבִיא אֲשֶׁר־אִתּוֹ חֲלוֹם
יְסַפֵּר חֲלוֹם
וַאֲשֶׁר דְּבָרִי אִתּוֹ
יְדַבֵּר דְּבָרִי אֱמֶת
מַה־לַתֶּבֶן אֶת־הַבָּר
נְאֻם־יְהֹוָה:
29 הֲלוֹא כֹה דְבָרִי
כָּאֵשׁ נְאֻם־יְהֹוָה
וּכְפַטִּישׁ יְפֹצֵץ סָלַע:
30 לָכֵן הִנְנִי עַל־הַנְּבִאִים נְאֻם־
יְהֹוָה מְגַנְּבֵי דְבָרַי אִישׁ מֵאֵת
31 רֵעֵהוּ: הִנְנִי עַל־הַנְּבִיאִם
נְאֻם־יְהֹוָה הַלֹּקְחִים לְשׁוֹנָם
32 וַיִּנְאֲמוּ נְאֻם: הִנְנִי עַל־נִבְּאֵי
חֲלֹמוֹת שֶׁקֶר נְאֻם־יְהֹוָה
וַיְסַפְּרוּם וַיַּתְעוּ אֶת־עַמִּי
בְּשִׁקְרֵיהֶם וּבְפַחֲזוּתָם וְאָנֹכִי

28. Let dreams be strictly distinguished from true prophecy. The former are compared with *straw* which contains no nourishment, the latter with *wheat* which provides the necessity for life (Kimchi).

29. The Divine word is not an inert force, but has dynamic power. It sweeps on and accomplishes its task, smashing any obstacle in its way as with a hammer. By that test the burning ardour of true prophecy may be distinguished from the complacency of the false (Kimchi).

30. *that steal My words.* They repeat as their own (but with variations) prophecies they heard from others who were truly inspired (Rashi).

31. *that use their tongues,* etc. That train their tongues to utter false prophecies prefaced by the formula *He saith (neum)* which was employed by genuine prophets (Rashi).

32. *their wantonness.* The noun *pachazuth* is derived from a root *pachaz* meaning 'to be hasty, unstable.' It may be translated, 'their frivolousness,' i.e.

I sent them not, nor commanded them; neither can they profit this people at all, saith the LORD.

33. And when this people, or the prophet, or a priest, shall ask thee, saying: 'What is the burden of the LORD?' then shalt thou say unto them: 'What burden! I will cast you off, saith the LORD.'   34. And as for the prophet, and the priest, and the people, that shall say: 'The burden of the LORD,' I will even punish that man and his house.   35. Thus shall ye say every one to his neighbour, and every one to his brother: 'What hath the LORD answered?' and: 'What hath the LORD spoken?' 36. And the burden of the LORD shall ye mention no more; for every man's own word shall be his burden; and would ye pervert the words of the living God, of the LORD of hosts our God?   37. Thus shalt thou say

לֹא־שְׁלַחְתִּים וְלֹא צִוִּיתִים
וְהוֹעֵיל לֹא־יוֹעִילוּ לָעָם־
33 הַזֶּה נְאֻם־יְהוָה: וְכִי־
יִשְׁאָלְךָ הָעָם הַזֶּה אוֹ־הַנָּבִיא
אוֹ־כֹהֵן לֵאמֹר מַה־מַשָּׂא
יְהוָה וְאָמַרְתָּ אֲלֵיהֶם אֶת־
מַה־מַשָּׂא וְנָטַשְׁתִּי אֶתְכֶם
34 נְאֻם־יְהוָה: וְהַנָּבִיא וְהַכֹּהֵן
וְהָעָם אֲשֶׁר יֹאמַר מַשָּׂא יְהוָה
וּפָקַדְתִּי עַל־הָאִישׁ הַהוּא
35 וְעַל־בֵּיתוֹ: כֹּה תֹאמְרוּ אִישׁ
עַל־רֵעֵהוּ וְאִישׁ אֶל־אָחִיו
מֶה־עָנָה יְהוָה וּמַה־דִּבֶּר
36 יְהוָה: וּמַשָּׂא יְהוָה לֹא
תִזְכְּרוּ־עוֹד כִּי הַמַּשָּׂא יִהְיֶה
לְאִישׁ דְּבָרוֹ וַהֲפַכְתֶּם אֶת־
דִּבְרֵי אֱלֹהִים חַיִּים יְהוָה
37 צְבָאוֹת אֱלֹהֵינוּ: כֹּה תֹאמַר

their irresponsibility in lightheartedly claiming to be God-inspired (Metsudath David).

33. The text is somewhat difficult, but the general sense is, *massa* signifying both *burden* and 'prophecy': When the people jeeringly ask you (Jeremiah), 'What prophecy (burden) have you now?' We are sure that your prophecy will be another tiresome burden!' answer them, '*What burden!* It is that God will cast you off, as one casts off a burden (Metsudath David). By an apparently different division and vocalization of the consonants *(attem hammas-*

sa), LXX and Vulgate render, 'Ye are the burden,' but Rashi derived the same interpretation from M.T.

34ff. Since the term *massa* can be so misused, let it no longer be employed in prophetic utterances.

35. *answered.* In response to an inquiry.

36. *for every man's own word shall be his burden.* This translation does not make much sense. The closest interpretation to it is Rashi's. 'For every man's word shall be a burden of retribution for the one who uses this expression.

to the prophet: 'What hath the LORD answered thee?' and: 'What hath the LORD spoken?' 38. But if ye say: 'The burden of the LORD'; therefore thus saith the LORD: Because ye say this word: 'The burden of the LORD,' and I have sent unto you, saying: 'Ye shall not say: The burden of the LORD'; 39. therefore, behold, I will utterly tear you out, and I will cast you off, and the city that I gave unto you and to your fathers, away from My presence; 40. and I will bring an everlasting reproach upon you, and a perpetual shame, which shall not be forgotten.

אֶל־הַנָּבִיא מֶה־עָנָךְ יְהֹוָה

38 וּמַה־דִּבֶּר יְהֹוָה: וְאִם־מַשָּׂא
יְהֹוָה תֹּאמֵרוּ לָכֵן כֹּה אָמַר
יְהֹוָה יַעַן אֲמָרְכֶם אֶת־הַדָּבָר
הַזֶּה מַשָּׂא יְהֹוָה וָאֶשְׁלַח
אֲלֵיכֶם לֵאמֹר לֹא תֹאמְרוּ

39 מַשָּׂא יְהֹוָה: לָכֵן הִנְנִי וְנָשִׁיתִי
אֶתְכֶם נָשֹׁא וְנָטַשְׁתִּי אֶתְכֶם
וְאֶת־הָעִיר אֲשֶׁר־נָתַתִּי
לָכֶם וְלַאֲבוֹתֵיכֶם מֵעַל פָּנָי:

40 וְנָתַתִּי עֲלֵיכֶם חֶרְפַּת עוֹלָם
וּכְלִמּוּת עוֹלָם אֲשֶׁר לֹא
תִשָּׁכֵחַ:

24	CHAPTER XXIV	כד

1. The LORD showed me, and behold two baskets of figs set before the temple of the LORD; after that

1 הִרְאַנִי יְהֹוָה וְהִנֵּה שְׁנֵי דּוּדָאֵי
תְאֵנִים מוּעָדִים לִפְנֵי הֵיכַל
יְהֹוָה אַחֲרֵי הַגְלוֹת

37. *the prophet.* i.e. the man who claims to be a messenger of God.

39. *I will utterly tear you out, and I will cast you off.* See on verse 33. Kimchi renders the first clause, followed by A.V. and R.V.: 'I will utterly forget you,' I will forget My covenant with you. Some Hebrew MSS. agree with the ancient Versions in pointing the consonant as *s* instead of *sh* which changes the sense to, 'I will lift up with a lifting.' There is still a play upon the double meaning of *massa* (see Abarbanel). [We cannot understand why so dire a punishment was merited, and have to assume that

false prophecy had reached such proportions as to constitute a major crime which endangered the existence as well as the spiritual state of the nation.]

CHAPTER XXIV

VISION OF THE TWO BASKETS OF FIGS

ITS message is that contrary to what might be expected, the Judeans who had been exiled, and not those who remained in the Holy Land, would meet with God's favour. No explicit reason is given for this differentiation, but it is hinted at in verse 7. The shock of cap-

Nebuchadrezzar king of Babylon had carried away captive Jeconiah the son of Jehoiakim, king of Judah, and the princes of Judah, with the craftsmen and smiths, from Jerusalem, and had brought them to Babylon. 2. One basket had very good figs, like the figs that are first-ripe; and the other basket had very bad figs, which could not be eaten, they were so bad. 3. Then said the LORD unto me: 'What seest thou, Jeremiah?' And I said: 'Figs; the good figs, very good; and the bad, very bad, that cannot be eaten, they are so bad.' 4. And the word of the LORD came unto me, saying: 5. 'Thus saith the LORD, the God of Israel: Like these good figs, so will I regard the captives of Judah, whom I have sent out of this place into the land of the Chaldeans, for

נְבוּכַדְרֶאצַּר מֶלֶךְ־בָּבֶל
אֶת־יְכָנְיָהוּ בֶן־יְהְוֹיָקִים
מֶלֶךְ־יְהוּדָה וְאֶת־שָׂרֵי יְהוּדָה
וְאֶת־הֶחָרָשׁ וְאֶת־הַמַּסְגֵּר
מִירוּשָׁלַם וַיְבִאֵם בָּבֶל:
2 הַדּוּד אֶחָד תְּאֵנִים טֹבוֹת מְאֹד
כִּתְאֵנֵי הַבַּכֻּרוֹת וְהַדּוּד אֶחָד
תְּאֵנִים רָעוֹת מְאֹד אֲשֶׁר לֹא־
3 תֵאָכַלְנָה מֵרֹעַ: וַיֹּאמֶר יְהוָֹה
אֵלַי מָה־אַתָּה רֹאֶה יִרְמְיָהוּ
וָאֹמַר תְּאֵנִים הַתְּאֵנִים הַטֹּבוֹת
טֹבוֹת מְאֹד וְהָרָעוֹת רָעוֹת
מְאֹד אֲשֶׁר לֹא־תֵאָכַלְנָה
4 מֵרֹעַ: וַיְהִי דְבַר־יְהוָֹה אֵלַי
5 לֵאמֹר: כֹּה־אָמַר יְהוָֹה
אֱלֹהֵי יִשְׂרָאֵל כַּתְּאֵנִים
הַטֹּבוֹת הָאֵלֶּה כֵּן אַבִּיר אֶת־
גָּלוּת יְהוּדָה אֲשֶׁר שִׁלַּחְתִּי
מִן־הַמָּקוֹם הַזֶּה אֶרֶץ כַּשְׂדִּים

---

tivity, entailing physical and spiritual uprooting from the Holy Land, had effected a change in the hearts of the exiles who were now ready to know and acknowledge God. Not so those who stayed at home: they remained obdurate and spiritually deaf and blind; hence they were doomed. For a vehement condemnation of those who had not gone into captivity, cf. Ezek. xxii., and for the hopeful future of the exiles, cf. Ezek. xi. 17–20, xx. 37ff.

1. *Jeconiah.* See on xxii. 24.

the craftsmen and smiths. The phrase is repeated in xxix. 2 and 2 Kings xxiv. 14. It is probably idiomatic denoting all skilled artisans. According to Targum, the craftsmen and the sentries of the gates.

2. *the figs that are first-ripe.* In June, considered to be a delicacy (cf. Isa. xxviii. 4; Hos. ix.10).

5. *for good.* To be connected with *will I regard.* God will look favourably upon them (Rashi).

good. 6. And I will set Mine eyes upon them for good, and I will bring them back to this land; and I will build them, and not pull them down; and I will plant them, and not pluck them up. 7. And I will give them a heart to know Me, that I am the LORD; and they shall be My people, and I will be their God; for they shall return unto Me with their whole heart. 8. And as the bad figs, which cannot be eaten, they are so bad; surely thus saith the LORD: So will I make Zedekiah the king of Judah, and his princes, and the residue of Jerusalem, that remain in this land, and them that dwell in the land of Egypt; 9. I will even make them a horror among all the kingdoms of the earth for evil; a reproach and a proverb, a taunt and a curse, in all places whither I shall drive them. 10. And I will send the sword, the famine, and the pestilence, among them, till they be consumed from off the land that I gave unto them and to their fathers.'

6 לְטוֹבָ֑ה וְשַׂמְתִּ֨י עֵינִ֤י עֲלֵיהֶם֙
לְטוֹבָ֔ה וַהֲשִׁבֹתִ֖ים עַל־הָאָ֣רֶץ
הַזֹּ֑את וּבְנִיתִים֙ וְלֹ֣א אֶהֱרֹ֔ס
7 וּנְטַעְתִּ֖ים וְלֹ֥א אֶתּֽוֹשׁ׃ וְנָתַתִּ֨י
לָהֶ֥ם לֵב֙ לָדַ֣עַת אֹתִ֔י כִּ֥י אֲנִ֖י
יְהֹוָ֑ה וְהָיוּ־לִ֣י לְעָ֗ם וְאָֽנֹכִ֗י
אֶהְיֶ֤ה לָהֶם֙ לֵֽאלֹהִ֔ים כִּֽי־
יָשֻׁ֥בוּ אֵלַ֖י בְּכָל־לִבָּֽם׃
8 וְכַתְּאֵנִים֙ הָֽרָע֔וֹת אֲשֶׁ֥ר לֹֽא־
תֵאָכַ֖לְנָה מֵרֹ֑עַ כִּֽי־כֹ֣ה ׀ אָמַ֣ר
יְהֹוָ֗ה כֵּ֣ן אֶתֵּ֞ן אֶת־צִדְקִיָּ֤הוּ
מֶֽלֶךְ־יְהוּדָה֙ וְאֶת־שָׂרָ֔יו וְאֵ֣ת ׀
שְׁאֵרִ֣ית יְרֽוּשָׁלִַ֗ם הַנִּשְׁאָרִים֙
בָּאָ֣רֶץ הַזֹּ֔את וְהַיֹּשְׁבִ֖ים בְּאֶ֥רֶץ
9 מִצְרָֽיִם׃ וּנְתַתִּ֨ים לְזַעֲוָ֤ה
לְרָעָ֔ה לְכֹ֖ל מַמְלְכ֣וֹת הָאָ֑רֶץ
לְחֶרְפָּ֤ה וּלְמָשָׁל֙ לִשְׁנִינָ֔ה
וְלִקְלָלָ֖ה בְּכָל־הַמְּקֹמ֖וֹת
10 אֲשֶׁר־אַדִּיחֵ֥ם שָֽׁם׃ וְשִׁלַּחְתִּ֣י
בָ֗ם אֶת־הַחֶ֙רֶב֙ אֶת־הָ֣רָעָ֔ב
וְאֶת־הַדָּ֑בֶר עַד־תֻּמָּם֙ מֵעַ֣ל
הָֽאֲדָמָ֔ה אֲשֶׁר־נָתַ֥תִּי לָהֶ֖ם
וְלַאֲבוֹתֵיהֶֽם׃

v. 9. לזעוה ק׳

---

6. *eyes.* The Hebrew is singular.

7. *for they shall return unto Me.* [Theoretical knowledge of God alone is of no value; it must be an activating force which leads man back to Him.]

8. *and them that dwell in the land of*

Egypt. They fled there with Johanan son of Kareah after the assassination of Gedaliah son of Ahikam (Kimchi) in defiance of God's command through Jeremiah.

9. Cf. Deut. xxviii. 37.

1. The word that came to Jeremiah concerning all the people of Judah in the fourth year of Jehoiakim the son of Josiah, king of Judah, that was the first year of Nebuchadrezzar king of Babylon; 2. which Jeremiah the prophet spoke unto all the people of Judah, and to all the inhabitants of Jerusalem, saying:

3. From the thirteenth year of Josiah the son of Amon, king of Judah, even unto this day, these three and twenty years, the word of the LORD hath come unto me, and I have spoken unto you, speaking betimes and often; but ye have not

א הַדָּבָר אֲשֶׁר־הָיָה עַל־־
יִרְמְיָהוּ עַל־כָּל־עַם יְהוּדָה
בַּשָּׁנָה הָרְבִעִית לִיהוֹיָקִים
בֶּן־יֹאשִׁיָּהוּ מֶלֶךְ יְהוּדָה
הִיא הַשָּׁנָה הָרִאשֹׁנִית
לִנְבוּכַדְרֶאצַּר מֶלֶךְ בָּבֶל:
ב אֲשֶׁר דִּבֶּר יִרְמְיָהוּ הַנָּבִיא
עַל־כָּל־עַם יְהוּדָה וְאֶל
כָּל־יֹשְׁבֵי יְרוּשָׁלָֽ͏ם לֵאמֹר:
ג מִן־שְׁלֹשׁ עֶשְׂרֵה שָׁנָה
לְיֹאשִׁיָּהוּ בֶן־אָמוֹן מֶלֶךְ
יְהוּדָה וְעַד ׀ הַיּוֹם הַזֶּה זֶה
שָׁלֹשׁ וְעֶשְׂרִים שָׁנָה הָיָה דְבַר־
יְהוָה אֵלָי וָאֲדַבֵּר אֲלֵיכֶם
אַשְׁכֵּים וְדַבֵּר וְלֹא שְׁמַעְתֶּם:

ע. 3. א׳ במקום ה׳

CHAPTER XXV

CHRONOLOGICALLY this chapter precedes the last four chapters which were Jeremiah's reply to Zedekiah's message (cf. xxi. 1f.). We now return to *the fourth year of Jehoiakim . . . that was the first year of Nebuchadrezzar.* The unusual precision of dating suggests the awareness of the prophet that the year was a turning-point in history. Its date is *c.* 604 B.C.E., after the Babylonian victory at Carchemish over Pharaoh-neco, king of Egypt (cf. xlvi. 2). In that victory Jeremiah detected the doom of Judea and of all nations that would not submit to the conqueror. Rashi comments: 'In this year their exile was finally decreed; yet before it was actualized, Jeremiah was

bidden to make one more appeal to the people that they might repent and avert their doom.'

1–7 THE PEOPLE'S HEEDLESSNESS OF DIVINE WARNINGS

2. *unto all the people of Judah.* Not merely to the princes and leaders; he appealed to the masses. At this stage he was still free and not in hiding (cf. xxxvi. 1ff.).

3. *these three and twenty years.* Jeremiah received his call in the thirteenth year of Josiah (i. 2) who reigned thirty-one years (2 Kings xxii. 1); so he prophesied for eighteen or nineteen years in that reign. To this must be added the three months of Jehoahaz's reign (2 Kings

hearkened. 4. And the LORD hath
sent unto you all His servants the
prophets, sending them betimes and
often—but ye have not hearkened,
nor inclined your ear to hear—
5. saying: 'Return ye now every one
from his evil way, and from the evil
of your doings, and dwell in the land
that the LORD hath given unto you
and to your fathers, for ever and
ever; 6. and go not after other gods
to serve them, and to worship them,
and provoke Me not with the work
of your hands; and I will do you no
hurt.' 7. Yet ye have not hearkened
unto Me, saith the LORD; that ye
might provoke Me with the work of
your hands to your own hurt.
8. Therefore thus saith the LORD of
hosts: Because ye have not heard
My words, 9. behold, I will send

4 וְשָׁלַח֩ יְהֹוָ֨ה אֲלֵיכֶ֜ם אֶת־כָּל־
עֲבָדָ֧יו הַנְּבִאִ֛ים הַשְׁכֵּ֥ם וְשָׁלֹ֖חַ
וְלֹ֣א שְׁמַעְתֶּ֑ם וְלֹֽא־הִטִּיתֶ֤ם
5 אֶת־אָזְנְכֶ֖ם לִשְׁמֹֽעַ׃ לֵאמֹ֗ר
שֽׁוּבוּ־נָ֞א אִ֣ישׁ מִדַּרְכּ֤וֹ הָֽרָעָה֙
וּמֵרֹ֣עַ מַעַלְלֵיכֶ֔ם וּשְׁבוּ֙ עַל־
הָ֣אֲדָמָ֔ה אֲשֶׁ֨ר נָתַ֧ן יְהֹוָ֛ה לָכֶ֖ם
וְלַאֲבֽוֹתֵיכֶ֑ם לְמִן־עוֹלָ֖ם
6 וְעַד־עוֹלָֽם׃ וְאַל־תֵּלְכ֗וּ
אַחֲרֵי֙ אֱלֹהִ֣ים אֲחֵרִ֔ים
לְעָבְדָ֖ם וּלְהִשְׁתַּחֲוֺ֣ת לָהֶ֑ם
וְלֹֽא־תַכְעִ֤יסוּ אוֹתִי֙ בְּמַעֲשֵׂ֣ה
7 יְדֵיכֶ֔ם וְלֹ֥א אָרַ֖ע לָכֶֽם׃ וְלֹֽא־
שְׁמַעְתֶּ֥ם אֵלַ֖י נְאֻם־יְהֹוָ֑ה
לְמַ֧עַן הַכְעִיסֵ֛נִי בְּמַעֲשֵׂ֥ה
8 יְדֵיכֶ֖ם לְרַ֥ע לָכֶֽם׃ לָכֵ֗ן כֹּ֤ה
אָמַר֙ יְהֹוָ֣ה צְבָא֔וֹת יַ֕עַן אֲשֶׁ֥ר
לֹֽא־שְׁמַעְתֶּ֖ם אֶת־דְּבָרָֽי׃
9 הִנְנִ֣י שֹׁלֵ֗חַ וְלָקַחְתִּי֙ אֶת־כָּל־

v. 7. קמץ בטרחא   v. 7. הכעיסני ק'

---

xxiii. 31) and the three years of Jehoiakim's (Kimchi).

speaking betimes and often. Cf. vii. 13.

4. *and the LORD hath sent.* [The verb
may be construed as pluperfect: 'now
the Lord had sent,' before Jeremiah
began his mission.]

5. *saying.* This follows on *speaking* and
sending in verses 3f. (Daath Mikra).

and dwell. i.e. and, as a consequence,
remain in possession of the land (Daath
Mikra).

6. *provoke Me not.* The prophets in
giving God's message would naturally
say, in His name, 'provoke Me not.'
There is no necessity to assume a
copyist's error for 'provoke Him not,'
as some commentators do. M.T. is
supported by LXX.

7. *the work of your hands.* The idols;
again in xxxii. 30 (Metsudath David).

to your own hurt. To provoke God is to
court disaster (Metsudath David).

165

and take all the families of the north, saith the LORD, and I will send unto Nebuchadrezzar the king of Babylon, My servant, and will bring them against this land, and against the inhabitants thereof, and against all these nations round about; and I will utterly destroy them, and make them an astonishment, and a hissing, and perpetual desolations. 10. Moreover I will cause to cease from among them the voice of mirth and the voice of gladness, the voice of the bridegroom and the voice of the bride, the sound of the mill-stones, and the light of the lamp. 11. And this whole land shall be a desolation, and a waste; and these nations shall serve the king of Babylon seventy years. 12. And it

מִשְׁפְּחוֹת צָפוֹן נְאֻם־יְהוָֹה
וְאֶל־נְבוּכַדְרֶאצַּר מֶלֶךְ־
בָּבֶל עַבְדִּי וַהֲבִאֹתִים עַל־
הָאָרֶץ הַזֹּאת וְעַל־יֹשְׁבֶיהָ
וְעַל כָּל־הַגּוֹיִם הָאֵלֶּה סָבִיב
וְהַחֲרַמְתִּים וְשַׂמְתִּים לְשַׁמָּה
וְלִשְׁרֵקָה וּלְחָרְבוֹת עוֹלָם:
10 וְהַאֲבַדְתִּי מֵהֶם קוֹל שָׂשׂוֹן
וְקוֹל שִׂמְחָה קוֹל חָתָן וְקוֹל
כַּלָּה קוֹל רֵחַיִם וְאוֹר נֵר:
11 וְהָיְתָה כָּל־הָאָרֶץ הַזֹּאת
לְחָרְבָּה וּלְשַׁמָּה וְעָבְדוּ הַגּוֹיִם
הָאֵלֶּה אֶת־מֶלֶךְ־בָּבֶל
12 שִׁבְעִים שָׁנָה: וְהָיָה כִמְלֹאות

v. 11.   v. 12. כצ״ל מלא ר׳

8—11 JUDAH WILL BE SUBJECT TO BABYLON SEVENTY YEARS

9. *families.* See on iii. 14.

My servant. Nebuchadnezzar was un-consciously carrying out God's pur-poses and therefore could appropriately be described as His *servant* (so again xxvii. 6, xliii. 10; cf. *His anointed* applied to Cyrus, Isa. xlv. 1) (Daath Mikra).

an astonishment, and a hissing. Cf. xviii. 16.

10. *the voice of mirth,* etc. From vii. 34.

the sound of the millstones. Grinding corn, because there will be none to grind. The Talmud (Sanh. 32b) under-stands it as the powdering of ingredients used to heal the wound caused by cir-cumcision. This interpretation makes it a sequel to *the voice of the bridegroom,* etc. There will be no marriage and no birth.

the light of the lamp. The Talmud refers this to the kindling of lamps at a domes-tic festivity. Kimchi explains that they would grind spices for festive occasions and light many candles. Jonathan renders: the sound of groups that praise with the light of many candles. Kara states: when the cities become desolate, it goes without saying that the mills will no longer be heard and the lights of the candles no longer seen. Hence, Daath Mikra explains this verse as depicting a gradual cessation of life. Not only will there be no sound of joy and mirth, but there will soon be no signs of life. Since the inhabitants will be exiled, the sound of the mills will no longer be heard, neither will the glimmer of the candles appear in the windows.

11. *these nations.* Round about Judea (verse 9) (Metsudath David).

seventy years. Reckoned from the

shall come to pass, when seventy years are accomplished, that I will punish the king of Babylon, and that nation, saith the LORD, for their iniquity, and the land of the Chaldeans; and I will make it perpetual desolations. 13. And I will bring upon that land all My words which I have pronounced against it, even all that is written in this book, which Jeremiah hath prophesied against all the nations. 14. For many nations and great kings shall make bondmen of them also; and I will recompense them according to their deeds, and according to the work of their own hands.

15. For thus saith the LORD, the God of Israel, unto me: Take this cup of the wine of fury at My hand, and cause all the nations, to whom

שִׁבְעִים שָׁנָה אֶפְקֹד עַל־
מֶלֶךְ־בָּבֶל וְעַל־הַגּוֹי הַהוּא
נְאֻם־יְהוָה אֶת־עֲוֹנָם וְעַל־
אֶרֶץ כַּשְׂדִּים וְשַׂמְתִּי אֹתוֹ
לְשִׁמְמוֹת עוֹלָם: וְהֵבֵאוֹתִי 13
עַל־הָאָרֶץ הַהִיא אֶת־כָּל־
דְּבָרַי אֲשֶׁר־דִּבַּרְתִּי עָלֶיהָ
אֵת כָּל־הַכָּתוּב בַּסֵּפֶר הַזֶּה
אֲשֶׁר־נִבָּא יִרְמְיָהוּ עַל־כָּל־
הַגּוֹיִם: כִּי עָבְדוּ־בָם גַּם־ 14
הֵמָּה גּוֹיִם רַבִּים וּמְלָכִים
גְּדוֹלִים וְשִׁלַּמְתִּי לָהֶם
כְּפָעֳלָם וּכְמַעֲשֵׂה יְדֵיהֶם:
כִּי כֹה אָמַר יְהוָה אֱלֹהֵי 15
יִשְׂרָאֵל אֵלַי קַח אֶת־כּוֹס
הַיַּיִן הַחֵמָה הַזֹּאת מִיָּדִי
וְהִשְׁקִיתָה אוֹתוֹ אֶת־כָּל־
הַגּוֹיִם אֲשֶׁר אָנֹכִי שֹׁלֵחַ אוֹתְךָ

v. 13. והבאתי ק'

fourth year of Jehoiakim (440 B.C.E.) to the assassination of Belshazzar (371 B.C.E.) (Kimchi).

12–14 THE FATE OF BABYLON

12. The prediction of Babylon's downfall interrupts the continuity of the passage. Nevertheless its insertion here is natural; it tells how Judah's exile will come to an end through Babylon's collapse (cf. xxix. 10).

13. *in this book.* In its concluding chapters, from xlvi. to the end (Rashi).

which Jeremiah hath prophesied. The mention of the prophet in the third person can be explained by the fact that the words are part of God's declaration.

14. *many nations.* The Medes and Persians (Rashi, Kimchi).

15–29 THE NATIONS MUST DRINK FROM THE CUP OF GOD'S FURY

15. The cup of wine as symbolizing disaster is a frequent figure in the Bible (cf. xiii. 12f., xlix. 12; Isa. li. 17, 22).

I send thee, to drink it. 16. And they shall drink, and reel to and fro, and be like madmen, because of the sword that I will send among them. —17. Then took I the cup at the LORD's hand, and made all the nations to drink, unto whom the LORD had sent me: 18. Jerusalem, and the cities of Judah, and the kings thereof, and the princes thereof, to make them an appalment, an astonishment, a hissing, and a curse; as it is this day; 19. Pharaoh king of Egypt, and his servants, and his princes, and all his people; 20. and all the mingled people; and all the kings of the land of Uz, and all the kings of the land of the Philistines, and Ashkelon, and Gaza,

אֲלֵיהֶֽם: וְשָׁתוּ וְהִֽתְגֹּֽעֲשׁוּ 16
וְהִתְהֹלָֽלוּ מִפְּנֵי הַחֶרֶב אֲשֶׁר
אָנֹכִי שֹׁלֵחַ בֵּֽינֹתָֽם: וָאֶקַּח 17
אֶת־הַכּוֹס מִיַּד יְהֹוָה וָאַשְׁקֶה
אֶת־כָּל־הַגּוֹיִם אֲשֶׁר־שְׁלָחַנִי
יְהֹוָה אֲלֵיהֶֽם: אֶת־יְרוּשָׁלַםִ 18
וְאֶת־עָרֵי יְהוּדָה וְאֶת־
מְלָכֶיהָ אֶת־שָׂרֶיהָ לָתֵת אֹתָם
לְחָרְבָּה לְשַׁמָּה לִשְׁרֵקָה
וְלִקְלָלָה כַּיּוֹם הַזֶּֽה: אֶת־ 19
פַּרְעֹה מֶֽלֶךְ־מִצְרַיִם וְאֶת־
עֲבָדָיו וְאֶת־שָׂרָיו וְאֶת־כָּל־
עַמּֽוֹ: וְאֵת כָּל־הָעֶרֶב וְאֵת 20
כָּל־מַלְכֵי אֶרֶץ הָעוּץ וְאֵת
כָּל־מַלְכֵי אֶרֶץ פְּלִשְׁתִּים
וְאֶת־אַשְׁקְלוֹן וְאֶת־עַזָּה

---

16. *be like madmen.* The terrors of war will make them frantic (Metsudath David).

17. *then took I the cup.* To be understood symbolically. He had a vision in which he did so (Kimchi).

18ff. Abarbanel explains that the nations are enumerated in the order they were conquered by Babylon. The first nation to be conquered was Judah, next Egypt, and next the mingled nations which presumably had no king, since no king is mentioned. Then he conquered the land of the Philistines. Ashkelon, Gaza, Ekron, and Ashdod are mentioned separately since they were individual kingdoms. It can be assumed that the other nations mentioned were conquered in the order they are enumerated.

the kings thereof. Jehoiakim, Jehoiachin and Zedekiah (Kimchi).

as it is this day. The phrase was added after the overthrow of Judah (Rashi).

20. *all the mingled people.* The foreigners settled in Egypt (Kara).

Uz. An Aramean tribe (Lam. iv. 21), probably east or north-east of Edom, not far from Egypt (see Daath Mikra).

Ashkelon. About ten miles north of Gaza (see Daath Mikra).

the remnant of Ashdod. Another of the Philistine cities, thirty-five miles north of Gaza. The word *remnant* implies that its inhabitants were either mostly slain or deported after its capture by the

and Ekron, and the remnant of
Ashdod; 21. Edom, and Moab, and
the children of Ammon; 22. and all
the kings of Tyre, and all the kings
of Zidon, and the kings of the isle
which is beyond the sea; 23. Dedan,
and Tema, and Buz, and all that
have the corners of their hair polled;
24. and all the kings of Arabia, and
all the kings of the mingled people
that dwell in the wilderness; 25. and
all the kings of Zimri, and all the
kings of Elam, and all the kings of

וְאֶת־עֶקְרוֹן וְאֵת שְׁאֵרִית
21 אַשְׁדּוֹד: אֶת־אֱדוֹם וְאֶת־
22 מוֹאָב וְאֶת־בְּנֵי עַמּוֹן: וְאֵת
כָּל־מַלְכֵי צֹר וְאֵת כָּל־
מַלְכֵי צִידוֹן וְאֵת מַלְכֵי הָאִי
23 אֲשֶׁר בְּעֵבֶר הַיָּם: אֶת־דְּדָן
וְאֶת־תֵּימָא וְאֶת־בּוּז וְאֵת
24 כָּל־קְצוּצֵי פֵאָה: וְאֵת כָּל־
מַלְכֵי עֲרָב וְאֵת כָּל־מַלְכֵי
הָעֶרֶב הַשֹּׁכְנִים בַּמִּדְבָּר:
25 וְאֵת | כָּל־מַלְכֵי זִמְרִי וְאֵת
כָּל־מַלְכֵי עֵילָם וְאֵת כָּל־

Egyptian king Psammetichus (see Herodotus).

22. *Zidon.* [About twenty miles south
of Beirut. It extended from the slopes of
Lebanon to the coast.]

the isle. The coastland, i.e. the Phoeni-
cian colonies along the shores of the
Mediterranean. According to Daath
Mikra, it is the island of Cyprus.

23. *Dedan.* A tribe dwelling south-
east of Edom, descended from Abraham and Keturah (Gen. xxv. 3), famed
as traders (Ezek. xxvii. 15, 20, xxxviii.
13).

Tema. An Arabian tribe (cf. Gen. xxv.
15) inhabiting a region towards the
Syrian desert.

Buz. A tribe descended from Nahor,
Abraham's brother (Gen. xxii. 21).

all that have . . . polled. See on ix. 25.

24. *Arabia.* The tribes occupying the

Arabian peninsula. These were nomadic
tribes, as described by Isaiah xiii. 20
(Kimchi).

*the mingled people that dwell in the wilder-
ness.* See on verse 20. Unlike the
mingled people mentioned above, these
dwelt in the wilderness (Kimchi). Abarbanel points out the aforementioned
were not governed by a king, whereas
these were governed by kings. According to Rashi, who renders, 'the allies,'
the aforementioned were the allies and
supports of Pharaoh, whereas these
were the allies of Arabia.

25. *Zimri.* As the name of a people it is
not found elsewhere. Kimchi conjectures that this Zimri may be Zimran, one
of Abraham's sons by Keturah (Gen.
xxv. 2) who became the ancestor of a
tribe bearing his name.

Elam. East of Babylon, it is now called
Chuzistan (see Carta's Atlas of the Bible,
Daath Mikra, Hertz, Gen. x. 22).

the Medes; 26. and all the kings of
the north, far and near, one with
another; and all the kingdoms of the
world, which are upon the face of
the earth.—And the king of Sheshach shall drink after them. 27.
And thou shalt say unto them:
Thus saith the LORD of hosts, the
God of Israel: Drink ye, and be
drunken, and spew, and fall, and rise
no more, because of the sword which
I will send among you. 28. And it
shall be, if they refuse to take the cup
at thy hand to drink, then shalt thou
say unto them: Thus saith the
LORD of hosts: Ye shall surely drink.
29. For, lo, I begin to bring evil on
the city whereupon My name is

26 מַלְכֵי מָדָי: וְאֵת ׀ כָּל־מַלְכֵי
הַצָּפוֹן הַקְּרֹבִים וְהָרְחֹקִים
אִישׁ אֶל־אָחִיו וְאֵת כָּל־
הַמַּמְלְכוֹת הָאָרֶץ אֲשֶׁר עַל־
פְּנֵי הָאֲדָמָה וּמֶלֶךְ שֵׁשַׁךְ יִשְׁתֶּה
27 אַחֲרֵיהֶם: וְאָמַרְתָּ אֲלֵיהֶם
כֹּה־אָמַר יְהֹוָה צְבָאוֹת אֱלֹהֵי
יִשְׂרָאֵל שְׁתוּ וְשִׁכְרוּ וּקְיוּ וְנִפְלוּ
וְלֹא תָקוּמוּ מִפְּנֵי הַחֶרֶב אֲשֶׁר
28 אָנֹכִי שֹׁלֵחַ בֵּינֵיכֶם: וְהָיָה כִּי
יְמָאֲנוּ לָקַחַת־הַכּוֹס מִיָּדְךָ
לִשְׁתּוֹת וְאָמַרְתָּ אֲלֵיהֶם כֹּה
אָמַר יְהֹוָה צְבָאוֹת שָׁתוֹ
29 תִשְׁתּוּ: כִּי הִנֵּה בָעִיר אֲשֶׁר־
נִקְרָא שְׁמִי עָלֶיהָ אָנֹכִי מֵחֵל

26. *all the kings of the north.* The kings of
the peoples dwelling in the mountains
north and northeast of Mesopotamia,
who dreaded the rise of Babylon.
Consequently, they were among the
peoples that attacked Babylon when she
fell by the hand of Cyrus, king of Persia.
See below l. 9, li. 48. Others explain this
as the kingdom of Aram, north of Eretz
Israel (see Ez. xxxii. 30, Daath Mikra).

26. *one with another.* To be attached to
what precedes: 'near to, or distant
from, one another' (Daath Mikra).

Sheshach. According to Jewish tradition the name is a cypher for Babel on
the system whereby the last letter of the
alphabet is substituted for the first, the
penultimate for the second, and so on.
Cf. li. 41 where Babel and Sheshach are
parallel synonyms. Another cypher of

this kind occurs in li. 1. Ibn Kaspi
asserts that the prophets sometimes
concealed their intention. Perhaps it
was not safe to mention the destined
downfall of Babylon at the time this
prophecy was recorded. Azulai explains
that the numerical value of Sheshach
coincides with that of *kether,* crown,
denoting that Babylon usurped a crown
not due her, i.e., Nebuchadnezzar was
overly haughty and did not ascribe his
conquests to God but to his own power.

shall drink after them. [His turn will
come too, after these have all suffered
humiliation and subjugation. Though
he was unwittingly acting as God's
servant (verse 9), he was consciously bent
on plunder and dominion, and therefore punishment will befall him.]

29. *the city whereupon My name is called.*

called, and should ye be utterly
unpunished? Ye shall not be unpunished; for I will call for a sword
upon all the inhabitants of the earth,
saith the LORD of hosts.

30. Therefore prophesy thou
against them all these words, and
say unto them:

The LORD doth roar from on
high,
And utter His voice from His
holy habitation;
He doth mightily roar because of
His fold;
He giveth a shout, as they that
tread the grapes,
Against all the inhabitants of the
earth.

31 A noise is come even to the end
of the earth;
For the LORD hath a controversy
with the nations,
He doth plead with all flesh;
As for the wicked, He hath given
them to the sword,
Saith the LORD.

32 Thus saith the LORD of hosts:
Behold, evil shall go forth
From nation to nation,

לְהָרֵעַ וְאַתֶּם הִנָּקֵה תִנָּקוּ לֹא
תִנָּקוּ כִּי חֶרֶב אֲנִי קֹרֵא עַל־
כָּל־יֹשְׁבֵי הָאָרֶץ נְאֻם יְהֹוָה
30 צְבָאוֹת: וְאַתָּה תִּנָּבֵא אֲלֵיהֶם
אֵת כָּל־הַדְּבָרִים הָאֵלֶּה
וְאָמַרְתָּ אֲלֵיהֶם
יְהֹוָה מִמָּרוֹם יִשְׁאָג
וּמִמְּעוֹן קָדְשׁוֹ יִתֵּן קוֹלוֹ
שָׁאֹג יִשְׁאַג עַל־נָוֵהוּ
הֵידָד כְּדֹרְכִים יַעֲנֶה
אֶל כָּל־יֹשְׁבֵי הָאָרֶץ:
31 בָּא שָׁאוֹן עַד־קְצֵה הָאָרֶץ
כִּי רִיב לַיהֹוָה בַּגּוֹיִם
נִשְׁפָּט הוּא לְכָל־בָּשָׂר
הָרְשָׁעִים נְתָנָם לַחֶרֶב
נְאֻם־יְהֹוָה:
32 כֹּה אָמַר יְהֹוָה צְבָאוֹת
הִנֵּה רָעָה יֹצֵאת
מִגּוֹי אֶל־גּוֹי

v. 30. קמץ בפשטא

Jerusalem which housed the Temple
bearing God's name (cf. vii. 10) and was
called 'the city of the Land' (Metsudath
David).

30-38 DIVINE JUDGMENT UPON ALL NATIONS

30. *from on high.* From His heavenly
abode (Metsudath David).

because of His fold. He roars in grief

over the destruction of Jerusalem and
the Temple (Rashi, Metsudath David).

31. *plead.* The verb *nishpat* is the
niphal conjugation of *shaphat*, 'to judge';
hence the meaning may be, 'He doth
bring Himself into judgment.' Not as a
capricious and cruel tyrant does He
decree all this desolation, but as a righteous Judge pronouncing sentence on
the guilty (see Kimchi).

32. *from nation to nation.* The sense is

And a great storm shall be raised
up
From the uttermost parts of the
earth.

33. And the slain of the LORD shall
be at that day from one end of the
earth even unto the other end of the
earth; they shall not be lamented,
neither gathered, nor buried; they
shall be dung upon the face of the
ground.

34 Wail, ye shepherds, and cry;
And wallow yourselves in the
dust, ye leaders of the flock;
For the days of your slaughter
are fully come,
And I will break you in pieces,
And ye shall fall like a precious
vessel.

35 And the shepherds shall have no
way to flee,
Nor the leaders of the flock to
escape.

36 Hark! the cry of the shepherds,
And the wailing of the leaders of
the flock!
For the LORD despoileth their
pasture.

וְסַעַר גָּדוֹל יֵעוֹר
מִיַּרְכְּתֵי־אָרֶץ׃

33 וְהָיוּ חַלְלֵי יְהוָה בַּיּוֹם הַהוּא
מִקְצֵה הָאָרֶץ וְעַד־קְצֵה
הָאָרֶץ לֹא יִסָּפְדוּ וְלֹא יֵאָסְפוּ
וְלֹא יִקָּבֵרוּ לְדֹמֶן עַל־פְּנֵי
הָאֲדָמָה יִהְיוּ׃

34 הֵילִילוּ הָרֹעִים וְזַעֲקוּ
וְהִתְפַּלְּשׁוּ אַדִּירֵי הַצֹּאן
כִּי־מָלְאוּ יְמֵיכֶם לִטְבוֹחַ
וּתְפוֹצוֹתִיכֶם
וּנְפַלְתֶּם כִּכְלִי חֶמְדָּה׃

35 וְאָבַד מָנוֹס מִן־הָרֹעִים
וּפְלֵיטָה מֵאַדִּירֵי הַצֹּאן׃

36 קוֹל צַעֲקַת הָרֹעִים
וִילֲלַת אַדִּירֵי הַצֹּאן
כִּי־שֹׁדֵד יְהוָה
אֶת־מַרְעִיתָם׃

v. 34. הפ׳ בחולם ובחירק הת׳

---

either that the evil will visit the nations
in succession (Metsudath David); or that
nations will war with and inflict evil
upon each other (Malbim).

33. Either the destruction will be universal so that there will be none left to
bewail and bury the dead (Daath
Mikra), or the slain will be too
numerous to receive these attentions
(Metsudath David).

34. *shepherds.* National rulers (Targum).

wallow yourselves. Cf. vi. 26.

and I will break you in pieces. Rashi,
Metsudath David and several ancient
Versions render: 'and your dispersions
(are close at hand.)' You will soon go
into exile.

like a precious vessel. Made of fragile
material which is shattered beyond
repair (Malbim).

35. Cf. Amos ii. 14.

36. Cf. Zech. xi. 3.

37 And the peaceable folds are brought to silence
Because of the fierce anger of the LORD.

38 He hath forsaken His covert, as the lion;
For their land is become a waste
Because of the fierceness of the oppressing sword,
And because of His fierce anger.

37 וְנָדַמּוּ נְאוֹת הַשָּׁלוֹם

מִפְּנֵי חֲרוֹן אַף־יְהֹוָה:

38 עָזַב כַּכְּפִיר סֻכּוֹ

כִּי־הָיְתָה אַרְצָם לְשַׁמָּה

מִפְּנֵי חֲרוֹן הַיּוֹנָה

וּמִפְּנֵי חֲרוֹן אַפּוֹ:

26	CHAPTER XXVI	כו

1. In the beginning of the reign of Jehoiakim the son of Josiah, king of Judah, came this word from the LORD, saying: 2. 'Thus saith the LORD: Stand in the court of the LORD's house, and speak unto all the cities of Judah, which come to worship in the LORD's house, all the

1 בְּרֵאשִׁית מַמְלְכוּת יְהוֹיָקִים

בֶּן־יֹאשִׁיָּהוּ מֶלֶךְ יְהוּדָה

הָיָה הַדָּבָר הַזֶּה מֵאֵת יְהֹוָה

2 לֵאמֹר: כֹּה אָמַר יְהֹוָה עֲמֹד

בַּחֲצַר בֵּית־יְהֹוָה וְדִבַּרְתָּ

עַל־כָּל־עָרֵי יְהוּדָה הַבָּאִים

לְהִשְׁתַּחֲוֹת בֵּית־יְהֹוָה אֵת

CHAPTER XXVI

37. *are brought to silence.* The peaceful pastoral regions are now reduced to silence because neither man nor flock is there any more (Daath Mikra).

38. *as the lion.* The section ends with the same simile as the one at its beginning (verse 30). Like a lion which seeks another when its lair is destroyed, so has God abandoned His land now that it is in ruins (Kimchi).

sword. This word is not in the text but is understood from the context. But many Hebrew MSS. agree with LXX and the Targum in reading *hachereb,* 'the sword,' for *charon,* 'the fierceness of,' as in xlvi. 16, l. 16.

BEGINNING with this chapter and extending to the end of xlv we have in the main a record of incidents in the life of Jeremiah. Since the prophet is generally referred to in the third person, it is probable that this section of the Book consists of extracts from the memoirs of Jeremiah compiled by Baruch. The present chapter is to be linked with vii and describes the sequel to the address in the Temple (see Abarbanel).

1-6 DOOM OF THE TEMPLE FORETOLD

1. *in the beginning,* etc. [The date is 607 B.C.E.]

2. *the court.* [The outer court where the people assembled.]

words that I command thee to speak unto them; diminish not a word.

3. It may be they will hearken, and turn every man from his evil way; that I may repent Me of the evil, which I purpose to do unto them because of the evil of their doings.

4. And thou shalt say unto them: Thus saith the LORD: If ye will not hearken to Me, to walk in My law, which I have set before you, 5. to hearken to the words of My servants the prophets, whom I send unto you, even sending them betimes and often, but ye have not hearkened; 6. then will I make this house like Shiloh, and will make this city a curse to all the nations of the earth'.

7. So the priests and the prophets and all the people heard Jeremiah speaking these words in the house of the LORD.

8. Now it came to pass, when

כָּל־הַדְּבָרִים אֲשֶׁר צִוִּיתִיךָ
לְדַבֵּר אֲלֵיהֶם אַל־תִּגְרַע
3 דָּבָר: אוּלַי יִשְׁמְעוּ וְיָשֻׁבוּ
אִישׁ מִדַּרְכּוֹ הָרָעָה וְנִחַמְתִּי
אֶל־הָרָעָה אֲשֶׁר אָנֹכִי חֹשֵׁב
לַעֲשׂוֹת לָהֶם מִפְּנֵי רֹעַ
4 מַעַלְלֵיהֶם: וְאָמַרְתָּ אֲלֵיהֶם
כֹּה אָמַר יְהֹוָה אִם־לֹא
תִשְׁמְעוּ אֵלַי לָלֶכֶת בְּתוֹרָתִי
5 אֲשֶׁר נָתַתִּי לִפְנֵיכֶם: לִשְׁמֹעַ
עַל־דִּבְרֵי עֲבָדַי הַנְּבִאִים
אֲשֶׁר אָנֹכִי שֹׁלֵחַ אֲלֵיכֶם
וְהַשְׁכֵּם וְשָׁלֹחַ וְלֹא שְׁמַעְתֶּם:
6 וְנָתַתִּי אֶת־הַבַּיִת הַזֶּה כְּשִׁלֹה
וְאֶת־הָעִיר הַזֹּאתה אֶתֵּן
לִקְלָלָה לְכֹל גּוֹיֵ הָאָרֶץ:
7 וַיִּשְׁמְעוּ הַכֹּהֲנִים וְהַנְּבִאִים
וְכָל־הָעָם אֶת־יִרְמִיָהוּ
מְדַבֵּר אֶת־הַדְּבָרִים הָאֵלֶּה
8 בְּבֵית יְהֹוָה: וַיְהִי | כְּכַלּוֹת

v. 6. יתיר ה׳　v. 6. חסר י׳

---

diminish not a word. Although the warning you have given to the people will endanger your life (see Daath Mikra).

3. *that I may repent Me.* See on xviii. 8.

4. *My law.* The law as embodied in the Pentateuch (Daath Soferim).

5. *to hearken to the words of My servants the prophets.* This is to be understood as, 'and to hearken' (Metsudath David).

6. *Shiloh.* See on vii. 12.

a curse. i.e. in cursing, people will say, 'May this place become like Jerusalem' (Metsudath David). [It is easy to appreciate the moral courage necessary to deliver such a message.]

7–9 JEREMIAH'S DEATH DEMANDED

7. *the prophets.* The false prophets (Rashi, Abarbanel, Metsudath David).

Jeremiah had made an end of speaking all that the LORD had commanded him to speak unto all the people, that the priests and the prophets and all the people laid hold on him, saying: 'Thou shalt surely die. 9. Why hast thou prophesied in the name of the LORD, saying: This house shall be like Shiloh, and this city shall be desolate, without an inhabitant?' And all the people were gathered against Jeremiah in the house of the LORD.

10. When the princes of Judah heard these things, they came up from the king's house unto the house of the LORD; and they sat in the entry of the new gate of the LORD's house. 11. Then spoke the priests and the prophets unto the princes and to all the people, saying: 'This man is worthy of death; for he hath prophesied against this city, as ye have heard with your ears.'

יִרְמְיָהוּ לְדַבֵּר אֵת כָּל־
אֲשֶׁר־צִוָּה יְהֹוָה לְדַבֵּר אֶל־
כָּל־הָעָם וַיִּתְפְּשׂוּ אֹתוֹ
הַכֹּהֲנִים וְהַנְּבִיאִים וְכָל־
הָעָם לֵאמֹר מוֹת תָּמוּת׃
9 מַדּוּעַ נִבֵּיתָ בְשֵׁם־יְהֹוָה
לֵאמֹר כְּשִׁלוֹ יִהְיֶה הַבַּיִת הַזֶּה
וְהָעִיר הַזֹּאת תֶּחֱרַב מֵאֵין
יוֹשֵׁב וַיִּקָּהֵל כָּל־הָעָם אֶל־
10 יִרְמְיָהוּ בְּבֵית יְהֹוָה׃ וַיִּשְׁמְעוּ
שָׂרֵי יְהוּדָה אֵת הַדְּבָרִים
הָאֵלֶּה וַיַּעֲלוּ מִבֵּית־הַמֶּלֶךְ
בֵּית יְהֹוָה וַיֵּשְׁבוּ בְּפֶתַח שַׁעַר־
11 יְהֹוָה הֶחָדָשׁ׃ וַיֹּאמְרוּ הַכֹּהֲנִים
וְהַנְּבִיאִים אֶל־הַשָּׂרִים וְאֶל־
כָּל־הָעָם לֵאמֹר מִשְׁפַּט־
מָוֶת לָאִישׁ הַזֶּה כִּי נִבָּא אֶל־
הָעִיר הַזֹּאת כַּאֲשֶׁר שְׁמַעְתֶּם

כצ״ל v. 9.

The LXX here and in verses 8, 11, 16 adds the word 'false'; but the context makes it clear that these are intended.

8. thou shalt surely die. For prophesying falsely in God's name in accordance with the law of Deut. xviii. 20. It was inconceivable to them that such a prediction could be from God (Abarbanel).

9. all the people. Here, apparently, the mass of the population sided with the priests and prophets, whereas in verse 16 they were sympathetic to Jeremiah. When they heard his defense, that he

was indeed speaking God's word, they repented (Metsudath David).

10–11 IMPEACHMENT AND ACQUITTAL OF JEREMIAH

10. princes. The civil rulers (Abarbanel).

11. this man is worthy of death. A paraphrase of the Hebrew which is literally 'judgment of death to this man.'

as ye have heard with your ears. This was true of the people, but not of the

12. Then spoke Jeremiah unto all the princes and to all the people, saying: 'The LORD sent me to prophesy against this house and against this city all the words that ye have heard. 13. Therefore now amend your ways and your doings, and hearken to the voice of the LORD your God; and the LORD will repent Him of the evil that He hath pronounced against you. 14. But as for me, behold, I am in your hand; do with me as is good and right in your eyes. 15. Only know ye for certain that, if ye put me to death, ye will bring innocent blood upon yourselves, and upon this city, and upon the inhabitants thereof; for of a truth the LORD hath sent me unto you to speak all these words in your ears.'

12 בְּאָזְנֵיכֶם: וַיֹּאמֶר יִרְמְיָהוּ
אֶל־כָּל־הַשָּׂרִים וְאֶל־כָּל־
הָעָם לֵאמֹר יְהוָה שְׁלָחַנִי
לְהִנָּבֵא אֶל־הַבַּיִת הַזֶּה וְאֶל־
הָעִיר הַזֹּאת אֵת כָּל־
הַדְּבָרִים אֲשֶׁר שְׁמַעְתֶּם:
13 וְעַתָּה הֵיטִיבוּ דַרְכֵיכֶם
וּמַעַלְלֵיכֶם וְשִׁמְעוּ בְּקוֹל
יְהוָה אֱלֹהֵיכֶם וְיִנָּחֵם יְהוָה
אֶל־הָרָעָה אֲשֶׁר דִּבֶּר
14 עֲלֵיכֶם: וַאֲנִי הִנְנִי בְיֶדְכֶם
עֲשׂוּ־לִי כַּטּוֹב וְכַיָּשָׁר
15 בְּעֵינֵיכֶם: אַךְ | יָדֹעַ תֵּדְעוּ
כִּי אִם־מְמִתִים אַתֶּם אֹתִי
כִּי־דָם נָקִי אַתֶּם נֹתְנִים
עֲלֵיכֶם וְאֶל־הָעִיר הַזֹּאת
וְאֶל־יֹשְׁבֶיהָ כִּי בֶאֱמֶת שְׁלָחַנִי
יְהוָה עֲלֵיכֶם לְדַבֵּר בְּאָזְנֵיכֶם
אֵת כָּל־הַדְּבָרִים הָאֵלֶּה:

princes who had not been in the Temple court when Jeremiah spoke. The words were doubtless addressed directly to the former to whom the accusers turned (Daath Mikra).

12. *the* LORD *sent me.* Jeremiah replies to the princes and to all the people that he is not an impostor, for God sent him to prophesy all that he prophesied. He is, therefore, not a false prophet (Abarbanel).

13. *Therefore now,* etc. Moreover, he is not a prophet of doom, for if they

repent and mend their ways, God will repent of the evil He has pronounced against them (Abarbanel).

14. *as is good and right.* The double expression indicates that the prophet recognizes that his fate depends not on what he feels is right, but on what his judges feel is right. He is as one who is delivered into the hands of his enemies with no way of extricating himself from his predicament. He, therefore, makes peace with the idea that he is helpless (Daath Mikra).

15. *only know ye,* etc. Be aware of the

16. Then said the princes and all the people unto the priests and to the prophets: 'This man is not worthy of death; for he hath spoken to us in the name of the LORD our God.' 17. Then rose up certain of the elders of the land, and spoke to all the assembly of the people, saying: 18. 'Micah the Morashtite prophesied in the days of Hezekiah king of Judah; and he spoke to all the people of Judah, saying: Thus saith the LORD of hosts:

Zion shall be plowed as a field,

And Jerusalem shall become heaps,

And the mountain of the house as the high places of a forest.

19. Did Hezekiah king of Judah and all Judah put him at all to death? did he not fear the LORD, and entreat the favour of the LORD, and the LORD repented Him of the evil which He had pronounced against them? Thus

16 וַיֹּאמְרוּ הַשָּׂרִים וְכָל־הָעָם
אֶל־הַכֹּהֲנִים וְאֶל־הַנְּבִיאִים
אֵין־לָאִישׁ הַזֶּה מִשְׁפַּט־מָוֶת
כִּי בְּשֵׁם יְהֹוָה אֱלֹהֵינוּ דִּבֶּר
17 אֵלֵינוּ: וַיָּקֻמוּ אֲנָשִׁים מִזִּקְנֵי
הָאָרֶץ וַיֹּאמְרוּ אֶל־כָּל־
18 קְהַל הָעָם לֵאמֹר: מִיכָה
הַמּוֹרַשְׁתִּי הָיָה נִבָּא בִּימֵי
חִזְקִיָּהוּ מֶלֶךְ־יְהוּדָה וַיֹּאמֶר
אֶל־כָּל־עַם יְהוּדָה לֵאמֹר
כֹּה־אָמַר ׀ יְהֹוָה צְבָאוֹת
צִיּוֹן שָׂדֶה תֵחָרֵשׁ
וִירוּשָׁלַיִם עִיִּים תִּהְיֶה
וְהַר הַבַּיִת לְבָמוֹת יָעַר:
19 הֶהָמֵת הֱמִתֻהוּ חִזְקִיָּהוּ מֶלֶךְ־
יְהוּדָה וְכָל־יְהוּדָה הֲלֹא יָרֵא
אֶת־יְהֹוָה וַיְחַל אֶת־פְּנֵי יְהֹוָה
וַיִּנָּחֶם יְהֹוָה אֶל־הָרָעָה
אֲשֶׁר־דִּבֶּר עֲלֵיהֶם וַאֲנַחְנוּ

v. 18. מיכה ק׳

---

fact that if you put me to death, *you* are bringing doom upon the city, not I (Abarbanel).

16. *and all the people.* They were convinced by Jeremiah's defence (Metsudath David).

17. *elders of the land.* Usually this term connotes men who held an official status in the community; but here it is better understood in its literal sense. These men of advanced age had themselves heard, or been told by their fathers, the statement made by the earlier prophet which corroborated the Divine origin of Jeremiah's words (see Kara).

18. *the Morashtite.* A native of Moresheth, a small town near Gath about twenty-three miles south-west of Jerusalem. It was also known as Moreshethgath (Micah i. 14).

19. *fear the* LORD. As the effect of Micah's warnings and Jerusalem was then spared; so here is a precedent to be

might we procure great evil against our own souls.'

20. And there was also a man that prophesied in the name of the LORD, Uriah the son of Shemaiah of Kiriath-jearim; and he prophesied against this city and against this land according to all the words of Jeremiah; 21. and when Jehoiakim the king, with all his mighty men, and all the princes, heard his words, the king sought to put him to death; but when Uriah heard it, he was afraid, and fled, and went into Egypt; 22. and Jehoiakim the king sent men into Egypt, Elnathan the son of Achbor, and certain men with him, into Egypt; 23. and they fetched forth Uriah out of Egypt, and brought him unto Jehoiakim the

עֹשִׂים רָעָה גְדוֹלָה עַל־
20 נַפְשֹׁתֵינוּ: וְגַם־אִישׁ הָיָה
מִתְנַבֵּא בְּשֵׁם יְהֹוָה אוּרִיָּהוּ
בֶּן־שְׁמַעְיָהוּ מִקִּרְיַת הַיְעָרִים
וַיִּנָּבֵא עַל־הָעִיר הַזֹּאת וְעַל־
הָאָרֶץ הַזֹּאת כְּכֹל דִּבְרֵי
21 יִרְמְיָהוּ: וַיִּשְׁמַע הַמֶּלֶךְ
יְהוֹיָקִים וְכָל־גִּבּוֹרָיו וְכָל־
הַשָּׂרִים אֶת־דְּבָרָיו וַיְבַקֵּשׁ
הַמֶּלֶךְ הֲמִיתוֹ וַיִּשְׁמַע אוּרִיָּהוּ
וַיִּרָא וַיִּבְרַח וַיָּבֹא מִצְרָיִם:
22 וַיִּשְׁלַח הַמֶּלֶךְ יְהוֹיָקִים אֲנָשִׁים
מִצְרָיִם אֶת־אֶלְנָתָן בֶּן־
עַכְבּוֹר וַאֲנָשִׁים אִתּוֹ אֶל־
23 מִצְרָיִם: וַיֹּצִיאוּ אֶת־אוּרִיָּהוּ
מִמִּצְרַיִם וַיְבִאֻהוּ אֶל־הַמֶּלֶךְ

---

followed in the present instance (Metsudath David).

thus might we procure, etc. Better, 'but we are doing great harm to ourselves,' if we condemn Jeremiah to death (Metsudath David).

20–23   URIAH SLAIN FOR HIS PROPHECY

The Siphrë maintains that this episode was cited by Jeremiah's accusers as a counter-precedent to that of Micah, to prove that Jeremiah's defence ought not to be accepted. Be that as it may, the incident demonstrates the grave danger incurred by the prophets who were charged with messages of national disaster.

20. *Uriah the son of Shemaiah.* Nothing

is known of him apart from what is here recorded. According to Rabbi Akiva, he is Uriah the priest, mentioned by Isaiah (viii. 2) (Mak. 24b).

21. *his mighty men.* The military chiefs as distinct from the *princes* who were civilian rulers (Daath Mikra).

22. *Elnathan the son of Achbor.* Again mentioned in xxxvi. 12, 25. If identical with the Elnathan of 2 Kings xxiv. 8, he was Jehoiachin's grandfather and Jehoiakim's father-in-law. He would be a person of high status to send to Egypt for Uriah's extradition.

23. *they fetched forth Uriah out of Egypt.* There may have been an extradition treaty between Egypt and Judah, such as Rameses II had in the four-

king; who slew him with the sword,
and cast his dead body into the graves
of the children of the people. 24.
Nevertheless the hand of Ahikam
the son of Shaphan was with
Jeremiah, that they should not give
him into the hand of the people to
put him to death.

יְהוֹיָקִים וַיַּכֵּהוּ בֶּחָרֶב וַיַּשְׁלֵךְ
אֶת־נִבְלָתוֹ אֶל־קִבְרֵי בְּנֵי
הָעָם: אַךְ יַד אֲחִיקָם בֶּן־ 24
שָׁפָן הָיְתָה אֶת־יִרְמְיָהוּ
לְבִלְתִּי תֵּת־אֹתוֹ בְיַד־הָעָם
לַהֲמִיתוֹ:

27   CHAPTER XXVII   כז

1. In the beginning of the reign of
Jehoiakim the son of Josiah, king of
Judah, came this word unto Jeremiah
from the LORD, saying: 2. 'Thus
saith the LORD to me: Make thee
bands and bars, and put them upon

בְּרֵאשִׁית מַמְלֶכֶת יְהוֹיָקִם 1
בֶּן־יֹאשִׁיָּהוּ מֶלֶךְ יְהוּדָה הָיָה
הַדָּבָר הַזֶּה אֶל־יִרְמְיָה מֵאֵת
יְהוָֹה לֵאמֹר: כֹּה־אָמַר יְהוָֹה 2
אֵלַי עֲשֵׂה לְךָ מוֹסֵרוֹת וּמֹטוֹת

v. 1. מלא ר'

---

teenth century B.C.E. with a Syrian king
named Chetta. Or, Jehoiakim, being
subject to the overlordship of Pharaoh,
made the demand in the interests of
national peace and stability.

the graves of the children of the people.   The
phrase is found again in 2 Kings xxiii. 6.
A form of degradation is obviously
meant; A.V. and R.V. 'the common
people' approximates to the meaning
(Metsudath David). A common ceme-
tery, as distinct from a family sepulchre,
is to be understood (Daath Mikra).
Torczyner identifies this narrative with a
passage in Letter XVI of the Lachish
Letters.

24. In spite of this precedent, which re-
influenced the people against Jeremiah,
Ahikam's protection saved him.

Ahikam the son of Shaphan.   One of the
men sent by Josiah to consult the
prophetess Huldah on the Scroll found

in the Temple (2 Kings xxii. 12). He was
the father of Gedaliah who was left in
charge in Judah after the Babylonian
invasion. The son also proved a friend
of Jeremiah (xxxix. 14).

CHAPTER XXVII

1–15   THE KING WARNED NOT TO JOIN IN
REVOLT AGAINST NEBUCHADNEZZAR

1. *Jehoiakim.*   From verses 3 and 12 it
would appear that the warning was
addressed to Zedekiah, and that is the
reading here of the Peshitta and some
Hebrew MSS. Retaining the present
text, Rashi and Kimchi explain that
although the prophecy concerns Zedekiah, it was communicated to Jeremiah
at the beginning of Jehoiakim's reign.
The plot to rebel happened in 593 B.C.E.

2. *bands and bars.*   To form a yoke
consisting of wooden bars held together
by leather bands. For the symbolism of

179

thy neck; 3. and send them to the king of Edom, and to the king of Moab, and to the king of the children of Ammon, and to the king of Tyre, and to the king of Zidon, by the hand of the messengers that come to Jerusalem unto Zedekiah king of Judah; 4. and give them a charge unto their masters, saying: Thus saith the LORD of hosts, the God of Israel: Thus shall ye say unto your masters: 5. I have made the earth, the man and the beast that are upon the face of the earth, by My great power and by My outstretched arm; and I give it unto whom it seemeth right unto Me. 6. And now have I given all these lands into the hand of Nebuchadnezzar the king of Babylon, My servant; and the beasts of the field also have I given

וּנְתַתָּם עַל־־צַוָּארֶךָ:
3 וְשִׁלַּחְתָּם אֶל־מֶלֶךְ אֱדוֹם
וְאֶל־מֶלֶךְ מוֹאָב וְאֶל־מֶלֶךְ
בְּנֵי עַמּוֹן וְאֶל־מֶלֶךְ צֹר וְאֶל־
מֶלֶךְ צִידוֹן בְּיַד מַלְאָכִים
הַבָּאִים יְרוּשָׁלַ͏ִם אֶל־־
4 צִדְקִיָּהוּ מֶלֶךְ יְהוּדָה: וְצִוִּיתָ
אֹתָם אֶל־אֲדֹנֵיהֶם לֵאמֹר
כֹּה־אָמַר יְהֹוָה צְבָאוֹת אֱלֹהֵי
יִשְׂרָאֵל כֹּה תֹאמְרוּ אֶל־
5 אֲדֹנֵיכֶם: אָנֹכִי עָשִׂיתִי אֶת־
הָאָרֶץ אֶת־הָאָדָם וְאֶת־
הַבְּהֵמָה אֲשֶׁר עַל־פְּנֵי הָאָרֶץ
בְּכֹחִי הַגָּדוֹל וּבִזְרוֹעִי הַנְּטוּיָה
וּנְתַתִּיהָ לַאֲשֶׁר יָשַׁר בְּעֵינָי:
6 וְעַתָּה אָנֹכִי נָתַתִּי אֶת־־
כָּל־הָאֲרָצוֹת הָאֵלֶּה בְּיַד
נְבוּכַדְנֶאצַּר מֶלֶךְ־בָּבֶל
עַבְדִּי וְגַם אֶת־חַיַּת הַשָּׂדֶה

the action, cf. the parallels in 1 Kings XXII. 11 and Ezek. vii. 23 (see Daath Soferim).

3. *and send them.* Probably duplicates of the yoke which the prophet himself was to wear (Daath Mikra).

Edom . . . Zidon. The nations planning to revolt (Abarbanel).

the messengers. Their envoys sent to Zedekiah with an invitation to join in the conspiracy (Abarbanel).

4. *thus saith the* LORD *of hosts.* It was not unusual for the Hebrew prophets to

address themselves to foreign nations, and their messages were heard with respect (cf. Judg. iii. 20; 1 Kings xix. 15; Isa. xviii. 2).

5. God's control over the destinies of peoples is justified by His act of creation which called nations and individuals alike into being.

6. *My servant.* See on xxv. 9.

the beasts of the field also. An idiom expressing the all-embracing extent of God's dominion (cf. xxviii. 14; Dan. ii. 38).

him to serve him. 7. And all the
nations shall serve him, and his son,
and his son's son, until the time of
his own land come; and then many
nations and great kings shall make
him their bondman.   8. And it shall
come to pass, that the nation and the
kingdom which will not serve the
same Nebuchadnezzar king of Babylon, and that will not put their neck
under the yoke of the king of
Babylon, that nation will I visit,
saith the LORD, with the sword, and
with the famine, and with the
pestilence, until I have consumed
them by his hand.   9. But as for
you, hearken ye not to your prophets,
nor to your diviners, nor to your
dreams, nor to your soothsayers, nor
to your sorcerers, that speak unto
you, saying: Ye shall not serve the
king of Babylon; 10. for they
prophesy a lie unto you, to remove

7 נָתַ֣תִּי ל֔וֹ לְעׇבְד֑וֹ׃ וְעׇ֣בְדוּ אֹת֣וֹ
כׇל־הַגּוֹיִם֙ וְאֶת־בְּנ֣וֹ וְאֶת־
בֶּן־בְּנ֔וֹ עַ֛ד בֹּא־עֵ֥ת אַרְצ֖וֹ
גַּם־ה֑וּא וְעׇ֣בְדוּ ב֔וֹ גּוֹיִ֖ם רַבִּ֑ים
8 וּמְלָכִ֖ים גְּדֹלִ֑ים׃ וְהָיָ֗ה הַגּ֤וֹי
וְהַמַּמְלָכָה֙ אֲשֶׁ֣ר לֹא־יַעַבְד֣וּ
אֹת֗וֹ אֶת־נְבֽוּכַדְנֶאצַּ֥ר מֶֽלֶךְ־
בָּבֶ֔ל וְאֵ֛ת אֲשֶׁ֥ר לֹֽא־יִתֵּ֖ן
אֶת־צַוָּאר֔וֹ בְּעֹ֖ל מֶ֣לֶךְ בָּבֶ֑ל
בַּחֶ֧רֶב וּבָרָעָ֛ב וּבַדֶּ֖בֶר אֶפְקֹ֥ד
עַל־הַגּ֧וֹי הַה֛וּא נְאֻם־יְהֹוָ֖ה
9 עַד־תֻּמִּ֥י אֹתָ֖ם בְּיָד֑וֹ׃ וְ֠אַתֶּ֠ם
אַל־תִּשְׁמְע֞וּ אֶל־נְבִֽיאֵיכֶ֗ם
וְאֶל־קֹֽסְמֵיכֶם֙ וְאֶ֣ל־
חֲלֹמֹֽתֵיכֶ֔ם וְאֶל־עֹֽנְנֵיכֶ֖ם
וְאֶֽל־כַּשָּׁפֵיכֶ֑ם אֲשֶׁר־הֵ֞ם
אֹמְרִ֤ים אֲלֵיכֶם֙ לֵאמֹ֔ר לֹ֥א
10 תַעַבְד֖וּ אֶת־מֶ֥לֶךְ בָּבֶֽל׃ כִּ֣י
שֶׁ֗קֶר הֵ֚ם נִבְּאִ֣ים לָכֶ֔ם לְמַ֛עַן
הַרְחִ֥יק אֶתְכֶ֖ם מֵעַ֥ל

---

7. *his son, and his son's son.* viz. Evil-
merodach and Belshazzar respectively
(cf. lii. 31; Dan. v. 1, 30). God commands the nations to serve the Babylonian monarchs until the destined
destruction of their land by Cyrus and
Darius (Metsudath David).

8. *famine . . . pestilence.* The usual con-
comitants of *the sword* (Daath Mikra).

9. *your prophets.* [Who advise you to
rebel against Nebuchadnezzar.]

your diviners, etc. [Who assure you of
the success of your conspiracy.]

10. *to remove you,* etc.   Not that this was
the intention of those who counselled in
favour of the plot; but it would be the
consequence (Metsudath David).

you far from your land; and that I should drive you out and ye should perish. 11. But the nation that shall bring their neck under the yoke of the king of Babylon, and serve him, that nation will I let remain in their own land, saith the LORD; and they shall till it, and dwell therein.'

12. And I spoke to Zedekiah king of Judah according to all these words, saying: 'Bring your necks under the yoke of the king of Babylon, and serve him and his people, and live. 13. Why will ye die, thou and thy people, by the sword, by the famine, and by the pestilence, as the LORD hath spoken concerning the nation that will not serve the king of Babylon? 14. And hearken not unto the words of the prophets that speak unto you, saying: Ye shall not serve the king of Babylon, for they prophesy a lie unto you. 15. For I have not sent them, saith the LORD, and they prophesy falsely in My name; that I might drive you out, and that ye might perish, ye, and the prophets that prophesy unto you.'

אַדְמַתְכֶם וְהִדַּחְתִּי אֶתְכֶם
11 וַאֲבַדְתֶּם: וְהַגּוֹי אֲשֶׁר יָבִיא
אֶת־צַוָּארוֹ בְּעֹל מֶלֶךְ־בָּבֶל
וַעֲבָדוֹ וְהִנַּחְתִּיו עַל־אַדְמָתוֹ
נְאֻם־יְהֹוָה וַעֲבָדָהּ וְיָשַׁב בָּהּ:
12 וְאֶל־צִדְקִיָּה מֶלֶךְ־יְהוּדָה
דִּבַּרְתִּי כְּכָל־הַדְּבָרִים
הָאֵלֶּה לֵאמֹר הָבִיאוּ אֶת־
צַוְּארֵיכֶם בְּעֹל מֶלֶךְ בָּבֶל
13 וְעִבְדוּ אֹתוֹ וְעַמּוֹ וִחְיוּ: לָמָּה
תָמוּתוּ אַתָּה וְעַמֶּךָ בַּחֶרֶב
בָּרָעָב וּבַדֶּבֶר כַּאֲשֶׁר דִּבֶּר
יְהֹוָה אֶל־הַגּוֹי אֲשֶׁר לֹא־
14 יַעֲבֹד אֶת־מֶלֶךְ בָּבֶל: וְאַל־
תִּשְׁמְעוּ אֶל־דִּבְרֵי הַנְּבִאִים
הָאֹמְרִים אֲלֵיכֶם לֵאמֹר לֹא
תַעַבְדוּ אֶת־מֶלֶךְ בָּבֶל כִּי
15 שֶׁקֶר הֵם נִבְּאִים לָכֶם: כִּי לֹא
שְׁלַחְתִּים נְאֻם־יְהֹוָה וְהֵם
נִבְּאִים בִּשְׁמִי לַשָּׁקֶר לְמַעַן
הַדִּיחִי אֶתְכֶם וַאֲבַדְתֶּם אַתֶּם
וְהַנְּבִאִים הַנִּבְּאִים לָכֶם:

11. *their neck.* lit. 'its neck,' *nation* having the force of 'each nation.'

12. The plural includes the nation (Abarbanel).

13. *that will not serve.* i.e. that will not willingly subordinate itself to the king of Babylon (Metsudath David).

16. Also I spoke to the priests and to all this people, saying: 'Thus saith the LORD: Hearken not to the words of your prophets that prophesy unto you, saying: Behold, the vessels of the LORD's house shall now shortly be brought back from Babylon; for they prophesy a lie unto you. 17. Hearken not unto them; serve the king of Babylon, and live; wherefore should this city become desolate? 18. But if they be prophets, and if the word of the LORD be with them, let them now make intercession to the LORD of hosts, that the vessels which are left in the house of the LORD, and in the house of the king of Judah, and at Jerusalem, go not to Babylon. 19. For thus saith the LORD of hosts concerning the pillars, and concerning the sea, and concerning the bases, and concerning the residue of the vessels that remain in this city, 20. which Nebuchadnezzar king of

16 וְאֶל־הַכֹּהֲנִים וְאֶל־כָּל־
הָעָם הַזֶּה דִּבַּרְתִּי לֵאמֹר כֹּה
אָמַר יְהֹוָה אַל־תִּשְׁמְעוּ אֶל־
דִּבְרֵי נְבִיאֵיכֶם הַנִּבְּאִים לָכֶם
לֵאמֹר הִנֵּה כְלֵי בֵית־יְהֹוָה
מוּשָׁבִים מִבָּבֶלָה עַתָּה מְהֵרָה
כִּי שֶׁקֶר הֵמָּה נִבְּאִים לָכֶם:
17 אַל־תִּשְׁמְעוּ אֲלֵיהֶם עִבְדוּ
אֶת־מֶלֶךְ בָּבֶל וִחְיוּ לָמָּה
תִהְיֶה הָעִיר הַזֹּאת חָרְבָּה:
18 וְאִם־נְבִאִים הֵם וְאִם־יֵשׁ
דְּבַר־יְהֹוָה אִתָּם יִפְגְּעוּ־נָא
בַּיהֹוָה צְבָאוֹת לְבִלְתִּי־בֹאוּ
הַכֵּלִים ׀ הַנּוֹתָרִים בְּבֵית־
יְהֹוָה וּבֵית מֶלֶךְ יְהוּדָה
19 וּבִירוּשָׁלַםִ בָּבֶלָה: כִּי כֹה
אָמַר יְהֹוָה צְבָאוֹת אֶל־
הָעַמֻּדִים וְעַל־הַיָּם וְעַל־
הַמְּכֹנוֹת וְעַל יֶתֶר הַכֵּלִים
20 הַנּוֹתָרִים בָּעִיר הַזֹּאת: אֲשֶׁר

16–22 THE WARNING REPEATED TO PRIESTS AND PEOPLE

16. *the vessels of the* LORD's *house.* Which were carried away by Nebuchadnezzar to Babylon in the reign of Jehoiachin (cf. 2 Kings xxiv. 13 and note verse 20 of this chapter). The assurance that the holy vessels are to be restored to the Temple would naturally make a strong appeal to the priests and gain their support to a policy of revolt (Daath Soferim).

18. *let them now make intercession.* If these men are truly endowed with prophecy and called by God, instead of their deluding the people with false hopes, let them pray that fresh disaster will not befall the nation, since, in fact, the remaining vessels are destined to be taken to Babylon (Abarbanel).

19. *the pillars,* etc. Described in 1 Kings vii. 15–39. They were broken up by the Chaldeans and carried to Babylon (lii. 17).

Babylon took not, when he carried away captive Jeconiah the son of Jehoiakim, king of Judah, from Jerusalem to Babylon, and all the nobles of Judah and Jerusalem; 21. yea, thus saith the LORD of hosts, the God of Israel, concerning the vessels that remain in the house of the LORD, and in the house of the king of Judah, and at Jerusalem: 22. They shall be carried to Babylon, and there shall they be, until the day that I remember them, saith the LORD, and bring them up, and restore them to this place.'

לֹא־לְקָחָם נְבוּכַדְנֶאצַּר מֶלֶךְ
בָּבֶל בַּגְלוֹתוֹ אֶת־יְכָנְיָה בֶן־
יְהוֹיָקִים מֶלֶךְ־יְהוּדָה
מִירוּשָׁלַם בָּבֶלָה וְאֵת כָּל־
21 חֹרֵי יְהוּדָה וִירוּשָׁלָם: כִּי כֹה
אָמַר יְהֹוָה צְבָאוֹת אֱלֹהֵי
יִשְׂרָאֵל עַל־־הַכֵּלִים
הַנּוֹתָרִים בֵּית יְהֹוָה וּבֵית
מֶלֶךְ־יְהוּדָה וִירוּשָׁלָם:
22 בָּבֶלָה יוּבָאוּ וְשָׁמָּה יִהְיוּ עַד
יוֹם פָּקְדִי אֹתָם נְאֻם־יְהֹוָה
וְהַעֲלִיתִים וַהֲשִׁבֹתִים אֶל־
הַמָּקוֹם הַזֶּה:

28   CHAPTER XXVIII   כח

1. And it came to pass the same year, in the beginning of the reign of Zedekiah king of Judah, in the fourth year, in the fifth month, that Hananiah the son of Azzur the prophet, who was of Gibeon, spoke

1 וַיְהִי | בַּשָּׁנָה הַהִיא בְּרֵאשִׁית
מַמְלֶכֶת צִדְקִיָּה מֶלֶךְ־
יְהוּדָה בַּשָּׁנָה הָרְבִעִית בַּחֹדֶשׁ
הַחֲמִישִׁי אָמַר אֵלַי חֲנַנְיָה בֶן־
עַזּוּר הַנָּבִיא אֲשֶׁר מִגִּבְעוֹן

v. 20. בשנה ק'   v. 1. יתיר ר'

---

22. *until the day that I remember them.* The predicted event happened in the reign of Cyrus (Ezra i. 7ff.).

CHAPTER XXVIII

HANANIAH OPPOSES JEREMIAH

1. *the same year.* As that to which the last chapter relates (see on xxvii. 1).

Hananiah. According to the Talmud (Sanh. 89a), his false predictions arose from an unwarranted deduction. Hav-

ing heard Jeremiah foretell the downfall of Elam (xlix. 34ff.), a satellite State of Babylon, he concluded that the prophecy would apply with even greater force to Babylon. Nothing is known of him beyond what is here recorded.

the prophet. i.e. the false prophet (Targum). Anyone who predicted the future was known as a prophet (Abarbanel).

Gibeon. One of the priestly cities (Josh.

184

unto me in the house of the Lord, in the presence of the priests and of all the people, saying: 2. 'Thus speaketh the Lord of hosts, the God of Israel, saying: I have broken the yoke of the king of Babylon. 3. Within two full years will I bring back into this place all the vessels of the Lord's house, that Nebuchadnezzar king of Babylon took away from this place, and carried them to Babylon; 4. and I will bring back to this place Jeconiah the son of Jehoiakim, king of Judah, with all the captives of Judah, that went to Babylon, saith the Lord; for I will break the yoke of the king of Babylon.' 5. Then the prophet Jeremiah said unto the prophet Hananiah in the presence of the priests, and in the presence of all the people that stood in the house of the Lord, 6. even the prophet Jeremiah

בְּבֵית יְהֹוָה לְעֵינֵי הַכֹּהֲנִים
2 וְכָל־הָעָם לֵאמֹר: כֹּה־אָמַר
יְהֹוָה צְבָאוֹת אֱלֹהֵי יִשְׂרָאֵל
לֵאמֹר שָׁבַרְתִּי אֶת־עֹל מֶלֶךְ
3 בָּבֶל: בְּעוֹד | שְׁנָתַיִם יָמִים
אֲנִי מֵשִׁיב אֶל־הַמָּקוֹם הַזֶּה
אֶת־כָּל־כְּלֵי בֵּית יְהֹוָה אֲשֶׁר
לָקַח נְבוּכַדְנֶאצַּר מֶלֶךְ־
בָּבֶל מִן־הַמָּקוֹם הַזֶּה וַיְבִיאֵם
4 בָּבֶל: וְאֶת־יְכָנְיָה בֶן־
יְהוֹיָקִים מֶלֶךְ־יְהוּדָה וְאֶת־
כָּל־גָּלוּת יְהוּדָה הַבָּאִים
בָּבֶלָה אֲנִי מֵשִׁיב אֶל־הַמָּקוֹם
הַזֶּה נְאֻם־יְהֹוָה כִּי אֶשְׁבֹּר
5 אֶת־עֹל מֶלֶךְ בָּבֶל: וַיֹּאמֶר
יִרְמְיָה הַנָּבִיא אֶל־חֲנַנְיָה
הַנָּבִיא לְעֵינֵי הַכֹּהֲנִים וּלְעֵינֵי
כָּל־הָעָם הָעֹמְדִים בְּבֵית
6 יְהֹוָה: וַיֹּאמֶר יִרְמְיָה הַנָּבִיא

---

xxi. 17), five milies north-west of Jerusalem.

2. *I have broken.* The prophetic perfect referring to the future (Daath Mikra).

the yoke. The words have an allusion to the symbolic yoke worn by Jeremiah on his neck (cf. verse 10) (Malbim).

3. *within two full years.* See above verse 1, the Talmudic explanation of Hananiah's prophecy. Abarbanel conjectures that Hananiah's prophecy was the result of a dream, which he believed to be a

message from God. Although he sincerely believed his dream to be prophetic, he was punished for not analyzing it with the proper care.

4. Hananiah contradicts the prediction of Jeremiah in xxii. 24–27.

6. Jeremiah replies that he hopes Hananiah's forecast of the future will be realized, knowing in his heart that events would falsify it. The Rabbis (Sotah 41b, 42a) take Jeremiah to task for flattering Hananiah. Because of this

said: 'Amen! the LORD do so! the LORD perform thy words which thou hast prophesied, to bring back the vessels of the LORD's house, and all them that are carried away captive, from Babylon unto this place! 7. Nevertheless hear thou now this word that I speak in thine ears, and in the ears of all the people: 8. The prophets that have been before me and before thee of old prophesied against many countries, and against great kingdoms, of war, and of evil, and of pestilence. 9. The prophet that prophesieth of peace, when the word of the prophet shall come to pass, then shall the prophet be known, that the LORD hath truly sent him.'

10. Then Hananiah the prophet took the bar from off the prophet Jeremiah's neck, and broke it. 11. And Hananiah spoke in the presence of all the people, saying: 'Thus saith the LORD: Even so will I break the yoke of Nebuchadnezzar

אָמֵן כֵּן יַעֲשֶׂה יְהֹוָה יָקֵם יְהֹוָה
אֶת־דְּבָרֶיךָ אֲשֶׁר נִבֵּאתָ
לְהָשִׁיב כְּלֵי בֵית־יְהֹוָה וְכָל־
הַגּוֹלָה מִבָּבֶל אֶל־הַמָּקוֹם
הַזֶּה: אַךְ שְׁמַע־נָא הַדָּבָר 7
הַזֶּה אֲשֶׁר אָנֹכִי דֹּבֵר בְּאָזְנֶיךָ
וּבְאָזְנֵי כָּל־הָעָם: הַנְּבִיאִים 8
אֲשֶׁר הָיוּ לְפָנַי וּלְפָנֶיךָ מִן־
הָעוֹלָם וַיִּנָּבְאוּ אֶל־אֲרָצוֹת
רַבּוֹת וְעַל־מַמְלָכוֹת גְּדֹלוֹת
לְמִלְחָמָה וּלְרָעָה וּלְדָבֶר:
הַנָּבִיא אֲשֶׁר יִנָּבֵא לְשָׁלוֹם 9
בְּבֹא דְּבַר הַנָּבִיא יִוָּדַע הַנָּבִיא
אֲשֶׁר־שְׁלָחוֹ יְהֹוָה בֶּאֱמֶת:
וַיִּקַּח חֲנַנְיָה הַנָּבִיא אֶת־ 10
הַמּוֹטָה מֵעַל צַוַּאר יִרְמְיָה
הַנָּבִיא וַיִּשְׁבְּרֵהוּ: וַיֹּאמֶר 11
חֲנַנְיָה לְעֵינֵי כָל־הָעָם לֵאמֹר
כֹּה אָמַר יְהֹוָה כָּכָה אֶשְׁבֹּר
אֶת־עֹל | נְבֻכַדְנֶאצַּר מֶלֶךְ־

v. 8. נ״א על v. 11. חצי הספר בפסוקים

flattery, Jeremiah later fell into the hands of Hananiah's grandson. See below xxxvii. 13.

8f. Jeremiah's argument is as follows: The fact that your prophecy is favorable while mine is unfavorable is no reason for yours to be believed more than mine. On the contrary, all our predecessors predicted evil. Should a prophet predict good, the only proof of his genuineness is the fulfillment of his words (Abarbanel). Others explain that Jeremiah argued that if his prophecy were not fulfilled, he could not be branded as a liar, for God sometimes repents of His evil decrees. Should Hananiah's prophecy not be fulfilled, however, he would definitely be branded a liar (Rashi from Tanhuma).

10. Hananiah makes no verbal reply,

king of Babylon from off the neck of all the nations within two full years.' And the prophet Jeremiah went his way. 12. Then the word of the LORD came unto Jeremiah, after that Hananiah the prophet had broken the bar from off the neck of the prophet Jeremiah, saying: 13. 'Go, and tell Hananiah, saying: Thus saith the LORD: Thou hast broken the bars of wood; but thou shalt make in their stead bars of iron. 14. For thus saith the LORD of hosts, the God of Israel: I have put a yoke of iron upon the neck of all these nations, that they may serve Nebuchadnezzar king of Babylon; and they shall serve him; and I have given him the beasts of the field also.' 15. Then said the prophet Jeremiah unto Hananiah the prophet: 'Hear now, Hananiah; the LORD hath not sent thee; but thou makest this people to trust in a lie.

בְּבֶל בְּעוֹד שְׁנָתַיִם יָמִים מֵעַל
צַוַּאר כָּל־הַגּוֹיִם וַיֵּלֶךְ יִרְמְיָה
12 הַנָּבִיא לְדַרְכּוֹ: וַיְהִי דְבַר־
יְהֹוָה אֶל־יִרְמְיָה אַחֲרֵי שְׁבוֹר
חֲנַנְיָה הַנָּבִיא אֶת־הַמּוֹטָה
מֵעַל צַוַּאר יִרְמְיָה הַנָּבִיא
13 לֵאמֹר: הָלוֹךְ וְאָמַרְתָּ אֶל־
חֲנַנְיָה לֵאמֹר כֹּה אָמַר יְהֹוָה
מוֹטֹת עֵץ שָׁבָרְתָּ וְעָשִׂיתָ
14 תַחְתֵּיהֶן מֹטוֹת בַּרְזֶל: כִּי
כֹה־אָמַר יְהֹוָה צְבָאוֹת אֱלֹהֵי
יִשְׂרָאֵל עֹל בַּרְזֶל נָתַתִּי עַל־
צַוַּאר | כָּל־הַגּוֹיִם הָאֵלֶּה
לַעֲבֹד אֶת־נְבֻכַדְנֶאצַּר
מֶלֶךְ־בָּבֶל וַעֲבָדֻהוּ וְגַם אֶת־
15 חַיַּת הַשָּׂדֶה נָתַתִּי לוֹ: וַיֹּאמֶר
יִרְמְיָה הַנָּבִיא אֶל־חֲנַנְיָה
הַנָּבִיא שְׁמַע־נָא חֲנַנְיָה לֹא־
שְׁלָחֲךָ יְהֹוָה וְאַתָּה הִבְטַחְתָּ
אֶת־הָעָם הַזֶּה עַל־שָׁקֶר:

but evidences his disagreement by breaking the yoke worn by Jeremiah to express his conviction that the Babylonian yoke would be similarly broken.

11. *went his way.* Jeremiah makes no retort to Hananiah, either because he was so astounded at the latter's audacity to make a prediction that would soon be disproved; or possibly, because God

had not instructed him to make any further statements (Daath Soferim).

13. *thou shalt make in their stead bars of iron.* By breaking the wooden bar, you are imposing a heavier yoke upon the people as the sequel of the revolt to which you incite them (Metsudath David).

14. *the beasts of the field.* See on xxvii. 6.

16. Therefore thus saith the LORD:
Behold, I will send thee away from
off the face of the earth; this year
thou shalt die, because thou hast
spoken perversion against the LORD.'
17. So Hananiah the prophet died
the same year in the seventh month.

16 לָכֵ֗ן כֹּ֚ה אָמַ֣ר יְהוָ֔ה הִנְנִ֥י
מְשַׁלֵּֽחֲךָ֙ מֵעַ֖ל פְּנֵ֣י הָאֲדָמָ֑ה
הַשָּׁנָה֙ אַתָּ֣ה מֵ֔ת כִּֽי־סָרָ֖ה
17 דִבַּ֥רְתָּ אֶל־־יְהֹוָֽה: וַיָּ֛מָת
חֲנַנְיָ֥ה הַנָּבִ֖יא בַּשָּׁנָ֣ה הַהִ֑יא
בַּחֹ֖דֶשׁ הַשְּׁבִיעִֽי:

29   CHAPTER XXIX   **כט**

1. Now these are the words of the
letter that Jeremiah the prophet sent
from Jerusalem unto the residue of
the elders of the captivity, and to
the priests, and to the prophets, and
to all the people, whom Nebuchadnezzar had carried away captive

1 וְאֵ֙לֶּה֙ דִּבְרֵ֣י הַסֵּ֔פֶר אֲשֶׁ֥ר שָׁלַ֖ח
יִרְמְיָ֣ה הַנָּבִ֑יא מִירוּשָׁלִָ֖ם אֶל־־
יֶ֣תֶר זִקְנֵ֣י הַגּוֹלָ֑ה וְאֶל־־
הַכֹּֽהֲנִ֗ים וְאֶל־הַנְּבִיאִים֙ וְאֶל־
כָּל־־הָעָ֔ם אֲשֶׁ֛ר הֶגְלָ֖ה

---

16. *perversion.* [You have perverted
God's message.]

17. *in the seventh month.* Two months
later (cf. verse 1).

CHAPTER XXIX

ALTHOUGH like other prophets Jeremiah
had taught that the exile was punishment for the people's sins, now that
many inhabitants of Judea were in
captivity (the allusion is to those who
were carried off with king Jeconiah in
597 B.C.E.), it was his duty to preach
hope and encouragement to them.
Though he smote his people with verbal
castigations, he also healed, reviving the
smitten with fresh confidence. But he
was at the same time realistic, and
deemed it his duty to warn the people
not to delude themselves into thinking
that the exile would come to a speedy

end, as some false prophets were assuring them. The letter was probably written in 595 B.C.E.

1. *residue.* The reference is obscure. Is
it possible that many elders of the
captivity had perished in some disaster
not recorded elsewhere? Daath Mikra
conjectures that many of the elders
perished during the trek from the Holy
Land to Babylon. Daath Soferim explains that this is in contradistinction to
those elders who believed that the exile
would be very short and refused to heed
the words of the prophet. Metsudath
David explains that it is in contradistinction to those who remained in
Jerusalem.

elders ... priests ... prophets. [The
enumeration suggests that a form of
communal organization had been
retained in exile similar to that which
existed in Judea. Jeremiah's epistle was

from Jerusalem to Babylon, 2. after that Jeconiah the king, and the queen-mother, and the officers, and the princes of Judah and Jerusalem, and the craftsmen, and the smiths, were departed from Jerusalem; 3. by the hand of Elasah the son of Shaphan, and Gemariah the son of Hilkiah, whom Zedekiah king of Judah sent unto Babylon to Nebuchadnezzar king of Babylon, saying:

4. Thus saith the LORD of hosts, the God of Israel, unto all the captivity, whom I have caused to be

נְבוּכַדְנֶאצַּר מִירוּשָׁלַ͏ִם

2 בָּבֶלָה: אַחֲרֵי צֵאת יְכָנְיָה
הַמֶּלֶךְ וְהַגְּבִירָה וְהַסָּרִיסִים
שָׂרֵי יְהוּדָה וִירוּשָׁלַ͏ִם וְהֶחָרָשׁ

3 וְהַמַּסְגֵּר מִירוּשָׁלָ͏ִם: בְּיַד
אֶלְעָשָׂה בֶן־שָׁפָן וּגְמַרְיָה בֶּן־
חִלְקִיָּה אֲשֶׁר שָׁלַח צִדְקִיָּה
מֶלֶךְ־יְהוּדָה אֶל־
נְבוּכַדְנֶאצַּר מֶלֶךְ בָּבֶל

4 בָּבֶלָה לֵאמֹר: כֹּה אָמַר יְהֹוָה
צְבָאוֹת אֱלֹהֵי יִשְׂרָאֵל לְכָל־
הַגּוֹלָה אֲשֶׁר־הִגְלֵיתִי

an 'open letter' addressed to all sections of the captives.]

2. *Jeconiah.* See on xxii. 24.

the queen-mother. Nehushta; see on xiii. 18.

the craftsmen, and the smiths. See on xxiv. 1.

were departed. Into exile (Metsudath David).

3. *Elasah the son of Shaphan.* Probably the brother of Ahikam the son of Shaphan who protected Jeremiah when the priests and the people demanded his death (xxvi. 24) (Daath Mikra).

Gemariah. The name, but of a different person, occurs again in xxxvi. 10ff.

Hilkiah. Possibly identical with the High Priest of that name mentioned in 2 Kings xxii. 4. However, it is not mentioned that he was a priest (Daath Mikra).

whom Zedekiah . . . sent unto Babylon. [The purpose of the mission is not

stated. Perhaps it was in connection with the affairs and problems of the exiles; or they bore tribute to the Babylonian king. It hardly seems likely that they were sent for the purpose of delivering Jeremiah's message, though it is not impossible, since its contents would have the approval of Nebuchadnezzar.]

saying. This refers back to the *letter* in verse 1 (Metsudath David).

4ff. Jeremiah's message contains a direction which was accepted by the Jewish people in subsequent ages. Since the overthrow of the State in 135 C.E., while the Jew never ceased to hope in an ultimate restoration to Zion, he modelled his relations to the land of his birth or domicile upon Jeremiah's advice. So far as he was permitted, he struck roots there, 'building houses and planting gardens,' and fully identifying himself with the interests of the country. Above all, he 'sought the peace of the city,' loyal citizenship being considered by him a religious duty. The fact that Jeremiah could urge this doctrine upon

carried away captive from Jerusalem unto Babylon:

5. Build ye houses, and dwell in them, and plant gardens, and eat the fruit of them; 6. take ye wives, and beget sons and daughters; and take wives for your sons, and give your daughters to husbands, that they may bear sons and daughters; and multiply ye there, and be not diminished. 7. And seek the peace of the city whither I have caused you to be carried away captive, and pray unto the LORD for it; for in the peace thereof shall ye have peace.

8. For thus saith the LORD of hosts, the God of Israel: Let not

5 מִירוּשָׁלַ͏ִם בָּבֶלָה׃ בְּנוּ בָתִּים
וְשֵׁבוּ וְנִטְעוּ גַנּוֹת וְאִכְלוּ אֶת־
6 פִּרְיָן׃ קְחוּ נָשִׁים וְהוֹלִידוּ
בָּנִים וּבָנוֹת וּקְחוּ לִבְנֵיכֶם
נָשִׁים וְאֶת־בְּנוֹתֵיכֶם תְּנוּ
לַאֲנָשִׁים וְתֵלַדְנָה בָּנִים וּבָנוֹת
וּרְבוּ־שָׁם וְאַל־תִּמְעָטוּ׃
7 וְדִרְשׁוּ אֶת־שְׁלוֹם הָעִיר
אֲשֶׁר הִגְלֵיתִי אֶתְכֶם שָׁמָּה
וְהִתְפַּלְלוּ בַעֲדָהּ אֶל־יְהֹוָה
כִּי בִשְׁלוֹמָהּ יִהְיֶה לָכֶם
8 שָׁלוֹם׃ כִּי כֹה אָמַר יְהֹוָה
צְבָאוֹת אֱלֹהֵי יִשְׂרָאֵל אַל־

---

the exiles, while at the same time assuring them of their restoration after seventy years (verse 10), indicates that in his mind no mutually exclusive dual loyalty was involved, but that on the contrary each fortified the other. This, too, has been the attitude of the Jewish people in the Diaspora.

5. *build ye houses,* etc. The exiles in Babylon did not suffer the restrictions which were imposed upon Jews in many countries in later times. They were permitted to own land and engage in agriculture. It is noteworthy that Jeremiah's advice did not include engaging in commerce, in which direction it is now thought that the ability of Jews chiefly lay. A variety of circumstances, such as the interdict upon their owning land, combined to force them from the soil and drive them into trade. In the first century C.E. Josephus wrote, 'As for ourselves, we neither inhabit a maritime country, nor delight in commerce, nor in such intercourse with other men as arises from it; but the cities we dwell in are remote from the sea, and as we have a fruitful country to dwell in, we take pains in cultivating it' (*Contra Apionem,* i. 12).

6. *take ye wives,* etc. Celibacy is foreign to Judaism, and the duty to propagate the species is regarded as the first of the precepts of the Torah (Gen. i. 28 and see on xvi. 2). From this duty, an indication of Judaism's robust optimism, not even the grief of the exile was to deflect them. The advice also reenforced the warning that the stay in Babylon would be of long duration (see Malbim).

7. *and pray unto the* LORD *for it.* Cf. Ezra vi. 10 where Cyrus asked for the prayers of the people and 1 Macc. vii. 33 which tells that a sacrifice was offered in the Temple for the Syrian monarchy. A Rabbi exhorted, 'Pray for the welfare of the government, since but for the fear of it men would swallow each other alive' (Aboth). Similar expressions of loyalty

your prophets that are in the midst of you, and your diviners, beguile you, neither hearken ye to your dreams which ye cause to be dreamed. 9. For they prophesy falsely unto you in My name; I have not sent them, saith the LORD.

10. For thus saith the LORD: After seventy years are accomplished for Babylon, I will remember you, and perform My good word toward you, in causing you to return to this place. 11. For I know the thoughts that I think toward you, saith the LORD, thoughts of peace, and not of evil, to give you a future and a hope. 12. And ye shall call upon Me, and go, and pray unto Me, and I will

יַשִּׁיאוּ לָכֶם נְבִיאֵיכֶם אֲשֶׁר־
בְּקִרְבְּכֶם וְקֹסְמֵיכֶם וְאַל־
תִּשְׁמְעוּ אֶל־חֲלֹמֹתֵיכֶם אֲשֶׁר
9 אַתֶּם מַחְלְמִים: כִּי בְשֶׁקֶר
הֵם נִבְּאִים לָכֶם בִּשְׁמִי לֹא
10 שְׁלַחְתִּים נְאֻם־יְהֹוָה: כִּי־
כֹה אָמַר יְהֹוָה כִּי לְפִי מְלֹאת
לְבָבֶל שִׁבְעִים שָׁנָה אֶפְקֹד
אֶתְכֶם וַהֲקִמֹתִי עֲלֵיכֶם אֶת־
דְּבָרִי הַטּוֹב לְהָשִׁיב אֶתְכֶם
11 אֶל־הַמָּקוֹם הַזֶּה: כִּי אָנֹכִי
יָדַעְתִּי אֶת־הַמַּחֲשָׁבֹת אֲשֶׁר
אָנֹכִי חֹשֵׁב עֲלֵיכֶם נְאֻם־יְהֹוָה
מַחְשְׁבוֹת שָׁלוֹם וְלֹא לְרָעָה
לָתֵת לָכֶם אַחֲרִית וְתִקְוָה:
12 וּקְרָאתֶם אֹתִי וַהֲלַכְתֶּם
וְהִתְפַּלַּלְתֶּם אֵלָי וְשָׁמַעְתִּי

---

to the State are recorded in Josephus, *The Jewish War*, II, xvii. 3 and *Contra Apionem*, ii. 6. To this day, the prayer for the king (or head of the State) and his advisers is part of the Service on Sabbaths and Festivals (cf. A.D.P.B., p. 153).

8. *which ye cause to be dreamed.* By asking the professional seers to reveal the future by means of oracles derived from dreams (Metsudath David).

10. *seventy years.* See on xxv. 11.

for Babylon. The time for her downfall will then have been reached (see on xxv. 12).

My good word. My promise of redemption as recorded in xxvii. 22.

11. *for I know.* The *I* is emphatic and indicates a contrast: however you may interpret the purpose of the exile, *I know*, etc. (Daath Mikra).

12. Just as predictions of disaster are conditional upon whether the people persist in their evil, so are God's promises of restoration dependent upon penitence. He will not show favour to Israel simply because they are His people; it must be deserved. The characteristic feature of this passage, as indeed of all the prophecies of redemp-

hearken unto you. 13. And ye shall seek Me, and find Me, when ye shall search for Me with all your heart. 14. And I will be found of you, saith the LORD, and I will turn your captivity, and gather you from all the nations, and from all the places whither I have driven you, saith the LORD; and I will bring you back unto the place whence I caused you to be carried away captive. 15. For ye have said: 'The LORD hath raised us up prophets in Babylon.' 16. For thus saith the LORD concerning the king that sitteth upon the throne of David, and concerning all the people

אֲלֵיכֶם: וּבִקַּשְׁתֶּם אֹתִי 13
וּמְצָאתֶם כִּי תִדְרְשֻׁנִי בְּכָל־
לְבַבְכֶם: וְנִמְצֵאתִי לָכֶם 14
נְאֻם־יְהֹוָה וְשַׁבְתִּי אֶת־
שְׁבִיתְכֶם וְקִבַּצְתִּי אֶתְכֶם
מִכָּל־הַגּוֹיִם וּמִכָּל־
הַמְּקֹמוֹת אֲשֶׁר הִדַּחְתִּי
אֶתְכֶם שָׁם נְאֻם־יְהֹוָה
וַהֲשִׁבֹתִי אֶתְכֶם אֶל־הַמָּקוֹם
אֲשֶׁר־הִגְלֵיתִי אֶתְכֶם מִשָּׁם:
כִּי אֲמַרְתֶּם הֵקִים לָנוּ יְהֹוָה 15
נְבִאִים בָּבֶלָה: כִּי־כֹה אָמַר 16
יְהֹוָה אֶל־הַמֶּלֶךְ הַיּוֹשֵׁב אֶל־
כִּסֵּא דָוִד וְאֶל־כָּל־הָעָם

v. 14. שבותכם ק׳ v. 16. נ״א על

tion, is the conviction on the part of the prophets that through suffering Israel would be purged of sin and thereby earn salvation.

13. *ye shall seek Me, and find Me.* 'This is a great pronouncement of Scripture, proclaiming the omnipotence of repentance. But the sinner must *seek* God; i.e. he must feel the "loss" of God, and take active measures to *find* Him and regain His favour. And that search must be with the sinner's whole heart and soul. Sincere repentance always and everywhere secures the Divine mercy. It would be so in the exile, if they sought God with a radical change of heart, and the devotion of the whole being. And indeed it was in the exile that repentant Israel found God, rediscovered the Torah, rediscovered itself' (Hertz, *The Pentateuch,* Soncino edition, p. 762).

14. *I will be found of you.* The literal

translation is probably 'and I will make Myself found unto you': God makes Himself readily accessible to those who seek Him in true repentance; cf. the Talmudic teaching, 'If one comes to cleanse himself (from sin), he is helped (by God)' (Shab. 104a).

15–19. A repeated admonition to the people not to allow themselves to be beguiled. They maintain that God has given them prophets in Babylon who predict a speedy return. So far from this being true, even they who are still in Judea are destined for destruction because they have not yet learned the grim lesson of the misfortune of the present captives and still refuse to hearken to God's word.

15. *prophets in Babylon.* Who prophesy a return in the near future (Kimchi).

16. *the king.* Zedekiah (Rashi).

that dwell in this city, your brethren that are not gone forth with you into captivity; 17. thus saith the LORD of hosts: Behold, I will send upon them the sword, the famine, and the pestilence, and will make them like vile figs, that cannot be eaten, they are so bad. 18. And I will pursue after them with the sword, with the famine, and with the pestilence, and will make them a horror unto all the kingdoms of the earth, a curse, and an astonishment, and a hissing, and a reproach, among all the nations whither I have driven them; 19. because they have not hearkened to My words, saith the LORD, wherewith I sent unto them My servants the prophets, sending them betimes and often; but ye would not hear, saith the LORD. 20. Hear ye therefore the word of the LORD, all ye of the

הַיּוֹשֵׁב בָּעִיר הַזֹּאת אֲחֵיכֶם
אֲשֶׁר לֹא־יָצְאוּ אִתְּכֶם
17 בַּגּוֹלָה: כֹּה אָמַר יְהֹוָה
צְבָאוֹת הִנְנִי מְשַׁלֵּחַ בָּם אֶת־
הַחֶרֶב אֶת־הָרָעָב וְאֶת־
הַדָּבֶר וְנָתַתִּי אוֹתָם כַּתְּאֵנִים
הַשֹּׁעָרִים אֲשֶׁר לֹא־תֵאָכַלְנָה
18 מֵרֹעַ: וְרָדַפְתִּי אַחֲרֵיהֶם
בַּחֶרֶב בָּרָעָב וּבַדָּבֶר וּנְתַתִּים
לְזַעֲוָה לְכֹל מַמְלְכוֹת הָאָרֶץ
לְאָלָה וּלְשַׁמָּה וְלִשְׁרֵקָה
וּלְחֶרְפָּה בְּכָל־הַגּוֹיִם אֲשֶׁר־
19 הִדַּחְתִּים שָׁם: תַּחַת אֲשֶׁר־
לֹא־שָׁמְעוּ אֶל־דְּבָרַי
נְאֻם־יְהֹוָה אֲשֶׁר שָׁלַחְתִּי
אֲלֵיהֶם אֶת־עֲבָדַי הַנְּבִאִים
הַשְׁכֵּם וְשָׁלֹחַ וְלֹא שְׁמַעְתֶּם
20 נְאֻם־יְהֹוָה: וְאַתֶּם שִׁמְעוּ
דְבַר־יְהֹוָה כָּל־הַגּוֹלָה

v. 18. לזעוה ק׳

this city. Jerusalem.

17. *like vile figs.* Cf. xxiv. 2-10.

18. *whither I have driven them.* The prophetic perfect (Metsudath David).

19. *because they have not hearkened.* i.e. all this punishment will befall them because they did not hearken, viz. your forefathers did not hearken (Abarbanel).

sending them betimes and often. Although

I sent them early and often, with great eagerness, they did not hearken to them (Metsudath David).

ye would not hear. Not only did your forefathers refuse to listen, but you too would not hear (Abarbanel).

20. *hear ye therefore.* The emphasis is on *ye*: they in Judea have refused to hear; then do *ye* in captivity hear my words and do not heed the false prophets (Abarbanel).

captivity, whom I have sent away from Jerusalem to Babylon: 21. Thus saith the LORD of hosts, the God of Israel, concerning Ahab the son of Kolaiah, and concerning Zedekiah the son of Maaseiah, who prophesy a lie unto you in My name: Behold, I will deliver them into the hand of Nebuchadrezzar king of Babylon; and he shall slay them before your eyes; 22. and of them shall be taken up a curse by all the captivity of Judah that are in Babylon, saying: 'The LORD make thee like Zedekiah and like Ahab, whom the king of Babylon roasted in the fire'; 23. because they have wrought vile deeds in Israel, and have committed adultery with their neighbours' wives, and have spoken words in My name falsely, which I commanded them not; but I am He that knoweth, and am witness, saith the LORD.

24. And concerning Shemaiah the Nehelamite thou shalt speak, saying:

אֲשֶׁר־שִׁלַּחְתִּי מִירוּשָׁלַם
21 בָּבֶלָה: כֹּה־אָמַר יְהֹוָה
צְבָאוֹת אֱלֹהֵי יִשְׂרָאֵל אֶל־
אַחְאָב בֶּן־קוֹלָיָה וְאֶל־
צִדְקִיָּהוּ בֶן־מַעֲשֵׂיָה הַנִּבְּאִים
לָכֶם בִּשְׁמִי שָׁקֶר הִנְנִי ׀ נֹתֵן
אֹתָם בְּיַד נְבוּכַדְרֶאצַּר
מֶלֶךְ־בָּבֶל וְהִכָּם לְעֵינֵיכֶם:
22 וְלֻקַּח מֵהֶם קְלָלָה לְכֹל גָּלוּת
יְהוּדָה אֲשֶׁר בְּבָבֶל לֵאמֹר
יְשִׂמְךָ יְהֹוָה כְּצִדְקִיָּהוּ וּכְאֶחָב
אֲשֶׁר־קָלָם מֶלֶךְ־בָּבֶל
23 בָּאֵשׁ: יַעַן אֲשֶׁר עָשׂוּ נְבָלָה
בְיִשְׂרָאֵל וַיְנַאֲפוּ אֶת־נְשֵׁי
רֵעֵיהֶם וַיְדַבְּרוּ דָבָר בִּשְׁמִי
שֶׁקֶר אֲשֶׁר לוֹא צִוִּיתִם וְאָנֹכִי
הַוֹּיֵדֵעַ וָעֵד נְאֻם־יְהֹוָה:
24 וְאֶל־שְׁמַעְיָהוּ הַנֶּחֱלָמִי

v. 23. היודע ק'

---

21. *Ahab . . . Zedekiah.* Nothing more is known of these men.

he shall slay them. They forfeited their lives because they issued messages to the Judeans in exile which were regarded as treason by the Babylonian king (Daath Mikra).

22. *a curse.* Since they will meet their death through fire, a very agonizing death, their name will serve as a curse among the exiles (Abarbanel). A play on the name Kolaiah is to be detected: it is

connected with *kelalah* (a curse) and the verb *kalah* (to roast) (Daath Mikra).

23. *vile deeds.* Hebrew *nebalah*, usually denoting a gross act of immorality (cf. Gen. xxxiv. 7; Deut. xxii. 21). This was a sin against God Who punished them by delivering them into the hand of Nebuchadnezzar as guilty of treasonous utterances, for which they paid the penalty of death by burning (Daath Mikra).

24. *the Nehelamite.* According to Tar-

25. Thus speaketh the Lord of hosts, the God of Israel, saying: Because thou hast sent letters in thine own name unto all the people that are at Jerusalem, and to Zephaniah the son of Maaseiah the priest, and to all the priests, saying: 26. 'The Lord hath made thee priest in the stead of Jehoiada the priest, that there should be officers in the house of the Lord for every man that is mad, and maketh himself a prophet, that thou shouldest put him in the stocks and in the collar. 27. Now therefore, why hast thou not rebuked Jeremiah of Anathoth, who maketh himself a prophet to you, 28. forasmuch as he hath sent unto us in Babylon, saying: The captivity is long; build ye houses, and dwell in them; and plant gardens, and eat the fruit of them?' 29. And Zephaniah the priest read this letter in the ears of Jeremiah the

25 תֹּאמַר לֵאמֹר׃ כֹּה־אָמַ֣ר
יְהוָ֤ה צְבָאוֹת֙ אֱלֹהֵ֣י יִשְׂרָאֵ֔ל
לֵאמֹ֑ר יַ֣עַן אֲשֶׁ֣ר אַתָּ֣ה שָׁלַ֣חְתָּ
בְשִׁמְכָ֣ה סְפָרִ֗ים אֶל־כָּל־
הָעָם֙ אֲשֶׁ֣ר בִּירוּשָׁלַ֔ם וְאֶל־
צְפַנְיָ֥ה בֶן־מַֽעֲשֵׂיָ֖ה הַכֹּהֵ֑ן
וְאֶל־כָּל־הַכֹּהֲנִ֖ים לֵאמֹֽר׃
26 יְהוָ֞ה נְתָנְךָ֣ כֹהֵ֗ן תַּ֚חַת יְהוֹיָדָ֣ע
הַכֹּהֵ֔ן לִהְי֞וֹת פְּקִדִים֙ בֵּ֣ית
יְהוָ֔ה לְכָל־אִ֥ישׁ מְשֻׁגָּ֖ע
וּמִתְנַבֵּ֑א וְנָתַתָּ֥ה אֹת֖וֹ אֶל־
הַמַּהְפֶּ֖כֶת וְאֶל־הַצִּינֹֽק׃
27 וְעַתָּ֗ה לָ֚מָּה לֹ֣א גָעַ֔רְתָּ
בְּיִרְמְיָ֖הוּ הָֽעֲנְּתֹתִ֑י הַמִּתְנַבֵּ֖א
28 לָכֶֽם׃ כִּ֣י עַל־כֵּ֞ן שָׁלַ֤ח אֵלֵ֙ינוּ֙
בָּבֶ֣ל לֵאמֹ֔ר אֲרֻכָּ֖ה הִ֑יא בְּנ֤וּ
בָתִּים֙ וְשֵׁ֔בוּ וְנִטְע֥וּ גַנּ֖וֹת וְאִכְל֥וּ
29 אֶת־פְּרִיהֶֽן׃ וַיִּקְרָ֛א צְפַנְיָ֥ה
הַכֹּהֵ֖ן אֶת־הַסֵּ֣פֶר הַזֶּ֑ה

v. 25. יתיר ה׳

gum and Rashi this is a place name, not otherwise known. Jeremiah's letter aroused bitter indignation in a leading captive who seeks to have him suppressed as a madman.

25. *in thine own name.* Without the authority of the exiles (Metsudath David). He pretended to be a true prophet and to represent the Babylonian exiles (Abarbanel).

Zephaniah. See on xxi. 1.

26. *thee.* Zephaniah. Verses 26–28 give the text of Shemaiah's letter.

Jehoiada. He mentions Jehoiada since he was a high priest and the greatest of his generation. This is Jehoiada who served during the reign of Jehoash king of Judah (2 Kings xi.) (Kimchi). From here we learn that his function was to maintain order there and suppress disturbances.

29. *read this letter,* etc. Zephaniah was

prophet. 30. Then came the word of the LORD unto Jeremiah, saying: 31. Send to all them of the captivity, saying: Thus saith the LORD concerning Shemaiah the Nehelamite: Because that Shemaiah hath prophesied unto you, and I sent him not, and he hath caused you to trust in a lie; 32. therefore thus saith the LORD: Behold, I will punish Shemaiah the Nehelamite, and his seed; he shall not have a man to dwell among this people, neither shall he behold the good that I will do unto My people, saith the LORD; because he hath spoken perversion against the LORD.

30 וַיְהִי אֶל־יִרְמְיָהוּ הַנָּבִיא: בְּאָזְנֵי
דְּבַר־יְהֹוָה אֶל־יִרְמְיָהוּ
31 לֵאמֹר: שְׁלַח עַל־כָּל־
הַגּוֹלָה לֵאמֹר כֹּה אָמַר יְהֹוָה
אֶל־שְׁמַעְיָה הַנֶּחֱלָמִי יַעַן
אֲשֶׁר נִבָּא לָכֶם שְׁמַעְיָה וַאֲנִי
לֹא שְׁלַחְתִּיו וַיַּבְטַח אֶתְכֶם
32 עַל־שָׁקֶר: לָכֵן כֹּה־אָמַר
יְהֹוָה הִנְנִי פֹקֵד עַל־שְׁמַעְיָה
הַנֶּחֱלָמִי וְעַל־זַרְעוֹ לֹא־
יִהְיֶה לוֹ אִישׁ ׀ יוֹשֵׁב ׀ בְּתוֹךְ־
הָעָם הַזֶּה וְלֹא־יִרְאֶה בַטּוֹב
אֲשֶׁר־אֲנִי עֹשֶׂה־לְעַמִּי נְאֻם־
יְהֹוָה כִּי־סָרָה דִבֶּר עַל־
יְהֹוָה:

30   CHAPTER XXX   ל

1. The word that came to Jeremiah from the LORD, saying: 2. 'Thus

1 הַדָּבָר אֲשֶׁר־הָיָה אֶל־
יִרְמְיָהוּ מֵאֵת יְהֹוָה לֵאמֹר:

evidently in sympathy with the prophet (Daath Mikra). Or, perhaps he read it as an indictment to Jeremiah. Zephaniah, however, was more moderate than the other priests of Jehoiakim's reign (Daath Soferim).

32. *the good.* The restoration of the people to their land (Metsudath David). As Shemaiah could not in any case have experienced this event, which was to take place seventy years hence, it must be understood as referring to his descendants. They would be denied the

happiness of returning to the ancestral home. Daath Soferim, however, explains that Shemaiah would not be granted the good life enjoyed by the Babylonian exiles.

perversion. Hebrew *sarah*; see on xxviii. 16.

CHAPTER XXX

PROMISE OF NATIONAL RESTORATION

THE biographical chapters are interrupted by the insertion of xxx and xxxi

speaketh the LORD, the God of
Israel, saying: Write thee all the
words that I have spoken unto thee
in a book.   3. For, lo, the days come,
saith the LORD, that I will turn the
captivity of My people Israel and
Judah, saith the LORD; and I will
cause them to return to the land
that I gave to their fathers, and they
shall possess it.'

4. And these are the words that
the LORD spoke concerning Israel
and concerning Judah.   5. For thus
saith the LORD:

> We have heard a voice of trembl-
> ing,
>
> Of fear, and not of peace.

6 Ask ye now, and see

2 כֹּה־אָמַ֞ר יְהֹוָ֤ה אֱלֹהֵי֙ יִשְׂרָאֵ֣ל
לֵאמֹ֑ר כְּתׇב־לְךָ֗ אֵ֣ת כׇּל־
הַדְּבָרִ֛ים אֲשֶׁר־דִּבַּ֥רְתִּי
3 אֵלֶ֖יךָ אֶל־סֵֽפֶר׃ כִּ֣י הִנֵּ֪ה
יָמִ֣ים בָּאִים֩ נְאֻם־יְהֹוָ֨ה וְשַׁבְתִּ֜י
אֶת־שְׁב֧וּת עַמִּ֛י יִשְׂרָאֵ֥ל
וִֽיהוּדָ֖ה אָמַ֣ר יְהֹוָ֑ה וַהֲשִׁבֹתִ֗ים
אֶל־הָאָ֛רֶץ אֲשֶׁר־נָתַ֥תִּי
4 לַאֲבוֹתָ֖ם וִֽירֵשֽׁוּהָ׃ וְאֵ֣לֶּה
הַדְּבָרִ֔ים אֲשֶׁ֛ר דִּבֶּ֥ר יְהֹוָ֖ה
אֶל־יִשְׂרָאֵ֣ל וְאֶל־יְהוּדָֽה׃
5 כִּי־כֹה֙ אָמַ֣ר יְהֹוָ֔ה
ק֥וֹל חֲרָדָ֖ה שָׁמָ֑עְנוּ
פַּ֖חַד וְאֵ֥ין שָׁלֽוֹם׃
6 שַׁאֲלוּ־נָ֣א וּרְא֗וּ

---

which develop the theme of national
restoration foretold at the end of the
last chapter. In the main they take the
exile for granted, and were apparently
written after the overthrow of Judah
(verse 18). The prophet had a twofold
duty: (i) to tell of impending disaster
consequent upon national sin; (ii) to
offer comfort and hope for the future
when the catastrophe had occurred.
There is nothing contradictory in the
two tasks; for as he has to be stern with
sinners and impress upon them the
inevitable consequences of their evil, so,
with the same goal of national amendment in view, he reassures the people
that they can be raised from their degradation since repentance is always within
their power. Passages such as this
demonstrate the falsity of the popular
conception of Jeremiah as a pessimist.
On the contrary, he was a realistic

optimist, clearly seeing the doom which
the Judeans were bringing upon themselves, and yet certain of their ultimate
recovery.

1–4   INTRODUCTORY

2. *write thee all the words . . . in a
book.* The implication is that the oracle
which follows forms a special and distinct prophecy, to be written in a
separate *book* or scroll (see Metsudath
David).

3. *Israel and Judah.* The restoration of
the whole nation of twelve tribes was the
prophetic ideal and hope (Metsudath
David).

5–9   THE NATION'S YOKE WILL BE BROKEN

5. *we have heard . . . peace.* This is a
quotation of the people's words, a

Whether a man doth travail with
child;
Wherefore do I see every man
With his hands on his loins, as a
woman in travail,
And all faces are turned into
paleness?

7 Alas! for that day is great,
So that none is like it;
And it is a time of trouble unto
Jacob,
But out of it shall he be saved.

8 And it shall come to pass in that
day,
Saith the LORD of hosts,
That I will break his yoke from
off thy neck,
And will burst thy bands;
And strangers shall no more make
him their bondman;

9 But they shall serve the LORD their
God,
And David their king,
Whom I will raise up unto them.

10 Therefore fear thou not, O Jacob
My servant, saith the LORD;

אִם־יֹלֵד זָכָר
מַדּוּעַ רָאִיתִי כָל־גֶּבֶר
יָדָיו עַל־חֲלָצָיו כַּיּוֹלֵדָה
וְנֶהֶפְכוּ כָל־פָּנִים לְיֵרָקוֹן:

7 הוֹי כִּי גָדוֹל הַיּוֹם הַהוּא
מֵאַיִן כָּמֹהוּ
וְעֵת־צָרָה הִיא לְיַעֲקֹב
וּמִמֶּנָּה יִוָּשֵׁעַ:

8 וְהָיָה בַיּוֹם הַהוּא
נְאֻם | יְהוָה צְבָאוֹת
אֶשְׁבֹּר עֻלּוֹ מֵעַל צַוָּארֶךָ
וּמוֹסְרוֹתֶיךָ אֲנַתֵּק
וְלֹא־יַעַבְדוּ־בוֹ עוֹד זָרִים:

9 וְעָבְדוּ אֵת יְהוָה אֱלֹהֵיהֶם
וְאֵת דָּוִד מַלְכָּם
אֲשֶׁר אָקִים לָהֶם:

10 וְאַתָּה אַל־תִּירָא
עַבְדִּי יַעֲקֹב נְאֻם־יְהוָֹה

---

phrase like 'ye say' being understood
before it. The verse expresses the popular fear and insecurity. It is followed by
words of Divine assurance (see Daath
Mikra).

6. The gestures which the men display
in their anguish are comparable with
the throes of a woman in childbirth.

7. *that day is great.* The day ushering in
the final deliverance will be great in
suffering and distress (Metsudath
David).

8. The change from the third to the
second person in this verse is not
unusual in Biblical literature.

9. *the* LORD *their God, and David their
king.* This is the true corollary to their
no longer serving strangers. They would
reach the highest form of liberty for
them, viz. the service of the LORD. His
Messianic regent on earth would be a
scion of the house of David (cf. Ezek.
xxxiv. 23; Hos. iii. 5).

10–11   GOD IS THEIR REDEEMER

Verse 10 is repeated almost *verbatim* in
xlvi. 27 and verse 11 is echoed in xlvi.
28.

10. *O Jacob My servant.* [A designation
of the people frequently used in the
second part of Isaiah.]

Neither be dismayed, O Israel;

For, lo, I will save thee from afar,

And thy seed from the land of
   their captivity;

And Jacob shall again be quiet
   and at ease,

And none shall make him afraid.

11 For I am with thee, saith the
   LORD, to save thee;

For I will make a full end of all
   the nations whither I have
   scattered thee,

But I will not make a full end of
   thee;

For I will correct thee in
   measure,

And will not utterly destroy thee.

12 For thus saith the LORD:

Thy hurt is incurable,

And thy wound is grievous.

13 None deemeth of thy wound that
   it may be bound up;

וְאַל־תֵּחַת יִשְׂרָאֵל

כִּי הִנְנִי מוֹשִׁיעֲךָ מֵרָחוֹק

וְאֶת־זַרְעֲךָ מֵאֶרֶץ שִׁבְיָם

וְשָׁב יַעֲקֹב וְשָׁקַט וְשַׁאֲנַן

וְאֵין מַחֲרִיד:

11 כִּי־אִתְּךָ אֲנִי

נְאֻם־יְהוָה לְהוֹשִׁיעֶךָ

כִּי אֶעֱשֶׂה כָלָה בְּכָל־הַגּוֹיִם ׀

אֲשֶׁר הֲפִצוֹתִיךָ שָּׁם

אַךְ אֹתְךָ לֹא־אֶעֱשֶׂה כָלָה

וְיִסַּרְתִּיךָ לַמִּשְׁפָּט

וְנַקֵּה לֹא אֲנַקֶּךָ:

12 כִּי כֹה אָמַר יְהוָה

אָנוּשׁ לְשִׁבְרֵךְ

נַחְלָה מַכָּתֵךְ:

13 אֵין־דָּן דִּינֵךְ לְמָזוֹר

---

from afar. The land of exile, no matter how distant it be (Kimchi).

11. *for I will make a full end of all the nations.* [This judgment is not pronounced in a spirit of partiality or vindictiveness. Israel alone of all those peoples possessed the recuperative power which enabled him to attain, through exile and suffering, spiritual and national regeneration. Not so the others, and a people that is irremediably corrupt must sooner or later perish. History has amply corroborated this prophecy: the great nations of antiquity, including those which drove Israel into exile, have disappeared, whereas he has suffered 'correction' but lives.]

I will correct thee in measure. See on x. 24

for *in measure.* Divine justice demands that Israel's sin shall not go unpunished; but he obtains pardon after being 'corrected' (Kara).

12–17   THEY WHO AFFLICTED ISRAEL WILL BE PUNISHED

The pronouns in this section are in the feminine as referring to the nation as a whole.

12. Jeremiah used somewhat similar language of himself in xv. 18.

13. *none deemeth of thy wound,* etc. A.J. reproduces the sense: the hurt done to thee. A.V. and R.V. render more literally: 'There is none to plead thy cause, that thou mayest be bound up.'

Thou hast no healing medicines.

14 All thy lovers have forgotten thee,
They seek thee not;
For I have wounded thee with the wound of an enemy,
With the chastisement of a cruel one;
For the greatness of thine iniquity,
Because thy sins were increased.

15 Why criest thou for thy hurt,
That thy pain is incurable?
For the greatness of thine iniquity, because thy sins were increased,
I have done these things unto thee.

16 Therefore all they that devour thee shall be devoured,
And all thine adversaries, every one of them, shall go into captivity;
And they that spoil thee shall be a spoil,
And all that prey upon thee will I give for a prey.

17 For I will restore health unto thee,
And I will heal thee of thy wounds, saith the LORD;
Because they have called thee an outcast:
'She is Zion, there is none that careth for her.'

רְפֻאוֹת תְּעָלָה אֵין לָךְ ׃

14 כָּל־מְאַהֲבַיִךְ שְׁכֵחוּךְ
אוֹתָךְ לֹא יִדְרֹשׁוּ
כִּי מַכַּת אוֹיֵב הִכִּיתִיךְ
מוּסַר אַכְזָרִי
עַל רֹב עֲוֹנֵךְ
עָצְמוּ חַטֹּאתָיִךְ ׃

15 מַה־תִּזְעַק עַל־שִׁבְרֵךְ
אָנוּשׁ מַכְאֹבֵךְ
עַל ׀ רֹב עֲוֹנֵךְ עָצְמוּ חַטֹּאתַיִךְ
עָשִׂיתִי אֵלֶּה לָךְ ׃

16 לָכֵן כָּל־אֹכְלַיִךְ יֵאָכֵלוּ
וְכָל־צָרַיִךְ כֻּלָּם בַּשְּׁבִי יֵלֵכוּ
וְהָיוּ שֹׁאסַיִךְ לִמְשִׁסָּה
וְכָל־בֹּזְזַיִךְ אֶתֵּן לָבַז ׃

17 כִּי אַעֲלֶה אֲרֻכָה לָךְ
וּמִמַּכּוֹתַיִךְ אֶרְפָּאֵךְ
נְאֻם־יְהוָה
כִּי נִדָּחָה קָרְאוּ לָךְ
צִיּוֹן הִיא דֹּרֵשׁ אֵין לָהּ ׃

v. 16. יתיר א'

---

14. *thy lovers.* See on xxii. 20. When Israel was still in his country, his allies proved but broken reeds. Now that he is in exile, they have forgotten him (Metsudath David).

15. *why criest thou . . . incurable?* The sufferings have not been without cause; they are the consequence of national sin (Metsudath David).

16. *therefore.* Because God's justice

has gone to the length of afflicting Israel so severely, his tormentors also will receive condign punishment (Metsudath David).

and they that spoil thee, etc. On the principle of measure for measure (Daath Mikra).

17. *I will restore health unto thee.* See on viii. 22.

she is Zion. Ill-wishers connected the

18 Thus saith the LORD:
   Behold, I will turn the captivity
      of Jacob's tents,
   And have compassion on his
      dwelling-places;
   And the city shall be builded
      upon her own mound,
   And the palace shall be in-
      habited upon its wonted place.
19 And out of them shall proceed
      thanksgiving
   And the voice of them that make
      merry;
   And I will multiply them, and
      they shall not be diminished,
   I will also increase them, and
      they shall not dwindle away.
20 Their children also shall be as
      aforetime,
   And their congregation shall be
      established before Me,
   And I will punish all that oppress
      them.
21 And their prince shall be of
      themselves,
   And their ruler shall proceed
      from the midst of them;
   And I will cause him to draw
      near, and he shall approach
      unto Me;
   For who is he that hath pledged
      his heart
   To approach unto Me? saith the
      LORD.

18 כֹּה ׀ אָמַר יְהוָֹה
הִנְנִי־שָׁב שְׁבוּת אָהֳלֵי יַעֲקוֹב
וּמִשְׁכְּנֹתָיו אֲרַחֵם
וְנִבְנְתָה עִיר עַל־תִּלָּהּ
וְאַרְמוֹן עַל־מִשְׁפָּטוֹ יֵשֵׁב:
19 וְיָצָא מֵהֶם תּוֹדָה
וְקוֹל מְשַׂחֲקִים
וְהִרְבִּתִים וְלֹא יִמְעָטוּ
וְהִכְבַּדְתִּים וְלֹא יִצְעָרוּ:
20 וְהָיוּ בָנָיו כְּקֶדֶם
וַעֲדָתוֹ לְפָנַי תִּכּוֹן
וּפָקַדְתִּי עַל כָּל־לֹחֲצָיו:
21 וְהָיָה אַדִּירוֹ מִמֶּנּוּ
וּמֹשְׁלוֹ מִקִּרְבּוֹ יֵצֵא
וְהִקְרַבְתִּיו וְנִגַּשׁ אֵלַי
כִּי מִי הוּא־זֶה עָרַב אֶת־לִבּוֹ
לָגֶשֶׁת אֵלַי נְאֻם־יְהוָֹה:

מלא ר׳ v. 18.

name Zion with *tsiyyah*, 'a desert' (see
Mandelkern).

18-22 JERUSALEM WILL BE REBUILT AND
         HAPPY

18. *his dwelling-places.* Which are now
desolate (Metsudath David).

her own mound. i.e. on the original site.
Cities were often built on hills or
mounds (Hebrew *tel*), to guard against a
sudden surprise attack. Also, because
the air was cooler and fresher (Daath
Mikra).

19. *thanksgiving.* Cf. xxxiii. 11.

20. *as aforetime.* They shall be dear to
Me as aforetime (Metsudath David).

shall be established before Me. God will
watch over and guard them (Metsudath
David).

21. *of themselves ... from the midst of
them.* They will no longer be subject to
foreign rule (Kimchi).

I will cause him to draw near. I will
inspire him to fear Me, and his fear of
Me will become more and more intense
(Metsudath David).

for who is he, etc. The clause is of
uncertain meaning. A.V. has 'for who is

22 And ye shall be My people,
   And I will be your God.

23 Behold, a storm of the LORD is
   gone forth in fury,
   A sweeping storm;
   It shall whirl upon the head of
   the wicked.

24 The fierce anger of the LORD
   shall not return,
   Until He have executed, and till
   He have performed
   The purposes of His heart;
   In the end of days ye shall
   consider it.

25 At that time, saith the LORD,
   Will I be the God of all the
   families of Israel,
   And they shall be My people.

וֶהְיִיתֶם לִי לְעָם 22
וְאָנֹכִי אֶהְיֶה לָכֶם לֵאלֹהִים׃

הִנֵּה ׀ סַעֲרַת יְהוָֹה חֵמָה יָצְאָה 23
סַעַר מִתְגּוֹרֵר
עַל רֹאשׁ רְשָׁעִים יָחוּל׃

לֹא יָשׁוּב חֲרוֹן אַף־יְהוָֹה 24
עַד־עֲשֹׂתוֹ וְעַד־הֲקִימוֹ
מְזִמּוֹת לִבּוֹ
בְּאַחֲרִית הַיָּמִים תִּתְבּוֹנְנוּ בָהּ׃

בָּעֵת הַהִיא נְאֻם־יְהוָֹה 25
אֶהְיֶה לֵאלֹהִים
לְכֹל מִשְׁפְּחוֹת יִשְׂרָאֵל
וְהֵמָּה יִהְיוּ־לִי לְעָם׃

31   CHAPTER XXXI   לא

1 Thus saith the LORD:
   The people that were left of the
   sword
   Have found grace in the wilderness,

כֹּה אָמַר יְהוָֹה 1
מָצָא חֵן בַּמִּדְבָּר
עַם שְׂרִידֵי חָרֶב

v. 25. בנ״א כאן תחלת סימן ל״א   v. 1. הפטרה ליום שני של ר״ה

---

this that engaged his heart to approach
unto Me?' i.e. who is worthy to
approach Me unless I have caused him
to draw near to Me? (Abarbanel,
Metsudath David).

23-25 GOD'S JUDGMENT WILL BE
EXECUTED UPON THE WICKED

These verses are almost identical with
xxiii. 19f. The general sense here is that
the punishment of the wicked, whether
of the oppressive nations or of the
sinners in Israel is uncertain, will
precede the restoration of Israel.

25. In the English Version this verse

begins chapter xxxi. It properly rounds
off chapter xxx and belongs there.

CHAPTER XXXI

1-21 PROMISED RESTORATION OF THE
NORTHERN KINGDOM

1. *that were left of the sword.* The survivors of the carnage which accompanied the overthrow of the Northern
Kingdom. The use of this phrase dis-
counts the interpretation that the
prophet is alluding to the exodus from
Egypt (Abarbanel).

the wilderness. The land of their exile.

Even Israel, when I go to cause
   him to rest.

2 'From afar the LORD appeared
   unto me.'
   'Yea, I have loved thee with an
     everlasting love;
   Therefore with affection have I
     drawn thee.

3 Again will I build thee, and thou
   shalt be built,
   O virgin of Israel;
   Again shalt thou be adorned with
     thy tabrets,
   And shalt go forth in the dances
     of them that make merry.

4 Again shalt thou plant vineyards
   upon the mountains of Samaria;
   The planters shall plant, and shall
     have the use thereof.

הָל֥וֹךְ לְהַרְגִּיע֖וֹ יִשְׂרָאֵֽל׃

2 מֵרָח֕וֹק יְהֹוָ֖ה נִרְאָ֣ה לִ֑י
וְאַהֲבַ֤ת עוֹלָם֙ אֲהַבְתִּ֔יךְ
עַל־כֵּ֖ן מְשַׁכְתִּ֥יךְ חָֽסֶד׃

3 ע֤וֹד אֶבְנֵךְ֙ וְֽנִבְנֵ֔ית
בְּתוּלַ֖ת יִשְׂרָאֵ֑ל
ע֚וֹד תַּעְדִּ֣י תֻפַּ֔יִךְ
וְיָצָ֖את בִּמְח֥וֹל מְשַׂחֲקִֽים׃

4 ע֚וֹד תִּטְּעִ֣י כְרָמִ֔ים
בְּהָרֵ֖י שֹׁמְר֑וֹן
נָטְע֥וּ נֹטְעִ֖ים וְחִלֵּֽלוּ׃

They will find favour in God's eyes. The verbs are in the prophetic past, although applying to the future. Although this interpretation seems to make sense, Abarbanel prefers to explain, 'have found favor with their speech,' meaning that God will accept their prayers when they pray to be restored to their land.

Israel. The Ten Tribes of the north (Abarbanel).

cause him to rest. When God restores him to his land (Rashi). An alternative rendering, given in R.V. margin, is: 'When he (Israel) went to find him rest' (Metsudath David).

2. *'from afar . . . me.' 'Yea,'* etc. A.J. puts the two clauses into separate inverted commas, thus dividing the verse into two distinct utterances: the people in distant exile proclaim that God appeared to them from afar, from the land of Egypt to redeem them and to give them rest from their exile. Therefore, they pray that God should again give them rest from their exile. To

this, God replies that this is so, because *I have loved thee with an everlasting love.*

have I drawn thee. Towards Me from Egyptian bondage and have given thee My Law and the Promised Land (Abarbanel).

3. *build.* Not only literally, but in the more general sense of 'restore thy fortunes' (cf. xii. 16).

O virgin of Israel. [Although others have had dominion over thee, yet thou art as beloved to Me as an unsullied virgin.]

4. *shall have the use thereof* (chillelu). For the first three years the fruit borne by a tree was termed *orlah,* lit. 'uncircumcised,' i.e. forbidden. In the fourth year it might be eaten, but only as 'holy' food in Jerusalem. But if it was too burdensome to carry, it was redeemed and its value spent there. The verb *chillel* is the technical term for such redemption (cf. Lev. xix. 23–25; Deut. xx. 6; in the last mentioned verse the verb *chillel* occurs).

5 For there shall be a day,
   That the watchmen shall call upon
     the mount Ephraim:
   Arise ye, and let us go up to Zion,
   Unto the LORD our God.'
6 For thus saith the LORD:
   Sing with gladness for Jacob,
   And shout at the head of the
     nations;
   Announce ye, praise ye, and say:
   'O LORD, save Thy people,
   The remnant of Israel.'
7 Behold, I will bring them from the
     north country,
   And gather them from the utter-
     most parts of the earth,
   And with them the blind and the
     lame,
   The woman with child and her
     that travaileth with child to-
     gether;
   A great company shall they
     return hither.
8 They shall come with weeping,
   And with supplications will I lead
     them;

כִּי יֶשׁ־יוֹם 5
קָרְאוּ נֹצְרִים בְּהַר אֶפְרָיִם
קוּמוּ וְנַעֲלֶה צִיּוֹן
אֶל־יְהֹוָה אֱלֹהֵינוּ:
כִּי־כֹה ׀ אָמַר יְהֹוָה 6
רָנּוּ לְיַעֲקֹב שִׂמְחָה
וְצַהֲלוּ בְּרֹאשׁ הַגּוֹיִם
הַשְׁמִיעוּ הַלְלוּ וְאִמְרוּ
הוֹשַׁע יְהֹוָה אֶת־עַמְּךָ
אֵת שְׁאֵרִית יִשְׂרָאֵל:
הִנְנִי מֵבִיא אוֹתָם מֵאֶרֶץ צָפוֹן 7
וְקִבַּצְתִּים מִיַּרְכְּתֵי־אָרֶץ
בָּם עִוֵּר וּפִסֵּחַ
הָרָה וְיֹלֶדֶת יַחְדָּו
קָהָל גָּדוֹל יָשׁוּבוּ הֵנָּה:
בִּבְכִי יָבֹאוּ 8
וּבְתַחֲנוּנִים אוֹבִילֵם

v. 7. קמץ בסגולתא

---

5. *the watchmen.* Who give the signal for the pilgrimage. Probably there were watch-towers by the cities on the route from Samaria to Jerusalem. As the watchmen saw the procession of pilgrims from the more distant cities approaching, they gave the signal to their own pilgrims to make ready to join the band (see Kimchi).

to Zion. An indication that the breach between Samaria and Judea will have been healed, and Jerusalem resume its rightful place as the religious centre of a reunited Israelite nation (Abarbanel).

6. *praise ye, and say: 'O* LORD, *save Thy*

people.' *Praise ye* (Hebrew *hallelu*) probably refers to the liturgical recitation of God's praises in religious worship (cf. Ps. cxviii. 25 which forms part of what is known in the Jewish liturgy as 'Hallel').

7. *the north country.* See on iii. 12.

the uttermost parts of the earth. All places where the Ten Tribes had been dispersed (Abarbanel, Metsudath David).

the blind, etc. Even those for whom the journey would be difficult will be brought back (Kimchi).

8. *with weeping . . . with supplications.* Their redemption will be consummated

I will cause them to walk by rivers of waters,
In a straight way wherein they shall not stumble;
For I am become a father to Israel,
And Ephraim is My first-born.

9 Hear the word of the LORD, O ye nations,
And declare it in the isles afar off, and say:
'He that scattered Israel doth gather him,
And keep him, as a shepherd doth his flock.'

10 For the LORD hath ransomed Jacob,
And He redeemeth him from the hand of him that is stronger than he.

11 And they shall come and sing in the height of Zion,
And shall flow unto the goodness of the LORD,
To the corn, and to the wine, and to the oil,
And to the young of the flock and of the herd;
And their soul shall be as a watered garden,

אוֹלִיכֵם אֶל־נַחֲלֵי מַיִם
בְּדֶרֶךְ יָשָׁר לֹא יִכָּשְׁלוּ בָּהּ
כִּי־הָיִיתִי לְיִשְׂרָאֵל לְאָב
וְאֶפְרַיִם בְּכֹרִי הוּא:

9 שִׁמְעוּ דְבַר־יְהֹוָה גּוֹיִם
וְהַגִּידוּ בָאִיִּים מִמֶּרְחָק
וְאִמְרוּ מְזָרֵה יִשְׂרָאֵל יְקַבְּצֶנּוּ
וּשְׁמָרוֹ כְּרֹעֶה עֶדְרוֹ:

10 כִּי־פָדָה יְהֹוָה אֶת־יַעֲקֹב
וּגְאָלוֹ מִיַּד חָזָק מִמֶּנּוּ:

11 וּבָאוּ וְרִנְּנוּ בִמְרוֹם־צִיּוֹן
וְנָהֲרוּ אֶל־טוּב יְהֹוָה
עַל־דָּגָן וְעַל־תִּירֹשׁ
וְעַל־יִצְהָר
וְעַל־בְּנֵי־צֹאן וּבָקָר
וְהָיְתָה נַפְשָׁם כְּגַן רָוֶה

v. 11. מלעיל

---

through the tears and prayers of a penitent people (Rashi).

I will cause . . . waters. God will guide them like a shepherd who leads his flocks to a river to quench their thirst (see Daath Soferim). Most exegetes take this passage literally, that God will lead the people in ways where they will find water and not suffer from thirst. Cf. Isa. xlix. 10. Abarbanel explains this figuratively, the intention being that God will teach them His Torah, for 'the entire world will be full of knowledge of the Lord as the water covers the seabed' (Isa. xi. 9).

father to Israel, and Ephraim is My first-born. Ephraim is called 'My first-

born,' either because of Jacob's blessing to Joseph giving him two shares, or because Ephraim was the first to go into exile (Abarbanel).

9. *the isles.* See on xxv. 22.

He that scattered Israel. The peoples who drove the two Kingdoms into captivity acted as God's agents (Kimchi).

as a shepherd doth his flock. A simile conveying the idea of great tenderness (cf. Isa. xl. 11).

10. *hath ransomed.* The prophetic perfect (Abarbanel).

11. *shall flow unto.* The verb has been explained as denoting that the popula-

And they shall not pine any more at all.

12 Then shall the virgin rejoice in the dance,
And the young men and the old together;
For I will turn their mourning into joy,
And will comfort them, and make them rejoice from their sorrow.

13 And I will satiate the soul of the priests with fatness,
And My people shall be satisfied with My goodness,
Saith the Lord.

14 Thus saith the Lord:
A voice is heard in Ramah,
Lamentation, and bitter weeping,
Rachel weeping for her children;
She refuseth to be comforted for her children,
Because they are not.

15 Thus saith the Lord:
Refrain thy voice from weeping,

וְלֹא־יוֹסִיפוּ לְדַאֲבָה עוֹד:

12 אָז תִּשְׂמַח בְּתוּלָה בְּמָחוֹל
וּבַחֻרִים וּזְקֵנִים יַחְדָּו
וְהָפַכְתִּי אֶבְלָם לְשָׂשׂוֹן
וְנִחַמְתִּים וְשִׂמַּחְתִּים מִיגוֹנָם:

13 וְרִוֵּיתִי נֶפֶשׁ הַכֹּהֲנִים דָּשֶׁן
וְעַמִּי אֶת־טוּבִי יִשְׂבָּעוּ
נְאֻם־יְהֹוָה:

14 כֹּה ׀ אָמַר יְהֹוָה
קוֹל בְּרָמָה נִשְׁמָע
נְהִי בְּכִי תַמְרוּרִים
רָחֵל מְבַכָּה עַל־בָּנֶיהָ
מֵאֲנָה לְהִנָּחֵם עַל־בָּנֶיהָ
כִּי אֵינֶנּוּ:

15 כֹּה ׀ אָמַר יְהֹוָה
מִנְעִי קוֹלֵךְ מִבֶּכִי

v. 13. קמץ בטרחא

tion will stream into Jerusalem to celebrate a feast in gratitude for their prosperity (Abarbanel). Daath Mikra suggests that the verb means here 'they will beam (with joy) at.'

goodness. i.e. the bounty (Metsudath David).

as a watered garden. Cf. Isa. lviii. 11. [In a country where water is scarce, the phrase is expressive of the highest good and contentment.]

shall not pine. As they had done in captivity (Metsudath David).

12. The dancing may be a general term for rejoicing in the happy state of the land, or apply more particularly to the vintage festivals.

13. *I will satiate.* So many sacrifices will be brought that the priests, to whom belonged *the breast of waving and the thigh of heaving* (Lev. vii. 34), will have all their needs abundantly supplied (Kimchi).

the soul. The Hebrew term *nephesh* frequently denotes the seat of desire, the appetite (Daath Mikra).

14. *Ramah.* Between Gibeon and Beeroth (Josh. xviii. 25), five miles north of Jerusalem (according to Malbim).

Rachel weeping for her children. Rachel, an ancestress of a section of the Israelite people, who had so longed for children as to regard herself as dead without them (Gen. xxx. 1), now weeps that they

And thine eyes from tears;
For thy work shall be rewarded,
saith the LORD;
And they shall come back from
the land of the enemy.

16 And there is hope for thy future,
saith the LORD;
And thy children shall return to
their own border.

17 I have surely heard Ephraim
bemoaning himself:
'Thou hast chastised me, and I
was chastised,
As a calf untrained;
Turn Thou me, and I shall be
turned,
For Thou art the LORD my God.

18 Surely after that I was turned,
I repented,
And after that I was instructed,
I smote upon my thigh;
I was ashamed, yea, even con-
founded,

וְעֵינַ֖יִךְ מִדִּמְעָ֑ה
כִּ֣י יֵ֥שׁ שָׂכָ֛ר לִפְעֻלָּתֵ֖ךְ
נְאֻם־יְהֹוָ֑ה
וְשָׁ֖בוּ מֵאֶ֥רֶץ אוֹיֵֽב׃

16 וְיֵשׁ־תִּקְוָ֥ה לְאַחֲרִיתֵ֖ךְ
נְאֻם־יְהֹוָ֑ה
וְשָׁ֥בוּ בָנִ֖ים לִגְבוּלָֽם׃

17 שָׁמ֣וֹעַ שָׁמַ֗עְתִּי
אֶפְרַ֙יִם֙ מִתְנוֹדֵ֔ד
יִסַּרְתַּ֙נִי֙ וָֽאִוָּסֵ֔ר
כְּעֵ֖גֶל לֹ֣א לֻמָּ֑ד
הֲשִׁיבֵ֣נִי וְאָשׁ֔וּבָה
כִּ֥י אַתָּ֖ה יְהֹוָ֥ה אֱלֹהָֽי׃

18 כִּֽי־אַחֲרֵ֤י שׁוּבִי֙ נִחַ֔מְתִּי
וְאַֽחֲרֵי֙ הִוָּ֣דְעִ֔י
סָפַ֖קְתִּי עַל־יָרֵ֑ךְ
בֹּ֙שְׁתִּי֙ וְגַם־נִכְלַ֔מְתִּי

are no more, slain or driven into exile.
Ramah is mentioned because her tomb
was in its vicinity. According to Gen.
Rabbah 82.10, Jacob intentionally
buried her there by the road-side,
because he foresaw that his descendants
would pass by on the way to exile and
she would weep and intercede for them.
Rashi and Metsudath David interpret:
'A voice is heard on high'; Rachel's
lamentation has ascended to the heights
of heaven.

15. *thy work.* i.e. the toil and care
spent in bearing and rearing her children. Their exile seemed to make all
this *work* futile; but let her take comfort
because they will come back and revive
their national life (Daath Soferim).

16. *there is hope for thy future.* [That has
been the sustaining thought in the long
night of the Jewish dispersion: hope,
amounting to conviction, of a restoration to Zion.]

17. *Ephraim.* The exiled Northern
Kingdom (Metsudath David).

Thou hast chastised me, and I was chastised.
The people accepted their chastisement
as proof that they had sinned and as
Divine judgment upon them. They have
learned the lesson to be derived from
their experience (Kimchi).

18. *I was turned.* The parallelism suggests that the meaning is 'turned from
my evil ways' (Kimchi).

Because I did bear the reproach
of my youth.'

19 Is Ephraim a darling son unto
Me?

Is he a child that is dandled?

For as often as I speak of him,

I do earnestly remember him
still;

Therefore My heart yearneth for
him,

I will surely have compassion
upon him, saith the LORD.

20 Set thee up waymarks,

Make thee guide-posts;

Set thy heart toward the highway,

Even the way by which thou
wentest;

Return, O virgin of Israel,

Return to these thy cities.

21 How long wilt thou turn away
coyly,

כִּי נָשָׂאתִי חֶרְפַּת נְעוּרָי:

19 הֲבֵן יַקִּיר לִי אֶפְרַיִם

אִם יֶלֶד שַׁעֲשׁוּעִים

כִּי־מִדֵּי דַבְּרִי בּוֹ

זָכֹר אֶזְכְּרֶנּוּ עוֹד

עַל־כֵּן הָמוּ מֵעַי לוֹ

רַחֵם אֲרַחֲמֶנּוּ נְאֻם־יְהֹוָה:

20 הַצִּיבִי לָךְ צִיֻּנִים

שִׂמִי לָךְ תַּמְרוּרִים

שִׁתִי לִבֵּךְ לַמְסִלָּה

דֶּרֶךְ הָלָכְתְּ

שׁוּבִי בְּתוּלַת יִשְׂרָאֵל

שֻׁבִי אֶל־עָרַיִךְ אֵלֶּה:

21 עַד־מָתַי תִּתְחַמָּקִין

v. 19. הלכת ק׳   v. 20. ע״כ

the reproach of my youth. The wicked
deeds perpetrated in early nationhood
which are a *reproach* (disgrace) (Kimchi).

19. It would be hard to surpass the
tender love which animates this verse.

is Ephraim a darling son unto Me? In
truth Ephraim has not so behaved that
God should regard him as such; yet His
thoughts are constantly turned to him
in yearning and compassion (Metsudath
David).

a child that is dandled. lit. 'a child of
delights,' one in whom his parent takes
intense pleasure (Kimchi).

as I speak of him. To my servants, the
prophets (Kimchi).

heart. lit. 'bowels,' the seat of the
emotions (cf. iv. 19).

20. *waymarks . . . guide-posts.* Mark

well the road you have travelled into
captivity, because by that road you will
return — a figure of speech emphasizing
the certainty of restoration (Rashi).

guideposts. This translation follows
Kimchi. Rashi renders 'small palms.'
Plant these to mark the way you traversed from Eretz Israel to Babylon.
Midrashically, Israel is exhorted to
remember the ways of his ancestors and
to pour out supplications with bitterness before God (Targum).

thou wentest. So the *kerë*; but the *kethib*
means 'I went': wherever Israel has
gone, God has accompanied him
(Rashi).

O virgin of Israel. As in verse 3. Though
thou hast had many masters, yet art
thou beloved to Me as a virgin bride.

21. *turn away coyly.* This translation

O thou backsliding daughter?
For the Lord hath created a new
  thing in the earth:
A woman shall court a man.

22 Thus saith the Lord of hosts,
  the God of Israel:
Yet again shall they use this
  speech
In the land of Judah and in the
  cities thereof,
When I shall turn their captivity:
'The Lord bless thee, O habita-
  tion of righteousness,
O mountain of holiness.'

23 And Judah and all the cities
  thereof
Shall dwell therein together:
The husbandmen, and they that
  go forth with flocks.

24 For I have satiated the weary
  soul,
And every pining soul have I
  replenished.

הַבַּת הַשּׁוֹבֵבָה
כִּי־בָרָא יְהֹוָה חֲדָשָׁה בָּאָרֶץ
נְקֵבָה תְּסוֹבֵב גָּבֶר:

22 כֹּה־אָמַר יְהֹוָה צְבָאוֹת
אֱלֹהֵי יִשְׂרָאֵל
עוֹד יֹאמְרוּ אֶת־הַדָּבָר הַזֶּה
בְּאֶרֶץ יְהוּדָה וּבְעָרָיו
בְּשׁוּבִי אֶת־שְׁבוּתָם
יְבָרֶכְךָ יְהֹוָה
נְוֵה־צֶדֶק הַר הַקֹּדֶשׁ:

23 וְיָשְׁבוּ בָהּ
יְהוּדָה וְכָל־עָרָיו יַחְדָּו
אִכָּרִים וְנָסְעוּ בַּעֵדֶר:

24 כִּי הִרְוֵיתִי נֶפֶשׁ עֲיֵפָה
וְכָל־נֶפֶשׁ דָּאֲבָה מִלֵּאתִי:

follows Rashi. The root *chamak* occurs in
Cant. v. 6, *my beloved had turned away*,
and the conjugation used in this verse
suggests 'turn hither and thither' (so
Kimchi), expressive of uncertainty of
action, viz. whether to turn to God or
not.

a woman shall court a man.   Whatever the
meaning of this obscure clause may be,
it must indicate something that is most
unusual *(a new thing in the earth)*. A
commonly accepted interpretation is
that, contrary to the normal procedure,
the woman will propose marriage to the
man she loves; and applied to the
context the sense is that Israel (the
female) will seek union with God.
Closer to the Hebrew verb is the
explanation: a female (by nature timid)
will turn into a man (i.e. manly in
character, the Hebrew being *geber* which

indicates the *strength* of the male).
Hence, Israel will cease to be hesitant in
returning to God but will be resolute.
Both interpretations are stated by Rashi.

22–25   PROMISED RESTORATION OF
        JUDAH

22. *yet again.* [The words presuppose
that the Southern Kingdom is in a state
of desolation.]

23. *Judah . . . cities.* i.e. the population will *dwell therein,* in a land distinguished for righteousness and holiness
(Metsudath David).

and they that go forth.   Kimchi renders:
'and they shall go about with the flocks,'
without fear of marauders.

24. *I have satiated.*   The prophetic perfect (Daath Mikra).

25 Upon this I awaked, and beheld;
    And my sleep was sweet unto me.
26. Behold, the days come, saith
the Lord, that I will sow the house
of Israel and the house of Judah
with the seed of man, and with the
seed of beast. 27. And it shall come
to pass, that like as I have watched
over them to pluck up and to break
down, and to overthrow and to
destroy, and to afflict; so will I
watch over them to build and to
plant, saith the Lord.
28 In those days they shall say no
    more:
    'The fathers have eaten sour
     grapes,
    And the children's teeth are set
     on edge.'
29. But every one shall die for his
own iniquity; every man that eateth

עַל־זֹאת הֱקִיצֹתִי וָאֶרְאֶה 25
וּשְׁנָתִי עָרְבָה לִּי:
הִנֵּה יָמִים בָּאִים נְאֻם־יְהֹוָה 26
וְזָרַעְתִּי אֶת־בֵּית יִשְׂרָאֵל
וְאֶת־בֵּית יְהוּדָה זֶרַע אָדָם
וְזֶרַע בְּהֵמָה: וְהָיָה כַּאֲשֶׁר 27
שָׁקַדְתִּי עֲלֵיהֶם לִנְתוֹשׁ
וְלִנְתוֹץ וְלַהֲרֹס וּלְהַאֲבִיד
וּלְהָרֵעַ כֵּן אֶשְׁקֹד עֲלֵיהֶם
לִבְנוֹת וְלִנְטוֹעַ נְאֻם־יְהֹוָה:
בַּיָּמִים הָהֵם לֹא־יֹאמְרוּ עוֹד 28
אָבוֹת אָכְלוּ בֹסֶר
וְשִׁנֵּי בָנִים תִּקְהֶינָה:
כִּי אִם־אִישׁ בַּעֲוֹנוֹ יָמוּת כָּל־ 29

25. 1. The speaker is the prophet, who
comments upon the vision of the future
which he had just experienced. A sleep
in which he beheld so glowing a
prospect must indeed have been *sweet* to
him (Metsudath David).

I awaked. The vision came to him
while he was in a trance of ecstasy,
from which he now awoke (Metsudath
David).

26–33   A NEW COVENANT TO BE MADE
WITH ISRAEL

26. *I will sow,* etc. In contrast to the
present state of the land, sparsely
populated and with few cattle in the
fields, God will, as it were, sow the soil
with seed which will produce men and
cattle in abundance (Metsudath David).
Similar imagery is employed in Ezek.
xxxvi. 9ff.

27. Cf. i. 10–12 to which the verse may
have reference.

28f. The same proverb receives comment in Ezek. xviii. 2–4. No more will it
be assumed that children are punished
for the sins of their fathers, but there
will be acknowledgment that when
people are punished, it is for their own
sins. This doctrine does not conflict with
Exod. xx. 5. That statement is clearly
qualified by the word 'of them who hate
Me,' indicating that only if the children
continue to commit the sins of the
fathers does God visit the iniquity of the
fathers upon the children. And even
then, only in the case of serious sins
such as idolatry. God promises Israel
that in the future they will worship
Him wholeheartedly, the earth will be
full of the knowledge of the Lord, and
there will be few sinners. Even the
sinners will not commit such serious

the sour grapes, his teeth shall be set on edge.

30. Behold, the days come, saith the Lord, that I will make a new covenant with the house of Israel, and with the house of Judah; 31. not according to the covenant that I made with their fathers in the day that I took them by the hand to bring them out of the land of Egypt; forasmuch as they broke My covenant, although I was a lord over them, saith the Lord. 32. But this is the covenant that I will make with the house of Israel after those days, saith the Lord, I will put My law in their inward parts, and in their heart will I write it; and I will be their God, and they shall

הָאָדָ֖ם הָאֹכֵ֣ל הַבֹּ֑סֶר תִּקְהֶ֖ינָה
30 שִׁנָּֽיו׃ הִנֵּ֛ה יָמִ֥ים בָּאִ֖ים נְאֻם־
יְהוָ֑ה וְכָרַתִּ֗י אֶת־בֵּ֤ית יִשְׂרָאֵל֙
וְאֶת־בֵּ֥ית יְהוּדָ֖ה בְּרִ֥ית
31 חֲדָשָֽׁה׃ לֹ֣א כַבְּרִ֗ית אֲשֶׁ֤ר
כָּרַ֙תִּי֙ אֶת־אֲבוֹתָ֔ם בְּיוֹם֙
הֶחֱזִיקִ֣י בְיָדָ֔ם לְהוֹצִיאָ֖ם
מֵאֶ֣רֶץ מִצְרָ֑יִם אֲשֶׁר־הֵ֜מָּה
הֵפֵ֣רוּ אֶת־בְּרִיתִ֗י וְאָנֹכִ֛י
32 בָּעַ֥לְתִּי בָ֖ם נְאֻם־יְהוָֽה׃ כִּ֣י
זֹ֣את הַבְּרִ֡ית אֲשֶׁ֣ר אֶכְרֹת֩ אֶת־
בֵּ֨ית יִשְׂרָאֵ֜ל אַחֲרֵ֧י הַיָּמִ֣ים
הָהֵ֗ם נְאֻם־יְהוָה֒ נָתַ֤תִּי אֶת־
תּֽוֹרָתִי֙ בְּקִרְבָּ֔ם וְעַל־לִבָּ֖ם
אֶכְתֲּבֶ֑נָּה וְהָיִ֤יתִי לָהֶם֙
לֵֽאלֹהִ֔ים וְהֵ֖מָּה יִֽהְיוּ־לִֽי

sins, and even they will be given respite until their old age, as in Isa. lxv. 20. Surely the son will not suffer for his father's sins (Kimchi).

30. God will make a new covenant with Israel which, unlike the old, will be permanent, because it will be inscribed on their hearts. There is nothing here to suggest that the new covenant would differ in nature from the old. No new revelation is intended, nor was it needed. The prophet only makes the assertion that, unlike the past, Israel will henceforth remain faithful to God, while He in turn will never reject them.

31. *that I took them by the hand.* Like a loving father guiding the steps of his young child (cf. Hos. xi. 3) (Daath Soferim).

32. *the house of Israel.* Here the designation of the whole nation, both Judah and Israel (the Northern Kingdom).

in their inward parts, and in their heart. I will no longer be something external to them, but so deeply ingrained in their consciousness as to be part of them. This, indeed, is the aim of all religious teaching (Malbim).

I will be . . . they shall be. *I* is not emphasized by the addition of the pronoun but *they* is (see note on preceding verse). The implication is that God will be what He has always been in His relationship to Israel; *they*, on the other hand, will now likewise permanently acknowledge Him and be His people. Permanence is the essence of the new covenant (see Daath Mikra).

be My people; 33. and they shall
teach no more every man his neighbour, and every man his brother,
saying: 'Know the LORD'; for they
shall all know Me, from the least of
them unto the greatest of them,
saith the LORD; for I will forgive
their iniquity, and their sin will I
remember no more.

34 Thus saith the LORD,

Who giveth the sun for a light by
day,

And the ordinances of the moon
and of the stars for a light by
night,

Who stirreth up the sea, that the
waves thereof roar,

The LORD of hosts is His name:

35 If these ordinances depart from
before Me,

Saith the LORD,

Then the seed of Israel also shall
cease

From being a nation before Me
for ever.

36 Thus saith the LORD:

If heaven above can be measured,

לְעָם: וְלֹא יְלַמְּדוּ עוֹד אִישׁ 33
אֶת־רֵעֵהוּ וְאִישׁ אֶת־אָחִיו
לֵאמֹר דְּעוּ אֶת־יְהוָה כִּי
כוּלָּם יֵדְעוּ אוֹתִי לְמִקְּטַנָּם
וְעַד־גְּדוֹלָם נְאֻם־יְהוָֹה כִּי
אֶסְלַח לַעֲוֹנָם וּלְחַטָּאתָם לֹא
אֶזְכָּר־עוֹד:
כֹּה | אָמַר יְהֹוָה 34
נֹתֵן שֶׁמֶשׁ לְאוֹר יוֹמָם
חֻקֹּת יָרֵחַ וְכוֹכָבִים
לְאוֹר לָיְלָה
רֹגַע הַיָּם וַיֶּהֱמוּ גַלָּיו
יְהוָֹה צְבָאוֹת שְׁמוֹ:
אִם־יָמֻשׁוּ הַחֻקִּים הָאֵלֶּה 35
מִלְּפָנַי
נְאֻם־יְהֹוָה
גַּם זֶרַע יִשְׂרָאֵל יִשְׁבְּתוּ
מִהְיוֹת גּוֹי לְפָנַי כָּל־הַיָּמִים:
כֹּה | אָמַר יְהֹוָה 36
אִם־יִמַּדּוּ שָׁמַיִם מִלְמַעְלָה

v. 33. דגש אחר שורק

33. *I will forgive their iniquity.* This
being the obstacle which prevented
them from 'knowing' God (Kimchi).

34–39 SURVIVAL OF ISRAEL AS CERTAIN
AS NATURE'S LAWS

34. Only God Who created the universe

and ordained the laws of Nature could
make the declaration that follows.

35. *cease from being a nation.* This is an
absolute promise, not dependent on
any world happenings (Daath Soferim).

36. *if heaven . . . beneath.* This is un-
thinkable; similarly beyond thought is
the complete and final rejection of
Israel by God (Rashi).

And the foundations of the earth
searched out beneath,
Then will I also cast off all the
seed of Israel
For all that they have done, saith
the LORD.

37. Behold, the days come, saith the
LORD, that the city shall be built to
the LORD from the tower of Hananel
unto the gate of the corner. 38. And
the measuring line shall yet go out
straight forward unto the hill Gareb,
and shall turn about unto Goah.
39. And the whole valley of the dead
bodies, and of the ashes, and all the
fields unto the brook Kidron, unto
the corner of the horse gate toward
the east, shall be holy unto the LORD;
it shall not be plucked up, nor
thrown down any more for ever.

וְיֵחָקְרוּ מוֹסְדֵי־אֶרֶץ לְמָטָּה
גַּם־אֲנִי אֶמְאַס
בְּכָל־זֶרַע יִשְׂרָאֵל
עַל־כָּל־אֲשֶׁר עָשׂוּ
נְאֻם־יְהֹוָה׃

37 הִנֵּה יָמִים ∴ נְאֻם־יְהֹוָה
וְנִבְנְתָה הָעִיר לַיהֹוָה מִמִּגְדַּל
38 חֲנַנְאֵל עַד־שַׁעַר הַפִּנָּה׃ וְיָצָא
עוֹד קַו הַמִּדָּה נֶגְדּוֹ עַל
39 גִּבְעַת גָּרֵב וְנָסַב גֹּעָתָה׃ וְכָל־
הָעֵמֶק הַפְּגָרִים ׀ וְהַדֶּשֶׁן וְכָל־
הַשְּׁרֵמוֹת עַד־נַחַל קִדְרוֹן
עַד־פִּנַּת שַׁעַר הַסּוּסִים
מִזְרָחָה קֹדֶשׁ לַיהֹוָה לֹא־
יִנָּתֵשׁ וְלֹא־יֵהָרֵס עוֹד
לְעוֹלָם׃

v. 37. באים קרי ולא כתיב v. 38. קו ק' v. 39. השדמות ק'

37. *come.* Inserted in the text by the *kerë* but omitted in the *kethib.*

the tower of Hananel . . . the gate of the corner. At the north-east (cf. Neh. iii. 1, xii. 39) and the north-west (cf. 2 Kings xiv. 13) of the city respectively. They are both mentioned in Zech. xiv. 10 and describe the ends of the north wall from east to west (Daath Mikra).

38. *Gareb . . . Goah.* Nothing is known of these, but apparently the verse indicates an extension of the city boundary on the south (Daath Mikra).

39. *the whole valley of the dead bodies,* etc. The *valley* is that where Sennacherib's hosts were miraculously slain by an angel (Targum and all traditional commentaries).

and of the ashes. Where the ashes of the sacrifices were cast outside. This place, too, will be augmented to Jerusalem and will be included within the walls. This prophecy will be fulfilled with the final redemption, since it was not fulfilled in the days of the Second Temple (Rashi).

the brook Kidron. Flowing east of Jerusalem.

the horse gate. Mentioned in Neh. iii. 28 and located at the south-east corner of the Temple (Daath Mikra).

holy unto the LORD. And added to the city (Metsudath David).

it shall not be plucked up, etc. [The permanence of the nation requires the permanence of their capital.]

32   CHAPTER XXXII   לב

1. The word that came to Jeremiah from the LORD in the tenth year of Zedekiah king of Judah, which was the eighteenth year of Nebuchadrezzar. 2. Now at that time the king of Babylon's army was besieging Jerusalem; and Jeremiah the prophet was shut up in the court of the guard, which was in the king of Judah's house. 3. For Zedekiah king of Judah had shut him up, saying:

1 הַדָּבָר אֲשֶׁר הָיָה אֶל־יִרְמְיָהוּ
מֵאֵת יְהֹוָה בִּשְׁנַת הָעֲשִׂרִית
לְצִדְקִיָּהוּ מֶלֶךְ יְהוּדָה הִיא
הַשָּׁנָה שְׁמֹנֶה־עֶשְׂרֵה שָׁנָה
2 לִנְבוּכַדְרֶאצַּר: וְאָז חֵיל
מֶלֶךְ בָּבֶל צָרִים עַל־
יְרוּשָׁלָ͏ִם וְיִרְמְיָהוּ הַנָּבִיא הָיָה
כָלוּא בַּחֲצַר הַמַּטָּרָה אֲשֶׁר
3 בֵּית־מֶלֶךְ יְהוּדָה: אֲשֶׁר
כְּלָאוֹ צִדְקִיָּהוּ מֶלֶךְ־יְהוּדָה

v. 1. בשנה ק׳

CHAPTER XXXII

JEREMIAH PURCHASES A FAMILY ESTATE

THIS chapter records a transaction revealing Jeremiah's faith in a future for his people. Jerusalem was under siege; God had foretold its downfall and the consequent exile of the nation. At such a time of confusion and uncertainty, Jeremiah, at God's bidding, purchases an estate in Anathoth from his kinsman, depositing the title-deeds with Baruch, in the firm conviction that the nation would again return to the homeland. This incident alone is sufficient to free Jeremiah from the charge of pessimism. He was a realist and had no doubt about the imminent collapse of the Judean State, but simultaneously his trust in God's word made him confident of rehabilitation.

1–5 INTRODUCTORY

1. *the tenth year of Zedekiah.* The siege of Jerusalem commenced in the ninth year of his reign (xxxix. 1), was raised on receipt of the news that an Egyptian army was advancing (xxxvii. 5), and subsequently resumed. During the interval Jeremiah left Jerusalem to visit his estate in Anathoth, was accused of defection to the Chaldeans and imprisoned in close confinement (xxxvii. 11–15), which imprisonment, however, was relaxed on his petitioning the king (xxxvii. 21). But this chapter describes him as still *shut up in the court of the guard* (verse 2), and is therefore later than the events enumerated. It is apparent that this section of the Book does not follow a strictly chronological order.

which was the eighteenth year of Nebuchadrezzar. Cf. xxv. 1.

2. *the court of the guard.* This was a court where prisoners were kept lest they escape. Perhaps this was an open place, where the prisoners confined therein were exposed to the elements. It was therefore called 'the court of the guard' rather than 'the house of the guard' (Daath Mikra). It is referred to again in Neh. iii. 25.

3. Verses 3–5 are a parenthesis to account for Jeremiah's detention.

'Wherefore dost thou prophesy, and say: Thus saith the LORD: Behold, I will give this city into the hand of the king of Babylon, and he shall take it; 4. and Zedekiah king of Judah shall not escape out of the hand of the Chaldeans, but shall surely be delivered into the hand of the king of Babylon, and shall speak with him mouth to mouth, and his eyes shall behold his eyes; 5. and he shall lead Zedekiah to Babylon, and there shall he be until I remember him, saith the LORD; though ye fight with the Chaldeans, ye shall not prosper?'

6. And Jeremiah said: 'The word of the LORD came unto me, saying: 7. Behold, Hanamel, the son of Shallum thine uncle, shall come unto thee, saying: Buy thee my field that is in Anathoth; for the right of redemption is thine to buy it.'

לֵאמֹר מַדּוּעַ אַתָּה נִבָּא לֵאמֹר
כֹּה אָמַר יְהֹוָה הִנְנִי נֹתֵן אֶת־
הָעִיר הַזֹּאת בְּיַד מֶלֶךְ־בָּבֶל
4 וּלְכָדָהּ׃ וְצִדְקִיָּהוּ מֶלֶךְ
יְהוּדָה לֹא יִמָּלֵט מִיַּד
הַכַּשְׂדִּים כִּי־הִנָּתֹן יִנָּתֵן בְּיַד
מֶלֶךְ־בָּבֶל וְדִבֶּר־פִּיו עִם־
פִּיו וְעֵינָיו אֶת־עֵינָו תִּרְאֶינָה׃
5 וּבָבֶל יוֹלִךְ אֶת־צִדְקִיָּהוּ וְשָׁם
יִהְיֶה עַד־פָּקְדִי אֹתוֹ נְאֻם־
יְהֹוָה כִּי תִלָּחֲמוּ אֶת־
הַכַּשְׂדִּים לֹא תַצְלִיחוּ׃
6 וַיֹּאמֶר יִרְמְיָהוּ הָיָה דְבַר־
7 יְהֹוָה אֵלַי לֵאמֹר׃ הִנֵּה
חֲנַמְאֵל בֶּן־שַׁלֻּם דֹּדְךָ בָּא
אֵלֶיךָ לֵאמֹר קְנֵה לְךָ אֶת־
שָׂדִי אֲשֶׁר בַּעֲנָתוֹת כִּי לְךָ
8 מִשְׁפַּט הַגְּאֻלָּה לִקְנוֹת׃ וַיָּבֹא

---

wherefore dost thou prophesy, etc. Although his imprisonment in the first place was due to the charge of defection (see on verse 1), his insistence that Jerusalem would fall was a contributory cause. It is noteworthy that he maintained the truth of his prediction when petitioning the king (xxxvii. 19).

5. *until I remember him.* The verb *pakad* is used in both a favourable and unfavourable sense. A.J. rather suggests the former. A.V. and R.V., 'visit him,' follow the Jewish commentators who explain: with the visitation that comes to all men, viz. death.

6-15 WHY JEREMIAH WAS TOLD TO BUY HANAMEL'S LAND

6. *the word of the* LORD *came unto me.* Repeated from verse 1 because of the lengthy digression which intervenes (Rashi).

7. *Hanamel, the son of Shallum thine uncle.* The comma printed in A.J. after *Hanamel* (omitted in A.V. and R.V.) is necessary, because *uncle,* as is clear from verses 8f., refers to Shallum, not to Hanamel (Kimchi).

Anathoth. Jeremiah's birthplace (i. 1).

the right of redemption is thine. As nearest

215

8. So Hanamel mine uncle's son came to me in the court of the guard according to the word of the LORD, and said unto me: 'Buy my field, I pray thee, that is in Anathoth, which is in the land of Benjamin; for the right of inheritance is thine, and the redemption is thine; buy it for thyself.' Then I knew that this was the word of the LORD. 9. And I bought the field that was in Anathoth of Hanamel mine uncle's son, and weighed him the money, even seventeen shekels of silver. 10. And I subscribed the deed, and sealed it, and called witnesses, and weighed him the money in the balances. 11. So I took the deed of the purchase, both that which was sealed, containing the terms and conditions, and that which was

אֵלַי חֲנַמְאֵל בֶּן־דֹּדִי כִּדְבַר
יְהוָה אֶל־חֲצַר הַמַּטָּרָה
וַיֹּאמֶר אֵלַי קְנֵה נָא אֶת־שָׂדִי
אֲשֶׁר־בַּעֲנָתוֹת אֲשֶׁר ׀ בְּאֶרֶץ
בִּנְיָמִין כִּי־לְךָ מִשְׁפַּט הַיְרֻשָּׁה
וּלְךָ הַגְּאֻלָּה קְנֵה־לָךְ וָאֵדַע
9 כִּי דְבַר־יְהוָה הוּא: וָאֶקְנֶה
אֶת־הַשָּׂדֶה מֵאֵת חֲנַמְאֵל
בֶּן־דֹּדִי אֲשֶׁר בַּעֲנָתֹת
וָאֶשְׁקֲלָה־לּוֹ אֶת־הַכֶּסֶף
שִׁבְעָה שְׁקָלִים וַעֲשָׂרָה
10 הַכָּסֶף: וָאֶכְתֹּב בַּסֵּפֶר
וָאֶחְתֹּם וָאָעֵד עֵדִים וָאֶשְׁקֹל
11 הַכֶּסֶף בְּמֹאזְנָיִם: וָאֶקַּח אֶת־
סֵפֶר הַמִּקְנָה אֶת־הֶחָתוּם
הַמִּצְוָה וְהַחֻקִּים וְאֶת־הַגָּלוּי:

kinsman (we must assume that Hanamel was childless), Jeremiah had the right of pre-emption, so that the estate might remain in the family (Lev. xxv. 25). This incident (cf. also Ruth iv. 1ff.) is an indication that this law of land-tenure was actually practised.

8. *the right of inheritance is thine.* As next of kin; therefore *the redemption is thine* too (Metsudath David).

then I knew . . . the LORD. This does not mean that he had any doubt about the genuineness of *the word of the* LORD which came to him. The phrase goes much deeper and signifies that Jeremiah at once perceived all that lay behind Hanamel's visit, namely that he purchase the field, and its import for the future of the nation — that the impend-

ing disaster would not end the existence of Israel (Abarbanel).

9. *seventeen shekels of silver.* lit. 'seven shekels and ten (pieces of) the silver.' The price appears to be very low, but the field may have been small. It should also be borne in mind that the purchase price was determined by the number of years still to run before the end of the Jubilee cycle when the estate would revert to the original owner. There is no suggestion in the text that the land was sold to Jeremiah at 'panic value' due to the political situation. According to Targum, the amount was seven *minas* and ten *selaim.* This amounts to 185 shekels, a considerable sum.

10. *I subscribed the deed.* lit. 'I wrote in the book,' i.e. set out all the particulars in the document (Metsudath David).

open; 12. and I delivered the deed of the purchase unto Baruch the son of Neriah, the son of Mahseiah, in the presence of Hanamel mine uncle['s son], and in the presence of the witnesses that subscribed the deed of the purchase, before all the Jews that sat in the court of the guard. 13. And I charged Baruch before them, saying: 14. 'Thus saith the LORD of hosts, the God of Israel: Take these deeds, this deed of the purchase, both that which is sealed, and this deed which is open, and put them in an earthen vessel; that

12 וָאֶתֵּן אֶת־הַסֵּפֶר הַמִּקְנָה
אֶל־בָּרוּךְ בֶּן־נֵרִיָּה בֶּן־
מַחְסֵיָה לְעֵינֵי חֲנַמְאֵל דֹּדִי
וּלְעֵינֵי הָעֵדִים הַכֹּתְבִים
בְּסֵפֶר הַמִּקְנָה לְעֵינֵי כָּל־
הַיְּהוּדִים הַיֹּשְׁבִים בַּחֲצַר
13 הַמַּטָּרָה: וָאֲצַוֶּה אֶת־בָּרוּךְ
14 לְעֵינֵיהֶם לֵאמֹר: כֹּה־אָמַר
יְהֹוָה צְבָאוֹת אֱלֹהֵי יִשְׂרָאֵל
לָקוֹחַ אֶת־הַסְּפָרִים הָאֵלֶּה
אֵת סֵפֶר הַמִּקְנָה הַזֶּה וְאֵת
הֶחָתוּם וְאֵת סֵפֶר הַגָּלוּי הַזֶּה
וּנְתַתָּם בִּכְלִי־חָרֶשׂ לְמַעַן

11. *both that which was sealed . . . and that which was open.* Kimchi explains that there were three documents: the deed that was sealed, the terms and conditions, and a duplicate of the deed which was open. Thus it would not be necessary to break the seal in order to read the deed. His father, Rabbi Joseph Kimchi, explains that 'that which was open' refers to a notice to all kinsmen that the field was up for sale, enabling them to purchase it. Rashi explains that this refers to the confirmation of the validity of the deed by the court. Hence, if the witnesses die, there will be no difficulty involved in claiming the field.

containing the terms and conditions. A paraphrase of the Hebrew which is literally 'the commandment and the statutes,' evidently used here in a technical sense (see Kimchi).

12. *Baruch.* Jeremiah's amanuensis mentioned now for the first time. To him we owe the compilation of the material of this Book in the main.

Hanamel mine uncle['s son]. The addition in brackets reconciles the Hebrew text with verse 8. It is supported by LXX, Peshitta and several Hebrew MSS., and this explanation is accepted by Kimchi. He refers to Gen. xiv. 14, where Lot is referred to as Abram's brother, although he was, in fact, his brother's son. Rashi and Kimchi both suggest that this Hanamel may not be the same man as previously mentioned. i.e. Jeremiah's father had a brother named Hanamel and a brother named Shallum. Shallum had a son named Hanamel. Hence, one Hanamel was Jeremiah's uncle and one was his cousin.

before all the Jews. It was customary to carry out a transfer of this kind with great publicity (cf. Ruth iv. 9).

14. *put them in an earthen vessel,* etc. That they be preserved and not rot (Abarbanel). This deed was to be preserved until the return from exile when the following prophecy would be

they may continue many days.
15. For thus saith the LORD of hosts,
the God of Israel: Houses and fields
and vineyards shall yet again be
bought in this land.'

16. Now after I had delivered the
deed of the purchase unto Baruch
the son of Neriah, I prayed unto the
LORD, saying: 17. 'Ah Lord GOD!
behold, Thou hast made the heaven
and the earth by Thy great power
and by Thy outstretched arm; there
is nothing too hard for Thee;
18. who showest mercy unto
thousands, and recompensest the
iniquity of the fathers into the
bosom of their children after them;
the great, the mighty God, the LORD
of hosts is His name; 19. great in

15 יַעַמְדוּ יָמִים רַבִּים׃ כִּי כֹה
אָמַר יְהֹוָה צְבָאוֹת אֱלֹהֵי
יִשְׂרָאֵל עוֹד יִקָּנוּ בָתִּים
וְשָׂדוֹת וּכְרָמִים בָּאָרֶץ הַזֹּאת׃

16 וָאֶתְפַּלֵּל אֶל־יְהֹוָה אַחֲרֵי
תִתִּי אֶת־סֵפֶר הַמִּקְנָה אֶל־

17 בָּרוּךְ בֶּן־נֵרִיָּה לֵאמֹר׃ אֲהָהּ
אֲדֹנָי יְהֹוִה הִנֵּה ׀ אַתָּה עָשִׂיתָ
אֶת־הַשָּׁמַיִם וְאֶת־הָאָרֶץ
בְּכֹחֲךָ הַגָּדוֹל וּבִזְרֹעֲךָ
הַנְּטוּיָה לֹא־יִפָּלֵא מִמְּךָ כָּל־

18 דָּבָר׃ עֹשֶׂה חֶסֶד לַאֲלָפִים
וּמְשַׁלֵּם עֲוֹן אָבוֹת אֶל־חֵיק
בְּנֵיהֶם אַחֲרֵיהֶם הָאֵל הַגָּדוֹל
הַגִּבּוֹר יְהֹוָה צְבָאוֹת שְׁמוֹ׃

fulfilled to be a sign for those dwelling
in exile that God had commanded them
to purchase the field as a consolation
for Israel, that they should not despair
of returning to their native land
(Kimchi).

15. *shall yet again be bought.* By Jews;
herein lay the significance of the transaction, which expressed in most forceful
manner God's promise of, and Jeremiah's confidence in, national revival
(Metsudath David).

16–25 REACTION OF DOUBT IN THE
          PROPHET

The pious men of the Bible are often
depicted as subject to human weak-
nesses. Though imbued with ardent
faith, they cannot always escape the
chilling winds of scepticism. It is,

indeed, this human quality of its heroes
that makes the Bible a help and inspiration to those who strive and aspire, fall
yet rise again. Such a wave of doubt now
passes over Jeremiah, when he contem-
plates how seemingly opposed his transaction is, not only to the tragic realities
of the situation, the city being about to
fall, but also to the messages he has so
often proclaimed in God's name of the
overthrow of the Judean State. In
anguish of spirit he prays to God and
receives a reassuring answer.

17. *Ah.* The Hebrew particle
expresses a cry of anguish (Metsudath
Zion).

18. *their children after them.* i.e. when
the children follow in their father's
footsteps, as did Jeremiah's generation
(Rashi).

counsel, and mighty in work; whose
eyes are open upon all the ways of
the sons of men, to give every one
according to his ways, and according
to the fruit of his doings; 20. who
didst set signs and wonders in the
land of Egypt, even unto this day,
and in Israel and among other men;
and madest Thee a name, as at this
day; 21. and didst bring forth Thy
people Israel out of the land of
Egypt with signs, and with wonders,
and with a strong hand, and with an
outstretched arm, and with great
terror; 22. and gavest them this
land, which Thou didst swear to
their fathers to give them, a land
flowing with milk and honey;
23. and they came in, and possessed
it; but they hearkened not to Thy
voice, neither walked in Thy law;
they have done nothing of all that
Thou commandedst them to do;
therefore Thou hast caused all this
evil to befall them; 24. behold the
mounds, they are come unto the city

19 גְּדֹל֙ הָֽעֵצָ֔ה וְרַ֖ב הָעֲלִֽילִיָּ֑ה
אֲשֶׁר־עֵינֶ֣יךָ פְקֻח֗וֹת עַל־
כָּל־דַּרְכֵי֙ בְּנֵ֣י אָדָ֔ם לָתֵ֤ת
לְאִישׁ֙ כִּדְרָכָ֔יו וְכִפְרִ֖י
20 מַעֲלָלָֽיו׃ אֲשֶׁר־שַׂ֣מְתָּ אֹת֣וֹת
וּמֹפְתִים֮ בְּאֶֽרֶץ־מִצְרַ֒יִם֒ עַד־
הַיּ֣וֹם הַזֶּ֗ה וּבְיִשְׂרָאֵל֙ וּבָֽאָדָ֔ם
וַתַּֽעֲשֶׂה־לְּךָ֥ שֵׁ֖ם כַּיּ֥וֹם הַזֶּֽה׃
21 וַתֹּצֵ֛א אֶת־עַמְּךָ֥ אֶת־יִשְׂרָאֵ֖ל
מֵאֶ֣רֶץ מִצְרָ֑יִם בְּאֹת֣וֹת
וּבְמֽוֹפְתִ֗ים וּבְיָ֤ד חֲזָקָה֙
וּבְאֶזְר֣וֹעַ נְטוּיָ֔ה וּבְמוֹרָ֖א
22 גָּדֽוֹל׃ וַתִּתֵּ֣ן לָהֶ֗ם אֶת־הָאָ֤רֶץ
הַזֹּאת֙ אֲשֶׁר־נִשְׁבַּ֣עְתָּ לַֽאֲבוֹתָ֔ם
לָתֵ֣ת לָהֶ֑ם אֶ֛רֶץ זָבַ֥ת חָלָ֖ב
23 וּדְבָֽשׁ׃ וַיָּבֹ֜אוּ וַיִּֽרְשׁ֣וּ אֹתָ֗הּ
וְלֹֽא־שָׁמְע֤וּ בְקוֹלֶ֙ךָ֙ וּבְתֹֽרוֹתְךָ֣
לֹֽא־הָלָ֔כוּ אֵת֩ כָּל־אֲשֶׁ֨ר
צִוִּ֧יתָה לָהֶ֛ם לַעֲשׂ֖וֹת לֹ֣א עָשׂ֑וּ
וַתַּקְרֵ֣א אֹתָ֔ם אֵ֥ת כָּל־הָרָעָ֖ה
24 הַזֹּֽאת׃ הִנֵּ֣ה הַסֹּֽלְל֞וֹת בָּ֣אוּ

v. 23. וּבְתוֹרֹתֶךָ ק׳ v. 23. קָמֵץ בז״ק

---

the great, the mighty God. Jeremiah
omitted *the awful* from Moses' description of God (cf. Deut. x. 17), because, he
said, 'With the heathen about to destroy
His Temple, where are His awful
deeds!' (Talmud, Yoma 69b).

19. *to give every one,* etc. Repeated
from xvii. 10.

20. *even unto this day.* The phrase is
variously explained as: 'which are
remembered to this day'; 'which continue to this day'; 'which are still spoken
of' (Kimchi).

21. A reminiscence of Deut. iv. 34, xxvi.
8.

22. Cf. xi. 5.

to take it; and the city is given into the hand of the Chaldeans that fight against it, because of the sword, and of the famine, and of the pestilence; and what Thou hast spoken is come to pass; and, behold, Thou seest it. 25. Yet Thou hast said unto me, O Lord GOD: Buy thee the field for money, and call witnesses; whereas the city is given into the hand of the Chaldeans.'

26. Then came the word of the LORD unto Jeremiah, saying: 27. 'Behold, I am the LORD, the God of all flesh; is there any thing too hard for Me? 28. Therefore thus saith the LORD: Behold, I will give this city into the hand of the Chaldeans, and into the hand of Nebuchad-rezzar king of Babylon, and he shall take it; 29. and the Chaldeans, that fight against this city, shall come

הָעִיר֙ לְלָכְדָ֔הּ וְהָעִ֣יר נִתְּנָ֗ה
בְּיַד֙ הַכַּשְׂדִּים֙ הַנִּלְחָמִ֣ים
עָלֶ֔יהָ מִפְּנֵ֛י הַחֶ֥רֶב וְהָרָעָ֖ב
וְהַדָּ֑בֶר וַאֲשֶׁ֥ר דִּבַּ֛רְתָּ הָיָ֖ה
וְהִנְּךָ֥ רֹאֶֽה׃ וְאַתָּ֛ה אָמַ֥רְתָּ אֵלַ֖י 25
אֲדֹנָ֣י יְהֹוִ֗ה קְנֵֽה־לְךָ֤ הַשָּׂדֶה֙
בַּכֶּ֔סֶף וְהָעֵ֖ד עֵדִ֑ים וְהָעִ֕יר
נִתְּנָ֖ה בְּיַ֥ד הַכַּשְׂדִּֽים׃ וַיְהִי֙ 26
דְבַר־יְהֹוָ֔ה אֶֽל־יִרְמְיָ֖הוּ
לֵאמֹֽר׃ הִנֵּה֙ אֲנִ֣י יְהֹוָ֔ה אֱלֹהֵ֖י 27
כָּל־בָּשָׂ֑ר הֲמִמֶּ֖נִּי יִפָּלֵ֥א כָּל־
דָּבָֽר׃ לָכֵ֗ן כֹּ֥ה אָמַ֖ר יְהֹוָ֑ה 28
הִנְנִ֣י נֹתֵן֩ אֶת־הָעִ֨יר הַזֹּ֜את
בְּיַ֣ד הַכַּשְׂדִּ֗ים וּבְיַ֛ד
נְבוּכַדְרֶאצַּ֥ר מֶֽלֶךְ־בָּבֶ֖ל
וּלְכָדָֽהּ׃ וּבָ֙אוּ֙ הַכַּשְׂדִּ֔ים 29
הַנִּלְחָמִים֙ עַל־הָעִ֣יר הַזֹּ֔את

ע״כ v.27.

---

24. *the mounds.* See on vi. 6.

is given. The perfect of certainty; the city had not yet been captured (Metsudath David).

the Chaldeans. [By this time Chaldea included the whole of Babylonia, although originally it was only the southern part of it.]

25. *yet Thou hast said.* Why then didst Thou inform me that Hanamel was coming? This informing was tantamount to commanding me to buy the field and to call witnesses as is customary when buying a field (Metsudath David).

26–44　GOD'S REPLY TO JEREMIAH

27. *is there any thing too hard for Me?* 'One of the great answers — and facts — of history (cf. Gen. xviii. 14). God gives back to Jeremiah his own words, *There is nothing too hard for Thee* (verse 17). He had come to God with the best thoughts about Him, and God gives him the answer that his thoughts are true' (Hertz).

28–44. After verse 27 gives the words of God, the prophecy of Jeremiah is resumed; hence *thus saith the* LORD.

28. *therefore.* Since He is *the God of all flesh,* it is He Who will deliver the city

and set this city on fire, and burn it, with the houses, upon whose roofs they have offered unto Baal, and poured out drink-offerings unto other gods, to provoke Me.   30. For the children of Israel and the children of Judah have only done that which was evil in My sight from their youth; for the children of Israel have only provoked Me with the work of their hands, saith the LORD.   31. For this city hath been to Me a provocation of Mine anger and of My fury from the day that they built it even unto this day, that I should remove it from before My face; 32. because of all the evil of the children of Israel and of the children of Judah, which they have done to provoke Me, they, their kings, their princes, their priests, and their

וְהִצִּיתוּ אֶת־הָעִיר הַזֹּאת
בָּאֵשׁ וּשְׂרָפוּהָ וְאֵת הַבָּתִּים
אֲשֶׁר קִטְּרוּ עַל־גַּגּוֹתֵיהֶם
לַבַּעַל וְהִסִּכוּ נְסָכִים
לֵאלֹהִים אֲחֵרִים לְמַעַן
הַכְעִסֵנִי: כִּי־הָיוּ בְנֵי־ 30
יִשְׂרָאֵל וּבְנֵי יְהוּדָה אַךְ עֹשִׂים
הָרַע בְּעֵינַי מִנְּעֻרֹתֵיהֶם כִּי
בְנֵי־יִשְׂרָאֵל אַךְ מַכְעִסִים
אֹתִי בְּמַעֲשֵׂה יְדֵיהֶם נְאֻם־
יְהוָה: כִּי עַל־אַפִּי וְעַל־ 31
חֲמָתִי הָיְתָה לִּי הָעִיר הַזֹּאת
לְמִן־הַיּוֹם אֲשֶׁר בָּנוּ אוֹתָהּ
וְעַד הַיּוֹם הַזֶּה לַהֲסִירָהּ מֵעַל
פָּנָי: עַל כָּל־רָעַת בְּנֵי־ 32
יִשְׂרָאֵל וּבְנֵי יְהוּדָה אֲשֶׁר עָשׂוּ
לְהַכְעִסֵנִי הֵמָּה מַלְכֵיהֶם
שָׂרֵיהֶם כֹּהֲנֵיהֶם וּנְבִיאֵיהֶם

---

into the hands of the enemy, and not the might of the foe that will lay it low. Consequently He, too, will have the power to redeem it when the time comes (Metsudath David).

29. *upon whose roofs . . . unto Baal.* See on xix. 13. The clause is not parenthetical but an essential part of the oracle, stating the reason for the city's fate (Malbim).

30. *from their youth.* From the nation's beginnings (Kimchi).

31. *from the day that they built it.* In fact the Israelites did not build Jerusalem but captured it from the Jebusites. The verb *banah* is something employed for 'enlarging, repairing' (cf. Josh. xix. 50; Judg. xxi. 23), and this seems to be its force in the verse. When Jerusalem passed into the hands of David, many alterations and additions were made, and the clause indicates that period (see Abarbanel, Daath Mikra).

32f. These verses recall ii. 26f., vii. 13, 25, xi. 17.

prophets, and the men of Judah, and the inhabitants of Jerusalem. 33. And they have turned unto Me the back, and not the face; and though I taught them, teaching them betimes and often, yet they have not hearkened to receive instruction. 34. But they set their abominations in the house whereupon My name is called, to defile it. 35. And they built the high places of Baal, which are in the valley of the son of Hinnom, to set apart their sons and their daughters unto Molech; which I commanded them not, neither came it into My mind, that they should do this abomination; to cause Judah to sin. 36. And now therefore thus saith the LORD, the God of Israel, concerning this city, whereof ye say: It is given into the hand of the king of Babylon by the sword, and by the famine, and by the pestilence: 37. Behold, I will gather them out of all the countries, whither I have driven them in Mine anger, and in My fury, and in great wrath; and I will bring them back unto this place, and I will cause them to dwell safely; 38. and they shall be My people, and I will be

וְאִישׁ יְהוּדָה וְיֹשְׁבֵי יְרוּשָׁלֵָם׃

33 וַיִּפְנוּ אֵלַי עֹרֶף וְלֹא פָנִים וְלַמֵּד אֹתָם הַשְׁכֵּם וְלַמֵּד וְאֵינָם שֹׁמְעִים לָקַחַת מוּסָר׃

34 וַיָּשִׂימוּ שִׁקּוּצֵיהֶם בַּבַּיִת אֲשֶׁר־נִקְרָא שְׁמִי־עָלָיו

35 לְטַמְּאוֹ׃ וַיִּבְנוּ אֶת־בָּמוֹת הַבַּעַל אֲשֶׁר ׀ בְּגֵיא בֶן־הִנֹּם לְהַעֲבִיר אֶת־בְּנֵיהֶם וְאֶת־ בְּנוֹתֵיהֶם לַמֹּלֶךְ אֲשֶׁר לֹא־ צִוִּיתִים וְלֹא עָלְתָה עַל־לִבִּי לַעֲשׂוֹת הַתּוֹעֵבָה הַזֹּאת לְמַעַן הַחֲטִי אֶת־יְהוּדָה׃

36 וְעַתָּה לָכֵן כֹּה־אָמַר יְהוָה אֱלֹהֵי יִשְׂרָאֵל אֶל־הָעִיר הַזֹּאת אֲשֶׁר ׀ אַתֶּם אֹמְרִים נִתְּנָה בְּיַד מֶלֶךְ־בָּבֶל בַּחֶרֶב

37 וּבָרָעָב וּבַדָּבֶר׃ הִנְנִי מְקַבְּצָם מִכָּל־הָאֲרָצוֹת אֲשֶׁר הִדַּחְתִּים שָׁם בְּאַפִּי וּבַחֲמָתִי וּבְקֶצֶף גָּדוֹל וַהֲשִׁבֹתִים אֶל־ הַמָּקוֹם הַזֶּה וְהֹשַׁבְתִּים

38 לָבֶטַח׃ וְהָיוּ לִי לְעָם וַאֲנִי

v. 35. החטיא ק׳

34f. Mainly reproduced from vii. 30f.

35. *Baal . . . Molech.* [The two are identified here, the former being a generic term and the latter specifying it.]

36-44 THE PROMISE OF RESTORATION
36. *and now.* A resumption of verse 27.

37. *I have driven them.* [The prophetic perfect.]

their God; 39. and I will give them one heart and one way, that they may fear Me for ever; for the good of them, and of their children after them; 40. and I will make an everlasting covenant with them, that I will not turn away from them, to do them good; and I will put My fear in their hearts, that they shall not depart from Me. 41. Yea, I will rejoice over them to do them good, and I will plant them in this land in truth with My whole heart and with My whole soul. 42. For thus saith the LORD: Like as I have brought all this great evil upon this people, so will I bring upon them all the good that I have promised them. 43. And fields shall be bought in this land, whereof ye say:

אֶהְיֶה לָהֶם לֵאלֹהִים: וְנָתַתִּי 39
לָהֶם לֵב אֶחָד וְדֶרֶךְ אֶחָד
לְיִרְאָה אוֹתִי כָּל־הַיָּמִים
לְטוֹב לָהֶם וְלִבְנֵיהֶם
אַחֲרֵיהֶם: וְכָרַתִּי לָהֶם בְּרִית 40
עוֹלָם אֲשֶׁר לֹא־אָשׁוּב
מֵאַחֲרֵיהֶם לְהֵיטִיבִי אוֹתָם
וְאֶת־יִרְאָתִי אֶתֵּן בִּלְבָבָם
לְבִלְתִּי סוּר מֵעָלָי: וְשַׂשְׂתִּי 41
עֲלֵיהֶם לְהֵטִיב אוֹתָם
וּנְטַעְתִּים בָּאָרֶץ הַזֹּאת בֶּאֱמֶת
בְּכָל־לִבִּי וּבְכָל־נַפְשִׁי: כִּי־ 42
כֹה אָמַר יְהוָה כַּאֲשֶׁר הֵבֵאתִי
אֶל־הָעָם הַזֶּה אֵת כָּל־
הָרָעָה הַגְּדוֹלָה הַזֹּאת כֵּן אָנֹכִי
מֵבִיא עֲלֵיהֶם אֶת־כָּל־
הַטּוֹבָה אֲשֶׁר אָנֹכִי דֹּבֵר
עֲלֵיהֶם: וְנִקְנָה הַשָּׂדֶה בָּאָרֶץ 43
הַזֹּאת אֲשֶׁר | אַתֶּם אֹמְרִים

38. None of the prophets looked forward only to physical restoration. The return was also to be spiritual (cf. xxxi. 32).

39. *one heart and one way.* Expressive of unanimity and singleness of purpose (Daath Mikra).

40. *I will not turn . . . good.* i.e. I will not cease doing them good (Metsudath David).

I will not put My fear in their hearts. If this is to be understood literally it would imply loss of free will which is implicit in the ethical teaching of the Bible. A Rabbinical maxim teaches, 'Everything is in the hands of Heaven (God) save the fear of Heaven.' Abarbanel explains that God will inspire them to fear Him through the many miracles and wonders He will perform in Messianic times.

41. *with My whole heart.* Nowhere else is this phrase applied to God.

42. The same thought as in xxxi. 27.

43. *fields.* The Hebrew is singular and to be distinguished from *fields* in the

It is desolate, without man or beast;
it is given into the hand of the
Chaldeans. 44. Men shall buy
fields for money, and subscribe the
deeds, and seal them, and call
witnesses, in the land of Benjamin,
and in the places about Jerusalem,
and in the cities of Judah, and in the
cities of the hill-country, and in the
cities of the Lowland, and in the
cities of the South; for I will cause
their captivity to return, saith the
Lord.'

שְׁמָמָה הִיא מֵאֵין אָדָם וּבְהֵמָה
44 נִתְּנָה בְּיַד הַכַּשְׂדִּים: שָׂדוֹת
בַּכֶּסֶף יִקְנוּ וְכָתוֹב בַּסֵּפֶר |
וְחָתוֹם וְהָעֵד עֵדִים בְּאֶרֶץ
בִּנְיָמִן וּבִסְבִיבֵי יְרוּשָׁלַ͏ִם
וּבְעָרֵי יְהוּדָה וּבְעָרֵי הָהָר
וּבְעָרֵי הַשְּׁפֵלָה וּבְעָרֵי הַנֶּגֶב
כִּי־אָשִׁיב אֶת־שְׁבוּתָם נְאֻם־
יְהֹוָה:

33   CHAPTER XXXIII   לֹג

1. Moreover the word of the Lord
came unto Jeremiah the second
time, while he was yet shut up in the
court of the guard, saying:

2 Thus saith the Lord the Maker
   thereof,

   The Lord that formed it to
   establish it,

1 וַיְהִי דְבַר־יְהֹוָה אֶל־
יִרְמְיָהוּ שֵׁנִית וְהוּא עוֹדֶנּוּ
עָצוּר בַּחֲצַר הַמַּטָּרָה לֵאמֹר:
2 כֹּה־אָמַר יְהֹוָה עֹשָׂהּ
יְהֹוָה יוֹצֵר אוֹתָהּ לַהֲכִינָהּ:

---

next verse which is plural. Although
here too the plural is meant, verse 44
emphasizes that very many fields will be
bought (Abarbanel).

44. *subscribe the deeds.* See on verse 10.
the land of Benjamin, etc. Kimchi understands this verse as an indication that
the return from Babylon is meant, when
only the tribes of Judah and Benjamin
would return. Abarbanel understands it
as a reference to the Messianic Era. The
land of Benjamin is mentioned because
that was the location of Hanamel's field
and there Jeremiah was prophesying,
but, in fact, the entire land of Israel is
meant.

CHAPTER XXXIII

1–13   RENEWED PROMISE OF REDEMPTION

The futility of resistance to the Chaldeans is again stressed, and the promise
of a return from captivity repeated.

1. *the second time.* The second message
must have come soon after the first as
the next clause implies (Daath Mikra).

the court of the guard. See on xxxii. 2.

2. *the Maker thereof.* i.e. He Who magnified and exalted Jerusalem (Metsudath David).

that formed it to establish it. He will

The LORD is His name:

3 Call unto Me, and I will answer thee,

And will tell thee great things, and hidden, which thou knowest not.

4. For thus saith the LORD, the God of Israel, concerning the houses of this city, and concerning the houses of the kings of Judah, which are broken down for mounds, and for ramparts; 5. whereon they come to fight with the Chaldeans, even to fill them with the dead bodies of men, whom I have slain in Mine anger and in My fury, and for all whose wickedness I have hid My face from this city: 6. Behold, I will bring it

יְהֹוָה ׀ שְׁמוֹ:

3 קְרָא אֵלַי וְאֶעֱנֶךָּ
וְאַגִּידָה לְךָ גְּדֹלוֹת וּבְצֻרוֹת
לֹא יְדַעְתָּם:

4 כִּי כֹה אָמַר יְהֹוָה אֱלֹהֵי
יִשְׂרָאֵל עַל־בָּתֵּי הָעִיר הַזֹּאת
וְעַל־בָּתֵּי מַלְכֵי יְהוּדָה
הַנְּתֻצִים אֶל־הַסֹּלְלוֹת וְאֶל־

5 הֶחָרֶב: בָּאִים לְהִלָּחֵם אֶת־
הַכַּשְׂדִּים וּלְמַלְאָם אֶת־פִּגְרֵי
הָאָדָם אֲשֶׁר־הִכֵּיתִי בְאַפִּי
וּבַחֲמָתִי וַאֲשֶׁר הִסְתַּרְתִּי פָנַי
מֵהָעִיר הַזֹּאת עַל כָּל־

6 רָעָתָם: הִנְנִי מַעֲלֶה־לָּהּ

renew it to establish it forever (Metsudath David).

the LORD *is His name.* [The Tetragrammaton in the text (the Hebrew consonants being JHWH) denotes God either under the aspect of eternity (hence some translate as 'the Eternal') or, according to the Rabbis, the attribute of mercy. This gives point to the introduction of the Name at this point: He is eternal and looks beyond the present darkness to future light; He is merciful, and when the demands of justice have been met by a period of exile, He will in His mercy restore Israel to his land and ancient glory.]

call unto Me, and I will answer thee. In contradistinction to what God had commanded him not to pray for the people (vii. 16), He now invites him to pray, promising to answer His prayers (Kimchi).

hidden. The Hebrew *betsuroth* elsewhere describes 'fortified' cities, difficult of access; hence 'secret things' which are beyond man's knowledge. A few Hebrew MSS. read *netsuroth, hidden things,* as in Isa. xlviii. 6; but the more unusual word of M.T. is likely to have stood in the original text of the present verse. The latter reading appears to be that of Targum Jonathan and Rashi.

4. *mounds.* For the word, see on vi. 6; but here the *mounds* indicate material heaped up to reinforce the city walls and strengthen the defences (Rashi).

5. *they come.* The subject is the Judean defenders of the besieged city (see Kimchi, Metsudath David).

even to fill them with the dead bodies of men. Their resistance, however heroic, is futile and only adds to the heaps of the slain (Kimchi, Metsudath David).

healing and cure, and I will cure them; and I will reveal unto them the abundance of peace and truth. 7. And I will cause the captivity of Judah and the captivity of Israel to return, and will build them, as at the first. 8. And I will cleanse them from all their iniquity, whereby they have sinned against Me; and I will pardon all their iniquities, whereby they have sinned against Me, and whereby they have transgressed against Me. 9. And this city shall be to Me for a name of joy, for a praise and for a glory, before all the nations of the earth, which shall hear all the good that I do unto them, and shall fear and tremble for all the good and for all the peace that I procure unto it.

10. Thus saith the LORD: Yet again there shall be heard in this place, whereof ye say: It is waste, without man and without beast, even in the cities of Judah, and in the streets of Jerusalem, that are desolate, without man and without

אַרְכָּה וּמַרְפֵּא וּרְפָאתִים
וְגִלֵּיתִי לָהֶם עֲתֶרֶת שָׁלוֹם
7 וֶאֱמֶת: וַהֲשִׁבֹתִי אֶת־שְׁבוּת
יְהוּדָה וְאֵת שְׁבוּת יִשְׂרָאֵל
וּבְנִתִים כְּבָרִאשֹׁנָה:
8 וְטִהַרְתִּים מִכָּל־עֲוֺנָם אֲשֶׁר
חָטְאוּ־לִי וְסָלַחְתִּי לְכָל־
עֲוֺנוֹתֵיהֶם אֲשֶׁר חָטְאוּ־לִי
9 וַאֲשֶׁר פָּשְׁעוּ בִי: וְהָיְתָה לִי
לְשֵׁם שָׂשׂוֹן לִתְהִלָּה וּלְתִפְאֶרֶת
לְכֹל גּוֹיֵי הָאָרֶץ אֲשֶׁר יִשְׁמְעוּ
אֶת־כָּל־הַטּוֹבָה אֲשֶׁר אָנֹכִי
עֹשֶׂה אֹתָם וּפָחֲדוּ וְרָגְזוּ עַל
כָּל־הַטּוֹבָה וְעַל כָּל־
הַשָּׁלוֹם אֲשֶׁר אָנֹכִי עֹשֶׂה לָּהּ:
10 כֹּה | אָמַר יְהוָה עוֹד יִשָּׁמַע
בַּמָּקוֹם־הַזֶּה אֲשֶׁר אַתֶּם
אֹמְרִים חָרֵב הוּא מֵאֵין אָדָם
וּמֵאֵין בְּהֵמָה בְּעָרֵי יְהוּדָה
וּבְחֻצוֹת יְרוּשָׁלַם הַנְּשַׁמּוֹת
מֵאֵין אָדָם וּמֵאֵין יוֹשֵׁב וּמֵאֵין

v. 8. ר' יתיר

6. *cure.* See on viii. 22.

truth. i.e. a permanent peace (Daath Mikra).

7. *as at the first.* Before the Kingdom was split into two after the death of Solomon (Abarbanel).

8. Cf. Ezek. xxxvi. 25.

9. *and shall fear and tremble for all the good,* etc. The love which God will display to His people, who acknowledge Him, will make the nations fear His displeasure for not acknowledging Him (Kimchi, Ibn Kaspi).

10. *whereof ye say.* [i.e. you will, when in captivity, say.]

inhabitant and without beast, 11. the voice of joy and the voice of gladness, the voice of the bridegroom and the voice of the bride, the voice of them that say: 'Give thanks to the LORD of hosts, for the LORD is good, for His mercy endureth for ever,' even of them that bring offerings of thanksgiving into the house of the LORD. For I will cause the captivity of the land to return as at the first, saith the LORD.

12. Thus saith the LORD of hosts: Yet again shall there be in this place, which is waste, without man and without beast, and in all the cities thereof, a habitation of shepherds causing their flocks to lie down. 13. In the cities of the hill-country, in the cities of the Lowland, and in the cities of the South, and in the land of Benjamin, and in the places about Jerusalem, and in the cities of Judah, shall the flocks again pass under the hands of him that counteth them, saith the LORD.

14. Behold, the days come, saith the LORD, that I will perform that good word which I have spoken concerning the house of Israel and

11 בְּהֵמָה: קוֹל שָׂשׂוֹן וְקוֹל
שִׂמְחָה קוֹל חָתָן וְקוֹל כַּלָּה
קוֹל אֹמְרִים הוֹדוּ אֶת־יְהוָה
צְבָאוֹת כִּי־טוֹב יְהוָה כִּי־
לְעוֹלָם חַסְדּוֹ מְבִאִים תּוֹדָה
בֵּית יְהוָה כִּי־אָשִׁיב אֶת־
שְׁבוּת־הָאָרֶץ כְּבָרִאשֹׁנָה
12 אָמַר יְהוָה: כֹּה אָמַר יְהוָה
צְבָאוֹת עוֹד יִהְיֶה | בַּמָּקוֹם
הַזֶּה הֶחָרֵב מֵאֵין־אָדָם וְעַד־
בְּהֵמָה וּבְכָל־עָרָיו נְוֵה רֹעִים
13 מַרְבִּצִים צֹאן: בְּעָרֵי הָהָר
בְּעָרֵי הַשְּׁפֵלָה וּבְעָרֵי הַנֶּגֶב
וּבְאֶרֶץ בִּנְיָמִן וּבִסְבִיבֵי
יְרוּשָׁלַ͏ִם וּבְעָרֵי יְהוּדָה עֹד
תַּעֲבֹרְנָה הַצֹּאן עַל־יְדֵי
14 מוֹנֶה אָמַר יְהוָה: הִנֵּה יָמִים
בָּאִים נְאֻם־יְהוָה וַהֲקִמֹתִי
אֶת־הַדָּבָר הַטּוֹב אֲשֶׁר
דִּבַּרְתִּי אֶל־בֵּית יִשְׂרָאֵל

---

11. *the voice of joy,* etc. Contrast vii. 34.

give thanks ... for ever. A liturgical refrain used in the Temple services (cf. Ps. cvi. 1, cxviii. 1, cxxxvi. 1; Ezra iii. 11).

that bring offerings. [Better, 'as they bring,' etc.]

12. *in this place.* Jerusalem (Metsudath David).

all the cities thereof. Of Israel (Metsudath David).

causing their flocks to lie down. An idyllic picture of undisturbed peace: the flocks will lie down without fear of attack (Kimchi).

13. *the cities of the hill-country,* etc. See on xvii. 26 and xxxii. 44.

him that counteth them. To see that none is missing; the old pastoral life of the country will be restored. This follows Metsudath David. Most exegetes, however, interpret this figuratively as concerning the house of Judah.

15. In those days, and at that time,
Will I cause a shoot of righteousness to grow up unto David;
And he shall execute justice and
righteousness in the land.

16 In those days shall Judah be
saved,
And Jerusalem shall dwell safely;
And this is the name whereby
she shall be called,
The LORD is our righteousness.

17. For thus saith the LORD: There
shall not be cut off unto David a
man to sit upon the throne of the
house of Israel; 18. neither shall
there be cut off unto the priests the
Levites a man before Me to offer
burnt-offerings, and to burn meal-
offerings, and to do sacrifice continually.

19. And the word of the LORD
came unto Jeremiah, saying: 20.
Thus saith the LORD:
If ye can break My covenant with
the day,
And My covenant with the night,
So that there should not be day
and night in their season;

וְעַל־בֵּית יְהוּדָה:

15 בַּיָּמִים הָהֵם וּבָעֵת הַהִיא
אַצְמִיחַ לְדָוִד צֶמַח צְדָקָה
וְעָשָׂה מִשְׁפָּט וּצְדָקָה בָּאָרֶץ:

16 בַּיָּמִים הָהֵם תִּוָּשַׁע יְהוּדָה
וִירוּשָׁלַם תִּשְׁכּוֹן לָבֶטַח
וְזֶה אֲשֶׁר־יִקְרָא־לָהּ
יְהוָה | צִדְקֵנוּ:

17 כִּי־כֹה אָמַר יְהוָה לֹא־יִכָּרֵת
לְדָוִד אִישׁ יֹשֵׁב עַל־כִּסֵּא
18 בֵּית־יִשְׂרָאֵל: וְלַכֹּהֲנִים
הַלְוִיִּם לֹא־יִכָּרֵת אִישׁ מִלְּפָנָי
מַעֲלֶה עוֹלָה וּמַקְטִיר מִנְחָה
19 וְעֹשֶׂה זֶּבַח כָּל־הַיָּמִים: וַיְהִי
דְּבַר־יְהוָה אֶל־יִרְמְיָהוּ
20 לֵאמוֹר: כֹּה אָמַר יְהוָה
אִם־תָּפֵרוּ אֶת־בְּרִיתִי הַיּוֹם
וְאֶת־בְּרִיתִי הַלָּיְלָה
וּלְבִלְתִּי הֱיוֹת יוֹמָם־וָלַיְלָה
בְּעִתָּם:

v. 19. יתיר ו

referring to Israel being governed by
the Messiah.

14-22 RESTORATION OF THE MONARCHY
AND PRIESTHOOD

15f. Repeated with variants from xxiii.
5f. Here *the LORD is our righteousness* is
applied to Jerusalem, not to the king. It
will be the watchword, as it were, of the
city's inhabitants (Kimchi).

17. *there shall not be cut off.* Permanently; should his dynasty cease, it will only
be temporarily, to be renewed in the
future (Rashi).

19f. The covenant with David is as
dependable as the sequence of day and
night (cf. Ps. lxxxix. 36–38).

20. *My covenant with the day . . . the night.*
An allusion to God's oath after the
Flood (Gen. viii. 22) (Rashi, Kimchi).

21 Then may also My covenant be
broken with David My ser-
vant,

That he should not have a son to
reign upon his throne;

And with the Levites the priests,
My ministers.

22 As the host of heaven cannot be
numbered,

Neither the sand of the sea
measured;

So will I multiply the seed of
David My servant,

And the Levites that minister
unto Me.

23. And the word of the LORD
came to Jeremiah, saying: 24. 'Con-
siderest thou not what this people
have spoken, saying: The two
families which the LORD did choose,
He hath cast them off? and they
contemn My people, that they
should be no more a nation before
them. 25. Thus saith the LORD:
If My covenant be not with day and
night, if I have not appointed the
ordinances of heaven and earth;
26. then will I also cast away the
seed of Jacob, and of David My

21 גַּם־בְּרִיתִי תֻפַר
אֶת־דָּוִד עַבְדִּי
מִהְיֽוֹת־לוֹ בֵן
מֹלֵךְ עַל־כִּסְאוֹ
וְאֶת־הַלְוִיִּם הַכֹּהֲנִים
מְשָׁרְתָֽי׃
22 אֲשֶׁר לֹא־יִסָּפֵר צְבָא הַשָּׁמַיִם
וְלֹא יִמַּד חוֹל הַיָּם
כֵּן אַרְבֶּה אֶת־זֶרַע דָּוִד עַבְדִּי
וְאֶת־הַלְוִיִּם מְשָׁרְתֵי אֹתִֽי׃
23 וַיְהִי דְּבַר־יְהֹוָה אֶל־יִרְמְיָהוּ
24 לֵאמֹֽר׃ הֲלוֹא רָאִיתָ מָה־
הָעָם הַזֶּה דִּבְּרוּ לֵאמֹר שְׁתֵּי
הַמִּשְׁפָּחוֹת אֲשֶׁר בָּחַר יְהֹוָה
בָּהֶם וַיִּמְאָסֵם וְאֶת־עַמִּי
יִנְאָצוּן מִהְיוֹת עוֹד גּוֹי
25 לִפְנֵיהֶֽם׃ כֹּה אָמַר יְהֹוָה אִם־
לֹא בְרִיתִי יוֹמָם וָלָיְלָה חֻקּוֹת
26 שָׁמַיִם וָאָרֶץ לֹא־שָֽׂמְתִּי׃ גַּם־
זֶרַע יַעֲקוֹב וְדָוִד עַבְדִּי אֶמְאַס
מלא ר v. 26.

---

21. *My covenant . . . with David.* Cf. 2
Sam. vii. 12–16 (Daath Mikra).

22. *and the Levites.* Perhaps an allusion to Num. xxv. 13 (Daath Mikra).

23-26 THE COVENANT ALSO APPLIED TO
THE NATION

24. *this people . . . My people.* [The first
alludes to the sceptical and faithless
section of the nation, the latter to the
community as a whole.]

two families. Some explain as Israel and
Judah (see Daath Mikra); others as the
royal house of David and the priesthood (Rashi, Kimchi).

before them. Rashi interprets this to
mean 'in their view.'

25f. A similar assurance is given with
regard to the nation as to the monarchy
and priesthood (verse 20).

26. *Isaac.* The Hebrew is spelt *yischak*

servant, so that I will not take of his seed to be rulers over the seed of Abraham, Isaac, and Jacob; for I will cause their captivity to return, and will have compassion on them.'

מִקַּחַת מִזַּרְעוֹ מֹשְׁלִים אֶל־
זֶרַע אַבְרָהָם יִשְׂחָק וְיַעֲקֹב
כִּי־אָשׁוֹב אֶת־שְׁבוּתָם
וְרִחַמְתִּים׃

---

34   CHAPTER XXXIV   לד

1. The word which came unto Jeremiah from the LORD, when Nebuchadrezzar king of Babylon, and all his army, and all the kingdoms of the land of his dominion, and all the peoples, fought against Jerusalem, and against all the cities thereof, saying:

2. Thus saith the LORD, the God of Israel: Go, and speak to Zedekiah king of Judah, and tell him: Thus saith the LORD: Behold, I will give this city into the hand of the king of Babylon, and he shall burn it with fire; 3. and thou shalt not escape out of his hand, but shalt surely be taken, and delivered into his hand; and thine eyes shall behold the eyes of the king of Babylon, and

1 הַדָּבָר אֲשֶׁר־הָיָה אֶל־
יִרְמְיָהוּ מֵאֵת יְהֹוָה
וּנְבוּכַדְרֶאצַּר מֶלֶךְ־בָּבֶל ו
וְכָל־חֵילוֹ וְכָל־מַמְלְכוֹת
אֶרֶץ מֶמְשֶׁלֶת יָדוֹ וְכָל־
הָעַמִּים נִלְחָמִים עַל־יְרוּשָׁלַ͏ִם
וְעַל־כָּל־עָרֶיהָ לֵאמֹר׃
2 כֹּה־אָמַר יְהֹוָה אֱלֹהֵי יִשְׂרָאֵל
הָלֹךְ וְאָמַרְתָּ אֶל־צִדְקִיָּהוּ
מֶלֶךְ יְהוּדָה וְאָמַרְתָּ אֵלָיו כֹּה
אָמַר יְהֹוָה הִנְנִי נֹתֵן אֶת־הָעִיר
הַזֹּאת בְּיַד מֶלֶךְ־בָּבֶל
3 וּשְׂרָפָהּ בָּאֵשׁ׃ וְאַתָּה לֹא
תִמָּלֵט מִיָּדוֹ כִּי תָּפֹשׂ תִּתָּפֵשׂ
וּבְיָדוֹ תִּנָּתֵן וְעֵינֶיךָ אֶת־עֵינֵי
מֶלֶךְ־בָּבֶל תִּרְאֶינָה וּפִיהוּ

אשיב ק׳ v. 26.

---

instead of the usual *yitschak*. So again in Amos vii. 9, 16; Ps. cv. 9.

CHAPTER XXXIV

THE biographical section of the Book is resumed and extends to the end of xxxix.

1–7   THE FATE OF JERUSALEM AND ITS KING

1. The verse refers to the siege during the years 588–586 B.C.E.

3. *and thine eyes shall behold.* Cf. xxxii. 4.

he shall speak with thee mouth to mouth, and thou shalt go to Babylon. 4. Yet hear the word of the LORD, O Zedekiah king of Judah: Thus saith the LORD concerning thee: Thou shalt not die by the sword; 5. thou shalt die in peace; and with the burnings of thy fathers, the former kings that were before thee, so shall they make a burning for thee; and they shall lament thee: 'Ah lord!' for I have spoken the word, saith the LORD.

6. Then Jeremiah the prophet spoke all these words unto Zedekiah king of Judah in Jerusalem, 7. when the king of Babylon's army fought against Jerusalem, and against all the cities of Judah that were left, against Lachish and against Azekah; for these alone remained of the cities of Judah as fortified cities.

8. The word that came unto Jeremiah from the LORD, after that

אֶת־פִּ֙יךָ֙ יְדַבֵּ֔ר וּבָבֶ֖ל תָּבֽוֹא׃

4 אַ֚ךְ שְׁמַ֣ע דְּבַר־יְהֹוָ֔ה צִדְקִיָּ֖הוּ מֶ֣לֶךְ יְהוּדָ֑ה כֹּֽה־אָמַ֤ר יְהֹוָה֙ עָלֶ֔יךָ לֹ֥א תָמ֖וּת בֶּחָֽרֶב׃

5 בְּשָׁל֣וֹם תָּמ֗וּת וּֽבְמִשְׂרְפ֣וֹת אֲבוֹתֶ֡יךָ הַמְּלָכִ֣ים הָרִֽאשֹׁנִ֣ים אֲשֶׁר־הָי֣וּ לְפָנֶ֗יךָ כֵּ֚ן יִשְׂרְפוּ־לָ֔ךְ וְה֥וֹי אָד֖וֹן יִסְפְּדוּ־לָ֑ךְ כִּֽי־דָבָ֥ר אֲנִֽי־דִבַּ֖רְתִּי נְאֻם־

6 יְהֹוָֽה׃ וַיְדַבֵּר֙ יִרְמְיָ֣הוּ הַנָּבִ֔יא אֶל־צִדְקִיָּ֖הוּ מֶ֣לֶךְ יְהוּדָ֑ה אֵ֛ת כׇּל־הַדְּבָרִ֥ים הָאֵ֖לֶּה

7 בִּירוּשָׁלָֽ͏ִם׃ וְחֵ֣יל מֶֽלֶךְ־בָּבֶ֗ל נִלְחָמִים֙ עַל־יְר֣וּשָׁלַ֔͏ִם וְעַ֛ל כׇּל־עָרֵ֥י יְהוּדָ֖ה הַנּֽוֹתָר֑וֹת אֶל־לָכִ֣ישׁ וְאֶל־עֲזֵקָ֔ה כִּ֣י הֵ֗נָּה נִשְׁאֲר֛וּ בְּעָרֵ֥י

8 יְהוּדָ֖ה עָרֵ֥י מִבְצָֽר׃ הַדָּבָ֞ר אֲשֶׁר־הָיָ֧ה אֶֽל־יִרְמְיָ֛הוּ מֵאֵ֥ת

---

v. 8. הפטרת משפטים

---

5. *thou shalt die in peace.* i.e. a natural death; he would not die in battle or by the executioner's sword (Kara).

with the burnings of thy fathers. The Talmud records that it was the custom to make a funeral pyre of the bed and other articles as a mark of honour to the deceased (Sanh. 52b). Aromatic spices were laid on the bed (cf. 2 Chron. xvi. 14).

'Ah lord!' See on xxii. 18.

7. *Lachish.* About thirty-five miles south-west of Jerusalem.

Azekah. About fifteen miles south-west of Jerusalem. The towns mark the limit of Nebuchadnezzar's advance southwards.

8-22 OATH TO FREE HEBREW SLAVES VIOLATED

The dire peril of the nation had caused a quickening of the national conscience

the king Zedekiah had made a covenant with all the people that were at Jerusalem, to proclaim liberty unto them; 9. that every man should let his man-servant, and every man his maid-servant, being a Hebrew man or a Hebrew woman, go free; that none should make bondmen of them, even of a Jew his brother; 10. and all the princes and all the people hearkened, that had entered into the covenant to let every one his man-servant, and every one his maid-servant, go free, and not to make bondmen of them any more; they hearkened, and let them go; 11. but afterwards they turned, and caused the servants and the handmaids, whom they had let go free, to return, and brought them into subjection for servants and for handmaids; 12. therefore the word of the LORD came to Jeremiah from the LORD, saying:

יְהֹוָה אַחֲרֵי כְּרֹת הַמֶּ֫לֶךְ
צִדְקִיָּ֫הוּ בְּרִית אֶת־כָּל־
הָעָם אֲשֶׁר בִּירוּשָׁלַ֫ם לִקְרֹא
9 לָהֶם דְּרוֹר: לְשַׁלַּח אִישׁ אֶת־
עַבְדּוֹ וְאִישׁ אֶת־שִׁפְחָתוֹ
הָעִבְרִי וְהָעִבְרִיָּה חָפְשִׁים
לְבִלְתִּי עֲבָד־בָּם בִּיהוּדִי
10 אָחִיהוּ אִישׁ: וַיִּשְׁמְעוּ כָל־
הַשָּׂרִים וְכָל־הָעָם אֲשֶׁר־
בָּאוּ בַבְּרִית לְשַׁלַּח אִישׁ אֶת־
עַבְדּוֹ וְאִישׁ אֶת־שִׁפְחָתוֹ
חָפְשִׁים לְבִלְתִּי עֲבָד־בָּם
11 עוֹד וַיִּשְׁמְעוּ וַיְשַׁלֵּחוּ: וַיָּשׁוּבוּ
אַחֲרֵי־כֵן וַיָּשִׁבוּ אֶת־
הָעֲבָדִים וְאֶת־הַשְּׁפָחוֹת
אֲשֶׁר שִׁלְּחוּ חָפְשִׁים וַיִּכְבְּשׁוּם
12 לַעֲבָדִים וְלִשְׁפָחוֹת: וַיְהִי
דְבַר־יְהֹוָה אֶל־יִרְמְיָ֫הוּ מֵאֵת

v. 11. יתיר י'

---

and some effort at repentance. Zedekiah had induced the owners under a solemn oath to free their slaves. When the danger from Babylon had been temporarily removed, the masters broke their oath and forcibly retook them. This act of perjury would have the effect of bringing the Babylonians back to attack Judea.

8. *and had made a covenant.* Which was ratified in the most solemn manner (cf. verses 18f.).

unto them. The slaves, mentioned in the next verse (Metsudath David, Kimchi).

9. *go free.* [It is noteworthy that national repentance took the form of respecting the rights of the weakest and most downtrodden of the people. This is characteristic of the Mosaic Code and of Judaism.] This verse involves two innovations; one, that all slaves, even those who had not worked for six years, were to be freed, and two, that thereafter no one was to make bondmen of their fellow Jews (Malbim).

10. *and all the princes ... hearkened.* Not only did the people obey, but also the princes. They agreed to enter the

13. Thus saith the Lord, the God of Israel: I made a covenant with your fathers in the day that I brought them forth out of the land of Egypt, out of the house of bondage, saying: 14. 'At the end of seven years ye shall let go every man his brother that is a Hebrew, that hath been sold unto thee, and hath served thee six years, thou shalt let him go free from thee'; but your fathers hearkened not unto Me, neither inclined their ear. 15. And ye were now turned, and had done that which is right in Mine eyes, in proclaiming liberty every man to his neighbour; and ye had made a covenant before Me in the house whereon My name is called; 16. but ye turned and profaned My name, and caused every man his servant, and every man his handmaid, whom ye had let go free at their pleasure, to return; and ye brought them into subjection, to be unto you for

13 יְהֹוָה לֵאמֹר: כֹּה־אָמַר יְהֹוָה
אֱלֹהֵי יִשְׂרָאֵל אָנֹכִי כָּרַתִּי
בְרִית אֶת־אֲבוֹתֵיכֶם בְּיוֹם
הוֹצִאִי אוֹתָם מֵאֶרֶץ מִצְרַיִם
14 מִבֵּית עֲבָדִים לֵאמֹר: מִקֵּץ
שֶׁבַע שָׁנִים תְּשַׁלְּחוּ אִישׁ אֶת־
אָחִיו הָעִבְרִי אֲשֶׁר־יִמָּכֵר לְךָ
וַעֲבָדְךָ שֵׁשׁ שָׁנִים וְשִׁלַּחְתּוֹ
חָפְשִׁי מֵעִמָּךְ וְלֹא־שָׁמְעוּ
אֲבוֹתֵיכֶם אֵלַי וְלֹא הִטּוּ אֶת־
15 אָזְנָם: וַתָּשֻׁבוּ אַתֶּם הַיּוֹם
וַתַּעֲשׂוּ אֶת־הַיָּשָׁר בְּעֵינַי
לִקְרֹא דְרוֹר אִישׁ לְרֵעֵהוּ
וַתִּכְרְתוּ בְרִית לְפָנַי בַּבַּיִת
אֲשֶׁר־נִקְרָא שְׁמִי עָלָיו:
16 וַתָּשֻׁבוּ וַתְּחַלְּלוּ אֶת־שְׁמִי
וַתָּשִׁבוּ אִישׁ אֶת־עַבְדּוֹ וְאִישׁ
אֶת־שִׁפְחָתוֹ אֲשֶׁר־שִׁלַּחְתֶּם
חָפְשִׁים לְנַפְשָׁם וַתִּכְבְּשׁוּ אֹתָם
לִהְיוֹת לָכֶם לַעֲבָדִים

covenant, to accept both innovations and then execute them by letting their slaves go free (Malbim).

13. *I made.* The *I* is emphatic and offers the contrast with *ye were now turned* in verse 15 where *ye* is also stressed (Daath Mikra).

out of the house of bondage. The reason for mentioning this is clear: the exodus, whereby they were liberated from slavery, was an assertion of man's right

to freedom. Just as God freed you from the house of bondage, so must you free your brethren from bondage (Malbim).

14. *seven years.* This includes the year of liberation. Actually the slave's servitude was limited to six years (Exod. xxi. 2; Deut. xv. 12).

15. *and ye.* See on verse 13.

16. *and profaned My name.* By violating the oath which must have included the

servants and for handmaids. 17. Therefore thus saith the LORD: Ye have not hearkened unto Me, to proclaim liberty, every man to his brother, and every man to his neighbour; behold, I proclaim for you a liberty, saith the LORD, unto the sword, unto the pestilence, and unto the famine; and I will make you a horror unto all the kingdoms of the earth. 18. And I will give the men that have transgressed My covenant, that have not performed the words of the covenant which they made before Me, when they cut the calf in twain and passed between the parts thereof; 19. the princes of Judah, and the princes of Jerusalem, the officers, and the priests, and all the people of the land, that passed *between the parts of the calf; 20. I will even give them into the hand of their enemies, and into the hand of them that seek their life; and their dead bodies shall be for food unto the fowls of the heaven, and to the beasts of the

17 וְלִשְׁפָחֽוֹת: לָכֵן כֹּה־אָמַר
יְהֹוָה אַתֶּם לֹא־שְׁמַעְתֶּם אֵלַי
לִקְרֹא דְרוֹר אִישׁ לְאָחִיו וְאִישׁ
לְרֵעֵהוּ הִנְנִי קֹרֵא לָכֶם דְּרוֹר
נְאֻם־יְהֹוָה אֶל־הַחֶרֶב אֶל־
הַדֶּבֶר וְאֶל־הָרָעָב וְנָתַתִּי
אֶתְכֶם לְזַוֲעָה לְכֹל מַמְלְכוֹת
18 הָאָרֶץ: וְנָתַתִּי אֶת־הָאֲנָשִׁים
הָעֹבְרִים אֶת־בְּרִתִי אֲשֶׁר
לֹא־הֵקִימוּ אֶת־דִּבְרֵי
הַבְּרִית אֲשֶׁר כָּרְתוּ לְפָנָי
הָעֵגֶל אֲשֶׁר כָּרְתוּ לִשְׁנַיִם
19 וַיַּעַבְרוּ בֵּין בְּתָרָיו: שָׂרֵי
יְהוּדָה וְשָׂרֵי יְרוּשָׁלַם
הַסָּרִסִים וְהַכֹּהֲנִים וְכֹל עַם
הָאָרֶץ הָעֹבְרִים בֵּין בִּתְרֵי
20 הָעֵגֶל: וְנָתַתִּי אוֹתָם בְּיַד
אֹיְבֵיהֶם וּבְיַד מְבַקְשֵׁי נַפְשָׁם
וְהָיְתָה נִבְלָתָם לְמַאֲכָל לְעוֹף
הַשָּׁמַיִם וּלְבֶהֱמַת הָאָרֶץ:

v. 17.   חסר י׳ לזעוה ק׳   v. 18.

Divine name (Abarbanel, Metsudath David).

17. *I proclaim for you a liberty.* Spoken ironically: you will be freed from My service and protection and fall a prey to the sword (Rashi, Kimchi).

18. *when they cut the calf in twain.* This was the ancient manner of making a covenant (cf. Gen. xv. 9f.). Its significance was probably that of an implied

oath: may the person who breaks the covenant be cut in two even as the calf is divided (Isaiah da Trani).

19. *the people of the land.* The entire populace had participated in this gala event (Daath Soferim).

20. *their dead bodies, etc.* The severity of the punishment is an index to the heinousness of the offence. Not only will the guilty be slain, but their bodies

234

earth. 21. And Zedekiah king of Judah and his princes will I give into the hand of their enemies, and into the hand of them that seek their life, and into the hand of the king of Babylon's army, that are gone up from you. **22.** Behold, I will command, saith the LORD, and cause them to return to this city; and they shall fight against it, and take it, and burn it with fire; and I will make the cities of Judah a desolation, without inhabitant.

21 וְאֶת־צִדְקִיָּהוּ מֶלֶךְ־יְהוּדָה
וְאֶת־שָׂרָיו אֶתֵּן בְּיַד אֹיְבֵיהֶם
וּבְיַד מְבַקְשֵׁי נַפְשָׁם וּבְיַד חֵיל
מֶלֶךְ בָּבֶל הָעֹלִים מֵעֲלֵיכֶם:
22 הִנְנִי מְצַוֶּה נְאֻם־יְהֹוָה
וַהֲשִׁבֹתִים אֶל־הָעִיר הַזֹּאת
וְנִלְחֲמוּ עָלֶיהָ וּלְכָדוּהָ
וּשְׂרָפֻהָ בָאֵשׁ וְאֶת־עָרֵי
יְהוּדָה אֶתֵּן שְׁמָמָה מֵאֵין יֹשֵׁב:

---

35   CHAPTER XXXV   לה

1. The word which came unto Jeremiah from the LORD in the days of Jehoiakim the son of Josiah, king of Judah, saying: **2.** 'Go unto the house of the Rechabites, and speak

1 הַדָּבָר אֲשֶׁר־הָיָה אֶל־
יִרְמְיָהוּ מֵאֵת יְהֹוָה בִּימֵי
יְהוֹיָקִים בֶּן־יֹאשִׁיָּהוּ מֶלֶךְ
2 יְהוּדָה לֵאמֹר: הָלוֹךְ אֶל־
בֵּית הָרֵכָבִים וְדִבַּרְתָּ אוֹתָם

---

will not receive honourable burial. Such a warning was most likely to evoke repentance (Daath Soferim).

21. *that are gone up from you.* The siege was temporarily broken off by Nebuchadnezzar at the news that an Egyptian army was advancing against him (xxxvii. 5). During this lull the slaves were retaken (see Daath Mikra).

22. *cause them to return.* Just as you caused your slaves to return, so will I cause your enemies to return and besiege the city. This is payment in kind (Alshich).

CHAPTER XXXV

THE INCIDENT OF THE RECHABITES

1–11 THE FIDELITY OF THE RECHABITES

1. *in the days of Jehoiakim.* This chapter

and the following chronologically precede xxxii–xxxiv and take us back to the latter part of Jehoiakim's reign in 598 B.C.E., when the Chaldeans attacked Judea and forced many of the inhabitants to take refuge in Jerusalem. These refugees included the Rechabites, who were forbidden by their principles to live in cities (verses 1–11).

2. *the house.* i.e. the tribe, as in verses 3, 5, 18 (see Targum).

Rechabites. The descendants of Jonadab the son of Rechab (verse 6). They were a nomadic tribe of Kenite descent and so connected with Jethro, the father-in-law of Moses who was a Kenite (Judg. i. 16, and cf. 1 Chron. ii. 55).

chambers. These were anterooms in the

unto them, and bring them into the house of the Lord, into one of the chambers, and give them wine to drink.' 3. Then I took Jaazaniah the son of Jeremiah, the son of Habazziniah, and his brethren, and all his sons, and the whole house of the Rechabites; 4. and I brought them into the house of the Lord, into the chamber of the sons of Hanan the son of Igdaliah, the man of God, which was by the chamber of the princes, which was above the chamber of Maaseiah the son of Shallum, the keeper of the door; 5. and I set before the sons of the house of the Rechabites goblets full of wine, and cups, and I said unto them: 'Drink ye wine.' 6. But they said: 'We will drink no wine; for Ionadab the son of Rechab our

וַהֲבֵאוֹתָם בֵּית יְהֹוָה אֶל־
אַחַת הַלְּשָׁכוֹת וְהִשְׁקִיתָ אוֹתָם
3 יָיִן: וָאֶקַּח אֶת־יַאֲזַנְיָה בֶן־
יִרְמְיָהוּ בֶּן־חֲבַצִּנְיָה וְאֶת־
אֶחָיו וְאֶת־כָּל־בָּנָיו וְאֵת
4 כָּל־בֵּית הָרֵכָבִים: וָאָבִא
אֹתָם בֵּית יְהֹוָה אֶל־לִשְׁכַּת
בְּנֵי חָנָן בֶּן־יִגְדַּלְיָהוּ אִישׁ
הָאֱלֹהִים אֲשֶׁר־אֵצֶל לִשְׁכַּת
הַשָּׂרִים אֲשֶׁר מִמַּעַל לְלִשְׁכַּת
מַעֲשֵׂיָהוּ בֶן־שַׁלֻּם שֹׁמֵר הַסַּף׃
5 וָאֶתֵּן לִפְנֵי | בְּנֵי בֵית־
הָרֵכָבִים גְּבִעִים מְלֵאִים יַיִן
וְכֹסוֹת וָאֹמַר אֲלֵיהֶם שְׁתוּ־
6 יָיִן: וַיֹּאמְרוּ לֹא נִשְׁתֶּה־יָּיִן
כִּי יוֹנָדָב בֶּן־רֵכָב אָבִינוּ צִוָּה

פתח בס"פ v. 4.

Temple for storing *the hallowed things* (1 Chron. xxviii. 12), and for the use of priests and Levites.

3. *Jaazaniah.* Probably the head of the tribe (Daath Mikra). His father, Jeremiah, is, of course, not to be identified with the prophet.

4. *into the house of the* Lord. To give the widest publicity to what was about to take place (Abarbanel).

the sons of. It is uncertain whether this is to be understood literally, or 'the disciples of.' Nothing more is recorded of Hanan (Daath Mikra).

the man of God. The prophet (Targum).

Maaseiah. Cf. xxi. 1.

the keeper of the door. More lit. 'of the threshold.' There were three such officers (cf. lii. 24; 2 Kings xxv. 18) who had charge of the funds for the repair of the Temple (2 Kings xii. 10). In lii. 24 they are mentioned alongside *the chief priest* and *the second priest,* which indicates that they were high-placed dignitaries (see Metsudath Zion).

5. *goblets.* Large flagons from which the wine was poured into the *cups* (Metsudath Zion).

6. *our father.* Our ancestor. He collaborated with Jehu in the abolition of Baal-worship (2 Kings x. 15ff.) (Kimchi).

ye shall drink no wine. As nomads they were to live a simple life and shun the luxuries of the cities (Daath Soferim).

father commanded us, saying: Ye
shall drink no wine, neither ye, nor
your sons, for ever; 7. neither shall
ye build house, nor sow seed, nor
plant vineyard, nor have any; but
all your days ye shall dwell in tents,
that ye may live many days in the
land wherein ye sojourn. 8. And
we have hearkened to the voice of
Jonadab the son of Rechab our
father in all that he charged us, to
drink no wine all our days, we, our
wives, our sons, nor our daughters;
9. nor to build houses for us to dwell
in, neither to have vineyard, or field,
or seed; 10. but we have dwelt in
tents, and have hearkened, and done
according to all that Jonadab our
father commanded us. 11. But it
came to pass, when Nebuchadrezzar
king of Babylon came up against the
land, that we said: Come, and let us
go to Jerusalem for fear of the army
of the Chaldeans, and for fear of the
army of the Arameans; so we dwell
at Jerusalem.'

12. Then came the word of the
Lord unto Jeremiah, saying:

עָלֵ֫ינוּ לֵאמֹ֖ר לֹא תִשְׁתּוּ־יַ֑יִן
אַתֶּ֥ם וּבְנֵיכֶ֖ם עַד־עוֹלָֽם׃
7 וּבַ֣יִת לֹֽא־תִבְנ֗וּ וְזֶ֤רַע לֹֽא־
תִזְרָ֙עוּ֙ וְכֶ֣רֶם לֹֽא־תִטָּ֔עוּ וְלֹ֖א
יִֽהְיֶ֣ה לָכֶ֑ם כִּ֠י בָּאֳהָלִ֤ים תֵּֽשְׁבוּ֙
כָּל־יְמֵיכֶ֔ם לְמַ֨עַן תִּֽחְי֜וּ יָמִ֣ים
רַבִּ֗ים עַל־פְּנֵ֤י הָֽאֲדָמָה֙ אֲשֶׁ֣ר
8 אַתֶּ֖ם גָּרִ֣ים שָׁ֑ם וַנִּשְׁמַ֗ע בְּק֞וֹל
יְהוֹנָדָ֤ב בֶּן־רֵכָב֙ אָבִ֔ינוּ לְכֹ֖ל
אֲשֶׁ֣ר צִוָּ֑נוּ לְבִלְתִּ֤י שְׁתֽוֹת־יַ֙יִן֙
כָּל־יָמֵ֔ינוּ אֲנַ֖חְנוּ נָשֵׁ֥ינוּ בָּנֵ֖ינוּ
9 וּבְנֹתֵֽינוּ׃ וּלְבִלְתִּ֤י בְּנ֣וֹת בָּתִּים֙
לְשִׁבְתֵּ֔נוּ וְכֶ֧רֶם וְשָׂדֶ֛ה וָזֶ֖רַע
10 לֹ֥א יִֽהְיֶה־לָּֽנוּ׃ וַנֵּ֖שֶׁב
בָּֽאֳהָלִ֑ים וַנִּשְׁמַ֣ע וַנַּ֔עַשׂ כְּכֹ֛ל
11 אֲשֶׁר־צִוָּ֖נוּ יוֹנָדָ֣ב אָבִֽינוּ׃ וַיְהִ֗י
בַּעֲל֨וֹת נְבוּכַדְרֶאצַּ֥ר מֶֽלֶךְ־
בָּבֶל֮ אֶל־הָאָרֶץ֒ וַנֹּ֗אמֶר בֹּ֜אוּ
וְנָב֣וֹא יְרוּשָׁלַ֗ם מִפְּנֵי֙ חֵ֣יל
הַכַּשְׂדִּ֔ים וּמִפְּנֵ֖י חֵ֣יל אֲרָ֑ם
12 וַנֵּ֖שֶׁב בִּירֽוּשָׁלָֽם׃ וַיְהִ֤י דְבַר־
יְהֹוָ֔ה אֶֽל־יִרְמְיָ֖הוּ לֵאמֹֽר׃

v. 7. קמץ בפשטא   v. 7. קמץ בז״ק

11. *let us go to Jerusalem.* They were
forced by circumstances to transgress
the law of their tribe not to dwell in
cities, but they would not drink wine
(Rashi).

Arameans. Allies of the Chaldeans
(2 Kings xxiv. 2).

12–17 MORAL OF THE INCIDENT FOR THE
JUDEANS

13. 'Thus saith the LORD of hosts, the God of Israel: Go, and say to the men of Judah and the inhabitants of Jerusalem: Will ye not receive instruction to hearken to My words? saith the LORD. 14. The words of Jonadab the son of Rechab, that he commanded his sons, not to drink wine, are performed, and unto this day they drink none, for they hearken to their father's commandment; but I have spoken unto you, speaking betimes and often, and ye have not hearkened unto Me. 15. I have sent also unto you all My servants the prophets, sending them betimes and often, saying: Return ye now every man from his evil way, and amend your doings, and go not after other gods to serve them, and ye shall dwell in the land which I have given to you and to your fathers; but ye have not inclined your ear, nor hearkened unto Me. 16. Because the sons of Jonadab the son of Rechab have performed the

13 כֹּה־אָמַר יְהֹוָה צְבָאוֹת אֱלֹהֵי
יִשְׂרָאֵל הָלֹךְ וְאָמַרְתָּ לְאִישׁ
יְהוּדָה וּלְיוֹשְׁבֵי יְרוּשָׁלָ͏ִם הֲלוֹא
תִקְחוּ מוּסָר לִשְׁמֹעַ אֶל־
14 דְּבָרַי נְאֻם־יְהֹוָה: הוּקַם
אֶת־דִּבְרֵי יְהוֹנָדָב בֶּן־רֵכָב
אֲשֶׁר־צִוָּה אֶת־בָּנָיו לְבִלְתִּי
שְׁתוֹת־יַיִן וְלֹא שָׁתוּ עַד־הַיּוֹם
הַזֶּה כִּי שָׁמְעוּ אֵת מִצְוַת
אֲבִיהֶם וְאָנֹכִי דִּבַּרְתִּי אֲלֵיכֶם
הַשְׁכֵּם וְדַבֵּר וְלֹא שְׁמַעְתֶּם
15 אֵלָי: וָאֶשְׁלַח אֲלֵיכֶם אֶת־
כָּל־עֲבָדַי הַנְּבִיאִים | הַשְׁכֵּם
וְשָׁלֹחַ | לֵאמֹר שֻׁבוּ־נָא אִישׁ
מִדַּרְכּוֹ הָרָעָה וְהֵיטִיבוּ
מַעַלְלֵיכֶם וְאַל־־תֵּלְכוּ
אַחֲרֵי אֱלֹהִים אֲחֵרִים
לְעָבְדָם וּשְׁבוּ אֶל־הָאֲדָמָה
אֲשֶׁר־נָתַתִּי לָכֶם וְלַאֲבֹתֵיכֶם
וְלֹא הִטִּיתֶם אֶת־אָזְנְכֶם וְלֹא
16 שְׁמַעְתֶּם אֵלָי: כִּי הֵקִימוּ בְּנֵי
יְהוֹנָדָב בֶּן־רֵכָב אֶת־מִצְוַת

v. 15. נ״א עַל

13. *will ye not receive . . . My words?* i.e. will you not follow this example of loyal obedience? (Metsudath David).

14. *are performed.* The Hebrew verb rather signifies 'are established,' i.e. have taken a firm hold on the Rechabites (Metsudath David).

unto this day. Although about three hundred years have passed since Jonadab instituted the law (Kimchi).

but I have spoken. The pronoun is emphasized in the Hebrew to mark a

commandment of their father which
he commanded them, but this people
hath not hearkened unto Me;
17. therefore thus saith the LORD,
the God of hosts, the God of Israel:
Behold, I will bring upon Judah and
upon all the inhabitants of Jerusalem
all the evil that I have pronounced
against them; because I have spoken
unto them, but they have not heard,
and I have called unto them, but
they have not answered.'

18. And unto the house of the
Rechabites Jeremiah said: 'Thus
saith the LORD of hosts, the God of
Israel: Because ye have hearkened
to the commandment of Jonadab
your father, and kept all his precepts,
and done according unto all that he
commanded you; 19. therefore thus
saith the LORD of hosts, the God of
Israel: There shall not be cut off
unto Jonadab the son of Rechab a
man to stand before Me for ever.'

אֲבִיהֶם אֲשֶׁר צִוָּם וְהָעָם הַזֶּה
17 לֹא שָׁמְעוּ אֵלָי: לָכֵן כֹּה־
אָמַר יְהוָֹה אֱלֹהֵי צְבָאוֹת
אֱלֹהֵי יִשְׂרָאֵל הִנְנִי מֵבִיא אֶל־
יְהוּדָה וְאֶל כָּל־יוֹשְׁבֵי
יְרוּשָׁלַם אֵת כָּל־הָרָעָה אֲשֶׁר
דִּבַּרְתִּי עֲלֵיהֶם יַעַן דִּבַּרְתִּי
אֲלֵיהֶם וְלֹא שָׁמֵעוּ וָאֶקְרָא
18 לָהֶם וְלֹא עָנוּ: וּלְבֵית
הָרֵכָבִים אָמַר יִרְמְיָהוּ כֹּה־
אָמַר יְהוָֹה צְבָאוֹת אֱלֹהֵי
יִשְׂרָאֵל יַעַן אֲשֶׁר שְׁמַעְתֶּם
עַל־מִצְוַת יְהוֹנָדָב אֲבִיכֶם
וַתִּשְׁמְרוּ אֶת־כָּל־מִצְוֹתָיו
וַתַּעֲשׂוּ כְּכֹל אֲשֶׁר־צִוָּה
19 אֶתְכֶם: לָכֵן כֹּה אָמַר יְהוָֹה
צְבָאוֹת אֱלֹהֵי יִשְׂרָאֵל לֹא־
יִכָּרֵת אִישׁ לְיוֹנָדָב בֶּן־רֵכָב
עֹמֵד לְפָנַי כָּל־הַיָּמִים:

contrast with Jonadab who was obeyed,
whereas God's commands are ignored
(Daath Mikra).

17. Cf. xix 15.

18–19   THE REWARD OF THE RECHABITES

18. As the disobedience of the Judeans
will involve them in ruin, so the faith-

fulness of the Rechabites will receive
recognition by God.

19. *to stand before Me for ever.*   See on
xv. 19. The phrase elsewhere usually
connotes service in the Temple. It is
uncertain whether such is the intention
here. For the Rabbinical interpretation
and alleged traces of them in subse-

1. And it came to pass in the fourth year of Jehoiakim the son of Josiah, king of Judah, that this word came unto Jeremiah from the LORD, saying: 2. 'Take thee a roll of a book, and write therein all the words that I have spoken unto thee against Israel, and against Judah, and against all the nations, from the day I spoke unto thee, from the days of Josiah, even unto this day. 3. It may be that the house of Judah will hear all the evil which I purpose to do unto them; that they may return every man from his evil way, and I

1 וַיְהִי בַּשָּׁנָה הָרְבִיעִת
לִיהוֹיָקִים בֶּן־יֹאשִׁיָּהוּ מֶלֶךְ
יְהוּדָה הָיָה הַדָּבָר הַזֶּה אֶל־
יִרְמְיָהוּ מֵאֵת יְהֹוָה לֵאמֹר:
2 קַח־לְךָ מְגִלַּת־סֵפֶר וְכָתַבְתָּ
אֵלֶיהָ אֵת כָּל־הַדְּבָרִים אֲשֶׁר
דִּבַּרְתִּי אֵלֶיךָ עַל־יִשְׂרָאֵל
וְעַל־יְהוּדָה וְעַל־כָּל־הַגּוֹיִם
מִיּוֹם דִּבַּרְתִּי אֵלֶיךָ מִימֵי
3 יֹאשִׁיָּהוּ וְעַד הַיּוֹם הַזֶּה: אוּלַי
יִשְׁמְעוּ בֵּית יְהוּדָה אֵת כָּל־
הָרָעָה אֲשֶׁר אָנֹכִי חֹשֵׁב
לַעֲשׂוֹת לָהֶם לְמַעַן יָשׁוּבוּ
אִישׁ מִדַּרְכּוֹ הָרָעָה וְסָלַחְתִּי

---

quent times, the reader may consult the article on 'Rechabites' in the Jewish Encyclopædia.

CHAPTER XXXVI

JEREMIAH DICTATES HIS PROPHECIES TO BARUCH

ABARBANEL explains that Jeremiah himself wrote all his prophecies, that the spirit of prophecy assisted him in their recording. The Scroll of Lamentations, however, was written only through divine inspiration, not through prophecy. It was this scroll that Jeremiah dictated to Baruch.

1–8 JEREMIAH COMMANDED TO COMMIT HIS UTTERANCES TO WRITING

1. *in the fourth year of Jehoiakim.* See on XXV. 1.

2. *a roll of a book.* Ancient books were in the form of scrolls, parchment skins being sewn together and attached to wooden rollers. The text was written in columns parallel to the rollers so that the *roll* was unwound as the reading proceeded.

against Israel, and against Judah. [Jeremiah's prophecies about Israel consisted only of promises (cf., e.g., iii. 12ff., xxxi. 1ff.) seeing that the Northern Kingdom no longer existed, and threats of further calamity would have been pointless. It is to be noted that the Hebrew preposition *al* may be rendered 'concerning' as well as 'against' and is perhaps to be so understood here.]

and against all the nations. Cf. xxv. 15–29, xlvi-li.

3. *it may be,* etc. God does not desire

may forgive their iniquity and their sin.'

4. Then Jeremiah called Baruch the son of Neriah; and Baruch wrote from the mouth of Jeremiah all the words of the LORD, which He had spoken unto him, upon a roll of a book. 5. And Jeremiah commanded Baruch, saying: 'I am detained, I cannot go into the house of the LORD; 6. therefore go thou, and read in the roll, which thou hast written from my mouth, the words of the LORD in the ears of the people in the LORD's house upon a fast-day; and also thou shalt read them in the ears of all Judah that come out of their cities. 7. It may be they will present their supplication before the LORD, and will return every one from his evil way; for great is the anger and the fury that the LORD hath pronounced against this people.' 8. And Baruch the son of Neriah did according to all that

וַיִּקְרָא לַעֲוֺנָם וּלְחַטָּאתָם:
4 יִרְמְיָהוּ אֶת־בָּרוּךְ בֶּן־נֵרִיָּה וַיִּכְתֹּב בָּרוּךְ מִפִּי יִרְמְיָהוּ אֵת כָּל־דִּבְרֵי יְהֹוָה אֲשֶׁר־דִּבֶּר אֵלָיו עַל־מְגִלַּת־סֵפֶר:
5 וַיְצַוֶּה יִרְמְיָהוּ אֶת־בָּרוּךְ לֵאמֹר אֲנִי עָצוּר לֹא אוּכַל
6 לָבוֹא בֵּית יְהֹוָה: וּבָאתָ אַתָּה וְקָרָאתָ בַמְּגִלָּה אֲשֶׁר־כָּתַבְתָּ מִפִּי אֶת־דִּבְרֵי יְהֹוָה בְּאָזְנֵי הָעָם בֵּית יְהֹוָה בְּיוֹם צוֹם וְגַם בְּאָזְנֵי כָל־יְהוּדָה הַבָּאִים
7 מֵעָרֵיהֶם תִּקְרָאֵם: אוּלַי תִּפֹּל תְּחִנָּתָם לִפְנֵי יְהֹוָה וְיָשֻׁבוּ אִישׁ מִדַּרְכּוֹ הָרָעָה כִּי־גָדוֹל הָאַף וְהַחֵמָה אֲשֶׁר־דִּבֶּר
8 יְהֹוָה אֶל־הָעָם הַזֶּה: וַיַּעַשׂ

the destruction of the wicked, but their repentance (cf. xviii. 8, xxvi. 3) (Abarbanel).

4. Baruch the son of Neriah. He is first mentioned in xxxii. 12f. as Jeremiah's attendant.

5. I am detained. The Hebrew verb atsur occurs in xxxiii. 1 and xxxix. 15 in the sense of 'imprisoned' and is interpreted in like manner in our verse by Targum, Rashi, and Metsudoth. Although verse 19 indicates that Jeremiah was able to escape, that was only because the princes allowed him to do so, not because he was free to come and go at will. Although it is not mentioned in other places that Jehoiakim impri-

soned Jeremiah, our verse implies it, so Metsudath David.

6. upon a fast-day. Possibly several fast-days were appointed for intercession on account of the grave position (cf. verse 9) and one of them to be selected for the reading because a large crowd would be present (Abarbanel).

7. present their supplication. lit. 'their supplication will fall.' When they learn of the fate that threatens them they may be in a repentant mood. Jeremiah had already warned them many times, yet he does not abandon hope of a last-minute change of heart (Malbim).

8. did. As described in detail in verses 9ff.

Jeremiah the prophet commanded him, reading in the book the words of the LORD in the LORD's house.

9. Now it came to pass in the fifth year of Jehoiakim the son of Josiah, king of Judah, in the ninth month, that they proclaimed a fast before the LORD, all the people in Jerusalem, and all the people that came from the cities of Judah unto Jerusalem. 10. Then did Baruch read in the book the words of Jeremiah in the house of the LORD, in the chamber of Gemariah the son of Shaphan the scribe, in the upper court, at the entry of the new gate of the LORD's house, in the ears of all the people. 11. And when Micaiah the son of Gemariah, the son of Shaphan, had heard out of the book all the words of the LORD,

בָּרוּךְ בֶּן־נֵרִיָּה כְּכָל אֲשֶׁר־
צִוָּהוּ יִרְמְיָהוּ הַנָּבִיא לִקְרֹא
בַסֵּפֶר דִּבְרֵי יְהֹוָה בֵּית יְהֹוָה׃
9 וַיְהִי בַשָּׁנָה הַחֲמִשִׁית
לִיהוֹיָקִים בֶּן־יֹאשִׁיָּהוּ מֶלֶךְ־
יְהוּדָה בַּחֹדֶשׁ הַתְּשִׁעִי קָרְאוּ
צוֹם לִפְנֵי יְהֹוָה כָּל־הָעָם
בִּירוּשָׁלַם וְכָל־הָעָם הַבָּאִים
מֵעָרֵי יְהוּדָה בִּירוּשָׁלָם׃
10 וַיִּקְרָא בָרוּךְ בַּסֵּפֶר אֶת־
דִּבְרֵי יִרְמְיָהוּ בֵּית יְהֹוָה
בְּלִשְׁכַּת גְּמַרְיָהוּ בֶן־שָׁפָן
הַסֹּפֵר בֶּחָצֵר הָעֶלְיוֹן פֶּתַח
שַׁעַר בֵּית־יְהֹוָה הֶחָדָשׁ בְּאָזְנֵי
כָּל־הָעָם׃ 11 וַיִּשְׁמַע מִכָיְהוּ
בֶן־גְּמַרְיָהוּ בֶן־שָׁפָן אֶת־
כָּל־דִּבְרֵי יְהֹוָה מֵעַל־

9–26 THE ROLL IS READ IN THE TEMPLE
AND TO THE KING AND BURNED

9. *in the fifth year.* About a year elapsed before the scroll was written and read in public. Baruch waited for the proper occasion, when a fast-day would be proclaimed and people would gather from all the cities of Judah to Jerusalem (Malbim).

in the ninth month. Later called Kislew; it corresponds roughly to December. No statutory Jewish fast is held in this month; so the occasion was special. From outside sources we learn that Nebuchadnezzar conquered and destroyed Ashkelon at that time, throw-

ing fright into Jehoiakim and his people (Daath Mikra).

10. *in the chamber.* [i.e. stood by the entrance of this chamber] (Daath Mikra).

Gemariah the son of Shaphan the scribe. *The scribe* may refer to either the father or the son. Shaphan was a scribe in the days of Josiah (2 Kings xxii. 3, 8). If the father is the Shaphan mentioned in xxvi. 24, then Gemariah was a brother of Ahikam who was friendly disposed towards Jeremiah. He may be the man of that name in xxix. 3 (Daath Mikra).

11. *Micaiah.* Gemariah was attending a council of *the princes* at the time of the

12. he went down into the king's house, into the scribe's chamber; and, lo, all the princes sat there, even Elishama the scribe, and Delaiah the son of Shemaiah, and Elnathan the son of Achbor, and Gemariah the son of Shaphan, and Zedekiah the son of Hananiah, and all the princes. 13. Then Micaiah declared unto them all the words that he had heard, when Baruch read the book in the ears of the people. 14. Therefore all the princes sent Jehudi the son of Nethaniah, the son of Shelemiah, the son of Cushi, unto Baruch, saying: 'Take in thy hand the roll wherein thou hast read in the ears of the people, and come.' So Baruch the son of Neriah took the roll in his hand, and came unto them. 15. And they said unto him: 'Sit down now, and read it in our ears.' So Baruch read it in their ears. 16. Now it came to pass, when

הַסֵּפֶר: וַיֵּרֶד בֵּית־הַמֶּלֶךְ 12
עַל־לִשְׁכַּת הַסֹּפֵר וְהִנֵּה־שָׁם
כָּל־הַשָּׂרִים יוֹשְׁבִים אֱלִישָׁמָע
הַסֹּפֵר וּדְלָיָהוּ בֶן־שְׁמַעְיָהוּ
וְאֶלְנָתָן בֶּן־עַכְבּוֹר וּגְמַרְיָהוּ
בֶן־שָׁפָן וְצִדְקִיָּהוּ בֶן־חֲנַנְיָהוּ
וְכָל־הַשָּׂרִים: וַיַּגֵּד לָהֶם 13
מִיכָיְהוּ אֵת כָּל־הַדְּבָרִים
אֲשֶׁר שָׁמֵעַ בִּקְרֹא בָרוּךְ
בַּסֵּפֶר בְּאָזְנֵי הָעָם: וַיִּשְׁלְחוּ 14
כָל־הַשָּׂרִים אֶל־בָּרוּךְ אֶת־
יְהוּדִי בֶּן־נְתַנְיָהוּ בֶּן־שֶׁלֶמְיָהוּ
בֶן־כּוּשִׁי לֵאמֹר הַמְּגִלָּה אֲשֶׁר
קָרָאתָ בָּהּ בְּאָזְנֵי הָעָם קָחֶנָּה
בְיָדְךָ וָלֵךְ וַיִּקַּח בָּרוּךְ בֶּן־
נֵרִיָּהוּ אֶת־הַמְּגִלָּה בְיָדוֹ וַיָּבֹא
אֲלֵיהֶם: וַיֹּאמְרוּ אֵלָיו שֵׁב 15
נָא וּקְרָאֶנָּה בְּאָזְנֵינוּ וַיִּקְרָא
בָרוּךְ בְּאָזְנֵיהֶם: וַיְהִי כְּשָׁמְעָם 16

reading and may have instructed his son to report the contents to him.

12. *he went down.* See on xxii. 1.

even Elishama the scribe. Scribes evidently held high rank. If identical with the Elishama of xli. 1 and 2 Kings xxv. 25, he was of royal blood.

Elnathan the son of Achbor. He was mentioned in xxvi. 22.

all the princes. [i.e. the rest of the princes who are unnamed.]

14. *Jehudi . . . Cushi.* The names signify 'Jew' and 'Ethiopian' respectively, and it has been conjectured that Ethiopian descent is implied. This supposition is unnecessary since the prophet Zephaniah had a father named Cushi (Zeph. i. 1) who was of pure Hebrew lineage.

15. *sit down.* The invitation to Baruch to sit in the presence of the princes is an indication of friendly disposition on their part towards him. Some ancient Versions read the verb as *shub* instead of

they had heard all the words, they turned in fear one toward another, and said unto Baruch: 'We will surely tell the king of all these words.' 17. And they asked Baruch, saying: 'Tell us now: How didst thou write all these words at his mouth?' 18. Then Baruch answered them: 'He pronounced all these words unto me with his mouth, and I wrote them with ink in the book.' 19. Then said the princes unto Baruch: 'Go, hide thee, thou and Jeremiah; and let no man know where ye are.' 20. And they went in to the king into the court; but they had deposited the roll in the chamber of Elishama the scribe; and they told all the words in the ears of the king. 21. So the king sent Jehudi to fetch the roll; and he

אֶת־כָּל־הַדְּבָרִים פָּחֲדוּ
אִישׁ אֶל־רֵעֵהוּ וַיֹּאמְרוּ אֶל־
בָּרוּךְ הַגֵּיד נַגֵּיד לַמֶּלֶךְ אֵת
17 כָּל־הַדְּבָרִים הָאֵלֶּה: וְאֶת־
בָּרוּךְ שָׁאֲלוּ לֵאמֹר הַגֶּד־נָא
לָנוּ אֵיךְ כָּתַבְתָּ אֶת־כָּל־
18 הַדְּבָרִים הָאֵלֶּה מִפִּיו: וַיֹּאמֶר
לָהֶם בָּרוּךְ מִפִּיו יִקְרָא אֵלַי
אֵת כָּל־הַדְּבָרִים הָאֵלֶּה וַאֲנִי
כֹּתֵב עַל־הַסֵּפֶר בַּדְּיוֹ:
19 וַיֹּאמְרוּ הַשָּׂרִים אֶל־בָּרוּךְ
לֵךְ הִסָּתֵר אַתָּה וְיִרְמְיָהוּ וְאִישׁ
20 אַל־יֵדַע אֵיפֹה אַתֶּם: וַיָּבֹאוּ
אֶל־הַמֶּלֶךְ חָצֵרָה וְאֶת־
הַמְּגִלָּה הִפְקִדוּ בְּלִשְׁכַּת
אֱלִישָׁמָע הַסֹּפֵר וַיַּגִּידוּ בְּאָזְנֵי
הַמֶּלֶךְ אֵת כָּל־הַדְּבָרִים:
21 וַיִּשְׁלַח הַמֶּלֶךְ אֶת־יְהוּדִי
לָקַחַת אֶת־הַמְּגִלָּה וַיִּקָּחֶהָ

sheb, i.e. 'return and read, read again'; Targum, too, appears to have had that reading.

16. *we will surely tell the king.* Better, 'we must certainly tell,' etc.; the contents of the document are considered to be of such importance that they feel obliged to let the king know (see Malbim).

17f. Before the matter is reported to the king, the princes make sure that Baruch wrote down the actual words of Jeremiah.

19. *thou and Jeremiah.* Such direful warnings spoken in public during a crisis endangered the life of both the man who wrote them and the man who delivered them; cf. what happened to Uriah (xxvi. 23).

let no man know where ye are. Kimchi explains that they were advised to hide in the court of the guard. Apparently he pictures it as a large place, where it is impossible to hide and avoid detection.

20. *the court.* i.e. the inner court where the king's residence was located (Metsudath David).

took it out of the chamber of
Elishama the scribe. And Jehudi
read it in the ears of the king, and
in the ears of all the princes that
stood beside the king. 22. Now the
king was sitting in the winter-house
in the ninth month; and the brazier
was burning before him. 23. And
it came to pass, when Jehudi had
read three or four columns, that he
cut it with the penknife, and cast it
into the fire that was in the brazier,
until all the roll was consumed in the
fire that was in the brazier. 24. Yet
they were not afraid, nor rent their
garments, neither the king, nor any
of his servants that heard all these
words. 25. Moreover Elnathan and

מִלִּשְׁכַּת אֱלִישָׁמָע הַסֹּפֵר
וַיִּקְרָאֶהָ יְהוּדִי בְּאָזְנֵי הַמֶּלֶךְ
וּבְאָזְנֵי כָּל־הַשָּׂרִים הָעֹמְדִים
22 מֵעַל הַמֶּלֶךְ: וְהַמֶּלֶךְ יוֹשֵׁב
בֵּית הַחֹרֶף בַּחֹדֶשׁ הַתְּשִׁיעִי
וְאֶת־הָאָח לְפָנָיו מְבֹעָרֶת:
23 וַיְהִי ׀ כִּקְרוֹא יְהוּדִי שָׁלֹשׁ
דְּלָתוֹת וְאַרְבָּעָה יִקְרָעֶהָ
בְּתַעַר הַסֹּפֵר וְהַשְׁלֵךְ אֶל־
הָאֵשׁ אֲשֶׁר אֶל־הָאָח עַד־תֹּם
כָּל־הַמְּגִלָּה עַל־הָאֵשׁ אֲשֶׁר
24 עַל־הָאָח: וְלֹא פָחֲדוּ וְלֹא
קָרְעוּ אֶת־בִּגְדֵיהֶם הַמֶּלֶךְ
וְכָל־עֲבָדָיו הַשֹּׁמְעִים אֵת
25 כָּל־הַדְּבָרִים הָאֵלֶּה: וְגַם

---

21. *beside the king.* lit. 'above the
king'; he was sitting and they were
standing (Ibn Nachmiash).

22. *the winter-house.* The king's palace
consisted of several buildings, as we
read in the text that a court separated
the chamber of Elishama the scribe
from the house where the king dwelt. In
addition to the winter-house, Jehoiakim also had a summer-house. See
above xxiv. 12. The summer-house had
large windows through which the wind
would blow and cool the house. Most
likely, the windows of the summer-
house faced the north so that the sun
would not warm it, and the winter-
house had small windows facing the
south. Such was the custom of the kings
and the wealthy, as in Amos (iii. 15)
(Daath Mikra).

in the ninth month. At a time of the year

when the king required the warmth
provided in the winter-house (Abarbanel).

and the brazier was burning. The LXX
reads *we-esh*, 'and the fire of the
brazier,' for *we-eth* which is the sign of
the accusative. Although the grammati-
cal construction of M.T. is difficult it is
attested by the Targum.

23. *when Jehudi,* etc. The Hebrew
means that as often as Jehudi read three
or four columns, he cut off that section
of the scroll, which was perhaps too
large to be consigned to the flames as a
whole (Daath Mikra).

penknife. lit. 'scribe's knife.'

24. *nor rent their garments.* In token of
grief and penitence (Kimchi). Contrast
the behaviour of king Josiah when he
heard the reading of the newly discovered *book of the Law* (2 Kings xxii. 11).

Delaiah and Gemariah had entreated the king not to burn the roll; but he would not hear them. 26. And the king commanded Jerahmeel the king's son, and Seraiah the son of Azriel, and Shelemiah the son of Abdeel, to take Baruch the scribe and Jeremiah the prophet; but the LORD hid them.

27. Then the word of the LORD came to Jeremiah, after that the king had burned the roll, and the words which Baruch wrote at the mouth of Jeremiah, saying: 28. 'Take thee again another roll, and write in it all the former words that were in the first roll, which Jehoiakim the king of Judah hath burned. 29. And concerning Jehoiakim king of Judah thou shalt say: Thus saith the LORD: Thou hast burned this roll, saying: Why hast thou written

אֶלְנָתָן וּדְלָיָהוּ וּגְמַרְיָהוּ
הִפְגִּעוּ בַמֶּלֶךְ לְבִלְתִּי שְׂרֹף
אֶת־הַמְּגִלָּה וְלֹא שָׁמַע
26 אֲלֵיהֶם: וַיְצַוֶּה הַמֶּלֶךְ אֶת־
יְרַחְמְאֵל בֶּן־הַמֶּלֶךְ וְאֶת־
שְׂרָיָהוּ בֶן־עַזְרִיאֵל וְאֶת־
שֶׁלֶמְיָהוּ בֶּן־עַבְדְּאֵל לָקַחַת
אֶת־בָּרוּךְ הַסֹּפֵר וְאֵת
יִרְמְיָהוּ הַנָּבִיא וַיַּסְתִּרֵם יְהוָה:
27 וַיְהִי דְבַר־יְהוָה אֶל־יִרְמְיָהוּ
אַחֲרֵי | שְׂרֹף הַמֶּלֶךְ אֶת־
הַמְּגִלָּה וְאֶת־הַדְּבָרִים אֲשֶׁר
כָּתַב בָּרוּךְ מִפִּי יִרְמְיָהוּ
28 לֵאמֹר: שׁוּב קַח־לְךָ מְגִלָּה
אַחֶרֶת וּכְתֹב עָלֶיהָ אֵת כָּל־
הַדְּבָרִים הָרִאשֹׁנִים אֲשֶׁר הָיוּ
עַל־הַמְּגִלָּה הָרִאשֹׁנָה אֲשֶׁר
שָׂרַף יְהוֹיָקִים מֶלֶךְ־יְהוּדָה:
29 וְעַל־יְהוֹיָקִים מֶלֶךְ־יְהוּדָה
תֹאמַר כֹּה אָמַר יְהוָה אַתָּה
שָׂרַפְתָּ אֶת־הַמְּגִלָּה הַזֹּאת
לֵאמֹר מַדּוּעַ כָּתַבְתָּ עָלֶיהָ

---

25. *not to burn the roll.* The roll, written through divine inspiration, was regarded as Holy Writ. Burning it was akin to burning a *sepher Torah* (see Kimchi verse 24).

26. *Jerahmeel the king's son.* [This may only mean a member of the royal household (cf. xxxviii. 6; 1 Kings xxii.

26; Zeph. i. 8). Less probable is the explanation that *Hammelech* is a name.]

27-32 JEREMIAH COMMANDED TO HAVE
THE SCROLL REWRITTEN

29. *saying: Why hast thou written,* etc. Jehoiakim had not actually spoken the words to Jeremiah, who was in hiding.

therein, saying: The king of Babylon shall certainly come and destroy this land, and shall cause to cease from thence man and beast? 30. Therefore thus saith the LORD concerning Jehoiakim king of Judah: He shall have none to sit upon the throne of David; and his dead body shall be cast out in the day to the heat, and in the night to the frost. 31. And I will visit upon him and his seed and his servants their iniquity; and I will bring upon them, and upon the inhabitants of Jerusalem, and upon the men of Judah, all the evil that I have pronounced against them, but they hearkened not.'

32. Then took Jeremiah another roll, and gave it to Baruch the scribe, the son of Neriah; who wrote therein from the mouth of Jeremiah all the words of the book which Jehoiakim king of Judah had burned in the fire; and there were added besides unto them many like words.

לֵאמֹר בֹּא יָבוֹא מֶלֶךְ בָּבֶל וְהִשְׁחִית אֶת־הָאָרֶץ הַזֹּאת וְהִשְׁבִּית מִמֶּנָּה אָדָם וּבְהֵמָה:

30 לָכֵן כֹּה־אָמַר יְהֹוָה עַל־ יְהוֹיָקִים מֶלֶךְ יְהוּדָה לֹא־ יִהְיֶה־לּוֹ יוֹשֵׁב עַל־כִּסֵּא דָוִד וְנִבְלָתוֹ תִּהְיֶה מֻשְׁלֶכֶת לַחֹרֶב בַּיּוֹם וְלַקֶּרַח בַּלָּיְלָה:

31 וּפָקַדְתִּי עָלָיו וְעַל־זַרְעוֹ וְעַל־עֲבָדָיו אֶת־עֲוֹנָם וְהֵבֵאתִי עֲלֵיהֶם וְעַל־יֹשְׁבֵי יְרוּשָׁלִַם וְאֶל־אִישׁ יְהוּדָה אֵת כָּל־הָרָעָה אֲשֶׁר־דִּבַּרְתִּי אֲלֵיהֶם וְלֹא שָׁמֵעוּ:

32 וְיִרְמְיָהוּ לָקַח ׀ מְגִלָּה אַחֶרֶת וַיִּתְּנָהּ אֶל־בָּרוּךְ בֶּן־נֵרִיָּהוּ הַסֹּפֵר וַיִּכְתֹּב עָלֶיהָ מִפִּי יִרְמְיָהוּ אֵת כָּל־דִּבְרֵי הַסֵּפֶר אֲשֶׁר שָׂרַף יְהוֹיָקִים מֶלֶךְ־יְהוּדָה בָּאֵשׁ וְעוֹד נוֹסַף עֲלֵיהֶם דְּבָרִים רַבִּים כָּהֵמָּה:

They express the thought in the king's mind (Daath Soferim).

30. *he shall have none to sit upon the throne of David.* His son Jehoiachin did in fact reign, but only for three months, a negligible period (Kimchi).

his dead body shall be cast out. See on xxii. 19.

32. *and there were added,* etc. The Rabbis, who understand the episode as referring to the Book of Lamentations, explain that the roll originally contained the first, second, and fourth chapters, each of which consists of one acrostic. To the second roll was added the third chapter, which itself consists of three acrostics (Rashi from Lamentations Rabbah, Proem 28).

37   CHAPTER XXXVII   לז

1. And Zedekiah the son of Josiah reigned as king, instead of Coniah the son of Jehoiakim, whom Nebuchadrezzar king of Babylon made king in the land of Judah. 2. But neither he, nor his servants, nor the people of the land, did hearken unto the words of the LORD, which He spoke by the prophet Jeremiah.

3. And Zedekiah the king sent Jehucal the son of Shelemiah, and Zephaniah the son of Maaseiah the priest, to the prophet Jeremiah, saying: 'Pray now unto the LORD our God for us.' 4. Now Jeremiah

וַיִּמְלׇךְ־מֶלֶךְ צִדְקִיָּהוּ בֶּן־ ‎1
יֹאשִׁיָּהוּ תַּחַת כׇּנְיָהוּ בֶּן־
יְהוֹיָקִים אֲשֶׁר הִמְלִיךְ
נְבוּכַדְרֶאצַּר מֶלֶךְ־בָּבֶל
בְּאֶרֶץ יְהוּדָה: וְלֹא שָׁמַע ‎2
הוּא וַעֲבָדָיו וְעַם הָאָרֶץ אֶל־
דִּבְרֵי יְהֹוָה אֲשֶׁר דִּבֶּר בְּיַד
יִרְמְיָהוּ הַנָּבִיא: וַיִּשְׁלַח ‎3
הַמֶּלֶךְ צִדְקִיָּהוּ אֶת־יְהוּכַל
בֶּן־שֶׁלֶמְיָה וְאֶת־צְפַנְיָהוּ
בֶן־מַעֲשֵׂיָה הַכֹּהֵן אֶל־
יִרְמְיָהוּ הַנָּבִיא לֵאמֹר
הִתְפַּלֶּל־נָא בַעֲדֵנוּ אֶל־
יְהֹוָה אֱלֹהֵינוּ: וְיִרְמְיָהוּ בָּא ‎4

CHAPTER XXXVII

1–10 ZEDEKIAH WARNED THAT THE BABYLONIANS WILL DESTROY JERUSALEM

1. *Zedekiah.* The last two chapters related to the reign of Jehoiakim. The present one treats of two incidents during Zedekiah's reign.

reigned as king. This is an unusual phrase instead of the normal 'reigned.' Because Jehoiachin (Coniah) reigned only three months, he was hardly to be regarded as a *king;* hence by contrast the text explicitly states that Zedekiah reigned *as king* (Kimchi).

whom Nebuchadrezzar, etc. Referring to Zedekiah (cf. 2 Kings xxiv. 17).

2. *the people of the land.* Whereas

Jehoiakim was a wicked king and his generation was righteous, as in the previous chapter, Zedekiah was a righteous king and his generation was wicked. He was, however, influenced by his subjects (Malbim).

3. *Zedekiah the king sent.* For a previous mission of this kind, cf. xxi. 1. The present deputation was sent when the siege had been raised on account of the Egyptian army's approach.

Jehucal. He was not friendly disposed to Jeremiah; in xxxviii. 4 he was one of those who demanded his death.

Zephaniah the son of Maaseiah the priest. He was a member of the earlier mission to Jeremiah (xxi. 1).

came in and went out among the
people; for they had not put him
into prison. 5. And Pharaoh's army
was come forth out of Egypt; and
when the Chaldeans that besiegea
Jerusalem heard tidings of them,
they broke up from Jerusalem.
6. Then came the word of the LORD
unto the prophet Jeremiah, saying:
7. 'Thus saith the LORD, the God of
Israel: Thus shall ye say to the king
of Judah, that sent you unto Me to
inquire of Me: Behold, Pharaoh's
army, which is come forth to help
you, shall return to Egypt into their
own land. 8. And the Chaldeans
shall return, and fight against this
city; and they shall take it, and
burn it with fire. 9. Thus saith the
LORD: Deceive not yourselves, saying: The Chaldeans shall surely
depart from us; for they shall not
depart. 10. For though ye had
smitten the whole army of the
Chaldeans that fight against you,
and there remained but wounded
men among them, yet would they

וַיֵּצֵא בְּתוֹךְ הָעָם וְלֹא־נָתְנוּ
5 אֹתוֹ בֵּית הַכְּלִיא׃ וְחֵיל
פַּרְעֹה יָצָא מִמִּצְרַיִם וַיִּשְׁמְעוּ
הַכַּשְׂדִּים הַצָּרִים עַל־
יְרוּשָׁלִַם אֶת־שִׁמְעָם וַיֵּעָלוּ
6 מֵעַל יְרוּשָׁלִָם׃ וַיְהִי דְּבַר־
יְהוָה אֶל־יִרְמְיָהוּ הַנָּבִיא
7 לֵאמֹר׃ כֹּה־אָמַר יְהוָה
אֱלֹהֵי יִשְׂרָאֵל כֹּה תֹאמְרוּ
אֶל־מֶלֶךְ יְהוּדָה הַשֹּׁלֵחַ
אֶתְכֶם אֵלַי לְדָרְשֵׁנִי הִנֵּה ׀
חֵיל פַּרְעֹה הַיֹּצֵא לָכֶם
לְעֶזְרָה שָׁב לְאַרְצוֹ מִצְרָיִם׃
8 וְשָׁבוּ הַכַּשְׂדִּים וְנִלְחֲמוּ עַל־
הָעִיר הַזֹּאת וּלְכָדֻהָ וּשְׂרָפֻהָ
9 בָאֵשׁ׃ כֹּה אָמַר יְהוָה אַל־
תַּשִּׁאוּ נַפְשֹׁתֵיכֶם לֵאמֹר הָלֹךְ
יֵלְכוּ מֵעָלֵינוּ הַכַּשְׂדִּים כִּי לֹא
10 יֵלֵכוּ׃ כִּי אִם־הִכִּיתֶם כָּל־
חֵיל כַּשְׂדִּים הַנִּלְחָמִים אִתְּכֶם
וְנִשְׁאֲרוּ־בָם אֲנָשִׁים
מְדֻקָּרִים אִישׁ בְּאָהֳלוֹ יָקוּמוּ

v. 4. הכלוא ק'

4. *came in and went out.* [This is mentioned to account for his arrest which
soon followed.]

5. *Pharaoh's army.* He was Pharaoh
Hophra (cf. xliv. 30) who reigned
590–571 B.C.E. and was an ally of the
Judean king.

7. *shall return to Egypt.* Without having

given any effective help to Judea. The
cause of the Egyptian army's retreat is
not stated; perhaps it was defeated (cf.
Ezek. xxx. 21), or turned back in fear of
the contest without giving battle
(Malbim).

10. *wounded men.* The Hebrew is literally 'thrust through' and can be under-

rise up every man in his tent, and burn this city with fire.'

11. And it came to pass, that when the army of the Chaldeans was broken up from Jerusalem for fear of Pharaoh's army, 12. then Jeremiah went forth out of Jerusalem to go into the land of Benjamin, to receive his portion there, in the midst of the people. 13. And when he was in the gate of Benjamin, a captain of the ward was there, whose name was Irijah, the son of Shelemiah, the son of Hananiah; and he laid hold on Jeremiah the prophet, saying: 'Thou fallest away to the Chaldeans.' 14. Then said Jeremiah: 'It is false; I fall not away to the Chaldeans'·

וְשָׂרְפוּ אֶת־הָעִיר הַזֹּאת
בָּאֵשׁ: וְהָיָה בְּהֵעָלוֹת חֵיל 11
הַכַּשְׂדִּים מֵעַל יְרוּשָׁלַ͏ִם מִפְּנֵי
חֵיל פַּרְעֹה: וַיֵּצֵא יִרְמְיָהוּ 12
מִירוּשָׁלַ͏ִם לָלֶכֶת אֶרֶץ בִּנְיָמִן
לַחֲלִק מִשָּׁם בְּתוֹךְ הָעָם:
וַיְהִי־הוּא בְּשַׁעַר בִּנְיָמִן וְשָׁם 13
בַּעַל פְּקִדֻת וּשְׁמוֹ יִרְאִיָּיה
בֶּן־שֶׁלֶמְיָה בֶּן־חֲנַנְיָה
וַיִּתְפֹּשׂ אֶת־יִרְמְיָהוּ הַנָּבִיא
לֵאמֹר אֶל־הַכַּשְׂדִּים אַתָּה
נֹפֵל: וַיֹּאמֶר יִרְמְיָהוּ שֶׁקֶר 14
אֵינֶנִּי נֹפֵל עַל־הַכַּשְׂדִּים

---

stood as 'slain men' (cf. Lam. iv. 9). The language is a rhetorical exaggeration which emphasizes the inevitableness of the fate in store for Jerusalem (Metsudath David).

every man in his tent. The intention may mean that, although these men are lying wounded in their tents, they will rise and burn the city (Metsudath David). It may also mean that those in their tents far from Jerusalem will nevertheless rise and burn the city (Malbim).

11–15 JEREMIAH IS ARRESTED

11. *was broken up from Jerusalem.* When the army left the siege on Jerusalem, and the inhabitants opened the gates of the city (Kara).

12. *to go into the land of Benjamin.* Doubtless his intended destination was his native town of Anathoth (cf. i. 1, xxxii. 8).

to receive his portion there. The meaning of the verb, literally 'to cause to divide,'

cannot be determined with certainty. A.J. follows Targum Jonathan and presupposes that a relative had died in Anathoth and it was necessary for Jeremiah to be there in connection with the inheritance. What is related in xxxii. happened at a later date. Kimchi renders: 'to escape thence into the midst of the people.' He anticipated arrest and attempted to avoid it. According to Pesikta Rabbathi, quoted by Kimchi, he went there to receive his portion of the priests' due among the priests of Anathoth. According to Rabbi Benjamin son of Levi, mentioned in Pesikta d'Rav Kahana, he went to disseminate his prophetic teachings among the people of Anathoth.

13. *in the gate of Benjamin.* The wall on the north side of the city leading to the territory of Benjamin (Kimchi, Daath Mikra).

14. *I fall not away to the Chaldeans.* Although he had counselled submission to Babylon (cf. xxi. 9), his personal

but he hearkened not to him; so Irijah laid hold on Jeremiah, and brought him to the princes. 15. And the princes were wroth with Jeremiah, and smote him, and put him in prison in the house of Jonathan the scribe; for they had made that the prison.

16. When Jeremiah was come into the dungeon-house, and into the cells, and Jeremiah had remained there many days; 17. then Zedekiah the king sent, and fetched him; and the king asked him secretly in his house, and said: 'Is there any word from the LORD?' And Jeremiah said: 'There is.' He said also: 'Thou shalt be delivered into the hand of the king of Babylon'. 18. Moreover Jeremiah said unto

וְלֹא שָׁמַע אֵלָיו וַיִּתְפֹּשׂ יִרְאִיָּיה
בְּיִרְמְיָהוּ וַיְבִאֵהוּ אֶל־
הַשָּׂרִים: וַיִּקְצְפוּ הַשָּׂרִים 15
עַל־יִרְמְיָהוּ וְהִכּוּ אֹתוֹ וְנָתְנוּ
אוֹתוֹ בֵּית הָאֵסוּר בֵּית יְהוֹנָתָן
הַסֹּפֵר כִּי־אֹתוֹ עָשׂוּ לְבֵית
הַכֶּלֶא: כִּי בָא יִרְמְיָהוּ אֶל־ 16
בֵּית הַבּוֹר וְאֶל־הַחֲנֻיוֹת
וַיֵּשֶׁב־שָׁם יִרְמְיָהוּ יָמִים
רַבִּים: וַיִּשְׁלַח הַמֶּלֶךְ 17
צִדְקִיָּהוּ וַיִּקָּחֵהוּ וַיִּשְׁאָלֵהוּ
הַמֶּלֶךְ בְּבֵיתוֹ בַּסֵּתֶר וַיֹּאמֶר
הֲיֵשׁ דָּבָר מֵאֵת יְהוָה וַיֹּאמֶר
יִרְמְיָהוּ יֵשׁ וַיֹּאמֶר בְּיַד־מֶלֶךְ
בָּבֶל תִּנָּתֵן: וַיֹּאמֶר יִרְמְיָהוּ 18

resolve was to remain in Judea and not surrender himself. Hence his repudiation of the charge.]

15. *the princes were wroth.* Their attitude towards Jeremiah was different from that of their predecessors in Jehoiakim's reign (xxvi. 16, xxxvi. 19) who were now exiles in Babylon. As mentioned above, the generation of Jehoiakim was righteous although the king was wicked. The generation of Zedekiah was wicked although the king was righteous. Jeremiah had compared them to bad figs (xxiv.).

Jonathan the scribe. No reason is given why his house was chosen for the prophet's detention. It has been suggested that the prisons were filled with political opponents (Daath Mikra).

16. *into the dungeon-house.* From verse 20 it appears that this dungeon was part of Jonathan's house. The dungeon-house was surrounded by the cells and was the worst prison of all (Abarbanel).

many days. [During which time the Chaldeans resumed the siege of the city. This event induced Zedekiah to communicate again with Jeremiah.]

17. *secretly.* Fearing the resentment of the princes (cf. xxxviii. 5, 24ff.). Nevertheless his action proves his faith in Jeremiah as a true prophet (Daath Soferim).

there is. Yes, there is a recent prophecy, and it concerns you (Malbim).

thou shalt be delivered, etc. Cf. xxxii. 3f., xxxiv. 2f.

king Zedekiah: 'Wherein have I sinned against thee, or against thy servants, or against this people, that ye have put me in prison? 19. Where now are your prophets that prophesied unto you, saying: The king of Babylon shall not come against you, nor against this land? 20. And now hear, I pray thee, O my lord the king: let my supplication, I pray thee, be presented before thee; that thou cause me not to return to the house of Jonathan the scribe, lest I die there.' 21. Then Zedekiah the king commanded, and they committed Jeremiah into the court of the guard, and they gave him daily a loaf of bread out of the bakers' street, until all the bread in the city was spent. Thus Jeremiah remained in the court of the guard.

אֶל־הַמֶּ֫לֶךְ צִדְקִיָּ֫הוּ מֶ֫ה
חָטָ֫אתִי לְךָ וְלַעֲבָדֶ֫יךָ וְלָעָם
הַזֶּ֫ה כִּי־נְתַתֶּ֫ם אוֹתִ֫י אֶל־
19 בֵּ֫ית הַכֶּ֫לֶא: וְאַיּ֫וֹ נְבִיאֵיכֶ֫ם
אֲשֶׁר־נִבְּא֫וּ לָכֶ֫ם לֵאמֹ֫ר לֹא־
יָבֹ֫א מֶ֫לֶךְ־בָּבֶ֫ל עֲלֵיכֶ֫ם וְעַל
20 הָאָ֫רֶץ הַזֹּ֫את: וְעַתָּ֫ה שְׁמַע־
נָ֫א אֲדֹנִ֫י הַמֶּ֫לֶךְ תִּפָּל־נָ֫א
תְחִנָּתִ֫י לְפָנֶ֫יךָ וְאַל־תְּשִׁבֵ֫נִי
בֵּ֫ית יְהוֹנָתָ֫ן הַסֹּפֵ֫ר וְלֹ֫א אָמ֫וּת
21 שָׁ֫ם: וַיְצַוֶּ֫ה הַמֶּ֫לֶךְ צִדְקִיָּ֫הוּ
וַיַּפְקִ֫דוּ אֶת־יִרְמְיָ֫הוּ בַּחֲצַ֫ר
הַמַּטָּרָ֫ה וְנָתֹ֫ן ל֫וֹ כִכַּר־לֶ֫חֶם
לַיּוֹם֫ מִח֫וּץ הָאֹפִ֫ים עַד־תֹּ֫ם
כָּל־הַלֶּ֫חֶם מִן־הָעִ֫יר וַיֵּ֫שֶׁב
יִרְמְיָ֫הוּ בַּחֲצַ֫ר הַמַּטָּרָ֫ה:

---

38   CHAPTER XXXVIII   לח

1. And Shephatiah the son of Mattan, and Gedaliah the son of Pashhur, and Jucal the son of

1 וַיִּשְׁמַ֫ע שְׁפַטְיָ֫ה בֶן־מַתָּ֫ן
וּגְדַלְיָ֫הוּ בֶן־פַּשְׁח֫וּר וְיוּכַל֫

v. 19. ואיה ק'

---

19. *that prophesied unto you.* Cf. xxviii. 2 ff.

20. *let my supplication,* etc. See on xxxvi. 7.

21. *court of the guard.* See on xxxii. 2.

the bakers' street. In the East each trade was usually confined to a particular street (Daath Mikra).

until all the bread, etc. Cf. lii. 6.

CHAPTER XXXVIII

1–13 JEREMIAH'S IMPRISONMENT AND ESCAPE

1. *Shephatiah.* He is not mentioned elsewhere.

Gedaliah the son of Pashhur. Possibly the same Pashhur who put Jeremiah in the stocks (xx. 1 f.).

Jucal. Identical with Jehucal of xxxvii. 3 (Daath Mikra).

Shelemiah, and Pashhur the son of
Malchiah, heard the words that
Jeremiah spoke unto all the people,
saying: 2. 'Thus saith the LORD: He
that remaineth in this city shall die
by the sword, by the famine, and
by the pestilence; but he that goeth
forth to the Chaldeans shall live,
and his life shall be unto him for a
prey, and he shall live. 3. Thus
saith the LORD: This city shall surely
be given into the hand of the army
of the king of Babylon, and he shall
take it.' 4. Then the princes said
unto the king: 'Let this man, we
pray thee, be put to death; forasmuch as he weakeneth the hands of
the men of war that remain in this
city, and the hands of all the people,
in speaking such words unto them;
for this man seeketh not the welfare
of this people, but the hurt.'
5. Then Zedekiah the king said:
'Behold, he is in your hand; for the
king is not he that can do any thing

בֶּן־שֶׁלֶמְיָהוּ וּפַשְׁחוּר בֶּן־
מַלְכִּיָּה אֶת־הַדְּבָרִים אֲשֶׁר
יִרְמְיָהוּ מְדַבֵּר אֶל־כָּל־
2 הָעָם לֵאמֹר: כֹּה אָמַר יְהֹוָה
הַיֹּשֵׁב בָּעִיר הַזֹּאת יָמוּת
בַּחֶרֶב בָּרָעָב וּבַדָּבֶר וְהַיֹּצֵא
אֶל־הַכַּשְׂדִּים יִחְיֶה וְהָיְתָה־
3 לּוֹ נַפְשׁוֹ לְשָׁלָל וָחָי: כֹּה אָמַר
יְהֹוָה הִנָּתֹן תִּנָּתֵן הָעִיר הַזֹּאת
בְּיַד חֵיל מֶלֶךְ־בָּבֶל וּלְכָדָהּ:
4 וַיֹּאמְרוּ הַשָּׂרִים אֶל־הַמֶּלֶךְ
יוּמַת נָא אֶת־הָאִישׁ הַזֶּה כִּי
עַל־כֵּן הוּא מְרַפֵּא אֶת־יְדֵי
אַנְשֵׁי הַמִּלְחָמָה הַנִּשְׁאָרִים ׀
בָּעִיר הַזֹּאת וְאֵת יְדֵי כָל־
הָעָם לְדַבֵּר אֲלֵיהֶם כַּדְּבָרִים
הָאֵלֶּה כִּי ׀ הָאִישׁ הַזֶּה אֵינֶנּוּ
דֹרֵשׁ לְשָׁלוֹם לָעָם הַזֶּה כִּי
5 אִם־לְרָעָה: וַיֹּאמֶר הַמֶּלֶךְ
צִדְקִיָּהוּ הִנֵּה־הוּא בְּיֶדְכֶם
כִּי־אֵין הַמֶּלֶךְ יוּכַל אֶתְכֶם

v. 2. וחיה ק׳

Pashhur the son of Malchiah. Mentioned
in xxi. 1.

*the words that Jeremiah spoke unto all the
people.* Jeremiah's transfer to the court
of the guard (xxxvii. 21) apparently gave
him an opportunity to address the
people (Metsudath David).

2. What Jeremiah told *all the people*
agreed with the message he had sent to
king Zedekiah (cf. xxi. 9).

4. *weakeneth the hands.* Discourages
(Metsudath David).

5. *the king is not,* etc. What a contrast
this confession of weakness makes with
the autocratic power which was normally wielded by an Oriental king!

against you.' 6. Then took they Jeremiah, and cast him into the pit of Malchiah the king's son, that was in the court of the guard; and they let down Jeremiah with cords. And in the pit there was no water, but mire; and Jeremiah sank in the mire.

7. Now when Ebed-melech the Ethiopian, an officer, who was in the king's house, heard that they had put Jeremiah in the pit; the king then sitting in the gate of Benjamin; 8. Ebed-melech went forth out of the king's house, and spoke to the king, saying: 9. 'My lord the king, these men have done evil in all that they have done to Jeremiah the prophet, whom they have cast into the pit; and he is like to die in the place where he is because of the famine;

6 דָּבֵר: וַיִּקְחוּ אֶת־יִרְמְיָהוּ
וַיַּשְׁלִכוּ אֹתוֹ אֶל־הַבּוֹר |
מַלְכִּיָּהוּ בֶן־הַמֶּלֶךְ אֲשֶׁר
בַּחֲצַר הַמַּטָּרָה וַיְשַׁלְּחוּ אֶת־
יִרְמְיָהוּ בַּחֲבָלִים וּבַבּוֹר אֵין־
מַיִם כִּי אִם־טִיט וַיִּטְבַּע

7 יִרְמְיָהוּ בַּטִּיט: וַיִּשְׁמַע עֶבֶד־
מֶלֶךְ הַכּוּשִׁי אִישׁ סָרִיס וְהוּא
בְּבֵית הַמֶּלֶךְ כִּי־נָתְנוּ אֶת־
יִרְמְיָהוּ אֶל־הַבּוֹר וְהַמֶּלֶךְ

8 יוֹשֵׁב בְּשַׁעַר בִּנְיָמִן: וַיֵּצֵא
עֶבֶד־מֶלֶךְ מִבֵּית הַמֶּלֶךְ
וַיְדַבֵּר אֶל־הַמֶּלֶךְ לֵאמֹר:

9 אֲדֹנִי הַמֶּלֶךְ הֵרֵעוּ הָאֲנָשִׁים
הָאֵלֶּה אֵת כָּל־אֲשֶׁר עָשׂוּ
לְיִרְמְיָהוּ הַנָּבִיא אֵת אֲשֶׁר־
הִשְׁלִיכוּ אֶל־הַבּוֹר וַיָּמָת
תַּחְתָּיו מִפְּנֵי הָרָעָב כִּי אֵין

Zedekiah does not explicitly authorize putting Jeremiah to death.

6. *pit.* More exactly, a 'cistern' dug underground for the storage of water (Daath Mikra).

the king's son. Others, including A.V., 'the son of Hammelech' (see on xxxvi. 26).

7. *Ebed-melech.* The name means 'king's servant.' As he was an Ethiopian and an alien, he would not be disturbed by Jeremiah's prediction, and apparently had respect for the prophet (Kara). According to the Rabbis, he was called

'Cushi' because his good deeds were as unusual as the skin coloring of an Ethiopian. Rashi quotes two midrashim that identify him as Baruch son of Neriah. According to one (Siphrë, Num. xii. 1), he was called Cushi because of his deeds and according to the other he is called 'the servant of the Cushite king,' namely Zedekiah, given this appellation because of *his* righteous deeds. This follows the Targum and the Talmud (*Moed Katan* 16b) as well.

9. *because of the famine.* Or, 'for hunger' (A.V.).

for there is no more bread in the city.' 10. Then the king commanded Ebed-melech the Ethiopian, saying: 'Take from hence thirty men with thee, and take up Jeremiah the prophet out of the pit, before he die.' 11. So Ebed-melech took the men with him, and went into the house of the king under the treasury, and took thence worn clouts and worn rags, and let them down by cords into the pit to Jeremiah. 12. And Ebed-melech the Ethiopian said unto Jeremiah: 'Put now these worn clouts and rags under thine armholes under the cords.' And Jeremiah did so. 13. So they drew up Jeremiah with the cords, and took

10 הַלֶּחֶם עוֹד בָּעִיר: וַיְצַוֶּה
הַמֶּלֶךְ אֶת־עֶבֶד־מֶלֶךְ הַכּוּשִׁי
לֵאמֹר קַח בְּיָדְךָ מִזֶּה שְׁלֹשִׁים
אֲנָשִׁים וְהַעֲלִיתָ אֶת־יִרְמְיָהוּ
הַנָּבִיא מִן־הַבּוֹר בְּטֶרֶם
11 יָמוּת: וַיִּקַּח | עֶבֶד־מֶלֶךְ
אֶת־הָאֲנָשִׁים בְּיָדוֹ וַיָּבֹא
בֵית־הַמֶּלֶךְ אֶל־תַּחַת
הָאוֹצָר וַיִּקַּח מִשָּׁם בְּלוֹיֵ
הַסְּחָבוֹת וּבְלוֹיֵ מְלָחִים
וַיְשַׁלְּחֵם אֶל־יִרְמְיָהוּ אֶל־
12 הַבּוֹר בַּחֲבָלִים: וַיֹּאמֶר
עֶבֶד־מֶלֶךְ הַכּוּשִׁי אֶל־
יִרְמְיָהוּ שִׂים נָא בְּלוֹאֵי
הַסְּחָבוֹת וְהַמְּלָחִים תַּחַת
אַצִּלוֹת יָדֶיךָ מִתַּחַת
לַחֲבָלִים וַיַּעַשׂ יִרְמְיָהוּ כֵּן:
13 וַיִּמְשְׁכוּ אֶת־יִרְמְיָהוּ בַּחֲבָלִים

v. 11. סחבות ק'

there is no more bread in the city. A natural exaggeration in a plea for Jeremiah's immediate release. Ebed-melech meant that the shortage was so great that no one would think of feeding Jeremiah who was hidden away in the pit (Kimchi).

10. *thirty men.* A surprisingly large number. Rashi and Kimchi explain that famine had so weakened the men of the city that thirty men were necessary to haul Jeremiah up. This is not very plausible, and more probably the king wished to forestall an attempt at resistance on the part of the prophet's enemies as Isaiah da Trani explains it.

11. *under the treasury.* i.e. into a room under the treasury.

worn clouts and worn rags. In the besieged city, during the two years of the siege there was a shortage of clothing. Ebed-melech searched for old clothes in order to make it easier and pleasanter for Jeremiah when he would be lifted from the pit. He found worn clouts and rags, an indication that any small, insignificant thing was kept during those trying times, perhaps it would be needed (Daath Soferim). This illustrates his thoughtfulness and his consideration for Jeremiah's feelings (Abarbanel).

him up out of the pit; and Jeremiah
remained in the court of the guard.

14. Then Zedekiah the king sent,
and took Jeremiah the prophet unto
him into the third entry that was in
the house of the LORD; and the king
said unto Jeremiah: 'I will ask thee
a thing; hide nothing from me.'
15. Then Jeremiah said unto Zedekiah: 'If I declare it unto thee, wilt
thou not surely put me to death?
and if I give thee counsel, thou wilt
not hearken unto me.' 16. So
Zedekiah the king swore secretly
unto Jeremiah, saying: 'As the LORD
liveth, that made us this soul, I will
not put thee to death, neither will I
give thee into the hand of these men
that seek thy life.'

17. Then said Jeremiah unto
Zedekiah: 'Thus saith the LORD,
God of hosts, the God of Israel: If
thou wilt go forth unto the king of
Babylon's princes, then thy soul

וַיַּעֲלוּ אֹתוֹ מִן־הַבּוֹר וַיֵּשֶׁב
יִרְמְיָהוּ בַּחֲצַר הַמַּטָּרָה:

14 וַיִּשְׁלַח הַמֶּלֶךְ צִדְקִיָּהוּ וַיִּקַּח
אֶת־יִרְמְיָהוּ הַנָּבִיא אֵלָיו
אֶל־מָבוֹא הַשְּׁלִישִׁי אֲשֶׁר
בְּבֵית יְהוָה וַיֹּאמֶר הַמֶּלֶךְ
אֶל־יִרְמְיָהוּ שֹׁאֵל אֲנִי אֹתְךָ
דָּבָר אַל־תְּכַחֵד מִמֶּנִּי דָּבָר:

15 וַיֹּאמֶר יִרְמְיָהוּ אֶל־צִדְקִיָּהוּ
כִּי אַגִּיד לְךָ הֲלוֹא הָמֵת
תְּמִיתֵנִי וְכִי אִיעָצְךָ לֹא תִשְׁמַע

16 אֵלָי: וַיִּשָּׁבַע הַמֶּלֶךְ צִדְקִיָּהוּ
אֶל־יִרְמְיָהוּ בַּסֵּתֶר לֵאמֹר
חַי־יְהוָה אֵת אֲשֶׁר עָשָׂה־לָנוּ
אֶת־הַנֶּפֶשׁ הַזֹּאת אִם־
אֲמִיתֶךָ וְאִם־אֶתֶּנְךָ בְּיַד
הָאֲנָשִׁים הָאֵלֶּה אֲשֶׁר

17 מְבַקְשִׁים אֶת־נַפְשֶׁךָ: וַיֹּאמֶר
יִרְמְיָהוּ אֶל־צִדְקִיָּהוּ כֹּה־
אָמַר יְהוָה אֱלֹהֵי צְבָאוֹת
אֱלֹהֵי יִשְׂרָאֵל אִם־יָצֹא תֵצֵא
אֶל־שָׂרֵי מֶלֶךְ־בָּבֶל וְחָיְתָה

v. 16. כתיב ולא קרי

14-28   ZEDEKIAH AGAIN CONSULTS
         JEREMIAH

14. *the third entry.* This is not mentioned elsewhere. Perhaps it is identical
with *the king's entry* of 2 Kings xvi. 18 as
Kimchi explains.

15. Aware of how weak-minded the
king was, Jeremiah feared that he would
again be imperilled by giving unwel-
come information.

17. *go forth.* i.e. surrender.

the king of Babylon's princes. Who were

shall live, and this city shall not be burned with fire; and thou shalt live, thou, and thy house; 18. but if thou wilt not go forth to the king of Babylon's princes, then shall this city be given into the hand of the Chaldeans, and they shall burn it with fire, and thou shalt not escape out of their hand.' 19. And Zedekiah the king said unto Jeremiah: 'I am afraid of the Jews that are fallen away to the Chaldeans, lest they deliver me into their hand, and they mock me.' 20. But Jeremiah said: 'They shall not deliver thee. Hearken, I beseech thee, to the voice of the LORD, in that which I speak unto thee; so it shall be well with thee, and thy soul shall live. 21. But if thou refuse to go forth, this is the word that the LORD hath shown me: 22. Behold, all the women that are left in the king of Judah's house shall be brought forth to the king of Babylon's princes, and those women shall say:

Thy familiar friends have set thee on,
And have prevailed over thee;

נַפְשֶׁךָ וְהָעִיר הַזֹּאת לֹא תִשָּׂרֵף
בָּאֵשׁ וְחָיִתָה אַתָּה וּבֵיתֶךָ׃
18 וְאִם־לֹא־תֵצֵא אֶל־שָׂרֵי מֶלֶךְ
בָּבֶל וְנִתְּנָה הָעִיר הַזֹּאת בְּיַד
הַכַּשְׂדִּים וּשְׂרָפוּהָ בָּאֵשׁ וְאַתָּה
19 לֹא־תִמָּלֵט מִיָּדָם׃ וַיֹּאמֶר
הַמֶּלֶךְ צִדְקִיָּהוּ אֶל־יִרְמְיָהוּ
אֲנִי דֹאֵג אֶת־הַיְּהוּדִים אֲשֶׁר
נָפְלוּ אֶל־הַכַּשְׂדִּים פֶּן־יִתְּנוּ
אֹתִי בְּיָדָם וְהִתְעַלְּלוּ־בִי׃
20 וַיֹּאמֶר יִרְמְיָהוּ לֹא יִתֵּנוּ שְׁמַע־
נָא ׀ בְּקוֹל יְהֹוָה לַאֲשֶׁר אֲנִי
דֹּבֵר אֵלֶיךָ וְיִיטַב לְךָ וּתְחִי
21 נַפְשֶׁךָ׃ וְאִם־מָאֵן אַתָּה
לָצֵאת זֶה הַדָּבָר אֲשֶׁר הִרְאַנִי
22 יְהֹוָה׃ וְהִנֵּה כָל־הַנָּשִׁים אֲשֶׁר
נִשְׁאֲרוּ בְּבֵית מֶלֶךְ־יְהוּדָה
מוּצָאוֹת אֶל־שָׂרֵי מֶלֶךְ בָּבֶל
וְהֵנָּה אֹמְרֹת הִסִּיתוּךָ וְיָכְלוּ
לְךָ אַנְשֵׁי שְׁלֹמֶךָ הָטְבְּעוּ בַבֹּץ

besieging Jerusalem; the king was apparently not there (cf. xxxix. 3, 5). According to the Rabbis (San. 96b and Lev. Rabbah 19:6), Nebuchadnezzar never came to Jerusalem. He feared that he would meet Sennacherib's fate. See below on lii. 12.

19. *and they mock me.* Zedekiah was indeed afraid that the Chaldeans would deliver him to the Jews who had already surrendered to them, and that they

would avenge themselves upon him since he would have slain them had he known of their defection to the enemy (Kimchi).

22. *all the women that are left.* The reference is probably to the ladies of the court who survived the invasion, since the next verse mentions the women of the royal household. Taunts and reproaches from such a source would be especially humiliating to the king (Malbim).

Thy feet are sunk in the mire,

And they are turned away back.

23. And they shall bring out all thy wives and thy children to the Chaldeans; and thou shalt not escape out of their hand, but shalt be taken by the hand of the king of Babylon; and thou shalt cause this city to be burned with fire.'

24. Then said Zedekiah unto Jeremiah: 'Let no man know of these words, and thou shalt not die.

25. But if the princes hear that I have talked with thee, and they come unto thee, and say unto thee: Declare unto us now what thou hast said unto the king; hide it not from us, and we will not put thee to death; also what the king said unto thee; 26. then thou shalt say unto

23 רַגְלֶךָ נָסֹגוּ אָחֽוֹר: וְאֶת־
כָּל־נָשֶׁיךָ וְאֶת־בָּנֶיךָ
מֽוֹצִאִים אֶל־הַכַּשְׂדִּים וְאַתָּה
לֹא־תִמָּלֵט מִיָּדָם כִּי בְיַד
מֶֽלֶךְ־בָּבֶל תִּתָּפֵשׂ וְאֶת־
הָעִיר הַזֹּאת תִּשְׂרֹף בָּאֵשׁ:
24 וַיֹּאמֶר צִדְקִיָּהוּ אֶל־יִרְמְיָהוּ
אִישׁ אַל־יֵדַע בַּדְּבָרִים־
25 הָאֵלֶּה וְלֹא תָמֽוּת: וְכִֽי־
יִשְׁמְעוּ הַשָּׂרִים כִּֽי־דִבַּרְתִּי
אִתָּךְ וּבָאוּ אֵלֶיךָ וְאָמְרוּ אֵלֶיךָ
הַגִּֽידָה־נָּא לָנוּ מַה־דִּבַּרְתָּ
אֶל־הַמֶּלֶךְ אַל־תְּכַחֵד מִמֶּנּוּ
וְלֹא נְמִיתֶךָ וּמַה־דִּבֶּר אֵלֶיךָ
26 הַמֶּֽלֶךְ: וְאָמַרְתָּ אֲלֵיהֶם

חסרי׳ v. 22.

thy familiar friends. lit. 'the men of thy peace,' i.e. the false prophets who prophesied peace (i.e. victory) to the last (Rashi and Kimchi); or the men who advised thee, as they thought, for thy welfare (Kimchi). The phrase occurs again in Obad. 7.

have set thee on. Incited thee to a suicidal resistance (Kara).

thy feet are sunk in the mire. A proverbial phrase with the meaning: you are caught in difficulties from which you can·ot extricate yourself, like a traveller who·s feet sink in a bog. It is very proba)le that the imagery was suggested to Jeremiah by his personal experience when his own feet *sank in the mire* (verse 6, but the noun is different). God caused him to be drawn out of it,

but that will not happen to the king (Daath Mikra).

23. *and thou shalt cause . . . fire.* Better and literally, 'and thou shalt burn this city with fire.' By following a policy against which Jeremiah had persistently but unsuccessfully warned him, Zedekiah was responsible for the city being destroyed by fire (Kimchi).

24. *thou shalt not die.* Not that Zedekiah would put him to death; but should the princes come to know of what transpired at the interview, they would certainly do so and the king be powerless to save him (Metsudath David).

25. *if the princes hear.* [As they probably would, since what happens at a court

them: I presented my supplication before the king, that he would not cause me to return to Jonathan's house, to die there.' 27. Then came all the princes unto Jeremiah, and asked him; and he told them according to all these words that the king had commanded. So they left off speaking with him; for the matter was not reported. 28. So Jeremiah abode in the court of the guard until the day that Jerusalem was taken.

And it came to pass, when Jerusalem was taken—

מַפִּיל־אֲנִי תְּחִנָּתִי לִפְנֵי
הַמֶּלֶךְ לְבִלְתִּי הֲשִׁיבֵנִי בֵּית
יְהוֹנָתָן לָמוּת שָׁם: וַיָּבֹאוּ כָל־ 27
הַשָּׂרִים אֶל־יִרְמְיָהוּ וַיִּשְׁאֲלוּ
אֹתוֹ וַיַּגֵּד לָהֶם כְּכָל־
הַדְּבָרִים הָאֵלֶּה אֲשֶׁר צִוָּה
הַמֶּלֶךְ וַיַּחֲרִשׁוּ מִמֶּנּוּ כִּי לֹא־
נִשְׁמַע הַדָּבָר: וַיֵּשֶׁב יִרְמְיָהוּ 28
בַּחֲצַר הַמַּטָּרָה עַד־יוֹם
אֲשֶׁר־נִלְכְּדָה יְרוּשָׁלָ͏ִם וְהָיָה
כַּאֲשֶׁר נִלְכְּדָה יְרוּשָׁלָ͏ִם:

| 39 | CHAPTER XXXIX | לט |

1. in the ninth year of Zedekiah king of Judah, in the tenth month, came Nebuchadrezzar king of Babylon and all his army against Jerusalem, and besieged it;

בַּשָּׁנָה הַתְּשִׁעִית לְצִדְקִיָּהוּ 1
מֶלֶךְ־יְהוּדָה בַּחֹדֶשׁ הָעֲשִׂרִי
בָּא נְבוּכַדְרֶאצַּר מֶלֶךְ־בָּבֶל
וְכָל־חֵילוֹ אֶל־יְרוּשָׁלַ͏ִם

v. 28. פסקא באמצע פסוק

---

can rarely be kept secret.] Kara renders: 'when the princes hear.'

26. *Jonathan's house.* Where Jeremiah had nearly died in the dungeon (xxxvii. 15). [Doubtless the prophet had made that petition of the king in the course of the interview.]

27. *according to all these words,* etc. [He told them as much of the conversation as the king permitted.]

for the matter was not reported. Referring to the political questions and answers in the interview (Abarbanel). [Jeremiah could not communicate these to the princes, even if he had wished to do so, without betraying a confidence.]

28. *and it came to pass ... taken.* As translated this clause must be connected with xxxix. 1 and commence the next chapter; but for that meaning we should expect the verb *wayyehi* instead of *wehayah.* Metsudath David renders: 'and he (Jeremiah) remained (there) when Jerusalem was taken.'

CHAPTER XXXIX

1–3 FALL OF JERUSALEM

1. *in the ninth,* etc. This and the following verse are in parenthesis. Verses 1–10 are paralleled by lii. 4–16 and 2 Kings xxv. 1–12.

2. in the eleventh year of Zedekiah, in the fourth month, the ninth day of the month, a breach was made in the city—3. that all the princes of the king of Babylon came in, and sat in the middle gate, even Nergal-sarezer, Samgar-nebo, Sarsechim Rab-saris, Nergal-sarezer Rab-mag, with all the residue of the princes of the king of Babylon. 4. And it came to pass, that when Zedekiah the king of Judah and all the men of war saw them, then they fled, and went forth out of the city by night, by the way of the king's garden, by the gate betwixt the two walls; and he went out the way of the Arabah. 5. But the army of the Chaldeans pursued after them, and overtook Zedekiah in the plains of Jericho; and when they had taken

2 וַיָּצֻרוּ עָלֶיהָ׃ בְּעַשְׁתֵּי־עֶשְׂרֵה
שָׁנָה לְצִדְקִיָּהוּ בַּחֹדֶשׁ
הָרְבִיעִי בְּתִשְׁעָה לַחֹדֶשׁ
3 הָבְקְעָה הָעִיר׃ וַיָּבֹאוּ כֹּל
שָׂרֵי מֶלֶךְ־בָּבֶל וַיֵּשְׁבוּ בְּשַׁעַר
הַתָּוֶךְ נֵרְגַל שַׁרְאֶצֶר סַמְגַּר־
נְבוּ שַׂרְסְכִים רַב־סָרִיס נֵרְגַל
שַׁרְאֶצֶר רַב־מָג וְכָל־
שְׁאֵרִית שָׂרֵי מֶלֶךְ־בָּבֶל׃
4 וַיְהִי כַּאֲשֶׁר רָאָם צִדְקִיָּהוּ
מֶלֶךְ־יְהוּדָה וְכֹל אַנְשֵׁי
הַמִּלְחָמָה וַיִּבְרְחוּ וַיֵּצְאוּ
לַיְלָה מִן־הָעִיר דֶּרֶךְ גַּן
הַמֶּלֶךְ בְּשַׁעַר בֵּין הַחֹמֹתָיִם
5 וַיֵּצֵא דֶּרֶךְ הָעֲרָבָה׃ וַיִּרְדְּפוּ
חֵיל־כַּשְׂדִּים אַחֲרֵיהֶם וַיַּשִּׂגוּ
אֶת־צִדְקִיָּהוּ בְּעַרְבוֹת יְרֵחוֹ

v. 3. כצ״ל בסין

2. lii. 6 adds that on this day the supply of food failed.

3. *the middle gate.* Probably, the central (chief) gate in the walls of Jerusalem (Metsudath David).

Nergal-sarezer. The name occurs twice, apparently borne by two different men (Metsudath Zion, Kimchi).

4-7 FATE OF ZEDEKIAH

4. *by the gate betwixt the two walls.* There was a place in Jerusalem known as 'betwixt the two walls' because it was surrounded by two high walls. It was situated in the south of the city. In Isa.

xx. 11, we learn that they made a 'basin' there to which the water of the pool of Siloam flowed through the tunnel made by Hezekiah. There was a gate through which it was possible to go out to the Kidron Valley. This side was perhaps watched less than the north where the army invaded the city (Daath Mikra).

the Arabah. The deep valley of the Jordan north of the Dead Sea. Zedekiah was evidently trying to reach Jordan where he may have hoped to find refuge (Daath Mikra).

5. *the plains of Jericho.* The west side of the Arabah (Daath Mikra).

him, they brought him up to Nebuchadrezzar king of Babylon to Riblah in the land of Hamath, and he gave judgment upon him. 6. Then the king of Babylon slew the sons of Zedekiah in Riblah before his eyes; also the king of Babylon slew all the nobles of Judah. 7. Moreover he put out Zedekiah's eyes, and bound him in fetters, to carry him to Babylon. 8. And the Chaldeans burned the king's house, and the house of the people, with fire, and broke down the walls of Jerusalem. 9. Then Nebuzaradan the captain of the guard carried away captive into Babylon the remnant of the people that remained in the city, the deserters also, that fell away to him, with the rest of the people that remained. 10. But

וַיִּקְחוּ אֹתוֹ וַיַּעֲלֻהוּ אֶל־
נְבוּכַדְרֶאצַּר מֶלֶךְ־בָּבֶל
רִבְלָתָה בְּאֶרֶץ חֲמָת וַיְדַבֵּר
6 אִתּוֹ מִשְׁפָּטִים: וַיִּשְׁחַט מֶלֶךְ
בָּבֶל אֶת־בְּנֵי צִדְקִיָּהוּ
בְּרִבְלָה לְעֵינָיו וְאֵת כָּל־חֹרֵי
יְהוּדָה שָׁחַט מֶלֶךְ בָּבֶל:
7 וְאֶת־עֵינֵי צִדְקִיָּהוּ עִוֵּר
וַיַּאַסְרֵהוּ בַּנְחֻשְׁתַּיִם לָבִיא
8 אֹתוֹ בָּבֶלָה: וְאֶת־בֵּית
הַמֶּלֶךְ וְאֶת־בֵּית הָעָם שָׂרְפוּ
הַכַּשְׂדִּים בָּאֵשׁ וְאֶת־חֹמֹת
9 יְרוּשָׁלַ͏ִם נָתָצוּ: וְאֵת יֶתֶר הָעָם
הַנִּשְׁאָרִים בָּעִיר וְאֶת־
הַנֹּפְלִים אֲשֶׁר נָפְלוּ עָלָיו וְאֵת
יֶתֶר הָעָם הַנִּשְׁאָרִים הֶגְלָה
נְבוּזַרְאֲדָן רַב־טַבָּחִים בָּבֶל:

v. 7. כצ״ל

Riblah. This lies between the mountain ranges of Lebanon and Hermon.

he gave judgment upon him. For having violated his oath of allegiance (Kimchi; cf. 2 Chron. xxxvi. 13).

6. *nobles.* The Hebrew word occurred in xxvii. 20.

7. *he put out Zedekiah's eyes.* A common form of punishment in ancient times. It is mentioned in the Code of Hammurabi.

8–10 FATE OF THE POPULATION OF JERUSALEM

8. *the house of the people.* The singular is used in a collective sense, the people's houses. The Rabbis interpret it as the synagogue (Kimchi).

9. *Nebuzaradan.* He arrived in Jerusalem a month after the fall of the city (lii. 12).

the captain of the guard. lit. 'the chief of the executioners'; the phrase is comparable with that in Gen. xxxix. 1 (Metsudath David).

that fell away to him. Before the final capture of the city (Daath Mikra).

the rest of the people. From the other cities of Judah (Abarbanel, Metsudath David).

Nebuzaradan the captain of the guard left of the poor of the people, that had nothing, in the land of Judah, and gave them vineyards and fields in that day. 11. Now Nebuchadrezzar king of Babylon gave charge concerning Jeremiah to Nebuzaradan the captain of the guard, saying: 12. 'Take him, and look well to him, and do him no harm; but do unto him even as he shall say unto thee.' 13. So Nebuzaradan the captain of the guard sent, and Nebushazban Rab-saris, and Nergal-sarezer Rab-mag, and all the chief officers of the king of Babylon; 14. they sent, and took Jeremiah out of the court of the guard, and committed him unto Gedaliah the son of Ahikam, the son of Shaphan, that he should carry him home; so he dwelt among the people.

10 וּמִן־הָעָם הַדַּלִּים אֲשֶׁר
אֵין־לָהֶם מְאוּמָה הִשְׁאִיר
נְבוּזַרְאֲדָן רַב־טַבָּחִים בְּאֶרֶץ
יְהוּדָה וַיִּתֵּן לָהֶם כְּרָמִים
11 וִיגֵבִים בַּיּוֹם הַהוּא: וַיְצַו
נְבוּכַדְרֶאצַּר מֶלֶךְ־־בָּבֶל
עַל־יִרְמְיָהוּ בְּיַד נְבוּזַרְאֲדָן
12 רַב־טַבָּחִים לֵאמֹר: קָחֶנּוּ
וְעֵינֶיךָ שִׂים עָלָיו וְאַל־תַּעַשׂ
לוֹ מְאוּמָה רָּע כִּי אִם כַּאֲשֶׁר
יְדַבֵּר אֵלֶיךָ כֵּן עֲשֵׂה עִמּוֹ:
13 וַיִּשְׁלַח נְבוּזַרְאֲדָן רַב־־
טַבָּחִים וּנְבוּשַׁזְבָּ֗ן רַב־סָרִיס
וְנֵרְגַל שַׂרְאֶצֶר רַב־מָג וְכֹל
14 רַבֵּי מֶלֶךְ־בָּבֶל: וַיִּשְׁלְחוּ
וַיִּקְחוּ אֶת־יִרְמְיָהוּ מֵחֲצַר
הַמַּטָּרָה וַיִּתְּנוּ אֹתוֹ אֶל־
גְּדַלְיָהוּ בֶּן־אֲחִיקָם בֶּן־שָׁפָן
לְהוֹצִאֵהוּ אֶל־הַבָּיִת וַיֵּשֶׁב

---

v. 12. ר׳ דגושה   v. 12. כתיב ולא קרי   v. 13. נון זעירא

---

10. *vineyards and fields.* He was confident that they would not rebel against him since he gave them vineyards and fields (Malbim).

11–14 NEBUCHADNEZZAR'S FRIENDLY TREATMENT OF JEREMIAH

12. *look well to him.* Nebuchadnezzar's favourable attitude to Jeremiah was doubtless due to the latter's counsel to Zedekiah to submit.

14. *Gedaliah.* He was subsequently appointed governor over the Jews who were left behind (xl. 5).

Ahikam, the son of Shaphan. See on xxvi. 24.

home. Gedaliah's house (Kimchi, Kara).

so he dwelt among the people. i.e. he was no longer in confinement and was now free to come and go. This verse anticipates the fuller narrative in the next chapter (Abarbanel).

15. Now the word of the LORD came unto Jeremiah, while he was shut up in the court of the guard, saying: **16.** 'Go, and speak to Ebed-melech the Ethiopian, saying: Thus saith the LORD of hosts, the God of Israel: Behold, I will bring My words upon this city for evil, and not for good; and they shall be accomplished before thee in that day. **17.** But I will deliver thee in that day, saith the LORD; and thou shalt not be given into the hand of the men of whom thou art afraid. **18.** For I will surely deliver thee, and thou shalt not fall by the sword, but thy life shall be for a prey unto thee; because thou hast put thy trust in Me, saith the LORD.'

15 בְּתוֹךְ הָעָם: וְאֶל־יִרְמְיָהוּ
הָיָה דְבַר־יְהֹוָה בִּהְיֹתוֹ עָצוּר
16 בַּחֲצַר הַמַּטָּרָה לֵאמֹר: הָלוֹךְ
וְאָמַרְתָּ לְעֶבֶד־מֶלֶךְ הַכּוּשִׁי
לֵאמֹר כֹּה־אָמַר יְהֹוָה
צְבָאוֹת אֱלֹהֵי יִשְׂרָאֵל הִנְנִי
מֵבִי אֶת־דְּבָרַי אֶל־הָעִיר
הַזֹּאת לְרָעָה וְלֹא לְטוֹבָה
וְהָיוּ לְפָנֶיךָ בַּיּוֹם הַהוּא:
17 וְהִצַּלְתִּיךָ בַיּוֹם־הַהוּא נְאֻם־
יְהֹוָה וְלֹא תִנָּתֵן בְּיַד הָאֲנָשִׁים
18 אֲשֶׁר־אַתָּה יָגוֹר מִפְּנֵיהֶם: כִּי
מַלֵּט אֲמַלֶּטְךָ וּבַחֶרֶב לֹא
תִפֹּל וְהָיְתָה לְךָ נַפְשְׁךָ לְשָׁלָל
כִּי־בָטַחְתָּ בִּי נְאֻם־יְהֹוָה:

v. 16. מביא ק׳

15–18 EBED-MELECH'S REWARD

15. *came.* Better, 'had come,' since this passage is chronologically earlier than the preceding. It is the sequel to xxxviii., and is stated to teach us that God does not withhold the reward for a good deed (Abarbanel).

16. *Ebel-melech the Ethiopian.* He had interceded with the king against the harsh conditions of Jeremiah's imprisonment (xxxviii. 7ff.). The present promise was his reward.

before thee. i.e. he will witness their happening (Rashi).

17. *of whom thou art afraid.* Either the princes who would have shown hostility to him on account of his intercession on Jeremiah's behalf (Ibn Nachmiash); or of the invading Chaldean army. Most commentators accept the latter.

18. *by the sword.* i.e. he will not die by violence.

for a prey. See on xxi. 9. The same promise was made to Baruch (xlv. 5).

because thou hast put thy trust in Me. Manifested by his effort to save Jeremiah, the messenger of God, at the risk of his life (Metsudath David).

40   CHAPTER XL   מ

1. The word which came to Jeremiah from the LORD, after that Nebuzaradan the captain of the guard had let him go from Ramah, when he had taken him being bound in chains among all the captives of Jerusalem and Judah, that were carried away captive unto Babylon. 2. And the captain of the guard took Jeremiah, and said unto him: 'The LORD thy God pronounced this evil upon this place; 3. and the LORD hath brought it, and done according as He spoke; because ye have sinned against the LORD, and have not hearkened to His voice, therefore

א הַדָּבָר אֲשֶׁר־הָיָה אֶל־יִרְמְיָהוּ
מֵאֵת יְהֹוָה אַחַר ׀ שַׁלַּח אֹתוֹ
נְבוּזַרְאֲדָן רַב־טַבָּחִים מִן־
הָרָמָה בְּקַחְתּוֹ אֹתוֹ וְהוּא־
אָסוּר בָּאזִקִּים בְּתוֹךְ כָּל־
גָּלוּת יְרוּשָׁלִַם וִיהוּדָה
ב הַמֻּגְלִים בָּבֶלָה: וַיִּקַּח רַב־
טַבָּחִים לְיִרְמְיָהוּ וַיֹּאמֶר אֵלָיו
יְהֹוָה אֱלֹהֶיךָ דִּבֶּר אֶת־
הָרָעָה הַזֹּאת אֶל־הַמָּקוֹם
ג הַזֶּה: וַיָּבֵא וַיַּעַשׂ יְהֹוָה כַּאֲשֶׁר
דִּבֵּר כִּי־חֲטָאתֶם לַיהֹוָה
וְלֹא־שְׁמַעְתֶּם בְּקוֹלוֹ וְהָיָה

v. 1. נחה א׳

CHAPTER XL

CHAPTERS xl-xliv. narrate incidents in Jeremiah's life after the fall of Jerusalem.

1–6   JEREMIAH DECIDES TO REMAIN IN JUDEA

1. *the word which came to Jeremiah from the* LORD. But no Divine utterance follows! The clause is to be understood as a general introduction to the whole narrative of events which immediately followed the capture of Jerusalem. The actual *word* comes later in xlii. 7. The purpose of presenting this history is to tell us the situation concerning which the *word* came to Jeremiah (Rashi, Kimchi).

Ramah. See on xxxi. 14. This was a halting-place for the captives on the journey to Babylon. Kimchi states that Nebuzaradan was stationed there. He had not entered Jerusalem with the other officers.

bound in chains. Although Nebuchadnezzar had ordered that the prophet was to be treated with consideration (xxxix. 12), it is easily understood how the command may have been overlooked in the prevailing confusion. At Ramah the mistake was rectified. The Rabbis declare that, on seeing the file of chained prisoners, Jeremiah voluntarily had himself fettered to demonstrate his complete identification with the sorrows of his people.

that were carried away. Better, 'who were being carried away.'

2. *the* LORD *thy God pronounced this evil upon this place.* This verse and the next

264

this thing is come upon you.
4. And now, behold, I loose thee
this day from the chains which are
upon thy hand. If it seem good
unto thee to come with me into
Babylon, come, and I will look well
unto thee; but if it seem ill unto thee
to come with me into Babylon,
forbear; behold, all the land is
before thee; whither it seemeth good
and right unto thee to go, thither go.
—5. Yet he would not go back.—
Go back then to Gedaliah the son of
Ahikam, the son of Shaphan, whom
the king of Babylon hath made
governor over the cities of Judah,
and dwell with him among the
people; or go wheresoever it seemeth
right unto thee to go.' So the
captain of the guard gave him an
allowance and a present, and let him
go. 6. Then went Jeremiah unto
Gedaliah the son of Ahikam to
Mizpah, and dwelt with him among

4 לָכֶם יַדָּבְר הַזֶּה: וְעַתָּה הִנֵּה
פִּתַּחְתִּיךָ הַיּוֹם מִן־הָאזִקִּים
אֲשֶׁר עַל־יָדֶךָ אִם־־טוֹב
בְּעֵינֶיךָ לָבוֹא אִתִּי בָבֶל בֹּא
וְאָשִׂים אֶת־עֵינִי עָלֶיךָ וְאִם־
רַע בְּעֵינֶיךָ לָבוֹא־אִתִּי בָבֶל
חֲדָל רְאֵה כָּל־הָאָרֶץ לְפָנֶיךָ
אֶל־טוֹב וְאֶל־הַיָּשָׁר בְּעֵינֶיךָ
5 לָלֶכֶת שָׁמָּה לֵךְ: וְעוֹדֶנּוּ לֹא־
יָשׁוּב וְשֻׁבָה אֶל־גְּדַלְיָה בֶן־
אֲחִיקָם בֶּן־שָׁפָן אֲשֶׁר הִפְקִיד
מֶלֶךְ־בָּבֶל בְּעָרֵי יְהוּדָה וְשֵׁב
אִתּוֹ בְּתוֹךְ הָעָם אוֹ אֶל־כָּל־
הַיָּשָׁר בְּעֵינֶיךָ לָלֶכֶת לֵךְ
וַיִּתֶּן־לוֹ רַב־טַבָּחִים אֲרֻחָה
6 וּמַשְׂאֵת וַיְשַׁלְּחֵהוּ: וַיָּבֹא
יִרְמְיָהוּ אֶל־גְּדַלְיָה בֶן־
אֲחִיקָם הַמִּצְפָּתָה וַיֵּשֶׁב אִתּוֹ

v. 3. נחה א׳ v. 4. הדבר ק׳

contain a statement which sounds
strange in the mouth of a heathen.
Nevertheless, Jeremiah's preaching,
which may well have reached his ears,
apparently, impressed Nebuzaradan.
According to the Rabbis (Gittin 57a),
Nebuzaradan felt remorse for the
massacre he had inflicted upon Israel
and became proselytized.

4. *I will look well unto thee.* See on
xxxix. 12.

5. *yet he would not go back,* etc. The
Hebrew is grammatically awkward and

forms a broken sentence. Perhaps the
general sense is: Jeremiah interrupted
Nebuzaradan with a remark that he did
not desire to go back (presumably, to
Jerusalem); whereupon the captain of
the guard, understanding from Jeremiah's demeanour that he did not wish
to accompany him to Babylon, bade
him go to Gedaliah (Kimchi).

6. *Mizpah.* [Situated on a hill about
four miles north-west of Jerusalem.
Jeremiah did not return to Jerusalem
because, no doubt, he felt that his place

the people that were left in the land.

7. Now when all the captains of the forces that were in the fields, even they and their men, heard that the king of Babylon had made Gedaliah the son of Ahikam governor in the land, and had committed unto him men, and women, and children, and of the poorest of the land, of them that were not carried away captive to Babylon; 8. then they came to Gedaliah to Mizpah, even Ishmael the son of Nethaniah, and Johanan and Jonathan the sons of Kareah, and Seraiah the son of Tanhumeth, and the sons of Ephai the Netophathite, and Jezaniah the son of the Maacathite, they and their men. 9. And Gedaliah the son of Ahikam the son of Shaphan swore unto them and to their men, saying: 'Fear not to serve the Chaldeans; dwell in the land, and

בְּתוֹךְ הָעָם הַנִּשְׁאָרִים בָּאָרֶץ׃

7 וַיִּשְׁמְעוּ כָל־־שָׂרֵי הַחֲיָלִים
אֲשֶׁר בַּשָּׂדֶה הֵמָּה וְאַנְשֵׁיהֶם
כִּי־הִפְקִיד מֶלֶךְ־בָּבֶל אֶת־
גְּדַלְיָהוּ בֶן־אֲחִיקָם בָּאָרֶץ
וְכִי | הִפְקִיד אִתּוֹ אֲנָשִׁים
וְנָשִׁים וָטַף וּמִדַּלַּת הָאָרֶץ
מֵאֲשֶׁר לֹא־הָגְלוּ בָּבֶלָה׃
8 וַיָּבֹאוּ אֶל־גְּדַלְיָה הַמִּצְפָּתָה
וְיִשְׁמָעֵאל בֶּן־נְתַנְיָהוּ וְיוֹחָנָן
וְיוֹנָתָן בְּנֵי־קָרֵחַ וּשְׂרָיָה בֶן־
תַּנְחֻמֶת וּבְנֵי | עֵיפַי הַנְּטֹפָתִי
וִיזַנְיָהוּ בֶּן־הַמַּעֲכָתִי הֵמָּה
9 וְאַנְשֵׁיהֶם׃ וַיִּשָּׁבַע לָהֶם
גְּדַלְיָהוּ בֶן־אֲחִיקָם בֶּן־שָׁפָן
וּלְאַנְשֵׁיהֶם לֵאמֹר אַל־־
תִּירְאוּ מֵעֲבוֹד הַכַּשְׂדִּים שְׁבוּ

עיפי ק׳   v. 8.

was by the side of Gedaliah to help him in his difficult task of governorship over a stricken land.]

7. *in the fields.* i.e. in the open country outside the cities. The *forces* were bands of people who had fled from Jerusalem to the villages and the open country. They had appointed captains over them to govern them. These captains heard that the king of Babylon had made Gedaliah governor of the land and had committed unto him etc., indicating that he did not intend to exile any more

Judeans, but to settle them in the land (Kimchi, Abarbanel).

8. *Ishmael.* He was of royal blood (cf. xli. 1); he was responsible for Gedaliah's murder.

Johanan. A loyal supporter of Gedaliah who warned him of a plot against his life (verses 13ff.) and led the expedition against Ishmael after the assassination (xli. 11f.).

9. *fear not to serve.* Fear not that you will be compelled to serve the Chaldeans; you will need only to serve the king of Babylon, and he will not impose

serve the king of Babylon, and it shall be well with you. 10. As for me, behold, I will dwell at Mizpah, to stand before the Chaldeans that may come unto us; but ye, gather ye wine and summer fruits and oil, and put them in your vessels, and dwell in your cities that ye have taken.' 11. Likewise when all the Jews that were in Moab, and among the children of Ammon, and in Edom, and that were in all the countries, heard that the king of Babylon had left a remnant of Judah, and that he had set over them Gedaliah the son of Ahikam, the son of Shaphan; 12. then all the Jews returned out of all places whither they were driven, and came to the land of Judah, to Gedaliah, unto Mizpah, and gathered wine and summer fruits in great abundance.

13. Moreover Johanan the son of

בָּאָרֶץ וְעִבְדוּ אֶת־מֶלֶךְ בָּבֶל
10 וְיִיטַב לָכֶם: וַאֲנִי הִנְנִי יֹשֵׁב
בַּמִּצְפָּה לַעֲמֹד לִפְנֵי
הַכַּשְׂדִּים אֲשֶׁר יָבֹאוּ אֵלֵינוּ
וְאַתֶּם אִסְפוּ יַיִן וָקַיִץ וְשֶׁמֶן
וְשִׂמוּ בִּכְלֵיכֶם וּשְׁבוּ בְּעָרֵיכֶם
11 אֲשֶׁר־תְּפַשְׂתֶּם: וְגַם כָּל־
הַיְּהוּדִים אֲשֶׁר־בְּמוֹאָב |
וּבִבְנֵי־עַמּוֹן וּבֶאֱדוֹם וַאֲשֶׁר
בְּכָל־הָאֲרָצוֹת שָׁמְעוּ כִּי־
נָתַן | מֶלֶךְ־בָּבֶל שְׁאֵרִית
לִיהוּדָה וְכִי הִפְקִיד עֲלֵיהֶם
אֶת־גְּדַלְיָהוּ בֶּן־אֲחִיקָם
12 בֶּן־שָׁפָן: וַיָּשֻׁבוּ כָל־
הַיְּהוּדִים מִכָּל־הַמְּקֹמוֹת
אֲשֶׁר נִדְּחוּ־שָׁם וַיָּבֹאוּ
אֶרֶץ־יְהוּדָה אֶל־גְּדַלְיָהוּ
הַמִּצְפָּתָה וַיַּאַסְפוּ יַיִן וָקַיִץ
13 הַרְבֵּה מְאֹד: וְיוֹחָנָן בֶּן־קָרֵחַ

---

hard labour upon you (Metsudath David).

10. *to stand before the Chaldeans.* As your representative, to protect your interests (Daath Mikra).

gather ye wine and summer fruits. [The debacle having taken place in the fifth month (2 Kings xxv. 8), about the beginning of August, the summer's harvest was yet to be gathered. Evidently the Babylonians had not cut down the vines and trees.]

your cities that ye have taken. With a great

part of the population deported, those who remained quickly settled in the derelict cities (Daath Mikra).

11. *in Moab ... Ammon ... Edom.* Whither they had fled during Nebuchadnezzar's invasion (Metsudath David).

12. *and came to the land of Judah.* Because of the mild treatment given them by Nebuchadnezzar (Daath Mikra).

to Gedaliah. Since the king appointed him as governor (Daath Mikra).

Kareah, and all the captains of the forces that were in the fields, came to Gedaliah to Mizpah, 14. and said unto him: 'Dost thou know that Baalis the king of the children of Ammon hath sent Ishmael the son of Nethaniah to take thy life?' But Gedaliah the son of Ahikam believed them not. 15. Then Johanan the son of Kareah spoke to Gedaliah in Mizpah secretly, saying: 'Let me go, I pray thee, and I will slay Ishmael the son of Nethaniah, and no man shall know it; wherefore should he take thy life, that all the Jews that are gathered unto thee should be scattered, and the remnant of Judah perish?' 16. But Gedaliah the son of Ahikam said unto Johanan the son of Kareah: 'Thou shalt not do this thing; for thou speakest falsely of Ishmael.'

וְכָל־שָׂרֵי הַחֲיָלִים אֲשֶׁר
בַּשָּׂדֶה בָּאוּ אֶל־גְּדַלְיָהוּ
14 הַמִּצְפָּתָה: וַיֹּאמְרוּ אֵלָיו
הֲיָדֹעַ תֵּדַע כִּי בַּעֲלִיס ׀ מֶלֶךְ
בְּנֵי־עַמּוֹן שָׁלַח אֶת־יִשְׁמָעֵאל
בֶּן־נְתַנְיָה לְהַכֹּתְךָ נָפֶשׁ
וְלֹא־הֶאֱמִין לָהֶם גְּדַלְיָהוּ
15 בֶּן־אֲחִיקָם: וְיוֹחָנָן בֶּן־קָרֵחַ
אָמַר אֶל־גְּדַלְיָהוּ בַסֵּתֶר
בַּמִּצְפָּה לֵאמֹר אֵלְכָה נָּא
וְאַכֶּה אֶת־יִשְׁמָעֵאל בֶּן־
נְתַנְיָה וְאִישׁ לֹא יֵדָע לָמָּה
יַכֶּכָּה נֶּפֶשׁ וְנָפֹצוּ כָּל־יְהוּדָה
הַנִּקְבָּצִים אֵלֶיךָ וְאָבְדָה
16 שְׁאֵרִית יְהוּדָה: וַיֹּאמֶר
גְּדַלְיָהוּ בֶן־אֲחִיקָם אֶל־
יוֹחָנָן בֶּן־קָרֵחַ אַל־תַּעֲשֵׂ
אֶת־הַדָּבָר הַזֶּה כִּי־שֶׁקֶר
אַתָּה דֹבֵר אֶל־יִשְׁמָעֵאל:

v. 16. תעשה ק'

13-16 GEDALIAH IGNORES A WARNING OF ISHMAEL'S PLOT

14. *Baalis.* His motive was probably to hinder the rehabilitation of the country which Gedaliah had inaugurated, so that Judea might fall an easy victim to his own expansionist plans (Abarbanel, Malbim).

Ishmael. Perhaps his jealousy of Gedaliah and resentment at being passed over as governor made him a ready tool in Baalis' hands (Kimchi, Rashi, Abarbanel).

believed them not. [It was incredible to him that for reasons of personal pique, Ishmael, knowing full well that the assassination of the governor appointed by Nebuchadnezzar might entail the destruction of the remnant of Judea, would nevertheless commit such an act of treason.]

15. *should be scattered.* As was indeed the effect of Gedaliah's murder.

16. *thou speakest falsely of Ishmael.* It is evidence of the nobility of Gedaliah's character that he refused to give cre-

41   CHAPTER XLI   מא

1. Now it came to pass in the seventh month, that Ishmael the son of Nethaniah, the son of Elishama, of the seed royal, and one of the chief officers of the king, and ten men with him, came unto Gedaliah the son of Ahikam to Mizpah; and there they did eat bread together in Mizpah. 2. Then arose Ishmael the son of Nethaniah, and the ten men that were with him, and smote Gedaliah the son of Ahikam the son of Shaphan with the sword, and slew him, whom the king of Babylon had made governor over the land. 3. Ishmael also slew

א וַיְהִי | בַּחֹדֶשׁ הַשְּׁבִיעִי בָּא
יִשְׁמָעֵאל בֶּן־נְתַנְיָה בֶן־
אֱלִישָׁמָע מִזֶּרַע הַמְּלוּכָה
וְרַבֵּי הַמֶּלֶךְ וַעֲשָׂרָה אֲנָשִׁים
אִתּוֹ אֶל־גְּדַלְיָהוּ בֶן־
אֲחִיקָם הַמִּצְפָּתָה וַיֹּאכְלוּ שָׁם
ב לֶחֶם יַחְדָּו בַּמִּצְפָּה: וַיָּקָם
יִשְׁמָעֵאל בֶּן־נְתַנְיָה וַעֲשֶׂרֶת
הָאֲנָשִׁים | אֲשֶׁר־הָיוּ אִתּוֹ וַיַּכּוּ
אֶת־גְּדַלְיָהוּ בֶן־אֲחִיקָם בֶּן־
שָׁפָן בַּחֶרֶב וַיָּמֶת אֹתוֹ אֲשֶׁר־
הִפְקִיד מֶלֶךְ־בָּבֶל בָּאָרֶץ:

dence to what was told him (Daath Soferim).

CHAPTER XLI

1–3   GEDALIAH MURDERED BY ISHMAEL

1. *in the seventh month.* Kimchi considers the new moon to be intended here. In the Jewish calendar the third of the seventh month is observed as the fast of Gedaliah, deferred to that day because the first and second are the New Year.

and one of the chief officers. One is not in the original. A.V. has 'and the princes of the king even ten men.' The Hebrew may mean, 'and some of the chief officers' (so Rashi and Kimchi), the *ten men* being of lower rank. Another possibility is to understand the whole as descriptive of Ishmael: 'one of the seed royal and (of) the chief officers' (Metsudath David).

they did eat bread together. Gedaliah

received them as guests and gave them hospitality (Abarbanel). [This made the subsequent crime all the more heinous.]

2. *and slew him.* Josephus, *Antiquities* X, ix. 4, relates that Gedaliah 'was immersed in his cups to the degree of insensibility, and had fallen asleep,' and while in this helpless condition he was killed. Either this story is true or Gedaliah's retinue must have been too small to protect him. In spite of the warning he had received (xl. 14), Gedaliah's trust in Ishmael was so great that he took no precautions. In the light of Ishmael's subsequent flight, it is not easy to see what his motive was. If it was mere pique at having been passed over for the governorship, he certainly went to extreme lengths to gratify it. It is more likely, perhaps, that he did not contemplate flight at first (see on the next verse), thinking to take Gedaliah's place as governor, either under Nebuchadnezzar or, if Baalis (see on xl. 14)

all the Jews that were with him, even with Gedaliah, at Mizpah, and the Chaldeans that were found there, even the men of war.

4. And it came to pass the second day after he had slain Gedaliah, and no man knew it, 5. that there came certain men from Shechem, from Shiloh, and from Samaria, even fourscore men, having their beards shaven and their clothes rent, and having cut themselves, with meal-offerings and frankincense in their hand to bring them to the house of

3 וְאֵת כָּל־הַיְּהוּדִים אֲשֶׁר־
הָיוּ אִתּוֹ אֶת־גְּדַלְיָהוּ בַּמִּצְפָּה
וְאֶת־הַכַּשְׂדִּים אֲשֶׁר נִמְצְאוּ
שָׁם אֵת אַנְשֵׁי הַמִּלְחָמָה הִכָּה
4 יִשְׁמָעֵאל: וַיְהִי בַּיּוֹם הַשֵּׁנִי
לְהָמִית אֶת־גְּדַלְיָהוּ וְאִישׁ לֹא
5 יָדָע: וַיָּבֹאוּ אֲנָשִׁים מִשְּׁכֶם
מִשִּׁלוֹ וּמִשֹּׁמְרוֹן שְׁמֹנִים אִישׁ
מְגֻלְּחֵי זָקָן וּקְרֻעֵי בְגָדִים
וּמִתְגֹּדְדִים וּמִנְחָה וּלְבוֹנָה
בְּיָדָם לְהָבִיא בֵּית יְהוָה:

should annex Judea, under him (see Daath Mikra).

whom the king of Babylon had made governor. Kimchi renders: 'because the king of Babylon had made him governor.' This rendering explicitly makes resentment the motive.

3. *and the Chaldeans.* [This deliberate act of provocation seems to be quite senseless, because Nebuchadnezzar would certainly avenge their death, thereby depriving Ishmael of whatever he thought to gain. Possibly it was not part of his original plan. The Chaldeans may have died in defence of the governor; or perhaps Ishmael became panic-stricken after the death of Gedaliah, and to cover up his deed, if only for a short time (cf. *and no man knew it,* verse 4), slew all present. His later conduct (cf. verses 7ff.) makes the second explanation probable. In any event, the soldiers must have been unarmed since so small a force sufficed to overwhelm them.]

4–10 FURTHER ATROCITIES OF ISHMAEL

5. *from Shechem, from Shiloh, and from Samaria.* Three towns in what was

formerly the Northern Kingdom which had been destroyed nearly 140 years earlier, in 722 B.C.E., and its inhabitants deported to Assyria (2 Kings xvii. 6). These pilgrims were either descendants of those Jews who were still left after the deportation of the population (cf. 2 Chron. xxxiv. 9 which records that a *remnant* stayed in the country), or Judeans who had settled there (Daath Mikra).

Shechem. Now the Arab town of Nablus; it lies in a valley between the mountains Gerizim and Ebal.

Shiloh. See on vii. 12.

Samaria. The capital of the former Northern Kingdom.

having their beards shaven, etc. In mourning for the destroyed Temple (Kimchi).

and having cut themselves. Likewise as a sign of mourning (see on xvi. 6) (Kimchi).

meal-offerings and frankincense. [Doubtless there were no longer facilities to slaughter animals as offerings.]

the LORD. 6. And Ishmael the son of Nethaniah went forth from Mizpah to meet them, weeping all along as he went; and it came to pass, as he met them, he said unto them: 'Come to Gedaliah the son of Ahikam.' 7. And it was so, when they came into the midst of the city, that Ishmael the son of Nethaniah slew them, and cast them into the midst of the pit, he, and the men that were with him. 8. But ten men were found among them that said unto Ishmael: 'Slay us not; for we have stores hidden in the field, of wheat, and of barley, and of oil, and of honey.' So he forbore, and slew them not among their brethren. 9. Now the pit wherein Ishmael cast all the dead bodies of the men whom he had slain by the side of Gedaliah was that which Asa the king had made for fear of Baasa king of Israel;

6 וַיֵּצֵא יִשְׁמָעֵאל בֶּן־נְתַנְיָה לִקְרָאתָם מִן־הַמִּצְפָּה הֹלֵךְ הָלֹךְ וּבֹכֶה וַיְהִי כִּפְגֹשׁ אֹתָם וַיֹּאמֶר אֲלֵיהֶם בֹּאוּ אֶל־ 7 גְּדַלְיָהוּ בֶּן־אֲחִיקָם: וַיְהִי כְּבוֹאָם אֶל־תּוֹךְ הָעִיר וַיִּשְׁחָטֵם יִשְׁמָעֵאל בֶּן־נְתַנְיָה אֶל־תּוֹךְ הַבּוֹר הוּא וְהָאֲנָשִׁים 8 אֲשֶׁר־אִתּוֹ: וַעֲשָׂרָה אֲנָשִׁים נִמְצְאוּ־בָם וַיֹּאמְרוּ אֶל־ יִשְׁמָעֵאל אַל־תְּמִתֵנוּ כִּי־ יֶשׁ־לָנוּ מַטְמֹנִים בַּשָּׂדֶה חִטִּים וּשְׂעֹרִים וְשֶׁמֶן וּדְבָשׁ וַיֶּחְדַּל וְלֹא הֱמִיתָם בְּתוֹךְ אֲחֵיהֶם: 9 וְהַבּוֹר אֲשֶׁר הִשְׁלִיךְ שָׁם יִשְׁמָעֵאל אֵת | כָּל־פִּגְרֵי הָאֲנָשִׁים אֲשֶׁר הִכָּה בְּיַד־ גְּדַלְיָהוּ הוּא אֲשֶׁר עָשָׂה הַמֶּלֶךְ אָסָא מִפְּנֵי בַּעְשָׁא מֶלֶךְ־

---

to bring them to the house of the LORD. In its ruins (Abarbanel). The Talmud (Meg. 10a) preserves a tradition that sacrifices could be offered in the first Temple even after it was destroyed.

6. *weeping all along as he went.* To gain their sympathy he mourned with them over the destruction of the Temple. In this way he averted suspicion (Metsudath David).

7. *slew them.* His motive is not certain. It may have been to keep the assassination of Gedaliah secret as long as pos-

sible (Metsudath David). [Another explanation, suggested by verse 8, was his lust for plunder.]

8. stores hidden in the field. These were hidden in the field to keep them safe from the Chaldeans. It is also possible that these stores were not hidden, but were of the type that are usually hidden. They were still out on the field, not yet gathered. With these, they offered bribes to Ishmael (Daath Mikra).

9. that which Asa the king had made. There is no record of this elsewhere in

the same Ishmael the son of Netha-niah filled with them that were slain. 10. Then Ishmael carried away captive all the residue of the people that were in Mizpah, even the king's daughters, and all the people that remained in Mizpah, whom Nebuzaradan the captain of the guard had committed to Gedaliah the son of Ahikam; Ishmael the son of Nethaniah carried them away captive, and departed to go over to the children of Ammon.

11. But when Johanan the son of Kareah, and all the captains of the forces that were with him, heard of all the evil that Ishmael the son of Nethaniah had done, 12. then they took all the men, and went to fight with Ishmael the son of Nethaniah, and found him by the great waters that are in Gibeon. 13. Now it came to pass, that when all the people that were with Ishmael saw Johanan the son of Kareah, and all

יִשְׂרָאֵל אֹתוֹ מִלֵּא יִשְׁמָעֵאל
10 בֶּן־נְתַנְיָהוּ חֲלָלִים: וַיִּשְׁבְּ ׀
יִשְׁמָעֵאל אֶת־כָּל־שְׁאֵרִית
הָעָם אֲשֶׁר בַּמִּצְפָּה אֶת־בְּנוֹת
הַמֶּלֶךְ וְאֶת־כָּל־הָעָם
הַנִּשְׁאָרִים בַּמִּצְפָּה אֲשֶׁר
הִפְקִיד נְבוּזַרְאֲדָן רַב־
טַבָּחִים אֶת־גְּדַלְיָהוּ בֶּן־
אֲחִיקָם וַיִּשְׁבֵּם יִשְׁמָעֵאל
בֶּן־נְתַנְיָה וַיֵּלֶךְ לַעֲבֹר אֶל־
11 בְּנֵי עַמּוֹן: וַיִּשְׁמַע יוֹחָנָן בֶּן־
קָרֵחַ וְכָל־שָׂרֵי הַחֲיָלִים אֲשֶׁר
אִתּוֹ אֵת כָּל־הָרָעָה אֲשֶׁר
עָשָׂה יִשְׁמָעֵאל בֶּן־נְתַנְיָה:
12 וַיִּקְחוּ אֶת־כָּל־הָאֲנָשִׁים
וַיֵּלְכוּ לְהִלָּחֵם עִם־יִשְׁמָעֵאל
בֶּן־נְתַנְיָה וַיִּמְצְאוּ אֹתוֹ אֶל־
13 מַיִם רַבִּים אֲשֶׁר בְּגִבְעוֹן: וַיְהִי
כִּרְאוֹת כָּל־הָעָם אֲשֶׁר אֶת־
יִשְׁמָעֵאל אֶת־יוֹחָנָן בֶּן־קָרֵחַ

the Bible; but commentators refer to 1 Kings xv. 22 and 2 Chron. xvi. 6. Possibly it was a kind of protective moat (Metsudath David).

10. *carried away captive.* [It seems impossible that he did all this with only ten men. He must have had a far larger band, but took only ten with him when he went to see Gedaliah in order not to arouse his suspicions.]

in Mizpah. Including Jeremiah presumably (cf. xl. 6).

the king's daughters. It is not known whether they were the daughters of Zedekiah, Jehoiakim, or Jehoiachin (Kimchi).

11–18 JOHANAN RESCUES THE CAPTIVES

12. *Gibeon.* See on xxviii. 1; it was about a mile north of Mizpah. The *great*

the captains of the forces that were
with him, then they were glad.
14. So all the people that Ishmael
had carried away captive from
Mizpah cast about and returned,
and went unto Johanan the son of
Kareah. 15. But Ishmael the son
of Nethaniah escaped from Johanan
with eight men, and went to the
children of Ammon.

16. Then took Johanan the son of
Kareah, and all the captains of the
forces that were with him, all the
remnant of the people whom he had
recovered from Ishmael the son of
Nethaniah, from Mizpah, after that
he had slain Gedaliah the son of
Ahikam, the men, even the men of
war, and the women, and the
children, and the officers, whom he
had brought back from Gibeon;
17. and they departed, and dwelt in
Geruth Chimham, which is by
Beth-lehem, to go to enter into
Egypt, 18. because of the Chaldeans;

וְאֵת כָּל־שָׂרֵי הַחֲיָלִים אֲשֶׁר

14 אִתּוֹ וַיִּשְׂמָחוּ: וַיָּסֹבּוּ כָּל־
הָעָם אֲשֶׁר־שָׁבָה יִשְׁמָעֵאל
מִן־הַמִּצְפָּה וַיָּשֻׁבוּ וַיֵּלְכוּ
אֶל־יוֹחָנָן בֶּן־קָרֵחַ:

15 וְיִשְׁמָעֵאל בֶּן־נְתַנְיָה נִמְלַט
בִּשְׁמֹנָה אֲנָשִׁים מִפְּנֵי יוֹחָנָן

16 וַיֵּלֶךְ אֶל־בְּנֵי עַמּוֹן: וַיִּקַּח
יוֹחָנָן בֶּן־קָרֵחַ וְכָל־שָׂרֵי
הַחֲיָלִים אֲשֶׁר־אִתּוֹ אֵת כָּל־
שְׁאֵרִית הָעָם אֲשֶׁר הֵשִׁיב מֵאֵת
יִשְׁמָעֵאל בֶּן־נְתַנְיָה מִן־
הַמִּצְפָּה אַחַר הִכָּה אֶת־
גְּדַלְיָה בֶּן־אֲחִיקָם גְּבָרִים
אַנְשֵׁי הַמִּלְחָמָה וְנָשִׁים וְטַף
וְסָרִסִים אֲשֶׁר הֵשִׁיב מִגִּבְעוֹן:

17 וַיֵּלְכוּ וַיֵּשְׁבוּ בְּגֵרוּת כמותם
אֲשֶׁר־אֵצֶל בֵּית לָחֶם לָלֶכֶת

18 לָבוֹא מִצְרָיִם: מִפְּנֵי

v. 17. כמהם ק׳

waters are perhaps identical with the *pool*
mentioned in 2 Sam. ii. 13 (Daath
Mikra).

14. *cast about.* [i.e. turned round.
While Ishmael's force had been large
enough to take this people captive (see
on verse 10), it was not sufficiently
strong to hold them when deliverance
was near.]

15. *to the children of Ammon.* Cf. xl. 14.

16. *from Mizpah.* i.e. these persons

had been in Mizpah before Ishmael
carried them away (Metsudath David).

17. *Geruth Chimham.* lit. 'the lodging-
place of Chimham.' He was the son of
Barzillai the Gileadite, and it is possible
that David made a grant of land to
Chimham in consideration of services
rendered by his father (cf. 2 Sam. xvii.
27ff., xix. 38ff.) (Targum, Metsudath
David).

273

for they were afraid of them, because
Ishmael the son of Nethaniah had
slain Gedaliah the son of Ahikam,
whom the king of Babylon made
governor over the land.

הַכַּשְׂדִּים כִּי יָרְאוּ מִפְּנֵיהֶם
כִּי־הִכָּה יִשְׁמָעֵאל בֶּן־נְתַנְיָה
אֶת־גְּדַלְיָהוּ בֶּן־אֲחִיקָם
אֲשֶׁר־הִפְקִיד מֶלֶךְ־בָּבֶל
בָּאָרֶץ׃

---

42   CHAPTER XLII   מב

1. Then all the captains of the forces,
and Johanan the son of Kareah, and
Jezaniah the son of Hoshaiah, and
all the people from the least even
unto the greatest, came near, 2. and
said unto Jeremiah the prophet:
'Let, we pray thee, our supplication
be accepted before thee, and pray
for us unto the LORD thy God, even
for all this remnant; for we are left
but a few of many, as thine eyes do
behold us; 3. that the LORD thy
God may tell us the way wherein we
should walk, and the thing that we

1 וַיִּגְּשׁוּ כָּל־שָׂרֵי הַחֲיָלִים וְיוֹחָנָן
בֶּן־קָרֵחַ וִיזַנְיָה בֶּן־הוֹשַׁעְיָה
וְכָל־הָעָם מִקָּטֹן וְעַד־גָּדוֹל׃
2 וַיֹּאמְרוּ אֶל־יִרְמְיָהוּ הַנָּבִיא
תִּפָּל־נָא תְחִנָּתֵנוּ לְפָנֶיךָ
וְהִתְפַּלֵּל בַּעֲדֵנוּ אֶל־יְהוָה
אֱלֹהֶיךָ בְּעַד כָּל־הַשְּׁאֵרִית
הַזֹּאת כִּי־נִשְׁאַרְנוּ מְעַט
מֵהַרְבֵּה כַּאֲשֶׁר עֵינֶיךָ רֹאוֹת
3 אֹתָנוּ׃ וְיַגֶּד־לָנוּ יְהוָה אֱלֹהֶיךָ
אֶת־הַדֶּרֶךְ אֲשֶׁר נֵלֶךְ־בָּהּ

CHAPTER XLII

IN xlii. 1-xliii. 7 we read that Jeremiah
is consulted by his brethren in Judea
about migration to Egypt. In spite of his
emphatic advice, given in God's name,
against the proposal, the people
migrate taking the prophet and Baruch
with them.

1-6 JEREMIAH ASKED TO SEEK GUIDANCE
FROM GOD

1. *Jezaniah the son of Hoshaiah.* Perhaps
the same Jezaniah mentioned in xl. 8,

but there called by his family name or
placename (Daath Mikra). It is also
possible that he was the brother of
Azariah the son of Hoshaiah mentioned
in xliii 2. (Daath Soferim).

2. *let . . . our supplication be accepted.*
For the idiom, see on xxxvi. 7.

3. *may tell us the way.* As often happens, their desire was not really for
guidance, but for Divine confirmation
of a decision which they had already
made, viz. to emigrate to Egypt. In his
reply, Jeremiah showed that he under-

274

should do.' 4. Then Jeremiah the
prophet said unto them: 'I have
heard you; behold, I will pray unto
the LORD your God according to
your words; and it shall come to
pass, that whatsoever thing the LORD
shall answer you, I will declare it
unto you; I will keep nothing back
from you.' 5. Then they said to
Jeremiah: 'The LORD be a true and
faithful witness against us, if we do
not even according to all the word
wherewith the LORD thy God shall
send thee to us. 6. Whether it be
good, or whether it be evil, we will
hearken to the voice of the LORD our
God, to whom we send thee; that it
may be well with us, when we
hearken to the voice of the LORD
our God.'

7. And it came to pass after ten
days, that the word of the LORD

וְאֶת־הַדָּבָר אֲשֶׁר נַעֲשֶׂה:

4 וַיֹּאמֶר אֲלֵיהֶם יִרְמְיָהוּ הַנָּבִיא
שָׁמַעְתִּי הִנְנִי מִתְפַּלֵּל אֶל־
יְהֹוָה אֱלֹהֵיכֶם כְּדִבְרֵיכֶם
וְהָיָה כָּל־הַדָּבָר אֲשֶׁר־יַעֲנֶה
יְהֹוָה אֶתְכֶם אַגִּיד לָכֶם לֹא־

5 אֶמְנַע מִכֶּם דָּבָר: וְהֵמָּה
אָמְרוּ אֶל־יִרְמְיָהוּ יְהִי יְהֹוָה
בָּנוּ לְעֵד אֱמֶת וְנֶאֱמָן אִם־לֹא
כְּכָל־הַדָּבָר אֲשֶׁר יִשְׁלָחֲךָ
יְהֹוָה אֱלֹהֶיךָ אֵלֵינוּ כֵּן נַעֲשֶׂה:

6 אִם־טוֹב וְאִם־רָע בְּקוֹל |
יְהֹוָה אֱלֹהֵינוּ אֲשֶׁר אֲנוּ שֹׁלְחִים
אֹתְךָ אֵלָיו נִשְׁמָע לְמַעַן אֲשֶׁר
יִיטַב־לָנוּ כִּי נִשְׁמַע בְּקוֹל

7 יְהֹוָה אֱלֹהֵינוּ: וַיְהִי מִקֵּץ
עֲשֶׂרֶת יָמִים וַיְהִי דְבַר־יְהֹוָה

v. 6. אנחנו ק׳

stood that this was the true position (cf.
xlii. 17).

4. *I have heard you.* i.e. I will do as you
wish (Metsudath David).

5. *against us.* May God punish us if we
act contrary to His will (Metsudath
David).

7-22 GOD WARNS AGAINST FLIGHT TO EGYPT

7. *after ten days.* Since they had asked
him to pray to God on their behalf
(Metsudath David). Abarbanel considers this very unusual for the Bible to
tell us how many days it took for the
prophet to receive a reply from God to

his request. We do not find it elsewhere
in Scripture. He, therefore, conjectures
that the intention is different. As stated
above, the assassination of Gedaliah
transpired on Rosh Hashanah, the first
of Tishri, or, as he asserts, on the
second day of Tishri. Immediately,
Johanan the son of Kareah pursued
Ishmael and rescued the captives. Then
they appealed to Jeremiah to pray to
God for His word whether they should
flee to Egypt to avoid the wrath of
Nebuchadnezzar. At the end of the
ten-day period, i.e. on Yom Kippur, the
last of the Ten Days of Penitence, God
gave him His answer. This was but one
or two days after his prayer.

came unto Jeremiah. 8. Then called he Johanan the son of Kareah, and all the captains of the forces that were with him, and all the people from the least even to the greatest, 9. and said unto them: 'Thus saith the LORD, the God of Israel, unto whom ye sent me to present your supplication before Him: 10. If ye will still abide in this land, then will I build you, and not pull you down, and I will plant you, and not pluck you up; for I repent Me of the evil that I have done unto you. 11. Be not afraid of the king of Babylon, of whom ye are afraid; be not afraid of him, saith the LORD; for I am with you to save you, and to deliver you from his hand. 12. And I will grant you compassion, that he may have compassion upon you, and cause you to return to your own land. 13. But if ye say: We will not

8 אֶל־יִרְמְיָהוּ: וַיִּקְרָא אֶל־
יוֹחָנָן בֶּן־קָרֵחַ וְאֶל כָּל־שָׂרֵי
הַחֲיָלִים אֲשֶׁר אִתּוֹ וּלְכָל־
הָעָם לְמִקָּטֹן וְעַד־גָּדוֹל:
9 וַיֹּאמֶר אֲלֵיהֶם כֹּה־אָמַר
יְהֹוָה אֱלֹהֵי יִשְׂרָאֵל אֲשֶׁר
שְׁלַחְתֶּם אֹתִי אֵלָיו לְהַפִּיל
10 תְּחִנַּתְכֶם לְפָנָיו: אִם־שׁוֹב
תֵּשְׁבוּ בָּאָרֶץ הַזֹּאת וּבָנִיתִי
אֶתְכֶם וְלֹא אֶהֱרֹס וְנָטַעְתִּי
אֶתְכֶם וְלֹא אֶתּוֹשׁ כִּי נִחַמְתִּי
אֶל־הָרָעָה אֲשֶׁר עָשִׂיתִי
11 לָכֶם: אַל־תִּירְאוּ מִפְּנֵי מֶלֶךְ
בָּבֶל אֲשֶׁר־אַתֶּם יְרֵאִים
מִפָּנָיו אַל־תִּירְאוּ מִמֶּנּוּ נְאֻם־
יְהֹוָה כִּי־אִתְּכֶם אָנִי לְהוֹשִׁיעַ
אֶתְכֶם וּלְהַצִּיל אֶתְכֶם מִיָּדוֹ:
12 וְאֶתֵּן לָכֶם רַחֲמִים וְרִחַם
אֶתְכֶם וְהֵשִׁיב אֶתְכֶם אֶל־
13 אַדְמַתְכֶם: וְאִם־אֹמְרִים

---

that the word of the Lord. This is the 'word of the Lord,' mentioned above (xl. 1) (Isaiah da Trani).

10. *then will I build you,* etc. Cf. xxiv. 6.

for I repent Me. An anthropomorphism: God's conduct towards the people would now be reversed, which in human eyes indicates regret over the past. In fact, however, there is no mental change in God; still less is there regret. Divine punishment is remedial, not vindictive; and now that suffering may have been supposed to convince

the people of the error of their ways, destruction could give way to reconstruction (Daath Soferim).

11. *of whom ye are afraid.* They feared the vengeance of Nebuchadnezzar for Gedaliah's murder (cf. xli. 18) (Metsudath David, Malbim).

12. *I will grant you compassion.* [By withholding the Babylonian king from violent action against you.]

and cause you to return. i.e. those of you (the word referring to the nation as a whole) who have been exiled (Kimchi).

abide in this land; so that ye hearken
not to the voice of the LORD your
God; 14. saying: No; but we will go
into the land of Egypt, where we
shall see no war, nor hear the sound
of the horn, nor have hunger of
bread; and there will we abide;
15. now therefore hear ye the word
of the LORD, O remnant of Judah:
Thus saith the LORD of hosts, the
God of Israel: If ye wholly set your
faces to enter into Egypt, and go to
sojourn there; 16. then it shall come
to pass, that the sword, which ye
fear, shall overtake you there in the
land of Egypt, and the famine,
whereof ye are afraid, shall follow
hard after you there in Egypt; and
there ye shall die. 17. So shall it be
with all the men that set their faces
to go into Egypt to sojourn there;
they shall die by the sword, by the
famine, and by the pestilence; and
none of them shall remain or escape
from the evil that I will bring upon

אַתֶּם לֹא נֵשֵׁב בָּאָרֶץ הַזֹּאת
לְבִלְתִּי שְׁמֹעַ בְּקוֹל יְהֹוָה
14 אֱלֹהֵיכֶם: לֵאמֹר לֹא כִּי אֶרֶץ
מִצְרַיִם נָבוֹא אֲשֶׁר לֹא־נִרְאֶה
מִלְחָמָה וְקוֹל שׁוֹפָר לֹא נִשְׁמָע
וְלַלֶּחֶם לֹא־נִרְעָב וְשָׁם נֵשֵׁב:
15 וְעַתָּה לָכֵן שִׁמְעוּ דְבַר־יְהֹוָה
שְׁאֵרִית יְהוּדָה כֹּה־אָמַר
יְהֹוָה צְבָאוֹת אֱלֹהֵי יִשְׂרָאֵל
אִם־אַתֶּם שׂוֹם תְּשִׂמוּן פְּנֵיכֶם
לָבֹא מִצְרַיִם וּבָאתֶם לָגוּר
16 שָׁם: וְהָיְתָה הַחֶרֶב אֲשֶׁר אַתֶּם
יְרֵאִים מִמֶּנָּה שָׁם תַּשִּׂיג אֶתְכֶם
בְּאֶרֶץ מִצְרָיִם וְהָרָעָב אֲשֶׁר־
אַתֶּם ׀ דְּאָגִים מִמֶּנּוּ שָׁם יִדְבַּק
אַחֲרֵיכֶם מִצְרַיִם וְשָׁם תָּמֻתוּ:
17 וְיִהְיוּ כָל־הָאֲנָשִׁים אֲשֶׁר־
שָׂמוּ אֶת־פְּנֵיהֶם לָבוֹא
מִצְרַיִם לָגוּר שָׁם יָמוּתוּ בַּחֶרֶב
בָּרָעָב וּבַדָּבֶר וְלֹא־יִהְיֶה
לָהֶם שָׂרִיד וּפָלִיט מִפְּנֵי
הָרָעָה אֲשֶׁר אֲנִי מֵבִיא

14. *where we shall see no war.* All other
lands were at war with Nebuchadnezzar,
who conquered all the lands of Syria
after the destruction of the Temple.
Only in Egypt was there neither war nor
famine (Malbim).

and there we will abide. Without fear of
exile (Metsudath David).

17. *from the evil that I will bring upon
them.* [Although *I repent Me of the evil
that I have done unto you* (verse 10),
should you migrate to Egypt in defiance
of My command, you prove that you
have still not learned to obey Me, and
further punishment is necessary.]

them. 18. For thus saith the LORD
of hosts, the God of Israel: As Mine
anger and My fury hath been poured
forth upon the inhabitants of Jerusalem, so shall My fury be poured
forth upon you, when ye shall enter
into Egypt; and ye shall be an
execration, and an astonishment, and
a curse, and a reproach; and ye shall
see this place no more. 19. The
LORD hath spoken concerning you,
O remnant of Judah: Go ye not into
Egypt; know certainly that I have
forewarned you this day. 20. For
ye have dealt deceitfully against
your own souls; for ye sent me unto
the LORD your God, saying: Pray
for us unto the LORD our God; and
according unto all that the LORD our
God shall say, so declare unto us,
and we will do it; 21. and I have this
day declared it to you; but ye have
not hearkened to the voice of the
LORD your God in any thing for

18 עֲלֵיהֶם : כִּי כֹה אָמַר יְהֹוָה
צְבָאוֹת אֱלֹהֵי יִשְׂרָאֵל כַּאֲשֶׁר
נִתַּךְ אַפִּי וַחֲמָתִי עַל־יֹשְׁבֵי
יְרוּשָׁלַם כֵּן תִּתַּךְ חֲמָתִי
עֲלֵיכֶם בְּבֹאֲכֶם מִצְרָיִם
וִהְיִיתֶם לְאָלָה וּלְשַׁמָּה
וְלִקְלָלָה וּלְחֶרְפָּה וְלֹא־
תִרְאוּ עוֹד אֶת־הַמָּקוֹם הַזֶּה :
19 דִּבֶּר יְהֹוָה עֲלֵיכֶם שְׁאֵרִית
יְהוּדָה אַל־תָּבֹאוּ מִצְרָיִם
יָדֹעַ תֵּדְעוּ כִּי־הַעִידֹתִי
20 בָכֶם הַיּוֹם : כִּי הִתְעֵתֶם
בְּנַפְשׁוֹתֵיכֶם כִּי־אַתֶּם
שְׁלַחְתֶּם אֹתִי אֶל־יְהֹוָה
אֱלֹהֵיכֶם לֵאמֹר הִתְפַּלֵּל
בַּעֲדֵנוּ אֶל־יְהֹוָה אֱלֹהֵינוּ
וּכְכֹל אֲשֶׁר יֹאמַר יְהֹוָה
אֱלֹהֵינוּ כֵּן הַגֶּד־לָנוּ וְעָשִׂינוּ :
21 וָאַגִּד לָכֶם הַיּוֹם וְלֹא שְׁמַעְתֶּם
בְּקוֹל יְהֹוָה אֱלֹהֵיכֶם וּלְכֹל

v. 20. התעיתם ק׳

---

18. *and ye shall see this place no more.*
These Judeans hoped that their stay in
Egypt would be only temporary, until
Nebuchadnezzar's anger had cooled
(Daath Mikra).

19. Jeremiah has delivered God's direction, but it is evident to him that the
command to remain in Judea is not
acceptable to his hearers; so he adds his
own admonition (Malbim).

20. *ye have dealt deceitfully against your
own souls.* You practised self-deceit
when you asked for God's guidance,
knowing in your hearts that your course
was already decided (Daath Mikra).
Kimchi renders: 'Ye have willfully
deceived (God).'

21. *in any thing.* lit. 'and in every
thing.' You have not hearkened in this
matter, and indeed in every matter on

which He hath sent me unto you.
22. Now therefore know certainly
that ye shall die by the sword, by the
famine, and by the pestilence, in the
place whither ye desire to go to
sojourn there.'

אֲשֶׁר־שְׁלָחַנִי אֲלֵיכֶם: וְעַתָּה 22
יָדֹעַ תֵּדְעוּ כִּי בַּחֶרֶב בָּרָעָב
וּבַדֶּבֶר תָּמוּתוּ בַּמָּקוֹם אֲשֶׁר
חֲפַצְתֶּם לָבוֹא לָגוּר שָׁם:

---

43   CHAPTER XLIII   מג

1. And it came to pass, that when
Jeremiah had made an end of
speaking unto all the people all the
words of the LORD their God,
wherewith the LORD their God had
sent him to them, even all these
words, 2. then spoke Azariah the son
of Hoshaiah, and Johanan the son of
Kareah, and all the proud men,
saying unto Jeremiah: 'Thou speakest falsely; the LORD our God hath
not sent thee to say: Ye shall not go
into Egypt to sojourn there; 3. but
Baruch the son of Neriah setteth
thee on against us, to deliver us into
the hand of the Chaldeans, that they
may put us to death, and carry us

וַיְהִי כְּכַלּוֹת יִרְמְיָהוּ לְדַבֵּר 1
אֶל־כָּל־הָעָם אֶת־כָּל־־
דִּבְרֵי יְהוָה אֱלֹהֵיהֶם אֲשֶׁר
שְׁלָחוֹ יְהוָה אֱלֹהֵיהֶם אֲלֵיהֶם
אֵת כָּל־הַדְּבָרִים הָאֵלֶּה:
וַיֹּאמֶר עֲזַרְיָה בֶן־הוֹשַׁעְיָה 2
וְיוֹחָנָן בֶּן־קָרֵחַ וְכָל־־
הָאֲנָשִׁים הַזֵּדִים אֹמְרִים אֶל־
יִרְמְיָהוּ שֶׁקֶר אַתָּה מְדַבֵּר לֹא
שְׁלָחֲךָ יְהוָה אֱלֹהֵינוּ לֵאמֹר
לֹא־תָבֹאוּ מִצְרַיִם לָגוּר שָׁם:
כִּי בָרוּךְ בֶּן־נֵרִיָּה מַסִּית אֹתְךָ 3
בָּנוּ לְמַעַן תֵּת אֹתָנוּ בְיַד־
הַכַּשְׂדִּים לְהָמִית אֹתָנוּ

---

which God has sent me to you (Metsudath David).

CHAPTER XLIII

1–7   FLIGHT TO EGYPT IN DEFIANCE
OF GOD

2. *Azariah.* See on xlii. 1.

proud men. Better, 'presumptuous
men,' who were determined to act con-

trary to the direction given by Jeremiah
(Daath Mikra).

3. *but Baruch,* etc. [Since Jeremiah was
by now an old man, they accused him of
having fallen under Baruch's influence
and expressing his views as a message of
God. To this charge Jeremiah does not
deign to make reply. He appreciates
that the leaders are determined on their
course of action and remonstration is
useless.]

away captives to Babylon.' 4. So Johanan the son of Kareah, and all the captains of the forces, and all the people, hearkened not to the voice of the LORD, to dwell in the land of Judah. 5. But Johanan the son of Kareah, and all the captains of the forces, took all the remnant of Judah, that were returned from all the nations whither they had been driven to sojourn in the land of Judah: 6. the men, and the women, and the children, and the king's daughters, and every person that Nebuzaradan the captain of the guard had left with Gedaliah the son of Ahikam, the son of Shaphan, and Jeremiah the prophet, and Baruch the son of Neriah; 7. and they came into the land of Egypt; for they hearkened not to the voice of the LORD; and they came even to Tahpanhes.

8. Then came the word of the LORD unto Jeremiah in Tahpanhes, saying: 9. 'Take great stones in thy

4 וּלְהַגְלוֹת אֹתָנוּ בָּבֶל: וְלֹא־
שָׁמַע יוֹחָנָן בֶּן־קָרֵחַ וְכָל־
שָׂרֵי הַחֲיָלִים וְכָל־הָעָם
בְּקוֹל יְהֹוָה לָשֶׁבֶת בְּאֶרֶץ
5 יְהוּדָה: וַיִּקַּח יוֹחָנָן בֶּן־קָרֵחַ
וְכָל־שָׂרֵי הַחֲיָלִים אֵת כָּל־
שְׁאֵרִית יְהוּדָה אֲשֶׁר־שָׁבוּ
מִכָּל־הַגּוֹיִם אֲשֶׁר נִדְּחוּ־שָׁם
6 לָגוּר בְּאֶרֶץ יְהוּדָה: אֶת־
הַגְּבָרִים וְאֶת־הַנָּשִׁים וְאֶת־
הַטַּף וְאֶת־בְּנוֹת הַמֶּלֶךְ וְאֵת
כָּל־הַנֶּפֶשׁ אֲשֶׁר הִנִּיחַ
נְבוּזַרְאֲדָן רַב־טַבָּחִים אֶת־
גְּדַלְיָהוּ בֶּן־אֲחִיקָם בֶּן־שָׁפָן
וְאֵת יִרְמְיָהוּ הַנָּבִיא וְאֶת־
7 בָּרוּךְ בֶּן־נֵרִיָּהוּ: וַיָּבֹאוּ אֶרֶץ
מִצְרַיִם כִּי לֹא שָׁמְעוּ בְּקוֹל
יְהֹוָה וַיָּבֹאוּ עַד־תַּחְפַּנְחֵס:
8 וַיְהִי דְבַר־יְהֹוָה אֶל־יִרְמְיָהוּ
9 בְּתַחְפַּנְחֵס לֵאמֹר: קַח בְּיָדְךָ

---

5. *that were returned ... the land of Judah.* Nearly two months had elapsed between the fall of Jerusalem and the assassination of Gedaliah. It is known that both before the Babylonian invasion and after its success, many Judeans had escaped from the doomed city and taken refuge in the surrounding countries of Ammon, Moab and Edom (cf. xl. 11f.). They returned during the two months, and to them the present verse refers. The Hebrew for *they had been driven* does not necessarily imply

compulsory deportation and may well mean voluntary flight.

6. *the king's daughters.* See on xli. 10.

Jeremiah ... Baruch. They were probably forced to join in the migration (Metsudath David), although it is not impossible that they felt it their duty to accompany their brethren to Egypt and be of service to them there (Daath Mikra).

7. *Tahpanhes.* On the Egyptian frontier; see on ii. 16.

hand, and hide them in the mortar
in the framework, which is at the
entry of Pharaoh's house in Tahpanhes, in the sight of the men of
Judah; 10. and say unto them:
Thus saith the LORD of hosts, the
God of Israel: Behold, I will send
and take Nebuchadrezzar the king
of Babylon, My servant, and will set
his throne upon these stones that
I have hid; and he shall spread his
royal pavilion over them. 11. And
he shall come, and shall smite the
land of Egypt; such as are for death
to death, and such as are for
captivity to captivity, and such as
are for the sword to the sword.
12. And I will kindle a fire in the
houses of the gods of Egypt; and
he shall burn them, and carry them

אֲבָנִים גְּדֹלוֹת וּטְמַנְתָּם בַּמֶּ֫לֶט
בַּמַּלְבֵּן אֲשֶׁר בְּפֶ֫תַח בֵּית־־
פַּרְעֹה בְּתַחְפַּנְחֵס לְעֵינֵי
אֲנָשִׁים יְהוּדִים: וְאָמַרְתָּ 10
אֲלֵיהֶם כֹּה־אָמַר יְהֹוָה
צְבָאוֹת אֱלֹהֵי יִשְׂרָאֵל הִנְנִי
שֹׁלֵחַ וְלָקַחְתִּי אֶת־־
נְבוּכַדְרֶאצַּר מֶֽלֶךְ־בָּבֶל
עַבְדִּי וְשַׂמְתִּי כִסְאוֹ מִמַּ֫עַל
לָאֲבָנִים הָאֵלֶּה אֲשֶׁר טָמָ֑נְתִּי
וְנָטָה אֶת־שַׁפְרִירוֹ עֲלֵיהֶם:
וּבָאה וְהִכָּה אֶת־אֶ֫רֶץ 11
מִצְרָיִם אֲשֶׁר לַמָּ֫וֶת לַמָּ֫וֶת
וַאֲשֶׁר לַשְּׁבִי לַשֶּׁ֫בִי וַאֲשֶׁר
לַחֶ֫רֶב לֶחָ֑רֶב: וְהִצַּתִּי אֵשׁ 12
בְּבָתֵּי אֱלֹהֵי מִצְרַיִם וּשְׂרָפָם

v. 10. שפרירו ק׳ v. 11. ובא ק׳

8–13 NEBUCHADNEZZAR'S CONQUEST OF EGYPT FORETOLD

9. *in the mortar in the framework.* The Egyptologist, Flinders Petrie, who carried out excavations at Tahpanhes, renders the Hebrew *malben* by 'pavement.' His account reads, 'When I came to clear the fort at Dafneh, there proved to be but one entry into Pharaoh's house; and in front of that was a wide paved area on the north of the fort. It was a place probably for the external guard, and for stacking goods, unloading camels, and such purposes of outdoor life in Egypt... This platform was a place exactly corresponding to Jeremiah's detailed account, and the identification of it is certain.'

10. *My servant.* See on xxv. 9.

will set his throne. When conducting a campaign against Egypt.

royal pavilion. The strange Hebrew noun does not occur elsewhere. It is apparently derived from a root found in Assyrian meaning, 'to spread out,' and some commentators have suggested 'carpet,' but A.J. is preferable, following Rashi. Targum renders: his palace.

12. *I will kindle.* The fire will be kindled by Nebuchadnezzar acting as God's agent (Daath Soferim).

burn them. i.e. the images of wood (Metsudath David).

carry them away captives. The gods of silver and gold, which are not

away captives; and he shall fold up
the land of Egypt, as a shepherd
foldeth up his garment; and he shall
go forth from thence in peace.
13. He shall also break the pillars of
Beth-shemesh, that is in the land of
Egypt; and the houses of the gods
of Egypt shall he burn with fire.'

וְשָׁבֵם וְעָטָה אֶת־אֶרֶץ
מִצְרַיִם כַּאֲשֶׁר־יַעֲטֶה הָרֹעֶה
אֶת־בִּגְדוֹ וְיָצָא מִשָּׁם בְּשָׁלוֹם:
וְשִׁבַּר אֶת־מַצְּבוֹת בֵּית שֶׁמֶשׁ 13
אֲשֶׁר בְּאֶרֶץ מִצְרָיִם וְאֶת־
בָּתֵּי אֱלֹהֵי מִצְרַיִם יִשְׂרֹף
בָּאֵשׁ:

---

44   CHAPTER XLIV   מד

1. The word that came to Jeremiah
concerning all the Jews that dwelt
in the land of Egypt, that dwelt at

הַדָּבָר אֲשֶׁר־הָיָה אֶל־ 1
יִרְמְיָהוּ אֶל כָּל־הַיְּהוּדִים
הַיֹּשְׁבִים בְּאֶרֶץ מִצְרָיִם

---

destroyed, will form part of the
triumphal procession of the conqueror.
This was a common practice in ancient
times (Metsudath David, Daath Mikra).

he shall fold up the land of Egypt. The
figure is of something being rolled up
and taken away. Nebuchadnezzar will
carry Egypt away (i.e. the spoil of Egypt)
as easily as a shepherd folds his garment
and walks off (Rashi, Kimchi).

in peace. He will carry away his spoil
unhindered (Metsudath David).

13. *Beth-shemesh.* lit. 'house of the
sun.' The Rabbis identify this city as
Heliopolis (the city of the sun) or On.
See on Isaiah xix. 18. This was one of
the cities peopled by Sennacherib's
captives from Egypt and Ethiopia who
embraced Judaism after Sennacherib's
downfall (Rashi). In later times, it
became an idolatrous city, the site of the
temple of Ra, the sun god, which had in

front of it an avenue of obelisks.
Nebuchadnezzar would destroy this
temple with its obelisks (Daath Soferim,
Daath Mikra).

CHAPTER XLIV

JEREMIAH DENOUNCES THE CULT OF THE
QUEEN OF HEAVEN

1–14   IDOLATRY BY EGYPTIAN JEWS
CONDEMNED

1. *the word that came to Jeremiah.* It is
not necessary to assume that this
prophecy is considerably later than the
events narrated in the last chapter. The
Jews may have dispersed as soon as they
arrived in Egypt, and quickly formed
communities in the cities named in this
verse. Moreover, there were Jewish
communities in Egypt before the
present immigration. Jeremiah would
naturally take the earliest opportunity
of protesting against heathen practices
by his co-religionists before these

Migdol, and at Tahpanhes, and at Noph, and in the country of Pathros, saying: 2. 'Thus saith the LORD of hosts, the God of Israel: Ye have seen all the evil that I have brought upon Jerusalem, and upon all the cities of Judah; and, behold, this day they are a desolation, and no man dwelleth therein; 3. because of their wickedness which they have committed to provoke Me, in that they went to offer, and to serve other gods, whom they knew not, neither they, nor ye, nor your fathers. 4. Howbeit I sent unto you all My servants the prophets, sending them betimes and often, saying: Oh, do not this abominable thing that I hate. 5. But they hearkened not, nor inclined their ear to turn from their wickedness, to forbear offering unto other gods. 6. Wherefore My fury and Mine anger was poured forth, and was kindled in the cities of Judah and in the streets of Jerusalem; and they are wasted and

הַיֹּשְׁבִים בְּמִגְדֹּל וּבְתַחְפַּנְחֵס וּבְנֹף וּבְאֶרֶץ פַּתְרוֹס לֵאמֹר:

2 כֹּה־אָמַר יְהוָה צְבָאוֹת אֱלֹהֵי יִשְׂרָאֵל אַתֶּם רְאִיתֶם אֵת כָּל־הָרָעָה אֲשֶׁר הֵבֵאתִי עַל־יְרוּשָׁלַ͏ִם וְעַל כָּל־עָרֵי יְהוּדָה וְהִנָּם חָרְבָּה הַיּוֹם הַזֶּה וְאֵין בָּהֶם יוֹשֵׁב:

3 מִפְּנֵי רָעָתָם אֲשֶׁר עָשׂוּ לְהַכְעִסֵנִי לָלֶכֶת לְקַטֵּר לַעֲבֹד לֵאלֹהִים אֲחֵרִים אֲשֶׁר לֹא יְדָעוּם הֵמָּה אַתֶּם

4 וַאֲבֹתֵיכֶם: וָאֶשְׁלַח אֲלֵיכֶם אֶת־כָּל־עֲבָדַי הַנְּבִיאִים הַשְׁכֵּים וְשָׁלֹחַ לֵאמֹר אַל־נָא תַעֲשׂוּ אֵת דְּבַר־הַתֹּעֵבָה

5 הַזֹּאת אֲשֶׁר שָׂנֵאתִי: וְלֹא שָׁמְעוּ וְלֹא־הִטּוּ אֶת־אָזְנָם לָשׁוּב מֵרָעָתָם לְבִלְתִּי קַטֵּר

6 לֵאלֹהִים אֲחֵרִים: וַתִּתַּךְ חֲמָתִי וְאַפִּי וַתִּבְעַר בְּעָרֵי יְהוּדָה וּבְחֻצוֹת יְרוּשָׁלָ͏ִם

became rooted among the recent settlers, although they were not new to them (cf. vii. 18). He hoped that the tragic catastrophe which they had suffered would recall them to their senses, and he would prevail upon them to abandon the pagan rites (see Daath Soferim, Daath Mikra).

Migdol. On the north-east border of Egypt, to the east of Tahpanhes (cf. Exod. xiv. 2).

Tahpanhes . . . Noph. See on ii. 16.

Pathros. The southern part of what is now Egypt, formerly claimed by Ethiopia. It starts a few miles south of Memphis and extends to Cyrene on the first cataract.

3. *and to serve.* Omit *and* which is not in the text.

4. Cf. vii. 25, xxv. 4.

6. *My fury and Mine anger was poured forth.* Cf. vii. 20, xlii. 18.

desolate, as at this day. 7. Therefore now thus saith the LORD, the
God of hosts, the God of Israel:
Wherefore commit ye this great evil
against your own souls, to cut off
from you man and woman, infant
and suckling, out of the midst of
Judah, to leave you none remaining;
8. in that ye provoke Me with the
works of your hands, offering unto
other gods in the land of Egypt,
whither ye are gone to sojourn; that
ye may be cut off, and that ye may
be a curse and a reproach among all
the nations of the earth? 9. Have
ye forgotten the wicked deeds of
your fathers, and the wicked deeds
of the kings of Judah, and the
wicked deeds of their wives, and
your own wicked deeds, and the
wicked deeds of your wives, which
they committed in the land of
Judah, and in the streets of Jerusalem? 10. They are not humbled
even unto this day, neither have
they feared, nor walked in My law,
nor in My statutes, that I set before
you and before your fathers. 11.
Therefore thus saith the LORD of

וַתִּהְיֶ֫ינָה לְחָרְבָּה לִשְׁמָמָה
7 כַּיּוֹם הַזֶּה: וְעַתָּה כֹּה־אָמַר
יְהֹוָה אֱלֹהֵי צְבָאוֹת אֱלֹהֵי
יִשְׂרָאֵל לָמָה אַתֶּם עֹשִׂים רָעָה
גְדוֹלָה אֶל־־נַפְשֹׁתֵכֶם
לְהַכְרִית לָכֶם אִישׁ־וְאִשָּׁה
עוֹלֵל וְיוֹנֵק מִתּוֹךְ יְהוּדָה
לְבִלְתִּי הוֹתִיר לָכֶם שְׁאֵרִית:
8 לְהַכְעִסֵ֫נִי בְּמַעֲשֵׂי יְדֵיכֶם
לְקַטֵּר לֵאלֹהִים אֲחֵרִים
בְּאֶרֶץ מִצְרַיִם אֲשֶׁר־אַתֶּם
בָּאִים לָגוּר שָׁם לְמַעַן הַכְרִית
לָכֶם וּלְמַעַן הֱיוֹתְכֶם לִקְלָלָה
וּלְחֶרְפָּה בְּכֹל גּוֹיֵי הָאָרֶץ:
9 הַשְׁכַחְתֶּם אֶת־רָעוֹת
אֲבוֹתֵיכֶם וְאֶת־רָעוֹת |
מַלְכֵי יְהוּדָה וְאֵת רָעוֹת נָשָׁיו
וְאֵת רָעֹתֵיכֶם וְאֵת רָעֹת
נְשֵׁיכֶם אֲשֶׁר עָשׂוּ בְּאֶרֶץ
10 יְהוּדָה וּבְחֻצוֹת יְרוּשָׁלָ֫ם: לֹא
דֻכְּאוּ עַד הַיּוֹם הַזֶּה וְלֹא יָרֵאוּ
וְלֹא־הָלְכוּ בְתוֹרָתִי וּבְחֻקֹּתַי
אֲשֶׁר־נָתַתִּי לִפְנֵיכֶם וְלִפְנֵי
11 אֲבוֹתֵיכֶם: לָכֵן כֹּה־אָמַר

---

7. *against your own souls.* i.e. against
yourselves, incurring severe penalties
(Metsudath David).

9. *wives.* Who instigated them to idol-
worship (cf. verse 15).

10. *they are not humbled.* The second
person is changed to the third for the
purpose of including the past generations (Kimchi).

hosts, the God of Israel: Behold, I will set My face against you for evil, even to cut off all Judah. 12. And I will take the remnant of Judah, that have set their faces to go into the land of Egypt to sojourn there, and they shall all be consumed; in the land of Egypt shall they fall; they shall be consumed by the sword and by the famine; they shall die, from the least even unto the greatest, by the sword and by the famine; and they shall be an execration, and an astonishment, and a curse, and a reproach. 13. For I will punish them that dwell in the land of Egypt, as I have punished Jerusalem, by the sword, by the famine, and by the pestilence; 14. so that none of the remnant of Judah, that are gone into the land of Egypt to sojourn there, shall escape or remain, that they should return into the land of Judah, to which they have a desire to return to dwell there; for none shall return save such as shall escape.'

15. Then all the men who knew

יְהֹוָה צְבָאוֹת אֱלֹהֵי יִשְׂרָאֵל
הִנְנִי שָׂם פָּנַי בָּכֶם לְרָעָה
וּלְהַכְרִית אֶת־כָּל־יְהוּדָה:
12 וְלָקַחְתִּי אֶת־שְׁאֵרִית יְהוּדָה
אֲשֶׁר־שָׂמוּ פְנֵיהֶם לָבוֹא
אֶרֶץ־מִצְרַיִם לָגוּר שָׁם וְתַמּוּ
כֹל בְּאֶרֶץ מִצְרַיִם יִפֹּלוּ
בַּחֶרֶב בָּרָעָב יִתַּמּוּ מִקָּטֹן
וְעַד־גָּדוֹל בַּחֶרֶב וּבָרָעָב
יָמֻתוּ וְהָיוּ לְאָלָה לְשַׁמָּה
13 וְלִקְלָלָה וּלְחֶרְפָּה: וּפָקַדְתִּי
עַל־הַיּוֹשְׁבִים בְּאֶרֶץ מִצְרַיִם
כַּאֲשֶׁר פָּקַדְתִּי עַל־יְרוּשָׁלִָם
14 בַּחֶרֶב בָּרָעָב וּבַדָּבֶר: וְלֹא
יִהְיֶה פָּלִיט וְשָׂרִיד לִשְׁאֵרִית
יְהוּדָה הַבָּאִים לָגוּר־שָׁם
בְּאֶרֶץ מִצְרַיִם וְלָשׁוּב ׀ אֶרֶץ
יְהוּדָה אֲשֶׁר־הֵמָּה מְנַשְּׂאִים
אֶת־נַפְשָׁם לָשׁוּב לָשֶׁבֶת שָׁם
כִּי לֹא־יָשׁוּבוּ כִּי אִם־
15 פְּלֵטִים: וַיַּעֲנוּ אֶת־יִרְמְיָהוּ
כָל־הָאֲנָשִׁים הַיֹּדְעִים כִּי־

11. *I will set My face.* Cf. xxi. 10.

all Judah. i.e. the Judeans who had come to Egypt with the exception of those mentioned in verses 14 and 28 (Ibn Nachmiash).

12. Cf. xlii. 18.

14. *save such as shall escape.* [It is significant that even while making so sweeping a prophecy of complete annihilation, the prophet still assumes that some would escape and return, since the connection of the Jews with the Land of Israel could never be finally severed.]

that their wives offered unto other
gods, and all the women that stood
by, a great assembly, even all the
people that dwelt in the land of
Egypt, in Pathros, answered Jeremiah, saying: 16. 'As for the word
that thou hast spoken unto us in the
name of the LORD, we will not
hearken unto thee. 17. But we
will certainly perform every word
that is gone forth out of our mouth,
to offer unto the queen of heaven,
and to pour out drink-offerings unto
her, as we have done, we and our
fathers, our kings and our princes,
in the cities of Judah, and in the
streets of Jerusalem; for then had
we plenty of food, and were well,
and saw no evil. 18. But since we
left off to offer to the queen of
heaven, and to pour out drink-
offerings unto her, we have wanted
all things, and have been consumed

מְקַטְּרוֹת נְשֵׁיהֶם לֵאלֹהִים
אֲחֵרִים וְכָל־הַנָּשִׁים
הָעֹמְדוֹת קָהָל גָּדוֹל וְכָל־
הָעָם הַיֹּשְׁבִים בְּאֶרֶץ־
מִצְרַיִם בְּפַתְרוֹס לֵאמֹר:
16 הַדָּבָר אֲשֶׁר־דִּבַּרְתָּ אֵלֵינוּ
בְּשֵׁם יְהוָה אֵינֶנּוּ שֹׁמְעִים
17 אֵלֶיךָ: כִּי עָשֹׂה נַעֲשֶׂה אֶת־
כָּל־הַדָּבָר ׀ אֲשֶׁר־יָצָא
מִפִּינוּ לְקַטֵּר לִמְלֶכֶת הַשָּׁמַיִם
וְהַסֵּיךְ־לָהּ נְסָכִים כַּאֲשֶׁר
עָשִׂינוּ אֲנַחְנוּ וַאֲבֹתֵינוּ מְלָכֵינוּ
וְשָׂרֵינוּ בְּעָרֵי יְהוּדָה וּבְחֻצוֹת
יְרוּשָׁלָםִ וַנִּשְׂבַּע־לֶחֶם וַנִּהְיֶה
18 טוֹבִים וְרָעָה לֹא רָאִינוּ: וּמִן־
אָז חָדַלְנוּ לְקַטֵּר לִמְלֶכֶת
הַשָּׁמַיִם וְהַסֵּךְ־לָהּ נְסָכִים
חָסַרְנוּ כֹל וּבַחֶרֶב וּבָרָעָב

v. 17. 'חסר א v. 18. 'חסר א

15. *their wives offered unto other
gods.* The cult of the queen of heaven
apparently had a special appeal to the
women; or perhaps it was confined to
them (cf. vii. 18). Although *other gods* are
mentioned in general terms, the answer
(verse 17) makes it clear that this particular cult is referred to. This may explain why prominence is given to *wives*
in verse 9.

17. *every word that is gone forth out of our
mouth.* These women had evidently
taken a vow to practise this cult (Metsudath David).

18. *since we left off.* The allusion is
doubtless to the reigns of Jehoiakim,
Jehoiachin, and Zedekiah (Abarbnel).

we have wanted all things, etc. They had
in mind the disasters which had befallen
the nation since Josiah's defeat and
death at Megiddo. This passage throws

by the sword and by the famine.
19. And is it we that offer to the
queen of heaven, and pour out
drink-offerings unto her? did we
make her cakes in her image, and
pour out drink-offerings unto her,
without our husbands?'

20. Then Jeremiah said unto all
the people, to the men, and to the
women, even to all the people that
had given him that answer, saying:
21. 'The offering that ye offered in
the cities of Judah, and in the streets
of Jerusalem, ye and your fathers,
your kings and your princes, and the
people of the land, did not the LORD
remember them, and came it not
into His mind? 22. so that the
LORD could no longer bear, because
of the evil of your doings, and
because of the abominations which
ye have committed; therefore is your
land become a desolation, and an

19 תֵּמַנּוּ: וְכִי־אֲנַחְנוּ מְקַטְּרִים
לִמְלֶכֶת הַשָּׁמַיִם וּלְהַסֵּךְ לָהּ
נְסָכִים הֲמִבַּלְעֲדֵי אֲנָשֵׁינוּ
עָשִׂינוּ לָהּ כַּוָּנִים לְהַעֲצִבָהּ
20 וְהַסֵּךְ לָהּ נְסָכִים: וַיֹּאמֶר
יִרְמְיָהוּ אֶל־כָּל־הָעָם עַל־
הַגְּבָרִים וְעַל־הַנָּשִׁים וְעַל־
כָּל־הָעָם הָעֹנִים אֹתוֹ דָּבָר
21 לֵאמֹר: הֲלוֹא אֶת־הַקִּטֵּר
אֲשֶׁר קִטַּרְתֶּם בְּעָרֵי יְהוּדָה
וּבְחֻצוֹת יְרוּשָׁלַם אַתֶּם
וַאֲבוֹתֵיכֶם מַלְכֵיכֶם וְשָׂרֵיכֶם
וְעַם הָאָרֶץ אֹתָם זָכַר יְהֹוָה
22 וַתַּעֲלֶה עַל־לִבּוֹ: וְלֹא־
יוּכַל יְהֹוָה עוֹד לָשֵׂאת מִפְּנֵי
רֹעַ מַעַלְלֵיכֶם מִפְּנֵי הַתּוֹעֵבֹת
אֲשֶׁר עֲשִׂיתֶם וַתְּהִי אַרְצְכֶם

v. 19. חסר א'   v. 19. הה' רפה

light on their mentality: far from attri-
buting their misfortunes to the judgment of God for their disloyalty to His
service, they saw in them the consequence which followed on the abandonment of the pagan cult (see
Abarbanel).

19. This verse is spoken by the women
and is their retort to Jeremiah's attack
upon them. The first question, like the
second, is governed by *without our husbands*. 'If, then,' the women reply to
Jeremiah, 'we have taken part in the
worship as the consequence of the vow

we made (see on verse 17), do not blame
us, but our husbands who approved it!'
(see vii. 18).

20-23   JEREMIAH RETORTS THAT IDOLA-
TRY IS THE CAUSE OF THEIR PLIGHT

22. *could no longer bear*. [God is long-
suffering, but there comes a time when
He must punish. That time came after
Josiah's reforms which had failed to
cleanse the nation of heathenish
influences and practices. Sin has been
accumulating during the generations
until the point was reached when retri-

astonishment, and a curse, without an inhabitant, as at this day. 23. Because ye have offered, and because ye have sinned against the LORD, and have not hearkened to the voice of the LORD, nor walked in His law, nor in His statutes, nor in His testimonies; therefore this evil is happened unto you, as at this day.'

24. Moreover Jeremiah said unto all the people, and to all the women: 'Hear the word of the LORD, all Judah that are in the land of Egypt: 25. Thus saith the LORD of hosts, the God of Israel, saying: Ye and your wives have both spoken with your mouths, and with your hands have fulfilled it, saying: We will surely perform our vows that we have vowed, to offer to the queen of heaven, and to pour out drink-offerings unto her; ye shall surely establish your vows, and surely perform your vows. 26. Therefore hear ye the word of the LORD, all Judah that dwell in the land of Egypt: Behold, I have sworn by

לְחָרְבָּה וּלְשַׁמָּה וְלִקְלָלָה
23 מֵאֵין יוֹשֵׁב כְּהַיּוֹם הַזֶּה: מִפְּנֵי
אֲשֶׁר קִטַּרְתֶּם וַאֲשֶׁר חֲטָאתֶם
לַיהֹוָה וְלֹא שְׁמַעְתֶּם בְּקוֹל
יְהֹוָה וּבְתֹרָתוֹ וּבְחֻקֹּתָיו
וּבְעֵדְוֹתָיו לֹא הֲלַכְתֶּם עַל־
כֵּן קָרָאת אֶתְכֶם הָרָעָה הַזֹּאת
24 כַּיּוֹם הַזֶּה: וַיֹּאמֶר יִרְמְיָהוּ
אֶל־כָּל־הָעָם וְאֶל כָּל־
הַנָּשִׁים שִׁמְעוּ דְּבַר־יְהֹוָה
כָּל־יְהוּדָה אֲשֶׁר בְּאֶרֶץ
25 מִצְרָיִם: כֹּה־אָמַר יְהֹוָה
צְבָאוֹת אֱלֹהֵי יִשְׂרָאֵל לֵאמֹר
אַתֶּם וּנְשֵׁיכֶם וַתְּדַבֵּרְנָה
בְּפִיכֶם וּבִידֵיכֶם מִלֵּאתֶם |
לֵאמֹר עָשֹׂה נַעֲשֶׂה אֶת־
נְדָרֵינוּ אֲשֶׁר נָדַרְנוּ לְקַטֵּר
לִמְלֶכֶת הַשָּׁמַיִם וּלְהַסֵּךְ לָהּ
נְסָכִים הָקֵים תְּקִימְנָה אֶת־
נִדְרֵיכֶם וְעָשֹׂה תַעֲשֶׂינָה אֶת־
26 נִדְרֵיכֶם: לָכֵן שִׁמְעוּ דְבַר־
יְהֹוָה כָּל־יְהוּדָה הַיֹּשְׁבִים
בְּאֶרֶץ מִצְרָיִם הִנְנִי נִשְׁבַּעְתִּי

v. 25. חסר א׳

butive action had to be taken. That punishment had not come sooner, while they were actually practising the rites, was only due to God's forbearance, and not to the protection of the queen of heaven.]

24-30 JEREMIAH CONCLUDES HIS WARNING

25. *ye shall surely establish*, etc. Spoken ironically. If you insist, then carry on with your rites! (Daath Mikra).

My great name, saith the Lord,
that My name shall no more be
named in the mouth of any man of
Judah in all the land of Egypt,
saying: As the Lord God liveth.
27. Behold, I watch over them for
evil, and not for good; and all the
men of Judah that are in the land of
Egypt shall be consumed by the
sword and by the famine, until there
be an end of them.   28. And they
that escape the sword shall return
out of the land of Egypt into the
land of Judah, few in number; and
all the remnant of Judah, that are
gone into the land of Egypt to
sojourn there, shall know whose
word shall stand, Mine, or theirs.
29. And this shall be the sign unto
you, saith the Lord, that I will
punish you in this place, that ye
may know that My words shall
surely stand against you for evil;
30. thus saith the Lord: Behold,
I will give Pharaoh Hophra king of

בִּשְׁמִי הַגָּדוֹל אָמַר יְהֹוָה אִם־
יִהְיֶה עוֹד שְׁמִי נִקְרָא | בְּפִי |
כָּל־אִישׁ יְהוּדָה אֹמֵר חַי־
אֲדֹנָי יֱהֹוִה בְּכָל־אֶרֶץ
27 מִצְרָיִם: הִנְנִי שֹׁקֵד עֲלֵיהֶם
לְרָעָה וְלֹא לְטוֹבָה וְתַמּוּ כָל־
אִישׁ יְהוּדָה אֲשֶׁר בְּאֶרֶץ
מִצְרַיִם בַּחֶרֶב וּבָרָעָב עַד־
28 כְּלוֹתָם: וּפְלִיטֵי חֶרֶב יְשֻׁבוּן
מִן־אֶרֶץ מִצְרַיִם אֶרֶץ יְהוּדָה
מְתֵי מִסְפָּר וְיָדְעוּ כָּל־
שְׁאֵרִית יְהוּדָה הַבָּאִים
לְאֶרֶץ־מִצְרַיִם לָגוּר שָׁם
דְּבַר־מִי יָקוּם מִמֶּנִּי וּמֵהֶם:
29 וְזֹאת לָכֶם הָאוֹת נְאֻם־יְהֹוָה
כִּי־פֹקֵד אֲנִי עֲלֵיכֶם בַּמָּקוֹם
הַזֶּה לְמַעַן תֵּדְעוּ כִּי קוֹם
יָקוּמוּ דְבָרַי עֲלֵיכֶם לְרָעָה:
30 כֹּה | אָמַר יְהֹוָה הִנְנִי נֹתֵן אֶת־
פַּרְעֹה חָפְרַע מֶלֶךְ־מִצְרַיִם

26. *My name shall no more be named.*
Because the men of Judah in Egypt will
perish (Metsudath David).

27. *all the men of Judah.* As the next
verse shows, this is not to be pressed too
strictly; it merely indicates widespread
destruction (Kimchi).

28. *they that escape . . . the land of
Judah.* [Nevertheless, in course of
time a flourishing Jewish community
grew in Egypt, worshippers of God and

not idolaters. This fact explains the
nonfulfilment of the prophecy which is
always conditional. By eventually abandoning the idolatrous practices they
averted their threatened fate.]

29. *the sign.* viz. when you see the
overthrow of Pharaoh Hophra you will
know that it presages your own doom
(Metsudath David, Kimchi, Abarbanel).

30. *Pharaoh Hophra.* The Greek Apries
who reigned from 589 to 570 B.C.E. 'It

Egypt into the hand of his enemies, and into the hand of them that seek his life; as I gave Zedekiah king of Judah into the hand of Nebuchadrezzar king of Babylon, his enemy, and that sought his life.'

בְּיַד אֹיְבָיו וּבְיַד מְבַקְשֵׁי נַפְשׁוֹ
כַּאֲשֶׁר נָתַתִּי אֶת־צִדְקִיָּהוּ
מֶלֶךְ־יְהוּדָה בְּיַד
נְבוּכַדְרֶאצַּר מֶלֶךְ־בָּבֶל
אֹיְבוֹ וּמְבַקֵּשׁ נַפְשׁוֹ:

45   CHAPTER XLV   מה

1. The word that Jeremiah the prophet spoke unto Baruch the son of Neriah, when he wrote these words in a book at the mouth of Jeremiah, in the fourth year of Jehoiakim the son of Josiah, king of Judah, saying: 2. 'Thus saith the LORD, the God of Israel, concerning thee, O Baruch:

3 Thou didst say:

Woe is me now!

1 הַדָּבָר אֲשֶׁר דִּבֶּר יִרְמְיָהוּ
הַנָּבִיא אֶל־בָּרוּךְ בֶּן־נֵרִיָּה
בְּכָתְבוֹ אֶת־הַדְּבָרִים הָאֵלֶּה
עַל־סֵפֶר מִפִּי יִרְמְיָהוּ בַּשָּׁנָה
הָרְבִעִית לִיהוֹיָקִים בֶּן־
יֹאשִׁיָּהוּ מֶלֶךְ יְהוּדָה לֵאמֹר:
2 כֹּה־אָמַר יְהֹוָה אֱלֹהֵי יִשְׂרָאֵל
עָלֶיךָ בָּרוּךְ:
3 אָמַרְתָּ
אוֹי־נָא לִי

may be noted that the Hebrew *Hophra* is very close to the Egyptian Haa-ab-ra which was pronounced Hoavra. The Greek form Apries is much less exact' (Petrie).

CHAPTER XLV
JEREMIAH'S ANSWER TO BARUCH'S LAMENT

THIS chapter goes back to the fourth year of the reign of Jehoiakim. It was found in Jeremiah's writings after the scroll described in chapter xxxvi. For the following reason, it was placed here after the prophecy of the fate of the Jews who fled to Egypt. As mentioned above (xliii. 3), the people suspected Jeremiah

of being influenced by Baruch in his prophecy of their doom if they should migrate to Egypt. Baruch, they claimed, wished to remain in the Holy Land in order to attain prophecy, which he could not were he to migrate to Egypt. In the following chapter, we find that Jeremiah had already revealed to Baruch that God had told him that because of the impending destruction of the Temple, he could not attain prophecy. That was already in the fourth year of Jehoiakim (Abarbanel).

1. *these words.* viz. the *roll* described in chapter xxxvi, as the date indicates (Abarbanel, Metsudath David).

For the LORD hath added sorrow
    to my pain;
I am weary with my groaning,
And I find no rest.

4. Thus shalt thou say unto him:
    Thus saith the LORD:
Behold, that which I have built
    will I break down,
And that which I have planted
    I will pluck up;
And this in the whole land.

5 And seekest thou great things for
    thyself?
    Seek them not;
for, behold, I will bring evil upon
all flesh, saith the LORD; but thy
life will I give unto thee for a prey
in all places whither thou goest.'

כִּי־יָסַף יְהוָה יָגוֹן
עַל־מַכְאֹבִי
יָגַעְתִּי בְּאַנְחָתִי
וּמְנוּחָה לֹא מָצָאתִי׃

4 כֹּה ׀ תֹּאמַר אֵלָיו
כֹּה אָמַר יְהוָה
הִנֵּה אֲשֶׁר־בָּנִיתִי אֲנִי הֹרֵס
וְאֵת אֲשֶׁר־נָטַעְתִּי אֲנִי נֹתֵשׁ
וְאֶת־כָּל־הָאָרֶץ לִי־הִיא׃

5 וְאַתָּה תְּבַקֶּשׁ־לְךָ גְדֹלוֹת
אַל־תְּבַקֵּשׁ
כִּי הִנְנִי מֵבִיא רָעָה עַל־כָּל־
בָּשָׂר נְאֻם־יְהוָה וְנָתַתִּי לְךָ
אֶת־נַפְשְׁךָ לְשָׁלָל עַל כָּל־
הַמְּקֹמוֹת אֲשֶׁר תֵּלֶךְ־שָׁם׃

v. 4. ‏במקצת ספרים לא נמצא מלת לי‎

3. hath added sorrow to my pain. For *sorrow* we should substitute 'anguish, anxiety.' Baruch was weighed down by anxiety about his own future in addition to pain at the calamities which were foretold for his people (Daath Mikra).

4. that which I have built, etc. Cf. i. 10. God is about to undo His work; what a grief it is to Him! But justice demands that it be done (Daath Mikra).

and this in the whole land. There are two readings of the text: 'even all the land which is Mine,' and 'even all the land it is.' If the former is adopted, the meaning is, 'My own land (of Israel) it is which will suffer destruction.' The alternative reading signifies: all the cities of the land (of Israel) come under this threat of destruction (Metsudath David).

5. *seekest thou great things for thyself?* In a time when God breaks down what He has built, it is unfitting that Baruch should seek personal greatness. Scripture does not record what form his aspirations took. According to Rabbinical interpretation, his complaint in verse 3 was that he had not been granted the gift of prophecy, as had the disciples of other great prophets, such as Joshua and Elisha, the disciples of Moses and Elijah respectively. He is rebuked and told that, at such a time, he must expect no personal aggrandisement, not even of the spiritual kind. He is told, 'If there is no vineyard, what is the necessity of a fence? If there is no flock, what is the necessity of a shepherd? for behold, I will bring evil upon all flesh.' Hence, prophets attain

46   CHAPTER XLVI   מו

1. The word of the LORD which came to Jeremiah the prophet concerning the nations.

2. Of Egypt: concerning the army of Pharaoh-neco king of Egypt, which was by the river Euphrates in Carchemish, which Nebuchadrezzar king of Babylon smote in the fourth year of Jehoiakim the son of Josiah, king of Judah.

3 Make ready buckler and shield,
   And draw near to battle.

4 Harness the horses, and mount,
   ye horsemen,

אֲשֶׁר הָיָה דְבַר־יְהֹוָה אֶל־ 1
יִרְמְיָהוּ הַנָּבִיא עַל־הַגּוֹיִם:
לְמִצְרַיִם עַל־חֵיל פַּרְעֹה נְכוֹ 2
מֶלֶךְ מִצְרַיִם אֲשֶׁר־הָיָה עַל־
נְהַר־פְּרָת בְּכַרְכְּמִשׁ אֲשֶׁר
הִכָּה נְבוּכַדְרֶאצַּר מֶלֶךְ בָּבֶל
בִּשְׁנַת הָרְבִיעִית לִיהוֹיָקִים
בֶּן־יֹאשִׁיָּהוּ מֶלֶךְ יְהוּדָה:
עִרְכוּ מָגֵן וְצִנָּה 3
וּגְשׁוּ לַמִּלְחָמָה:
אִסְרוּ הַסּוּסִים 4
וַעֲלוּ הַפָּרָשִׁים

---

prophecy only in the merit of Israel (Rashi and Kimchi from Mechilta).

CHAPTER XLVI

JUDGMENT UPON EGYPT

JEREMIAH felt deeply that he was the eye-witness of world-shattering events. Not only the fate of his own people was hanging in the balance, but likewise the destiny of the surrounding nations. Chapters xlvi-li. form a well-defined and separate section with which the prophecies of Jeremiah conclude (cf. li. 64). A similar series of judgments upon contemporary peoples is to be found in other prophets (cf. Isa. xiii-xxiii.; Ezek. xxv-xxxii; Amos i. 3-ii. 3).

1. *concerning the nations.* See on i. 5. This verse is the introduction to the whole section to the end of it.

2. *Pharaoh-neco.* He had defeated and slain king Josiah at Megiddo in 608

B.C.E., whose successor, Jehoahaz, he deposed after a reign of only three months, and set Jehoiakim upon the throne (2 Kings xxiii. 29-34). Extending his conquests eastwards, he clashed with Nebuchadnezzar who overthrew him at Carchemish in 605 B.C.E. This decisive victory, which ensured the widespread Babylonian supremacy over neighbouring nations, was the occasion of this oracle (Kimchi).

3. *make ready,* etc. A warning to the Egyptians to prepare for a critical contest which would decide the fate of their country. A note of irony can be detected in the words, since the prophet knew that resistance would prove useless (Metsudath David).

4. *harness the horses.* To the chariots; the same verb, lit. 'bind,' as in Exod. xiv. 6 (Metsudath David).

mount, ye horsemen. Most moderns

And stand forth with your helmets;
Furbish the spears, put on the
coats of mail.
5 Wherefore do I see them dismayed and turned backward?
And their mighty ones are beaten
down,
And they are fled apace, and look
not back;
Terror is on every side, saith the
LORD.
6 The swift cannot flee away,
Nor the mighty man escape;
In the north by the river
Euphrates
Have they stumbled and fallen.
7 Who is this like the Nile that
riseth up,
Like the rivers whose waters toss
themselves?
8 Egypt is like the Nile that riseth
up,
And like the rivers whose waters
toss themselves;
And he saith: 'I will rise up,
I will cover the earth,

וְהִתְיַצְּבוּ בְּכוֹבָעִים
מִרְקוּ הָרְמָחִים
לִבְשׁוּ הַסִּרְיֹנֹת:
5 מַדּוּעַ רָאִיתִי הֵמָּה חַתִּים
נְסֹגִים אָחוֹר
וְגִבּוֹרֵיהֶם יֻכַּתּוּ
וּמָנוֹס נָסוּ וְלֹא הִפְנוּ
מָגוֹר מִסָּבִיב נְאֻם־יְהוָה:
6 אַל־יָנוּס הַקַּל
וְאַל־יִמָּלֵט הַגִּבּוֹר
צָפוֹנָה עַל־יַד נְהַר־פְּרָת
כָּשְׁלוּ וְנָפָלוּ:
7 מִי־זֶה כַּיְאֹר יַעֲלֶה
כַּנְּהָרוֹת יִתְגָּעֲשׁוּ מֵימָיו:
8 מִצְרַיִם כַּיְאֹר יַעֲלֶה
וְכַנְּהָרוֹת יִתְגֹּעֲשׁוּ מָיִם
וַיֹּאמֶר אֶעֱלֶה אֲכַסֶּה־אֶרֶץ

prefer the translation, 'mount the steeds,' as Schoraschim, Ibn Ganah.

stand forth with your helmets. i.e. wearing your helmets, which were set upon the head only in actual battle (Kimchi).

5. wherefore do I see, etc. All the elaborate preparations are made to withstand the Babylonian army in accordance with the prophet's advice; immediately he continues with ironical surprise that the formidable host of Egypt is in precipitate flight (Daath Mikra).

terror is on every side. See on vi. 25.

6. Utter defeat overtakes them; neither swift retreat nor a brave stand is of avail.

7f. The former onward sweep of the Egyptian armies, overrunning the countries of their invasion, is likened to the irresistible overflowing of the Nile as its waters inundate the country through which it flows (cf. Isa. viii. 7f.). What a contrast to their present helplessness and dismay! (Kimchi).

8. *he saith.* Pharaoh (Targum), or Egypt personified, is the subject (Metsudath David).

I will cover the earth. With my waters,

I will destroy the city and the
inhabitants thereof.'

9 Prance, ye horses, and rush
madly, ye chariots;

And let the mighty men go forth:
Cush and Put, that handle the
shield,

And the Ludim, that handle and
bend the bow.

10 For the Lord GOD of hosts shall
have on that day

A day of vengeance, that He may
avenge Him of His adversaries;

And the sword shall devour and
be satiate,

And shall be made drunk with
their blood;

For the Lord GOD of hosts hath
a sacrifice

In the north country by the river
Euphrates.

11 Go up into Gilead, and take
balm,

O virgin daughter of Egypt;

In vain dost thou use many
medicines;

אֹבִ֫ידָה עִ֖יר וְיֹ֥שְׁבֵי בָֽהּ׃

9 עֲלוּ הַסּוּסִ֗ים
וְהִתְהֹלְל֣וּ הָרֶ֔כֶב
וְיֵצְא֖וּ הַגִּבּוֹרִ֑ים
כּ֤וּשׁ וּפוּט֙ תֹּפְ֣שֵׂי מָגֵ֔ן
וְלוּדִ֕ים תֹּפְשֵׂ֖י דֹּ֥רְכֵי קָֽשֶׁת׃

10 וְֽהַיּ֨וֹם הַה֜וּא
לַאדֹנָ֧י יֱהֹוִ֣ה צְבָא֗וֹת
י֤וֹם נְקָמָה֙ לְהִנָּקֵ֣ם מִצָּרָ֔יו
וְאָכְלָ֤ה חֶ֨רֶב֙ וְשָׂ֣בְעָ֔ה
וְרָוְתָ֖ה מִדָּמָ֑ם
כִּ֣י זֶ֠בַח לַאדֹנָ֨י יֱהֹוִ֧ה צְבָא֛וֹת
בְּאֶ֥רֶץ צָפ֖וֹן אֶל־נְהַר־פְּרָֽת׃

11 עֲלִ֤י גִלְעָד֙ וּקְחִ֣י צֳרִ֔י
בְּתוּלַ֖ת בַּת־מִצְרָ֑יִם
לַשָּׁוְא֙ הרביתי רְפֻא֔וֹת

ק׳ הרבית .v. 11

---

i.e. I will cover it with my great armies
(Metsudath David).

the city. The singular is used in a collective sense (Daath Mikra).

9. *prance, ye horses.* Better, 'advance,'
lit. 'go up.' The verse is probably the
continuation of *he saith* (verse 8). A.J.,
which ends the inverted commas in the
preceding verse, understands it as the
ironical urging of the prophet.

Cush and Put . . . and the Ludim. These
were mercenary troops who formed
part of the Egyptian forces. Cush (the
Ethiopians) and Put were descended
from Ham, one of the sons of Noah
(Gen. x. 6). The situation of Put is
uncertain. Some place it on the north

coast of Africa, west of Egypt; others
identify it with 'Punt,' a district on the
Red Sea (see Bieberfeld, Universal
Jewish History, vol. 1, p. 88). The
Ludim were also Africans (Gen. x. 13).
These three peoples are again spoken of
as mercenaries in Ezek. xxx. 5.

10. *a day of vengeance.* For the defeat
and death of Josiah at Megiddo (Kimchi).

hath a sacrifice. By God's decree a
general 'slaughter' (so the Hebrew may
be translated) will take place (Metsudath
David).

11. *Gilead.* See on viii. 22.

medicines. Egypt was noted for its

There is no cure for thee.

12 The nations have heard of thy shame,
And the earth is full of thy cry;
For the mighty man hath stumbled against the mighty,
They are fallen both of them together.

13. The word that the LORD spoke to Jeremiah the prophet, how that Nebuchadrezzar king of Babylon should come and smite the land of Egypt.

14 Declare ye in Egypt, and announce in Migdol,
And announce in Noph and in Tahpanhes;
Say ye: 'Stand forth, and prepare thee,
For the sword hath devoured round about thee.'

15 Why is thy strong one overthrown?
He stood not, because the LORD did thrust him down.

תְּעָלָה אֵין לָךְ׃

12 שָׁמְעוּ גוֹיִם קְלוֹנֵךְ
וְצִוְחָתֵךְ מָלְאָה הָאָרֶץ
כִּי־גִבּוֹר בְּגִבּוֹר כָּשָׁלוּ
יַחְדָּו נָפְלוּ שְׁנֵיהֶם׃

13 הַדָּבָר אֲשֶׁר דִּבֶּר יְהוָה
אֶל־יִרְמְיָהוּ הַנָּבִיא לָבוֹא
נְבוּכַדְרֶאצַּר מֶלֶךְ בָּבֶל
לְהַכּוֹת אֶת־אֶרֶץ מִצְרָיִם׃

14 הַגִּידוּ בְמִצְרַיִם
וְהַשְׁמִיעוּ בְמִגְדּוֹל
וְהַשְׁמִיעוּ בְנֹף וּבְתַחְפַּנְחֵס
אִמְרוּ הִתְיַצֵּב וְהָכֵן לָךְ
כִּי־אָכְלָה חֶרֶב סְבִיבֶיךָ׃

15 מַדּוּעַ נִסְחַף אַבִּירֶיךָ
לֹא עָמַד כִּי יְהוָה הֲדָפוֹ׃

v. 12. קמץ בז״ק v. 13. הפטרת בא

knowledge of medicine. Here it is figurative of the aid expected from Put, Cush, and Lud (Kimchi).

12. *thy shame.* Thy defeat, which puts thy boasted power to shame (Metsudath David).

the mighty man, etc. In the panic of their flight even their mighty warriors stumble against one another (Rashi).

13. *how that Nebuchadnezzar . . . should come,* etc. This oracle is separate from the preceding and probably dates from the time of Jeremiah's residence in Egypt (cf. xliii. 8ff.; Ezek. xxix. 17ff.) (Rashi, Kimchi).

14. *Egypt.* This is first mentioned

generally and then specific cities are enumerated (Kimchi).

Migdol. See on xliv. 1.

Noph . . . Tahpanhes. See on ii. 16.

stand forth. The Babylonians have overrun the neighbouring peoples; let Egypt prepare for the advance into its territory (Abarbanel).

15. *thy strong one.* The noun is apparently in the plural although the verb is in the singular. In that case the meaning is, 'Why are thy strong ones, every one of them, overthrown?' (Kimchi). But many Hebrew MSS. omit the second *yad* which makes the noun singular. By dividing the verb *nischaph* (overthrown)

295

16 He made many to stumble;

    Yea, they fell one upon another,

    And said: 'Arise, and let us
        return to our own people,

    And to the land of our birth,

    From the oppressing sword.'

17 They cried there: 'Pharaoh king
        of Egypt is but a noise;

    He hath let the appointed time
        pass by.'

18 As I live, saith the King,

    Whose name is the LORD of hosts,

    Surely like Tabor among the
        mountains,

    And like Carmel by the sea, so
        shall he come.

16 הִרְבָּה כּוֹשֵׁל

גַּם־נָפַל אִישׁ אֶל־רֵעֵהוּ

וַיֹּאמְרוּ קוּמָה |

וְנָשֻׁבָה אֶל־עַמֵּנוּ

וְאֶל־אֶרֶץ מוֹלַדְתֵּנוּ

מִפְּנֵי חֶרֶב הַיּוֹנָה:

17 קָרְאוּ שָׁם

פַּרְעֹה מֶלֶךְ־מִצְרַיִם שָׁאוֹן

הֶעֱבִיר הַמּוֹעֵד:

18 חַי־אָנִי נְאֻם־הַמֶּלֶךְ

יְהוָה צְבָאוֹת שְׁמוֹ

כִּי כְּתָבוֹר בֶּהָרִים

וּכְכַרְמֶל בַּיָּם יָבוֹא:

into two words, *nas chaph,* the LXX reads, 'Why is Apis fled? Thy mighty one stood not.' Apis was the sacred bull worshipped at Memphis and called Egypt's *strong one,* in the same way that God is described as *the Mighty One of Jacob* (Gen. xlix. 24). The text as rendered in A.J. might therefore be understood, 'Why is thy strong one (the god Apis upon whose protection Egypt relied) overthrown?' The defeat of a people, symbolized by that of their god, is a common idea in the Bible.

16. *they fell one upon another.* The subject may be the mercenary troops or, as some suppose, the foreigners in Egypt (Ibn Nachmiash). Either in their panic they each fell over the other as they fled, which makes this a sequel to *stumble;* or, they 'joined with each other' (cf. *thou fallest away to the Chaldeans,* xxxvii. 13, where the verb is used in that sense) *and said,* etc. (Kimchi, Metsudath David).

17. *there.* On the battlefield, if the subject is the mercenaries, or in Egypt, if it is the foreigners (Metsudath David, Ibn Nachmiash).

but a noise, Pharaoh's pomp and display of power are but an empty noise with no reality behind them (so some commentators). *But,* however, is not in the original, and it is doubtful whether *shaon* (the Hebrew for *noise*) is used in this sarcastic way. The meaning may be the reverse: 'Although Pharaoh makes such a tumult, being the king of a great army', yet *he hath let the appointed time pass by';* either in the sense that he failed to make the necessary preparation while there was time, or, in his cowardice, he refused the challenge to give battle at the time appointed by his generals. (see Kimchi, Abarbanel, Isaiah da Trani).

18. *like Tabor . . . like Carmel.* As Tabor is fast among the mountains, and as Tabor is fast upon the sea, so is it true

19 O thou daughter that dwellest in
   Egypt,
   Furnish thyself to go into cap-
   tivity;
   For Noph shall become a de-
   solation,
   And shall be laid waste, without
   inhabitant.

20 Egypt is a very fair heifer;
   But the gadfly out of the north is
   come, it is come.

21 Also her mercenaries in the
   midst of her
   Are like calves of the stall,
   For they also are turned back,
   they are fled away together,
   They did not stand;
   For the day of their calamity is
   come upon them,
   The time of their visitation.

22 The sound thereof shall go like
   the serpent's;

19 כְּלֵי גוֹלָה עֲשִׂי לָךְ
יוֹשֶׁבֶת בַּת־מִצְרָיִם
כִּי־נֹף לְשַׁמָּה תִהְיֶה
וְנִצְּתָה מֵאֵין יוֹשֵׁב:
20 עֶגְלָה יְפֵה־פִיָּה מִצְרָיִם
קֶרֶץ מִצָּפוֹן בָּא בָא:
21 גַּם־שְׂכִרֶיהָ בְקִרְבָּהּ
כְּעֶגְלֵי מַרְבֵּק
כִּי־גַם־הֵמָּה הִפְנוּ
נָסוּ יַחְדָּיו לֹא עָמָדוּ
כִּי יוֹם אֵידָם בָּא עֲלֵיהֶם
עֵת פְּקֻדָּתָם:
22 קוֹלָהּ כַּנָּחָשׁ יֵלֵךְ

that this thing will befall Egypt (Rashi).
i.e. just as Tabor is fast among the
mountains and Carmel is fast by the sea,
so that neither one will move, so is it
sure that Nebuchadnezzar will come
upon Egypt and will not change his
plans (Metsudath David). Rabbi Joseph
Kimchi explains: Just as nets are spread
on Mt. Tabor to hunt wild beasts, and
just as the trees of the forested plain are
transported by the sea, so will the Egyptians be captured and carried away by
Nebuchadnezzar.

19. *thou daughter.* Poetically used for
the population (Targum).

furnish . . . captivity. lit. 'vessels of
captivity make for thee,' i.e. provide
food and other necessities required for
the journey into captivity. The same
phrase occurs in Ezek. xii. 3 (Metsudath
David).

20. *a very fair heifer.* i.e. is comparable
to a well-nourished and finely developed animal.

21. *her mercenaries.* This follows Kara
and Kimchi. Targum and Rashi render:
her princes.

like calves of the stall. Well-fed and
vigorous; yet they proved cowardly and
useless in battle (Abarbanel, Kimchi).
Malbim emphasizes the point that they
fattened themselves at the expense of
Egypt, yet failed her in time of emergency. Metsudath David explains the
comparison to be that they are alike in
that they are destined to be slaughtered.

For they also are turned back. Although
princes are usually brave warriors, they
were not so, for they turned back and
fled together from the scene of the
battle (Metsudath David).

22. *the sound . . . like the serpent's.* The
sound of the cry of Egypt shall go like
the sound of a serpent that goes far and
is heard at a distance (Kimchi, Metsudath David). The Rabbis explain that
when God decreed upon the serpent
that he walk on his belly and his feet

For they march with an army,

And come against her with axes,

As hewers of wood.

23 They cut down her forest, saith
the LORD,

Though it cannot be searched;

Because they are more than the
locusts,

And are innumerable.

24 The daughter of Egypt is put to
shame;

She is delivered into the hand of
the people of the north.

25. The LORD of hosts, the God of
Israel, saith: Behold, I will punish
Amon of No, and Pharaoh, and
Egypt, with her gods, and her kings;

כִּי־בְחַיִל יֵלֵכוּ

וּבְקַרְדֻּמּוֹת בָּאוּ לָהּ

כְּחֹטְבֵי עֵצִים:

23 כָּרְתוּ יַעְרָהּ נְאֻם־יְהֹוָה

כִּי לֹא יֵחָקֵר

כִּי רַבּוּ מֵאַרְבֶּה

וְאֵין לָהֶם מִסְפָּר:

24 הֹבִישָׁה בַּת־מִצְרָיִם

נִתְּנָה בְּיַד עַם־צָפוֹן:

25 אָמַר יְהֹוָה צְבָאוֹת אֱלֹהֵי

יִשְׂרָאֵל הִנְנִי פוֹקֵד אֶל־אָמוֹן

מִנֹּא וְעַל־פַּרְעֹה וְעַל־

מִצְרַיִם וְעַל־אֱלֹהֶיהָ וְעַל־

---

were cut off, the serpent's cry was heard
from one end of the world to the other.
The prophet compares the cry of Egypt
to this cry (Rashi).

they march. The subject is the enemy
(Metsudath David).

with an army. Or, 'with might' (Daath
Mikra).

as hewers of wood. Like a band of wood-
cutters hewing trees in a forest, so does
the enemy cut down the dense population of Egypt. (Malbim).

23. *they cut down.* Kimchi quotes
authorities who parse the verb as the
imperative, thus rendering: 'cut down.'
Metsudath David, too, appears to
follow that interpretation.

her forest. i.e. the trees of her forest.
This may refer to the people of Egypt or
to her leaders. Jonathan follows the
latter interpretation (Kimchi).

though it cannot be searched. If *though* is

retained, the meaning is: though the
forest is so dense that it cannot be
penetrated, i.e. in spite of Egypt's
innumerable population, *it* referring to
the forest (Egypt). R.V. margin,
however, renders: 'for it cannot be
searched,' *it* then alluding to the
Chaldean army (equals *they* at the beginning of the verse); the Chaldeans cut
down the Egyptian host because their
army is so numerous that its numbers
cannot be counted (so Rashi and
Kimchi). The parallelism of the second
half of the verse is in favour of the latter
interpretation.

locusts. The Hebrew word means
'multiplier' with reference to the vast
swarms of the locusts (Kimchi, Shorashim).

25. *Amon of No.* The god Amon
worshipped in No, i.e. Thebes, now
Luxor, the ancient capital of Upper
Egypt (cf. Nahum iii. 8) (Malbim, Daath
Mikra).

even Pharaoh, and them that trust
in him; 26. and I will deliver them
into the hand of those that seek
their lives, and into the hand of
Nebuchadrezzar king of Babylon,
and into the hand of his servants;
and afterwards it shall be inhabited,
as in the days of old, saith the LORD.

27 But fear not thou, O Jacob My
servant,

Neither be dismayed, O Israel;

For, lo, I will save thee from afar,

And thy seed from the land of
their captivity;

And Jacob shall again be quiet
and at ease,

And none shall make him afraid.

28 Fear not thou, O Jacob My
servant, saith the LORD,

For I am with thee;

For I will make a full end of all
the nations whither I have
driven thee,

But I will not make a full end of
thee;

And I will correct thee in
measure,

But will not utterly destroy thee.

מַלְכֶּיהָ וְעַל־פַּרְעֹה וְעַל

26 הַבֹּטְחִים בּוֹ: וּנְתַתִּים בְּיַד

מְבַקְשֵׁי נַפְשָׁם וּבְיַד

נְבוּכַדְרֶאצַּר מֶלֶךְ־בָּבֶל

וּבְיַד־עֲבָדָיו וְאַחֲרֵי־כֵן תִּשְׁכֹּן

כִּימֵי־קֶדֶם נְאֻם־יְהוָה:

27 וְאַתָּה אַל־תִּירָא עַבְדִּי יַעֲקֹב

וְאַל־תֵּחַת יִשְׂרָאֵל

כִּי הִנְנִי מוֹשִׁעֲךָ מֵרָחוֹק

וְאֶת־זַרְעֲךָ מֵאֶרֶץ שִׁבְיָם

וְשָׁב יַעֲקֹב וְשָׁקַט וְשַׁאֲנַן

וְאֵין מַחֲרִיד:

28 אַתָּה אַל־תִּירָא

עַבְדִּי יַעֲקֹב נְאֻם־יְהוָה

כִּי אִתְּךָ אָנִי

כִּי אֶעֱשֶׂה כָלָה בְּכָל־הַגּוֹיִם ׀

אֲשֶׁר הִדַּחְתִּיךָ שָׁמָּה

וְאֹתְךָ לֹא־אֶעֱשֶׂה כָלָה

וְיִסַּרְתִּיךָ לַמִּשְׁפָּט

וְנַקֵּה לֹא אֲנַקֶּךָּ: ׃

v. 27 מלא ר' v. 28 עד כא'

them that trust in him. Egypt's satellites
(Metsudath David); or perhaps the
Judeans who trusted in Egypt against
Babylon (Daath Mikra).

26. *and afterwards it shall be inhabited.*
After destruction by Babylon, Egypt will
be restored and repopulated (cf. Ezek.
xxix. 13f.).

27f. Almost identical with xxx. 10f. As
so often happens, the prophet ends with
a message of hope, to a degree reversing
the somberness of what goes before. He
assures them that even though many of
the nations among whom they were
driven will cease to exist, Israel will
never be utterly destroyed.

299

47   CHAPTER XLVII   מז

1. The word of the LORD that came to Jeremiah the prophet concerning the Philistines, before that Pharaoh smote Gaza.

2 Thus saith the LORD:

Behold, waters rise up out of the north,

And shall become an overflowing stream,

And they shall overflow the land and all that is therein,

The city and them that dwell therein;

And the men shall cry,

And all the inhabitants of the land shall wail.

3 At the noise of the stamping of the hoofs of his strong ones,

At the rushing of his chariots, at the rumbling of his wheels,

The fathers look not back to their children

For feebleness of hands;

אֲשֶׁ֣ר הָיָ֧ה דְבַר־יְהֹוָ֛ה אֶל־ 1
יִרְמְיָ֥הוּ הַנָּבִ֖יא אֶל־פְּלִשְׁתִּ֑ים
בְּטֶ֛רֶם יַכֶּ֥ה פַרְעֹ֖ה אֶת־עַזָּֽה:

כֹּ֚ה ׀ אָמַ֣ר יְהֹוָ֔ה 2
הִנֵּה־מַ֙יִם֙ עֹלִ֣ים מִצָּפ֔וֹן
וְהָיוּ֙ לְנַ֣חַל שׁוֹטֵ֔ף
וְיִשְׁטְפוּ֙ אֶ֣רֶץ וּמְלוֹאָ֔הּ
עִ֖יר וְיֹ֣שְׁבֵי בָ֑הּ
וְזָעֲקוּ֙ הָֽאָדָ֔ם
וְהֵילִ֕ל כֹּ֖ל יוֹשֵׁ֥ב הָאָֽרֶץ:

מִקּ֗וֹל שַׁעֲטַת֙ פַּרְס֣וֹת אַבִּירָ֔יו 3
מֵרַ֣עַשׁ לְרִכְבּ֔וֹ הֲמ֖וֹן גַּלְגִּלָּ֑יו
לֹֽא־הִפְנ֤וּ אָבוֹת֙ אֶל־בָּנִ֔ים
מֵרִפְי֖וֹן יָדָֽיִם:

CHAPTER XLVII

JUDGMENT UPON THE PHILISTINES

1. *before that Pharaoh smote Gaza.* It is not clear to what this refers. Rashi and other Jewish commentators quote the *Seder Olam* as follows: In the tenth year of Zedekiah's reign, while Nebuchadnezzar was besieging Jerusalem, Pharaoh marched from Egypt with a relief force. On the way, however, he was informed that the siege had been raised, whereupon he returned to Egypt, and in the course of his return attacked Gaza. Herodotus (II. 159) records the capture of 'Kadytis,' probably Gaza, by Pharaoh-neco after the battle of Megiddo. In any event, this would not be the same disaster as that mentioned in verse 5 which is described as coming from the north (verse 2), unless it is assumed that

the whole prophecy refers to the return of Pharaoh who, on this occasion, would have been coming from the north; but this is unlikely. Abarbanel understands this to mean that they were attacked by Egypt from the south and by Babylon from the north. Pharaoh attacked only Gaza, whereas Babylon attacked the remainder of the country.

Gaza. See on xxv. 20. [Its situation on the edge of the Egyptian desert, at the junction of the caravan routes from Egypt and Arabia, made it important from a military as well as a trading point of view.]

2. *waters rise up.* Cf. xlvi. 8, where the advance of the Egyptian army is similarly described.

the north. Babylonia (Abarbanel).

3. *to their children.* To save them

4 Because of the day that cometh
  To spoil all the Philistines,
  To cut off from Tyre and Zidon
  Every helper that remaineth;
  For the LORD will spoil the
    Philistines,
  The remnant of the isle of
    Caphtor.

5 Baldness is come upon Gaza,
  Ashkelon is brought to nought,
    the remnant of their valley;
  How long wilt thou cut thyself?

6 O thou sword of the LORD,
  How long will it be ere thou be
    quiet?
  Put up thyself into thy scabbard,
  Rest, and be still.

7 How canst thou be quiet?
  For the LORD hath given it a
    charge;
  Against Ashkelon, and against the
    sea-shore,
  There hath He appointed it.

עַל־הַיּ֣וֹם הַבָּ֗א 4
לִשְׁד֖וֹד אֶת־כָּל־פְּלִשְׁתִּ֑ים
לְהַכְרִ֣ית לְצֹ֤ר וּלְצִידוֹן֙
כֹּ֚ל שָׂרִ֣יד עֹזֵ֔ר
כִּֽי־שֹׁדֵ֤ד יְהֹוָה֙ אֶת־פְּלִשְׁתִּ֔ים
שְׁאֵרִ֖ית אִ֥י כַפְתּֽוֹר׃
בָּ֤אָה קָרְחָה֙ אֶל־עַזָּ֔ה 5
נִדְמְתָ֥ה אַשְׁקְל֖וֹן
שְׁאֵרִ֣ית עִמְקָ֑ם
עַד־מָתַ֖י תִּתְגּוֹדָֽדִי׃
ה֗וֹי חֶ֚רֶב לַֽיהֹוָ֔ה 6
עַד־אָ֖נָה לֹ֣א תִשְׁקֹ֑טִי
הֵאָֽסְפִי֙ אֶל־תַּעְרֵ֔ךְ
הֵרָגְעִ֖י וָדֹֽמִּי׃
אֵ֣יךְ תִּשְׁקֹ֔טִי 7
וַֽיהֹוָ֖ה צִוָּה־לָ֑הּ
אֶֽל־אַשְׁקְל֛וֹן וְאֶל־ח֥וֹף הַיָּ֖ם
שָׁ֥ם יְעָדָֽהּ׃

(Rashi); so intense is the panic that even natural affections are forgotten, and it is each man for himself (Kimchi).

4. *Tyre and Zidon.* The allies of the Philistines (Rashi).

the isle of Caphtor. Probably to be identified with Crete (cf. Amos ix. 7). Only a *remnant* of its former population was left after the wars between Egypt and Assyria (Daath Mikra).

5. *baldness is come upon Gaza.* Gaza is completely razed to the ground, for which baldness is a simile (Targum,

Kimchi). Or, baldness is mentioned as a symbol of mourning (see on xvi. 6) (Daath Mikra).

Ashkelon. See on xxv. 20.

their valley. Abarbanel explains *valley* as 'the whole Philistine plain.'

6f. The prophet apostrophizes the *sword of the* LORD and appeals to it to cease raging, but admits that it cannot do so because God has charged it to destroy.

7. *the sea-shore.* Philistia (Metsudath David).

מח

48   CHAPTER XLVIII

1 Of Moab.

Thus saith the LORD of hosts, the
God of Israel:

Woe unto Nebo! for it is spoiled;

Kiriathaim is put to shame, it is
taken;

Misgab is put to shame and dismayed.

2 The praise of Moab is no more;

In Heshbon they have devised evil
against her:

'Come, and let us cut her off from
being a nation.'

Thou also, O Madmen, shalt be
brought to silence;

The sword shall pursue thee.

1 לְמוֹאָב

כֹּה־אָמַר יְהֹוָה צְבָאוֹת

אֱלֹהֵי יִשְׂרָאֵל

הוֹי אֶל־נְבוֹ כִּי שֻׁדָּדָה

הֹבִישָׁה נִלְכְּדָה קִרְיָתַיִם

הֹבִישָׁה הַמִּשְׂגָּב וָחָתָּה׃

2 אֵין עוֹד תְּהִלַּת מוֹאָב

בְּחֶשְׁבּוֹן חָשְׁבוּ עָלֶיהָ רָעָה

לְכוּ וְנַכְרִיתֶנָּה מִגּוֹי

גַּם־מַדְמֵן תִּדֹּמִּי

אַחֲרַיִךְ תֵּלֶךְ חָרֶב׃

CHAPTER XLVIII

JUDGMENT UPON MOAB

THIS chapter has many affinities with
other prophetic oracles on Moab, viz.
Amos ii. 1–3, Obadiah, Zeph. ii. 8ff.
and especially Isa. xvf.

1. *Moab.* The country situated on the
tableland east of the Dead Sea.

Nebo. Not the mountain of that name,
but the city mentioned in Num. xxxii.
38, built by the Reubenites, where other
cities occur which are referred to in this
chapter. The Moabite Stone records
how it was taken by Mesha, king of
Moab (*c.* 895 B.C.E.). Kiriathaim,
Kerioth, Jahzah, Dibon, Aroer, Bozrah
(Bezer), Beth-diblathaim, Baal-meon
and Horonaim (cf. Num. xxxii. 34–38)
are also named on the inscription.

Kiriathaim. Probably Kureyat, ten
miles north of the Dead Sea.

Misgab. As a place-name this is
unknown. The translation may be 'the
high fortress' as in Isa. xxv. 12.

2. *in Heshbon they have devised ... O
Madmen, shalt be brought to silence.* There
is a play on the name of each of the
cities: *Heshbon* is connected with the
verb *chashab*, 'to devise,' and *Madmen*
with *damam*, 'to be silent' (Rashi,
Kimchi). Heshbon, one of the chief
cities of Moab, lay to the north-east of
the Dead Sea, and marked the northern
boundary of Moab until the Reubenites
claimed the territory lying between it
and the Arnon, which flows into the
Dead Sea about the middle of its eastern
border. Many of the cities mentioned in
this chapter as part of Moab were
assigned to the Reubenites by Moses
(Num. xxxii. 33ff.; Josh. xiii. 15ff.) and
proved a source of hostility in the early
days (cf. Judg. iii. 12ff.; 1 Sam. xiv. 47);
but the sympathy of the prophet with
Moab's misfortunes (verse 31; cf. also
Isa. xv. 5) is perhaps an indication that
Israel had long acquiesced in their
seizure. The site of Madmen is
unknown; so far as the name is concerned, it may be compared with
Madmannah, a city of Judah (Josh. xv.
31) and Madmenah (Isa. x. 31) a Ben-
jamite city.

3 Hark! a cry from Horonaim,
   Spoiling and great destruction!

4 Moab is destroyed;
   Her little ones have caused a cry
   to be heard.

5 For by the ascent of Luhith
   With continual weeping shall they
   go up;
   For in the going down of Horonaim
   They have heard the distressing
   cry of destruction.

6 Flee, save your lives,
   And be like a tamarisk in the
   wilderness.

7 For, because thou hast trusted
   In thy works and in thy treasures,
   Thou also shalt be taken;
   And Chemosh shall go forth into
   captivity,
   His priests and his princes to-
   gether.

3 קוֹל צְעָקָה מֵחֹרֹנָיִם
שֹׁד וָשֶׁבֶר גָּדוֹל:

4 נִשְׁבְּרָה מוֹאָב
הִשְׁמִיעוּ זְּעָקָה צְעוֹרֶיהָ:

5 כִּי מַעֲלֵה הַלֻּחוֹת
בִּבְכִי יַעֲלֶה־בֶּכִי
כִּי בְּמוֹרַד חוֹרֹנַיִם
צָרֵי צַעֲקַת־שֶׁבֶר שָׁמֵעוּ:

6 נֻסוּ מַלְּטוּ נַפְשְׁכֶם
וְתִהְיֶינָה כַּעֲרוֹעֵר בַּמִּדְבָּר:

7 כִּי יַעַן בִּטְחֵךְ בְּמַעֲשַׂיִךְ
וּבְאוֹצְרוֹתַיִךְ
גַּם־אַתְּ תִּלָּכֵדִי
וְיָצָא כְמוֹשׁ בַּגּוֹלָה
כֹּהֲנָיו וְשָׂרָיו יַחְדָּו:

v. 4. צעוריה ק׳   v. 5. הלחית ק׳   v. 7. כמוש ק׳   v. 7. יחדיו ק׳

3. *Horonaim.* This town appears on the Moabite Stone on Horonen. Some scholars maintain that it was in the south of Moab; others, in the north, not far from Heshbon.

4. *her little ones,* etc. For the noun, cf. xiv. 3. Here the word may perhaps be connected with *tsa'ar,* 'her distressed ones.' However, this root is not found in Scriptures in this sense.

5. With this verse, cf. Isa. xv. 5.

the ascent of Luhith. [Between Zoar and Rabbath-Moab.]

with continual weeping shall they go up. lit. 'with weeping shall go up weeping,' i.e. one crowd of refugees in tears will succeed another.

6. *be like a tamarisk in the wilderness.* See on xvii. 6. The point is probably: flee to some isolated place; be lonely and forlorn like the tamarisk, so that you save your lives (Metsudath David).

7. *thy works.* The fruit of thy works, viz. flocks and herds (Metsudath David); or, thy merchandise (Daath Mikra).

thou also. Not only will your possessions be plundered, but you will be taken captive (Metsudath David).

Chemosh. Moab's principal deity (Num. xxi. 29). The downfall of a people was thought also to involve their gods. For a description of idols being carried in a triumphal procession, cf. xliii. 12 and Isa. xlvi. 1f.

8 And the spoiler shall come upon
every city,
And no city shall escape;
The valley also shall perish, and
the plain shall be destroyed;
As the LORD hath spoken.

9 Give wings unto Moab,
For she must fly and get away;
And her cities shall become a
desolation,
Without any to dwell therein.

10 Cursed be he that doeth the work
of the LORD with a slack hand,
And cursed be he that keepeth
back his sword from blood.

11 Moab hath been at ease from his
youth,
And he hath settled on his lees,
And hath not been emptied from
vessel to vessel,
Neither hath he gone into
captivity;
Therefore his taste remaineth in
him,

8 וּבָא שֹׁדֵד אֶל־כָּל־עִיר
וְעִיר לֹא תִמָּלֵט
וְאָבַד הָעֵמֶק וְנִשְׁמַד הַמִּישֹׁר
אֲשֶׁר אָמַר יְהוָה:

9 תְּנוּ־צִיץ לְמוֹאָב
כִּי נָצֹא תֵּצֵא
וְעָרֶיהָ לְשַׁמָּה תִהְיֶינָה
מֵאֵין יוֹשֵׁב בָּהֵן:

10 אָרוּר עֹשֶׂה
מְלֶאכֶת יְהוָה רְמִיָּה
וְאָרוּר מֹנֵעַ חַרְבּוֹ מִדָּם:

11 שַׁאֲנַן מוֹאָב מִנְּעוּרָיו
וְשֹׁקֵט הוּא אֶל־שְׁמָרָיו
וְלֹא־הוּרַק מִכְּלִי אֶל־כֶּלִי
וּבַגּוֹלָה לֹא הָלָךְ
עַל־כֵּן עָמַד טַעְמוֹ בּוֹ

8. *the valley.* The valley of the Jordan
towards the Dead Sea.

the plain. The tableland which was the
site of Moab.

9. *wings.* The noun *tsits* is unusual,
although it has this meaning in later
usage. It is, however, found in Num. xv.
37 in the word *tsitsith*, denoting a fringe
hanging from a garment, also in Ezekiel
viii. 4, 'and I was taken by a lock of
(*tsitsith*) my head.' In Aramaic too we
find the word *tsitsin* used for 'fins,'
similar to wings. Thus, *tsits* denotes an
appendage (Rashi, Kimchi, Kara). It
may have been chosen for its assonance
with the verbs that follow, *natso tētsē*
(Kimchi). Targum renders: Remove the
crown from Moab. i.e. give others the
crown that belonged to Moab (Rashi).

10. *the work of the* LORD. Moab's
destruction is a Divine decree and must
therefore be executed with zeal. The
vindictive spirit of the verse is called
forth by the bitter experience of Israel at
Moab's hand (Kimchi).

11. *Moab hath been at ease,* etc. Since
Moab became a people, it never experienced exile, but always remained in its
place like wine that has settled on its lees
and has not been emptied from one
vessel to another. To make the matter
clearer, the prophet explains: Neither
hath he gone into captivity (Metsudath
David).

his taste remaineth. i.e. he did not
weaken (Kimchi).

And his scent is not changed.

12 Therefore, behold, the days come,

Saith the LORD,

That I will send unto him them that tilt up,

And they shall tilt him up;

And they shall empty his vessels,

And break their bottles in pieces.

13 And Moab shall be ashamed of Chemosh,

As the house of Israel was ashamed

Of Beth-el their confidence.

14 How say ye: 'We are mighty men,

And valiant men for the war'?

15 Moab is spoiled, and they are gone up into her cities,

And his chosen young men are gone down to the slaughter,

Saith the King,

Whose name is the LORD of hosts.

16 The calamity of Moab is near to come,

And his affliction hasteth fast.

וְרֵיחוֹ לֹא נָמָר׃

12 לָכֵן הִנֵּה־יָמִים בָּאִים֙

נְאֻם־יְהֹוָה

וְשִׁלַּחְתִּי־לוֹ צֹעִים

וְצֵעֻהוּ

וְכֵלָיו יָרִיקוּ

וְנִבְלֵיהֶם יְנַפֵּצוּ׃

13 וּבֹשׁ מוֹאָב מִכְּמוֹשׁ

כַּאֲשֶׁר־בֹּשׁוּ בֵּית יִשְׂרָאֵל

מִבֵּית אֵל מִבְטֶחָם׃

14 אֵיךְ תֹּאמְרוּ גִּבּוֹרִים אֲנָחְנוּ

וְאַנְשֵׁי־חַיִל לַמִּלְחָמָה׃

15 שֻׁדַּד מוֹאָב וְעָרֶיהָ עָלָה

וּמִבְחַר בַּחוּרָיו יָרְדוּ לַטָּבַח

נְאֻם־הַמֶּלֶךְ

יְהֹוָה צְבָאוֹת שְׁמוֹ׃

16 קָרוֹב אֵיד־מוֹאָב לָבוֹא

וְרָעָתוֹ מִהֲרָה מְאֹד׃

---

12. *them that tilt up.* Instead of the wine being decanted with care so that the lees are not mixed with it, the jars will be broken after the contents are carelessly poured out. In plain language, the Moabites will be driven out as exiles and their land made desolate (Malbim).

13. *Moab shall be ashamed of Chemosh.* The Moabites will suffer bitter disillusionment for having put trust in their god which had proved helpless to protect them (Metsudath David).

14. Moab had trusted in her strength to spare her the terrors of invasion.

15. *and they are gone up into her cities.* Others render: 'and her cities have gone up' in flame. The former is to be preferred, because the verbs, as in verse 18, are contrasted: as they who came to spoil Moab went up into her cities, the defenders deserted them and took to flight. This follows Abarbanel and Rabbi Joseph Kimchi.

16. For the language, cf. Deut. xxxii. 35.

17 Bemoan him, all ye that are
round about him,
And all ye that know his name;
Say: 'How is the strong staff
broken,
The beautiful rod!'

18 O thou daughter that dwellest in
Dibon,
Come down from thy glory, and
sit in thirst;
For the spoiler of Moab is come
up against thee,
He hath destroyed thy strong-
holds.

19 O inhabitant of Aroer,
Stand by the way, and watch;
Ask him that fleeth, and her that
escapeth;
Say: 'What hath been done?'

20 Moab is put to shame, for it is
dismayed;
Wail and cry;
Tell ye it in Arnon,
That Moab is spoiled.

17 נֻ֣דוּ ל֗וֹ כָּל־סְבִיבָ֔יו
וְכֹ֖ל יֹדְעֵ֣י שְׁמ֑וֹ
אִמְר֗וּ אֵיכָ֤ה נִשְׁבַּר֙ מַטֵּה־עֹ֔ז
מַקֵּ֖ל תִּפְאָרָֽה׃

18 רְדִ֤י מִכָּבוֹד֙ ישְׁבִ֣י בַצָּמָ֔א
ישֶׁ֖בֶת בַּת־דִּיב֑וֹן
כִּי־שֹׁדֵ֤ד מוֹאָב֙ עָ֣לָה בָ֔ךְ
שִׁחֵ֖ת מִבְצָרָֽיִךְ׃

19 אֶל־דֶּ֛רֶךְ עִמְדִ֥י וְצַפִּ֖י
יוֹשֶׁ֣בֶת עֲרוֹעֵ֑ר
שַׁאֲלִי־נָ֣ס וְנִמְלָ֔טָה
אִמְרִ֖י מַה־נִּהְיָֽתָה׃

20 הֹבִ֥ישׁ מוֹאָ֛ב כִּֽי־חַ֖תָּה
הֵילִ֣ילוּ ׀ וּֽזְעָ֔קִי
הַגִּ֖ידוּ בְאַרְנ֑וֹן
כִּ֥י שֻׁדַּ֖ד מוֹאָֽב׃

v. 18. ושבי ק׳   v. 20. הלילו ק׳   v. 20. וזעקו ק׳

17. *round about him.* i.e. peoples in Moab's vicinity, and *all ye that know his name* describes the nations which lived far away but had heard of Moab by repute (Daath Mikra).

the strong staff . . . the beautiful rod. The strength and glory of the nation (Metsudath David).

18. *daughter . . . Dibon.* i.e. inhabitants of Dibon, now called Diban. It is four miles north of the Arnon and thirteen east of the Dead Sea. The town stands on two hills and possibly that is why the prophet uses the verb *come down*. On the other hand, *come down from thy glory* is a natural expression

which may have no reference to physical situation. The Moabite Stone was discovered in Diban in 1868.

sit in thirst. This may be understood figuratively: you will thirst for all the things you once enjoyed (Kimchi); or literally: in your humbled condition as captives, you will sit on the ground and thirst (Metsudath David).

19. *Aroer.* A few miles south-east of Dibon close to the Arnon. It is the Gadite city of that name mentioned in Num. xxxii. 34, not the Judahite city of 1 Sam. xxx. 28.

20. *for it is dismayed.* [In the Hebrew the verb *is put to shame* is masculine and

21. And judgment is come upon the country of the Plain; upon Holon, and upon Jahzah, and upon Mephaath; 22. and upon Dibon, and upon Nebo, and upon Beth-diblathaim; 23. and upon Kiria-thaim, and upon Beth-gamul, and upon Beth-meon; 24. and upon Kerioth, and upon Bozrah, and upon all the cities of the land of Moab, far or near.

25 The horn of Moab is cut off,
And his arm is broken,
Saith the LORD.

26 Make ye him drunken,
For he magnified himself against the LORD;

וּמִשְׁפָּט בָּא אֶל־אֶרֶץ הַמִּישֹׁר 21
אֶל־־חֹלוֹן וְאֶל־יַהְצָה
וְעַל־מֵופָעַת: וְעַל־דִּיבוֹן 22
וְעַל־נְבוֹ וְעַל־בֵּית
דִּבְלָתָיִם: וְעַל קְרִיָתַיִם 23
וְעַל־בֵּית גָּמוּל וְעַל־בֵּית
מְעוֹן: וְעַל־קְרִיּוֹת וְעַל־ 24
בָּצְרָה וְעַל כָּל־עָרֵי אֶרֶץ
מוֹאָב הָרְחֹקוֹת וְהַקְּרֹבוֹת:
נִגְדְּעָה קֶרֶן מוֹאָב 25
וּזְרֹעוֹ נִשְׁבָּרָה
נְאֻם יְהֹוָה:
הַשְׁכִּירֻהוּ 26
כִּי עַל־יְהֹוָה הִגְדִּיל

v. 21. מיפעת ק׳

---

is dismayed is feminine. The meaning may be, 'Moab is put to shame, for it (Dibon) is dismayed.']

21. *the country of the Plain.* i.e. the territory of Moab, an enumeration of whose chief towns follows (Abarbanel).

Jahzah. A Levitical city (called Jahaz in Josh. xxi. 36). There Moses defeated the Amorite king Sihon (Num. xxi. 23f.). Its site was probably north-east of Dibon.

Mephaath. Another Levitical city (Josh. xxi. 37).

22. *Dibon.* See on verse 18.

Nebo. See on verse 1.

Beth-diblathaim. lit. 'the house of the two figs.' It is probably identical with Almon-diblathaim, one of the stages in Israel's journeyings through the wilderness (Num. xxxiii. 46), near Dibon-Gad, but its location is unknown.

23. *Kiriathaim.* See on verse 1.

Beth-gamul. Not mentioned elsewhere. Some authorities identify it with Umm el Jemal, south of Bozrah.

Beth-meon. The Baal-meon of Num. xxxii. 38, built by the Gadites; it lies about five miles south-west of Medeba.

24. *Kerioth.* Mentioned in Amos ii. 2. It has been conjecturally identified with Ar of Moab (Num. xxi. 28).

Bozrah. Possibly the Bezer of Deut. iv. 43; Josh. xx. 8, xxi. 36; it lay between Dibon and Aroer. The town of the same name in xlix. 13 was in Edom.

25. *horn.* The symbol of dominion, while *arm* signifies strength (Metsudath David).

26. *drunken.* Figurative of bewilderment (cf. xxv. 15) (Metsudath David).

he magnified himself. See on verses 29f.

And Moab shall wallow in his
    vomit,
And he also shall be in derision.

27 For was not Israel a derision
    unto thee?
Was he found among thieves?
For as often as thou speakest of
    him,
Thou waggest the head.

28 O ye that dwell in Moab,
Leave the cities, and dwell in the
    rock;
And be like the dove that maketh
    her nest
In the sides of the pit's mouth.

29 We have heard of the pride of
    Moab;
He is very proud;
His loftiness, and his pride, and
    his haughtiness,
And the assumption of his heart.

30 I know his arrogancy, saith the
    LORD,
That it is ill-founded;
His boastings have wrought
    nothing well-founded.

וְסָפַק מוֹאָב בְּקִיאוֹ
וְהָיָה לִשְׂחֹק גַּם־הוּא׃
27 וְאִם ׀ לוֹא הַשְּׂחֹק
הָיָה לְךָ יִשְׂרָאֵל
אִם־בְּגַנָּבִים נִמְצָאֹה
כִּי־מִדֵּי דְבָרֶיךָ
בּוֹ תִּתְנוֹדָד׃
28 עִזְבוּ עָרִים וְשִׁכְנוּ בַסֶּלַע
יֹשְׁבֵי מוֹאָב
וִהְיוּ כְיוֹנָה תְּקַנֵּן
בְּעֶבְרֵי פִי־פָחַת׃
29 שָׁמַעְנוּ גְאוֹן־מוֹאָב
גֵּאֶה מְאֹד
גָּבְהוֹ וּגְאוֹנוֹ וְגַאֲוָתוֹ
וְרֻם לִבּוֹ׃
30 אֲנִי יָדַעְתִּי נְאֻם־יְהֹוָה
עֶבְרָתוֹ וְלֹא־כֵן
בַּדָּיו לֹא־כֵן עָשׂוּ׃

נמצא ק׳ v. 27.

27. *was he found among thieves?* That
Moab treated him with such contempt!
(Kimchi).

waggest the head. In scorn (Metsudath
David).

28. *be like the dove,* etc. 'The wild
rock-pigeon invariably selects . . . deep
ravines for its nesting and roosting
place' (Tristram). The Moabites will
now lead a hunted and precarious existence (cf. iv. 29).

29f. Cf. Isa. xvi. 6. The passage has a
proverbial ring and probably both

Isaiah and Jeremiah were loosely
quoting a current saying about Moab's
pride which was notorious (cf. Isa. xxv.
11; Zeph. ii. 8ff. *He magnified himself
against the* LORD in verse 26 may also
refer to his inordinate pride.

29. *we have heard.* The subject is the
nations generally (Kimchi).

30. *I know his arrogancy.* The correct
translation is: I know his wrath. Rashi
explains: I know his wrath toward
Israel. Kimchi explains: I know his
wrath toward the nations, his neigh-
bors, because of his haughtiness.

31 Therefore will I wail for Moab;
Yea, I will cry out for all Moab;
For the men of Kir-heres shall
my heart moan.

32 With more than the weeping of
Jazer will I weep for thee,
O vine of Sibmah;
Thy branches passed over the
sea,
They reached even to the sea of
Jazer;
Upon thy summer fruits and
upon thy vintage
The spoiler is fallen.

עַל־כֵּן עַל־מוֹאָב אֲיֵלִיל 31
וּלְמוֹאָב כֻּלֹּה אֶזְעָק
אֶל־אַנְשֵׁי קִיר־חֶרֶשׂ יֶהְגֶּה:
מִבְּכִי יַעְזֵר אֶבְכֶּה־לָּךְ 32
הַגֶּפֶן שִׂבְמָה
נְטִישֹׁתַיִךְ עָבְרוּ יָם
עַד יָם יַעְזֵר נָגָעוּ
עַל־קֵיצֵךְ וְעַל־בְּצִירֵךְ
שֹׁדֵד נָפָל:

31ff. [The strong sympathy of the prophet with Moab should be noted. It is likewise met with in Isaiah and expressed in almost identical words. Evidently there was a close bond between Moab and Judah, notwithstanding the apparently exultant tones of part of this chapter; and this in spite of the fact that when Nebuchadnezzar attacked Judea in Jehoiakim's reign, he was assisted by the Moabites (2 Kings xxiv. 2). It may well be that the prophets, with their sense of universalism, felt this sympathy with the sufferings of the peoples whose downfall they had to announce even where their choice of language suggests satisfaction. A distinction is probably to be drawn between their official utterances, as it were, and their personal feelings.]

31. *therefore will I wail.* Isa. xvi. 7 has *therefore shall Moab wail for Moab;* but verse 11 of that chapter reads, *Wherefore my heart moaneth like a harp for Moab, and mine inward parts for Kir-heres.*

the men of (anshë) *Kir-heres.* The reading of the parallel passage in Isa. xvi. 7 is, *the sweet cakes of* (ashishë) *Kir-haresheth.* The version in Jeremiah seems to be a free adaptation of the other. Kir-heres is the modern Kerak, eight miles south of the Dead Sea.

32. Based on Isa. xvi. 8f. with variations.

Jazer . . . Sibmah. The former was ten miles north and the latter two and a half north-west of Heshbon. The district was famed for its vineyards, and remains of wine-presses and vineyard towers have been found in its ruins.

thy branches passed over the sea. Having mentioned the vines, the prophet makes use of a metaphor in which the whole nation is likened to a huge vine, the branches of which (i.e. portions of the nation) go over the sea into captivity (Rashi, Kimchi). In fact, no sea would have to be crossed, but the phrase may be idiomatic for going into captivity.

the sea of Jazer. There is no sea (or lake) in the vicinity of Jazer. Daath Mikra identifies the sea of Jazer with the Dead Sea. This is difficult, however, since Sibmah is nearer to the Dead Sea than Jazer. See *Carta's Atlas of the Bible.* The phrase may be metaphorical for the sea of corn which grew in the district, although this is not mentioned elsewhere. Perhaps the passage should be rendered, disregarding the accents: 'Thy branches passed over the sea even unto the sea; they reached to Jazer.' The first clause will then be idiomatic, indicating deportation to a great distance.

33 And gladness and joy is taken
away
From the fruitful field, and from
the land of Moab;
And I have caused wine to cease
from the winepresses;
None shall tread with shouting;
The shouting shall be no shouting.

34 From the cry of Heshbon even
unto Elealeh,
Even unto Jahaz have they
uttered their voice,
From Zoar even unto Horonaim,
A heifer of three years old;
For the Waters of Nimrim also
Shall be desolate.

35 Moreover I will cause to cease in
Moab,
Saith the LORD,
Him that offereth in the high
place,
And him that offereth to his gods.

33 וְנֶאֶסְפָה שִׂמְחָה וָגִיל
מִכַּרְמֶל וּמֵאֶרֶץ מוֹאָב
וְיַיִן מִיקָבִים הִשְׁבַּתִּי
לֹא־יִדְרֹךְ הֵידָד
הֵידָד לֹא הֵידָד:
34 מִזַּעֲקַת חֶשְׁבּוֹן עַד־אֶלְעָלֵה
עַד־יַהַץ נָתְנוּ קוֹלָם
מִצֹּעַר עַד־חֹרֹנַיִם
עֶגְלַת שְׁלִשִׁיָּה
כִּי גַּם־מֵי נִמְרִים
לִמְשַׁמּוֹת יִהְיוּ:
35 וְהִשְׁבַּתִּי לְמוֹאָב
נְאֻם־יְהֹוָה
מַעֲלֶה בָמָה
וּמַקְטִיר לֵאלֹהָיו:

---

33. Cf. Isa. xvi. 10.

the shouting shall be no shouting. It will
not be the joyous shouting of grape-
treading, but the grim shout of defeat.
The noun *hedad* signifies both sounds
(see on xxv. 30) (Kara, Isaiah da Trani).

34. Cf. Isa. xv. 4–6 of which this verse is
an abbreviation.

Elealeh. About two miles north of
Heshbon (see on verse 2).

even unto Jahaz. The cry of Heshbon to
Elealeh is heard even to Jahaz, as is the
cry of Zoar to Horonaim. As mentioned
above, Heshbon and Elealeh were in the
north of the country, and Zoar and
Horonaim were in the south. Yahaz was
in the middle. Thus, the prophet pre-
dicts that the cries will be heard

throughout the entire country of Moab
(Metsudath David).

a heifer of three years old. Apparently
Moab is likened to a heifer which is fully
grown and developed. It possessed
everything, but now only cries of
anguish are heard (Rashi, Kimchi). [The
Hebrew may also mean 'the third
Eglath' and is then to be understood as
another place-name, 'third' distinguishing it from two other towns called
Eglath in that neighbourhood.]

Nimrim. Probably the modern Wadi
Numeirah at the south-east end of the
Dead Sea (Daath Mikra).

desolate. [Dried up because their
sources had been dammed.]

35. Cf. Isa. xvi. 12.

36 Therefore my heart moaneth for
   Moab like pipes,
   And my heart moaneth like pipes
   for the men of Kir-heres;
   Therefore the abundance that he
   hath gotten is perished.

37 For every head is bald,
   And every beard clipped;
   Upon all the hands are cuttings,
   And upon the loins sackcloth.

38 On all the housetops of Moab
   and in the broad places thereof
   There   is   lamentation   every
   where;
   For I have broken Moab like a
   vessel wherein is no pleasure,
   Saith the LORD.

39 'How is it broken down!' wail ye!
   'How hath Moab turned the back
   with shame!'
   So shall Moab become a derision
   and a dismay
   To all that are round about him.

40 For thus saith the LORD:
   Behold, he shall swoop as a
   vulture,

36 עַל־כֵּן לִבִּי לְמוֹאָב
כַּחֲלִלִים יֶהֱמֶה
וְלִבִּי אֶל־אַנְשֵׁי קִיר־חֶרֶשׂ
כַּחֲלִילִים יֶהֱמֶה
עַל־כֵּן יִתְרַת עָשָׂה אָבָדוּ:

37 כִּי כָל־רֹאשׁ קָרְחָה
וְכָל־זָקָן גְּרֻעָה
עַל כָּל־יָדַיִם גְּדֻדֹת
וְעַל־מָתְנַיִם שָׂק:

38 עַל כָּל־גַּגּוֹת מוֹאָב
וּבִרְחֹבֹתֶיהָ כֻּלֹּה מִסְפֵּד
כִּי־שָׁבַרְתִּי אֶת־מוֹאָב כִּכְלִי
אֵין־חֵפֶץ בּוֹ
נְאֻם־יְהוָה:

39 אֵיךְ חַתָּה הֵילִילוּ
אֵיךְ הִפְנָה־עֹרֶף מוֹאָב בּוֹשׁ
וְהָיָה מוֹאָב לִשְׂחֹק וְלִמְחִתָּה
לְכָל־סְבִיבָיו:

40 כִּי־כֹה אָמַר יְהוָה
הִנֵּה כַנֶּשֶׁר יִדְאֶה

---

36. *like pipes.* Used for playing dirges
at funerals (Daath Mikra).

37f. Cf. Isa. xv. 2f.

37. All display various signs of mourning (see on xvi. 6).

40. *he shall swoop.* The subject is the
enemy (Rashi).

The simile is apt for the Babylonian
armies, which would not be detained at
the borders of the country they wish to
invade, but would resemble a mighty
eagle, or vulture, that swoops down and
spreads its wings in the middle of a
country. So will it spread its wings over
Moab, which will immediately be under
them (Malbim).

And shall spread out his wings
against Moab.

41 The cities are taken,
And the strongholds are seized,
And the heart of the mighty men
of Moab at that day
Shall be as the heart of a woman
in her pangs.

42 And Moab shall be destroyed
from being a people,
Because he hath magnified himself against the Lord.

43 Terror, and the pit, and the trap,
Are upon thee, O inhabitant of
Moab,
Saith the Lord.

44 He that fleeth from the terror
Shall fall into the pit;
And he that getteth up out of the
pit
Shall be taken in the trap;
For I will bring upon her, even
upon Moab,
The year of their visitation,
saith the Lord.

45 In the shadow of Heshbon the
fugitives
Stand without strength;

וּפָרַשׂ כְּנָפָיו אֶל־מוֹאָב׃

41 נִלְכְּדָה הַקְּרִיּוֹת
וְהַמְּצָדוֹת נִתְפָּשָׂה
וְהָיָה לֵב גִּבּוֹרֵי מוֹאָב
בַּיּוֹם הַהוּא
כְּלֵב אִשָּׁה מְצֵרָה׃

42 וְנִשְׁמַד מוֹאָב מֵעָם
כִּי עַל־יְהוָה הִגְדִּיל׃

43 פַּחַד וָפַחַת וָפָח
עָלֶיךָ יוֹשֵׁב מוֹאָב
נְאֻם־יְהוָה׃

44 הַנָּס מִפְּנֵי הַפַּחַד
יִפֹּל אֶל־הַפַּחַת
וְהָעֹלֶה מִן־הַפַּחַת
יִלָּכֵד בַּפָּח
כִּי־אָבִיא אֵלֶיהָ אֶל־מוֹאָב
שְׁנַת פְּקֻדָּתָם נְאֻם־יְהוָה׃

45 בְּצֵל חֶשְׁבּוֹן
עָמְדוּ מִכֹּחַ נָסִים

v. 44. הנס ק׳

41. *the cities.* In Hebrew *ha-kerioth,*
with a possible play on *Kerioth* (verse 24).

42. This was completely fulfilled. After
going into exile the Moabites practically
disappeared as a people.

43f. Based in the main upon Isa. xxiv.
17f.

43. *terror, and the pit, and the trap.* The
assonance of the Hebrew is striking:
pachad wa-phachath wa-phach.

44. *the year of their visitation.* The day of
reckoning for them (Metsudath David).

45f. Derived from Num. xxi. 28f., xxiv.
17.

45. *without strength.* The sense of the
whole verse is that the fugitives of Moab
will seek refuge in the shelter of
Heshbon for they will have no strength
to run farther (Metsudath David).

For a fire is gone forth out of
    Heshbon,
And a flame from the midst of
    Sihon,
And it devoureth the corner of
    Moab,
And the crown of the head of the
    tumultuous ones.
46 Woe unto thee, O Moab!
The people of Chemosh is un-
    done;
For thy sons are taken away
    captive,
And thy daughters into captivity.
47 Yet will I turn the captivity of
    Moab
In the end of days, saith the
    LORD.
Thus far is the judgment of
    Moab.

כִּי־אֵשׁ יָצָא מֵחֶשְׁבּוֹן
וְלֶהָבָה מִבֵּין סִיחֹן
וַתֹּאכַל פְּאַת מוֹאָב
וְקָדְקֹד בְּנֵי שָׁאוֹן׃
46 אוֹי־לְךָ מוֹאָב
אָבַד עַם־כְּמוֹשׁ
כִּי־לֻקְּחוּ בָנֶיךָ בַּשֶּׁבִי
וּבְנֹתֶיךָ בַּשִּׁבְיָה׃
47 וְשַׁבְתִּי שְׁבוּת־מוֹאָב
בְּאַחֲרִית הַיָּמִים
נְאֻם־יְהֹוָה
עַד־הֵנָּה מִשְׁפַּט מוֹאָב׃

49   **CHAPTER XLIX**   מט

1 Of the children of Ammon.

Thus saith the LORD:

Hath Israel no sons?

1 לִבְנֵי עַמּוֹן
כֹּה אָמַר יְהֹוָה
הֲבָנִים אֵין לְיִשְׂרָאֵל

v. 45. סבירין יצאה

for a fire is gone forth. They fell there for
a fire went forth out of Heshbon; i.e.
the Chaldeans emerged from there to
destroy them (Metsudath David).

from the midst of Sihon. i.e. from the city
that had once belonged to Sihon, the
Amorite conqueror (Metsudath David).
See Num. xxi. 28.

the tumultuous ones. The Moabite warriors (Kara).

46. *Chemosh.* See on verse 13. The
people of Chemosh is synonymous with
Moab; i.e. the people who worship
Chemosh (Metsudath David).

47. *turn the captivity.* [After the long
prediction of disaster, the note of comfort is heard, as in the case of Israel.
This accords with the universalism of
the prophets.]

in the end of days. In the days of the
Messiah (Kimchi).

CHAPTER XLIX

1–6 JUDGMENT UPON AMMON

THE Ammonites were Moab's neighbour on the north and of the tribe of
Gad on the east.

Hath he no heir?

Why then doth Malcam take possession of God,

And his people dwell in the cities thereof?

2 Therefore, behold, the days come, saith the LORD,

That I will cause an alarm of war to be heard

Against Rabbah of the children of Ammon;

And it shall become a desolate mound,

And her daughters shall be burned with fire;

Then shall Israel dispossess them that did dispossess him,

Saith the LORD.

3 Wail, O Heshbon, for Ai is undone;

Cry, ye daughters of Rabbah, gird you with sackcloth;

אִם־יוֹרֵשׁ אֵין לוֹ

מַדּוּעַ יָרַשׁ מַלְכָּם אֶת־גָּד

וְעַמּוֹ בְּעָרָיו יָשָׁב:

2 לָכֵן הִנֵּה יָמִים בָּאִים

נְאֻם־יְהוָֹה

וְהִשְׁמַעְתִּי

אֶל־רַבַּת בְּנֵי־עַמּוֹן

תְּרוּעַת מִלְחָמָה

וְהָיְתָה לְתֵל שְׁמָמָה

וּבְנֹתֶיהָ בָּאֵשׁ תִּצַּתְנָה

וְיָרַשׁ יִשְׂרָאֵל אֶת־יֹרְשָׁיו

אָמַר יְהוָֹה:

3 הֵילִילִי חֶשְׁבּוֹן כִּי שֻׁדְּדָה־עַי

צְעַקְנָה בְּנוֹת רַבָּה

חֲגֹרְנָה שַׂקִּים

v. 2. פתח באתנח

1. *Malcam.* The Ammonite deity. In 1 Kings xi. 5 the name is pointed Milcom. The god, as often, is named to represent the people who worship it.

take possession of Gad. When the Gadites, together with other peoples on the east side of the Jordan, were carried off by Tiglath-pileser (2 Kings xv. 29), the Ammonites took possession of their territory. They are denounced for this action because it was based on the assumption that the land would never be occupied again by its owners. The question is asked of them, 'Although it is true that the Gadites have been deported and will die in exile; but will they not have *heirs* who will return and claim the land?'

2. *Rabbah.* The Ammonite capital, on the river Jabbok, fourteen miles north-east of Heshbon; now Amman the capital of Jordan.

her daughters. The villages (Targum) again in verse 3 (cf. Num. xxi. 25 where *towns* is literally 'daughters').

3. *Heshbon . . . Ai.* Although an Ammonite town, Ai is otherwise, unknown. We may assume there was one with the same name as the town mentioned in Josh. vii. 2. There is nothing inherently improbable in two countries having cities similarly named. Possibly the same applies to Heshbon, as we know that there was a Heshbon in Moab (xlviii. 2). In that case the meaning is plain: the fate which overtook Ai will befall Heshbon in turn. If, however, the Heshbon of Moab is intended here,

Lament, and run to and fro
among the folds;
For Malcam shall go into captivity,
His priests and his princes together.

4 Wherefore gloriest thou in the
valleys,
Thy flowing valley, O backsliding
daughter?
That didst trust in thy treasures:
'Who shall come unto me?'

5 Behold, I will bring a terror upon
thee,
Saith the Lord GOD of hosts,
From all that are round about
thee;
And ye shall be driven out every
man right forth,
And there shall be none to gather
up him that wandereth.

6 But afterward I will bring back the
captivity of the children of
Ammon,
Saith the LORD.

סָפְדָנָה וְהִתְשׁוֹטַטְנָה בַּגְּדֵרוֹת
כִּי מַלְכָּם בַּגּוֹלָה יֵלֵךְ
כֹּהֲנָיו וְשָׂרָיו יַחְדָּיו:

4 מַה־תִּתְהַלְלִי בָּעֲמָקִים
זָב עִמְקֵךְ הַבַּת הַשּׁוֹבֵבָה
הַבֹּטְחָה בְּאֹצְרֹתֶיהָ
מִי יָבוֹא אֵלָי:

5 הִנְנִי מֵבִיא עָלַיִךְ פַּחַד
נְאֻם־אֲדֹנָי יְהוִה צְבָאוֹת
מִכָּל־סְבִיבָיִךְ
וְנִדַּחְתֶּם אִישׁ לְפָנָיו
וְאֵין מְקַבֵּץ לַנֹּדֵד:

6 וְאַחֲרֵי־כֵן אָשִׁיב
אֶת־שְׁבוּת בְּנֵי־עַמּוֹן
נְאֻם־יְהוָה:

---

the verse is to be explained: In his
march of conquest, Nebuchadnezzar
passed first through Ammon and then
Moab. Heshbon, city of Moab, is bidden to see what happened to Ai and
lament, because that will also be her
doom. Although the whole prophecy
refers to Ammon, Heshbon is addressed
in order to underline the fate of Ai (see
Kimchi).

among the folds. Where the sheep are
enclosed in the open fields, since the
cities will no longer afford protection
(Malbim).

Malcam shall go into captivity. See on
xliii. 12. The latter part of the verse is
derived from Amos i. 15.

4. *thy flowing valley.* The expression is
strange. Perhaps it means a well-
watered valley, Rabbah being described

as *the city of waters* (2 Sam. xii. 27)
(Malbim).

backsliding. Normally this term refers
to apostasy from the worship of God. In
connection with the Ammonites, who
were heathens, that is inappropriate. It
is to be understood in the sense of
flagrant disregard of the ordinary laws
of humanity and decency (called in Talmudic literature 'the seven precepts of
the sons of Noah,' Sanh. 56a) obligatory
upon all men.

treasures. i.e. ample supplies from the
fertility of the land (Malbim).

5. *right forth.* Every man will flee
wherever he can, without a thought for
his neighbour; so great will be the
terror (Kimchi).

6. See on xlviii. 47.

<table>
<tr><td>

7 Of Edom.

Thus saith the LORD of hosts:

Is wisdom no more in Teman?

Is counsel perished from the prudent?

Is their wisdom vanished?

8 Flee ye, turn back, dwell deep,

O inhabitants of Dedan;

For I do bring the calamity of Esau upon him,

The time that I shall punish him.

9 If grape-gatherers came to thee,

Would they not leave some gleaning grapes?

If thieves by night,

Would they not destroy till they had enough?

10 But I have made Esau bare,

</td><td dir="rtl">

לֶאֱדוֹם 7

כֹּה אָמַר יְהוָה צְבָאוֹת

הַאֵין עוֹד חָכְמָה בְּתֵימָן

אָבְדָה עֵצָה מִבָּנִים

נִסְרְחָה חָכְמָתָם:

נֻסוּ הָפְנוּ הֶעְמִיקוּ לָשֶׁבֶת 8

יֹשְׁבֵי דְּדָן

כִּי אֵיד עֵשָׂו הֵבֵאתִי עָלָיו

עֵת פְּקַדְתִּיו:

אִם־בֹּצְרִים בָּאוּ לָךְ 9

לֹא יַשְׁאִרוּ עוֹלֵלוֹת

אִם־גַּנָּבִים בַּלַּיְלָה

הִשְׁחִיתוּ דַיָּם:

כִּי־אֲנִי חָשַׂפְתִּי אֶת־עֵשָׂו 10

</td></tr>
</table>

7-22 JUDGMENT UPON EDOM

There is close similarity between this section and Obadiah, verses 7, 9, 10a and 14–16 corresponding to Obadiah 8, 5f., 1–4 respectively.

7. *is wisdom no more in Teman?* Has all the wisdom and counsel of Edom vanished that disaster finds her so helpless? Teman was a district in the north of Edom, but the name is sometimes used as a synonym for the whole country (Hab. iii. 3) (see Kimchi).

8. *turn back.* Turn your backs on your enemies in flight. Cf. above xlviii. 36 (Daath Soferim, Daath Mikra).

dwell deep. Seek inaccessible and hidden places where the enemy will not be able to find you (Rashi).

Dedan. See on xxv. 23.

Esau. Edom was the country inhabited by Esau's descendants (cf. Gen. xxxvi. 1). Although Dedan is distinguished from Edom in xxv. 21, 23, they were both parts of Esau's territory.

9f. The general meaning is clear, although the exact rendering is doubtful. According to A.J. the sense is: Surely grape-gatherers leave something over and even thieves destroy only until their rage is satiated; but a clean sweep will be made of Edom. R.V. margin renders: 'If grape-gatherers came to thee, they will leave no gleaning grapes; if thieves by night, they will destroy till they have enough, etc. A.J., however, is preferable, since it follows all Jewish exegetes and matches Obad. i. 5, which reads: 'If thieves came to thee, if robbers by night — How art thou cut off! — Would they not steal till they had enough? If grape-gatherers came to thee, would they not leave some gleaning grapes?'

I have uncovered his secret
places,
And he shall not be able to hide
himself;
His seed is spoiled, and his
brethren,
And his neighbours, and he is
not.

11 Leave thy fatherless children,
I will rear them,
And let thy widows trust in Me.

12. For thus saith the LORD: Behold,
they to whom it pertained not to
drink of the cup shall assuredly
drink; and art thou he that shall
altogether go unpunished? thou
shalt not go unpunished, but thou
shalt surely drink. 13. For I have
sworn by Myself, saith the LORD,
that Bozrah shall become an
astonishment, a reproach, a waste,
and a curse; and all the cities thereof
shall be perpetual wastes.

14 I have heard a message from the
LORD,

גִּלֵּיתִי אֶת־מִסְתָּרָיו
וְנֶחְבָּה לֹא יוּכָל
שֻׁדַּד זַרְעוֹ וְאֶחָיו
וּשְׁכֵנָיו וְאֵינֶנּוּ:

11 עָזְבָה יְתֹמֶיךָ אֲנִי אֲחַיֶּה
וְאַלְמְנֹתֶיךָ עָלַי תִּבְטָחוּ:

12 כִּי־כֹה ׀ אָמַר יְהֹוָה הִנֵּה
אֲשֶׁר־אֵין מִשְׁפָּטָם לִשְׁתּוֹת
הַכּוֹס שָׁתוֹ יִשְׁתּוּ וְאַתָּה הוּא
נָקֹה תִּנָּקֶה לֹא תִנָּקֶה כִּי שָׁתֹה
תִשְׁתֶּה:

13 כִּי בִי נִשְׁבַּעְתִּי נְאֻם־
יְהֹוָה כִּי־לְשַׁמָּה לְחֶרְפָּה
לְחֹרֶב וְלִקְלָלָה תִּהְיֶה בָצְרָה
וְכָל־עָרֶיהָ תִהְיֶינָה לְחָרְבוֹת
עוֹלָם:

14 שְׁמוּעָה שָׁמַעְתִּי מֵאֵת יְהֹוָה

---

10. *his secret places.* His hidden retreats
and fastnesses (Metsudath David).

his seed is spoiled. The next verse shows
that this is not meant literally in the
sense of total extermination, but rather
as denoting widespread destruction of
young and old (Daath Mikra).

11. *I will rear them,* etc. A tender verse.
Stern justice demands the suffering
predicted in the previous verses;
nevertheless, even when punishing, God
does not abandon His love for His
creatures, and the fatherless and widows
who survive the holocaust may safely be
left to His care. Maybe, too, this is an
exhortation to spare the women and
children from the horrors of war. This
is in accordance with Daath Mikra.

12. *they to whom it pertained not to drink,*
etc. Other nations will also be punished for gloating over Israel's downfall, although no fraternal ties bound
them. How much more so Edom, who
has a close affinity and blood relationship with Israel, being descended from
Esau, Jacob's brother! He should have
been grief-stricken and eager to render
assistance, instead of rejoicing at and
taking advantage of Israel's catastrophe,
and even intensifying it (cf. Obad. 1,
10–14) (Rashi, Kimchi).

13. *I have sworn by Myself.* See on xxii.
5.

Bozrah. See on xlviii. 24. It is usually
identified with Busaireh, twenty miles
south-east of the Dead Sea (Daath
Mikra).

And an ambassador is sent
among the nations:
'Gather yourselves together, and
come against her,
And rise up to the battle.'

15 For, behold, I make thee small
among the nations,
And despised among men.

16 Thy terribleness hath deceived
thee,
Even the pride of thy heart,
O thou that dwellest in the clefts
of the rock,
That holdest the height of the
hill;
Though thou shouldest make thy
nest as high as the eagle,
I will bring thee down from
thence, saith the LORD.

17 And Edom shall become an
astonishment;
Every one that passeth by it
Shall be astonished and shall
hiss at all the plagues thereof.

18 As in the overthrow of Sodom
and Gomorrah
And the neighbour cities thereof,
saith the LORD,

וְצִיר בַּגּוֹיִם שָׁלוּחַ
הִתְקַבְּצוּ וּבֹאוּ עָלֶיהָ
וְקוּמוּ לַמִּלְחָמָה:

15 כִּי־הִנֵּה קָטֹן נְתַתִּיךָ בַּגּוֹיִם
בָּזוּי בָּאָדָם:

16 תִּפְלַצְתְּךָ הִשִּׁיא אֹתָךְ
זְדוֹן לִבֶּךָ
שֹׁכְנִי בְּחַגְוֵי הַסֶּלַע
תֹּפְשִׂי מְרוֹם גִּבְעָה
כִּי־תַגְבִּיהַ כַּנֶּשֶׁר קִנֶּךָ
מִשָּׁם אוֹרִידְךָ נְאֻם־יְהוָה:

17 וְהָיְתָה אֱדוֹם לְשַׁמָּה
כֹּל עֹבֵר עָלֶיהָ
יִשֹּׁם וְיִשְׁרֹק
עַל־כָּל־מַכּוֹתֶהָ:

18 כְּמַהְפֵּכַת סְדֹם וַעֲמֹרָה
וּשְׁכֵנֶיהָ אָמַר יְהוָה

14. *a message ... an ambassador is sent.* The message (or, report) is that *an ambassador is sent,* etc. (Metsudath David). It is as though an ambassador is sent among the nations, urging them to gather and wage war against Edom (Kimchi). Kara explains that the prophet is the ambassador to the nations to give them God's message to wage war against Edom.

15. Edom lost her independence in the second century B.C.E. when she was conquered by John Hyrcanus and became part of Judea. In the rebellion against Rome, the Edomites (Idumeans as they were then called) played an important part.

16. *thy terribleness hath deceived thee.* The very strength which Edom at one time enjoyed and made her terrible in the eyes of her neighbours has deceived her and led to her ultimate downfall (Metsudath David).

as high as the eagle. Who makes his nest in a lofty place (Metsudath David).

I will bring thee down. To earth and deliver thee into the hand of the enemy (Metsudath David).

17. The language resembles that of xix. 8.

18. *and the neighbour cities thereof.* Cf. Deut. xxix. 22, where Admah and

No man shall abide there,
Neither shall any son of man
    dwell therein.

19 Behold, he shall come up like a
    lion from the thickets of the
    Jordan
Against the strong habitation;
For I will suddenly make him
    run away from it,
And whoso is chosen, him will I
    appoint over it;
For who is like Me? and who will
    appoint Me a time?
And who is that shepherd that
    will stand before Me?

20 Therefore hear ye the counsel
    of the Lord,
That He hath taken against
    Edom;
And His purposes, that He hath
    purposed against the inhabit-
    ants of Teman:
Surely the least of the flock shall
    drag them away,

לֹא־יֵשֵׁב שָׁם אִישׁ
וְלֹא־יָגוּר בָּהּ בֶּן־אָדָם׃
19 הִנֵּה כְּאַרְיֵה יַעֲלֶה
מִגְּאוֹן הַיַּרְדֵּן
אֶל־נְוֵה אֵיתָן
כִּי־אַרְגִּיעָה אֲרִיצֶנּוּ מֵעָלֶיהָ
וּמִי בָחוּר אֵלֶיהָ אֶפְקֹד
כִּי מִי כָמוֹנִי וּמִי יֹעִידֶנִּי
וּמִי־זֶה רֹעֶה
אֲשֶׁר יַעֲמֹד לְפָנָי׃
20 לָכֵן שִׁמְעוּ עֲצַת־יְהֹוָה
אֲשֶׁר יָעַץ אֶל־אֱדוֹם
וּמַחְשְׁבוֹתָיו אֲשֶׁר חָשַׁב
אֶל־יֹשְׁבֵי תֵימָן
אִם־לֹא יִסְחָבוּם
צְעִירֵי הַצֹּאן

Zeboiim are mentioned as the cities overthrown together with Sodom and Gomorrah (cf. also Gen. x. 19, xix. 24f.). The verse is substantially repeated in l. 40.

19-21. Cf. l. 44-46 where the verses are applied almost *verbatim* to Babylon.

19. *he shall come up.* Edom's enemy and conqueror is the subject (Metsudath David).

the thickets of the Jordan. See on xii. 5.

the strong habitation. Edom, which thought herself so strong to withstand attackers (Kara).

I will suddenly make him run away. The meaning is obscure and may be: I will make him (the enemy) run away from

Edom, not in defeat, but because in one moment (*suddenly*) he will have overrun and destroyed her, so that he now leaves her for further conquests. Alternatively, the text may be rendered: 'suddenly I will make him run over her.' Both are suggested by Rashi.

who will appoint Me a time? To contend with Me; [i.e. who can dispute My will? In former days the commanders of opposing armies mutually arranged the time for battle] (Rashi, Kimchi).

shepherd. i.e. king or leader (cf. iii. 15, vi. 3); which king of Edom can withstand Me? (Kimchi).

20. *the least of the flock.* A nation which is now regarded as weak. The Rabbis apply it to the Persians. Although they

Surely their habitation shall be
appalled at them.

21 The earth quaketh at the noise
of their fall;
There is a cry, the noise whereof
is heard in the Red Sea.

22 Behold, he shall come up and
swoop down as the vulture,
And spread out his wings against
Bozrah;
And the heart of the mighty men
of Edom at that day
Shall be as the heart of a woman
in her pangs.

23 Of Damascus.
Hamath is ashamed, and Arpad;
For they have heard evil tidings,
they are melted away;
There is trouble in the sea;
It cannot be quiet.

אִם־לֹא־יַשִּׁים
עֲלֵיהֶם נְוֵהֶם:

21 מִקּוֹל נִפְלָם רָעֲשָׁה הָאָרֶץ
צְעָקָה בְּיַם־סוּף
נִשְׁמַע קוֹלָהּ:

22 הִנֵּה כַנֶּשֶׁר יַעֲלֶה וְיִדְאֶה
וְיִפְרֹשׂ כְּנָפָיו עַל־בָּצְרָה
וְהָיָה לֵב גִּבּוֹרֵי אֱדוֹם
בַּיּוֹם הַהוּא
כְּלֵב אִשָּׁה מְצֵרָה:

23 לְדַמֶּשֶׂק
בּוֹשָׁה חֲמָת וְאַרְפָּד
כִּי־שְׁמֻעָה רָעָה שָׁמְעוּ נָמֹגוּ
בַּיָּם דְּאָגָה
הַשְׁקֵט לֹא יוּכָל:

נ״א קולם v. 21.

became a great Power, their ancestor,
Tiras, was the youngest of the sons of
Japheth, and might with justice be
described as *the least of the flock* (Rashi).

shall be appalled. The land is personified and represented as being horror-
stricken at the catastrophe which has
befallen the inhabitants. Jewish exegetes, however, explain this as an
expression of desolation. "Shall be
desolate because of them."

21. *there is a cry ... Red Sea.* This
translation follows Kimchi, Abarbanel,
Isaiah da Trani, and Metsudath David.
Malbim renders: "Such a cry, the sound
thereof was heard by the Red Sea." i.e.
such a cry was emitted by the Egyptians
when they were overwhelmed at the Red
Sea.

22. Cf. xlviii. 40f.

23-27 JUDGMENT UPON DAMASCUS

23. *Damascus.* The capital of Syria.

Hamath. The modern Hama, on the
Orontes, 110 miles north of Damascus.

is ashamed. i.e. filled with dismay at the
news of Nebuchadnezzar's conquests
(Abarbanel).

Arpad. Tel Erfad, 95 miles north of
Hamath. These three cities of Syria are
mentioned together in Isa. x. 9 (cf. also
Isa. xxxvi. 19, xxxvii. 13).

melted away. Helpless through fear (cf.
Exod. xv. 15).

there is trouble in the sea. This must be
understood metaphorically, there being

24 Damascus is waxed feeble, she
   turneth herself to flee,
   And trembling hath seized on
   her;
   Anguish and pangs have taken
   hold of her, as of a woman in
   travail.
25 'How is the city of praise left
   unrepaired,
   The city of my joy?'
26 Therefore her young men shall
   fall in her broad places,
   And all the men of war shall be
   brought to silence in that day,
   Saith the LORD of hosts.
27 And I will kindle a fire in the wall
   of Damascus,
   And it shall devour the palaces
   of Ben-hadad.
28. Of Kedar, and of the kingdoms
of Hazor, which Nebuchadrezzar
king of Babylon smote.
   Thus saith the LORD:
   Arise ye, go up against Kedar,

רָפְתָה דַמֶּשֶׂק הִפְנְתָה לָנוּס 24
וְרֶטֶט הֶחֱזִיקָה
צָרָה וַחֲבָלִים
אֲחָזָתָה כַּיּוֹלֵדָה:
אֵיךְ לֹא־עֻזְּבָה עִיר תְּהִלָּה 25
קִרְיַת מְשׂוֹשִׂי:
לָכֵן יִפְּלוּ בַחוּרֶיהָ בִּרְחֹבֹתֶיהָ 26
וְכָל־אַנְשֵׁי הַמִּלְחָמָה יִדַּמּוּ
בַּיּוֹם הַהוּא
נְאֻם יְהוָה צְבָאוֹת:
וְהִצַּתִּי אֵשׁ בְּחוֹמַת דַּמָּשֶׂק 27
וְאָכְלָה אַרְמְנוֹת בֶּן־הֲדָד:
לְקֵדָר | וּלְמַמְלְכוֹת חָצוֹר 28
אֲשֶׁר הִכָּה נְבוּכַדְרֶאצּוֹר
מֶלֶךְ־בָּבֶל
כֹּה אָמַר יְהוָה
קוּמוּ עֲלוּ אֶל־קֵדָר

v. 25 יתיר ו׳ .28 .v תהלת ק׳

no sea at Damascus. The sense is: trouble is brewing. For this figure of the sea as typifying restlessness, cf. Isa. lvii. 20 where the Hebrew for *it cannot be quiet* occurs *verbatim* (so Rashi and Kimchi).

25. *how is . . . my joy?* The prophet puts the sentence into the mouth of a citizen (or perhaps, the king) of Damascus. The Hebrew verb translated *unrepaired* is differently interpreted. Rashi explains: How was it that there was neglect in fortifying the city's walls? Metsudath David, taking the verb in its literal sense, interprets: Why was this famous city not 'forsaken,' i.e. left untouched, by the Babylonians?

26. *therefore.* Better, 'nevertheless,' i.e. notwithstanding the question in the preceding verse.

27. *it shall devour the palaces of Ben-hadad.* Quoted from Amos i. 4. The name Ben-hadad was borne by several kings of Syria (cf. 1 Kings xv. 18, xx. 1; 2 Kings vi. 24, viii. 7, xiii. 3).

28-33 JUDGMENT UPON KEDAR AND HAZOR

28. *Kedar.* See on ii. 10. The name denominates the nomadic Arabs (Rashi).

kingdoms of Hazor. Several modern

And spoil the children of the east.

29 Their tents and their flocks shall
they take,
They shall carry away for themselves their curtains,
And all their vessels, and their
camels;
And they shall proclaim against
them a terror on every side.

30 Flee ye, flit far off. dwell deep,
O ye inhabitants of Hazor, saith
the LORD;
For Nebuchadrezzar king of
Babylon hath taken counsel
against you,
And hath conceived a purpose
against you.

31 Arise, get you up against a
nation that is at ease,
That dwelleth without care, saith
the LORD;
That have neither gates nor bars,
That dwell alone.

32 And their camels shall be a booty,
And the multitude of their cattle
a spoil;

וְשָׁדְדוּ אֶת־בְּנֵי־קֶדֶם:

29 אָהֳלֵיהֶם וְצֹאנָם יִקָּחוּ
יְרִיעוֹתֵיהֶם וְכָל־כְּלֵיהֶם
וּגְמַלֵּיהֶם יִשְׂאוּ לָהֶם
וְקָרְאוּ עֲלֵיהֶם מָגוֹר מִסָּבִיב:

30 נֻסוּ נֻּדוּ מְאֹד הֶעְמִיקוּ לָשֶׁבֶת
יֹשְׁבֵי חָצוֹר נְאֻם־יְהֹוָה
כִּי־יָעַץ עֲלֵיכֶם נְבוּכַדְרֶאצַּר
מֶלֶךְ־בָּבֶל עֵצָה
וְחָשַׁב עֲלֵיהֶם מַחֲשָׁבָה:

31 קוּמוּ עֲלוּ אֶל־גּוֹי שְׁלֵיו
יוֹשֵׁב לָבֶטַח נְאֻם־יְהֹוָה
לֹא־דְלָתַיִם וְלֹא־בְרִיחַ
לוֹ בָּדָד יִשְׁכֹּנוּ:

32 וְהָיוּ גְמַלֵּיהֶם לָבַז
וַהֲמוֹן מִקְנֵיהֶם לְשָׁלָל

v. 29. עליכם ק׳ v. 30. קמץ בז״ק

---

scholars hold that the word is here
connected with *chatser* 'an unwalled
town, a village,' and denotes Arabs
living in settlements, as distinct from
nomads. Cf. Isa. xlii. 11. The plural
kingdoms indicates various tribes which
Nebuchadnezzar smote (Daath Mikra).

the children of the east. The Arabian
tribes located east of Canaan (Kimchi).

29. *tents . . . flocks . . . curtains*, etc. All
the terms used in the verse are appro-
priate to nomads and villagers.

curtains. The tent-hangings, as in iv.
20.

they shall proclaim against them, etc. A.J.
appears to mean that the Babylonians

will bring havoc upon the inhabitants of
Kedar. The clause may be more probably translated: 'They (the inhabitants)
shall announce, because of them, (the
Babylonians), "Terror on every side"'
so that they will all flee (Malbim).

30. *dwell deep.* See on verse 8.

counsel . . . a purpose. He has planned
to conquer you (Malbim).

31. *arise.* Addressed to the Babylonians by God at Whose will they *conceived a purpose* (Malbim).

that dwelleth without care, etc. The
Babylonians are encouraged to under-
take this campaign because their
opponents *dwelleth without care,* i.e.

And **I** will scatter unto all winds
   them that have the corners
   polled;
And I will bring their calamity
   from every side of them, saith
   the Lord.

33 And Hazor shall be a dwelling-
   place of jackals,
   A desolation for ever;
   No man shall abide there,
   Neither shall any son of man
   dwell therein.

34. The word of the Lord that
came to Jeremiah the prophet
concerning Elam in the beginning of
the reign of Zedekiah king of Judah,
saying:

35 Thus saith the Lord of hosts:
   Behold, I will break the bow of
   Elam,
   The chief of their might.

36 And I will bring against Elam the
   four winds
   From the four quarters of
   heaven,
   And will scatter them toward all
   those winds;

וְזֵרִתִים לְכָל־רוּחַ
קְצוּצֵי פֵאָה
וּמִכָּל־עֲבָרָיו אָבִיא
אֶת־אֵידָם נְאֻם־יְהֹוָה:
33 וְהָיְתָה חָצוֹר לִמְעוֹן תַּנִּים
שְׁמָמָה עַד־עוֹלָם
לֹא־יֵשֵׁב שָׁם אִישׁ
וְלֹא־יָגוּר בָּהּ בֶּן־אָדָם:
34 אֲשֶׁר הָיָה דְבַר־יְהֹוָה אֶל־
יִרְמְיָהוּ הַנָּבִיא אֶל־עֵילָם
בְּרֵאשִׁית מַלְכוּת צִדְקִיָּה
מֶלֶךְ־יְהוּדָה לֵאמֹר:
35 כֹּה אָמַר יְהֹוָה צְבָאוֹת
הִנְנִי שֹׁבֵר אֶת־קֶשֶׁת עֵילָם
רֵאשִׁית גְּבוּרָתָם:
36 וְהֵבֵאתִי אֶל־עֵילָם
אַרְבַּע רוּחוֹת
מֵאַרְבַּע קְצוֹת הַשָּׁמַיִם
וְזֵרִתִים לְכֹל הָרֻחוֹת הָאֵלֶּה

thinking themselves secure from attack,
they have made no preparations for
defence; *they have neither gates nor bars,*
i.e. they live in open villages without
fortifications and can be easily overrun;
and they *dwell alone* and have no
alliances with neighbouring peoples to
come to their aid (Malbim).

32. *the corners polled.* See on ix. 25.

33. *dwelling-place of jackals.* Cf. ix. 10.

dwell. Even temporarily (Metsudath
David).

34-39 JUDGMENT UPON ELAM

34. *Elam.* Now called Chuzistan, a
country east of Babylonia from which it
is separated by the Tigris.

35. *the bow.* The Elamites were famous
for their skill in archery (cf. Isa. xxii. 6);
but inasmuch as the same phrase is used
of the Northern Kingdom of Israel
(Hos. i. 5), the phrase may signify
nothing more than 'the might,' as in
Targum Jonathan.

36. *the four winds.* Attacks will be

And there shall be no nation whither the dispersed of Elam shall not come.

וְלֹא־יִהְיֶה הַגּוֹי אֲשֶׁר
לֹא־יָבוֹא שָׁם נִדְחֵי עֵילָם׃

37 And I will cause Elam to be dismayed before their enemies,
And before them that seek their life;
And I will bring evil upon them,
Even My fierce anger, saith the LORD;
And I will send the sword after them,
Till I have consumed them;

37 וְהַחְתַּתִּי אֶת־עֵילָם
לִפְנֵי אֹיְבֵיהֶם
וְלִפְנֵי ׀ מְבַקְשֵׁי נַפְשָׁם
וְהֵבֵאתִי עֲלֵיהֶם ׀ רָעָה
אֶת־חֲרוֹן אַפִּי נְאֻם־יְהוָה
וְשִׁלַּחְתִּי אַחֲרֵיהֶם
אֶת־הַחֶרֶב
עַד כַּלּוֹתִי אוֹתָם׃

38 And I will set My throne in Elam,
And will destroy from thence king and princes, saith the LORD.

38 וְשַׂמְתִּי כִסְאִי בְּעֵילָם
וְהַאֲבַדְתִּי מִשָּׁם מֶלֶךְ וְשָׂרִים
נְאֻם־יְהוָה׃

39 But it shall come to pass in the end of days,
That I will bring back the captivity of Elam, saith the LORD.

39 וְהָיָה ׀ בְּאַחֲרִית הַיָּמִים
אָשִׁיב אֶת־שְׁבִית עֵילָם
נְאֻם־יְהוָה׃

1. The word that the LORD spoke

1 הַדָּבָר אֲשֶׁר דִּבֶּר יְהוָה אֶל־

v. 36. סבירין יבואו ק׳   v. 36. עילם ק׳   v. 39. אשיב ק׳   v. 39. שבות ק׳

made upon Elam from every side (Targum).

38. *I will set My throne in Elam.* A phrase signifying that God will sit in judgment upon the nation. Kimchi interprets metaphorically: the widespread destruction will prove that God alone is King. The Rabbis (Meg. 10b, 11a), identifying Elam with Persia, refer the fulfilment of this prophecy to the days of Haman: the chain of events which led to the deliverance of the Jews from Haman's machinations, though natural in themselves, was none the less forged by God, whereby He displayed His Sovereignty.

39. See on xlviii. 47.

CHAPTER L

JUDGMENT UPON BABYLON

The exceptional length of this oracle (l. 1-li. 58) as compared with the

concerning Babylon, concerning the land of the Chaldeans, by Jeremiah the prophet.

2 Declare ye among the nations and announce,
And set up a standard;
Announce, and conceal not;
Say: 'Babylon is taken,
Bel is put to shame, Merodach is dismayed;
Her images are put to shame, her idols are dismayed.'

3 For out of the north there cometh up a nation against her,
Which shall make her land desolate,
And none shall dwell therein;
They are fled, they are gone, both man and beast.

בָּבֶל אֶל־אֶרֶץ כַּשְׂדִּים בְּיַד
יִרְמְיָהוּ הַנָּבִיא:
2 הַגִּידוּ בַגּוֹיִם וְהַשְׁמִיעוּ
וּשְׂאוּ־נֵס
הַשְׁמִיעוּ אַל־תְּכַחֵדוּ
אִמְרוּ נִלְכְּדָה בָבֶל
הֹבִישׁ בֵּל חַת מְרֹדָךְ
הֹבִישׁוּ עֲצַבֶּיהָ חַתּוּ גִּלּוּלֶיהָ:
3 כִּי עָלָה עָלֶיהָ גּוֹי מִצָּפוֹן
הוּא־יָשִׁית אֶת־אַרְצָהּ לְשַׁמָּה
וְלֹא־יִהְיֶה יוֹשֵׁב בָּהּ
מֵאָדָם וְעַד־בְּהֵמָה
נָדוּ הָלָכוּ:

judgments pronounced upon other nations is explained by the prophet's deeper interest in Babylon as his country's conqueror. This explanation also accounts for the sharper and more vindictive tone. It is mere pedantry to urge that Jeremiah regarded Babylon as the agent designated by God for punishing his countrymen. That was true; yet as a patriot he could not but cherish hatred against the ravisher of his land, just as he bewailed his people's fate in spite of having foretold it as just retribution for their sins. His hatred found expression in his joy at Babylon's downfall, a joy further occasioned by the conviction that it was well merited, since 'the virtuous are appointed the agents for reward, whereas the wicked are the agents for retribution' (Talmud).

1. *Babylon . . . the land of the Chaldeans.* Chaldea was originally the southern portion of Babylonia. The Chaldeans gradually became masters of the whole country.

2. *among the nations.* Who had suffered from Babylon's aggressive expansionism (Kimchi).

set up a standard. To summon the people to hear the news (Metsudath David).

Bel . . . Merodach. Babylonian deities. The latter is better known as Marduk.

put to shame . . . dismayed. By their inability to protect their devotees from disaster. [The language, of course, is figurative, and does not imply that the prophet ascribed any reality to these deities] (Kimchi).

3. *out of the north.* An allusion to the Persians (Rashi). Persia is not geographically north of Babylonia; nevertheless its use is easy to understand. To the Jews *the north* was a phrase of sinister import and became a colloquialism to describe the direction from which invasion by a foreign enemy would come. On the other hand, the

4 In those days, and in that time,
saith the LORD,
The children of Israel shall come,
They and the children of Judah
together;
They shall go on their way weep-
ing,
And shall seek the LORD their
God.

5 They shall inquire concerning
Zion
With their faces hitherward:
'Come ye, and join yourselves to
the LORD
In an everlasting covenant that
shall not be forgotten.'

6 My people hath been lost sheep;
Their shepherds have caused them
to go astray,
They have turned them away on
the mountains;
They have gone from mountain
to hill,
They have forgotten their resting-
place.

7 All that found them have devoured
them;
And their adversaries said: 'We
are not guilty';

4 בַּיָּמִים הָהֵמָּה וּבָעֵת הַהִיא
נְאֻם־יְהֹוָה
יָבֹאוּ בְנֵי־יִשְׂרָאֵל
הֵמָּה וּבְנֵי־יְהוּדָה יַחְדָּו
הָלוֹךְ וּבָכוֹ יֵלֵכוּ
וְאֶת־יְהֹוָה אֱלֹהֵיהֶם יְבַקֵּשׁוּ׃

5 צִיּוֹן יִשְׁאָלוּ
דֶּרֶךְ הֵנָּה פְנֵיהֶם
בֹּאוּ וְנִלְווּ אֶל־יְהֹוָה
בְּרִית עוֹלָם לֹא תִשָּׁכֵחַ׃

6 צֹאן אֹבְדוֹת הָיָה עַמִּי
רֹעֵיהֶם הִתְעוּם
הָרִים שׁוֹבֵבִים
מֵהַר אֶל־גִּבְעָה הָלָכוּ
שָׁכְחוּ רִבְצָם׃

7 כָּל־מוֹצְאֵיהֶם אֲכָלוּם
וְצָרֵיהֶם אָמְרוּ לֹא נֶאְשָׁם

v. 5. קמץ בז״ק　v. 6. היו ק׳　v. 6. שובבום ק׳　v. 6. קמץ בז״ק

reference may be to the Medo-Persian
empire, and the Medes lived on the
north-west of Babylonia (Daath Mikra).

4. Cf. iii. 21–25. The overthrow of
Babylon will arouse a feeling of penitence within the hearts of the people of
Israel, now reunited by their common
suffering.

5. *hitherward.* This is an indication
that Jeremiah was in the Holy Land
(Isaiah da Trani).

join yourselves to the LORD. The return
would not merely be to the land as a
nation, but to God as a religious
community (Metsudath David).

an everlasting covenant. Cf. xxxii. 40.

6. *lost sheep.* Better, 'straying sheep'
(see on xxiii. 1).

*they have turned them away on the moun-
tains.* The parallelism of the first half
of the verse suggests that the meaning
is: they have turned them adrift on the
trackless mountains, i.e. have led them
into spiritual dangers (idolatry) with
none to guide them. Rashi comments:
They have led them to idolatrous
worship which was most frequently
practised on mountains.

7. *we are not guilty.* Israel is so worth-
less that no guilt attaches to one who

Because they have sinned against the LORD, the habitation of justice,
Even the LORD, the hope of their fathers.

8 Flee out of the midst of Babylon,
And go forth out of the land of the Chaldeans,
And be as the he-goats before the flocks.

9 For, lo, I will stir up and cause to come up against Babylon
An assembly of great nations from the north country;
And they shall set themselves in array against her,
From thence she shall be taken;
Their arrows shall be as of a mighty man that maketh childless;
None shall return in vain.

10 And Chaldea shall be a spoil;
All that spoil her shall be satisfied, saith the LORD.

11 Because ye are glad, because ye rejoice,
O ye that plunder My heritage,

תַּחַת אֲשֶׁר חָטְאוּ לַיהוָה
נְוֵה־צֶדֶק
וּמִקְוֵה אֲבוֹתֵיהֶם יְהוָה:

8 נֻדוּ מִתּוֹךְ בָּבֶל
וּמֵאֶרֶץ כַּשְׂדִּים יֵצֵאוּ
וִהְיוּ כְּעַתּוּדִים לִפְנֵי־צֹאן:

9 כִּי הִנֵּה אָנֹכִי מֵעִיר
וּמַעֲלֶה עַל־בָּבֶל
קְהַל־גּוֹיִם גְּדֹלִים
מֵאֶרֶץ צָפוֹן
וְעָרְכוּ לָהּ מִשָּׁם תִּלָּכֵד
חִצָּיו כְּגִבּוֹר מַשְׁכִּיל
לֹא יָשׁוּב רֵיקָם:

10 וְהָיְתָה כַשְׂדִּים לְשָׁלָל
כָּל־שֹׁלְלֶיהָ יִשְׂבָּעוּ
נְאֻם־יְהוָה:

11 כִּי תִשְׂמְחוּ כִּי תַעֲלְזוּ
שֹׁסֵי נַחֲלָתִי

v. 8. צאו ק' v. 9. נ״א מַשְׁכִּיל v. 10. קמץ בטרחא v. 11. תשמחו ק' v. 11. תעלזו ק'

destroys him (Kimchi, Kara). This plea is refuted in ii. 3.

8. *flee*, etc. Hurry back to your own country (Kara).

as the he-goats before the flocks. When a gate of the enclosure is opened, the he-goats press forward to pass through first (Rashi, Metsudath David). Let the Judeans be the first of Babylon's captive peoples to go into freedom (Kara).

9. *an assembly of great nations.* They are enumerated in li. 27f.

none shall return in vain. If so translated,

the meaning must be that every arrow will find its mark (Kimchi). Preference is perhaps to be given to the rendering: '(a warrior) not returning empty-handed,' without spoil. However, all Jewish exegetes, as well as Targum, explain in the former manner.

11. *because ye are glad.* The verse may be understood in two ways. On the translation of A.J., it tells the Chaldeans that what is foretold in verse 12 is the sequel to their gloating over the plunder carried away from Judea. Alternatively, the introductory conjunction

327

Because ye gambol as a heifer at grass,
And neigh as strong horses;

12 Your mother shall be sore ashamed,
She that bore you shall be confounded;
Behold, the hindermost of the nations
Shall be a wilderness, a dry land, and a desert.

13 Because of the wrath of the LORD it shall not be inhabited,
But it shall be wholly desolate;
Every one that goeth by Babylon
Shall be appalled and hiss at all her plagues.

14 Set yourselves in array against Babylon round about,
All ye that bend the bow,
Shoot at her, spare no arrows;
For she hath sinned against the LORD.

15 Shout against her round about, she hath submitted herself;

כִּי תָפוּשִׁי כְּעֶגְלָה דָשָׁה
וְתִצְהֲלִי כָּאַבִּרִים:

12 בּוֹשָׁה אִמְּכֶם מְאֹד
חָפְרָה יוֹלַדְתְּכֶם
הִנֵּה אַחֲרִית גּוֹיִם
מִדְבָּר צִיָּה וַעֲרָבָה:

13 מִקֶּצֶף יְהוָה לֹא תֵשֵׁב
וְהָיְתָה שְׁמָמָה כֻּלָּהּ
כֹּל עֹבֵר עַל־בָּבֶל
יִשֹּׁם וְיִשְׁרֹק
עַל־כָּל־מַכּוֹתֶיהָ:

14 עִרְכוּ עַל־בָּבֶל | סָבִיב
כָּל־דֹּרְכֵי קֶשֶׁת
יְדוּ אֵלֶיהָ
אַל־תַּחְמְלוּ אֶל־חֵץ
כִּי לַיהוָה חָטָאָה:

15 הָרִיעוּ עָלֶיהָ סָבִיב נָתְנָה יָדָהּ

v. 11. תפושי ק׳　v. 11. נ״א דשא　v. 11. ותצהלו ק׳

may be rendered 'as,' and the sense will then be that, to the extent of Babylon's rejoicing when gathering spoil from their victims, so will God deliver them into the hands of their spoilers (Kara).

gambol . . . neigh. The first verb describes satiety, the latter the shout of joy. Filled with loot, the Chaldeans had behaved like the animals named (Metsudath David).

12. your mother. The nation of Babylon, personified as mother of the people (Targum).

behold, the hindermost of the nations, etc. A.J. has adopted the translation of A.V.;

but Jewish exegetes render: 'behold, the end of the nations shall be a wilderness,' etc., meaning that the end of the nations, i.e. the end of the kingdom of Babylon, shall be that their country will be a wilderness since all the people will be slain, leaving the country a wasteland (Kimchi).

13. Cf. xviii. 16 where the language is used of Judea.

14. A summons to the enemy to begin the attack.

15. shout. In order to frighten them as Joshua did in the battle of Jericho (Kimchi).

Her buttresses are fallen, her
   walls are thrown down;
For it is the vengeance of the
   LORD, take vengeance upon
   her;
As she hath done, do unto her.

16 Cut off the sower from Babylon,
   And him that handleth the sickle
     in the time of harvest;
For fear of the oppressing sword
   they shall turn every one to
   his people,
And they shall flee every one to
   his own land.

17 Israel is a scattered sheep,
   The lions have driven him away;
First the king of Assyria hath
   devoured him,
And last this Nebuchadrezzar
   king of Babylon hath broken
   his bones.

18 Therefore thus saith the LORD of
   hosts, the God of Israel:
Behold, I will punish the king of
   Babylon and his land,

נָפְלוּ אָשְׁוִיתֶיהָ

נֶהֶרְסוּ חוֹמוֹתֶיהָ

כִּי נִקְמַת יְהֹוָה הִיא הִנָּקְמוּ בָהּ

כַּאֲשֶׁר עָשְׂתָה עֲשׂוּ־לָהּ:

16 כִּרְתוּ זוֹרֵעַ מִבָּבֶל

וְתֹפֵשׂ מַגָּל בְּעֵת קָצִיר

מִפְּנֵי חֶרֶב הַיּוֹנָה

אִישׁ אֶל־עַמּוֹ יִפְנוּ

וְאִישׁ לְאַרְצוֹ יָנֻסוּ:

17 שֶׂה פְזוּרָה יִשְׂרָאֵל

אֲרָיוֹת הִדִּיחוּ

הָרִאשׁוֹן אֲכָלוֹ מֶלֶךְ אַשּׁוּר

וְזֶה הָאַחֲרוֹן עִצְּמוֹ

נְבוּכַדְרֶאצַּר מֶלֶךְ בָּבֶל:

18 לָכֵן כֹּה־אָמַר יְהֹוָה צְבָאוֹת

אֱלֹהֵי יִשְׂרָאֵל

הִנְנִי פֹקֵד אֶל־מֶלֶךְ בָּבֶל

וְאֶל־אַרְצוֹ

v. 15. אשיותיה ק׳

---

she hath submitted herself. lit. 'she hath
given her hand,' i.e. she has capitulated
(Kimchi).

buttresses. The Hebrew word is not
found again in the Bible except,
perhaps in Isa. xvi. 7. All Jewish
exegetes translate it as 'foundations,'
following the cognate noun in Aramaic.
In Isa., Rashi renders: walls.

her walls are thrown down. After the
foundations were dug under, the walls
were thrown down (Daath Mikra).

vengeance of the LORD. Upon Babylon

for the ill-treatment of God's people
(Metsudath David).

16. *cut off the sower.* Babylon being left
a wilderness (verse 12), all agricultural
operations come to an end (Metsudath
David).

17. *first the king of Assyria devoured
him.* A reference to the exile of the Ten
Tribes by Shalmaneser (Rashi, Kimchi).

hath broken his bones. The two remaining tribes of Judah and Benjamin
(Rashi, Kimchi, Metsudath David).

As I have punished the king of
Assyria.

19 And I will bring Israel back to
his pasture,

And he shall feed on Carmel and
Bashan,

And his soul shall be satisfied
upon the hills of Ephraim and
in Gilead.

20 In those days, and in that time,
saith the LORD,

The iniquity of Israel shall be
sought for, and there shall be
none,

And the sins of Judah, and they
shall not be found;

For I will pardon them whom I
leave as a remnant.

21 Go up against the land of
Merathaim, even against it,

And against the inhabitants of
Pekod;

Waste and utterly destroy after
them, saith the LORD,

And do according to all that I
have commanded thee.

כַּאֲשֶׁר פָּקַדְתִּי
אֶל־מֶלֶךְ אַשּׁוּר׃

19 וְשֹׁבַבְתִּי אֶת־יִשְׂרָאֵל
אֶל־נָוֵהוּ
וְרָעָה הַכַּרְמֶל וְהַבָּשָׁן
וּבְהַר אֶפְרַיִם וְהַגִּלְעָד
תִּשְׂבַּע נַפְשׁוֹ׃

20 בַּיָּמִים הָהֵם וּבָעֵת הַהִיא
נְאֻם־יְהֹוָה
יְבֻקַּשׁ אֶת־עֲוֹן יִשְׂרָאֵל וְאֵינֶנּוּ
וְאֶת־חַטֹּאת יְהוּדָה
וְלֹא תִמָּצֶאינָה
כִּי אֶסְלַח לַאֲשֶׁר אַשְׁאִיר׃

21 עַל־הָאָרֶץ מְרָתַיִם
עֲלֵה עָלֶיהָ
וְאֶל־יוֹשְׁבֵי פְּקוֹד
חֲרֹב וְהַחֲרֵם אַחֲרֵיהֶם
נְאֻם־יְהֹוָה
וַעֲשֵׂה כְּכֹל אֲשֶׁר צִוִּיתִךָ׃

v. 20. יתיר י׳

---

18. *Assyria.* [By this time the land had
been invaded and the power of the
nation shattered.]

19. *his pasture.* The Land of Israel in
its earlier dimensions, including even
the territory east of the Jordan.

Carmel. Its name signified fertility (cf.
the Hebrew of iv. 26).

Bashan . . . hills of Ephraim . . . Gilead.
Famous for their forests and herds of
cattle (l. 19; Deut. xxxii. 14; Isa. ii. 13;
Mic. vii. 14; Zech. xi. 2).

20. Cf. xxxi. 33.

21. *go up.* An exhortation to Babylon's conqueror (Metsudath David).

Merathaim . . . Pekod. lit. 'double
rebellion . . . visitation.' The destroyer
is bidden to attack Babylon, the country
which had so grievously rebelled against
God, now due to receive punishment.
The names are a play on actual locali-
ties. In south Babylonia there was a
place called *Mat Marratim,* and a Babylonian people was known as the *Pukudu*

22 Hark! battle is in the land,
And great destruction.

23 How is the hammer of the whole
earth
Cut asunder and broken!
How is Babylon become
A desolation among the nations!

24 I have laid a snare for thee, and
thou art also taken, O Babylon,
And thou wast not aware;
Thou art found, and also caught,
Because thou hast striven against
the LORD.

25 The LORD hath opened His
armoury,
And hath brought forth the
weapons of His indignation;
For it is a work that the Lord
GOD of hosts
Hath to do in the land of the
Chaldeans.

26 Come against her from every
quarter, open her granaries,
Cast her up as heaps, and destroy
her utterly;
Let nothing of her be left.

27 Slay all her bullocks, let them go
down to the slaughter;

קוֹל מִלְחָמָה בָּאָרֶץ 22
וְשֶׁבֶר גָּדוֹל:

אֵיךְ נִגְדַּע וַיִּשָּׁבֵר 23
פַּטִּישׁ כָּל־הָאָרֶץ
אֵיךְ הָיְתָה לְשַׁמָּה
בָּבֶל בַּגּוֹיִם:

יָקֹשְׁתִּי לָךְ וְגַם־נִלְכַּדְתְּ בָּבֶל 24
וְאַתְּ לֹא יָדָעַתְּ
נִמְצֵאת וְגַם־נִתְפַּשְׂתְּ
כִּי בַיהוָה הִתְגָּרִית:

פָּתַח יְהוָה אֶת־אוֹצָרוֹ 25
וַיּוֹצֵא אֶת־כְּלֵי זַעְמוֹ
כִּי־מְלָאכָה הִיא
לַאדֹנָי יֱהֹוִה צְבָאוֹת
בְּאֶרֶץ כַּשְׂדִּים:

בֹּאוּ־לָהּ מִקֵּץ 26
פִּתְחוּ מַאֲבֻסֶיהָ
סָלּוּהָ כְמוֹ־עֲרֵמִים
וְהַחֲרִימוּהָ
אַל־תְּהִי־לָהּ שְׁאֵרִית:

חִרְבוּ כָּל־פָּרֶיהָ יֵרְדוּ לַטָּבַח 27

(cf. Ezek. xxiii. 23) (Rashi, Kimchi,
Daath Mikra).

23. *the hammer*. Babylon which shattered other nations (cf. li. 20ff.) (Rashi).

24. *thou wast not aware*. Babylon fell by
a surprise attack (Abarbanel).

25. *the weapons of His indignation*. The
Persians and Medes who are the
weapons wherewith God wreaks His

indignation upon the Chaldeans
(Metsudath David; cf. Isa. xiii. 5).

26. *cast her up as heaps*. Pile up her
treasures and make an end of them by
carrying them off as spoil or destroying
them (Kimchi).

27. *her bullocks*. Her nobles and
princes (Rashi), or her mighty warriors
(cf. Isa. xxxiv. 7; Ps. xxii. 13) (Targum,
Kimchi).

Woe unto them! for their day is come, The time of their visitation.	הוֹי עֲלֵיהֶם כִּי־בָא יוֹמָם עֵת פְּקֻדָּתָם׃
28 Hark! they flee and escape out of the land of Babylon, To declare in Zion the vengeance of the LORD our God, The vengeance of His temple.	28 קוֹל נָסִים וּפְלֵטִים מֵאֶרֶץ בָּבֶל לְהַגִּיד בְּצִיּוֹן אֶת־נִקְמַת יְהֹוָה אֱלֹהֵינוּ נִקְמַת הֵיכָלוֹ׃
29 Call together the archers against Babylon, All them that bend the bow; Encamp against her round about, Let none thereof escape; Recompense her according to her work, According to all that she hath done, do unto her: For she hath been arrogant against the LORD, Against the Holy One of Israel.	29 הַשְׁמִיעוּ אֶל־בָּבֶל ׀ רַבִּים כָּל־דֹּרְכֵי קֶשֶׁת חֲנוּ עָלֶיהָ סָבִיב אַל־יְהִי־ לָ֯הּ פְּלֵטָה שַׁלְּמוּ־לָהּ כְּפָעֳלָהּ כְּכֹל אֲשֶׁר עָשְׂתָה עֲשׂוּ־לָהּ כִּי אֶל־יְהֹוָה זָדָה אֶל־קְדוֹשׁ יִשְׂרָאֵל׃
30 Therefore shall her young men fall in her broad places, And all her men of war shall be brought to silence in that day, Saith the LORD.	30 לָכֵן יִפְּלוּ בַחוּרֶיהָ בִּרְחֹבֹתֶיהָ וְכָל־אַנְשֵׁי מִלְחַמְתָּהּ יִדַּמּוּ בַּיּוֹם הַהוּא נְאֻם־יְהֹוָה׃
31 Behold, I am against thee, O thou most arrogant, Saith the Lord GOD of hosts; For thy day is come, The time that I will punish thee.	31 הִנְנִי אֵלֶיךָ זָדוֹן נְאֻם־אֲדֹנָי יֱהֹוִה צְבָאוֹת כִּי בָּא יוֹמְךָ עֵת פְּקַדְתִּיךָ׃
32 And the most arrogant shall stumble and fall,	32 וְכָשַׁל זָדוֹן וְנָפַל

v. 29. לה קרי ולא כתיב.

---

28. *they flee.* The Jews who return to their homeland (Kimchi).

the vengeance of His temple. For having been burnt by the Chaldeans (Metsu-dath David).

30. Repeated *verbatim* from xlix. 26 where it applies to Damascus.

31f. Cf. xxi. 13f.

And none shall raise him up;
And I will kindle a fire in his
    cities,
And it shall devour all that are
    round about him.

33 Thus saith the LORD of hosts:
The children of Israel and the
    children of Judah are op-
    pressed together;
And all that took them captives
    hold them fast;
They refuse to let them go.

34 Their Redeemer is strong,
The LORD of hosts is His name;
He will thoroughly plead their
    cause,
That He may give rest to the
    earth,
And disquiet the inhabitants of
    Babylon.

35 A sword is upon the Chaldeans,
    saith the LORD,
And upon the inhabitants of
    Babylon, and upon her princes,
    and upon her wise men.

36 A sword is upon the boasters,
    and they shall become fools;
A sword is upon her mighty
    men, and they shall be dis-
    mayed.

37 A sword is upon their horses,
    and upon their chariots,

וְאֵין לוֹ מֵקִים
וְהִצַּתִּי אֵשׁ בְּעָרָיו
וְאָכְלָה כָּל־סְבִיבֹתָיו׃

33 כֹּה אָמַר יְהוָה צְבָאוֹת
עֲשׁוּקִים בְּנֵי־יִשְׂרָאֵל
וּבְנֵי־יְהוּדָה יַחְדָּו
וְכָל־שֹׁבֵיהֶם הֶחֱזִיקוּ בָם
מֵאֲנוּ שַׁלְּחָם׃

34 גֹּאֲלָם ׀ חָזָק
יְהוָה צְבָאוֹת שְׁמוֹ
רִיב יָרִיב אֶת־רִיבָם
לְמַעַן הִרְגִּיעַ אֶת־הָאָרֶץ
וְהִרְגִּיז לְיֹשְׁבֵי בָבֶל׃

35 חֶרֶב עַל־כַּשְׂדִּים נְאֻם־יְהוָה
וְאֶל־יֹשְׁבֵי בָבֶל
וְאֶל־שָׂרֶיהָ וְאֶל־חֲכָמֶיהָ׃

36 חֶרֶב אֶל־הַבַּדִּים וְנֹאָלוּ
חֶרֶב אֶל־גִּבּוֹרֶיהָ וָחָתּוּ׃

37 חֶרֶב אֶל־סוּסָיו וְאֶל־רִכְבּוֹ

---

34. *their Redeemer.* [The Hebrew *goël*
signifies a near kinsman who has the
duty to avenge a murder and act as
protector (cf. Lev. xxv. 25; Num. xxxv.
21). God is represented as Israel's *goël*
Who will avenge and rescue.]

give rest to the earth. As the sequel to
Babylon's downfall (Rashi).

35. *wise men.* Perhaps the astrologers
who advised the national rulers (Daath
Mikra).

36. *boasters.* A.V. 'liars' follows Rashi
and Kimchi. It refers to the diviners who
assured Babylon of permanent domination (Abarbanel). [The order of these
verses is noteworthy: the princes, wise
men and diviners are the first to fall.
They nourish the spirit and morale of a
people, the imponderable essentials for
a successful war. Accordingly it is stated
that the will to victory will be destroyed
at its source, after which the demoral-
ization of the army follows as a matter of
course.]

And upon all the mingled people
that are in the midst of her,
And they shall become as
women;
A sword is upon her treasures,
and they shall be robbed.

38 A drought is upon her waters,
and they shall be dried up;
For it is a land of graven images,
And they are mad upon things of
horror.

39 Therefore the wild-cats with the
jackals shall dwell there,
And the ostriches shall dwell
therein;
And it shall be no more inhabited for ever,
Neither shall it be dwelt in from
generation to generation.

40 As when God overthrew Sodom
and Gomorrah
And the neighbour cities thereof,
saith the LORD;
So shall no man abide there,
Neither shall any son of man
dwell therein.

41 Behold, a people cometh from
the north,
And a great nation, and many
kings
Shall be roused from the uttermost parts of the earth.

וְאֶל־כָּל־הָעֶרֶב
אֲשֶׁר בְּתוֹכָהּ
וְהָיוּ לְנָשִׁים
חֶרֶב אֶל־אוֹצְרֹתֶיהָ וּבֻזָּזוּ:

38 חֹרֶב אֶל־מֵימֶיהָ וְיָבֵשׁוּ
כִּי אֶרֶץ פְּסִלִים הִיא
וּבָאֵימִים יִתְהֹלָלוּ:

39 לָכֵן יֵשְׁבוּ צִיִּים אֶת־אִיִּים
וְיָשְׁבוּ בָהּ בְּנוֹת יַעֲנָה
וְלֹא־תֵשֵׁב עוֹד לָנֶצַח
וְלֹא תִשְׁכּוֹן עַד־דּוֹר וָדֹר:

40 כְּמַהְפֵּכַת אֱלֹהִים
אֶת־סְדֹם וְאֶת־עֲמֹרָה
וְאֶת־שְׁכֵנֶיהָ נְאֻם־יְהֹוָה
לֹא־יֵשֵׁב שָׁם אִישׁ
וְלֹא־יָגוּר בָּהּ בֶּן־אָדָם:

41 הִנֵּה עַם בָּא מִצָּפוֹן
וְגוֹי גָּדוֹל וּמְלָכִים רַבִּים
יֵעֹרוּ מִיַּרְכְּתֵי־אָרֶץ:

---

37. *the mingled people.* This may mean
foreign traders or mercenaries (cf. xxv.
20).

38. *drought.* The Hebrew *choreb*
(drought) has the same consonants as
chereb (sword) in the preceding
two verses and was no doubt suggested by it.

her waters. Upon which the commer-
cial prosperity of Babylon depends
(Metsudath David).

things of horror. The idols, so-called
because of their terrifying grotesqueness
(Malbim).

39. These verses are reminiscent of Isa.
xiii. 19–22, while verse 40 is an almost
verbal repetition of xlix. 18. I will send
there horrible creatures resembling the
horrible beasts whose likeness they
made for idols (Malbim).

41–43. A repetition of vi. 22–24 with
the necessary changes, since there Jerusalem is the subject, while here Babylon
is threatened.

41. *a people.* The Persians and the
Medes (Metsudath David).

the north. See on verse 3.

42 They lay hold on bow and spear,
They are cruel, and have no
compassion;
Their voice is like the roaring
sea,
And they ride upon horses;
Set in array, as a man for war,
Against thee, O daughter of
Babylon.

43 The king of Babylon hath heard
the fame of them,
And his hands wax feeble;
Anguish hath taken hold of him,
And pain, as of a woman in
travail.

44 Behold, he shall come up like a
lion from the thickets of the
Jordan
Against the strong habitation;
For I will suddenly make them
run away from it,
And whoso is chosen, him will I
appoint over it;
For who is like Me? and who will
appoint Me a time?
And who is that shepherd that
will stand before Me?

45 Therefore hear ye the counsel of
the LORD,
That He hath taken against
Babylon,
And His purposes, that He hath
purposed against the land of
the Chaldeans:
Surely the least of the flock shall
drag them away,

42 קֶ֤שֶׁת וְכִידֹן֙ יַחֲזִ֔יקוּ
אַכְזָרִ֥י הֵ֖מָּה וְלֹ֣א יְרַחֵ֑מוּ
קוֹלָם֙ כַּיָּ֣ם יֶהֱמֶ֔ה
וְעַל־סוּסִ֖ים יִרְכָּ֑בוּ
עָר֗וּךְ כְּאִישׁ֙ לַמִּלְחָמָ֔ה
עָלַ֖יִךְ בַּת־בָּבֶֽל׃

43 שָׁמַ֧ע מֶֽלֶךְ־בָּבֶ֛ל אֶת־שִׁמְעָ֖ם
וְרָפ֣וּ יָדָ֑יו
צָרָה֙ הֶחֱזִיקַ֔תְהוּ
חִ֖יל כַּיּוֹלֵדָֽה׃

44 הִ֠נֵּה כְּאַרְיֵ֞ה יַעֲלֶ֗ה
מִגְּאוֹן֙ הַיַּרְדֵּ֔ן
אֶל־נְוֵ֖ה אֵיתָ֑ן
כִּֽי־אַרְגִּ֤עָה אֲרֹצֵם֙ מֵעָלֶ֔יהָ
וּמִ֥י בָח֖וּר אֵלֶ֣יהָ אֶפְקֹ֑ד
כִּ֣י מִ֤י כָמ֙וֹנִי֙ וּמִ֣י יֹעִידֶ֔נִּי
וּמִי־זֶ֣ה רֹעֶ֔ה
אֲשֶׁ֥ר יַעֲמֹ֖ד לְפָנָֽי׃

45 לָכֵ֞ן שִׁמְע֣וּ עֲצַת־יְהוָ֗ה
אֲשֶׁ֤ר יָעַץ֙ אֶל־בָּבֶ֔ל
וּמַ֣חְשְׁבוֹתָ֔יו אֲשֶׁ֥ר חָשַׁ֖ב
אֶל־אֶ֣רֶץ כַּשְׂדִּ֑ים
אִם־לֹ֤א יִסְחָבוּם֙
צְעִירֵ֣י הַצֹּ֔אן

אריצם ק׳ v. 44.

44-46. Almost a repetition of xlix.
19-21; there it applies to Edom, here to
Babylon.

44. *he shall come up.* The subject is
Cyrus; in xlix. 19 it is Nebuchadnezzar.
[The language which was used to

335

Surely their habitation shall be
appalled at them,

46 At the noise of the taking of
Babylon the earth quaketh,
And the cry is heard among the
nations.

אִם־לֹא יַשִּׁים עֲלֵיהֶם נָוֶה:

מִקּוֹל נִתְפְּשָׂה בָבֶל 46
נִרְעֲשָׁה הָאָרֶץ
וּזְעָקָה בַּגּוֹיִם נִשְׁמָע:

51　　　　　CHAPTER LI　　　　　**נא**

1 Thus saith the LORD:

Behold, I will raise up against
Babylon,
And agaInst them that dwell in
Leb-kamai, a destroying wind

2 And I will send unto Babylon
strangers, that shall fan her,
And they shall empty her land;
For in the day of trouble they
shall be against her round about.

3 Let the archer bend his bow
against her,
And let him lift himself up against
her in his coat of mail;

כֹּה אָמַר יְהֹוָה 1
הִנְנִי מֵעִיר עַל־בָּבֶל
וְאֶל־יֹשְׁבֵי לֵב קָמָי
רוּחַ מַשְׁחִית:
וְשִׁלַּחְתִּי לְבָבֶל ׀ זָרִים וְזֵרוּהָ 2
וִיבֹקְקוּ אֶת־אַרְצָהּ
כִּי־הָיוּ עָלֶיהָ מִסָּבִיב
בְּיוֹם רָעָה:
אֶל־יִדְרֹךְ יִדְרֹךְ 3
הַדֹּרֵךְ קַשְׁתּוֹ
וְאֶל־יִתְעַל בְּסִרְיֹנוֹ

v. 3. נ״א אֶל—וְאֶל כתיב ולא קרי v. 3.

describe the latter's overwhelming
might is now applied to his conqueror.
Military power, no matter how seemingly permanent, is but ephemeral.]

46. *the cry.* Of Babylon's anguish
(Metsudath David).

CHAPTER LI

1–58 JUDGMENT UPON BABYLON
CONTINUED

1. *Leb-kamai.* lit. 'the heart of them
that rise up against Me.' According to

tradition, the name is a cypher for
Casdim, Chaldea (see on xxv. 26).

a destroying wind. An allusion to Cyrus
(Rashi).

2. *strangers, that shall fan her.* There is a
play on the words *zarim (strangers)* and
zeruha (fan her) (Kimchi). For the verb,
see on xv. 7.

3. The verse is difficult, and for *el* and
we-el there is a variant reading *al* and
we-al. The translation of A.J. follows
Metsudath David who interprets *el* as
eleha, 'to her,' or 'against her.' This may

And spare ye not her young men,
Destroy ye utterly all her host.

4 And they shall fall down slain in
the land of the Chaldeans,
And thrust through in her streets.

5 For Israel is not widowed, nor
Judah,
Of his God, of the LORD of hosts;
For their land is full of guilt
Against the Holy One of Israel.

6 Flee out of the midst of Babylon,
And save every man his life,
Be not cut off in her iniquity;
For it is the time of the LORD's
vengeance;
He will render unto her a recom-
pense.

7 Babylon hath been a golden cup
in the LORD's hand,

וְאַל־תַּחְמְלוּ אֶל־בַּחֻרֶיהָ
הַחֲרִימוּ כָּל־צְבָאָהּ:

4 וְנָפְלוּ חֲלָלִים בְּאֶרֶץ כַּשְׂדִּים
וּמְדֻקָּרִים בְּחוּצוֹתֶיהָ:

5 כִּי לֹא־אַלְמָן
יִשְׂרָאֵל וִיהוּדָה מֵאֱלֹהָיו
מֵיְהֹוָה צְבָאוֹת
כִּי אַרְצָם מָלְאָה אָשָׁם
מִקְּדוֹשׁ יִשְׂרָאֵל:

6 נֻסוּ ׀ מִתּוֹךְ בָּבֶל
וּמַלְּטוּ אִישׁ נַפְשׁוֹ
אַל־תִּדַּמּוּ בַּעֲוֺנָהּ
כִּי עֵת נְקָמָה הִיא לַיהֹוָה
גְּמוּל הוּא מְשַׁלֵּם לָהּ:

7 כּוֹס־זָהָב בָּבֶל בְּיַד־יְהֹוָה

be the Targum's translation as it is explained by Kimchi and Ibn Nachmiash. In that case, we would have to emend the words *lah* and *ve-lah* spelled with an *aleph* to the same words spelled with a *he* although we do not find this reading in Kimchi or in Ibn Nachmiash. Kimchi and Abarbanel explain: '[God commands] to the archer who bends his bow and to him who boasts with his coat of mail: Spare ye not her young men, etc.' According to this interpretation, the word order is inverted. Some of the ancient Versions and several Hebrew MSS. support the variant *al* which is adopted by R.V., 'Let not the archer bend his bow, and let him not lift himself up.' This may be Targum Jonathan's interpretation according to our editions. On this interpretation, the Babylonian soldiers guarding the city

are told that resistance is useless. The difficulty in this explanation is that the second half of the verse is obviously spoken to the attackers.

5. *Israel is not widowed.* Has not lost her Protector. The language is based on the imagery common in the Bible of God as Israel's 'husband' (Daath Mikra).

their land. viz. of the Chaldeans (Rashi).

against the Holy One of Israel. The wrongs committed against Israel are sins against Israel's God (Kimchi).

6. *flee.* Addressed to the Judeans (cf. verse 45, l. 8) (Rashi).

the LORD's vengeance. See on l. 15.

7. *a golden cup.* Cf. xxv. 15f. where

That made all the earth drunken;

The nations have drunk of her wine,

Therefore the nations are mad.

8 Babylon is suddenly fallen and destroyed,

Wail for her;

Take balm for her pain,

If so be she may be healed.

9 We would have healed Babylon, but she is not healed;

Forsake her, and let us go every one into his own country;

For her judgment reacheth unto heaven,

And is lifted up even to the skies.

10 The LORD hath brought forth our victory;

Come, and let us declare in Zion

The work of the LORD our God.

11 Make bright the arrows,

מְשַׁכֶּרֶת כָּל־הָאָרֶץ

מִיֵּינָהּ שָׁתוּ גוֹיִם

עַל־כֵּן יִתְהֹלְלוּ גוֹיִם׃

8 פִּתְאֹם נָפְלָה בָבֶל וַתִּשָּׁבֵר

הֵילִילוּ עָלֶיהָ

קְחוּ צֳרִי לְמַכְאוֹבָהּ

אוּלַי תֵּרָפֵא׃

9 רִפִּאנוּ אֶת־בָּבֶל וְלֹא נִרְפָּתָה

עִזְבוּהָ וְנֵלֵךְ אִישׁ לְאַרְצוֹ

כִּי־נָגַע אֶל־הַשָּׁמַיִם מִשְׁפָּטָהּ

וְנִשָּׂא עַד־שְׁחָקִים׃

10 הוֹצִיא יְהֹוָה אֶת־צִדְקֹתֵינוּ

בֹּאוּ וּנְסַפְּרָה בְצִיּוֹן

אֶת־מַעֲשֵׂה יְהֹוָה אֱלֹהֵינוּ׃

11 הָבֵרוּ הַחִצִּים

v. 9. חסר א'

Jeremiah was bidden to make the nations drink of God's wrath. Babylon was God's agent for this purpose (*in the* LORD's *hand*). Kimchi understands the phrase as 'a goblet of wine clear as gold,' comparing 'the golden oil' in Zech. iv. 12. *Golden* possibly typifies the luxury and splendour of the Babylonian empire (Abarbanel).

are mad. Cf. xxv. 16. Intoxicated and bereft of their sense, not knowing how to defend themselves (Metsudath David).

8. *take balm,* etc. Spoken in sarcasm to the nations under Babylon's sway (Kimchi, Malbim).

9. *we would have healed Babylon.* It is as though the foreigners sojourning in Babylon reply, 'We have attempted to heal Babylon, but she is not healed. Therefore, forsake her and engage no longer in healing her.' This too is sarcasm (Metsudath David).

and let us go. Lest we catch the disease (Metsudath David).

10. *our victory.* lit. 'our righteousness' (so A.V.). 'Vindication' is the nearest equivalent. In Babylon's overthrow God has demonstrated the rightness of Israel's cause. Nebuchadnezzar exceeded the punishment due to the Judeans for their sins, and he now pays the penalty.

11. *make bright the arrows.* Polishing would increase their power of penetration (Kimchi). Targum renders: 'sharpen,' Rashi: 'clean.'

Fill the quivers,

The Lord hath roused the spirit
of the kings of the Medes;

Because His device is against
Babylon, to destroy it;

For it is the vengeance of the
Lord,

The vengeance of His temple.

12 Set up a standard against the
walls of Babylon,

Make the watch strong,

Set the watchmen, prepare the
ambushes;

For the Lord hath both devised
and done

That which He spoke concerning
the inhabitants of Babylon.

13 O thou that dwellest upon many
waters,

Abundant in treasures,

Thine end is come,

The measure of thy covetousness.

מִלְאוּ הַשְּׁלָטִים
הֵעִיר יְהֹוָה
אֶת־רוּחַ מַלְכֵי מָדַי
כִּי־עַל־בָּבֶל מְזִמָּתוֹ
לְהַשְׁחִיתָהּ
כִּי־נִקְמַת יְהֹוָה הִיא
נִקְמַת הֵיכָלוֹ:
12 אֶל־חוֹמֹת בָּבֶל שְׂאוּ־נֵס
הַחֲזִיקוּ הַמִּשְׁמָר
הָקִימוּ שֹׁמְרִים
הָכִינוּ הָאֹרְבִים
כִּי גַם־זָמַם יְהֹוָה גַּם־עָשָׂה
אֵת אֲשֶׁר־דִּבֶּר
אֶל־יֹשְׁבֵי בָבֶל:
13 שֹׁכַנְתְּ עַל־מַיִם רַבִּים
רַבַּת אוֹצָרֹת
בָּא קִצֵּךְ
אַמַּת בִּצְעֵךְ:

v. 13. שכנת ק׳

fill the quivers. The Hebrew *shelatim* is
of uncertain meaning. The translation
quivers is given by Rashi; A.V. and R.V.
'shields' follow Kimchi. If the latter is
right, the verb *fill* means 'gather the
shields.' Another rendering proposed is
'armour' in which there is a place for
arrows (Malbim).

the kings. Cyrus and Darius (Metsudath
David).

the vengeance of His temple. See on l. 28.

12. *make the watch strong.* To cut off any
who tried to escape (Abarbanel).

13. *many waters.* i.e. the Euphrates
and the numerous canals. Babylon
relied upon them for agriculture
(Metsudath David).

abundant in treasures. Treasures of grain
or treasures of silver and gold (Kimchi).

the measure of thy covetousness. Or, 'the
measure of thy spoil.' With the measure
that thou meted out and spoiled Jerusalem, wilt thou be spoiled (Kimchi). An
alternative rendering is 'the cubit at
which thou shalt be cut off,' a metaphor
taken from weaving. Rashi mentions
both explanations.

14 The LORD of hosts hath sworn by
    Himself:
    Surely I will fill thee with men,
      as with the canker-worm,
    And they shall lift up a shout
      against thee.

15 He that hath made the earth by
    His power,
    That hath established the world
      by His wisdom,
    And hath stretched out the
      heavens by His discernment;

16 At the sound of His giving a
    multitude of waters in the
    heavens,
    He causeth the vapours to ascend
      from the ends of the earth;
    He maketh lightnings at the time
      of the rain,
    And bringeth forth the wind out
      of His treasuries;

17 Every man is proved to be
    brutish, for the knowledge—
    Every goldsmith is put to shame
      by the graven image—
    That his molten image is false-
      hood, and there is no breath
      in them.

18 They are vanity, a work of
    delusion;
    In the time of their visitation
      they shall perish.

19 The portion of Jacob is not like
    these;
    For He is the former of all things,
    And [Israel] is the tribe of His
      inheritance;
    The LORD of hosts is His name.

20 Thou art My maul and weapons
    of war,

14 נִשְׁבַּע יְהֹוָה צְבָאוֹת בְּנַפְשׁוֹ

כִּי אִם־מִלֵּאתִיךְ אָדָם כַּיֶּלֶק

וְעָנוּ עָלַיִךְ הֵידָד׃

15 עֹשֵׂה אֶרֶץ בְּכֹחוֹ

מֵכִין תֵּבֵל בְּחָכְמָתוֹ

וּבִתְבוּנָתוֹ נָטָה שָׁמָיִם׃

16 לְקוֹל תִּתּוֹ הֲמוֹן מַיִם בַּשָּׁמַיִם

וַיַּעַל נְשִׂאִים מִקְצֵה־אָרֶץ

בְּרָקִים לַמָּטָר עָשָׂה

וַיּוֹצֵא רוּחַ מֵאֹצְרֹתָיו׃

17 נִבְעַר כָּל־אָדָם מִדַּעַת

הֹבִישׁ כָּל־צֹרֵף מִפָּסֶל

כִּי שֶׁקֶר נִסְכּוֹ וְלֹא־רוּחַ בָּם׃

18 הֶבֶל הֵמָּה מַעֲשֵׂה תַּעְתֻּעִים

בְּעֵת פְּקֻדָּתָם יֹאבֵדוּ׃

19 לֹא־כְאֵלֶּה חֵלֶק יַעֲקוֹב

כִּי־יוֹצֵר הַכֹּל הוּא

וְשֵׁבֶט נַחֲלָתוֹ

יְהֹוָה צְבָאוֹת שְׁמוֹ׃

20 מַפֵּץ־אַתָּה לִי כְּלֵי מִלְחָמָה

v. 19. מלא ר׳

---

14. *sworn by Himself.* See on xxii. 5.

as with the canker-worm. [Numerous as
locusts and destructive like them.]

a shout. For the Hebrew term *hedad,*
see on xxv. 30.

15-19. This passage is almost a *verbatim*
repetition of x. 12-16, on which see the
notes. It emphasizes how impotent

Babylon's idols are against God, and
therefore the certain fulfilment of His
judgment upon the Chaldeans.

20. *Thou.* Babylon. The present tense
in this verse, and the imperfect (future)
in this and the following verses (21-23)
are all to be understood as referring to
continuous acts in the past: this is the
role that Babylon has hitherto played
(after Rashi).

And with thee will I shatter the
nations,
And with thee will I destroy
kingdoms;
21 And with thee will I shatter the
horse and his rider,
And with thee will I shatter the
chariot and him that rideth
therein;
22 And with thee will I shatter man
and woman,
And with thee will I shatter the
old man and the youth,
And with thee will I shatter the
young man and the maid;
23 And with thee will I shatter the
shepherd and his flock,
And with thee will I shatter the
husbandman and his yoke of
oxen,
And with thee will I shatter
governors and deputies.
24 And I will render unto Babylon
and to all the inhabitants of
Chaldea
All their evil that they have done
in Zion, in your sight,
Saith the LORD.
25 Behold, I am against thee,
O destroying mountain, saith
the LORD,
Which destroyest all the earth;
And I will stretch out My hand
upon thee,

וּנְפַצְתִּי בְךָ גּוֹיִם

וְהִשְׁחַתִּי בְךָ מַמְלָכוֹת:

21 וְנִפַּצְתִּי בְךָ סוּס וְרִכְבּוֹ

וְנִפַּצְתִּי בְךָ רֶכֶב וְרֹכְבוֹ:

22 וְנִפַּצְתִּי בְךָ אִישׁ וְאִשָּׁה

וְנִפַּצְתִּי בְךָ זָקֵן וָנָעַר

וְנִפַּצְתִּי בְךָ בָּחוּר וּבְתוּלָה:

23 וְנִפַּצְתִּי בְךָ רֹעֶה וְעֶדְרוֹ

וְנִפַּצְתִּי בְךָ אִכָּר וְצִמְדּוֹ

וְנִפַּצְתִּי בְךָ פַּחוֹת וּסְגָנִים:

24 וְשִׁלַּמְתִּי לְבָבֶל

וּלְכֹל ׀ יוֹשְׁבֵי כַשְׂדִּים

אֵת כָּל־רָעָתָם

אֲשֶׁר־עָשׂוּ בְצִיּוֹן לְעֵינֵיכֶם

נְאֻם יְהֹוָה:

25 הִנְנִי אֵלֶיךָ

הַר הַמַּשְׁחִית נְאֻם־יְהֹוָה

הַמַּשְׁחִית אֶת־כָּל־הָאָרֶץ

וְנָטִיתִי אֶת־יָדִי עָלֶיךָ

maul. A war-club, mace (Daath Mikra).
Kimchi and Kara define it as a sledge-
hammer. For the figure, cf. l. 23. A
similar thought is expressed in Isa. x. 5
where it is applied to Assyria.

23. *governors and deputies.* Hebrew
pachoth u-seganim, found together again
in Ezek. xxiii. 6, 12, 23 where it is translated *governors and rulers.* The former is
cognate with 'pasha' and denotes the
governor appointed over a province (cf.
Hag. i. 1; Ezra v. 6; Neh. v. 14). The
latter denotes a subordinate official

(Daath Mikra). In Rabbinical Hebrew it
is used for the High Priest's deputy.
24. *in Zion, in your sight.* A comma is
rightly placed after *Zion,* as *in your sight* is
to be connected with the beginning of
the verse: *And I will render ... in your
sight. You* refers to the Judeans who will
have the satisfaction of witnessing the
downfall of their oppressors (after
Metsudath David).

25. *O destroying mountain.* Though
Babylon lay in a plain, she is described
as a *mountain* to indicate her towering
strength (Kimchi).

And roll thee down from the rocks,

And will make thee a burnt mountain.

26 And they shall not take of thee a stone for a corner,

Nor a stone for foundations;

But thou shalt be desolate for ever, saith the LORD.

27 Set ye up a standard in the land,

Blow the horn among the nations,

Prepare the nations against her,

Call together against her the kingdoms of Ararat, Minni, and Ashkenaz;

Appoint a marshal against her;

Cause the horses to come up as the rough canker-worm.

28 Prepare against her the nations, the kings of the Medes,

The governors thereof, and all the deputies thereof,

וְגִלְגַּלְתִּיךָ מִן־הַסְּלָעִים
וּנְתַתִּיךָ לְהַר שְׂרֵפָה:
26 וְלֹא־יִקְחוּ מִמְּךָ אֶבֶן לְפִנָּה
וְאֶבֶן לְמוֹסָדוֹת
כִּי־שִׁמְמוֹת עוֹלָם
תִּהְיֶה נְאֻם־יְהוָה:
27 שְׂאוּ־נֵס בָּאָרֶץ
תִּקְעוּ שׁוֹפָר בַּגּוֹיִם
קַדְּשׁוּ עָלֶיהָ גּוֹיִם
הַשְׁמִיעוּ עָלֶיהָ מַמְלְכוֹת
אֲרָרַט מִנִּי וְאַשְׁכְּנַז
פִּקְדוּ עָלֶיהָ טִפְסָר
הַעֲלוּ־סוּס כְּיֶלֶק סָמָר:
28 קַדְּשׁוּ עָלֶיהָ גוֹיִם
אֶת־מַלְכֵי מָדַי
אֶת־פַּחוֹתֶיהָ
וְאֶת־כָּל־סְגָנֶיהָ

נ״א מלחמה .v. 27

---

26. *a stone for a corner,* etc. It is customary to place large stones in the foundation of a building and also for cornerstones. This is figurative, as Jonathan paraphrases: 'They shall not take of thee a king for a kingdom or a governor for a rulership.'

27. *set ye up a standard.* To rally the nations which will join in the attack upon Babylon (Metsudath David).

prepare. See on vi. 4.

Ararat. The Assyrian Urartu, north-west of Lake Van, a district which included part of Armenia (Daath Mikra).

Minni. Occurs on Assyrian inscriptions as 'Mannai'; not far from Lake Van (see Daath Mikra).

Ashkenaz. Cf. Gen. x. 3; probably near the two former, but not known definitely (Daath Mikra).

28. *kings.* See on verse 11.

governors . . . deputies. See on verse 23.

342

And all the land of his dominion.

29 And the land quaketh and is in
pain;
For the purposes of the LORD are
performed against Babylon,
To make the land of Babylon a
desolation, without inhabitant.

30 The mighty men of Babylon have
forborne to fight,
They remain in their strongholds;
Their might hath failed, they are
become as women;
Her dwelling-places are set on
fire;
Her bars are broken.

31 One post runneth to meet another,
And one messenger to meet
another,
To tell the king of Babylon
That his city is taken on every
quarter;

32 And the fords are seized,
And the castles they have burned
with fire,
And the men of war are af-
frighted.

33 For thus saith the LORD of hosts,
The God of Israel:

וְאֵת כָּל־אֶרֶץ מֶמְשַׁלְתּֽוֹ׃

29 וַתִּרְעַשׁ הָאָרֶץ וַתָּחֹל
כִּי קָמָה עַל־בָּבֶל
מַחְשְׁבוֹת יְהֹוָה
לָשׂוּם אֶת־אֶרֶץ בָּבֶל
לְשַׁמָּה מֵאֵין יוֹשֵׁב׃

30 חָדְלוּ גִבּוֹרֵי בָבֶל לְהִלָּחֵם
יָשְׁבוּ בַּמְּצָדוֹת
נָשְׁתָה גְבוּרָתָם הָיוּ לְנָשִׁים
הִצִּיתוּ מִשְׁכְּנֹתֶיהָ
נִשְׁבְּרוּ בְרִיחֶֽיהָ׃

31 רָץ לִקְרַאת־רָץ יָרוּץ
וּמַגִּיד לִקְרַאת מַגִּיד
לְהַגִּיד לְמֶלֶךְ בָּבֶל
כִּי־נִלְכְּדָה עִירוֹ מִקָּצֶֽה׃

32 וְהַמַּעְבָּרוֹת נִתְפָּשׂוּ
וְאֶת־הָאֲגַמִּים שָׂרְפוּ בָאֵשׁ
וְאַנְשֵׁי הַמִּלְחָמָה נִבְהָֽלוּ׃

33 כִּי כֹה אָמַר יְהֹוָה צְבָאוֹת
אֱלֹהֵי יִשְׂרָאֵל

v. 32. קמץ בז״ק

all the land of his dominion. The king of
Media is to gather men from the
peoples over whom he rules.

30. *are set on fire.* lit. 'they (the enemy)
have burnt her dwelling-places' (A.V.
after Kimchi).

31. *to meet another.* The messengers
with news of defeat after defeat converge
as they approach the king's palace from
all sides (Malbim). Or, as one mes-

senger who has already given his
message leaves, he is met by another
bringing further tidings of disaster
(Kimchi).

32. *fords.* Modern authorities prefer
the translation 'ferries' (Daath Mikra).

the castles. This translation follows Ibn
Ganah who derives this meaning from
the cognate noun in Arabic. Normally
agam signifies 'a pool of water'; but

The daughter of Babylon is like
a threshing-floor
At the time when it is trodden;
Yet a little while, and the time of
harvest
Shall come for her.

34 Nebuchadrezzar the king of
Babylon hath devoured me,
He hath crushed me,
He hath set me down as an
empty vessel,
He hath swallowed me up like a
dragon,
He hath filled his maw with my
delicacies;
He hath washed me clean.

35 'The violence done to me and to
my flesh be upon Babylon,'
Shall the inhabitant of Zion say;
And: 'My blood be upon the
inhabitants of Chaldea,'
Shall Jerusalem say.

36 Therefore thus saith the LORD:
Behold, I will plead thy cause,
And take vengeance for thee;
And I will dry up her sea,
And make her fountain dry.

37 And Babylon shall become heaps,

בַּת־בָּבֶל כְּגֹרֶן עֵת הִדְרִיכָהּ
עוֹד מְעַט
וּבָאָה עֵת־הַקָּצִיר לָהּ:
34 אֲכָלַנוּ הֲמָמַנוּ
נְבוּכַדְרֶאצַּר מֶלֶךְ בָּבֶל
הִצִּיגַנוּ כְּלִי רִיק
בְּלָעַנוּ כַּתַּנִּין
מִלָּא כְרֵשׂוֹ מֵעֲדָנָי
הֱדִיחָנוּ:
35 חֲמָסִי וּשְׁאֵרִי עַל־בָּבֶל
תֹּאמַר יֹשֶׁבֶת צִיּוֹן
וְדָמִי אֶל־יֹשְׁבֵי כַשְׂדִּים
תֹּאמַר יְרוּשָׁלָ͏ִם:
36 לָכֵן כֹּה אָמַר יְהֹוָה
הִנְנִי־רָב אֶת־רִיבֵךְ
וְנִקַּמְתִּי אֶת־נִקְמָתֵךְ
וְהַחֲרַבְתִּי אֶת־יַמָּהּ
וְהֹבַשְׁתִּי אֶת־מְקוֹרָהּ:
37 וְהָיְתָה בָבֶל | לְגַלִּים

v. 34. אכלני ק׳ v. 34. הממני ק׳ v. 34. הציגני ק׳ v. 34. בלעני ק׳ v. 34. הדיחני ק׳

---

since this cannot be 'burned' Ibn Ganah
and Kimchi suggest 'reeds.' These were
the reeds growing on the river bank to
block the way of the invaders. They
would set it afire in order to gain access
to the city. These authorities, however,
prefer the former translation.

33. *at the time . . . trodden.* So has her
time come to be trodden down
(Kimchi).

dragon. The Hebrew *tannin* denotes
any great sea monster.

he hath washed me clean. He has made a
clean sweep of my possessions, leaving
me with nothing (Kimchi).

35. *the violence done to me . . . be
upon.* The same idiomatic phrase
occurs in Gen. xvi. 5, *my wrong be upon
thee.*

36. *her sea . . . her fountain.* The allusion may be to the Euphrates (Daath
Mikra) or the great reservoir, 420
furlongs in circumference, made by

A dwelling-place for jackals,
An astonishment, and a hissing,
Without inhabitant.

38 They shall roar together like
young lions;
They shall growl as lions' whelps.

39 With their poison I will prepare
their feast,
And I will make them drunken,
that they may be convulsed,
And sleep a perpetual sleep, and
not wake,
Saith the LORD.

40 I will bring them down like
lambs to the slaughter,
Like rams with he-goats.

41 How is Sheshach taken!
And the praise of the whole earth
seized!
How is Babylon become an
astonishment
Among the nations!

42 The sea is come up upon
Babylon;
She is covered with the multi-
tude of the waves thereof.

43 Her cities are become a desolation,

מְעוֹן־תַּנִּים
שַׁמָּה וּשְׁרֵקָה
מֵאֵין יוֹשֵׁב׃

38 יַחְדָּו כַּכְּפִרִים יִשְׁאָגוּ
נָעֲרוּ כְּגוֹרֵי אֲרָיוֹת׃

39 בְּחֻמָּם אָשִׁית אֶת־מִשְׁתֵּיהֶם
וְהִשְׁכַּרְתִּים לְמַעַן יַעֲלֹזוּ
וְיָשְׁנוּ שְׁנַת־עוֹלָם וְלֹא יָקִיצוּ
נְאֻם יְהוָה׃

40 אוֹרִידֵם כְּכָרִים לִטְבוֹחַ
כְּאֵילִים עִם־עַתּוּדִים׃

41 אֵיךְ נִלְכְּדָה שֵׁשַׁךְ
וַתִּתָּפֵשׂ תְּהִלַּת כָּל־הָאָרֶץ
אֵיךְ הָיְתָה לְשַׁמָּה
בָּבֶל בַּגּוֹיִם׃

42 עָלָה עַל־בָּבֶל הַיָּם
בַּהֲמוֹן גַּלָּיו נִכְסָתָה׃

43 הָיוּ עָרֶיהָ לְשַׁמָּה

Queen Nitocris, or the lake constructed
by Nebuchadnezzar.

38. they shall roar. The subject may be
the Babylonians: they will cry out in
distress as young lions roar when
hungry. Alternatively *they* refers to the
enemy. The latter is more plausible in
itself, but it involves an abrupt change
of subject, since the preceding and
following verses certainly have reference
to the Babylonians. Hence the former is
perhaps preferable. Kimchi suggests
both.

39. with their poison. More accurately,
'in their heat' (A.V.) or 'when they are

heated' (R.V.), inflamed with desire.
While they are reveling and carousing,
God will introduce something into their
feast which will induce a sleep from
which they will never awake. Cf. the
story of Belshazzar's banquet (Dan. v.)
(Kimchi).

40. lambs . . . rams . . . he-goats. [Typify-
ing the various sections of the
population, the last-named representing the leaders (see on l. 8).]

41. Sheshach. A cryptic name of Babylon (see on xxv. 26).

42. the sea. The flood of enemy troops
(cf. xlvi. 7f.) (Metsudath David).

345

A dry land, and a desert,
A land wherein no man dwelleth,
Neither doth any son of man
    pass thereby.
44 And I will punish Bel in Babylon,
And I will bring forth out of his
    mouth that which he hath
    swallowed up,
And the nations shall not flow
    any more unto him;
Yea, the wall of Babylon shall
    fall.
45 My people, go ye out of the
    midst of her,
And save yourselves every man
From the fierce anger of the
    LORD.
46 And let not your heart faint,
    neither fear ye,
For the rumour that shall be
    heard in the land;
For a rumour shall come one
    year,
And after that in another year a
    rumour,
And violence in the land, ruler
    against ruler.
47 Therefore, behold, the days
    come,

אֶרֶץ צִיָּה וַעֲרָבָה
אֶרֶץ לֹא־יֵשֵׁב בָּהֵן כָּל־אִישׁ
וְלֹא־יַעֲבֹר בָּהֵן בֶּן־אָדָם:
44 וּפָקַדְתִּי עַל־בֵּל בְּבָבֶל
וְהֹצֵאתִי אֶת־בִּלְעוֹ מִפִּיו
וְלֹא־יִנְהֲרוּ אֵלָיו עוֹד גּוֹיִם
גַּם־חוֹמַת בָּבֶל נָפָלָה:
45 צְאוּ מִתּוֹכָהּ עַמִּי
וּמַלְּטוּ אִישׁ אֶת־נַפְשׁוֹ
מֵחֲרוֹן אַף־יְהוָה:
46 וּפֶן־יֵרַךְ לְבַבְכֶם וְתִירְאוּ
בַּשְּׁמוּעָה הַנִּשְׁמַעַת בָּאָרֶץ
וּבָא בַשָּׁנָה הַשְּׁמוּעָה
וְאַחֲרָיו בַּשָּׁנָה הַשְּׁמוּעָה
וְחָמָס בָּאָרֶץ מֹשֵׁל עַל־מֹשֵׁל:
47 לָכֵן הִנֵּה יָמִים בָּאִים

---

44. *I will punish Bel in Babylon.* For Bel, cf. l. 2. The nation is identified with its deity, so that the disaster which overwhelms the former also involves the latter, and in despoiling the nation the deity will be broken and carried off. Cf. Isa. xlvi. (Kimchi).

that which he hath swallowed up. The riches of conquered peoples (Daath Soferim).

shall not flow any more unto him. Bel's impotence having been made manifest, none will pay it further homage (Metsudath David).

the wall of Babylon. Its defence against attack. With the wall gone, the city is open to the invader (Metsudath David).

45. Cf. verse 6.

46. A picture of the disquiet which will precede Babylon's final dissolution: rumour following on rumour and internecine war between her leaders. The Jews are bidden to remain calm and confident throughout the anxious period.

and let not your heart faint. More lit. 'and (beware) lest your heart faint.'

one year . . . another year. Belshazzar ruled for three years. In the first year, rumours spread that Media would attack Babylon, and so in the second, and so in the third year. This accounts for the repetition (Kimchi).

and violence in the land. That plunderers were coming to the land of the Chaldeans (Kimchi).

That I will do judgment upon the graven images of Babylon,
And her whole land shall be ashamed;
And all her slain shall fall in the midst of her.

48 Then the heaven and the earth, and all that is therein,
Shall sing for joy over Babylon;
For the spoilers shall come unto her
From the north, saith the LORD.

49 As Babylon hath caused the slain of Israel to fall,
So at Babylon shall fall the slain of all the land.

50 Ye that have escaped the sword,
Go ye, stand not still;
Remember the LORD from afar,
And let Jerusalem come into your mind.

51 'We are ashamed, because we have heard reproach,

וּפָקַדְתִּי עַל־פְּסִילֵי בָבֶל
וְכָל־אַרְצָהּ תֵּבוֹשׁ
וְכָל־חֲלָלֶיהָ יִפְּלוּ בְתוֹכָהּ:
48 וְרִנְּנוּ עַל־בָּבֶל שָׁמַיִם וָאָרֶץ
וְכֹל אֲשֶׁר בָּהֶם
כִּי מִצָּפוֹן
יָבוֹא־לָהּ הַשּׁוֹדְדִים
נְאֻם־יְהוָה:
49 גַּם־בָּבֶל לִנְפֹּל חַלְלֵי יִשְׂרָאֵל
גַּם־לְבָבֶל נָפְלוּ
חַלְלֵי כָל־הָאָרֶץ:
50 פְּלֵטִים מֵחֶרֶב
הִלְכוּ אַל־תַּעֲמֹדוּ
זִכְרוּ מֵרָחוֹק אֶת־יְהוָה
וִירוּשָׁלַ͏ִם
תַּעֲלֶה עַל־לְבַבְכֶם:
51 בֹּשְׁנוּ כִּי־שָׁמַעְנוּ חֶרְפָּה

v. 48. סבירין יבואו

---

47. The verse resembles verse 52.

48. *the heaven and the earth.* They are similarly called upon to rejoice over Israel's redemption in Isa. xliv. 23.

over Babylon. Over her discomfiture (Kimchi, Metsudath David).

from the north. Alluding to the Persians (Kimchi).

49. *as Babylon hath caused,* etc. This rendering, in which Rashi and Kimchi concur, assumes that the Hebrew is elliptical, the equivalent of *hath caused* being omitted, or that the *kal* conjugation of the verb is used with the force of

the *hiphul.* Targum renders: 'Also in Babylon have fallen the slain of Israel, also in Babylon shall fall the slain of all the land.' Daath Mikra renders: 'have fallen the slain of all the earth.' As the slain of all the earth have fallen at Babylon, it is fitting that now her own shall fall there.

50. The verse is addressed to the Judeans in Babylon who had survived the overthrow of their land (Rashi).

go ye. Back to Judea (Metsudath David).

51. *we are ashamed,* etc. The answer of the Judean exiles: they feel keenly the

347

Confusion hath covered our
faces;
For strangers are come
Into the sanctuaries of the LORD's
house.'

52 Wherefore, behold, the days
come, saith the LORD,
That I will do judgment upon
her graven images;
And through all her land the
wounded shall groan.

53 Though Babylon should mount
up to heaven,
And though she should fortify
the height of her strength,
Yet from Me shall spoilers come
unto her, saith the LORD.

54 Hark! a cry from Babylon,
And great destruction from the
land of the Chaldeans!

55 For the LORD spoileth Babylon,
And destroyeth out of her the
great voice;
And their waves roar like many
waters,
The noise of their voice is
uttered;

56 For the spoiler is come upon her,
even upon Babylon,
And her mighty men are taken,
Their bows are shattered;
For the LORD is a God of
recompenses,
He will surely requite.

בָּסְתָה כְלִמָּה פָּנֵינוּ

כִּי בָּאוּ זָרִים

עַל־מִקְדְּשֵׁי בֵּית יְהוָה׃

52 לָכֵן הִנֵּה־יָמִים בָּאִים

נְאֻם־יְהוָה

וּפָקַדְתִּי עַל־פְּסִילֶיהָ

וּבְכָל־אַרְצָהּ יֶאֱנֹק חָלָל׃

53 כִּי־תַעֲלֶה בָבֶל הַשָּׁמַיִם

וְכִי תְבַצֵּר מְרוֹם עֻזָּהּ

מֵאִתִּי יָבֹאוּ שֹׁדְדִים

לָהּ נְאֻם־יְהוָה׃

54 קוֹל זְעָקָה מִבָּבֶל

וְשֶׁבֶר גָּדוֹל מֵאֶרֶץ כַּשְׂדִּים׃

55 כִּי־שֹׁדֵד יְהוָה אֶת־בָּבֶל

וְאִבַּד מִמֶּנָּה קוֹל גָּדוֹל

וְהָמוּ גַלֵּיהֶם כְּמַיִם רַבִּים

נִתַּן שְׁאוֹן קוֹלָם׃

56 כִּי בָא עָלֶיהָ עַל־בָּבֶל שׁוֹדֵד

וְנִלְכְּדוּ גִּבּוֹרֶיהָ

חִתְּתָה קַשְּׁתוֹתָם

כִּי אֵל גְּמֻלוֹת יְהוָה

שַׁלֵּם יְשַׁלֵּם׃

כצ"ל v. 56.

taunt that their Temple in ruins is
evidence that the gods of Babylon had
overpowered their God (Rashi).

52. *I will do judgment upon her graven
images.* Thus silencing the reproaches
of the Babylonians (Abarbanel).

53. Cf. the language used against Edom
in xlix. 16, and against Babylon in Isa.
xiv. 13ff.

55. *the great voice.* The clamour of the
thronged population (Kimchi).

their waves. Kimchi understands this of

57 And I will make drunk her
princes and her wise men,
Her governors and her deputies,
and her mighty men;
And they shall sleep a perpetual
sleep, and not wake,
Saith the King, whose name is
the LORD of hosts.

58 Thus saith the LORD of hosts:
The broad walls of Babylon shall
be utterly overthrown,
And her high gates shall be
burned with fire;
And the peoples shall labour for
vanity,
And the nations for the fire;
And they shall be weary.

59. The word which Jeremiah the
prophet commanded Seraiah the son
of Neriah, the son of Mahseiah,
when he went with Zedekiah the

וְהִשְׁכַּרְתִּי שָׂרֶיהָ וַחֲכָמֶיהָ 57
פַּחוֹתֶיהָ וּסְגָנֶיהָ וְגִבּוֹרֶיהָ
וְיָשְׁנוּ שְׁנַת־עוֹלָם וְלֹא יָקִיצוּ
נְאֻם־הַמֶּלֶךְ
יְהוָה צְבָאוֹת שְׁמוֹ:
כֹּה־אָמַר יְהוָה צְבָאוֹת 58
חֹמוֹת בָּבֶל הָרְחָבָה
עַרְעֵר תִּתְעַרְעָר
וּשְׁעָרֶיהָ הַגְּבֹהִים בָּאֵשׁ יִצַּתּוּ
וְיִגְעוּ עַמִּים בְּדֵי־רִיק
וּלְאֻמִּים בְּדֵי־אֵשׁ
וְיָעֵפוּ:
הַדָּבָר אֲשֶׁר־צִוָּה | יִרְמְיָהוּ 59
הַנָּבִיא אֶת־שְׂרָיָה בֶן־
נֵרִיָּה בֶּן־מַחְסֵיָה בְּלֶכְתּוֹ
אֶת־צִדְקִיָּהוּ מֶלֶךְ־יְהוּדָה

פתח באתנח v. 58.

the Chaldeans; Kara, however, explains
that it refers to the tumult of the attacking enemy which will drown the noise
within the doomed city.

57. *And I will make drunk.* i.e. I will
confuse them so that they will be like
drunk. The wise men will not help with
their counsel, neither will the mighty
men help with their might. They will all
be as drunken men, until they sleep a
perpetual sleep; i.e. until they die
(Abarbanel). Malbim, however, interprets this verse literally as an allusion to
the night when Belshazzar became
drunk when drinking from the holy
vessels of the Temple.

saith the King. For God is the King over
all kings, and the power is His to
remove the kingdom from one king and
to give it to another, for He is the Lord
of the hosts of heaven and earth
(Kimchi).

58. *the broad walls of Babylon.* Both the
inner wall and the outer wall. Their
sturdy construction will not avail them
(Kimchi)

59-64 JEREMIAH'S INSTRUCTION TO
SERAIAH

59. *the son of Neriah.* Accordingly,
Seraiah was Baruch's brother (cf. xxxii.
12).

349

king of Judah to Babylon in the fourth year of his reign. Now Seraiah was quartermaster. 60. And Jeremiah wrote in one book all the evil that should come upon Babylon, even all these words that are written concerning Babylon. 61. And Jeremiah said to Seraiah: 'When thou comest to Babylon, then see that thou read all these words, 62. and say: O LORD, Thou hast spoken concerning this place, to cut it off, that none shall dwell therein, neither man nor beast, but that it shall be desolate for ever. 63. And it shall be, when thou hast made an end of reading this book, that thou shalt bind a stone to it, and cast it into

בְּבֶל בִּשְׁנַת הָרְבִעִית לְמָלְכוֹ
60 וּשְׂרָיָה שַׂר־מְנוּחָה: וַיִּכְתֹּב
יִרְמְיָהוּ אֵת כָּל־הָרָעָה
אֲשֶׁר־תָּבוֹא אֶל־בָּבֶל אֶל־
סֵפֶר אֶחָד אֵת כָּל־הַדְּבָרִים
הָאֵלֶּה הַכְּתֻבִים אֶל־בָּבֶל:
61 וַיֹּאמֶר יִרְמְיָהוּ אֶל־שְׂרָיָה
כְּבֹאֲךָ בָבֶל וְרָאִיתָ וְקָרָאתָ
אֵת כָּל־הַדְּבָרִים הָאֵלֶּה:
62 וְאָמַרְתָּ יְהוָה אַתָּה דִבַּרְתָּ
אֶל־הַמָּקוֹם הַזֶּה לְהַכְרִיתוֹ
לְבִלְתִּי הֱיוֹת־בּוֹ יוֹשֵׁב
לְמֵאָדָם וְעַד־בְּהֵמָה כִּי־
63 שִׁמְמוֹת עוֹלָם תִּהְיֶה: וְהָיָה
כְּכַלֹּתְךָ לִקְרֹא אֶת־הַסֵּפֶר
הַזֶּה תִּקְשֹׁר עָלָיו אֶבֶן

to Babylon. This visit of Zedekiah is not recorded elsewhere. He may have gone to pay homage to Nebuchadnezzar and clear himself from the suspicion of being implicated in the revolt which was then brewing (Daath Mikra).

in the fourth year of his reign. Cf. xxviii. 1ff. If Hananiah's prophecy of speedy liberation from the Babylonian yoke represented popular hopes and expectations, as it probably did, it would make it all the more necessary for Zedekiah to assure Nebuchadnezzar of his loyalty (Daath Mikra).

quartermaster. A questionable translation. According to Targum, he was the 'prince of tribute,' the king's receptionist. Anyone bringing tribute to Zedekiah

to be granted audience with him would seek admittance through Seraiah. Accordingly, we explain *menuchah* as *munchah,* a gift (Rashi, Kara).

60. *in one book.* i.e. on a separate roll of parchment.

61. *then see that thou read.* Better as R.V. margin: 'and shalt see and read,' i.e. thou shalt look at the scroll and read the prophecy (Metsudath David). [The reading could not have been done in public since it would have been a dangerous thing to do; he was to read it to himself or to a few of the leading Judeans in Babylon.]

63. Jeremiah's prophecies were often re-enforced by symbolical action (cf. xiii. 1ff., xix. 1ff., xxvii. 2ff., xliii. 9ff.).

the midst of the Euphrates; 64. and thou shalt say: Thus shall Babylon sink, and shall not rise again because of the evil that I will bring upon her; and they shall be weary.'

Thus far are the words of Jeremiah.

וְהִשְׁלַכְתּוֹ אֶל־תּוֹךְ פְּרָת:
64 וְאָמַרְתָּ כָּכָה תִּשְׁקַע בָּבֶל
וְלֹא־תָקוּם מִפְּנֵי הָרָעָה אֲשֶׁר
אָנֹכִי מֵבִיא עָלֶיהָ וְיָעֵפוּ
עַד־הֵנָּה דִּבְרֵי יִרְמְיָהוּ:

---

52   CHAPTER LII   נב

1. Zedekiah was one and twenty years old when he began to reign; and he reigned eleven years in Jerusalem; and his mother's name was Hamutal the daughter of Jeremiah of Libnah. 2. And he did that which was evil in the sight of the LORD, according to all that Jehoiakim had done. 3. For through the anger of the LORD did it come to pass in Jerusalem and Judah, until He had cast them out from His presence. And Zedekiah rebelled against the king of Babylon. 4. And it came to pass in the ninth year of his reign, in the tenth month, in the tenth day of

1 בֶּן־עֶשְׂרִים וְאַחַת שָׁנָה
צִדְקִיָּהוּ בְמָלְכוֹ וְאַחַת עֶשְׂרֵה
שָׁנָה מָלַךְ בִּירוּשָׁלָ͏ִם וְשֵׁם אִמּוֹ
חֲמִיטַל בַּת־יִרְמְיָהוּ
2 מִלִּבְנָה: וַיַּעַשׂ הָרַע בְּעֵינֵי
יְהוָה כְּכֹל אֲשֶׁר־עָשָׂה
3 יְהוֹיָקִים: כִּי | עַל־אַף יְהוָה
הָיְתָה בִּירוּשָׁלַ͏ִם וִיהוּדָה עַד־
הִשְׁלִיכוֹ אוֹתָם מֵעַל פָּנָיו
וַיִּמְרֹד צִדְקִיָּהוּ בְּמֶלֶךְ בָּבֶל:
4 וַיְהִי בַשָּׁנָה הַתְּשִׁעִית לְמָלְכוֹ
בַּחֹדֶשׁ הָעֲשִׂירִי בֶּעָשׂוֹר

v. 1. חמוטל ק'

---

64. *and they shall be weary.* This is the conclusion of verse 58.

thus far are the words of Jeremiah. This implies that the chapter which follows is not by Jeremiah's hand. It is taken largely from 2 Kings xxiv. 18-xxv. 30 (Metsudath David).

CHAPTER LII

THE FALL OF JERUSALEM

1. *when he began to reign.* In the year 597 B.C.E.

Hamutal. He was a full brother of Jehoahaz but half brother of Jehoiakim (2 Kings xxiii. 31, 36).

3. *did it come to pass.* For since the LORD's anger was set against Jerusalem and Judah to cast them out from His presence, He inspired Zedekiah to rebel against Nebuchadnezzar in order to bring this about (Metsudath David).

4-16 This is paralleled by xxxix. 1-10.

4. *in the tenth month, in the tenth day of the month.* This date marked the begin-

the month, that Nebuchadrezzar king of Babylon came, he and all his army, against Jerusalem, and encamped against it; and they built forts against it round about. 5. So the city was besieged unto the eleventh year of king Zedekiah. 6. In the fourth month, in the ninth day of the month, the famine was sore in the city, so that there was no bread for the people of the land. 7. Then a breach was made in the city, and all the men of war fled, and went forth out of the city by night by the way of the gate between the two walls, which was by the king's garden—now the Chaldeans were against the city round about—and they went by the way of the Arabah. 8. But the army of the Chaldeans pursued after the king, and overtook Zedekiah in the plains of Jericho; and all his army was scattered from him. 9. Then they took the king, and carried him up unto the king of Babylon to Riblah in the land of Hamath; and he gave

לַחֹדֶשׁ בָּא נְבוּכַדְרֶאצַּר
מֶלֶךְ־בָּבֶל הוּא וְכָל־חֵילוֹ
עַל־יְרוּשָׁלַם וַיַּחֲנוּ עָלֶיהָ
5 וַיִּבְנוּ עָלֶיהָ דָּיֵק סָבִיב: וַתָּבֹא
הָעִיר בַּמָּצוֹר עַד עַשְׁתֵּי־
עֶשְׂרֵה שָׁנָה לַמֶּלֶךְ צִדְקִיָּהוּ:
6 בַּחֹדֶשׁ הָרְבִיעִי בְּתִשְׁעָה
לַחֹדֶשׁ וַיֶּחֱזַק הָרָעָב בָּעִיר
וְלֹא־הָיָה לֶחֶם לְעַם הָאָרֶץ:
7 וַתִּבָּקַע הָעִיר וְכָל־אַנְשֵׁי
הַמִּלְחָמָה יִבְרְחוּ וַיֵּצְאוּ
מֵהָעִיר לַיְלָה דֶּרֶךְ שַׁעַר בֵּין־
הַחֹמֹתַיִם אֲשֶׁר עַל־גַּן הַמֶּלֶךְ
וְכַשְׂדִּים עַל־הָעִיר סָבִיב
8 וַיֵּלְכוּ דֶּרֶךְ הָעֲרָבָה: וַיִּרְדְּפוּ
חֵיל־כַּשְׂדִּים אַחֲרֵי הַמֶּלֶךְ
וַיַּשִּׂגוּ אֶת־צִדְקִיָּהוּ בְּעַרְבֹת
יְרֵחוֹ וְכָל־חֵילוֹ נָפֹצוּ מֵעָלָיו:
9 וַיִּתְפְּשׂוּ אֶת־הַמֶּלֶךְ וַיַּעֲלוּ
אֹתוֹ אֶל־מֶלֶךְ בָּבֶל רִבְלָתָה
בְּאֶרֶץ חֲמָת וַיְדַבֵּר אִתּוֹ

ning of the siege. In commemoration the day was proclaimed a public fast (cf. Zech. viii. 19) and is still so observed by Jews.

6. *in the fourth month, in the ninth day.* This day was also instituted as a fast (Zech. viii. 19); but it was later replaced by a fast observed on the seventeenth of the month on which day the walls of the Second Temple were

breached by Titus (Kara from Taanith 28b).

the people of the land. From the description in *Lamentations* it is evident that this term embraces all classes of the population.

7. *between the two walls,* etc. See on xxxix. 4.

9. *Riblah.* See on xxxix. 5.

judgment upon him. 10. And the king of Babylon slew the sons of Zedekiah before his eyes; he slew also all the princes of Judah in Riblah. 11. And he put out the eyes of Zedekiah; and the king of Babylon bound him in fetters, and carried him to Babylon, and put him in prison till the day of his death.

12. Now in the fifth month, in the tenth day of the month, which was the nineteenth year of king Nebuchadrezzar, king of Babylon, came Nebuzaradan the captain of the guard, who stood before the king of Babylon, into Jerusalem; 13. and he burned the house of the LORD, and the king's house; and all the houses of Jerusalem, even every great man's house, burned he with fire. 14. And all the army of the Chaldeans, that were with the captain of the guard, broke down all the walls of Jerusalem

מִשְׁפָּטִים: וַיִּשְׁחַט מֶלֶךְ־ 10
בָּבֶל אֶת־בְּנֵי צִדְקִיָּהוּ לְעֵינָיו
וְגַם אֶת־כָּל־שָׂרֵי יְהוּדָה
שָׁחַט בְּרִבְלָתָה: וְאֶת־עֵינֵי 11
צִדְקִיָּהוּ עִוֵּר וַיַּאַסְרֵהוּ
בַנְחֻשְׁתַּיִם וַיְבִאֵהוּ מֶלֶךְ־
בָּבֶל בָּבֶלָה וַיִּתְּנֵהוּ בְבֵית־
הַפְּקֻדֹּת עַד־יוֹם מוֹתוֹ:
וּבַחֹדֶשׁ הַחֲמִישִׁי בֶּעָשׂוֹר 12
לַחֹדֶשׁ הִיא שְׁנַת תְּשַׁע־
עֶשְׂרֵה שָׁנָה לַמֶּלֶךְ
נְבוּכַדְרֶאצַּר מֶלֶךְ־בָּבֶל בָּא
נְבוּזַרְאֲדָן רַב־טַבָּחִים עָמַד
לִפְנֵי מֶלֶךְ־בָּבֶל בִּירוּשָׁלָם:
וַיִּשְׂרֹף אֶת־בֵּית־יְהֹוָה וְאֶת־ 13
בֵּית הַמֶּלֶךְ וְאֵת כָּל־בָּתֵּי
יְרוּשָׁלַם וְאֶת־כָּל־בֵּית
הַגָּדוֹל שָׂרַף בָּאֵשׁ: וְאֶת־ 14
כָּל־חֹמוֹת יְרוּשָׁלַם סָבִיב

v. 11. בית ק׳

---

10. *he slew also . . . Riblah.* Omitted in 2 Kings xxv. 7.

11. *and put him in prison . . . death.* Not included in 2 Kings.

12. *the tenth day of the month.* 2 Kings xxv. 8 has *the seventh day.* The interval of three days may be accounted for as representing the date of Nebuzaradan's arrival on the scene and the commencement of operations. The Rabbis (Ta'anith 29a) explained that Nebuzaradan entered the Temple on the seventh,

set it on fire on the ninth and it burned until the tenth. Since the destruction of the Second Temple, a fast is kept on the ninth of the month.

the nineteenth year. i.e. 586 B.C.E.

13. *even every great man's house.* Omitted in xxxix. 8; the mansions of the rich (Metsudath David).

14. *broke down all the walls of Jerusalem.* In 2 Kings xxv. 10, the word 'all' is absent. There the intention is that they

round about. 15. Then Nebuzaradan the captain of the guard carried away captive of the poorest sort of the people, and the residue of the people that remained in the city, and those that fell away, that fell to the king of Babylon, and the residue of the multitude. 16. But Nebuzaradan the captain of the guard left of the poorest of the land to be vinedressers and husbandmen. 17. And the pillars of brass that were in the house of the LORD, and the bases and the brazen sea that were in the house of the LORD, did the Chaldeans break in pieces, and carried all the brass of them to Babylon. 18. The pots also, and the shovels,

נָתְצוּ כָל־חֵיל כַּשְׂדִּים אֲשֶׁר
15 אֶת־רַב־טַבָּחִים: וּמִדַּלּוֹת
הָעָם וְאֶת־יֶתֶר הָעָם |
הַנִּשְׁאָרִים בָּעִיר וְאֶת־
הַנֹּפְלִים אֲשֶׁר נָפְלוּ אֶל־מֶלֶךְ
בָּבֶל וְאֵת יֶתֶר הָאָמוֹן הֶגְלָה
נְבוּזַרְאֲדָן רַב־טַבָּחִים:
16 וּמִדַּלּוֹת הָאָרֶץ הִשְׁאִיר
נְבוּזַרְאֲדָן רַב־טַבָּחִים
17 לְכֹרְמִים וּלְיֹגְבִים: וְאֶת־
עַמּוּדֵי הַנְּחֹשֶׁת אֲשֶׁר לְבֵית־
יְהֹוָה וְאֶת־הַמְּכֹנוֹת וְאֶת־יָם
הַנְּחֹשֶׁת אֲשֶׁר בְּבֵית־יְהֹוָה
שִׁבְּרוּ כַשְׂדִּים וַיִּשְׂאוּ אֶת־
18 כָּל־נְחֻשְׁתָּם בָּבֶלָה: וְאֶת־
הַסִּרוֹת וְאֶת־הַיָּעִים וְאֶת־

broke down the main walls of Jerusalem. Here the word 'all' is added to include the auxilliary walls that were added to reinforce the main walls (Daath Soferim).

15. *of the poorest sort of the people.* But not all the inhabitants, as the next verse makes clear (Daath Soferim).

that remained in the city. Who had not been killed in the final attack. This seems to imply very heavy casualties (Daath Mikra).

and those that fell away. Better, 'and those that had fallen away'; i.e. those who had defected previously (Daath Soferim).

16. *the poorest of the land.* And in v. 15, 'the poorest sort of the people.'

Nebuzaradan, apparently, searched throughout the population of Jerusalem and throughout the entire land, for the simplest people, those who could be trusted to be faithful vassals to Babylon and not rebel (Daath Soferim).

17-23. A description of the sacred vessels which were carried away. The account is fuller than that given in 2 Kings xxv. 13-17, and is altogether absent from the corresponding passage in chapter xxxix. above.

17. *break in pieces.* They were too large to be carried away whole (Daath Mikra).

18f. The vessels were of pure gold (1 Kings vii. 50; cf. Exod. xxv. 29).

18. *the pots.* In which the ashes of the

and the snuffers, and the basins, and
the pans, and all the vessels of brass
wherewith they ministered, took
they away. 19. And the cups, and
the fire-pans, and the basins, and the
pots, and the candlesticks, and the
pans, and the bowls—that which was
of gold, in gold, and that which was
of silver, in silver—the captain of
the guard took away. 20. The two
pillars, the one sea, and the twelve
brazen bulls that were under the
bases, which king Solomon had
made for the house of the LORD—
the brass of all these vessels was

הַמְזַמְּר֗וֹת וְאֶת־הַמִּזְרָקֹת־
וְאֶת־הַכַּפּוֹת וְאֵת כָּל־כְּלֵי
הַנְּחֹשֶׁת אֲשֶׁר־יְשָׁרְתוּ בָהֶם
לָקָחוּ: וְאֶת־הַסִּפִּים וְאֶת־ 19
הַמַּחְתּוֹת וְאֶת־הַמִּזְרָקוֹת
וְאֶת־הַסִּירוֹת וְאֶת־הַמְּנֹרוֹת
וְאֶת־הַכַּפּוֹת וְאֶת־הַמְּנַקִּיּוֹת
אֲשֶׁר זָהָב זָהָב וַאֲשֶׁר־כֶּסֶף
כָּסֶף לָקַח רַב טַבָּחִים:
הָעַמּוּדִים | שְׁנַיִם הַיָּם אֶחָד֗ 20
וְהַבָּקָר שְׁנֵים־עָשָׂר נְחֹשֶׁת
אֲשֶׁר־תַּחַת הַמְּכֹנוֹת אֲשֶׁר
עָשָׂה הַמֶּלֶךְ שְׁלֹמֹה לְבֵית
יְהֹוָה לֹא־הָיָה מִשְׁקָל
לִנְחֻשְׁתָּם כָּל־הַכֵּלִים

v. 20. כצ״ל כתיב וקרי

altar of burnt-offerings were removed
(Exod. xxvii. 3).

snuffers. For the lamps (Exod. xxv. 38;
Num. iv. 9; 1 Kings vii. 50). Classic
Jewish exegetes define this as musical
instruments.

basins. In which the blood of the
sacrifices was caught (Kimchi, Shorashim).

pans. [Perhaps used in connection with
the incense.]

19. *cups.* Rashi conjectures that they
were jars for receiving (or storing) the
blood, and quotes Exod. xii. 22 where
the Hebrew word rendered *basin* is the
singular of the noun used here.

basin . . . pots . . . pans. These are
enumerated in the preceding verse;
presumably they were different vessels,

although called by the same name.
Metsudath David conjectures that one
group was made of silver and the other
group was made of gold.

the candlesticks. Cf. 1 Kings vii. 49.

bowls. According to the Rabbis, these
were the supports upon which the
showbread was held up over the table
(Rashi).

that which was of gold . . . in silver. Idiomatic for 'whether of gold or silver'
(Metsudath David).

20. *two pillars.* Cf. 1 Kings vii. 15ff.

*the one sea, and the twelve brazen
bulls.* Cf. 1 Kings vii. 23ff.

that were under the bases. In Solomon's
Temple the bases were under the lavers,

without weight. 21. And as for the pillars, the height of the one pillar was eighteen cubits; and a line of twelve cubits did compass it; and the thickness thereof was four fingers; it was hollow. 22. And a capital of brass was upon it; and the height of the one capital was five cubits, with network and pomegranates upon the capital round about, all of brass; and the second pillar also had like unto these, and pomegranates. 23. And there were ninety and six pomegranates on the outside; all the pomegranates were a hundred upon the network round about.

24. And the captain of the guard took Seraiah the chief priest, and Zephaniah the second priest, and the three keepers of the door; 25. and

21 הָאֵלֶּה: וְהָעַמּוּדִים שְׁמֹנֶה
עֶשְׂרֵה אַמָּה קוֹמָה֙ הָעַמֻּד
הָאֶחָ֔ד וְחוּט שְׁתֵּים־עֶשְׂרֵה
אַמָּה יְסֻבֶּ֑נּוּ וְעָבְי֛וֹ אַרְבַּע
22 אֶצְבָּעוֹת נָבוּב: וְכֹתֶרֶת עָלָיו
נְחֹ֗שֶׁת וְקוֹמַת הַכֹּתֶרֶת הָאַחַת֙
חָמֵשׁ אַמּוֹת֙ וּשְׂבָכָה וְרִמּוֹנִים
עַל־הַכּוֹתֶרֶת סָבִיב הַכֹּל
נְחֹ֑שֶׁת וְכָאֵלֶּה לָעַמּוּד הַשֵּׁנִי
23 וְרִמּוֹנִים: וַיִּֽהְיוּ֙ הָרִמֹּנִים
תִּשְׁעִים וְשִׁשָּׁה רוּחָה כָּל־
הָרִמּוֹנִים מֵאָה עַל־הַשְּׂבָכָה
24 סָבִיב: וַיִּקַּח רַב־טַבָּחִים
אֶת־שְׂרָיָה֙ כֹּהֵן הָרֹאשׁ וְאֶת־
צְפַנְיָ֖ה כֹּהֵן הַמִּשְׁנֶה וְאֶת־
25 שְׁלֹשֶׁת שֹׁמְרֵי הַסַּף: וּמִן־

v. 21. קומת ק'

---

whilst the bulls supported the sea. Rashi tries to get over the difficulty by suggesting that *tachath* here signifies 'near by.' Metsudath David refers to 2 Kings xvi. 17 where it is narrated that king Ahaz *cut off the borders of the bases, and removed the laver from off them; and took down the sea from off the brazen oxen that were under it, and put it upon a pavement of stone*; and he conjectures that Ahaz set the laver upon the oxen instead of the bases, understanding *tachath* here as 'instead of.'

21. *cubits.* A cubit was eighteen inches.

22. *capital.* The ornamental head of the pillar.

pomegranates. A common form of decoration in the East which also figured upon the High Priest's vestment (Exod. xxviii. 33).

23. Comparing this verse with the parallel account in 1 Kings vii. 20, Rashi concludes that each pillar had two rows each of a hundred pomegranates, but that four of them were hidden owing to the closeness of the pillars to the wall of the porch.

24–27. This passage is not included in chapter xxxix, but has its parrallel in 2 Kings xxv. 18–21.

24. *Seraiah.* [In Ezra vii. 1 Ezra is described as *the son of Seraiah*, where *son* probably means 'descendant.']

out of the city he took an officer that
was set over the men of war; and
seven men of them that saw the
king's face, who were found in the
city; and the scribe of the captain of
the host, who mustered the people of
the land; and threescore men of the
people of the land, that were found
in the midst of the city. 26. And
Nebuzaradan the captain of the
guard took them, and brought them
to the king of Babylon to Riblah.
27. And the king of Babylon smote
them, and put them to death at
Riblah in the land of Hamath. So
Judah was carried away captive out
of his land.

28. This is the people whom
Nebuchadrezzar carried away captive: in the seventh year three

הָעִיר לָקַח סָרִיס אֶחָד אֲשֶׁר־
הָיָה פָקִיד ׀ עַל־אַנְשֵׁי
הַמִּלְחָמָה וְשִׁבְעָה אֲנָשִׁים
מֵרֹאֵי פְנֵי־הַמֶּלֶךְ אֲשֶׁר־
נִמְצְאוּ בָעִיר וְאֵת סֹפֵר שַׂר
הַצָּבָא הַמַּצְבִּא אֶת־עַם
הָאָרֶץ וְשִׁשִּׁים אִישׁ מֵעַם
הָאָרֶץ הַנִּמְצְאִים בְּתוֹךְ
26 הָעִיר: וַיִּקַּח אוֹתָם נְבוּזַרְאֲדָן
רַב־טַבָּחִים וַיֹּלֶךְ אוֹתָם אֶל־
27 מֶלֶךְ בָּבֶל בְּרִבְלָתָה: וַיַּכֶּה
אוֹתָם מֶלֶךְ בָּבֶל וַיְמִתֵם
בְּרִבְלָה בְּאֶרֶץ חֲמָת וַיִּגֶל
28 יְהוּדָה מֵעַל אַדְמָתוֹ: זֶה הָעָם
אֲשֶׁר הֶגְלָה נְבוּכַדְרֶאצַּר
בִּשְׁנַת־שֶׁבַע יְהוּדִים שְׁלֹשֶׁת

the chief priest. His ancestry is traced
back in a direct descent from Aaron in 1
Chron. v. 29–40. The Hebrew for *chief
priest* is not the usual term for 'High
Priest' but that office is doubtless
intended (Metsudath David).

Zephaniah. See on xxi. 1.

the second priest. Presumably the deputy
High Priest (Metsudath David, Rashi).

keepers of the door. See on xxxv. 4.

25. *an officer.* For the Hebrew *saris,* see
on xxxviii. 7.

seven men. 2 Kings xxv. 19 has *five men.*
Rashi conjectures that two of these
seven were men of lesser importance (cf.
Esther i. 14 where it appears that seven
men occupied the position referred to
here in the Persian court).

*the people of the land . . . the people of the
land.* Although the phrase is repeated,
the probability is that different mean-
ings are to be attached to each. The first
describes the general population of the
country, from whom the army would be
naturally drawn. The second refers to
the esteemed citizens (Metsudath
David).

28–30. ENUMERATION OF THE DEPORTEES.

28. *in the seventh year.* 2 Kings xxiv. 12
reads *eighth year.* The deportation commenced at the end of the seventh and
lasted into the eighth year (Kimchi).
Rashi explains that it was the eighth
year of Nebuchadnezzar's reign, but
only the seventh of his suzerainty over
Judea which he reduced to vassalage a
year after ascending the throne. See the
next note.

thousand Jews and three and twenty; 29. in the eighteenth year of Nebuchadrezzar, from Jerusalem, eight hundred thirty and two persons; 30. in the three and twentieth year of Nebuchadrezzar Nebuzaradan the captain of the guard carried away captive of the Jews seven hundred forty and five persons; all the persons were four thousand and six hundred.

31. And it came to pass in the seven and thirtieth year of the captivity of Jehoiachin king of Judah, in the twelfth month, in the five and twentieth day of the month,

אֲלָפִים וְעֶשְׂרִים וּשְׁלֹשָׁה:

29 בִּשְׁנַת שְׁמוֹנֶה עֶשְׂרֵה לִנְבוּכַדְרֶאצַּר מִירוּשָׁלַ͏ִם נֶפֶשׁ שְׁמֹנֶה מֵאוֹת שְׁלֹשִׁים

30 וּשְׁנָיִם: בִּשְׁנַת שָׁלֹשׁ וְעֶשְׂרִים לִנְבוּכַדְרֶאצַּר הֶגְלָה נְבוּזַרְאֲדָן רַב־טַבָּחִים יְהוּדִים נֶפֶשׁ שְׁבַע מֵאוֹת אַרְבָּעִים וַחֲמִשָּׁה כָּל־נֶפֶשׁ אַרְבַּעַת אֲלָפִים וְשֵׁשׁ מֵאוֹת:

31 וַיְהִי בִשְׁלֹשִׁים וָשֶׁבַע שָׁנָה לְגָלוּת יְהוֹיָכִין מֶלֶךְ־יְהוּדָה בִּשְׁנֵים עָשָׂר חֹדֶשׁ בְּעֶשְׂרִים וַחֲמִשָּׁה לַחֹדֶשׁ נָשָׂא אֱוִיל

---

three thousand Jews and three and twenty. 2 Kings xxiv. 14 gives the number as 10,000. *Jews* denotes members of the tribe of Judah, whereas the larger number in Kings includes captives of all tribes living in Judea at the time. In this way Rashi seeks to explain the discrepancy in 2 Kings between verses 14 and 16. In Kings, Rashi quotes this reconcilement of the three verses from Seder Olam. Abarbanel, however, questions this solution, for if the author of Kings stated the number of exiles from the tribe of Benjamin and other tribes, why did he not state the number of exiles from Judah as well? Moreover, it is not plausible that the smaller tribe of Benjamin should have had seven thousand warriors whereas the larger tribe of Judah only three thousand. He, therefore, concludes that the entire captivity was 10,000, whereas the warriors equalled 7,000. The general populace, including King Jehoiachin,

his mother, his wives, his officers, etc. and the thousand craftsmen and sentries of the gates, equalled 3,000.

29. *eighteenth year.* Cf. verse 12 and 2 Kings xxv. 8, both of which read *nineteenth year.* According to *Seder Olam,* the conquest of Jehoiachin took place in the seventh year from the conquest of Jehoiakim, which was the eighth year of Nebuchadnezzar's reign (Rashi, Kimchi).

30. *in the three and twentieth year.* This third deportation is not recorded in 2 Kings, but we know from Josephus (*Antiquities* X, ix. 7) that in that year Nebuchadnezzar waged war in Syria, Ammon, Moab and Egypt and carried off captives. *Seder Olam* states that Tyre was finally reduced in that year, and the Jews in the countries bordering on the Holy Land were driven into captivity.

31. *in the five and twentieth day of the month.* 2 Kings xxv. 27 has *seven and*

that Evil-merodach king of Babylon,
in the first year of his reign, lifted up
the head of Jehoiachin king of Judah,
and brought him forth out of prison.
32. And he spoke kindly to him, and
set his throne above the throne of
the kings that were with him in
Babylon. 33. And he changed his
prison garments, and did eat bread
before him continually all the days of
his life. 34. And for his allowance,
there was a continual allowance
given him of the king of Babylon,
every day a portion until the day of
his death, all the days of his life.

מְרֹדַךְ מֶלֶךְ בָּבֶל בִּשְׁנַת
מַלְכֻתוֹ אֶת־רֹאשׁ יְהוֹיָכִין
מֶלֶךְ־יְהוּדָה וַיֹּצֵא אֹתוֹ מִבֵּית
הַכְּלִיא: וַיְדַבֵּר אִתּוֹ טֹבוֹת 32
וַיִּתֵּן אֶת־כִּסְאוֹ מִמַּעַל לְכִסֵּא
מְלָכִים אֲשֶׁר אִתּוֹ בְּבָבֶל:
וְשִׁנָּה אֵת בִּגְדֵי כִלְאוֹ וְאָכַל 33
לֶחֶם לְפָנָיו תָּמִיד כָּל־יְמֵי
חַיָּו: וַאֲרֻחָתוֹ אֲרֻחַת תָּמִיד 34
נִתְּנָה־לּוֹ מֵאֵת מֶלֶךְ־בָּבֶל
דְּבַר־יוֹם בְּיוֹמוֹ עַד־יוֹם
מוֹתוֹ כֹּל יְמֵי חַיָּו:

v. 31. הכלוא ק' v. 32. המלכים ק' v. 33. חסר י'

twentieth. Rashi suggests that Nebuchadnezzar died on the twenty-fifth, was buried on the twenty-sixth, and the following day his successor released Jehoiachin.

Evil-merodach. The name (in the Babylonian language Amil-Marduk) means 'servant of Marduk,' Babylonia's chief deity (see Daath Mikra).

lifted up the head. This may mean that he exalted him and aggrandized him. It may also mean that he counted him among the other kings (Rashi).

32. *the kings.* Apparently, the height of the thrones of the king's intimates reflected their esteem. We find the same practice in Persia in the kingdom of Ahasuerus (Esther iii. 1). Apparently, the captured kings in Babylon dwelt in the capital city and served as advisers to the king. Now Jehoiachin joined their ranks and became the most esteemed of

them all. The Judean exiles in Babylon perceived in this honour a sign of the coming redemption (Daath Mikra).

33. *changed his prison garments.* As was done to Joseph (Gen. xli. 14).

did eat bread before him. Was admitted to the privilege of sitting at the king's table (Metsudath David).

34. *all the days of his life.* This clause is apparently superfluous and may have been added to avoid closing the Book with the word *death.* Daath Soferim conjectures that the connotation is that Jehoiachin was blessed with longevity and enjoyed this privilege during all his remaining years. The Midrash (Lev. Rabbah 19) relates that Jehoiachin repented his evil ways while in prison and died a righteous man. He was therefore granted the privilege of receiving a portion from the king for the rest of his life.

Abarbanel, Isaac (1437–1509), Bible Commentator.
Aboth — *Pirke Aboth, Sayings of the Fathers*: Mishnaic tractate.
Alschich, Moses (sixteenth century Bible Commentator), *Maroth Hatsoveoth*.
Amos — One of the Minor Prophets.
Aruch — Lexicon of Talmud, Midrash, Targum, by Nathan of Rome (10th century).
Azulai, Chaim Joseph David (1727–1807) *Homath Anach*.
Baruch — A book of the Apochrypha.
Berakhoth — Talmudic tractate.
Biberfeld, Philip (Contemporary Jewish Historian) Universal Jewish History.
Canticum — Song of Songs, a Book of the Bible.
Chagigah — Talmudic tractate.
Chotam Tochnit — Hebrew Synonyms, by Abraham Bedarschi (13th century Scholar).
Chronicles — Book of the Bible.
Cohen, Hermann, Jewish Philosopher, *Jüdische Schriften*.
Daath Mikra (1983, Contemporary Jewish Commentary) Mosad HaRav Kook.
Daath Soferim (1969, Contemporary Jewish Commentary) Chaim D. Rabinowitz.
Deuteronomy — Last Book of the Pentateuch.
Dunash (10th century Grammarian) Teshuboth Dunash.
Ecclesiastes — Book of the Bible.
Esther — Book of the Bible.
Exodus — Second Book of the Pentateuch.
Ezekiel — Book of the Bible.
Ezra — Book of the Bible.
Genesis — First Book of the Pentateuch.
Gittin — Talmudic tractate.
Habakkuk — One of the Minor Prophets.
Haggai — One of the Minor Prophets.
Herodotus (Greek Historian, 5th century B.C.E.).
Hertz, J.H. (Late Chief Rabbi of England), *The Pentateuch and Haphtorahs*.
Hirsch, Mendel (19th century Educator) *The Haphtoroth*.
Hosea — One of the Minor Prophets.
Ibn Ezra, Abraham (1092–1167, Bible Commentator).
Ibn Ganah, Jona (11th century Grammarian and Lexicographer) *Schoraschim*.
Ibn Kaspi, Joseph (1279–1340, Bible Commentator) *Adne Keseph*.
Ibn Nachmiash (14th century Bible Commentator) *Commentary on Jeremiah*.
Isaiah da Trani (13th century Bible Commentator).
Job — Book of the Bible.
Jonah — One of the Minor Prophets.
Jonathan — author of the Targum, early Tanna (first century B.C.E.).
Josephus Flavius — (Jewish Historian, 1st century C.E.).
Joshua — First Book of the Prophets.
Judges — Book of the Bible.
Kara, Joseph (1060–1130, Bible Commentator).
Kethuboth — Talmudic tractate.
Kings — Book of the Bible.
Leviticus — Book of the Bible.
Makkoth — Talmudic tractate.
Mandelkern, Solomon (Bible Concordancem 1896).

AUTHORITIES QUOTED

Metsudat David, ('Tower of David'), *Commentary on Jeremiah* by David Altschul (17th century).

Metsudath Zion ('Tower of Zion'), Definitions of words of the Bible (same author as preceding).

Minchath Shai (Mantua 1742), Clarification of Masoretic Text, by Jedidiah Solomon of Nozri, Italy, sixteenth century Scholar and Grammarian.

Nahum — One of the Minor Prophets.

Nedarim — Talmudic tractate.

Nehemiah — Book of the Bible.

Numbers — Book of the Bible.

Obadiah — One of the Minor Prophets.

Petrie, Flinders (Egyptologist), *Egypt and Israel.*

Proverbs — Book of the Bible.

Psalms — Book of the Bible.

Ruth — Book of the Bible.

Siphré — Ancient Rabbinic Commentary on Numbers and Deuteronomy.

Sotah — Talmudic tractate.

Ta'anith — Talmudic tractate.

Talmud — Corpus of Jewish Law and Thought (compiled at the end of the 5th century C.E.).

Urim Vethummim (Commentary on Isaiah and Jeremiah, Venice 1602), Meir Aramah, Bible Commentator 1460–1545.

Zechariah — One of the Minor Prophets.

Zephaniah — One of the Minor Prophets.

TERMS AND ABBREVIATIONS

A.D.P.B. *Authorized Daily Prayer Book,* ed. S. Singer.

A.J. American-Jewish translation of the Scriptures.

A.V. Authorized Version.

B.C.E. Before the Christian era.

Ber. *Berachoth,* Talmudical tractate.

c. About.

C.E. Common era.

Cf. Compare, refer to.

Chag. *Chagigah,* Talmudical tractate.

ed. Editor, or edited by.

e.g. For example.

etc. Et cetera.

f. Following verse or chapter (plural ff.).

i.e. That is.

kerë. The Hebrew as it is to be read according to the Masoretes.

Keth. *Kethuboth,* Talmudical tractate.

kethib. The Hebrew as it is written according to tradition.

lit. Literally.

LXX. Septuagint (see Authorities Quoted).

Meg. *Megillah,* Talmudical tractate.

MS. Manuscript (plural MSS.).

M.T. Masoretic text.

R.V. Revised Version.

Sanh. *Sanhedrin,* Talmudical tractate.

Shab. *Shabbath,* Talmudical tractate.

sic. Thus (drawing attention to a remarkarble reading or statement).

viz. Namely.